PAYING THE PRICE

DATE DUE

PAYING THE PRICE

*Ignacio Ellacuría
and the
Murdered Jesuits of El Salvador*

TERESA WHITFIELD

Temple University Press, Philadelphia

Temple University Press, Philadelphia 19122
Copyright © 1995 by Temple University
All rights reserved
Published 1994

⊖ The paper used in this publication meets the minimum
requirements of American National Standard for Information
Sciences—Permanence of Paper for Printed Library Materials,
ANSI Z39.48-1984

Printed in the United States of America

Library of Congress Cataloging-in-Publication Data

Whitfield, Teresa.
    Paying the price : Ignacio Ellacuría and the murdered Jesuits of El Salvador / Teresa Whitfield.
      p. cm.
    Includes bibliographical references and index.
    ISBN 1-56639-252-7. — ISBN 1-56639-253-5 (pbk.)
    1. El Salvador—Politics and government—1979–1992. 2. El Salvador—Politics and
government—1944–1979. 3. Ellacuría, Ignacio. 4. Jesuits—El Salvador—Political
activity—History—20th century. 5. Universidad Centroamericana José Simeón Cañas.
6. Assassination—El Salvador—History—20th century. 7. Victims of state sponsored terrorism—
El Salvador—History—20th century. 8. El Salvador—Relations—United States. 9. United
States—Relations—El Salvador. 10. El Salvador—Church history—20th century. I. Ellacuría,
Ignacio. II. Title.
F1488.3.W48   1995
272'.9'097284—dc20
                                     94-20361
                                         CIP

To Jon Sobrino
and the staff
of the Monsignor Romero
Pastoral Center

The union of the spirit of the Gospel and the demands of history will always be subversive and revolutionary. And from that springs the attempt to temper one or the other, and particularly their combination.

Ignacio Ellacuría

CONTENTS

ILLUSTRATIONS

FOREWORD

I remember the moment when I learned of Ignacio Ellacuría's murder as
vividly as I do the assassination of John F. Kennedy and the death of
Ernesto "Che" Guevara. This, I suspect, pigeonholes me as a member of a
certain class and generation of Latin Americans. This cultural identity may
also explain my reaction upon hearing the news—from a Guatemalan
diplomat, in the ornate Council Chamber of the Pan-American Union in
Washington, D.C. What shot into my mind were the words of the fascist
general Millán Astray at a rally during the Spanish Civil War: "*¡Viva la
Muerte! ¡Abajo la Inteligencia!*"

As the U.N. secretary-general's representative, I devoted the better
part of 1990 and 1991 to conducting the negotiations between the
government of El Salvador and the *Frente Farabundo Martí para la
Liberación Nacional* (FMLN) that culminated in the comprehensive peace
accord signed on January 16, 1992 at Chapultepec Castle, in Mexico City.
The negotiations had an ambitious, four-fold purpose: to end the armed
conflict, promote democratization, guarantee unrestricted respect for
human rights, and reunify Salvadoran society.

El Salvador has come a long way since then. As part of a radical
reform involving unprecedented constitutional amendments, the Salvadoran armed forces have been restricted to defense from external threats,
and deprived of their previous roles in public security matters and as
the ultimate arbiter of national political life. They have been purged of

---

Disclaimer: The opinions expressed in this foreword do not necessarily reflect the views or position of
the United Nations.

officers judged unfit to serve in the reformed armed forces. A pioneering national civilian police force has been created and deployed throughout the country. Important changes to the electoral system have been adopted, to be followed by further improvements as a result of the lackluster 1994 performance. A national ombudsman for human rights has been established. A reform of the judiciary has been initiated. A program for transfer of land to former combatants and farmers who worked plots in the conflict areas is underway, as part of an effort to reintegrate them into legal society. One-quarter of the seats in the legislative assembly are now occupied by leaders of the FMLN after the March elections.

It is premature at this writing to assess how far the goals of the negotiations have been achieved. Delays and distortions occurred in the implementation of the peace agreements, including important ones such as those related to the police and the transfer of land. The report of the Truth Commission, which examined the most egregious crimes of the war years, was greeted with hostility and even slightly smothered by the government, thus impairing the salutary therapeutic exercise it was meant to produce. In addition, a number of specific reforms proposed by the Truth Commission have yet to be implemented. During the electoral campaign, political leaders were killed. At the very least, however, it can be said that, as a result of the peace agreements, the foundations of a more just society have been laid, and steps have been taken to build—on those foundations—a framework within which justice and human rights have a chance to prevail over intolerance and violence.

In her profound and deeply moving book, Teresa Whitfield seeks answers to two questions: Why were Ignacio Ellacuría SJ and his UCA brothers murdered, and what have their deaths meant? In providing these answers, she has largely succeeded in explaining why peace negotiations addressing the underlying causes of the armed conflicts were needed. She has also brought out the pivotal role played by the investigation of the Jesuit murders in keeping negotiations on track and at times propelling them forward.

Teresa Whitfield's book is replete with references to the negotiating process. In the same way, the story of the negotiation, yet to be written, will have to interlock with the Jesuit murder story from which it cannot be separated.

Without United States support, it is difficult to imagine that the El Salvador negotiations could have succeeded. Official support was voiced from the beginning at the highest levels of the U.S. government. In private, particularly at the sub-Cabinet level, the support was less enthusiastic. There was never any wavering, however, in the leadership of the U.S. Congress, and I agree with the author that this is in large part attributable to the moral outrage at the murder of the Jesuits. The U.S. Congress, with Representative Joseph Moakley in the lead, never let up its pressure. In the concluding rounds of the negotiations in New York, in September and December of 1991, Thomas Pickering, a former U.S. ambassador to El Salvador then serving as permanent representative to the United Nations, and his deputy, Alexander Watson, currently assistant secretary of state for inter-American affairs, played a critical role in support of U.N. efforts.

I met Ellacuría twice, once over *chipirones en su tinta,* a Basque specialty, at my favorite San Salvador restaurant, with my (Catalan) colleague Francesc Vendrell; the second time alone for two hours in his austere but airy office at the UCA, on the eve of President Cristiani's June 1, 1989 inauguration. I missed a third appointment in October—weeks before Ellacuria's death—having lingered too long at a meeting with Cristiani during a San Salvador stopover on my way to Church-sponsored talks in Costa Rica.

It would be presumptuous to claim Ellacuría's friendship on such frail grounds. I do know that on that second occasion he shared with me information that I have not heard anywhere else, and that in light of what is known today, sends shivers up my spine. I have no doubt that, had he lived, Ellacuría would have played a central role in the negotiations. In retrospect, I have the eerie feeling that in confiding in me at that early date, Ellacuría was somehow depositing valuables for safekeeping in a bank, or—who knows—sensing the worst, passing the baton.

Teresa Whitfield's apt title refers to "paying the price" in the sense of enduring a punishment, suffering a penalty—for the misdeed of promoting justice. I would like to suggest, from my perspective as a negotiator, that there is another, perhaps unintended dimension to this title. When we speak of paying a price, we allude to a transaction, an exchange, *do ut des.* But Ellacuría and his Jesuit brothers did not freely offer their lives for justice in El Salvador. There was no commerce, no deal was struck; the invisible, magic hand of the market did not operate. The lives of Ellacuría and his companions were expeditiously snatched away from them in a coldly planned military operation; their cook and her daughter fell because there could be no witnesses.

At a certain cosmic level, far above our heads, there may have been just such a sophisticated, one might say Jesuitical, transaction. The Jesuits had to lose their lives to provoke the moral outrage that kept the Salvadoran armed forces on the defensive and forced the concessions at the negotiating table, without which a durable peace could not possibly have been built.

My own moral outrage was difficult to restrain. On one occasion, after I had harangued the government delegation on the grave danger confronting the negotiating process, David Escobar Galindo, the intellectual leader of the delegation, referred in private to my admittedly passionate performance as "the apocalypse according to St. Alvaro."

I used to think, sporadic Catholic that I am, that if Ellacuría was contemplating from the heavens the zigzags of the investigation into the UCA murders, he would have been pleased at the fact that there was so much covering up, foot-dragging, and general dissembling, for thanks to that, the pressure at the negotiating table continued to the end. The investigation and the negotiations interwove in a fugue worthy of Bach; it seemed inspired in heaven.

Alvaro de Soto
May 1994

PREFACE

I had planned to be in El Salvador in late 1989, researching a documentary about Archbishop Oscar Romero. The film's point of departure was a photograph taken in March 1980, a year before his assassination, in which he stood amid a group of youths. His hands rested lightly on the shoulders of two small girls in front of him and all were caught wide-eyed, forever challenging the attention of the viewer. I had hoped to find the survivors pictured in the photograph and learn what they remembered of the man in their midst. Over the months it had become something of an obsession, a quest for both myself and the documentary's director, Peter Chappell. We had located the photographer and I was to return that November, but when November came it was not a month for the searching of the streets and back alleys of San Salvador.

The capital city was a battle zone, with the government combating the largest guerrilla offensive of the war with conventional ground forces, aerial bombardment, and a clampdown on organizations of the opposition. I was in Chile when I first heard that six Jesuit priests and two women had been murdered in the early hours of November 16, 1989. From New York and then from Nicaragua, I followed the news from El Salvador. I learned there was to be a memorial mass for the Jesuits on December 16 at the University of Central America (UCA), the institution to which they had dedicated their lives. I made sure I could be there.

At the mass I was moved by the number and variety of people who had come to pay tribute to the murdered Jesuits, by the poignancy of the service, and by the strength and humanity of what was said. Particularly striking were the words printed on a card given out as a memento of the occasion: "What does it mean to be a Jesuit today? To commit oneself beneath the standard of the cross in the crucial struggle of our time: the struggle for faith and the struggle for justice that that same faith demands." In the following days I sought out a meeting with José María Tojeira, father provincial of the Jesuits of Central America. Tentatively, for San Salvador was still reeling from the violence of the past few weeks, I suggested that I raise the money necessary to produce some kind of documentary about the murdered Jesuits.

Eleven months later I returned to San Salvador for the fifth time within a year, on the occasion of the first anniversary of the Jesuits' deaths and the screening of the documentary about them that I had produced and Ilan Ziv had directed. It played repeatedly through the night-long vigil held in the grounds of the UCA, but I maintained a low profile, anxious not to be publicly associated with a film criticizing the Salvadoran armed forces and those elements responsible for the Jesuits' murder. I had begun work on a book and feared jeopardizing the contacts I would need for its research, which would keep me in El Salvador for the next year and a half. Like the words that had so struck me at the memorial mass the previous year, the book's title came from the documents of the Jesuits' thirty-second General Congregation in 1975: "We shall not work for the promotion of justice without having to pay a price." The phrase is now inscribed on the Jesuits' tomb in the UCA chapel.

Fathers Ignacio Ellacuría, rector of the University of Central America, Ignacio Martín-Baró, its vice-rector, Segundo Montes, Amando López, Juan Ramón Moreno, and Joaquín López y López were murdered, together with their housekeeper and her daughter, Elba and Celina Ramos, by members of the Salvadoran army, funded and trained by the United States. Why were they killed and what have their deaths meant? I felt these two questions should be answered in closely related narratives. And as my research developed I realized that this book, in a synthesis of the two questions, would be stronger for featuring the life of Ignacio Ellacuría. As his brother Jesuit Jon Sobrino pointed out, it was Ellacuría "who most often put into words what these Jesuits accepted as fundamental in their life and work." But it was also undeniable that Ellacuría had been for two decades at the forefront of events that soon appeared to me like steps taken toward the dark night of November 16, 1989.

Ellacuría played an integral role in the radical change of direction undertaken by the Jesuits of Central America in the late 1960s and early 1970s and in the emergence of the UCA as what he called "a different kind of university." As the university's rector during the civil war Ellacuría was a force in El Salvador's politics, engendering from some sectors of Salvadoran society a uniquely visceral hatred. His voice emerged as one of the most consistent and articulate champions of a negotiated solution to the conflict. Even after their deaths Ellacuría and the slain Jesuits influenced the negotiation of a peaceful settlement, because progress (or the lack of it) in the investigation into their murders became one of the defining features of the period that culminated in the signing of the peace agreements in January 1992.

The form I chose for this book, then, is something of a hybrid—neither straight biography, nor political or ecclesiastical history. To answer my original two questions I interweave the two narratives from a common starting point: the events of November 15 and 16, 1989. Together the narratives demonstrate that the killings were not an arbitrary act, but sadly expressive of the Salvadoran reality within which the Jesuits lived, and an act which, paradoxically, strengthened and prolonged the impact of their lives. From the description of the murders themselves one narrative returns to the beginning of this story, Ellacuría's arrival from Spain as a young novice, and traces the evolution of the Jesuits and the UCA over the next forty years. The other tells how the unfolding of the Jesuit case, painful and embarrassing as the murder had been for a U.S. administration eager to justify the flow of military aid on the grounds that it came hand in glove with improvements in human rights, contributed to the gradual emergence of a new realism in U.S. policy toward El Salvador. Ultimately, the murder of the Jesuits and all that the subsequent investigation and prosecution of the crime revealed, allowed for negotiations conducted under the auspices of the United Nations to prosper and for the foundations to be laid for a durable peace in El Salvador. For this peace, still precarious at the time of writing, the Jesuits lived and died.

Teresa Whitfield
August 1994

ACKNOWLEDGMENTS

The research for *Paying the Price* was conducted with the assistance of a grant from the William M. Keck Jr. Foundation.

My first acknowledgment must go to my sources. Since I began work on this book in 1990 I have undertaken almost two hundred interviews with a wide range of individuals: Jesuits, politicians, military officers, members of the FMLN, U.S. officials, other diplomats, congressmen, their aides, church workers, lawyers, judges, human rights campaigners, university professors, and journalists among them. To these individuals, some of whom I returned to again and again, I express my deepest gratitude. No books or archival resources could have provided what they were able to teach me about El Salvador.

Among those who have followed this book from its very beginnings I must thank my agent, Lizzie Grossman, who was brave enough to take me on sight almost unseen, and Charlie Currie, who helped me make a start. Hugh Lacey proved vital at key stages of the manuscript's evolution. Both Cynthia Arnson and Margaret Crahan gave invaluable encouragement and criticism. I should also like to thank Robert Kimzey for his efforts to find my manuscript a home, Doris Braendel and Temple University Press for providing one, and Scott Pass of P. M. Gordon Associates for seeing it through production.

My debt to the Jesuits of Central America, past and present, is an obvious one. The generosity with which they and the lay men and women of the UCA shared memories and analysis was a source of inspiration in itself. Here there is only the space to thank the Jesuit provincial, José María Tojeira, UCA Rector Miguel Francisco Estrada, and director of

UCA Editores Rodolfo Cardenal for their support, and for the access to and permission to quote from their own publications, archive materials, and photographs they extended to me. My gratitude to Jon Sobrino and the staff of the Monsignor Romero Pastoral Center is expressed by the dedication: without the provision of office space, coffee, and cheerful encouragement during my time in El Salvador this book would not have been possible.

Quite apart from the specialist archives I drew upon for much of my research, I should like to pay public tribute to the success of the UCA in ensuring, through its research, documentation, and publications, that the task of those who seek to write on the recent history of El Salvador is greatly facilitated. Like all who have worked and will work in the future on the Jesuit case, I am indebted to the rigor and dedication with which Martha Doggett, Maggi Popkin, and the Lawyers Committee for Human Rights have followed its every development.

For support and accommodation during the months of research and writing thanks must go, first and foremost, to Nancy Boye, Andrea Stoutland, and Antonio Luzi in San Salvador; Gretta Siebentritt and Rafael Tovar in Washington; and Donna DeCesare, Ossi Lubrani, Joel Millman, Deborah Shaffer, and Chris Walker in New York. Among those friends who have been most constant in their encouragement of this enterprise I should like to thank Peter Chappell and Ilan Ziv, with whom I first worked, most memorably, in El Salvador, and Saskia Baron, Chuck Call, and Elizabeth Wood. Particular thanks are due to Michael Dodson for the maps, and to Rob McChesney of the U.S. Jesuit Conference. The confidence displayed by my parents, Lucy Warrack and Adrian Whitfield, that somehow I knew what I was doing, has been a mainstay of this whole venture. For that, as for so much else, I am very grateful. Finally, I should like to thank Jason Rosenbaum for being there to see me through the final year.

Pedro Armada SJ, Cynthia Arnson, Michael Campbell-Johnston SJ, Rodolfo Cardenal SJ, Margaret Crahan, Charles Currie SJ, Luis De Sebastián, Tom Gibb, Juan Hernández Pico SJ, David Holiday, Robert Kimzey, Hugh Lacey, Román Mayorga, Jim McGovern, Iain Murray, Gene Palombo, Maggi Popkin, Jon Sobrino SJ, Andrea Stoutland, Lucy Warrack, Adrian Whitfield, and Elizabeth Wood read part or all of the manuscript. I am grateful for their comments and corrections, while remaining wholly responsible for any errors that may remain.

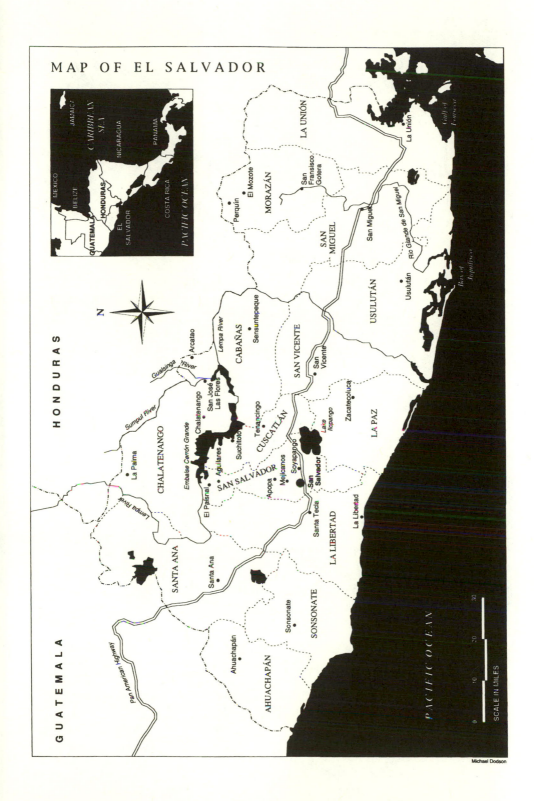

MAP OF EL SALVADOR

CARIBBEAN SEA

JAMAICA

MEXICO
BELIZE
GUATEMALA
HONDURAS
EL SALVADOR
NICARAGUA
COSTA RICA
PANAMA

PACIFIC OCEAN

GUATEMALA

HONDURAS

N

LA UNIÓN

La Unión

Gulf of Fonseca

El Mozote

San Fransisco Gotera

MORAZÁN

Perquín

SAN MIGUEL

San Miguel

Río Grande de San Miguel

USULUTÁN

Usulután

Bay of Jiquilisco

Lempa River

Arcatao

Gualsinga River

Sumpul River

CABAÑAS

Sensuntepeque

SAN VICENTE

San Vicente

Lempa River

San José Las Flores

Chalatenango

Embalse Cerrón Grande

Tenancingo

CUSCATLÁN

Zacatecoluca

Lake Ilopango

LA PAZ

CHALATENANGO

Lempa River

La Palma

Aguilares

Suchitoto

Melicanos

Soyapango

San Salvador

San Salvador

SAN SALVADOR

El Paisnal

Apopa

Santa Tecla

La Libertad

LA LIBERTAD

Pan American Highway

SANTA ANA

Santa Ana

Sonsonate

SONSONATE

AHUACHAPÁN

Ahuachapán

PACIFIC OCEAN

SCALE IN MILES

0   10   20   30

Michael Dodson

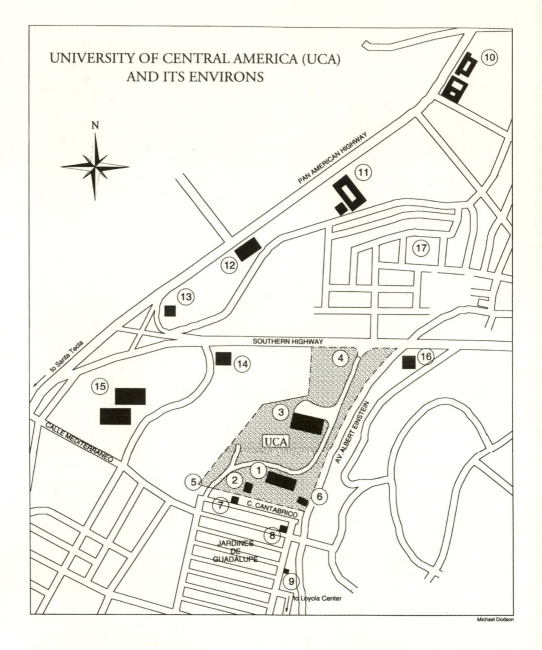

UNIVERSITY OF CENTRAL AMERICA (UCA) AND ITS ENVIRONS

1. Monsignor Romero Pastoral Center,
   new Jesuit residence
2. Chapel
3. Rectory
4. Main entrance
5. Pedestrian entrance
6. Gatehouse
7. Jesuit residence, 16, Calle Cantábrico
8. Jesuit residence, 50, Calle Mediterráneo

9. Curia, Jesuit Provincial's office
10. Estado Mayor, Army General Staff HQ
11. Military Academy
12. National Intelligence Directorate
13. Guadalupe Church
14. Mortgage Bank
15. Uninhabited apartment buildings
16. Democracy Tower
17. Military housing

INTRODUCTION

ONE NIGHT IN NOVEMBER

All this blood of martyrs spilled in El Salvador and throughout Latin America, far from bringing discouragement or despair, inspires a new spirit of struggle and new hope in our people. In this sense if we are not a "new world" nor a "new continent" at least we are clearly and verifiably—if perhaps not by those from beyond our shores—a continent of hope. And this is a particularly interesting symptom of something that may be new in the future, different from other continents that have no hope, as all they really have is fear.[1]

Ignacio Ellacuría, 1989

THE grounds of the university were unnaturally quiet that morning. On other weekdays students and staff began arriving soon after half past seven. Classes began at eight and the daily rhythm of a busy campus, host to some seven thousand students, took over. Ranged south from San Salvador's Southern Highway, the University of Central America "José Simeón Cañas" stretches across slopes rising away from the city. The university's functional, somewhat austere concrete buildings are scattered in a campus of gardens and trees, on this Wednesday fresh from the recent months of rain and brilliant green in the bright November sunlight. But there were no students, no staff to be seen, and from inside the university the only sounds were the whistles and trills of the birds in the trees, interrupted by the occasional shrill squawk of a parrot.[2]

From outside came the sounds of scattered gunfire, the dull thud of intermittent explosions, and, every now and then, the rumbling of an armored vehicle as the military patrolled the streets of Jardines de Guadalupe, the residential neighborhood behind the university. For while the silent classrooms, empty cafeteria, and network of steps and passages connecting the UCA's twenty-three buildings spoke of peace, the country outside was at war. This was the fourth day of an all-out military offensive launched by the guerrillas of the Farabundo Martí National Liberation Front (FMLN). It had started with a coordinated series of attacks on Saturday evening, and in the days following, the FMLN had made their most significant gains of the ten-year-old civil war. They were in control of entire sectors of the city and entrenched in some of the hardest fighting yet seen in the capital as the government and armed forces responded with

1

heavy artillery fire and air power, truly frightened that they might "lose" San Salvador to the rebels, or see it deteriorate into a Central American Beirut.

The concerns of the Jesuit priests running the university spanned the quiet inside and the turbulence beyond the boundaries of the UCA. As teachers and administrators, organizers of timetables and examinations, they were worried by the loss of at least a week's classes by the entire university. On Monday, with the university already surrounded by the army and its Southern Highway entrance closed to all vehicles, they had placed signs outside both this entrance and the pedestrian entrance in the southwestern corner of the campus. The signs read: "No classes today." Now it was Wednesday and no one knew how long those signs would have to stay there.

But the UCA had long been a university where teaching forms but one element of a triple-threaded activity. Without belittling the importance of teaching, the Jesuits, with university rector Ignacio Ellacuría at their head, dedicated the resources, time, and energy of the entire institution to what they termed "social projection" into the tragic reality of El Salvador. More than just teachers and priests, the men gathered on the third-floor of the building known by all as the "rectory" for a meeting of the university's board of directors were social scientists and political analysts with an unrivaled knowledge of the complex set of problems assailing the country. In its twenty-five-year history, the university they ran had assumed a strong sense of purpose within a society in crisis. In an interview on Spanish television years earlier, Ellacuría had explained that the university he led had "a very clear idea of what it has to do. . . . More than mold students, more than carry out research—although we do these two things—what the university has to do is set about solving the unacceptable problem of injustice in countries throughout Central America."[3]

Presiding over the meeting, Ignacio Ellacuría was a philosopher and theologian and the editor of the UCA's most prestigious publication, the monthly magazine *Estudios Centroamericanos (Central American Studies, or ECA)*. Even among his fellow Jesuits his bearing was of one accustomed to leadership: the slight tilt of his head as he listened, the focused concentration in his eyes, the measured authority and undoubted brilliance of what he had to say commanded attention from those who met him. The academic vice-rector, Ignacio Martín-Baró, or "Nacho" as he was most commonly known, spread his activities throughout the university. An innovative social psychologist, he had founded and now directed the Institute of Public Opinion, an enterprise whose polling and canvasing many had thought impossible in El Salvador's traumatized society. Segundo Montes had come down to this meeting from his office in the Institute for Human Rights, from where he also directed the university's Sociology Department. With his flowing beard, deep-set eyes, and direct and forceful energy, Montes cut a distinctive figure. Religious superior of this university community, within the UCA Montes was known as "Zeus."

With theologian Jon Sobrino, who was away at a conference in Thailand, Ellacuría, Martín-Baró, and Montes were the best known of the Jesuits of the UCA. The papers and books they had written, briefings and television appearances they had made, and interviews with local and foreign journalists they had given constituted a formidable body of work. But the commitment to "solving the unacceptable problem of injustice" in El Salvador was shared by the entire community, from the directors of the UCA's publishing and printing operations, Rodolfo Cardenal and Rogelio Pedraz, to theologians Amando López and Juan Ramón Moreno, economist Francisco Javier Ibisate, and administrator Miguel Francisco "Paco" Estrada.

It was not surprising then that the crisis facing the country should have been the Jesuits' prime concern at the Wednesday meeting. Like most of well-informed San Salvador, they had known an FMLN offensive was imminent, but the extent of the gains made in the first few days had taken them by surprise. As a body of analysts and observers they were convinced that what Martín-Baró had called, in an interview the week before the launching of the offensive, "the objective conditions for popular insurrection" did not exist.[4] Most worrying was the situation faced by the vast majority of the Salvadoran people, civilians already worn down by the war and economic attrition, unaligned with either side, and now in the midst of a battle zone. For the moment the FMLN occupied areas that were poor and heavily populated. All feared the civilian cost of the armed forces' counteroffensive. Artillery and aerial bombardment had left some families trapped in their homes without food, water or power; others were fleeing their neighborhoods, running through the streets beneath the paltry protection of white flags.

One of the Jesuits' employees, Lucía Barrera de Cerna, had telephoned to say that she and her family were evacuating their home in Soyapango, where the fighting was at its fiercest. Since 1981 Lucía had worked as a janitor in the rectory and in the *curia,* the Jesuit provincial's office some 200 meters uphill from the UCA in Jardines de Guadalupe. With her was her husband Jorge, a baker, and their four-year-old daughter.

Martín-Baró, who answered the telephone, immediately offered the family a room in the old residence of one of the two communities of UCA Jesuits, a house at number 16, Calle Cantábrico that backed onto the university chapel. This house was empty at the moment because the Jesuits who had been living there had recently completed their move into their new residence, inside the UCA on the second floor of the Monsignor Romero Pastoral Center.

Other employees, the cook Elba Ramos and her husband, night watchman, and gardener, Obdulio, lived with their daughter, Celina, in a house at the southeastern extreme of the university grounds. The family's house backed onto a street where the sounds of fighting and bombs kept them awake at night and this sent Elba to seek help from the Jesuits. "I'm sorry, Father," she explained to Francisco Javier Ibisate, "but in our house we can't sleep with all the noise there is in the night. You wouldn't have a little room where my daughter and I could come and sleep?" Ibisate went to Amando López, who oversaw the running of the buildings. "Heavens yes, let them sleep in there," was his answer, indicating an empty room alongside the new residence. "In there they'll get more peace and quiet."[5]

An inevitable topic of conversation at the meeting was the Jesuits' own security. Over the years the university had been the target of no less than sixteen bomb attacks, with abuse, threats, and wild accusations heaped on individual Jesuits and on the UCA as a whole by members of extreme right-wing organizations, the military, and the local press. The UCA was commonly labeled a hotbed of Marxist ideas where the minds of the Salvadoran youth were "poisoned" and guerrilla operations plotted. No evidence had ever been produced to support such accusations. But this was El Salvador, and everyone in the UCA that morning knew that lack of evidence did not necessarily provide an obstacle: tens of thousands of civilians had been murdered in the last ten years with scant regard for the law.

On Saturday night, soon after the launch of the offensive, three or four members of the FMLN on the run from the army had burst into the UCA. They blew open the gate at the southeastern corner of the university with a small bomb, fled through the new Jesuit residence, and disappeared into the night. The next morning a military patrol asked for and was given permission to inspect the damage done by the guerrilla unit. From that moment the UCA was placed under heavy military guard, with all who entered or left checked and the entry and exit of vehicles forbidden.

On Monday the Jesuits had worried about Ellacuría or "Ellacu," as he was known, getting caught by the curfew and having to spend a night at the airport. He was returning from a trip to Europe that evening, shortly before the six o'clock curfew began. Many of them may have been thinking about the 1980 murder and rape of the four American church-women on the road to La Libertad; the women had been followed from the airport by a pickup truck belonging to the National Guard. In the end, Ellacuría had arrived safely back at the UCA. The soldiers on the Southern Highway gate had stopped his car, but only until they realized who he was. Then they let him through. The Jesuits in the new residence were relieved to have the rector home. They quickly called the other community in number 50, Calle Mediterráneo, a few meters away in Jardines de Guadalupe, with news of his arrival. Then they listened to his account of the successes of his trip, which included the receipt of a $5,000 prize for the UCA he had brought back with him in a light brown case.

Scarcely half an hour after Ellacuría's return on Monday, the grounds of the UCA were invaded by a large military force and the new residence subjected to a detailed search. It was this search that was discussed when the conversation at the Wednesday meeting turned to the Jesuits' safety. While Rodolfo Cardenal had been deeply unsettled and had decided to sleep in Santa Tecla, a few kilometers south of the city, the others followed the line taken by Ellacuría: "They've come, they've searched us, and they've seen that we've got no weapons, nothing incriminating—we're safer for the fact that they have searched us." (Among those who stayed was 71-year-old Joaquín López y López—the oldest of the Jesuits and suffering from cancer, he was the only one not to work in the university he had helped to found twenty-five years earlier.) More frightening, they agreed, were the threats put out on the government-controlled radio station on Sunday, not twenty-four hours after the offensive began.

Facing a national emergency, the government and armed forces had assumed control of the airwaves from late Saturday evening. While this "national channel" allowed those who were unable to get home, or had lost track of a relative, to telephone in details of their whereabouts, other telephone calls, allegedly from members of the public, broadcast messages of a very different kind: "The Jesuits are communists—kill them!" "Get Ellacuría—off with his head!" "The Jesuits of the UCA are subversives and should be killed," and so on.[6] The Jesuits were not the only targets. Similar threats were broadcast against leaders of the FMLN, members of the democratic opposition, and even against the archbishop, Monsignor Arturo Rivera Damas, but this was hardly reassuring. "The threats," as one Jesuit put it, "were really something that induced you to go out and kill."

These worries aside, the Jesuits agreed that they were safe inside the UCA, in premises that had been searched and found "clean" by the army, and in a zone of the city too thoroughly and conspicuously militarized for "accidents" to occur. One of the Jesuits in the university that morning, Rogelio Pedraz, lived in a house in San Antonio Abad on the other side of the city and was of two minds as to whether to return home. At the base of the San Salvador volcano, San Antonio Abad is a poor neighborhood where makeshift huts cluster tightly against crumbling buildings. Long known for political activism, its proximity to guerrilla redoubts on the flanks of the volcano meant there had been plenty of fighting there since the offensive began. "I thought I'd be safer here in the UCA, but in the end I decided to go," he remembered. "I have this mania about clean clothes in the morning, and I hadn't a spare set with me." The others agreed that it was too risky for him to try to take his car out through the army cordon closing the university entrance, so Amando López and Juan Ramón Moreno drove him home at midday, across a tense, almost deserted San Salvador. The few vehicles in the streets had white flags protruding from their front windows or jammed into the antenna sockets. The people had their heads low as they hurried home, their faces drawn and frightened.

The university remained strangely quiet. That afternoon, Ibisate thought he would take advantage of the lack of students and get on with some of his own work at one of the concrete tables scattered under the trees in the upper levels of the campus. For several hours he worked away undisturbed. While the occasional sounds of conflict could still be heard, he was barely conscious of them until, at about four thirty, he became aware that the fighting was coming closer. Now it was obvious that there was a violent confrontation in Antiguo Cuscatlán, the neighborhood behind Jardines de Guadalupe. Soon stray bullets were skimming the buildings behind the UCA and whistling through the leaves of the trees above his head. He decided it was time to go home. Ibisate was one of those who lived in the Mediterráneo house; as he made his way out through the back of the UCA a neighbor called out a greeting, adding, "I should get home quick if I were you."

There is no curfew breaking in El Salvador. By six o'clock, under the stringent emergency measures introduced on Sunday, the streets were deserted as families and households together faced a long and frightening, and, in many cases, dark and hungry night. The Jesuits ate supper, continued the discussions of the day, answered a few telephone calls from friends and pupils, and went to bed.

But it was a noisy night, and Ibisate for one found it difficult to sleep. He was awakened at midnight by a low-flying airplane, then drifted back to sleep until a barrage of gunfire at about two in the morning stirred him once again. Wide awake now, he got up and went into the kitchen to make himself a cup of coffee. As he sat there drinking his coffee and smoking a cigarette he tried to work out where the shooting was. He thought it most likely that it came from the corner near the supermarket a block from the house. He was tempted to look through the keyhole to see what he could make out, but decided against it. He could hear the sound of breaking glass and remembered that on Saturday, as the offensive started, an attack had been launched on that same corner. It had been close enough for a stray bullet to come hissing through a second-floor window. Better not to risk the chance of another such bullet with his eye at the keyhole. Before three o'clock the shooting died down. Ibisate drained his coffee and went back to bed, determined to try to get some rest before morning.

IN a version of events released to the public in January 1990, Lieutenant José Ricardo Espinoza would remember that he received the order over his radio at about 10:15 P.M. that Wednesday. He was to gather his unit at the Captain General Gerardo Barrios Military Academy, named after the general who was president of the country at the time of its founding in 1867. Like every other officer in the Salvadoran army, Espinoza had been formed by what he learned within its walls. Unlike most other officers, but not all, when he entered the academy he was a graduate of a high school run by Jesuits, the *Externado San José.*[7]

A statue of the portly Barrios presides over the forecourt of the academy that bears his name. He is still invoked in a maneuver that seems strange to the eyes of a visitor. In normal times the academy swarms with lithe, pristinely turned out cadets. At any moment an officer may call one to attention. Before receiving the order the cadet executes a distinctive jump, landing squarely on his feet, legs slightly bent, while shouting the one word, "Barrios!" In their four years at the academy the cadets learn absolute loyalty to an institution whose motto is prominently displayed: "As long as the institution lives, the republic lives." The first and last proof of this loyalty is obedience to any and all orders.

Twenty-eight-year-old Espinoza was the commander of a commando unit within the elite Atlacatl Battalion. With the dark complexion and compact build typical of his native Sonsonate, he had benefited from some of the most specialized training available to any young officer. When he was younger he had wanted to study engineering at the UCA, but it had not been easy for his family to support his brother through medical school and so they had encouraged him to enter the armed forces. He had originally planned to become a pilot and then leave and work for a commercial airline, but in 1986 that had all gone wrong. He had run into trouble and been dismissed for what his military record had called "serious errors committed within the service."[8] The English he learned for flying school, however, had stood him in good stead; he had been given responsibility in the Atlacatl—where he had been since 1987—and had spent several months in the last year on an advanced commando course at the Special Warfare Center at Fort Bragg, North Carolina.

Until the previous Monday, Espinoza's entire company had been involved in a training exercise overseen by thirteen U.S. Special Forces experts flown in from Fort Bragg. The exercise was suspended when the army High Command called all available troops into active service to combat the FMLN offensive. Moving into the capital from the Atlacatl base in La Libertad, Espinoza and his sublieutenant Gonzalo Guevara Cerritos had reported directly to the general staff headquarters, the *estado mayor.* The commando unit was assigned to the military academy, under its director Colonel Guillermo Benavides. This was the operational center of a newly created security zone that included all the central military installations, nearby residential neighborhoods, and the UCA, a kilometer away to the south. The search of the university had been their first assignment.

Two days after that search, Espinoza would remember, he received his orders and returned to the academy with four of his eight patrols— those under the command of soldiers nicknamed Satan, Cursed, Streak, and Lightning. Nahum, Savage, Samson, and Lizard's patrols had been beyond radio contact. Shortly after 11:00 P.M. he had been ordered to present himself to Colonel Benavides in the operations center. He was joined by Guevara, and a lieutenant from his own *tanda,* or graduating class from the military academy, Yusshy Mendoza Vallecillos, currently posted to the academy itself.

Benavides was a relatively undistinguished member of the armed forces' most powerful *tanda.* The class of '66 had been larger than the classes before and after it and had always been known as the *tandona,* the "big class." But it was also unusual in containing a remarkably high proportion of the sons, nephews, and godsons of the ranking colonels of the day. Behind-the-scenes influence had helped ensure that these boys from the most tightly-knit military families should be put together and, following the time-honored loyalty of *tanda* members to each other, thereafter forever stick together. Members of the *tandona* now dominated the military hierarchy, from Chief of Staff Colonel René Emilio Ponce on down.

Colonel Benavides had returned from a crisis meeting in the *estado mayor* attended by around twenty-five of the armed forces' most senior commanders. In all the years of this war, things had never looked worse for the army. According to their accounts, Benavides suggested to the three young officers in front of him that they would have more privacy in his office. Once there he came straight to the point, ordering the assassination of those he described as "the intellectual leaders" of the guerrillas: "This is a situation in which it is them or us. We're going to begin at the top. Within our sector there is the university and Ellacuría is in there." Turning to Espinoza he added, "You did the search and your men know the site. Use the same layout as on the day of the search. He must be eliminated—and I don't want witnesses." Lieutenant Mendoza was to accompany them to make sure there were "no problems." Espinoza pointed out the seriousness of what he was being ordered to do. "Don't worry," answered Benavides. "You have my support."

Mendoza withdrew to his quarters while Espinoza and Guevara went to brief their men. Patrol leader Antonio Ramiro Avalos Vargas, nick-named "Satan" or "Toad," would remember being told that they were going to carry out a delicate mission—one that had been ordered by the "higher-ups." They were to find and kill some priests inside the UCA, because the priests were the leaders of the "delinquent terrorists" (as most members of the armed forces refer to the FMLN). The priests, he learned, were in it up to the hilt; backing up the terrorists with logistical assistance as well as masterminding their operations against military targets and the civilian population.

After midnight the commandos gathered outside the academy's central guard post. There were about thirty-six of them, but not all could fit into the two beige Ford pickups they were to use for transport. Those left behind would have to be collected on a return trip. As the men sat waiting for their officers to order the departure, Lieutenant Yusshy Mendoza emerged from inside. He carried an AK47 rifle and its loading chambers and the army's standard issue M16. "Which of you knows and can handle this weapon?" he asked, approaching the pickups and brandishing the AK47. "Pilijay!" they chorused back, referring to Oscar Mariano Amaya Grimaldi by his nickname. "Pilijay can handle that weapon."[9] A private in Avalos's patrol, Amaya climbed out of the pickup and went to collect his weapon. He had some three months' experience with an AK47, although it was not a usual combat weapon. To most of El Salvador, a Russian-made AK47 had "FMLN" written all over it, so its use within the army tended to be reserved for special operations such as this one. Amaya was not impressed with this particular AK47; from the most rudimentary checking over he considered it so dirty as to be inoperable. Sergeant Oscar Solorzano Esquivel immediately climbed down from a pickup and offered him oil, a rod, and a cloth to clean it up.

The pickups pulled out of the military academy and turned left up the highway toward Santa Tecla. Espinoza and Mendoza were in the lead vehicle, while Guevara was at the wheel of the one behind. The men were tense. They all knew they were being sent to kill, but some were unclear as to who they would be killing. Clutching the newly cleaned AK47, Amaya reckoned that, given the situation the country was in, it must be terrorist leaders they were after.

Turning left at Guadalupe Church, the trucks followed the access road onto the Southern Highway, then uphill to the Mortgage Bank behind the UCA. The men were unloaded beside some uninhabited apartment buildings, to the west of the university. Espinoza whistled and they were soon joined by twenty to twenty-five more men, the rest of the commando section and some additional reinforcements. Gathering around their commander, they learned that they had received an order to eliminate the intellectual leaders of the guerrillas. These men were inside the UCA and it was Pilijay who would actually kill them. Pilijay understood the importance of his role in the operation for the first time; as Lieutenant Mendoza told him, "You're the key man." At the moment of withdrawal there would be a flare, and the men would simulate a confrontation between themselves and the terrorists.

It was a clear night with a bright moon. Across the city, units like theirs were out in force, but it was only in this area that the electricity was out. They had never thought things would get so bad. Only months ago their colonel, León Linares, had assured them that the terrorists were on the retreat, which was why they wanted to negotiate. And now this! But they would show them, they were the Atlacatl, after all, "El Salvador's best," as their battalion chant went. "Who are you?" the officers demanded several times a day. "Special Forces of the Atlacatl, El Salvador's best!" came the answer. "How long for?" "All our lives! All our lives!" "Until when?" "Always, always, always, Atlacatl!" They were the Atlacatl. People were afraid of the Atlacatl.

At approximately 1:00 A.M. Espinoza gave the order to march and, forming a column, the entire unit headed toward the UCA, crossing Calle

Mediterráneo to reach its entrance. Espinoza turned to Amaya who was walking beside him with his AK47: "Hide that shit!" The gates were quickly forced open. Inside the grounds all was quiet. The men walked down some steps, along a path bordered by tall trees whose leaves rustled faintly in the still night. Turning right, they followed a road that curves around the southern side of the university. They passed a covered parking lot, then a line of low buildings on their right. Next to them the steep angles of the chapel roof shone white in the moonlight.

As they approached a two-story building beyond the chapel, the lieutenants told their men that this was the residence of the "terrorist priests." Turning right beyond the chapel and up some steps, Avalos was one of the first to come to a locked door. Next to it was a high fence of meshed wire, easy to climb over, surrounding a garden. On the other side, a covered passageway with rooms opening off to the left led toward some steps at the far end. To the right and beyond the building, the garden was open, with a wide expanse of grass.

By the time Sergeant Tomás Zarpate Castillo got to the door, it was already open. He walked through and, a few meters into the passageway, turned as he heard a sound from inside one of the rooms. He looked in and a shaft of moonlight glancing through the open door showed two women, one older and larger than the other. The older one was seated on one of two divan beds while the other was lying, covered, beside her. Mendoza was just behind him with a lamp that helped them make out the form of the younger woman. He ordered Zarpate to stay there and not let anyone leave. Mendoza then continued to search the building, moving through a kitchen, a dining room, and a sort of laundry area with a clothesline strung across it. All the rooms were empty.

The other commandos completely surrounded the building. To the left of the steps at the end of the passageway was the corridor they had searched on Monday. They knew that the priests' bedrooms were off this corridor, which led directly out into the wide grassy area at the front. At the far end of the corridor one soldier had found a piece of wood with which he was forcing a door that led onto a balcony above the road. Amaya came up behind him and saw that there was a hammock slung across the balcony. At that moment a man in a coffee-colored nightshirt came out and stopped beside the hammock, saying, "Wait, I'll open up, but stop making such a racket," and then disappeared inside again. From the front of the building, Amaya heard someone call out to him, "Hey, Pilijay, they're coming out here."

When he got to the door at the other end of the corridor, Amaya saw that the man in the nightshirt was already outside, near Sergeant Solorzano, "Hercules" Avalos, and another soldier from their unit. Four other residents of the building were coming out of the corridor onto the grassy area in front of the building. Solorzano took some men from his patrol inside, leaving Amaya and Avalos alone with the five. Realizing that it was just the two of them covering five men, Avalos ordered them to lie down and spread out on the ground. While they did not look dangerous—they were quite old and unarmed, some wore pajamas with slippers or sandals, some had trousers and shoes—Amaya knew that it was their brains that counted. At that moment, as he would remember later, he was sure they were delinquent terrorists.

Lieutenants Espinoza and Mendoza were over near the steps, a few meters away from where the men had the priests on the ground. Espinoza called Avalos over to him and asked, "When are you going to proceed?" Avalos understood this as an order to eliminate the five men. He crossed back over to where Amaya stood watch at the head of the first three, who were stretched out in a line. Leaning toward him, he whispered into his ear, "Let's proceed."

Some thirty meters away, in the room at the back of the number 16, Calle Cantábrico house lent them by Martín-Baró earlier that day, Lucía and Jorge Cerna were awakened by gunfire. They thought it came from the trees to the west of where they were, but then they heard the sounds of banging, breaking glass, and voices coming from the Pastoral Center. Leaving her husband to watch over their little girl, Geraldina, Lucía went into the room next door. Peering through the curtains she had a partial view of the passageway that led from the gate to the chapel up toward where the Jesuits were sleeping—not that there was any chance they'd be sleeping now. Lucía could see five men standing near the gate. Three of them were in shadow, but the other two were lit by the moon. Their faces were hidden by caps and visors, but she saw their camouflage uniforms and the guns they were carrying. At that moment she heard the voice of Father Nacho cry out, "This is an injustice! This is an abomination!"[10]

"Quick, quick, give it to them quickly!" Amaya began to fire at the three men he had in front of him. He could see that he was getting them in their heads. Avalos shot at the heads and bodies of the two closest to him with his M16. Amaya then opened up at all five, although some of his shots at Avalos's two went wild, hitting the wall behind.

Espinoza remembered that he felt bad about what was happening, that he tried to move away from the shooting, and that his eyes were filled with tears. One of the men on the ground, Segundo Montes, had been his headmaster at the *Externado*. Another, Ignacio Ellacuría, he would recognize anywhere; his father used to switch the channel when he appeared on television. But he had his orders. "Put them inside, even if you have to drag them," he told a corporal, Cota Hernández, standing nearby. Cota only had time to drag one body into the corridor, leaving it in the second bedroom on the right. He did not notice the shoe that fell off in the doorway, nor the book that slid from the bookshelf inside the bedroom and fell into the blood still flowing from the body. The book was by a German theologian, Jürgen Moltmann. Its title, *The Crucified God.*

Still guarding the two women down the passageway, Zarpate heard someone shouting, "Now!" and then a volley of shooting. He fired at the women in front of him, shot after shot. When the women were silent, and he was sure that they were dead, he turned and left through the door that led toward the chapel.

The shots were also heard by the soldiers downstairs in the Pastoral Center. They had broken the glass door, entered the building, and begun to burn computers, books, and documents. In one room they found a large portrait of Archbishop Romero. They aimed at his heart.

Leaving his soldiers in the downstairs offices, Corporal Angel Pérez Vásquez climbed up the steep bank on the road side of the building to the corridor above. He went around to the front and saw bodies lying on the grass. At that moment a sixth man emerged into the corridor. He was older than the others, thin, quite frail looking, and wearing a white undershirt. He came out, saw his companions lying dead on the grass and turned to go back in again, saying, as he went, "Don't kill me. I don't belong to any organization." Several of the soldiers called out to him, "Out you come, *compa!*" but he paid no attention. As he turned to enter a room on the left, a soldier fired at him. Pérez saw him fall and moved in to search the room. As he stepped over the old man, a hand reached out and groped for his feet. Pérez stepped back and fired at him twice. Then again and again.

Avalos and Jorge Alberto Sierra Ascencio were heading down the passageway toward the gate leading to the chapel when Avalos heard muffled sounds coming from a room on his right. Standing in the doorway he lit a match and saw that there were two women lying on the floor, embracing and moaning in a widening pool of blood. He ordered Sierra to finish them off. The soldier fired off a round of cartridges from his M16 until both women were quiet.

Once the main business of the operation was completed, the men began to draw back. Amaya was in the parking lot drinking a Pilsner beer when the lieutenants arrived. Espinoza asked the soldiers with him whether they had seen the flare they had agreed would be the signal for the retreat. As nobody was sure whether the flare had gone up, Cota fired his 40mm grenade launcher into the air as a sign for the others that it was time to go. Most of the unit now began to withdraw through the same entrance they had used earlier. One of the soldiers had a light brown case belonging to the priests in his hand. His beer finished, the can cast aside, Amaya volunteered to stay behind with Sergeant "Savage's" patrol to feign a confrontation between themselves and the terrorists. They fired at the building and at the cars parked in the lot with everything they had. By 3:00 A.M. they too were back in the military academy.

On their way out, the commandos noticed the sign hanging on the front of the gate. "No classes today," it read. They took it down, turned it over, wrote "The FMLN executed the enemy spies. Victory or death, FMLN," and hung it back on the gate.

It was November 16, 1989.

CHAPTER ONE

EARLY DAYS IN A NEW WORLD

A small stain of color on the map of America, a small rectangle in the Central American isthmus, drew my attention most particularly one day in Washington toward the end of November 1947. I had just received the order to move to El Salvador, where I had been destined to our Legation in the capital of this diminutive Spanish American country. Until then the republic had meant for me only a few geographical and historical facts. Around 25,000 square kilometers, some two million inhabitants. Coffee was its principal product. A mountain range of volcanoes . . . .[1]

Dr. Alberto de Mestas
Secretary of the Spanish Legation in El Salvador, 1949

FORTY years earlier Ignacio Ellacuría was among the six novices in black wool soutanes and black felt hats who stepped gingerly out of an airplane into the white heat of El Salvador's dry season. Behind them came the novice master who had shepherded this small group of boys on train, boat, and finally airplane from the old world to the new, from Spain to Spanish America, to this dusty airport on the outskirts of San Salvador.

The journey had been a long one. They had left Bilbao nearly a month before, on February 26, 1949, traveling by train across northern Spain to Barcelona. They took time there for a brief pilgrimage to the cave in nearby Manresa where, in 1522, St. Ignatius, the founder of the Society of Jesus, experimented in prayer, meditation, and penances in a painful process toward the key conversion of his life. After that had come an Atlantic crossing to Barranquilla in Colombia and then flights to Panama and El Salvador.

Their families had come to the station to see them off, but it had been a difficult parting for all of them. Bravado fought with emotion as one young Jesuit kissed his mother goodbye, saying *"Hasta el cielo!"*—"I'll see you in heaven!"[2] They had only been novices a year, but they were being sent to found a new novitiate in the vice-province of Central America. They had very little idea of what they would find when they got there, but there was something romantic, mystical even, about the idea of their "mission." They knew, moreover, that they would be the first of many from their province to make the long journey west: while vocations abounded in intensely Catholic Spain, the countries of Latin America had relatively few aspirants to the priesthood and a rapidly growing population in need of education and pastoral attention. Although it wouldn't be a question of conversion, they thought of the people they would find there as primitive, with the number of children born out of wedlock, for example, indicative of the challenges that would face them in the years ahead. "We saw our mission," a Jesuit who arrived in the mid-1950s put it, "as being to make good European Catholics of the Salvadorans—although perhaps second class ones at that."[3]

As the train pulled away on the first leg of the long journey to El Salvador, they leaned out of the window and waved. Nobody commented on the tears they saw run down the face of Señor Ellacuría, an oculist from Portugalete outside Bilbao. Born on November 9, 1930, his son Ignacio was the fourth of his five boys, and also the fourth to enter the religious life. He was a reserved and somewhat intense youth and his teachers at the Jesuit school of Tudela did not immediately think of him when it came to considering which of their pupils might have vocations. At the end of their seventh year in school, a small group of likely candidates was gathered together by the senior boys' spiritual father. Ignacio was not among them, but came forward of his own accord to join the Jesuits the following year.[4] On September 14, 1947 he had entered the Jesuit novitiate in Loyola, the home of St. Ignatius.

It would have been difficult for the six novices to determine whether they volunteered or were ordered to go to Central America. According to the Jesuits' own laws—the Constitutions of the Society of Jesus, first approved in 1558—novices could not be obliged to fulfill the orders of their Jesuit superiors before taking their vows of poverty, chastity, and obedience at the end of the two-year novitiate. Some months earlier the novice master had asked the assembled novices for volunteers to go to Central America. He had advised the eager young men gathered before him to consider it seriously for a couple of days and then, if they felt such a mission to be in line with their particular vocation, to put their name on a piece of paper and return it to him.

Three or four days later Fabián Zarrabe was summoned by the novice master: "Fabián, what's the matter with you? Everyone else has put their names on pieces of paper and you haven't given me anything. What is it? Don't you want to go to America?" Somewhat confused, the novice explained, "But you said that if God wanted one of us to go he'd make it clear—nothing's happened. He hasn't sent me any sign." "But you'd go?"

"Yes, of course." A week or so later the novice master gathered the novices together and read out a list of six names, among them that of Fabián Zarrabe.[5] "We had a very simple understanding of obedience back then," Ellacuría would remember, decades later, in an interview with a Spanish newspaper. "It wasn't a sacrifice or heroism. And I have never regretted having begun an American life."[6]

Although drawn from the provinces of Eastern and Western Castile, novice master Miguel Elizondo, Ellacuría, and the other young Spaniards who arrived with him were from the Basque region, the area spreading from southern France and the western end of the Pyrenees into Spain. Of distinct history, language, and culture to the rest of Spain, and indeed the rest of Europe, the Basques' independence of mind and spirit had combined with their intense sense of regional identity in their opposition to the forces of General Franco during the Spanish Civil War. Franco's triumph had brought the consolidation of "national catholicism," with its union of the army, the political power of the Falange, and the institutionalized Catholic Church, but the Basques had continued to challenge the monolithic structures of Franco's Spain. The position of the Basque Jesuits was a curious one. While Franco rapidly reinstated the Society, which had been expelled from the Spanish Republic in 1931, and surrounded himself with Jesuit advisers, in 1948 he had called upon his close relationship with the Jesuit authorities to have the Basque Jesuits, in what had been the Province of Castile, divided into two separate provinces.

But for the novices who on March 22, 1949, were driven from the airport to the new novitiate beside the Church of the Carmen in Santa Tecla, a market town a few kilometers to the south of San Salvador, as for those who followed them out from Spain in the following years, this political history receded quickly. A new life lay before them and the long journey only increased their sense of adventure. The violent contrasts of Central America that awaited them—the clear light and tropical climate, volcanoes, lakes, and palm-fringed coastline—were quite different from anything they had experienced before.

IN 1949 tiny El Salvador, just over 21,000 kilometers square, was in the midst of a period of spectacular growth in its population. With only 783,000 inhabitants in 1900, Salvadorans would number over 1.8 million by 1960 and 5 million by the early 1980s.[7] Infant mortality was running at 93 per 1,000 births and illiteracy at 86 percent, yet nowhere in the Americas was the population more densely packed, nor the scant resources of land more tirelessly worked.[8] The Spanish diplomat Alberto de Mestas was torn between his wonder at the majesty of the country's landscape and the sheer quantity and industriousness of its people as he chronicled his first impressions as a visitor to El Salvador: "Every inch of land accessible to the hand of man is cultivated, at times not without the great risk that by extending the cultivation to some areas erosion or drought will lead to the exhaustion of the fertile soils."[9]

Land in El Salvador meant one thing: coffee. Since the mid-nineteenth century, when the European taste for coffee led it to replace El Salvador's traditional crop of indigo, no country in Central America had become more dependent on any single crop, no oligarchy more identified with the production and trade of any one product. "Coffee," in the words of David Browning in his definitive study of Salvadoran land and society, "was king; it earned the country's foreign exchange, paid for its imports, provided the revenue for central and local government, financed the construction of roads, ports, and railways, gave employment—permanent or seasonal—to a large part of the population, and made the fortunes of a few."[10] The "few" were indeed very few; while the famous "fourteen families" of the Salvadoran oligarchy is something of an exaggeration, a small number of families comprising this coffee-producing elite did effectively run the country.

Seventeen years before the novices' arrival there had been an uprising of Indians too long exploited by their *cafetelero* masters in western El Salvador. They were joined by small groups of workers led by Augustín Farabundo Martí and the nascent Communist Party. No one, not then and not later, could forget what had happened next as General Maximiliano Hernández Martínez suppressed the rebellion. While estimates vary as to how many were killed in the ensuing *matanza* or massacre, 30,000 is the number most frequently cited. The army and security forces took to the streets and killed virtually all who crossed their paths. Martí himself was captured and shot by a firing squad; years later he would rise again in a revolutionary movement that would take his name. The killing—for fighting it could not be called—lasted only a few days, yet "1932" as the uprising and its suppression are commonly referred to, is with El Salvador still. "We all were born half-dead in 1932," the poet Roqué Dalton would write. "We survived but half alive."[11]

The year 1932 also heralded a period in Salvadoran history in which the oligarchy found its interests safeguarded by successive generations of the armed forces. General Martínez was finally ousted in 1944. The ensuing years saw internal struggle between conservatives and modernizers as some individuals recognized that the price of stability might be some kind of change. Among such men was Colonel Oscar Osorio, who came to power in December 1948 as the leader of a successful coup. Consistently high coffee prices had so far prevented serious unrest, but Osorio and the more progressive elements of the ruling elite were moving towards at least tacit agreement with the observations made only a few months earlier by U.S. Ambassador Albert F. Nufer: "El Salvador's economy, which is based on a single crop, coffee, is necessarily unstable. This, together with the fact that the bulk of the population exists on a bare subsistence level, creates conditions favorable to periodic political disturbance; has at times detracted from the effectiveness of El Salvador's cooperation in international affairs; and affords fertile soil for the seeds of communism."[12]

Santa Tecla was a small town of, in 1949, approximately 26,000 people.[13] Thirteen kilometers south of San Salvador and at a greater altitude, it was cooler and greener than the capital. Its population, like that of most of El Salvador, was largely *mestizo,* of mixed Spanish and Indian blood. Unlike neighboring Guatemala, Spanish was spoken throughout the country. But the poverty the novices saw all about them was qualitatively different from anything they had seen before. The children ran barefoot in the dust and stones of the street. The women spent long hours working, carrying water, grinding corn to make the heavy corn dough or *masa,* patting the warm round wedges of dough flat into thick *tortillas,* and cooking them as the staple of every meal.

El Salvador, as the young Jesuits soon discovered on their visits to the local prisons and hospitals and their "pilgrimages" through the country-side with the archbishop, Monsignor Luis Chávez y González, was a deeply religious country. Dressed like priests in their soutanes, the novices were welcomed as "little fathers," *padrecitos,* wherever they went. Once away from the city, the archbishop would send them around the villages, begging door to door for food. The generosity of the *campesinos* who gave a banana, some beans or a *tortilla,* a couple of mangos or a slice of melon, was something that deeply impressed them. No less obvious was the extravagant wealth and the easy assumption of power over others' lives taken for granted by the Salvadoran elite. One young Jesuit had been shocked by the boys studying at the Jesuits' high school, the *Externado San José.* As a novice he had been sent to help oversee the senior boys' retreat. He had listened in amazement as the priest in charge began the session by calmly asking all the boys to "hand in their pistols" and within a few minutes he found himself standing guard over a pile of twenty-odd weapons. And why did they have the pistols in the first place? Because "all those Indians," the boys and their families believed, might do them some harm, and they had a "right" to self-defense.[14]

The Society of Jesus was well established in Central America. Jesuits had first arrived in Guatemala in 1579, only seven years after they came to Mexico, and three decades after the first Jesuits in the New World landed in Brazil in 1549.[15] During the seventeenth and eighteenth centuries the Jesuits' influence spread throughout the continent. Missions, schools, universities, and houses of religious retreat and formation sprang up from California to Chile. But the Jesuits became best known for the success of the "reductions" of the Guaraní Indians in Paraguay and Brazil. By the mid-eighteenth century these autonomous, highly disciplined communities had a population of between 150,000 and 300,000 people. Thirty separate missions formed a "republic" of some 390,000 square kilometers—an area greater than that of half of France.[16] In 1768, however, in a climate of increasing hostility toward the Jesuits that would culminate in the suppression of the entire Society in 1773, Carlos III of Spain signed a decree banishing all Jesuits from Paraguay. The terms of his order leave no doubt as to the depth of his hatred of the Society: "If, after the embarkation, there is left a single Jesuit, be he ill or dying, you shall be punished with death. I, the King."[17]

A small number of Jesuits came from Guatemala to El Salvador in 1864. They did not stay long. In 1872 all Jesuits were expelled from El Salvador as part of a wave of Jesuit expulsions throughout Central America. There was time only to found the residence and chapel dedicated to the Sacred Heart in San Salvador and start missions in Sonsonate and Izalco. They would not return to the country until August 1914 when a small boat, aptly titled "Salvador," docked at the port of Acajutla. It carried a group of Mexican Jesuits fleeing the religious persecution unleashed by the Mexican revolution. The Jesuits were quickly installed in a building beside the Church of San José; by March of the following year they had undertaken the administration of El Salvador's seminary. Six years later, they responded to the demand for education with the founding of a school, the Colegio San José. It soon became known as the *Externado San José*, to distinguish it from the seminary or *Internado*, where seminarians were "interned" throughout the year.

The Jesuits in Central America were limited to the status of "mission" until February 7, 1937, when the Vice-Province of Central America—embracing Guatemala, El Salvador, Nicaragua, Panama, and Costa Rica—was created as a dependency of the Spanish Province of Castile.[18] Little by little the Mexican Jesuits returned to their country; by

1949 there were only 7 Mexicans left in Central America and 103 of the total of 150 Jesuits were from Spain. While relations between the Spaniards and the Central Americans were generally good, the mature Jesuits arriving from "the mother country" at times brought their political differences with them: in the words of one Basque Jesuit, there were occasions when, in these early years, "to be a Basque was to be a heretic."[19]

But for the six young Spaniards who arrived in El Salvador in 1949, for the "generations" who would follow them in subsequent years, and for the Central American novices they joined, their experience of each other and their life as Central American Jesuits was perpetually marked by their youth. "Those who came here as priests," remarked one Jesuit who had lived in Central America since he was a teenager, "died as Spaniards— something it would be hard to say of those of us who came here as eighteen-year-olds."[20]

IN Miguel Elizondo, the novices had a master of enormous common sense and profound spirituality. These two characteristics provided a foundation for the young Jesuits who passed through his hands that they would carry with them through their lives. Elizondo had embarked on the journey to Central America with "general and anecdotal ideas" about what he might find there. The existing "dependency" of the Central American vice-province on the province in Spain had promoted a certain amount of exchange, both of Jesuits and of information, between the two regions. But the uniformity of the teaching of the Catholic Church in those days had not led him, or anyone else, to expect anything of the Central American Church other than, "the only thing that existed, traditional European Catholicism, which was what we supposed had been brought over."[21]

Elizondo brought with him the freedom of spirit that is an essential component of the Jesuit's "availability" for the mission that might be asked of him "*Ad maiorem Dei gloriam*"—the motto of the Society of Jesus meaning, "for the greater glory of God." "I felt totally free of my past, of my antecedents as a Jesuit and as novice master, although I was a 'novice' in that myself." This freedom was something he was at pains to instill in his novices, constantly picking up on the Spaniards who, fresh from their year in the novitiate in Loyola, would begin sentences "But in Spain we—" "None of that, none of that. We're not in Spain now. Just because something is one way in Spain, it does not have to be the same in El Salvador." With what a Guatemalan Jesuit would describe as "a great capacity to understand that we tropicals were different,"[22] Elizondo would insist that it was the Spaniards who had to work the hardest. Far from being treated as superior, the burden was on them to assume the identity of their Central American *compañeros*. From now on, Central America would be their common home.

For the Spaniards, there were many things that were different about their daily life in Santa Tecla. In Spain their lives had been constricted by a complicated series of rules and regulations. Novices lived in a world apart, their very isolation made clear to all by their shaved heads and black soutanes. But Elizondo quickly reordered the novitiate's priorities. "What's important here?" one Jesuit remembers him saying. "This isn't about making you all look ridiculous by shaving your hair—and with this heat, well, if the clothes must go, then the clothes must go."[23] Novices in Spain had not been allowed to play soccer—a great deprivation in a country where soccer is the national sport. Basketball and handball were allowed, but had to be played within the restrictions imposed by the flowing material of the full-length soutane. Many of the novices were keen sportsmen, sharing with Ellacuría a devotion to the local team, Athlétic Bilbao.[24] And in El Salvador, to their great delight, soccer was allowed— without soutane, of course. Segundo Montes, a novice who had arrived from Valladolid in 1951, was remembered by his novice master as "somewhat adolescent," as his wild exertions brought the novitiate's roof tiles clattering into the courtyard.

Common sense also marked Elizondo's approach to the novices' spiritual development. "Well, you want to be Jesuits. What is it that St. Ignatius wanted the Jesuits to be?" he would ask new novices. "Have you read the Constitutions? No? Well, then, let's read them."[25] Wanting to form Jesuits with the greatest sense of the spirit of St. Ignatius that he could, Elizondo began by stripping away "the many things they were supposed to do in order to be a good Jesuit—the many rules to obey, virtues to practice, devotions to keep, and so on in order to reach what one can consider essential in the vocation to the Society."[26] Some of the novices were surprised by the fluidity of the timetable, the concentration on interior development rather than more traditional forms of physical mortification (although for the tougher ones there was some of that too), but pleased to find that it was possible to spend hours just talking in a spirit of real *compañerismo* with Elizondo and the others as each novice came to learn the importance given by St. Ignatius to his "companions of Jesus" being a true community of "friends in the Lord."[27]

Although there existed a freedom from some of the formalities, to imagine the life of the novices as easy, in any sense, would be quite wrong.

They were being prepared for the peculiar rigor of the spirituality St. Ignatius outlined in a slim volume titled *The Spiritual Exercises*. This rigor is necessary to sustain what the present general of the Jesuits, Peter Kolvenbach, has called "a spirituality of tensions": "The Society is simultaneously contemplative and active, universal yet part of a specific culture, organized as a community, yet orientated toward mission. There is always a danger of losing a proper balance between these values in tension."[28] Born of St. Ignatius's conception of the Society at a moment of profound historical crisis, these tensions and the very difficulties involved in maintaining a balance between them have been fundamental to the Society's capacity to survive nearly five centuries of a changing world.

The *Exercises* form an "open" text in the most contemporary sense of the word. Written by St. Ignatius from the experience of his own spiritual journey, they may be read by a reader, but not in any way understood as the components of an essay on spirituality. The *Exercises* are both "given"—in the case of novices by the novice master—and then "experienced" by each individual participant or "practicant." They are structured around a four-week period that charts a path by which each practicant may be prepared to fulfill what St. Ignatius established as the central tenet of the Jesuit life: "to search and find the will of God so that, once it is found, it may be completed."[29] When recruiting his first "companions" in the early days of the Society, the first thing St. Ignatius would do was personally give them the *Exercises*. A Jesuit will return to the *Exercises* throughout his life in annual retreats (usually compressing the full four weeks into one) for a renewal of all that is most specifically "Ignatian" about his identity and his mission.

The preparation for the vows of poverty, chastity, and obedience that end the two-year novitiate was one that brought the tensions of Ignatian spirituality alive: it was a preparation for the difficult and lifelong task of living these vows as a liberation rather than a series of restrictions that jeopardize the possibility of a fulfilled humanity. Out of the Constitutions and the *Exercises,* for example, comes an understanding of the Jesuit idea of obedience that must bind all the vows infinitely more complex than that supposed by the notorious demand for it to be "corpselike"—*perinde ac cadaver*. Far from passive in their obedience to "rules," the men forged by the spirituality of St. Ignatius are men ultimately bound by their vows, but men for whom obedience is not the negation of liberty but, through constant consultation with the superior in a process of "discernment," a channel through which a "greater service" may be rendered to others and to God.

Elizondo knew his novices well and set high standards for them. Forty years later he would remember: "I wanted to prepare in them the openness that is necessary for what the future will bring, without ever knowing what the future may be."[30] One of Elizondo's novices—and one who, as a future provincial in Central America, would have reason to appreciate the value of the lesson—would remark that, quite simply, "he taught us not to be afraid."[31]

SINCE the days of St. Ignatius, the Society of Jesus has had a commitment to the apostolic life, to taking the Gospel message out to the people of the world. "Wherever in the Church there has been or there is confrontation between man's most pressing needs and the Christian message," Pope Paul VI would say in 1974, "in regions beset by the worst crises, out there on the frontline, at the crossroads of ideologies, and in the social trenches, there have been and there are Jesuits."[32] The preparation for such a life has traditionally been long and demanding, with an emphasis on academic excellence. The novitiate was followed by five years dedicated to the humanities and philosophy, then a period known as "regency" in which the young Jesuit was given practical experience in one of the Society's works, four years of theology mandatory to ordination to the priesthood, and optional years of specialized study. Only then did the Jesuit reach "tertianship"—the third year of novitiate completed by ordained priests before the taking of the final vows. Although even a Jesuit who entered the novitiate in his late teens will not be fully formed until his mid-thirties, this extensive "investment" in its own is one of the Society of Jesus' greatest strengths. Besides developing each Jesuit's intellectual capabilities, such a training proved essential for individual Jesuits scattered to the far corners of the world and working in all quarters of life to feel themselves part of the "body in mission" that is the Society as a whole.

Throughout the 1950s, it was not possible for the Central American Jesuits to be trained within Central America. Instead, after the novitiate they experienced lengthy periods of absence punctuated by the years of regency—most commonly spent teaching in one of the Jesuits' schools— but otherwise extending until they returned as fully formed priests at the end of the 1960s. The "scholastics," as Jesuits in training are known, began their work in Quito, Ecuador, studying at the Catholic University. These five years were crucial as a period of intellectual development and as a time in which the Central American Jesuits could grow together as a group, defined by their experience with Elizondo in Santa Tecla.

Gathered in Quito at the time were young Jesuits from a variety of

Latin American countries—Ecuador, obviously, but also Bolivia and Paraguay, Mexico and Venezuela. As the years passed, the self-styled "Central American colony" grew to be the largest, and among the most dominant, of the different national groupings, whether on the sports field, in the classroom, or in the almost continual meetings held to discuss news from Central America. Over the years the "colony" had its problems with some of their Jesuit superiors, whose idea of formation they found considerably more restrictive than what they had been accustomed to with Elizondo. "We demanded," one Jesuit would remember, "in the name of Ignatian spirituality, that we should not have our training, our work, and our relaxation impaired by the monastic sort of structures that existed in Ecuador."[33] While the conservatism of some of the Jesuit authorities in Ecuador troubled Elizondo—and at one point led him to place several scholastics elsewhere for a year—from Santa Tecla he impressed upon his charges that the best thing about Ecuador was the quality of its teachers. And no young Jesuit was more able to make the most of all that his teachers could offer him than Ignacio Ellacuría.

Ellacuría's intelligence had been self-evident in Santa Tecla. But it was in Quito, and particularly under the tutelage of humanities professor Father Aurelio Espinoza Pólit, that his exceptional abilities as a critical, creative, and conceptualizing thinker really began to emerge. Other scholastics—some of whom were struggling with intensive classes in Latin and Greek grammar for the first time in their lives—soon became aware of the friendship that grew between Aurelito, as the diminutive Espinoza Pólit was affectionately known, and his questioning, debating, and constantly reading pupil. Ellacuría would encourage the newly arrived, as in later years he would tell those on their way south to Quito for the first time, "to make the most of Aurelito,"[34] to give themselves up to him with the fullest confidence that they would be formed and educated "by osmosis."[35]

Aurelio Espinoza Pólit was a distinguished classical scholar who had studied at Oxford University; he was a worldwide authority on the Greek dramatist Sophocles and the Latin poet Virgil. But he was perhaps most remarkable as a humanist in the fullest sense of the word. A man of enormous energy, Espinoza Pólit was the author of studies on a range of ancient and contemporary Ecuadoran authors and a number of articles on strictly religious matters, philosophy, and the theory of education. He was an occasional poet and, as rector of the Catholic University, adviser to the Ecuadoran government on cultural affairs. The young Central American Jesuits were particularly impressed by the attention Espinoza Pólit paid to the largely indigenous staff of their residence and, in marked contrast to the aristocratic and elitist Ecuadoran Jesuit province, to the problems of the Indian population. In an article he wrote in 1963 on the occasion of the death of his mentor, Ellacuría would say of him that, "he was in everything the opposite of a lightweight, of someone who superficially samples each subject like a butterfly."[36]

Espinoza Pólit was above all a teacher, a man who poured his whole being into his love of the texts under discussion and his passionate will to communicate the moral, religious, and human values he found within them. Remembering his days in the classroom, Ellacuría would acknowledge the lack of orthodoxy in methods that had Espinoza Polit teach works carefully selected for their absolute values, yet celebrate his subsequent revelation of "the human dilemma in its full spectrum of fulfillment, depths of feeling and emotion and psychological experience." In later years the teacher in Ellacuría would carry with him the excitement with the process of learning that he described in Espinoza Pólit: "What was fundamental in his teaching, and followed boldly and consistently without any room for discussion, was the preferring of education to erudition, of the vitality of the forms themselves to their material contents . . . The classes were totally creative, without any preplanned structures. He was constantly searching for the new insight, the vivid detail, the unsuspected discovery. There was much of spiritual adventure about those classes and for that reason they all seemed different."[37]

AFTER Elizondo, Espinoza Pólit was the second of the five men who made a lasting impression on Ellacuría's intellectual and spiritual formation. Other Central American Jesuits were exposed to some of them, but, as one who followed Ellacuría from Santa Tecla to Quito in 1950 remarked, "what happened is that Ellacu made the most of them."[38] From Quito Ellacuría returned to San Salvador, where he spent the three years of his regency teaching in the seminary and reacquainting himself with Central America before embarking on an extended period in Europe. His years of theological study in Innsbruck and his specialization in philosophy in Madrid would bring him into contact with his two great *maestros:* the Jesuit theologian Karl Rahner and the Spanish philosopher Xavier Zubiri. Under them and within the context of a Catholic Church in crisis, he would lay the foundations of an intellectual identity that only would be fully realized later in El Salvador.

Those who knew Ellacuría in the seminary remember him as a compelling and demanding presence, not unaware of his own intellectual abilities. As he published articles in the Jesuit magazine *ECA,* his contacts extended beyond Jesuits of his own generation to the priests and seminarians he lived among and the lay Salvadorans who came to the seminary for classes or conferences.[39] Stimulating for those who were not alarmed by his acid criticism, Ellacuría's classes were keenly followed by students seeking relief from more traditional methods of teaching rendered moribund by an unquestioning reverence for the material under discussion. One young seminarian, Rubén Zamora, remembered Ellacuría as "the first person who really made me investigate anything seriously—he was also the first person in my life I heard make fun of the texts we were studying." Asked to write a critique of a particular text, Zamora had been surprised to have his efforts dismissed by Ellacuría's comment that he "already knew" what the text said—what interested him was what his students thought of it.[40]

After regency there came a period in which the Jesuits in training for the Central American vice-province were dispersed throughout Europe and the United States for theology and, in some cases, a period of special studies. While each Jesuit's program was devised through consultation with his superiors, there was a group of Jesuits, a few years younger than Ellacuría, whose formation was coordinated more directly by and with each other. These were Jesuits destined to the Center of Investigation and Social Action (CIAS). Among them was the Guatemalan who had been so appreciative of Elizondo's sensitivity to "us tropicals," César Jerez. They had first heard of the Society's intention to found branches of CIAS throughout Latin America in Quito, where they had met Jesuits from the original CIAS, the Centro Bellarmino in Santiago, Chile. Preoccupation with their potential for usefulness to the poor of Central America was increased by their regency in Panama; assigned to a traditional school of the Panamanian elite, they took the boys under their supervision out to the poor *barrios* so as to open their eyes to a reality different from that of their comfortable homes and Jesuit-run school. In the future the training of these Jesuits would be planned with the CIAS in mind, with each one either studying economics or working toward a doctoral thesis on Central America.

The years spent in Innsbruck (1958 to 1962) were never a period that Ellacuría remembered warmly. After Central America, Austria was cold and dark. Missing too, as his contemporaries were spread throughout Europe, was the spirit of the Central American "colony" in Ecuador. From Espinoza Pólit, recovering from a near fatal illness in Quito, came a letter of encouragement and affection, expressing his approval that

Ellacuría should be studying in Innsbruck, but warning against becoming overly "Germanic" in his intellectual orientation. "I consider it a great advantage for you to be there with a mind to make the most of all the Germans have contributed to science and to criticism," he wrote, "but I would think it a disaster if you should become so subordinate to their work as to lose your freedom of spirit and the serene confidence in your own criteria and in the aesthetic perspicuity in which I do not believe we Latins are lacking."[41] Espinoza Pólit had little to worry about. The Spanish-speaking students formed a tightly knit group that gathered around the figure of Ellacuría to express their discontent both with what they saw as the outdated restrictions contained within the daily life of their Jesuit residence and with the surprisingly low calibre of much of the teaching.

Some found Ellacuría's controlled, ironic intellect arrogant and off-putting. There was a lofty disdain about him that would earn him—in his brilliance and his inaccessibility—the nickname "the Sun King."[42] Although his dissent was always rational and calm in its analysis, it was also piercing and unrelentingly critical. It did not go unnoticed by his superiors. The report on his four years in Innsbruck was in the form of a multiple choice (in Latin). While rated *eximia,* "excellent," for intelligence, the assessment of his *virtus,* "virtue" or "behavior," was only *mediocris,* and the conclusion to the report reads: "While he is highly talented, his character is one that is potentially difficult; his own spirit of critical judgment is persistent and not open to others; he separates himself from the community in small groups amongst whom he exercises a strong influence."[43]

Although the Jesuits lived in their own college, as students they attended the School of Theology of Innsbruck University and were able to participate in some of the usual activities of university life. Soccer, as ever, provided a welcome escape. Together with a couple of Austrians and a German, the Spanish-speaking Jesuits put together a team that was, in the eyes of their Jesuit superiors, rather alarmingly successful. With Ellacuría at center, the team easily won the Innsbruck University championship and then moved up a league to the Austrian National University Championships in Vienna. There too, the Jesuits carried all before them. Two players were selected to play in the Austrian National University team at the European championships before wind of this rather unlikely—and, some considered, unseemly—success reached Rome and the Jesuit father general. Letters were exchanged and the authorities in Innsbruck put a premature end to some promising soccer careers, explaining that they did not think that the playing of soccer in public was a suitable pursuit for those dedicated to the religious life.[44]

There were, of course, compensating factors in Innsbruck, and they were of an order that easily validated what was otherwise a mixed experience: the teaching of theologians Andres Jürgmann, Hugo, and in particular Karl Rahner, and the very fact of being *in* Innsbruck *with* Karl Rahner in the years leading up to Second Vatican Council.

Rahner believed that Vatican II, by any analysis of the most significant developments in the history of the Catholic Church, was one of the Church's two key transformations—the other being the moment when the early Christians first began to take the word of God out to the pagans in the beginning of the long process toward Christianity's establishment throughout Europe. While there followed centuries of missions and crusades under the name of the Church, it was not until Vatican II, in Rahner's view, that the Church moved beyond an essentially Eurocentric position toward its identity as the "world Church." Convoked by Pope John XXIII in response to the Church's need for *aggiornamento* or updating, the three years of the Council, from 1962 to 1965, saw the Church respond to the modern world with a series of institutional reforms that gave bishops greater liberty in their dealings with the Vatican and the laity more participation in church life. Among the most far-reaching of its innovations was a modification of the hierarchical structures of old and a recognition that the Church was a community of equals, a "people of God," bound together by Christian faith and practice. The Latin mass was relinquished and the Church as a whole gained a new tolerance and respect for cultural diversity both within its ranks and in other world religions.

The Council itself was the product, and the necessary reply to, a period of acute crisis in which Karl Rahner as a speculative theologian and his brother Hugo and their colleague Jürgmann, from their respective specialties of the church fathers and the liturgy, had played key roles in daring to respond to the challenge presented to faith by science, and the consequent process of secularization—and atheism—in a rapidly changing world. Jon Sobrino points out that Rahner did not shrink from new ideas, even when they meant a fundamental rethinking of God, a proposition considered little short of heretical by some in the Catholic Church and the Society of Jesus from the 1930s to the 1950s: "As a theologian he was not afraid of the new, whether it came from Kant or Hegel, Heidegger or Teilhard de Chardin; nor was he afraid of the new in history, be it the tragic realities of war or the environment of secularization, or, on the other hand, the positive 'new' of Vatican II. The new was not for him, as it is for others, in the first place a threat or an attack on theology; it was rather a profound question for theology, which while it might in itself raise difficulties, is also something positive, because in the last instance it is also through the new that God may be speaking His Word."[45]

For Ellacuría and the others studying in Innsbruck at this time (Segundo Montes was to arrive in 1961), there were both historical and spiritual experiences to witness, intimately connected by the occurrence of Vatican II, and of lasting importance in their progress towards the priesthood. There was, in the first place, the undeniable excitement of being there. A contemporary remembered that "Karl Rahner would give us a class one day, finish the class and get on an airplane to Rome in order to repeat this same class to 2,000 bishops. And after he'd given this class to the 2,000 bishops he'd come back to us and tell us what the bishops had asked him."[46] A less quantifiable experience at Innsbruck was that of seeing in Rahner something of what is difficult about faith in the modern world. To one whose formation was, with one obvious exception, within the intellectual climate of the radically atheist philosophy of the late twentieth century, this was of great value. Ellacuría communicated some of this to Sobrino in 1969 when he remarked of Rahner that, "he wore his doubts with great elegance."[47] A simple yet disturbing observation only possible from one who has been there too; it says as much about Ignacio Ellacuría as it does about Karl Rahner.

ELLACURÍA was ordained a priest on July 26, 1961. A few months later he was passing through Bilbao on a visit to his family when he decided to try to meet the Spanish philosopher Xavier Zubiri. An admirer from afar, Ellacuría wanted to ask for Zubiri's approval of his plans to write his doctoral thesis on the older man's work.

Xavier Zubiri held a unique position in European philosophy—not least because he was in his early sixties and had yet to publish a book. A deeply Christian man, he was, by his own admission, a philosopher more satisfied by theology than philosophy. He had been a pupil of Heidegger and of José Ortega y Gasset; in the universities of Louvain, Rome, Madrid, Freiburg, Berlin, and Paris he studied philosophy, theology, physics and mathematics, classical philology, oriental languages, and ancient history. From 1926 to 1936 he held the Chair of History of Philosophy in the Central University of Madrid in the face of considerable academic controversy and constant political crisis. He withdrew from a Spanish university life he no longer believed to be worthy of the name "university," and had the reputation of something of an ogre.[48]

Ellacuría had already written Zubiri a series of letters asking for a meeting and some response to his proposed thesis. He received no answer and so, with some trepidation, turned up on the philosopher's doorstep in Bilbao. Zubiri's sister-in-law answered the door and told him that Zubiri was out at mass and that while he did not generally like to receive visitors, he made an exception for priests. Ellacuría returned later that day to a reception "of great simplicity and spontaneity" that he would later describe to his provincial in Central America: "I told him immediately that I wanted to do my thesis with him and on him. It went down well; I'm not sure that I didn't flatter him. He made a few modest sounding remarks and then straight away asked me what I wanted to do. I briefly told him that I saw in him a juncture between the classical and the modern, between the essential and the existential. He smiled and said that that actually had been the intention of his work. He then assured me that he would put himself entirely at my disposition for everything that I might need."[49]

Zubiri had been as excited by his meeting as Ellacuría and wrote to his wife Carmen Castro, in Madrid at the time, to tell her that he had met "a brilliant young Jesuit," who not only knew Greek, in which he felt himself to be weaker than he should be, but *really* knew Greek—he had given a conference in Greek in Munich.[50] The meeting was the beginning of a friendship that was to have an effect well beyond the death of Zubiri in 1983—or even that of Ellacuría six years later. In the University of Central America philosophy students and Jesuit scholastics alike still follow a curriculum in which the influence of Zubirian thought can clearly be traced.

Ellacuría began work for his doctoral thesis in Madrid's Complutense University in 1962. Unimpressed by the philosophy faculty there and delighted by the exception that Zubiri was prepared to make to his usual rejection of all prospective students, between the two of them they were able to arrange that Zubiri should have sole supervision of his work, even though Zubiri had no formal relationship with the university. There had, indeed, been problems in getting the thesis admitted at all: the authorities had initially rejected a thesis on Zubiri as a living philosopher. Zubiri was furious—as he would be on the thesis's completion when it was only awarded the grade of *sobresaliente*, "excellent," rather than the superlative *cum laude*. Full of enthusiasm for his "unique situation," in early 1963 Ellacuría wrote to his provincial to explain that he would need two years to complete his work; formal conditions of the university could be met by finding a professor willing to take on the thesis at an official level, "without meddling in any way."[51]

Zubiri's enthusiasm for Ellacuría and for his thesis came from the realization that in Ellacuría he had found not just a disciple but a potential collaborator. Over the years they would endlessly analyze and discuss Zubiri's lectures and texts, with the old man increasingly impatient for Ellacuría's visits to his book-lined apartment in Madrid. Each night he would read Ellacuría the pages he had written during the day, asking "not for intellectual therapy, but that I should tell him the truth, the whole truth, with all of my criticisms."[52] When Ellacuría received a copy of Zubiri's first book, *Sobre la esencia,* he wrote to thank him for its warm dedication and, above all for the book itself, "for what it says that is in the service not only of philosophy and truth but also, and especially, for what is says that is in the service of Christianity and truth." He added, "This is what I feel, and I say it without any limitation whatsoever."[53]

Ellacuría's admiration for Zubiri stemmed from a profound appreciation of what he would call the older man's "life's task, the sweet yet costly task . . . the investigation of the truth of what seemed to him to be the fundamentals in human life."[54] From the solid basis of his own training in the material sciences, Zubiri maintained the conviction that philosophy "is never born of itself," but is, "a concrete operation, carried out from a specific situation."[55] He then developed a body of work that was, in an oft-repeated phrase of Ellacuría's, "pure philosophy, but not purely philosophy." In the future it would prove enormously fruitful for Ellacuría's construction of a philosophy encompassing a very different reality from that of Xavier Zubiri: Latin America and El Salvador in the years of revolution and war to come.

REVOLUTION and war, however, seemed far away when, in 1964, the Jesuits in San Salvador celebrated the fiftieth anniversary of their return to El Salvador in 1914. The anniversary was commemorated on August 18 with a solemn mass held in the church of the *Externado San José* and attended by the flower of Salvadoran society. In the absence of the archbishop the mass was celebrated by his auxiliary, Monsignor Arturo Rivera Damas. The anniversary address was given by a priest from San Miguel, Father Oscar Romero, who was one of the many Salvadoran clergy to have studied with the Jesuits in the seminary.

The country was in the midst of a period of remarkable economic growth fueled, in part, by the initiative launched in 1961 by the Kennedy administration, the Alliance for Progress. Over a ten-year period a massive $20 billion injection of funds was to finance the combination of economic development and social reform the Alliance's authors believed necessary to prevent repetitions of Fidel Castro's 1959 revolutionary victory occurring throughout Latin America. A parallel program supporting counterinsurgency, police, and military aid would ensure that governments meeting U.S. approval were adequately equipped for their own protection—and for the suppression of any political dissent. El Salvador was perfectly positioned to reap the benefits of a policy that made few attempts to hide the ulterior motives of its social concern. Its military rule had been briefly interrupted by a civilian-military junta brought to power in a 1960 coup led by junior officers. For some, however, the moderate reforms the junta had proposed smacked dangerously of communism. Within months it was toppled by a group of colonels and malleable civilians behind Colonel Julio Rivera and backed up by the U.S. embassy.

Praise from the United States was unstinting. Kennedy considered that, "Governments of the civil-military type of El Salvador are the most effective in containing communist penetration in Latin America."[56] But what civilian input there had been in Rivera's ruling *Directorio* was eclipsed by the colonel's triumph: in presidential elections in 1962 he was the sole candidate of the National Conciliation Party (PCN) he created. By 1964, with El Salvador in the process of receiving half of all foreign investment made since 1900, the economy was growing at the remarkable rate of 12 percent a year. Within the decade, multinational corporations were flocking to open up subsidiaries and in an April CIA Survey, the country was hailed as "one of the hemisphere's most stable, progressive republics."[57]

Besides a celebration of past achievements, the Jesuits' fiftieth anniversary came at a moment in which a number of Jesuits, under the direction of Vice-Provincial Luis Achaerandio, were pouring all of their energies towards their most ambitious project to date: the founding of a university. It would be named after the Salvadoran priest José Simeón Cañas, rector of San Carlos University in Guatemala, who, in December 1823, while recovering from a serious disease, had dragged himself before the assembly to ensure the abolition of slavery in Central America.

Jesuit universities in Central America had long been a topic of discussion. In the late 1950s, Miguel Elizondo, who became vice-provincial after leaving the novitiate in Santa Tecla in 1956, had invited an eminent visitor from Rome, Father Paolo Dezza, to assess where the new university should be established. Dezza visited Guatemala, Nicaragua, and

El Salvador and was greeted with great fanfare and blatant lobbying by the interested social elites, each of which wanted the university in their country. His solution was one in which reason overruled the prevailing reality of Central American politics: there should be one Central American University with distinct but interconnected faculties established in the different countries. When national interests proved an insurmountable hurdle, efforts to launch the universities became concentrated within each country, leading to the founding in 1960 of the University of Central America in the very "jesuitical" Nicaragua, with the help of a gift of land from President Somoza, and in 1961 the founding of the Rafael Landívar University in Guatemala.[58]

In El Salvador, pressure for the founding of a Catholic university had grown with the increasing radicalization of the National University. The Church hierarchy and monied elite of parents, politicians, and private educators such as the Jesuits looked on with increasing alarm at what they viewed as "communist infiltration" designed to exercise "an ideological influence on the intellectual minority in whose hands would rest the future of the country."[59] The public outcry coincided with a period of intense university reform initiated in 1963 by the National University's rector Fabio Castillo (in 1960 a civilian member of the short-lived junta) with new science departments and renewed investment in the university library.[60] It reached a crescendo when Castillo traveled to the Soviet Union to establish a program of academic exchange with the University of Moscow. "A group of philo-communist teachers," railed an editorial in *ECA*, "was converting the university into a center of Marxist agitation, its authorities preparing to launch the students for the conquest of power through a frontal attack on the democratic institutions of the country."[61]

As both the newly influential Christian Democratic Party (PDC) and the Catholic Parents Association began drafting laws that would allow for the opening of private universities, Archbishop Chávez, other bishops, and representatives of the religious congregations in El Salvador debated the merits of a Catholic university more formally tied to the Church hierarchy and to Rome. In the end, at a meeting on November 17, 1964, Monsignor Chávez, delegates from the Bishops' Conference, and the Papal Nuncio formally asked the Jesuits, represented by Fathers Achaerandio and Joaquín López y López, to take charge of the administration of the university. A Jesuit-run university, they explained, would be in accordance with the wishes "of the ecclesiastic hierarchy, the Catholic Parents Association, the representatives of capital, and explicitly, of the president of the republic himself."[62]

A modified version of the Law of Public Universities proposed by the opposition Christian Democratic Party was passed in the National Assembly on March 12, 1965. It established that the new universities would have the legal standing of "corporations of public utility" and would enjoy "autonomy within their teaching, administrative and economic management." As the frenetic fund-raising and administrative preparation for the new university moved forward toward the founding ceremony on September 15, El Salvador's Independence Day, and the opening of the university the following year, the implications of this law became clear: the university would legally be the property of its corporation—the board of directors—rather than the Society of Jesus, but in practice it would be under the moral and administrative control of the Jesuits who made up that board.[63]

The university's inaugural ceremony in the Darío cinema was a prestigious affair at which the guest list was headed by President Rivera. The product of long months of work by the Jesuits and their benefactors, the inauguration was an occasion of thanks and well-wishing. In his welcoming address, Florentino Idoate, the university's first rector, explained that the institution he led shared with Rivera and his government a commitment to "the concentrated development we are experiencing." During the planning of the university, he explained, staff had carried out a study to establish exactly what the country most needed. The answers had been clear: El Salvador faced an acute shortage of the technicians necessary for the economic and social development it pursued. These, then, would be the men and women that the university would educate in its initial faculties of industrial engineering and economics, men and women who, "privileged for having received a greater culture, would then be the natural leaders of others."[64]

THE UCA was founded on the crest of a wave of what, throughout Latin America, became known as *desarrollismo*, "developmentalism." In the 1950s, the Economic Commission on Latin America (ECLA), a United Nations agency with its headquarters in Chile, had produced a paradigmatic analysis of the economic ills facing the continent. It argued that since 1880 the world economy had developed to the progressive disadvantage of countries, like those of Latin America, overly dependent on the production and export of primary products, whether copper and minerals in Chile, beef in Argentina or coffee, bananas, and sugar in the various countries of Central America. The proposed solution had been regional integration for the smaller countries and then the introduction of international agreements protecting the prices of commodities and allowing for import substitution industrialization, or ISI. It was an analysis and a model whose logic had been adopted by the Alliance for Progress, but as the 1960s advanced there were already indications to suggest that the model was not working.

In 1964 the reform-minded government of President João Goulart was overthrown by the Brazilian military. As Penny Lernoux has pointed out, Goulart's planning minister, Celso Furtado, "was among the first to put his finger on the problem by insisting that 'development' was a myth invented by the industrialized nations to con the third world into footing the bill for the American (and European) way of life."[65] Rather than fostering real "development," Furtado and others who became known as "dependency theorists" would later argue, the initiative had deepened the structural dependency of the third world countries on the industrialized powers without resolving the third world's own economic ills. El Salvador was a case in point: it had been one of the prime beneficiaries of the Central American Common Market (CACM) formed in 1961 with Washington's blessing, and light industry had flourished to such an extent that the country became known as the "Ruhr of Central America."[66] The growth achieved through regional integration, however, had been at the expense of internal reform. The problems of the countryside had been ignored as the number of landless peasants increased from 12 percent of the rural population in 1961 to 30 percent ten years later.[67] By the end of the "decade of development" one in every eight Salvadorans—300,000 people—had fled their "stable and progressive" republic to try their chances in neighboring Honduras.

In 1968, the crisis of developmentalism contributed to what was as defining a moment for the Latin American Church as Vatican II had been for the Catholic Church as a whole: the Second Conference of the Latin American Bishops held in Medellín, Colombia. More a reinterpretation of Vatican II within the specific economic, social, and political circumstances of Latin America than an application of the Second Vatican Council's conclusions, the bishops assembled in Medellín proclaimed to the world that they could not "remain indifferent in the face of the tremendous social injustices existent in Latin America which keep the majority of our peoples in dismal poverty."[68]

Medellín came, as the Chilean theologian Pablo Richard has pointed out, as the "point of convergence" of two historical currents active within the Latin American Church in the 1960s.[69] One of them was constituted by a more or less attentive reception first of the great encyclicals of Pope

John XXIII, *Mater et Magistra* (1961), and particularly his statement on human rights, *Pacem in Terris* (1963),[70] then of the documents of Vatican II, and finally of the ground-breaking *Populorum Progressio* (1967), the Church's own pronunciation, "On the Development of Peoples." With a vehemence yet unseen in any document of the Church's magisterium, the encyclical admitted that "there are situations whose injustice cries to the heavens" (n.30) and called for "integral development": "Development is not reduced to simple economic growth. To be authentic it must be integral, that is to say, promote the good of all men and of all of man" (n.14). The other no less important current was the Christian movement emerging throughout Latin America (with understandably different characteristics in the different countries) alongside the rise of the Latin American political left in widely varying forms of popular organization.

The triumph of the Cuban revolution in 1959 not only served as an example to revolutionaries throughout the continent, but also encouraged university students and professors to reach out to the poor with marxist interpretations of their circumstances. Occurring simultaneously was the dissemination of the methods of "conscientization" pioneered by Paolo Freire for literacy training in northeastern Brazil.[71] These were adopted by new organizations within the Church, formed at the grass-roots level for discussion of the Gospel and a reflection on what it might mean to those confronting the hardships of the daily life of most Latin Americans. Members of these "base ecclesiastic communities" did not need Medellín to open their eyes to the poverty they lived in. Through discussion and reflection, however, they came to see that the Gospel was not something remote from their own lives, part of the fabric of what Medellín would denounce as the "structural injustice"[72] historically sustained and rationalized by the Latin American state and Church, but something alive and real and radical.

CHANGE for the Jesuits, in Latin America as elsewhere, was heralded by the 1965 election of a new father general, Pedro Arrupe, in a General Congregation (GCXXXI) that paved the way for the renovation of the Society of Jesus in the years to come. Only the second Basque general since Ignatius himself, Arrupe had studied in the United States as a young man, traveled widely, and spent twenty-seven years in Japan. On August 6, 1945, he was novice master in Nagatsuka, six miles from Hiroshima, when the atom bomb was dropped. At five o'clock the next morning, as he would recall years later, he was saying mass before attending to the carnage that lay before him. People were wounded and scorched in a way none had seen before; amid blackened, burning ruins, the city was littered with dead. "The Lord be with you," he began, and then stopped. How could he go on? Was the Lord really *with* these people? "I couldn't move, I was paralyzed, with my arms stretched out, contemplating that human tragedy." Yet the mass went on.[73]

Arrupe was a man whom Ellacuría described as "open to history and within history to the 'signs of the times.' "[74] As father general he was dedicated to a renewal of the Society of Jesus' commitment to justice, not in the abstract, but as a real involvement with the people who actually suffer *in*justice. In his first major letter to the Jesuits of Latin America, the "Letter of the Social Apostolate" written at the end of 1966 to endorse the conclusions of a meeting of the Latin American CIAS in Lima the previous July, he addressed the problem with characteristic directness: "It is a fact that the Society is not sufficiently orientated toward social justice; rather it has always been focused, in accordance with a strategy justified mainly by historical conditions, toward exercising an impact on the dominant social classes and in the training of their leaders. It is extremely sad that there are still, even among those who fill posts of great responsibility, people in the Society who have not realized the urgency and prevalence of the problem."[75]

The letter was eagerly welcomed by the Central American Jesuits now nearing the end of their formation in Europe and looking forward to their return to Central America and the practical application of their studies. The Central American CIAS was founded in 1965 at a meeting in Paris attended by Vice-Provincial Luis Achaerandio. Over the next few years periodic meetings were held as the group worked toward a coherent understanding of their Christian and sociological mission. In late 1966 Ignacio Ellacuría, extending the leadership he had shown over his closest contemporaries throughout the years of his formation to a leadership of "the younger generation" as a whole, spoke at a meeting of the CIAS at Versailles. He welcomed the CIAS as not only an expression of the "new historical age" addressed by Vatican II and by the Jesuit General Congregation, but also as something that for being "inexorably born of real needs and not from a received and dead tradition" had every chance of "representing a new kind of religious community capable of fulfilling in itself an authentic renovation."[76]

Arrupe visited Latin America in May 1968 to attend a meeting of all the Jesuit provincials for Latin America, held in Rio de Janeiro. The timing of the meeting was crucial: the conference in Medellín was due to begin at the end of August. Arrupe would be in attendance, as would Pope

Paul VI, in the first visit of a pope to Latin America. Like the documents drafted at Medellín, the "Rio Letter" formulated at this meeting and signed by all of the Latin American provincials, began with an analysis of the reality within which the Latin American Church—and Jesuits—were living, before moving on to reflection and then more concrete directives about what can and must be done: "Most Latin Americans find themselves in a state of poverty. . . . The alienated masses in the rural and urban areas are increasing at an accelerated rate. Native groups are subject to *de facto* racial discrimination. The same dialectic of violence is encouraged by those who reject the thoroughgoing reforms needed as by those who despair of a peaceful solution." The letter proposes "a profound transformation" of the Jesuits by claiming "the social problem in Latin America" to be "the problem of humankind itself."[77]

The bishops in Medellín—aided for the first time in such a conference by priests and Christians beneath episcopal rank—reviewed the role of the Church in the world described by Vatican II on a continent whose defining characteristic was the poverty of the majority of its people. The documents of Medellín would commit the Latin American Church to the words of Christ in the Gospel of St. Matthew—"whatever you do unto the least of my brothers, you do to me"[78]—in an acknowledgement that the mission of the Church in Latin America could only be accomplished through service to and a solidarity with its poor. Out of a spirit of service of those Latin Americans with a "hunger and thirst for justice," Medellín called for a "profound conversion" necessary for "true liberation" from "sin, ignorance, hunger, misery, and oppression."[79]

The epistemological shift away from the ubiquitous "development," with its ill-defined hopes of trickle-down improvement for all, to the more radical political and theological demand for "liberation" was institutionalized by Medellín, but did not come from Medellín alone. The Rio Letter before it had called for the "liberation of humankind from every sort of servitude that oppresses it," and in the coastal town of Chimbote, Peru, just a month before he traveled to Medellín to advise the assembled bishops, a Peruvian theologian named Gustavo Gutiérrez had given a talk titled "Towards a Theology of Liberation."[80] While the term would not become widespread until the publication of Gutiérrez' book *A Theology of Liberation* in 1971, much of what was happening in the Latin American Church in the 1960s can be seen as moving "toward" this new theology. "Poverty means death," Gutiérrez has asserted with a starkness as shocking as the fact, and it is here that liberation theology had its real origin. It is a theology that both drew on and fed the experience of the base communities, a theology born of "the contrast between the urgent task of proclaiming the life of the risen Jesus and the conditions of death in which the poor of Latin America were living."[81]

In Rio, the Jesuit provincials had known that what they were asking of their provinces would be difficult. A change that would integrate all of the Society's activities, be they in education or elsewhere, into the social apostolate in accordance with a goal of liberation not only demanded personal conversion, but also would "almost certainly arouse reactions" from outside the Society. Underlying the seriousness of what was being asked is the knowledge, stated clearly in the Rio Letter as in the introduction to the Final Documents at Medellín, that "the epoch we are living in is a critical moment in the history of salvation."[82] A moment, in biblical terms, of *kairos,* propitious and demanding at once, in which man is called upon to bear a very specific witness. And in the following decades there would be few places in which the events to be witnessed would prove more dramatic than El Salvador.

CHAPTER TWO

CHOOSING FOR THE POOR

The third world is the prophetic denunciation of how badly arranged are the things of this world. A society that makes possible the third world is an unjust society, an inhuman society, a society appallingly badly arranged. This is the case of the consumer society, which is that which has led to the constitution of the third world as it is. . . . It is not just that the third world demands a return to the poor. It demands it urgently and immediately at the same time as it offers the conditions for an authentic Christianity. As a task, it is one of the greatest and most worthy of enthusiasm that one might humanly imagine. It is an enormous task without abstractions and without need of purity of intentions because it is a task that is essentially pure and purifying; it is a task of protest, of rebellion against injustice, a task of solidarity and sacrifice, of the construction of a new world that is truly human.[1]

Ignacio Ellacuría, 1969

IGNACIO Ellacuría returned to El Salvador in 1967 to work in a university that was little more than an extension of a Catholic high school. Doors to a temporary home in the Don Rúa building had opened in February 1966 to 357 students. A handful of Jesuits, some secretaries, and a few teachers—in the main former pupils of the Jesuits giving classes free "to do the Fathers a favor"—made up the university staff. The students were graduates of the country's elite Catholic schools, their parents pleased by the prospect of a higher education safely in the hands of the Jesuits and free from contamination by the "Marxists" at the National University.

The university started "with absolutely nothing, no teachers, site nor money, only the prestige of the Society of Jesus,"[2] according to Román Mayorga, one of the *Externado* old boys who arrived to give classes on the first day; but it did surprisingly well. Applications for enrollment poured in and the Jesuits administering the university threw all of their energies into raising funds for a new campus. Long years at the *Externado* had fostered friendships between rector Florentino Idoate, treasurer José María Gondra, and general secretary Joaquín López y López and some of the wealthiest families in El Salvador. As these were precisely the families who were hoping to benefit from the new university, they were readily persuaded to join with the Jesuits in the purchase of the coffee-growing Finca Palermo, sprawled across a hill just south of the city. By early 1969

41

the university was able to move into the modest beginnings of its present campus.

Ellacuría was named to the controlling five-man board of directors within a year of his return, but he could find scant reflection of the preoccupations he had brought back from Europe, either in the path the university was taking or in the Jesuits who were guiding it. The vice-province as a whole had been taken by surprise by Vatican II, as it would be by Medellín. There was little of the conversion demanded by Vatican II in its call for the Church to "examine the signs of the times and interpret them in the light of the Gospel,"[3] or by Arrupe in the Letter of the Social Apostolate. In 1968 the signs of the times were clearly visible, whether one looked to increasing indications of the failure of reform in El Salvador, the revolutionary movements springing up all over Latin America, or to the students taking to the streets of North American and European cities. The questions being asked were urgent, necessary; yet the Central American Jesuits and the new university appeared not even to be trying to provide the answers.

And Ellacuría was not yet sure that he was here to stay. Early in 1968 Zubiri, missing his disciple and collaborator, had written to Father Arrupe in Rome to ask whether he might not consider allowing Ellacuría to leave the university in El Salvador and continue working in Madrid with him. Arrupe had been impressed by this petition and had written to Ellacuría's vice-provincial, by this time Segundo Azcue, to say that, as Ellacuría would describe it in a letter to Zubiri, "it seemed to him that your work was of extraordinary importance, and that therefore I should stay and work with you, even though there is great need here."[4] In a correspondence of true Ignatian discernment Arrupe insisted that he did not want to impose his decision before consulting the advisers in the vice-province's government. The advisers referred the matter to the university and then all the reports were returned to Rome. They landed on the desk not of Arrupe, but of Paolo Dezza, Arrupe's adviser on matters to do with education. "The definitive absence of Father Ellacuría would constitute a serious loss for the Salvadoran University," wrote Dezza to Azcue. "Considering everything, the most advisable course would be for him to help Don Xavier Zubiri during the summer vacations."[5]

Visits to Spain were important not only for the continuing work with Zubiri but also because they allowed Ellacuría to maintain contact with the large number of increasingly restless Central American Jesuits finishing their years of theology in Europe. It was with Jesuits such as these, and with CIAS members now in final stages of their formation—in

1968 César Jerez and Juan Hernández Pico, for example, began to spend their vacations from the University of Chicago working in El Salvador—that he found coincidence in a demand for radical change within the Central American vice-province.

Things came to a head in 1969. Medellín had joined the documents of Vatican II in being welcomed, as Hernández Pico remembered, "as an energizing rain after a long drought,"[6] but for those studying theology across Europe, "the new" that was being offered by these official Church documents provoked a profound dissatisfaction with courses structured along wholly preconciliar lines. This dissatisfaction was but one expression of the crisis that was, by the end of the decade, affecting not just the Jesuits but priests and religious orders across the world. While the most obvious result of this crisis was the number of priests seeking release from the priesthood—one Vatican study found that 7,370 individuals, over 1.7 percent of all priests, asked to be laicized between 1963 and 1968[7]—the malaise within the ranks of many orders, and the Jesuits were certainly no exception, was one that questioned the point and validity of the religious life itself.

Many of these concerns were voiced at a meeting of the younger Jesuits of the vice-province held in Madrid at the end of June 1969. The meeting followed a strike at the University of Comillas called by students to protest the conservatism of their theology classes. Ellacuría had lent his active support to the strike (which did not go unnoticed by Rome) and now played a leading role in the June meeting.

"Where and how to find the way to rediscover and renew the religious life?" was the question with which he launched an impassioned address. The answer outlined the seeds of ideas that were to recur throughout the lives of many of the forty-nine Jesuits present in a commitment to "the historic conditions expressed in the third world."[8] Finding in the concrete miseries of the third world a denunciation of the structures of the first world, and in the religious life, through the vows of poverty, chastity, and obedience, a liberating freedom from the values of that same (first) world, Ellacuría argued for the religious life's "resurrection" into a "new life" in the third world: "It is the old ideal of being in the world without being of the world." The very existence of the poor in the third world, he insisted, and the challenge this poverty presented when understood in terms of the Gospel's denunciation *of* poverty, but message *to* the poor, offered the best conditions for a religious life. In the third world it made sense to be a priest and it made sense to be a Jesuit.

But it was not going to be easy. "It is to be noted," Vice-Provincial

Azcue read from a letter of Arrupe at the beginning of the meeting, "that Jesuits are concerned to renew our way of life and work, and are making efforts to adapt their mentality to the new times. For this reason, the least they can expect is a certain amount of internal tension."[9] Out of the Madrid meeting came two concrete suggestions, one that there should soon be a meeting of the entire vice-province to address the growing pressures for change, and the other that the vice-province should finish the survey of all its works that Arrupe had asked of each province and vice-province when he first became general. From this detailed account of exactly what they were doing, it was hoped that Jesuits would consider whether their works conformed to the spirituality they professed, and, even more crucially, to the new directions taken by the Church and the Society of Jesus.

It was then that Ellacuría had a really inspired idea. The vice-province should hold a meeting that took the form and content of St. Ignatius's *Spiritual Exercises,* with the "subject" of the *Exercises* the vice-province itself: it was the vice-province in its entirety that was in need of a renovation of Ignatian spirituality as it moved toward a new, more socially committed period of its history. The idea provoked no small sense of alarm among some of the older members of the vice-province, particularly when it became known that the major contributions to the meeting would be made by Miguel Elizondo, who was now based in Medellín and clearly aligned with those pressing for change, and by Ellacuría, whose leadership a large section of the vice-province had learned to suspect for the content of his ideas and to fear for the potency with which these ideas were expressed. Azcue, who was elderly, nearly blind, and, while greatly respected, not well suited to conflict, became increasingly nervous of the coming storm. Word had got out that, following the scheme of the *Spiritual Exercises,* which begins with a week devoted to the examination of the practicant's sin, Ellacuría was preparing to speak on the "sins of the vice-province."

The more conservative of the Jesuits had their fears confirmed by the December meeting in San Salvador's seminary. While Ellacuría insisted that the form of the meeting "was not designed to attack anybody," there was no escaping the vehemence with which the "young," represented by Ellacuría and others who spoke for them, protested that they were "marginalized and alienated from Central American reality," nor the resentment of older Jesuits who felt their life's work was being invalidated. In an extension of his position in Madrid, Ellacuría asked the Society of Jesus to free itself of the values and structures of the first world,

responsible—with the "possible collaboration of the Society of Jesus"—
for the very existence of the third world, in order to live and work with
"effective action in the third world."[10]

THE meeting of December 1969 had some immediate consequences. In
response to the novices' complaint that the average age of the Jesuits
responsible for their formation was "around 77,"[11] a new novice master,
Juan Ramón Moreno, was appointed. More controversial was the choice
of Ellacuría to be responsible for the formation of all Jesuits in the
vice-province. Azcue wrote rather nervously to Arrupe to explain "it was
almost a necessary consequence of the Christmas meeting."[12] Arrupe's
answer confirmed that the nerves had been justified; while Ellacuría had
recently been in Rome and had made a generally favorable impression, he
was considered "a little radicalized with some explosive ideas . . .
controversial and without sound elements of judgment."[13] The appointment was approved "*ad experimentum.*" The spirit of change sweeping
through the Central American Jesuits was to complete the transformation
of their government when a new vice-provincial, Miguel Francisco
Estrada, emerged from the Congregation held the following April.

At thirty-six, Estrada was not only the youngest superior Central
America had ever had, but also, as a Salvadoran, the first Central
American. Without the intellectual fire of Ellacuría, he was nevertheless
clearly identified with "the young" and their demands for renovation
within the vice-province. Robust, practical, and determined, Estrada spent
the first months of his tenure in preparation for the meeting in September
1970 at which the completed survey was to be presented and the new
guidelines for the future of the Central American vice-province formally
discussed and established.

The twelve volumes of the survey followed the documents of
Medellín in turning first to the objective problems of Central America.
Citing statistics from the Salvadoran government and the Inter-American
Development Bank, the survey noted that El Salvador's population in
1970, with 168 people per square kilometer and an annual growth rate of
3.8 percent, was the densest and most rapidly growing in the continent. Its
income could hardly be more unfairly distributed: 8 percent of the
population received approximately 50 percent of the gross national
product, while the remaining 92 percent had to survive on the other 50
percent.[14] Any doubts that the situation was explosive were dispelled by
the events of 1969, as the demographic pressures of Salvadoran emigration
to Honduras combined with Honduran frustration at its deepening trade

deficit to trigger a five-day war in July. When Honduras evicted tens of thousands of Salvadorans to a country where the government of Colonel Fidel Sánchez Hernández was under siege from the opposition and un- and under-employment were running at 20 percent and 40 percent respectively, something had to give. The costs were great: before a truce mediated by the Organization of American States was reached two thousand people had been killed and four thousand wounded.[15] The Central American Common Market founded in 1961 was in tatters and the "decade of development" was over.

In 1970 the vice-province under Estrada's government was, at 316 Jesuits, more than double its size in 1949. El Salvador was home not only to the *curia,* or vice-provincial's office, but also to a larger number of active Jesuits than any other country. More revealing, however, and a reflection of the weight within the vice-province of the three major high-schools and three universities in El Salvador, Guatemala, and Nicaragua, was the fact that 84 percent of the Jesuits were concentrated in these three countries.[16] The contrast between the survey's analysis of the needs of Central America and the Jesuits' response struck "the young" of the vice-province as "a situation scandalous in the light of Vatican II, Medellín and Rio."[17] Within the September meeting they pushed with renewed urgency not just for reform, but also for a clear option by the vice-province for a future structured around the principal of "liberation."

The debate on the Jesuits' universities was particularly heated. It reflected both an intense ideological crisis taking place within El Salvador's UCA and a more general fear of Ellacuría as a proponent of "intellectual terrorism" within the vice-province. He was clearly both extraordinarily gifted and a natural leader, yet there were aspects of his character that won him only opposition: his ideas were so radical, so seemingly coherent, the strength of his dialectic so impregnable and at times shot through with a streak of aggression, that his opponents found themselves unable to reply and were left with the impression that they had been objects of an assault. The other members of the UCA board of directors were nervous about where his ideas were leading and considered that his views were attracting undesirable attention: the preceding April the director of immigration had taken declarations made by Ellacuría to the ministry of the interior, accused him of interfering in politics, and called for his expulsion.[18]

This was a time when, as Román Mayorga would write, "for those who believed that the university had no point if it was not at the service of the poor majority, the university as it existed had no point."[19] Save for the UCA's participation in the first national Congress on Agrarian Reform in

1970, the university's impact in or on the country had been almost entirely restricted to teaching. While Ellacuría and those behind him had first produced a special edition of *ECA* dedicated to the conflict with Honduras and then gained control of it as "a magazine of cultural diffusion of the UCA," their real influence was limited. They held that unless the UCA changed, and changed soon and radically, the Jesuits had no business running the university and it should be closed.

As a small team, with Mayorga among them, worked on a proposal for a $2 million loan from the Inter-American Development Bank (IADB), the debate intensified. A focal point for the arguments became the UCA's physical structure and its suitability for a third world university. Ellacuría produced a scathing dismissal of the survey's largely positive report on the UCA as rendering an image that is "triumphal, confusing desire with reality . . . in a disgraceful lack of self-criticism." He recounted how in a meeting of the UCA board of directors it had been argued that the IADB loan would have to be paid back with the students' fees, and that these students would not come to a university that was not equipped with facilities such as parking lots—in a country where the average annual income of ninety-two percent of the population was $141. "The idea latent in this affirmation," he added, "is of extraordinary seriousness with respect to the orientation of our university."[20]

The orientation of "our university" was to receive a major fillip from the official speech prepared for the reception of the IADB loan. Assigned to write it, Ellacuría had conferred with Mayorga as the principal architect of the proposal. Mayorga described how he felt they should be working toward "a new kind of university in Central America, a university that puts its whole self at the service of social change but *as a university*—that is to say, through the specific functions of the institution of a university."[21] Ellacuría assured him that these ideas coincided with the position he had been articulating theologically, and went away to write a document that they both reworked. Its approval by the board of directors represented a significant victory: it was a clear statement of a shift away from the framework of "development" within which the university had opened, through the "integral development" of *Populorum Progressio* to "liberation": "To work within an autonomous concept of liberation, free of clichés and of analyses divorced from the reality we live in, is the mission of a university that modestly seeks the creation of a new man, in whom liberty should not be a political attribute but an essential part of his being."[22] Years later Mayorga would recount how, on the airplane to Washington, a nervous Father Gondra, who was to deliver the speech to the assembled powers of the IADB, turned to him to ask, "Are you *sure* the Bank will like it? It's not too revolutionary for them?" "No, Father," he had answered, "don't you worry."[23]

Similar doubts were present at the final session of the meeting held in September 1970, but the arguments and demographic advantage of "the young" in the vice-province were too much for the older Jesuits. Unanimous approval for the final document assumed "liberation" as the direction to be taken by the vice-province as a whole. From this decision, the document calmly stated, "we see that there will follow a series of practical consequences for our lives, different, at least in part, and sometimes directly opposed to those that would have followed if we had chosen for the direction of 'development.' "[24]

WITHIN El Salvador the Jesuits were not, of course, living in an ecclesiastical vacuum. They worked alongside priests of the dioceses and other religious orders, all of whom had been, like them, challenged by the currents of change within the Latin American Church. Reactions were varied, as perhaps could be expected from El Salvador's social and economic extremes, but an openness on the part of the elderly Archbishop Chávez laid the basis for the remarkable dynamism of the more progressive sectors of the Salvadoran Church during the 1970s. An early move in this direction was made by a Salvadoran priest named José Inocencio Alas who, in 1969, began weekly courses in the town of Suchitoto based on Medellín's understanding of justice and peace. Later that year priests working with base communities throughout the country came together to form the "Pastoral Reflection Group." The opposition of the majority of the Salvadoran bishops to this undertaking was clearly expressed in June 1970. Only the archbishop and his closest collaborator, Monsignor Rivera Damas, were present as some two hundred priests, nuns, and lay people met for a Pastoral Week establishing a framework for the renovation of their work in the community. Opposition soon came from beyond the Church hierarchy as well: Alas's work in Suchitoto caught the attention of the army, which laid siege to the town twice during his first year's activity in an early indication of the repression that this area of the Church's work would face in the future.[25]

Resistance by the conservative bishops to the changes heralded by Vatican II and Medellín also lay behind the visit that the Jesuit provincial received from the archbishop and from the secretary of the Bishops' Conference, Monsignor Oscar Romero, late in September 1972. They had come to inform Estrada that the Jesuits' services in San Salvador's seminary, where they had been responsible for the training of the country's priests since 1915, would no longer be required.

At Estrada's request the dismissal of the Jesuits was put in writing, in a letter from Romero explaining that the return of the seminary to the diocesan clergy formed a part of the "process of maturity of the ecclesiastic life of the country."[26] The letter made no allusion to the fact that the Jesuits' departure from the seminary was the culmination of a process that began in 1967 when the Jesuits first sought a contract stating that they would be following the directions indicated by Vatican II for the Formation of the Clergy. A contract had eventually been signed in 1969, supposedly good for five years and giving the Jesuits "full autonomy in all that refers to the spiritual, academic and disciplinary direction of the seminary."[27] But only a year later, when the Jesuits' candidate for new seminary rector, Rutilio Grande—a Salvadoran priest who had been prefect of discipline since 1965 and was a close friend of the archbishop— was vetoed, did it become clear that this "full autonomy" was something of a misnomer. Grande's mistake had been to preach the sermon at the solemn mass on El Salvador's national holiday on the questionable validity of the claim staked by the Salvadoran flag to "God, Union, and Liberty."

Names of potential candidates were bandied back and forth between the bishops and the Jesuit vice-provincial until Estrada suggested that of Amando López, a Spanish-born Jesuit who had just completed a doctorate in theology in Strasbourg and Rome. Impressed by these credentials, the bishops accepted him. "I could make him rector," Estrada remembered, "because he was unknown to the Bishops' Conference—but *I* knew him and I knew who I was putting in there."[28]

Besides being a theologian firmly committed to the renewal of the Central American vice-province, López had always been distinguished for his gift for friendship and ease of communication. In the seminary he assembled a team that was young, well prepared, and open to the human needs of the seminarians. To the bishops' alarm, changes were introduced and the seminarians were allowed a life that more closely resembled that of other students: they traveled across the city for their philosophy classes in the UCA, and inside the seminary played soccer and established relation- ships of greater confidence with the Jesuits than had been permitted before. "But the bishops," remembered Estrada, "kept asking me to form the seminarians as they had been formed. 'We're going to form them as the Church says we should, as it was set out by Vatican II—and here is the document,' I told them, but it was no good."

The final blow for the bishops came in July 1972 when the

seminarians refused an invitation by the archbishop to sing and serve at a solemn mass in the cathedral. In addition to objecting that masses of this type were attended by dignitaries and diplomats fulfilling a "social obligation," rather than by the Salvadoran people attending for reasons of faith, the seminarians drew attention to the fact that the mass followed close upon the inauguration of the new president, Colonel Arturo Molina, whose government they considered to have been "rejected by the majority of the people."[29] Their concern that the Church should not be granting legitimacy to the "elected" government only confirmed the bishops' worst fears that the Jesuits had let the seminary run wild. The decision to demand their departure from the seminary was taken the following month.

IN retrospect, the seminarians' refusal to sing seems a modest reaction to the elections of 1972. A coalition of Christian Democrats, Social Democrats (in the National Revolutionary Movement, MNR), and an electoral front for the illegal Communist Party (the Nationalist Democratic Union, UDN), had drawn together in the National Opposition Union (UNO) to campaign for the presidency of San Salvador's popular Christian Democratic mayor, Napoleón Duarte, against President Sánchez Hernández's handpicked successor, Molina. Making much of the presence of the UDN on the ticket, rabid anticommunism, intimidation, and harassment of the UNO during the campaign matured into blatant fraud on election day itself. When the administration of the fraud broke down and a UNO victory was announced, a news blackout was imposed and Molina and the ruling PCN emerged victorious. Duarte went into hiding, but was abducted by the National Police, badly beaten up, and flown to Guatemala. With him went the hopes of El Salvador's democratic opposition.

On July 19, less than a fortnight after the cathedral mass, the National University suffered a military intervention. Explaining that the university had "fallen into the hands of the Communist Party of El Salvador and another small group of opportunists,"[30] President Molina sent in the tanks, troops, and air power. Eight hundred people were arrested that day, and on July 22 the rector Rafael Menjívar and fourteen other staff members were forcibly bundled into an airplane and taken to Nicaragua. The university would remain closed for more than a year.

Within the UCA's board of directors, where his hand had been strengthened by the presence of Román Mayorga, Ellacuría pushed hard for fulfillment of the university's role as El Salvador's critical conscience. As a university, he argued, the proper response to the events surrounding the 1972 elections was a full and detailed interdisciplinary study. Ideally suited to coordinate such a project were César Jerez and Juan Hernández Pico, now back from Chicago for good.

The study, which would be published in July 1973 as *El Salvador: Año Político 1971–1972,* became the focus of extreme tension among the Jesuits. Lines were drawn between those who saw in the publication of the book a test case of whether the university was able to live up to its rhetoric and those more conservative Jesuits, still in a majority on the board of directors and including the rector Luis Achaerandio, who feared the political and financial consequences that publication would bring with it. Their fears were understandable. In 1971 the UCA had published a study of a national teachers strike. The book had been a disaster on all fronts: badly printed, and even then issued only after considerable delays, it was largely unread, except by some members of the government who ensured that the 1972 state subsidy for the UCA, already presented to the Legislative Assembly, disappeared "as if by magic."[31] Representatives of the UCA had met with Molina between his "election" and his inauguration—to the criticism of some sectors of the university students and staff—with a view to defining the nature of the future relationship between the UCA and the government, but talk of the university's mission was very different from the publication of a book whose obvious conclusion was that the president of the republic was not the legitimate occupant of his presidency.

Fundamental differences of opinion reflected in the positions taken around the publication of *Año Político* were acknowledged in Estrada's division of the UCA community into two houses, UCAI and UCAII, in the Cantábrico and Mediterráneo streets behind the UCA. The formal division had followed a unilateral walkout of three Jesuits, led by Ellacuría, who was no longer on speaking terms with at least one of the older Jesuits they left behind. In Rome this division was regretted and criticized, and all the more so when Estrada expressed his own allegiance by moving into the UCAII residence, where he aligned himself with the forceful group of Jesuits who would form the nucleus of this community for years to come. Perhaps closest to Ellacuría was Luis de Sebastián, who had arrived in El Salvador in 1968 after finishing a doctorate at the London School of Economics. While others—most notably Jon Cortina, a Basque engineer and Jon Sobrino, both of whom returned to El Salvador in 1974—were to join UCAII in the future, that first community was completed by the anthropologist Jesús Arroyo; Amando López, who was now working in the UCA; Segundo Montes, who divided his time between the UCA and the

Externado San José; and a young Jesuit from Valladolid, Spain, still in his years of formation, Ignacio Martín-Baró.

The fact that the book was to be published in Guatemala—both to avoid a repetition of the experience suffered by the study of the teachers' strike and for reasons of security—spread the conflict into the neighboring country. The Jesuits of the Rafael Landívar University, who were watching the changes in El Salvador with alarm, sent an anonymous letter to the UCA to express their opposition to the printing of the book in their country. They argued that it "put in serious danger their legitimate right to enjoy a good name."[32] Publication in Guatemala also brought with it the logistical problem of bringing the printed books into El Salvador. After copies of the book were distributed to friends in countries outside Central America, batches of the book were brought in overland, many of them hidden in the car of César Jerez's uncle.

FAR from abating after the Jesuits' departure from the seminary and successful publication of *Año Político*, the problems with the Church hierarchy and controversy within the Jesuits exacerbated when an episode that became known as the "*Externado* affair" propelled the Jesuits onto the public stage. For many decades the *Externado San José* had been, with the Marist brothers' Liceo Salvadoreño, one of the two schools of choice for the upper echelons of Salvadoran society. As powerful schools in a small country they educated the business, intellectual, and political elites. But after Medellín's call for "liberating education" the influence wielded by the *Externado* could no longer be held up as a criterium for success. The school only offered its services to the 8 percent of the population that could afford its fees, and that fact alone was worthy of outrage.[33] While individual ex-pupils would fall on either side of the political divide that was to emerge with the revolution and civil war of the 1970s and 1980s, the social function of the school was clearly providing for the continuation of structures the Jesuits denounced as unjust.

The altering of an institution so deeply entwined with the most powerful sectors of society was not easy. As early as 1966 Arrupe had insisted on "the moral obligation of the Society to rethink all its ministries and apostolates"[34] and had warned that this would be necessary even for the Society's many schools. Two years later he had been more direct, maintaining that if this "rethinking" was not possible in an individual school, "it is better to shut it."[35] In 1970 the Mexican provincial had done just that, closing the Instituto Patria, a school that was 2,500 strong and widely regarded as one of the best in the country.[36] In El Salvador the rethinking of the *Externado* created simmering disagreement between a small group of Jesuits pushing hard for change and older Jesuits who considered that their long years of experience in the school had proved that they knew what they were doing. Concern to take education out to the poor had led to the founding in 1970 of *Fe y Alegría* by one of the Jesuits most closely associated with the *Externado,* Joaquín López y López. Part of a continentwide initiative of the years of development, as its name "Faith and Happiness" suggests, *Fe y Alegría* had opened with three schools supported by a mixture of donations, government aid, and an annual raffle. While it expanded rapidly, it was never really coordinated within the Jesuits' wider demands for "liberation."

In 1972 the *Externado* introduced heavily subsidized classes and began to effect a series of modifications to its curriculum. Sociology classes in the senior years examined the different interpretations of the problems of Latin America, many of which used Marxist terminology as a tool of analysis, and took pupils out on field trips into a world that, until now, they had lived in and looked at but not seen. Conflict among the *Externado* Jesuits grew increasingly bitter despite Estrada's efforts to maintain at least a norm of civility between them; with the intervention of the *Externado* parents, however, it rapidly escalated out of control. On April 27, 1973, after a stormy session of the parents' association, a letter was written to the school's rector, Francisco Javier Colino, with copies forwarded to Estrada and to Arrupe in Rome. The parents' complaints centered around the new sociology classes and in particular those of five young teachers—two of them Jesuits—working part time at the *Externado* while completing their studies at the UCA. They charged that their sons were being turned against them: they returned from field trips, "excursions that should be realized with a Christian spirit and not orientated by the doctrine of class struggle, and repeatedly accuse their families of living like bourgeois, as if the effort to maintain an economic well-being was a crime."[37]

The two groups of Jesuits found encouragement in their respective views from opposing factions in the parents. Colino, who had originally backed the reforms, now took the side of the reactionary parents, ran into opposition from Estrada, and, lacking the support of his vice-provincial, took himself off to Rome. In his place Estrada appointed Juan Ramón Moreno as "interim rector," responsible for investigating the validity of the parents' charges. A careful, intelligent, and sensitive man, Moreno was novice master at the time and unused to the sort of battlefield he had entered. When a novice himself he had been so retiring that Elizondo had made him hold conversations with a wall to overcome his shyness.[38] As the conflict escalated in the following months he suffered greatly from the stress of meeting after meeting of yet more tempestuous parents. Painstakingly, he explained the political orientation of authors taught in sociology classes ("Pope Paul VI is a non-Marxist author") and the validity of the opinion that if their sons found the level of poverty in El Salvador shocking it probably owed more to the fact that it was shocking than to the evil influence of the Jesuits. For all this he was accused of having "wrapped in the words of the Gospel, theology, and the sweet figure of Christ, the bitter pill of communism."[39]

The escalation had been triggered by an editorial in the semiofficial magazine of the San Salvador archdiocese, *Orientación,* written by Monsignor Romero. The editorial was a direct attack on a "certain school" whose Marxist teachers had perverted the principles of Medellín with "pamphlets and literature of known red origin."[40] Rapidly reprinted throughout the press as the authentic opinion of the Salvadoran Church, it touched off an unprecedented campaign against the Jesuits as "communists in sheep's clothing" and "a threat to peace and social order."[41] On June 11 the prosecutor general himself weighed in to charge the *Externado* with "teaching classes of Marxist orientation." Jesuits, staff, and parents of the *Externado* were called upon to testify, hour after hour and day after day, as the scandal absorbed the nation.

While Archbishop Chávez appointed an investigating commission that completely exonerated the *Externado* from the accusations made against it,[42] a furious Estrada confronted Romero and asked him to retract his charges: "My superior here is the archbishop. As provincial I advised the Archbishop of everything that we were going to do and of all that we are doing now. On what do you base your attack?" "I am well informed, Father," answered Romero in a monotone. "By whom? The official informant is the Jesuit provincial, no one else."[43] Two mothers satisfied with their sons' education wanted to have what they believed to be the correct version of events presented to the bishops and so paid a call on Monsignor Castro y Ramírez, the bishop of Santiago de María. Their protestations of confidence in the Jesuits were hopeless: "No, ladies, those Jesuits are poisoning the young. They spend their whole time going to the cinema and visiting women . . . but I've still got the strength to grab a pistol and kill the lot of them."[44] The women left in tears.

In response to the barrage of ill-informed abuse filling the newspapers and radio stations during the months of May, June, and July, the Jesuits, on the initiative of Ellacuría, published a six-part explanation of their work in the *Externado,* "*El Externado piensa así*" ("The *Externado* Thinks like This") in the local press. Besides refuting the charges of Marxist indoctrination, political demagogy, causing family conflict, and lack of Christian spirit, the document was important for the clarity of the framework it gave to others attempting to introduce change to El Salvador's Catholic schools. For the parents whose desire it had been to drive the Jesuits from "their" school, the document provided little cause for hope. Indeed, the product, in the main, of the pens of the residents of UCAII, its tone is one of level confidence, from Ellacuría's explanation of the theological basis for the *Externado*'s change, to Martín-Baró's somewhat cheeky quotation of Galileo at the document's conclusion: "The *Externado San José* knows that a creative, nationalist, and Christian education will be a cause of scandal for some. Precisely, for those who for their own interests would like the world, or at least this scrap of the world that is El Salvador, not to turn. *Eppur se muove!* (But turn it does!)"[45]

THE "*Externado* affair" gradually died down when a referendum of the parents revealed overwhelming support for the Jesuits, but the impression it left on some of El Salvador's most privileged classes that the Jesuits had betrayed their former social allegiances in order to spread communism and poison the minds of the young would not be forgotten.

The prosecutor general had not been able to prove anything against the teaching of the *Externado* although he found that three of the Jesuits—one a priest and the others the students from the UCA—had violated the Salvadoran constitution. In a meeting with Estrada and Archbishop Chávez in July, however, President Molina had been unable to explain exactly how the violation had occurred. Rather he had insisted that the three, all of whom were Nicaraguan, should leave the country, if not expelled by the government then under the orders of their Jesuit superior. Discussion of the three Jesuits' future was taken up at a second meeting with the president, held the following month over dinner at the home of Román Mayorga. Backed up by Ellacuría, Estrada explained that the work of the Jesuits and the government was "along similar lines, preparing the terrain for social reforms."[46] They would not accept the expulsion, as they considered it unjust, and instead asked for the president's vote of confidence. Molina accepted their position and even admitted that the Jesuits had been right about the *Externado.* The dinner ended in a spirit almost of reconciliation, with Molina promising to give the Jesuits the material that had been gathered during the course of the prosecutor's investigation.

He did not keep his word, but the two meetings were indicative of a curious relationship forming between the president and the Jesuits of the UCA, with Mayorga's presence as vice-rector—a Salvadoran, a layman, a former employee of the government development office, and a nephew of Molina's vice-president[47]—a reassuring factor. A little over a year after Molina assumed power in July 1972, the *ECA* editorial of September 1973, "*El Salvador se mueve*" ("El Salvador in Motion"), took note of advances made by the government in monetary reform, negotiations with Honduras, and a new consciousness of the urgency of agrarian reform and tentatively gave the Molina government its endorsement. But a genuine wish to lend the institutional powers of the university to the government's program of reforms was to run into problems on two counts: the lack of material progress in the government's promises and a suspicion of the Jesuits that was only increased by their criticisms both of the absence of reform and of the government's growing tendency to control the opposition this created with repression.

For several years these tensions did not prove insurmountable. Rather, at meetings between Jesuits and the government of Molina in May and June 1974, active collaboration was sought by both sides. Ministers were anxious to have the UCA's technical support in their analysis of the problems they were facing, while the Jesuits believed that through such concrete cooperation they could effect real change that would work in the favor of the country as a whole. There is no doubt that direct contact also provided an opportunity for the Jesuits to demand answers as to why they had, for example, been subjected to blacklists, delays at border control, and threats of expulsion. They tried to explain to the government that it had to distinguish between the useful and the agreeable, "the UCA is perhaps disagreeable for the government, but it also might be useful." They argued that all of the Jesuits working in the UCA felt themselves Salvadoran— they had after all, first arrived as disinterested eighteen year olds—and were "upset to be on lists—the greatest harm you could do us is to throw us out of El Salvador."[48]

One of the criticisms of the UCA was that it had become the "hotbed of subversion" that had previously existed in the National University. As such it was part of an international network run from Moscow, Peking, and Rome by Christian Democrats.[49] These charges originated in the government's observation of the swelling of the ranks of the UCA staff and students after the closure of the National University. This had coincided with the severe limitation of the space available for political opposition, and the effects on the UCA community were long-lasting. As president of the MNR, Guillermo Ungo had been Duarte's vice-presidential candidate. At the end of November 1972 he had returned from a brief exile to become the UCA's director of investigations. Other members of staff included economist Héctor Dada, one of the founders of the Christian Democratic Party; Hector Oquelí Colindres, Ungo's deputy in the MNR; and Rubén Zamora, who had left the seminary far behind him to spend two years in Chile witnessing the rise of Eduardo Frei, study law at the National University, and emerge as the unacknowledged leader of the younger generation of Christian Democrats.

These were men who had been intimately connected with the attempts to create a democratic opposition in the 1960s. Although of differing ages and political positions at the moment of the UCA's founding,[50] as progressive intellectuals they had been unanimous in their opposition to the UCA in its earliest years. Conscious of the changes that the UCA had experienced since then, they, and others besides, had been pleased to be given the opportunity to work within an institution that allowed for divergence of opinion while it maintained a clear vision of its own role in society. Their presence throughout the 1970s enriched the life and work of the university enormously, but was not without problems that increased with the complexity of the political decisions demanded of it. The Jesuits were committed to social change, but wary of the UCA's autonomy being jeopardized by individual political interests. The lay politicians thought that the Jesuits were anything from "naive" to "Machiavellian" and that in 1973 they were moving the UCA toward a role as "political counselor" to Molina that was a grave mistake.[51]

FROM Rome "Central America always seemed to be the eye of the storm,"[52] remembered Father Vincent O'Keefe, one of Arrupe's four assistant generals during a period in which Jesuit provinces throughout the world were experiencing upheaval. The "*Externado* affair" played out as one of a series of the internal crises that beset the Central American Vice-Province throughout the first half of the 1970s. The individual dramas were painful and probably inevitable: the changes needed to bring the work of the vice-province in line with the directions agreed upon in 1970 were drastic enough in themselves and they were taking place in a region, Central America, that was approaching political boiling point. From El Salvador the relationship with Arrupe and the Jesuit authorities in Rome was a further complicating factor. Estrada and his advisers were aware that Rome's impression of disunity among the Central American Jesuits was only exacerbated by the amount of "back channel" informa-

tion provided by Jesuits opposed to the direction in which Estrada was
leading the vice-province. At the same time Estrada's own communication
with Rome was on occasions not as prompt or complete as it might have
been, in part because he did not believe that Rome had really appreciated
that the conflict was "the least that Arrupe could have expected from his
documents."[53]

The culmination came with the Vice-Provincial Congregation held
in April 1974 in preparation for the Jesuits' thirty-second General
Congregation. This Congregation (GCXXXII) was due to open in Rome
at the end of the year; it would work toward redefining "the Society's
response to the call of our age."[54] A milestone in the history of the Jesuits,
the General Congregation was not achieved without pain, division, and
dissent among Jesuits throughout the world. All this and more was true of
Central America where the Vice-Provincial Congregation would be
described as "the longest and most conflictive in the history of the
province . . . a forum in which were aired resentments, suspicions,
aggressions and calumnies."[55] Attempts to define or express the "mission"
of the Jesuits provoked the bitterest arguments as the more conservative
Jesuits sought to halt the process of change, and the more progressive to
have their views enshrined in the Society's decrees. Estrada suffered a
humiliating defeat when it came to the vote necessary in a vice-province to
select who should go to Rome on their behalf. In a secret ballot he was
defeated by the conservative Luis Achaerandio. The margin was that of a
single vote.

Rome looked on in horror, appalled to find from the documents
forwarded from El Salvador that the vice-province was so divided that it
had not even been able to concelebrate the mass with which the
Congregation ended. Although the GCXXXII, with its public commitment of the entire Society to "the service of faith and the promotion of
justice," would both vindicate the more progressive Jesuits and provide
them with a firm basis upon which to act in the future, it seemed necessary
for something to be done about Central America. Amid threats to remove
Estrada from his position as vice-provincial, Rome stepped in to reorga-
nize the government with an express ban on Ellacuría's holding any
position of responsibility within the vice-province other than that of
director of the newly founded Center for Theological Reflection (CRT).
The thinking behind this authoritarian measure—which Ellacuría always
believed to have originated from Dezza rather than Arrupe himself[56]—was
that Ellacuría exerted too strong an influence over Estrada and that the
strength of his character was such that "the government was polarized by

his very presence."[57] While there is no doubt that Ellacuría did exert a strong influence over Estrada, it was an influence that Estrada, a pragmatic man given to government through consultation and in need of all the support he could get from "those who could help me do what I wanted to do," had actively sought and would continue to seek even when Ellacuría was out of the government.

A further factor in Ellacuría's demise from the government was the intense criticism to which his responsibility for the formation of the Jesuits had been subjected, both by his opponents in Central America, and in Rome (most notably by Dezza in a bitter argument at the end of 1971). With a serious commitment to the formation of the young of the vice-province within Central America, Ellacuría's program had been approved at the meeting in September 1970 without many of those who gave their approval paying it much attention. If they had they would have realized that the "liberation" and "effective action" he sought implied a total transformation of their existing ideas of formation for the Society of Jesus. It also implied a maturity of faith and a knowledge of how to live a vocation for the priesthood within a secular environment that Ellacuría perhaps overestimated in his charges. Caught up in the demands of the world in which they were living, many young Jesuits left for reasons of love, politics, or both.

There is no doubt that dismissal from the government was a severe blow for Ellacuría. But at the same time his liberation from the increasingly difficult ping-pong between the vice-province and Rome came at a moment that well suited developments within the UCA. The year 1974 had seen the foundation of the CRT, which, as a center specifically dedicated to the study and production of theology in and for Central America, had been a project close to Ellacuría since its first discussion at the meeting in Madrid in 1969. It also was a year that brought with it important institutional changes: as Achaerandio left El Salvador bound for Rome and the General Congregation, Román Mayorga was named the new rector. Not a Jesuit, and, at thirty-three years old, young for the position, he was nevertheless the logical choice. Intimately associated with the UCA since its first day, Mayorga had been, as vice-rector, a key figure in its subsequent evolution. He was also one of the few people in the university who had the respect and affection of both Jesuit factions necessary for what was inevitably delicate intra-Jesuit mediation. When in 1975 the board of directors was revised to fill the place of Achaerandio with Luis de Sebastián as the new vice-rector, the transformation was complete: the proponents of change within the UCA were for the first time in the majority on the university's principle decision-making body.

As wounds from the debacle of 1974 healed, relations with Rome at the level of the vice-province gradually improved. The year 1976 saw both the transition to a new vice-provincial, César Jerez, committed to reinforcing the changes made at the beginning of the decade, and then elevation to the status of a full province. It had been "a painful gestation" Arrupe told the members of the new province he addressed in Guatemala, but the elevation itself was "a recognition of maturity" and a manner in which to express "the profound esteem I have for this province, for its dynamism, for its apostolic zeal, and for its realism."[58] Years later, from the sick bed in which he would spend the last ten years of his life, Arrupe would struggle to whisper to Ellacuría: "We"—he was referring to himself and the Central American Jesuits—"began separated and far apart, but little by little we came together; we suffered a great deal, but at the end we came to understand each other and reach a level of deep agreement; God wanted it like that."[59]

A GRADUAL easing of difficulties among the Jesuits working in El Salvador coincided with mounting tensions within the country as a whole. Three months before the newly confident UCA celebrated its tenth anniversary in September 1975, events forced *ECA* to retract the guarded optimism it had expressed in its 1973 editorial "El Salvador in Motion." On July 30 government troops had opened fire on a peaceful demonstration in downtown San Salvador, killing and wounding scores of students. They had been demonstrating against the Salvadoran government's hosting of the $1.5 million Miss Universe contest in a country of widespread poverty. In an editorial whose title, *El Salvador se conmueve,* consciously echoed that of 1973, *ECA* argued that the "commotion" so tragically expressed by the massacre of the students was caused not only by El Salvador's lack of motion—no progress had been made in the implementation of reforms called for in the previous editorial—but also because any natural movement forward had been impeded, "braked." And the natural result of that braking would be some kind of explosion.[60]

Many of those who had their political expression frustrated and their personal frustrations unanswered had sought alternative forms of organization. The nucleus of the two major political-military organizations, the FPL (Popular Liberation Forces) and the ERP (People's Revolutionary Army) had been formed in 1970 and 1972 respectively as the former general secretary of the Communist Party, Salvador Cayetano Carpio

("Marcial"), resigned from his post and took the first FPL cell underground and a mixture of dissident Christian Democrats, students, and religious activists came together to form the ERP. To begin with neither organization had a visible impact on the country as a whole; maintaining strict clandestinity they developed their own infrastructures, ideology, and identity. Military actions, such as attacks on government installations and convoys, were kept to a minimum. But as the decade wore on and the government countered these actions (and the kidnapping of officials and businessmen that financed them) with unprecedented repression, so their incidence, and the strength of the political-military organizations themselves, increased.[61]

The evolution of the revolutionary movement, however, was never straightforward. Fundamental ideological differences between the organizations—most simply explained as being between the FPL's commitment to a "prolonged popular struggle" and the more insurrectional tendencies of the ERP—were compounded by the complexity of each organization's internal development. With time, for example, the FPL moved away from Marcial's hard-line Marxist-Leninist atheism toward the conscious collaboration with the politicized Christians of El Salvador's countryside articulated in the 1974 "Letter from the FPL–Farabundo Martí to Progressive Christians."[62] For its part, the ERP was racked by internal problems that culminated in May 1975 with the execution of the poet Roqué Dalton. Dalton had been accused by his own comrades of being a "Soviet-Cuban and CIA double agent." His followers broke with the ERP to form a new organization, the FARN (the Armed Forces of National Resistance, often known simply as the RN), which advocated closer ties to the increasingly mobilized Salvadoran people as it criticized the overly militaristic bent of the ERP.

The spontaneous reaction to the students' massacre took much of San Salvador by surprise. After a memorial mass the following day a diverse group of student, labor, and *campesino* associations calmly took possession of the city's cathedral.[63] Strongly represented was FECCAS, the Christian Peasants' Federation founded in the mid-1960s, but largely dormant until the revitalization of the Church in the years following Medellín. Also inside the cathedral were a number of priests, leaders of the Christian base communities flourishing throughout the archdiocese, and several Jesuit scholastics active in the parish of Aguilares. After a drawn-out and inconclusive series of negotiations—some of which had been mediated by Román Mayorga—the occupants emerged from the cathedral on August 5 to announce the formation of a broad front for the masses, the *Bloque*

Popular Revolucionario (Popular Revolutionary Block), BPR or *Bloque,* as it was almost always known.[64]

By 1977 each of the three revolutionary groups would be backed by an umbrella-like popular organization bringing together the myriad of federations, unions, and associations evolving among students and workers in the cities and *campesinos* empowered by the work of the Church in the countryside: the FPL by the BPR, the RN by FAPU (Front for Unified Popular Action), and the ERP by the LP-28 (People's Leagues of February 28). Taken together the mass organizations constituted a popular movement that would be a defining characteristic of the revolution and war to come.

FOR the Jesuits participation within the rapidly changing circumstances of the country was at its most direct within the team of priests and other collaborators working alongside Rutilio Grande in the parish of Aguilares. The extent and nature of this participation, however, far exceeded anything foreseen when Grande first embarked on his pastoral experiment in 1972. Back then there had been little to the hard life of the *campesinos* of Aguilares to distinguish it from that of the vast majority of the inhabitants of rural El Salvador. A small, hot town 30 kilometers to the north of San Salvador, Aguilares's major product was sugar. Covering an area of 170 square kilometers around the town, the parish had a population of 30,000. The land was divided into 35 *haciendas* dominated by three sugar plantations and the *campesinos* lived off the meager daily wage for seasonal work (around $3) and whatever they could grow on the rocky scraps of land they rented from the landowners.[65]

Inspired by a course in pastoral work he had just completed in Quito, Grande and his original team of three priests initiated a concentrated period of "mission" work quite unlike that of any traditional missionaries. The objective was to transcend the idea of a patriarchal priest overseeing a religion expressed through formal adoration and practices and create, instead, "a community of brothers committed to the construction of a new world, without oppressors or oppressed, according to the plan of God." Intensive work with small groups of people related the Bible and an idea of God to everyday experience in Aguilares, stressing, in unison with Medellín-influenced pastoral leaders throughout Latin America, that the miserable conditions in which people lived could not be accepted with passive resignation as "God's will": "God is not in the clouds lying in a hammock. God does things and wants you to build his Kingdom here on earth."[66]

"Aguilares was always a crisis of growth," remembered Salvador Carranza, who accompanied Grande throughout the experiment. "I don't think there was ever the peace to say, 'isn't this going well!' "[67] The process assumed a momentum that took the Jesuits by surprise as the parish quickly developed a core of over three hundred committed and motivated delegates of the Word, coordinating catechism classes and "conscientization" at every level. This momentum accelerated rapidly in 1974 with the arrival of an auxiliary team of Jesuits studying theology at the Center for Theological Reflection, reinforced by visits from slightly younger Jesuit students who lived in a community in Antiguo Cuscatlán behind the UCA and a group of UCA students. Some of these "collaborators" threw all their energies into the reorganization of FECCAS—which had had only a minimal presence in the parish until their arrival—with consequences that would have a profound effect on the parish and its role in the political development of the country.

The young Jesuits were of a generation whose formation had been at the epicenter of change. The majority were Central American and from backgrounds comfortable enough to have separated them from the hard realities of their own countries. The slightly older theology students had been novices at the end of the old regime. During years spent studying in Quito and then living in a small community in a poor neighborhood in Mexico City they had come into direct contact with the poor of Latin America for the first time. This experience combined with the study of the works of Paulo Freire, Marx, and the Latin American dependency theorists to awaken a profound commitment to working with the people of Central America to counter the injustice of their lives. This commitment was shared by the younger students who, as the first generation to benefit from Ellacuría's "formation for liberation," had remained in Central America, absorbing the grievances of the people they had worked among in hospitals, on building sites or in agricultural cooperatives. As both groups of Jesuits moved away from their privileged backgrounds they "began to discover," as one of them put it, "that we had lived a history of our countries that was not true."[68]

The new Center for Theological Reflection took shape, with Ellacuría joined by a team of theologians including Jon Sobrino, and it was decided that the young Jesuits, under the supervision of the Mexican Rafael Moreno, would form a community in Aguilares and come in to the UCA for their studies. The exchange between the work of the parish and the CRT was a process of mutual enrichment paradigmatic of the experience of other centers for liberation theology throughout the continent. Sobrino's writing on "The Historical Jesus" (the title of an article he published in *ECA* in 1975), for example, would be complemented by and rooted in what was real and necessary by the students' close relationship to *campesinos* who had in Aguilares discovered the relevance of the historical Jesus to their own lives. "For me Jesus is our guide," explained a *campesino* to Carlos Cabarrús, who would use the experience of Aguilares as the basis of his doctoral thesis. "He is a leader who gave us a good example with his life. He was in favor of the poor. He wanted there to be justice, love, understanding, and peace. He spoke really strongly against those who had power and exploited the people. He persuaded the hard of heart, took the powerful down from their thrones, and all the time was in favor of the poor. He is the first person I obey and I shall follow him always, even if that means giving up my life."[69]

But the presence of these collaborators in Aguilares quickly became complicated by the nature of their circumstances. The foundations laid by Grande and the original parish team had acted as a form of political yeast: from organization for the preparation for the Kingdom of God on earth to demands for more direct political organization, the step was a small one. The step, moreover, was sanctioned by Medellín's guidelines for the pastoral activity of the Latin American clergy. As the Document on Peace made clear, priests were encouraged to favor the efforts of the people "to create and develop their own base organizations for the revindication and consolidation of their rights and for the search of true justice."[70] But then things got more complicated: when repression of this activity—largely by the paramilitary organization ORDEN—mounted, the space for political protest closed and armed struggle emerged for many as the necessary tool for political liberation.[71] "The *campesino* has three options," concluded Cabarrús, "dying of hunger, as indeed happens when there is no work nor land and a lot of repression; dying fighting, in the worst instances; or the hope of living in a different society, a society that will be good for himself and his sons. He has chosen the third, with the risk of falling into the second."[72]

A distinction within the young Jesuits quickly emerged. While the parish team as a whole remained committed to a pastoral "accompaniment" of the people in this crucial period of their history, a small group believed this represented an insufficient response to the urgency of the moment. This group of two Guatemalans, Alberto Enríquez and Fernando Ascoli, and the Nicaraguan Antonio Cardenal, realized that they shared a conviction that the Christian commitment awakened in the people of Aguilares would need to move toward armed revolution if the injustice of their lives was to be redressed. Inspired by their contacts with the outstanding *campesino* leader Apolinario Serrano or "Polín," as he was known, the three threw all their energies into FECCAS, which had its first national seminar at the UCA in December 1974. Their tireless activity became further separated from that of the parish as they set about the organization of what they called simply "the Movement." Never meant to challenge the political vanguards existing in the FPL and ERP, Antonio Cardenal explained the Movement as "an organization for the support of the emergence of a broad front of the masses."[73]

The activities of the three young Jesuits created a series of conflicts both in Aguilares with Rutilio Grande and his team and in the UCA, where during the rapid acceleration of the process in 1975 (the three had been inside the cathedral among the founders of the BPR) Ellacuría would argue that they were making a grave mistake. Deeply distressed by the situation, Grande worried that the parish was losing some of its best delegates to FECCAS. "In some way the seed has been sown by our work," he complained to Antonio Cardenal. "And if they leave too quickly we shall never arrive at the harvest."[74] A lengthy document prepared by other Jesuits in his support assessed the experience of Aguilares and found doctrinal justification for the mobilization of the *campesinos* in the documents of Vatican II and Medellín. But the justification made Grande's position no easier to bear: Grande felt himself so caught between a total respect for the *campesino's* right to organize and his worry about what was happening to the parish that at one point he offered his resignation to the archbishop.[75]

From the UCA Ellacuría argued strongly against the three young Jesuits' progression toward leading roles within the development of the popular movement. He took them to task for the neglect of academic studies he believed a fundamental base from which analysis, free from any one ideology, could be constructed. Then he argued that by actively assuming a role within the political process they would be absorbed by it, becoming just a few more individuals in a mass of actors. His position was that the university and the Society of Jesus were entities capable of playing an important and original role in the process of change, but that that capability was dependent on their autonomy. While the arguments became, with time, increasingly bitter, these were not arguments the three could lightly dismiss even as they were convinced that Ellacuría's lack of direct contact with the people of El Salvador had led him to underestimate the strength of their organizations. In their view the demands of the Salvadoran reality were such that it was, quite simply, impossible to stay on the outside.

The Movement's first meeting with the FPL was held at the McDonald's on Boulevard de los Héroes, San Salvador's central thoroughfare. Worried about infiltration and the possibility that the meeting might turn out to be a setup, Alberto Enríquez had not wanted to go alone. The lengthy figure of Toño Cardenal had sat hunched over a table a few meters away, a kitchen knife tucked inside his shirt "just in case" ("not that I would have known what to do with it," he had remarked with a grin nearly seventeen years later, an FMLN *comandante* in Chalatenango), but their worries proved unnecessary. Coincidence of positions on the strength of the popular movement as a broad and fluid base upon which to build a revolution grew through a series of clandestine meetings with the FPL's second-in-command Felipe Peña until the nature of the decision they were facing became clear to all three of them. There was never any doubt for them, the organization they would eventually join, or the Jesuits they left behind that a decision to take up arms in a revolution was totally incompatible with a life as a Jesuit priest.[76]

Juan Hernández Pico succeeded Ellacuría as the Jesuit responsible for the formation of the younger generations. Writing of Toño Cardenal in particular (although not excluding the other two) Hernández Pico would remember how Cardenal's decision to leave the Jesuits had "destroyed" both himself and Ellacuría, even as they "respected it": "it was taken with the rectitude of conscience that characterized his whole life. But we couldn't avoid the sadness of seeing a young Nicaraguan leave the Jesuits, one of those in whom we had sown the hope of the progressive Central Americanization of the Society of Jesus."[77] For some their departure had been the final "proof" of the failings of Ellacuría's innovations in the Jesuits' formation. "All we are doing with our formation is losing the young," Gondra complained to the Regional Congregation in 1978. The Jesuits in the congregation were seated around a single table at the time and had looked up in surprise as Ellacuría rose to his feet. "We may have lost them for the Society," he said with driving emphasis, "but they are not a loss for the people of El Salvador." The Jesuits sat in startled silence, then burst into applause.[78]

THE year 1976 was a watershed for the UCA. It began with the explosion of a bomb placed outside the building housing *ECA*. This first physical attack, it was believed, had been in reaction to *ECA's* publication of a special edition for August–September 1975, dedicated to theology. This was not the first time that the UCA's theological production had caught the attention of the darker forces within the country: in late 1975 the existence of a threat to kill a politician, a nun, and a priest had been announced on television. Ellacuría had discovered that the priest in question was, perhaps surprisingly, not himself but the recently arrived Jon Sobrino. The reason? His dense theological treatise on "The Historical Jesus."[79] *ECA*'s response to the attack in early 1976 was succinct: "Neither bombs nor any other type of violence can silence the liberating word of *ECA*, committed as a university should be to the Salvadoran people and only to them."[80]

The greatest drama of 1976, however, began with a telephone call in June from Atilio Vieytez, a former professor at the UCA and now minister of planning in Molina's government. The call came to ask for the UCA's support of a proposed project of agrarian transformation. The university had been a consistent advocate of agrarian reform since its participation in the Agrarian Reform Congress in 1970—when the UCA delegation had been led by Vieytez—and the Molina government knew it would have few friends elsewhere. The left would demand more extensive reform while the right would demand none at all. The oligarchy and private interests represented by ANEP (National Association of Private Enterprise) held that agrarian reform was a communist plot. In 1970, for example, their delegates to the congress had withdrawn on the first day and then expressed horror and surprise that the UCA contingent, in the university's first expression of institutional independence, had not done the same. A few hours after José Inocencio Alas, the Church's representative at the congress, had spoken for agrarian reform, he was abducted from outside the National Palace, beaten, drugged, and left naked on the edge of a cliff.[81]

To say that reform was overdue would be a gross understatement. Between 1961 and 1975 landless peasants had increased from 12 percent to 41 percent of the rural population; 92 percent of properties covered 27 percent of the cultivatable land while at the other extreme a mere 0.7 percent covered 39 percent.[82] The "transformation" proposed by Molina ("We don't use the term agrarian reform," he had explained, "because that is communist terminology"[83]) was initially for an area of abject poverty in the cotton-growing lowlands of San Miguel and Usulután. This area was dominated by five major landholders, each of whom had an income equivalent to that of almost 7,000 local families. Illiteracy was running at 65 percent, lack of sanitation at 98 percent, drinking water at 50 percent, and adequate housing at 35 percent. Employment expectations were about 141 days of work a year. The area covered less than 4 percent of El Salvador's workable land.[84]

The government proposed to redistribute small parcels of land to 12,000 *campesino* families. The landowners would be able to keep up to thirty-five hectares and would be reimbursed at market value for whatever land they lost. The pilot project would have taken up to five years to complete and decades if applied to the entire country at the same rate, yet it caused uproar among landholders throughout the country. A new group calling itself FARO (Agricultural Front of the Eastern Region) material-ized to join ANEP in flooding the pages of the national press with articles, advertisements, and fliers denouncing Molina, and all who backed him, for their subversive intentions.

Opposition from the left had fed on the political inconsistencies inherent in a piece of legislation drawn up by a government trying to hedge its bets. Molina tried to pacify the landowners by assuring them that the reform was a "life insurance policy that your children will one day be grateful for" as it defused the mounting tension in the countryside without too radical a change. In stark contrast, however, was his claim that it was "not for the benefit of a small and privileged group of people . . . but principally for the great majority."[85] The Christian Democrats, no doubt with an eye on the presidential elections due the following year, warned the Salvadoran people not to be tricked by "campaigns and controversies of the powerful" and called for "a true agrarian reform," while the popular organizations, noting the positive noises being made by the United States, denounced the transformation as a plot hatched in collusion with the Organization of American States in order to modernize a capitalist state facing crisis.[86]

The debate within the UCA went, as did all major political decisions, to its Upper Council. The lay politicians were among those who argued vehemently against the UCA's lending its name to the proposed reform. "We didn't think that there existed the real conditions for agrarian reform," remembered Guillermo Ungo, on the council at the time, "but Ellacuría thought that was because of a dogmatic and sectarian position we held as the opposition."[87] When it came to the vote the position of the Jesuits and of Mayorga, who believed that the "rational and Christian" reaction was to welcome the reform as a significant improvement on *no* reform and "an indispensable first step" (in the strengthening of the State over the oligarchy as much as in agrarian reform itself), held the day. It had not been an easy decision, but they were convinced it was one that had the real interests of the country at heart. The council released a public statement in July to say that the university looked "with hope" on the proposed agrarian transformation.[88]

The position was a lonely one. Besides the U.S. embassy the only other forces to give the transformation their public support were the Communist Party and the Salvadoran Communal Union (UCS), a U.S.-backed *campesino* organization that stood to gain directly from its implementation. In August, as the propaganda campaign intensified, a bomb came close to destroying the offices of *ECA*. Work continued toward the September–October edition of the magazine, slated, under the editorial hand of Ignacio Martín-Baró, to be dedicated to a wide-ranging exposition of the agrarian question in El Salvador. Ellacuría's contribution was a lengthy analysis of the concept of property as a principle of de-ideologization that grounded support for the agrarian transformation in moral, ethical, and philosophical principles as much as in the socioeconomic reality of the country. Ambiguous as the proposed reform was, in it he believed there lay "the common good, which is the best form of finding the good of all, even though . . . the good of all cannot be achieved without an ill for some."[89] In early September came more bombs, this time containing anti-Jesuit propaganda material, just in case the message was not getting through.

But before the special edition of the magazine could appear, Molina—who had vowed, "not one step back"[90]—caved in. The oligarchy had turned to the military for reinforcement of their position and had found a key ally in Defense Minister General Carlos Humberto Romero (within a matter of months the presidential candidate for the PCN). On October 20, the assembly introduced changes to the original legislation sufficient to be denounced as "not one step back but a 180° turn and a headlong rush of thousands of paces."[91]

The UCA was left high and dry. It had risked its name and reputation to assume the position it believed to be correct and had now been left on its own. As the politicians inside the UCA had their worst suspicions confirmed—"You see? Those poor Jesuits went in with the government and believed that everything was rational and now they've gotten trapped"[92]—Ignacio Ellacuría took to the typewriter. He produced a brilliant, scorching editorial, *¡A sus órdenes, mi Capital!*, "At your orders, Capital!", denouncing the pressure the oligarchy and private enterprise had been able to bring to bear on the government as proof that El Salvador was living under "a dictatorship of the bourgeoisie": "The government has given in to the pressure of national capitalism, and it may well be to that of Central American capitalism as well; the government has given in, the government has submitted, the government has obeyed. After so much hot-air of foresight, strength, and decision, the government has ended up saying: *At your orders, Capital!*"[93]

THE animosity of capital toward the UCA was demonstrated again in early December when a large bomb exploded in its central administrative building, almost blowing Ibisate through a wide hole in the wall. "Why do they bomb us?" asked the *ECA* editorial. "Because the university represents a serious danger for those who live alienated from reason and justice and represents, in the other extreme, a real support for the oppressed majorities growing in consciousness of their necessities and in the possibility of the self-determination of their destinies."[94]

"Internal tension," Arrupe had promised his Jesuits in 1967. "Serious practical consequences" had been what the Jesuits of Central America had foreseen from their option for liberation taken in September 1970. Tension they had suffered aplenty in the last seven years, and the bombs in El Salvador represented practical consequences of the most dangerous kind. Yet there was an undeniable sense, both in the assured reaction of the Jesuits themselves and in a letter that arrived from Rome for the new provincial, César Jerez, that the public opprobrium and physical assault confirmed that they were on the right track, whatever the consequences. "I cannot be less than pleased and congratulate you most sincerely," wrote Arrupe, "for having defended the cause of the poor and for suffering persecution for this reason."[95]

CHAPTER THREE

How Much More Does It Take?

After ten years of bankrolling failure, it is time we altered our policy. Ten years ago four nuns were tortured and murdered, and Archbishop Romero was felled by an assassin's bullet. Five days ago six priests were dragged from their beds and shot, and in between 70,000 Salvadoran men, women, and children have died. How much more does it take?

Senator Mark Hatfield, 1989

AT 6:00 A.M. on November 16, 1989 Pedro Arévalo Coreas, an agent with the National Police in San Salvador, noticed some interference on his radio. Since the FMLN guerrillas launched their offensive on the night of November 11, his orders had been to supervise the distribution of food to active duty agents from his radio car. This Thursday morning he was gathering up the pans he had given out full of food the night before when his radio crackled into life. "We've killed Ellacuría," said the voice on his radio. "Enjoy!"[2]

THE Jesuit provincial looked in the mirror. His face was split in two. One half was clean shaven, fresh, well rested, the other thick with soap, awaiting attention from the razor he held in his hand. At that moment Paco Estrada appeared beside him. "Chema," he said. "Obdulio's here. He says they've killed Ellacuría and the others."

It was 6:45 A.M.

"Chema"—for José María—Tojeira, provincial of the Central American Jesuits since 1988, looked younger than his forty-two years. Born in Galicia in northwestern Spain, he was a naturalized Honduran with a warm, easy manner, a laugh that could be heard a block away from his office, and a strength and authority respected throughout the province. The moment stuck like a knife in his memory, pierced through by the look in Estrada's eyes: sunken, furrowed by lines and shadows, the look came from a place that neither had been before.

As Estrada left his room and Tojeira finished shaving, he felt himself consumed by emptiness, a physical sense of loneliness swelling upward

71

from the pit of his stomach that threatened to make him faint. Calling out
to another of the Jesuits living with him in Calle Mediterráneo, he began
to speak out aloud the things that needed to be done: "I have to finish
shaving. And then I'll get dressed. And then we'll go and see. Tell them to
wait so that I'm with the first to go." The sentences were spoken not so
much from a need to communicate what they contained as from a need to
be reminded through speech, through simple contact with another, "that
life continues, with all its ordinary and most basic functions, with the
ability to talk, to look, to explain, to move . . . that the internal slide
toward emptiness can be controlled."[3]

OBDULIO Ramos had wondered where his wife and daughter were. For
the second night of this offensive they had been sleeping in the room
loaned to them by the Jesuits. Away from the road and the noise of trucks
and tanks, the bursts of gunfire or the thud of bombs, they thought they
would get more sleep in one of the guest rooms at the back of the Jesuits'
new residence. The noise had been terrible the night before. Obdulio had
been so scared he had lost all sense of where the noise had been coming
from and had hidden under his bed. But when his wife and daughter
didn't appear in the morning, he left their gatehouse and followed the
path around through the garden he tended and up toward the residence to
find them.

There is a mango tree where the path crests the slope up to the
residence. Beside it Obdulio came to a sudden stop. The door to the
corridor of Jesuit bedrooms was wide open, the white wall to its right
splashed red with blood. On the patch of grass in front lay four bodies, face
down, unmoving. Ignacio Ellacuría, Segundo Montes, Ignacio Martín-
Baró, and Amando López. Blood, brains, and spent cartridges covered the
ground. A darkening trail led in through the doorway. Within it lay a
single lifeless shoe. Instinctively, Obdulio looked to the left, down the
steps toward the covered passage that ran perpendicular to the Jesuits'
bedrooms. In one of those rooms his wife and daughter had sought peace
and quiet. The doors to all three gaped open.

The two women lay embracing on the floor, the face of the
15-year-old Celina a mask of tranquility amid senseless destruction. Her
mother, Obdulio's wife, Elba, was completely unrecognizable; her face
and most of her head had been blown away. One leg lay across the body of
her daughter, with her blue dress hitched up around her thighs. The floor,
walls, and twin divan beds were splattered with blood and pieces of skull.

Obdulio turned away. He had to go and tell Father Chema what had happened.[4]

Lucía Cerna was awakened by a nightmare. She had crept back to bed after she saw the uniformed men near the gate to the Jesuits' residence. After Father Nacho cried out she had heard him no more. But in the nightmare that jolted her out of her sleep he was downstairs, standing on the doorstep under where they were sleeping, and laughing. She got up, got her little girl Geraldina ready, and saw that her husband was talking through the door to some of the UCA watchmen. They told him they'd seen what looked like bundles, lying on the grass outside the Jesuits' residence. Lucía combed her hair and turned to her husband, Jorge. "Let's go and see."

Skirting around the chapel they entered the residence's garden through the gate Lucía had been able to see the night before. On their left they passed a room with two women in it. Lucía was frightened but continued along the pathway, until, looking up the steps in front of them, she saw the bundles lying on the grass. One of them was wearing the blue shirt that Martín-Baró had been wearing the evening before. "Look," she said to Jorge. "Look at that. That looks like Father Nacho." "Take the little girl back," Jorge told her. "She shouldn't be seeing this." Lucía took Geraldina back to the chapel and waited for the men. Then she gathered up her identity documents, put them in a small bag, and set off to find the Jesuits in Calle Mediterráneo.[5]

Lucía arrived, tears streaming down her face, a few minutes after Obdulio. Ibisate, who had been curious to try to locate the origin of the shooting he had heard in the night, had met Obdulio in the street outside on his way to find them. He was crying and had both hands raised to his head as he broke the news. "Father, last night they killed all the priests, my wife, and her daughter." Ibisate helped him inside the house and was telling the other Jesuits, sleepily emerging from their bedrooms, when Lucía arrived: "Something terrible has happened. That shooting yesterday—it was inside. Go. You must go. Go and see the others."[6]

Chema Tojeira came down the stairs buttoning up his shirt. It seemed safer for the seven Jesuits to split up into two groups. Four skirted around to the right to come in through the gate by Obdulio's gatehouse, while the other three turned left on Calle Cantábrico to enter the university grounds through the back of number 16. It was not yet seven o'clock.

SINCE the launching of the FMLN offensive it had been bedlam inside the
estado mayor's Operations Center, COCFA, the usual command structures
having been superceded by the crisis. One officer whose duties took him in
and out of the center on a constant basis pinched the forefinger and thumb
of his right hand together to describe it being "like this—thick with
colonels. They were always in there, falling asleep on their feet." This
officer had been sent to COCFA on an errand soon after six o'clock on the
morning of November 16. He had been surprised by the casual tone with
which another officer had asked "How did it go in the UCA last night?"[7]

"We knew it was the army that had killed the Jesuits by about 8:00
A.M.," one captain in military intelligence would come forward to say a
year and a half later.[8] Captain Luis Parada had been present at the morning
meeting of the National Intelligence Directorate (DNI) when it was
interrupted, twice, by Captain Carlos Herrera Carranza. Located a few
hundred yards up the hill from the military academy and the *estado mayor*,
the DNI was created by the CIA and shared its office space. During the
offensive, when it was under the command of Colonel Carlos Guzmán
Aguilar, the DNI had been meeting at 7:30 A.M., half an hour earlier than
its usual 8:00 A.M. start.

The first interruption came as Herrera announced that Ellacuría had
been killed resisting arrest. The word "arrest," as Parada would testify,
suggested that "those responsible . . . were members of the armed forces."
Some present at the meeting remember that officers "cheered and
clapped" at this news. Herrera left the room, but reappeared a few minutes
later with an update: it was not just Ellacuría, but "eight priests" who had
been killed resisting arrest. This was serious. No one kills, or can say they
killed, *eight* priests making an arrest. One of the most senior officers
present, Colonel Roberto Pineda Guerra, a former director of the National
Intelligence School, put a damper on the celebratory mood by berating the
officers around him. "Idiots! Don't you realize we've just lost the war?"[9]

Shortly after the meeting ended two Salvadoran officers, together
with one of their counterparts from the CIA, made the short journey over
to the UCA, half a mile to the southeast of the DNI offices. They were on
the scene early, but the news had traveled fast, and people were gathering
from all over the city. When the press—with their cameras—appeared, the
CIA agent quietly slipped away. He would catch up with one of the DNI
officers later to tell him: "We believe that the military did this."[10]

Consternation among some of those who had attended the early
morning meeting only increased when they heard the broadcasts beginning at about 10:00 A.M. on the army-controlled National Radio channel.

Again and again the radio told the nation that the murders had been committed by the FMLN: "The Communists kill all those who don't serve them. . . . The government and armed forces condemn these assassinations . . . committed by the FMLN in an attempt to destablize democracy."[11] These broadcasts indicated that a high-level decision had been taken to cover up what could only have been a military action. Officers were uncertain of what would happen next. Would the United States and the foreign press buy the version that the FMLN had killed the priests? Pressure on the army to investigate the deaths of villagers in San Sebastián in 1988 had led to the detention of three officers—and that had been for the death of *campesinos,* not well-known Jesuits.

News reached U.S. Ambassador William Walker during the daily meeting of the Country Team of the U.S. Mission to El Salvador. Since the offensive began, these key staff meetings had been held every morning, at first at the ambassador's residence in the exclusive San Benito district, while embassy and military officials evaluated the security risk involved in traveling in to the embassy in the center of town. The meetings had been, as Walker remembered with a grin more than a year later, "well focused."[12] Even a self-confessed "crisis junkie"[13] could never have expected things could be so bad: nearly ten years and some $4 billion worth of United States aid expended, and the FMLN rebels were quite clearly not just undefeated, but capable of launching the largest offensive of the entire civil war. Whole sectors of the city were under rebel control, while small units operated freely, it appeared, wherever they pleased. Earlier in the week guards and marines posted outside the ambassador's residence had almost become involved in a serious confrontation between the Salvadoran army and the FMLN on the ambassador's doorstep. Within the embassy, jokes on the lines of "I'll see you on the roof" (shades of Saigon), were not appreciated.

Walker was an affable career diplomat in his fifties who had worked in and around Central America since the mid-1970s. Until becoming deputy to Elliot Abrams—Reagan's hard-line assistant secretary for inter-American affairs—in the mid-1980s, Walker had a reputation as something of a liberal among U.S. diplomats in the region. By the time he left his position as political counselor in 1977, he had been "virtually *persona non grata"* in El Salvador, according to one colleague, for the fuss he had made about the escalating human rights' abuses.[14] But Washington had paid him little attention. After a stint at the Council on Foreign Relations in New York and a couple of years in Honduras from 1980 to

1982, Walker had returned to El Salvador in August 1988, proving his mettle with a parachute jump at the air force's Ilopango base in a none too auspicious start. The ambassador's broken leg was in a plaster cast for weeks.

Only the day before, as opposition leaders Guillermo Ungo and Rubén Zamora stayed holed up in friendly Latin American embassies and reports of searches and detentions carried out in the offices and homes of church workers, union leaders, and prominent members of the popular movement came flooding in, Walker had assured reporters that he had "every confidence that the democratic left will have the same [political] space it had before."[15] And now at nine o'clock in the morning, in the middle of a meeting, he was being handed a piece of paper that said there had been an announcement that Ellacuría had been killed. He had two reactions: the first was that Ellacuría was, he believed, in Spain, and so it couldn't be true; the second that he hoped it didn't refer to some other Jesuit. Asking for more information he was told that it was not just Ellacuría, but four or five others as well. Still thinking, "impossible," he allowed now for the possibility that, "if it's true then it is going to be big."[16]

Also present at the Country Team meeting was Richard Chidester, who filled the sensitive position of legal officer. Chidester too had made the rounds of Reagan's Central America: he had previously been a political officer in the embassy in Honduras, responsible for liaison with the *contras,* and before that had worked with the Drug Enforcement Agency in Mexico City. His brief in San Salvador was to exert pressure on legal cases of particular importance to U.S. policy as they made their way through the Salvadoran legal system. As such he was the embassy's point man with the Special Investigative Unit, the SIU.

Together with a forensic unit, the SIU had been founded in 1985 to constitute a new Commission on Investigations that was introduced as part of El Salvador's U.S.-funded Judicial Reform Program.[17] Initially established with a mandate to investigate crimes deemed sensitive to military pressures, such as allegations of human rights abuses committed by members of the armed forces, the commission and the SIU had never acquired formal independence from the military structure. Despite technical training, financial aid, and its own permanent U.S. adviser, the SIU could not, or would not, overcome one of the most imposing of the barriers to real and lasting judicial reform in El Salvador: the impunity of Salvadoran military officers. Judges had been bought off, terrified into resignation, had fled into exile, and been killed, but not a single officer had ever been convicted of a human rights–related crime. The man Chidester called as soon as the Country Team meeting was over, Lieutenant Colonel Manuel Antonio Rivas, wore civilian clothes as he went about his duties, as did the thirty-odd detectives subordinate to him within the SIU, but all were active-duty members of the security forces.[18] As such they were answerable to military discipline and open to advancement or reward only within the military.

"I SAW it all, Father, it was them," sobbed Lucía Cerna to Tojeira, as she stood with the Jesuits over the bodies of their murdered brothers. "There were a lot of them. Maybe thirty or forty. I don't know. I saw some of them. They made a lot of noise, shooting, breaking doors and windows." "Who are 'they'?" came the question, gently. "Soldiers, Father."[19]

There was plenty to do that morning. Telephone calls to be made, people to be told, questions to be answered. Tojeira was running through a list—someone should call the other Jesuit communities; someone should go and tell the archbishop; they would need to call the father general in Rome, the "provincial of provincials," the senior Jesuit in Spain, the families—when they realized that they could smell burning. They checked back along the corridor, through the Jesuits' bedrooms, but found nothing. The trail in through the open door led to the second bedroom on the right—Jon Sobrino's. The peripatetic theologian was giving a conference in Thailand; his friend and colleague Juan Ramón Moreno lay stretched out on his bedroom floor, blood from his head flowing into the pages of books knocked from the bookshelf to the right of the bedroom door. In the room across the corridor lay the body of Joaquín López y López, face up, a gaping hole in his chest. But no burning.

Someone came to call them to the ground floor offices of the Monsignor Romero Pastoral Center. They followed the covered pathway, past the room where the two women lay, through the gate behind the chapel, and around to the right and the front of the building. Pieces of mortar shell and cartridges lay like fallen leaves in autumn. The building itself was pockmarked with gunfire, its windows broken. Inside, the entrance and nearby offices had been gutted. The walls and floor were coated with ash, the furniture twisted out of shape by raw heat. Some kind of flammable liquid had been thrown over books, documents, and computers. It was still burning. A large portrait of Monsignor Romero hung on a wall to the left of the entrance; it was scorched and crinkled out of shape. The expression on his face was one of tranquil preoccupation; characteristically, he had his hands clasped in his lap, his left hand fiddling with his bishop's ring on the right. Recoiling from the heat directed at the center of the picture, the covering glass had melted and crystallized into smoky curtains on either side of the murdered archbishop.[20]

"They were assassinated with lavish barbarity," Tojeira told the journalists who had rapidly gathered from all points of the city. "These people never touched a weapon, and they came here to kill them with bullets."[21] Clusters of reporters gathered around Tojeira and the other Jesuits, probing for what they knew, rapidly assembling brief biographical information for the stories that would run on front pages across the world. During the last few days the journalists had been working around the clock. Even those resident in the country, conscious for months of the rumors that "something big" was in the air, had been taken by surprise by the scale of the offensive. They were a tough, experienced lot. You can't cover Central America without having seen your fair share of bodies. But many were in tears that morning. One photographer actually could not take any photographs. Some of them had known some of the Jesuits well: any rookie reporter arriving in El Salvador knew of the Jesuits' reputation for rational, intelligent, and compassionate analysis of a highly complex political situation. And now they lay before them on the grass, the flies gathering in the spilled blood with the heat of the sun.

Reporters, Jesuits, colleagues from the UCA, and friends gathered around to hear the words of Archbishop Rivera Damas. Ashen and drawn, he was accompanied by his auxiliary bishop, Monsignor Gregorio Rosa Chávez, and María Julia Hernández, director of *Tutela Legal,* the archdiocese's legal aid office. The three had been in a meeting when the news arrived, discussing the need for the Church to reiterate its condemnation of the air force's indiscriminate bombing of the poor residential areas ringing the city. The FMLN guerrillas were operating from these neighborhoods, but it was the civilian residents who were taking the brunt of the bombing. "We're Christians," Rivera said at once. "We must go and pray."[22] Like Ellacuría and the Jesuits, the two bishops had been threatened by the anonymous callers on the government radio a few days earlier. "The same hatred that killed Monsignor Romero has now killed these Jesuits," Rivera told those gathered around the bodies. "This should not serve as a reason for more bloodshed . . . their sacrifice must signify an end to the violence."[23]

IT was nighttime in Thailand when Jon Sobrino was called to the telephone. Eleven o'clock in the morning in San Salvador. Since Monday, November 13 he had been in Hua Hin, about two hundred kilometers from Bangkok, giving a short theological course. From there he had followed the news of the offensive in El Salvador and had even managed to call home to see how the other Jesuits were doing. They had told him that Ellacuría had returned from Europe and that their new residence and Sobrino's Pastoral Center had been searched by the army, but they were fine. On the night of November 16 he was asleep when an Irish priest with him heard something on the BBC's World Service about some Jesuit in El Salvador getting killed. He telephoned Julian Filochowski, the director of the aid agency CAFOD in London, to ask him whether it was true and exactly what had happened. Filochowski explained and then asked— surprised at the long distance phone call—"but why do you want to know?" "Sobrino's here with me," the priest answered, "he's asleep." "Get him," said Filochowski, a trusted friend of the Central American Jesuits for many years.

Sobrino walked to the telephone thinking, "They've killed Ella-curía." It was almost like Monsignor Romero, he thought, something that had always seemed possible, something for which they were, if not prepared, then not totally unprepared either. "Something terrible has happened," Filochowski began. "I know," answered Sobrino, "Ellacuría." But he didn't know. Filochowski asked if he was sitting down, if he had a pencil. And then he told him what had happened. "They have murdered Ignacio Ellacuría." Sobrino remained silent, but did not write anything as it was this that he had half-expected. But Filochowski went on: "They have murdered Segundo Montes, Ignacio Martín-Baró, Amando López, Juan Ramón Moreno, and Joaquín López y López." Sobrino wrote in silence, hoping the list would end as each name reverberated like a hammer blow he could only receive in total helplessness. Together with two women seeking only a restful night's sleep, his community had been murdered. They had murdered his entire community.[24]

"I HAVE difficulty in imagining what sort of animals would, in cold blood, execute priests and other innocents," Ambassador Walker told journalists in a briefing. "This is a crime of such repugnance that to say that I condemn or deplore it seems inadequate. It is a barbarous act that has not only brought shame to El Salvador, but will leave a gaping hole in this country's intellectual and academic community."[25] His words, although stronger than most, expressed a condemnation that came from all sectors of Salvadoran society and, as the day wore on, from friends, church authorities, universities, and governments around the world. As the U.S. embassy offered protection for any witnesses who might come forward,

President Cristiani committed his government to investigate this crime thoroughly and punish the guilty, whoever they might be: "If there are people involved who turn out to be members of the armed forces, then the weight of the law must fall upon them."[26]

In the privacy of a meeting with Tojeira and Bishops Rivera and Rosa Chávez, Cristiani admitted the possibility that lay behind his public statements: the crime could have been committed by a military unit acting beyond its orders. "But I can assure you," he told the three men, "that the *estado mayor* has nothing to do with this murder. I have spent a lot of time with them in these days and I have been in constant contact with them."[27] A confidential cable released under the Freedom of Information Act suggests that a similar message was conveyed to Walker in a visit "a subdued but calm President Cristiani" paid to the ambassador's residence on November 18. Explaining the steps he was taking to ensure "a serious investigation into the murders of the UCA Jesuits"—steps that included a request for help from the UK and Spain—the president launched into what appears to have been his assessment of the role played by the army in the killing of the Jesuits. Although this section was deleted before its release, immediately following the deletion the cable reads: "He reiterated that despite all of this, he is still very proud of the job that the ESAF (El Salvadoran Armed Forces) has done this far, and noted that the UCA murders are the only important black spot on its record." The cable was signed "Walker."[28]

Senior officials of Cristiani's government followed the position not of their president but of a communiqué from the armed forces which held that the "treacherous murder" was "committed by the FMLN guerrillas."[29] On a visit to the grounds of the UCA, the deputy minister for foreign affairs told all who would listen that the murders had been committed by FMLN guerrillas wanting to make the country even more ungovernable than it already was. His source, he claimed, was the FMLN's *Radio Venceremos.* This opinion was repeated by the foreign minister himself, José Manuel Pacas Castro, in interviews with two U.S. television journalists and insinuated over the following days by Attorney General Mauricio Colorado's affirmation to the Salvadoran press that the finding of evidence of the use of Soviet-made AK47s at the scene of the crime could be interpreted as a sign that the FMLN was responsible.[30] The explanation of this theory was that the relationship of "friendship, respect, and mutual help" between Ellacuría and President Cristiani provided an incentive for the FMLN to purge itself of someone who was no longer an asset.[31] Those who supported this theory pointed to the initials FMLN scrawled on a wall within the Pastoral Center and the crudely lettered sign left on the university's back entrance claiming that it was the FMLN that had, in killing the Jesuits, brought justice to the "enemy spies."[32]

The circumstantial evidence, however, strongly suggested that this was not the case. The UCA had been surrounded by military units for several days; a twenty-four-hour surveillance post on the top of the optimistically named Democracy Tower just to the northeast of the university commands an admirable view of the whole campus; the entire city was under a dawn-to-dusk curfew; the assault on the Jesuits and their building had lasted a minimum of half an hour and had been carried out by a large unit that in its firing of grenades and antitank missiles had clearly not placed stealth high on the list of operational priorities. There was a witness claiming to have seen "soldiers."

And none of this took into account the more speculative evidence of a history of hatred and persecution of Jesuit priests stretching back to the 1970s; the threats on the radio at the start of the offensive; the military search of the residence on the Monday evening; the voice heard at three o'clock on the afternoon of November 16 by Bishops Rivera and Rosa Chávez trumpeting from a passing military vehicle, "Ignacio Ellacuría and Martín-Baró have fallen. We'll continue killing communists. We're soldiers from the First Brigade;" the whispered suggestion by one army officer who, early that Thursday morning, had turned to the Jesuit at his side, surveying the remnants of his brother priests, to say "It could have been us, Father."[33]

PRESIDENT Bush was being heckled. In the midst of a speech at a fund-raising lunch in Chicago, there was a woman in the audience shouting at him. "Why are we sending money to El Salvador?" The president tried to strike a deal: "I'll give her an answer if you promise to be quiet after I'm done. Promise? Word of honor?" But the woman was not to be deflected. "Why are we killing priests in El Salvador?"[34]

"The answer is—we're not. Now you be quiet. And here's the answer to your question." But it is doubtful whether the answer he gave satisfied his questioner: "We are supporting El Salvador because it had certifiably free elections. President Cristiani is trying to do a job for democracy. And the left-wing guerrillas must not take over El Salvador." What is the point of "certifiably free elections" if the victor cannot govern? What kind of "job for democracy" must it be if the president has to order his country's air force to bomb its own capital city in order to save it? Surely it is of questionable wisdom that in the age of *perestroika* the foreign policy of a great and powerful nation toward a small and unimportant country should rest only on the bedrock conviction that "the left-wing guerrillas must not take over."

In the days preceding this November 20 statement the FMLN offensive and the killing of the Jesuits had given U.S. policy towards El Salvador a serious buffeting. The triumph of Napoleón Duarte's Christian Democratic Party in the presidential elections of 1984 had contributed to a bipartisan consensus that, in Central American terms, El Salvador was a success story and the dollars should flow. The endless battles over Nicaragua and then the Iran-*contra* debacle had distracted congressional attention away from El Salvador, but toward the end of the Reagan administration cracks in the consensus were beginning to appear. Duarte's terminal cancer became a sad symbol for the fortunes of his government. Alarming for some in the Democratic party and among the moderate Republicans was the prospect of an ARENA government in power. The party had its origin in the death squads rampant in El Salvador at the end of the 1970s and in the early 1980s, and while presidential candidate Alfredo Cristiani—a graduate of Washington's own (Jesuit-run) Georgetown University—was not part of the extreme right wing, the shadowy figure of ex-major and ARENA party founder Roberto D'Aubuisson was thought by many to be the power behind the throne.[35] Charismatic and undeniably in possession of a large popular following, this was a man whom a CIA profile of 1981 had portrayed as "egocentric, reckless, and perhaps mentally unstable." Since then he had been described as a "psychopathic killer" by one U.S. ambassador to El Salvador, had publicly threatened another, and plotted to kill a third.[36]

The view of President Bush was that "Mr. Cristiani should be given the chance to prove his dedication to democracy, peace, and human rights."[37] The pragmatic approach to the resolution of problems in Central America adopted by Secretary of State James Baker had been in marked contrast to that of his predecessors. Within a few months that policy appeared to be bearing fruit as a Bipartisan Accord with Congress was signed at the White House on March 24. The agreement defused Nicaragua as a contentious issue and endorsed "an open consultative process with bipartisanship as the watchword" for policy toward the entire region just five days after Cristiani's 1989 electoral victory in El Salvador.[38]

But while Washington gave Cristiani the benefit of the doubt, a lingering unease brought El Salvador back on the agenda for congressional discussion. In June an amendment to the foreign aid bill had tried, without success, to introduce provisions for Congress to review the conduct of the new Cristiani government the following April.[39] More dramatic were events in the Senate in September when the Bush administration scored a major victory in a vote for an amendment that gave the administration a virtually free hand in its support of Cristiani. Both Senators Christopher Dodd and Patrick Leahy had been pillars of the opposition to the Reagan policy in Central America. Now, for the first time on a Central American issue, they found themselves on opposite sides, as Dodd, "very reluctantly," rose to argue that the political moment for Leahy's provision to allow for the introduction of minor "strings" to the military aid was not right, that in the wake of the recently initiated negotiations between the Cristiani government and the FMLN guerrillas, Cristiani must be given a chance.[60] Many senators followed Dodd in defeating Leahy and voting 82 to 18 for the passage of an amendment different only from his own, in Leahy's view, in that what it did was to "throw on an extra $5 million and take all the strings out."[41]

THE offensive was launched two days after the Berlin Wall began to come down. There was a sense in Congress, as voices were raised to protest the FMLN offensive and express concern for the "fragile democracy under siege by extremes of both right and left," that "the ancient rites of barbarism have no place in today's world, not even in El Salvador."[42] And then came the Jesuits.

Shock, revulsion and horror at the atrocity were compounded by a sense of *déjà vu*. Nearly ten years earlier it had been Archbishop Romero, murdered on the altar. Nine years ago four American churchwomen had been raped and murdered on a roadside, and now, $4 billion later, the Jesuits. "In many ways I feel like saying 'a pox on both your houses.' " railed Leahy in the Senate, ". . . on the Government of El Salvador and on the FMLN. The United States sends $1.5 million a day in aid to El Salvador . . . What do we see? Brutality, murder, and atrocities on both sides."[43] A telegram drafted by Congressman Joe Moakley, appealing to both sides in the conflict to bring an end to the violence, gathered 115 signatures during the course of November 16. Catholics formed the largest single denominational group with Congress; many congressmen had been educated by Jesuits and some had known *these* Jesuits personally. As protest and demands for action flooded in from constituents, more than one congressional aide was in tears: "Some of us have been working on Central America for years and years. And some of the best people we met and had been inspired by had just been shot in the head."[44]

Hearings on "The Current Political Situation in El Salvador" opened before Christopher Dodd's subcommittee in a packed hearing room on the afternoon of November 17.[45] A lot had changed since September. Dodd warned that Cristiani would need to show that he "is either in control of his government or he is not"—otherwise he would find that "the U.S. support will be restricted and, I would predict, eventually eliminated." With feelings running high, members of the public protesting U.S. involvement in El Salvador interrupted repeatedly. Circumstantial evidence surrounding the killing of the Jesuits—and the prompt reaction of organizations such as Human Rights Watch, which had written to Secretary of State Baker to express their "very grave presumption" of the Salvadoran army's responsibility—had convinced many that the killers had come from the right.[46] Among them was Assistant Secretary of State Bernard Aronson, who was careful to avoid any mention of the army, but told the senators, press, and public, "My guts tell me that they were killed by the right. . . . The people responsible for this crime are barbarians and murderers. They must be brought to justice and punished for their crimes."

Aware of the skepticism with which many in the room greeted promises of "justice" from the Salvadoran government, Aronson acknowledged that "there are two kinds of investigations in El Salvador." The kind "where innocents are murdered and the guilty go free" was so much more common than the other kind, that Aronson's citing of just one case—the San Sebastián massacre—in which U.S. pressure including a March 1989 trip to El Salvador by Vice-President Dan Quayle helped precipitate the detention of three army officers, one of them a major, did little to dent the senators' pessimism.

On November 20 and 21, both chambers of Congress adopted resolutions deploring the escalating violence in El Salvador. "Why do we all of a sudden give a hoot about that country," asked Senator Hatfield of his colleagues, "when for 10 years we have tolerated—no, more than that—silently endorsed a U.S. policy which has done nothing but bankroll the guaranteed failure of any potential for peace?" The answer was not difficult to find. Republican David Dreier congratulated his fellow members of the House for their joint response to the "terrible situation" in El Salvador, while reminding them how "unfortunate" it was that it was the brutal killing of the Jesuits that should have brought them to this point, "but it did, it brought us in a bipartisan way to face this issue." It also led to the introduction of wording that would make the prosecution of that crime a key factor in the future relationship between the two countries: "a satisfactory resolution of this case is a pivotal test of El Salvador's democratic and judicial institutions and will be instrumental in determining continued U.S. support for the Government of El Salvador."[47]

Although the strongly worded resolutions followed the defeat of attempts by liberals to introduce restrictions on military aid, the resolutions themselves, the vehemence of the debates, and the margins on the votes, particularly in the House, suggested that a major battle over aid to El Salvador could be expected in the following year.[48] A measure of the seriousness with which the Democratic leadership listened not just to the voices of the congressmen, but also to the voices of the American people they represented, was the decision by Speaker of the House Thomas Foley—himself Jesuit educated—to appoint a high-level task force to "gather all available information about the murders, those responsible and the process undertaken to bring them to justice." In a letter dated December 5, Speaker Foley invited Boston Democrat Joe Moakley, chair of the powerful House Rules Committee, to be the task force's chairman.[49]

LUCÍA Cerna returned to work on the Monday following the Jesuits' murder. Fighting in the city appeared to have died down and it was only a short walk from her mother's home to the provincial's office where she worked as a janitor. She was already working when Tojeira opened the door to his room and invited her to come in and meet María Julia Hernández. Tojeira encouraged Lucía to tell Hernández what she had seen and heard from the window of number 16, Calle Cantábrico. Hernández listened and then recommended that she should both give her testimony to the court and seek asylum in an embassy. What Lucía had seen was not conclusive proof in itself—five men, two of them in camouflage uniform, "like the soldiers I see in the street"—but she was the only witness to come forward and her testimony pointed toward the Salvadoran army.[50]

Lucía, her husband, and daughter took refuge in the Spanish embassy, where Lucía began to give her testimony on the afternoon of Wednesday, November 22. Among those present were the investigating judge, Ricardo Zamora, and Attorney General Mauricio Colorado. The Salvadoran flag was briefly raised over the Spanish embassy to ensure the testimony's compliance with Salvadoran law. Lucía and her family had been offered a choice of flying to safety in Spain, France, or Miami. They had never left El Salvador before and chose Miami because, "looking at a map, that doesn't look as far away from El Salvador if once we decide to go back."[51] They had planned to leave on the next morning's early TACA airline flight, but as the afternoon wore on, it became clear that it would not be possible to finish the testimony that day.

Late on the Wednesday evening Ambassador Walker was awakened by a telephone call from Washington. The State Department had heard there was a witness leaving El Salvador in the morning for Spain or France and wanted further details.[52] Walker got no reply from either the Spanish or French embassies, so called his legal officer and told him to find out what was going on. With Washington thinking the witness is leaving the country, he remembered telling Chidester, "We must make sure the witness would give a testimony to a judge." Chidester called Tojeira and had a telephone conversation that would set off a chain of events from which relations between the Jesuits and the U.S. embassy in El Salvador—historically characterized by more or less guarded antipathy, born of the Jesuits' criticism of U.S. policy and the U.S. embassy's suspicion of the Jesuits as being involved in some ways with the FMLN—would not recover.[53]

Tojeira had himself been telephoned by Fermín Saínz, the Jesuit who was with the Cernas, and told that the testimony was running long. He had understood this to mean that Lucía and her family would no longer be leaving in the morning.[54] He was not told that Lucia was by now in the French embassy or that they were going to restart the testimony at the crack of dawn in an attempt to catch the 8:50 A.M. TACA flight to Miami. And so he replied to Chidester's inquiry about a witness leaving the following morning by telling him he was "acting on old information" and that they would talk in the morning. Interviewed more than year after this telephone conversation Chidester would insist that Tojeira had deliberately lied to him as he "tried to get Lucía out, avoiding the U.S. embassy."[55]

The next day saw a mad scramble to the airport from all quarters of San Salvador, a number of missed airplanes, and increasingly frayed nerves. As the three Cernas would be landing in Miami without any visas or documentation, the Jesuits had been amenable to the suggestion that Chidester should go with them in order to help them clear immigration. Worried about the curfew, more worried still about the Cernas' safety in a heavily militarized airport, a cavalcade of French and American security accompanied them out to the airport and onto a French military aircraft summoned especially from Belize. And that appeared to be that. The Jesuits felt a sense of relief that the Cernas' ordeal was over: they would be helped through immigration by State Department officials and handed over to the Jesuits in Miami waiting to meet them.

What happened in Miami became the subject of heated controversy, but there are several incontrovertible facts: Lucía had already given her testimony under circumstances compliant with Salvadoran law; the Miami Jesuits were less than enthusiastic about becoming embroiled in the whole operation and readily acceded to the suggestion that the family should remain in the "care" of the State Department; such "care" was contrary to anything agreed to or discussed with the Jesuits in El Salvador; over a period of eight days Lucía and her husband were subjected to lengthy interrogations by two FBI agents and Lieutenant Colonel Rivas of the SIU, an officer of the Salvadoran army Lucía's testimony implicated; the Cernas were accompanied only by Chidester and were not asked if they wanted a lawyer or priest to be present during the interrogation; in a foreign country for the first time, alone, scared, and totally unsure of her future, Lucía panicked and changed her story because she felt her original one was not believed; she changed her story several times and was finally polygraphed repeatedly; she failed the polygraphs.

As soon as the Cernas were released into the care of the Jesuits in Miami, the latter asked members of the Lawyers Committee for Human Rights to interview Lucía and "provide them with a report evaluating her testimony and its utility to the Salvadoran criminal proceedings."[56] From witnesses they believed to be "forthcoming and highly credible," the Lawyers Committee heard how the Cernas had been bullied, intimidated, and humiliated. Lucía and Jorge felt they were being interrogated under the shadow of a threat to be returned to El Salvador, where they believed they would be killed. At one point Rivas had asked Lucia about Estrada, who had just been named rector of the UCA: "This Estrada, is he or isn't he a guerrilla?" At another she was asked to tell her investigators the name of the priest who had told her to say she saw soldiers. Frightened and lonely, and unwilling to give the name of one of the priests she had worked for for eight years, Lucía gave them the name of María Julia Hernández.[57]

In El Salvador the Jesuits were furious. Anger at what they believed to be deception by U.S. authorities and at the treatment meted out to the Cerna family only increased when the political implications of what had happened in Miami emerged. On December 9 President Cristiani gave a press conference in which he maintained that Lucía Cerna "had accepted that the statement she gave to the Fourth Criminal Court Judge here in San Salvador was false and that the truth was that she had only heard shots and explosions but that she had seen absolutely nothing."[58] Journalists receiving "deep background" briefings from U.S. embassy officials—including Walker—attributable only as "sources close to the investigation," were told that Lucía Cerna had failed "six FBI lie-detector tests," had changed her story three times, and was "not a credible witness."[59] The opportunity was not lost to smear María Julia Hernández's role as source of Lucia's testimony; over a year later Chidester would still maintain this thesis, stating, "I can see why María Julia might have wanted her witness."[60]

And in the United States the Jesuits were furious as well. Throughout the week of the interrogations the Jesuit Conference in Washington had been told by the State Department, "five, if not ten, times that they were simply doing an assessment of Lucía's safety."[61] The FBI, who would assure the Jesuits that the Cerna family was treated in "a courteous and professional manner," maintained that they could not do a risk assessment, because she was not "in the right category."[62] Paul Tipton, the president of the Association of Jesuit Colleges and Universities, was present at two of the Lawyers Committee interviews with the Cernas and had helped settle the family into temporary lodgings in his home state of Alabama. A garrulous southerner with a reputation for shooting from the hip, he was to become known by the Jesuits in El Salvador as "John Wayne." On Sunday, December 10 he fired off a letter to Secretary of State James Baker that was a direct attack on Walker and his embassy: "Ambassador Walker's apparent participation in efforts to discredit the testimony of this courageous witness is a shocking betrayal of the responsibilities of our official representative in El Salvador."[63]

Flying back from Alabama that evening, an exhausted Tipton—who had upgraded his ticket in order to try and get some sleep—found himself sitting next to the chairman of the Republican party, Lee Atwater. Atwater had been cutting a record in Nashville and was still in full Western clothes. Tipton had never met him, but introduced himself, gave him a copy of his letter to Baker, and spent the next hour and a half letting off steam about the U.S.'s handling of Lucía Cerna. "I told him that he needed to get the guys in the policy committee to get the National Security Council on to it." The next morning Tipton received telephone calls from Atwater himself and from the National Security Council and news that "the good ole' boys" in the Senate were besieging the assistant secretary of state with questions about the performance of the FBI and their ambassador to El Salvador.[64]

"THE unfortunate part of all this is that Lucía never had anything," was Chidester's analysis in an attempt to explain the episode. "There was no reason for her to leave. She left because the Jesuits were following some political agenda."[65] A team from London's New Scotland Yard, which traveled to the United States and El Salvador in January 1990 to monitor the progress of the investigation, had the opportunity to interview the Cernas and were given an account they believed "as accurate as could be expected." They concluded that the Cernas saw "very little of the circumstances surrounding the killings, but what little they did see is most accurately described in Mrs. Cerna's statement in San Salvador and in the New Scotland Yard interview."[66] "We thought it was our big break," Chidester argued in self-defense, "that she was an eye witness for the killings." But he had no explanation as to why, when it became patently clear that Lucia wasn't "our big break," the combined forces of the Department of State, the FBI, and the Salvadoran SIU has not been able to bring the interrogations to a close and get on with the investigation elsewhere.

At the time, Ambassador Walker answered criticisms of the embassy's role in the episode by asking, "Why does anyone think we'd go to all this trouble just to discredit her?"[67] But it was a question posed at a moment when the credibility of his own embassy was at a low. As the offensive tailed off into a backlash of persecution of the opposition, with churches and political organizations ransacked and searched and individuals threatened, detained, mistreated, and deported—or just sent running for the border—the embassy emerged as an apologist for the Cristiani government.[66] The State Department had not been pleased by a combination of silence from official Salvadoran sources and what they perceived as a pro-FMLN bias in much of the journalism coming out of San Salvador. "Due to the failings of the Salvadorans' own public relations," explained one embassy official working with the press at the time, "we became the spokesperson for the Salvadoran government."[69]

A lengthy profile of Walker published in the *Washington Post* on December 19, 1989 describes a man whom some reporters were beginning to refer to as "Ambassador Sunshine" for the consistently upbeat versions of the government's conduct he was giving in briefings. "He sought to justify the raids by government forces on churches and refugee centers," wrote *Washington Post* correspondent Lee Hockstader, "comparing them to the United States' internment of Japanese Americans after Pearl Harbor."[70] While Aronson had allowed his "gut feeling" that the Jesuits' killers came from the right to go on the record, Walker "seemed to dismiss evidence that pointed at right-wing military involvement." And this after his November 18 conversation with Cristiani and despite the view he expressed to Tojeira, in a private meeting a few days later, that "some special military unit of which we have no control" had most likely carried out the murders.[71] When asked whether the United States would hold the

Salvadoran government responsible for abuses it had committed during and after the offensive, Walker had become "visibly annoyed." "Management control problems exist in a situation like this. And it's not a management control problem that would lend itself to a Harvard Business School analysis. I mean, this is war. It's fighting, it's death. . . . I really think President Cristiani is under barrage from all sides and all sorts of events. I think some things are happening that he would prefer not to happen."[72]

With Walker prepared to defend what he described as "a weak vacillating government that maybe isn't all it should be" in order to make sure that the "violent left never comes to power here," it was not difficult for critics to see in the United States' treatment of Lucía Cerna a deliberate attempt to discredit the only witness to come forward with testimony against an army massively funded by the United States. In retrospect Walker would groan at the memory of his relationship with the press during the offensive and argue that, with respect to the killings of the Jesuits, "my point from the beginning was that the city is in a state of war . . . let us not jump to conclusions. I said it the first day, I say it today, as long as the Jesuit case remains unsolved the government of El Salvador and the people of El Salvador are going to suffer the consequences."[73] But whatever way one looked at it, the "optics" on the Lucía Cerna episode, in State Department jargon, were not good.

IN a cable dated December 15 the State Department would describe how "President Cristiani and his top military leadership are committed to a speedy, thorough, and impartial investigation."[74] The SIU had arrived at the UCA shortly after nine o'clock on the morning of November 16. They began to take photographs and gather physical evidence such as fingerprints, spent cartridges, and fragments of mortars and shells, but they did not seal off the scene of the crime—despite a State Department report to the contrary—until the following Saturday morning.[75] Some leads were produced by inquiries made at the very beginning of the investigation. On November 17, for example, the SIU spoke to troops in the area who indicated that the Atlacatl Battalion had been patrolling Jardines de Guadalupe behind the UCA on the evening of November 15, and to two members of the National Police who had been on watch on top of the Democracy Tower. They remembered seeing "troops and tanks of the Atlacatl Battalion" pass by on the Southern Highway at around midnight on the night of November 15 and then hearing "bombs and shooting" around 2:00 A.M.[76] But the troops' mention of the Atlacatl was not followed up nor recorded in the SIU's official report, and formal statements from the two policemen were not taken until December 11 and 12, by which time their memories had become curiously vague. One did not remember seeing or hearing military vehicles or troops, while the other had heard the vehicles but seen nothing. Treasury Police who had been with them on the Tower, when interviewed in early December, remembered having a similarly troublefree night.

As assistance in the more technical aspects of the investigation was offered from all sides, the SIU dawdled in its investigation of possible military involvement. By November 16, the search of the Jesuits' residence two days before the murder was public knowledge. On November 21, Paco Estrada told the SIU that he had been informed by a Jesuit present at the search that it had been carried out by the Atlacatl. Witnesses to the intense militarization of the area surrounding the UCA at the time of the crime abounded. Yet obvious questions took a long time to be asked, in part because Rivas was in Miami "discovering" that the one eyewitness to have come forward and given legal testimony in El Salvador was "not credible." What was the military up to in the area surrounding the UCA from the beginning of the offensive until the night of November 15–16? The question was not asked of Chief of Staff Colonel René Emilio Ponce until December 4. Who carried out the search on November 13? In went the letter on December 5. Did the ammunition gathered from beside the Jesuits' bodies on November 16 come from the armed forces? The question was not asked until December 7 and ballistic tests were not begun for another two weeks.

Overall, the Salvadoran judiciary's role in the investigation was, at this stage, limited, partly because the two court prosecutors who had been assigned to work alongside the SIU were—illegally—denied access to the SIU investigation and repeatedly told that Rivas "had no time to see them."[77] But even so, prompted by declarations made by two Jesuits on November 28—one told how the Loyola Center, a Jesuit retreat center on the hill above the UCA, had been occupied by about 120 members of the Atlacatl on the afternoon of the November 15[78]—the court requested further information on troop movements from Colonel Ponce. Ponce answered in a sworn declaration that entered the court record on December 11. It included a number of anomalies: the Atlacatl had carried out the Monday search of the residence, but, he claimed, at 8:50 P.M., nearly two and a half hours after the 6:30 P.M. time given by Martín-Baró in an account he left in his computer, and a full fifty minutes after the Jesuits in Calle Mediterráneo had been advised by telephone that the search had ended; it had been the Treasury Police, not the Atlacatl, that had carried out the search of the Loyola Center and indeed the Atlacatl did not appear on his list of troops in the area of the UCA that night. Most perplexing of all was Ponce's inclusion of an entry from the High Command's log that described how at 12:30 A.M. "delinquent terrorists" had damaged the very theology building within the UCA campus outside which the Jesuits had been shot shortly afterward, "without any casualties reported."[79]

The SIU's request for an account of military activity around the UCA was finally answered on December 18. The answers brought yet another entry for 12:30 A.M. on the November 16: this time the "delinquent terrorists" had assassinated the "Jesuit fathers," an employee and her daughter—and the names were given—"inside the installations" of the university.[80] This entry was all the more questionable for its inclusion of the victims' names: the military could have had no knowledge of the presence of the two women, as they had not been there during the Monday search, yet the recorded time was at least an hour before the operation at the UCA took place.

COLONEL Carlos Armando Avilés was a gregarious officer a couple of years younger than the officers of the High Command. An ex-pupil of the Jesuits in the *Externado San José,* like many of those in the upper ranks of the Salvadoran army, he had studied psychological warfare in Taiwan. In the mid-1980s he was the director of the army's press office COPREFA, where he seemed genuinely to enjoy the contact with foreign journalists and the chance it gave him to show off his excellent English. Patently ambitious and a consistent critic of the powerful *tandona* officers above him, Avilés was found by journalists and congressional investigators to be one of the most forthcoming of army sources. He became director of C-5, the army's Department of Psychological Operations in mid-1988, from which he answered challenges to the army's human rights record by holding out his small white hands and saying, in English, "Look—no blood on these hands!"[81]

Avilés took an active interest in the Jesuit case and was instrumental in setting up a briefing by Rivas for Fathers Tojeira and Estrada on the progress being made by the SIU. He had known some of the murdered Jesuits personally and also had a paternal interest in the work of the SIU, whose commanding officer he had been before he was appointed to "PsyOps." U.S. embassy officials remember him in December being "very cocky, saying the case would be wrapped up within a week or ten days—he told the FBI and

SIU that it was just a case of 'dotting the "i"'s and crossing the "t"'s.' "[82] As they arrived for their December 22 meeting the Jesuits had been displeased to find that Chidester had expected to be present throughout; Tojeira lost no time in having him excluded. Within the briefing the Jesuits (and Avilés) were told that the investigation was still divided between the army and the FMLN, although the unit that conducted the search of the Jesuit residence had been identified as being from the Atlacatl. As this information came a full month after Estrada had himself testified to the SIU that he believed the search to have been carried out by the Atlacatl, this did not come as a great surprise. In Rivas's opinion "a spirit of full cooperation" between the Jesuits and the SIU emerged from this meeting. The State Department would describe it as "full and detailed."[83] Neither view was shared by the Jesuits.

Among the things not said at the briefing was that the investigation was now focussing on the Atlacatl commando unit that had carried out the search. The SIU had questioned first its two lieutenants and then the enlisted men under their command. As more and more commandos were interviewed the contradictions in their testimony multiplied: they differed crucially as they referred to circumstances—lack of electric light for example—true of the night of November 15 but not of the night of November 13. They could not agree on how they had entered the UCA on the evening of November 13—one commando remembered having achieved the physically impossible by sliding under the main entrance gate—nor on what they had done between the two dates. While others in the army claimed to have heard news of the Jesuits through the public media within hours, the Atlacatl commandos did not hear it for days; one would tell his interrogators, six weeks after news of the Jesuits' death had circled the world, that he "learned about the deaths of the Jesuits at the moment of his interrogation."[84]

Major Eric Buckland did not have a good Christmas. Like many U.S. officers at this "hardship posting," he was in El Salvador without his family. But it wasn't just homesickness that bothered Buckland, as he explained in a letter he wrote to his sister Carol, a journalist with CNN. Five days before Christmas his closest Salvadoran friend, and the officer he was supposed to advise, Carlos Avilés, had told him that he knew who ordered the killing of the Jesuits: Colonel Guillermo Benavides, director of the military academy and on the night of November 15 commanding officer of the security zone stretching from the *estado mayor* to the UCA. Benavides had given the order and it had been carried out by a commando unit of the Atlacatl led by a young lieutenant. Benavides had apparently panicked and gone to Rivas saying, "I did it, what are you going to do to help me?" Rivas had been scared by the conversion with Benavides, a *tandona* member and several years his senior, and the investigation had slowed. At that point another colonel, Ivan López y López (like Avilés a former head of the SIU), who had been assigned to assist Rivas with the case from the beginning of December, asked Rivas what was going on and Rivas had told him. López y López told Avilés. And Avilés told Buckland on a basis of "break in case of emergency . . . not as a Salvadoran officer to an American Major—it's Carlos to Eric."[85]

Buckland had understood "break in case of emergency" to mean that if Benavides was not held accountable or if Avilés should be killed for what he knew, then he, Buckland, should step forward and "somehow get the truth out." He was immediately plunged into a tangled conflict of loyalties and fears. He knew that as a U.S. military officer he should inform his superiors of what was the first real break on the case, yet he felt himself deeply bound to Avilés, whom he believed to be the finest colonel he had ever served under. He knew that the pressures on the case were such that "somebody up the chain had to take a fall," but he also believed, from what Avilés had told him, that the case was about to be broken and the facts made public. He considered that it would be better for the Salvadorans and the future of the armed forces if they were seen to solve the case on their own. Yet he was worried and frightened, convinced that the information that Avilés had just given him put his own life at risk as well as that of Avilés. Although he realized it was incautious to use the heavily bugged Salvadoran telephone system, on the following day he called his sister and outlined what he knew—again on a "break in case of emergency" basis. He promised to put the details in a letter.

But as the days passed his worries were not allayed—"everything just kept eating and eating and eating at me." Although Avilés had told him that a lieutenant from the Atlacatl had been polygraphed two or three times "and was flunking," nothing had happened with Benavides. He knew that ballistic tests were beginning to show similarities between the cartridges found at the UCA and weapons belonging to the Atlacatl, but at the same time he was troubled that the Jesuits, in their briefing on December 22, had not been told about the conversation between Benavides and Rivas. And Avilés seemed worried. Buckland had asked him if Colonel Ponce knew. "Colonel Ponce?" Avileés had answered, "I don't know, I don't think so. I don't know who knows, and what if the higher-ups ordered it?"[86]

By January 2 Buckland was so afraid that he had taken to patrolling his house in his pajamas, an automatic rifle slung over his shoulder, an overturned couch against the door. When his immediate superior, Colonel William Hunter, dropped by his office on some other errand, he sent his secretary out of the room and told him. Hunter went straight to the senior U.S. officer stationed in El Salvador, the head of "MilGroup," Colonel Milton Menjívar. But telling left Buckland feeling no better— "Once I told him, I felt as if I had really betrayed Colonel Avilés." And in the course of the day things got very definitely worse.

Without consulting either the ambassador, who was in Washington, or the Deputy Chief of Mission Jeff Dietrich, Menjívar took Janice Elmore, a political officer with special responsibility for liaison with the Salvadoran military, and went straight to Colonel Ponce. Ponce reacted with disbelief, disappointment, and then outrage and asked to be given the source of this information. Menjívar decided, according to testimony he would give a year and a half later, that for his allegations to have validity, he would have to tell Ponce where they came from. It wasn't, he would explain, "one of those I heard it through the grapevine type rumors."[87] And so he told him, soldier to soldier—Major Buckland says that Colonel Avilés told him. Both officers were summoned straight to Ponce.

"I was an instant basket case," was how Buckland described his reaction to the summons. He walked into the meeting and found the others waiting for him; Avilés had already been told what Buckland had said. Buckland went over to Menjívar and asked if he could talk to him privately before he talked to Ponce, but Menjívar replied that, "we're beyond talking in private up here." The first person to speak was Avilés. Buckland "felt terrible" and more terrible still when Avilés denied everything. Sitting on a sofa feeling "like there were a thousand buffaloes sitting on me," Buckland realized that it had to be clear to those in the room with them that either he, or this man he liked, admired, and trusted was a liar. As Buckland gave the assembled officers his story, Avilés was "just hopping around in his chair . . . just bouncing, dancing around in his chair."[88] Buckland met Ponce's "gut-check" of a look square in the eyes ("He's got these real soft eyes, it's hard to explain but he's almost kind of a teddy bear in a way when you look at him. He's normally a very soft and kind of a gentle-looking guy"). He had let down Avilés and his own superiors had served him up to the Salvadorans.

Ponce had wanted Colonel López y López, to come and account for his part in the story. When he failed to reach him on the telephone Avilés volunteered to go and find him. Strangely, it did not occur to any of those present that perhaps López y López should be confronted *before* he had

had the advantage of a briefing from Avilés on exactly what was going on. Avilés was gone from Ponce's office for about an hour. He returned with López y López in tow—and López y López also denied all knowledge of anything Buckland had been talking about.[89]

JANUARY 2 was not a good day for Ambassador Walker either. The first major break in a case upon which hung the future relations between his country and El Salvador, and he was not just out of the country, but out of the loop. An American military officer, a member of his Mission, had had information for ten days and had done nothing with it; when he did come forward another military officer, flying in the face of diplomatic protocol and common sense, had taken the information to the Salvadoran chief of staff when it could perfectly well have awaited Walker's return. All chances of working with Avilés as a highly placed informant and potential witness were blown.

Over the next few months public statements of a rather facetious nature—"unlike newspaper men who feel they'd rather die then reveal a source, we are not in the same game"[90]—would be offered in defense in Menjívar's actions. But off the record, officials would be more forthcoming. Menjívar, whom colleagues believe would "not have had the gall to go ahead" if the ambassador had been in the country, had sidestepped Walker's deputy and the case officer Chidester, neither of whom were informed until around noon on the following day. Other U.S. officials would maintain that Menjívar—Salvadoran born, and more successful than most in establishing close ties to the Salvadoran High Command—was "on some kind of personal crusade—there was no rationalization whatsoever for him doing what he did. It was really stupid." Or, put more succinctly, "Milt flipped."[91]

Matters were not improved by what Walker had been doing in Washington on January 2; in a meeting with Congressman Moakley, whose staff were preparing a fact-finding trip to El Salvador for the following week, Walker had insisted that there was no evidence to implicate any particular group or individuals in the killings. Interviewed by the New York Times, Moakley would remember that a "congenial" Walker had thought it possible that the priests had been killed by guerrillas dressed up in army uniforms, because "anybody can get army uniforms."[92] One congressional aide present at the briefing remembered that "although he didn't say the FMLN had done it, what he did was accord equal weight to a variety of theories to a point that defied common sense."[93]

Back in El Salvador things began to move rather quickly. On January

3, as Dietrich briefed Cristiani and Menjívar briefed the full High Command on Buckland's allegations, Chidester spoke to Rivas. Rivas denied having had any conversation with Benavides in which the senior colonel admitted guilt, but insisted the he believed they were making progress with the investigation of the Atlacatl, and that "if the Atlacatl is guilty, then Benavides is guilty."[94] If this was the case it is curious that there was no mention of Benavides's name in any of the SIU records up until this moment. Benavides had been responsible for the security zone including the UCA at the time of the Jesuits' murder. Yet he had neither been questioned about his possible involvement in the crime nor investigated for what, in the event of his ignorance of the murder, must surely have been gross incompetence.

Two days later the results of Rivas's ballistic tests became available. As both Avilés and Buckland failed polygraph examinations on their respective stories, the SIU investigation, it appeared, was closing in to confirm exactly the information that Buckland claimed to have been given him by Avilés.

ON Salvadoran television public statements by the president are preceded by the playing of the national anthem over scenic vistas of a green and pleasant land full of smiling people that does not have a lot to do with the hard reality of daily life. On January 7, 1990 expectation was high. Cristiani's audience was not disappointed as he announced that "we have determined that there was some involvement of the military" in the killing of the Jesuits. A special "Honor Commission" made up of officers of different ranks and civilian lawyers had been set up to determine the "exact circumstances" in which the murders took place and to "clarify the crime in all respects."[95]

Forty-seven members of the Atlacatl Battalion were detained at once in a military garrison in San Salvador, and by January 13 Cristiani was able to return to the airwaves to announce the detention of Colonel Guillermo Benavides, three lieutenants, including Lieutenant José Ricardo Espinoza of the Atlacatl's commando unit, and five enlisted men, one of whom had already deserted. The process by which these nine men—and these nine alone—were "placed at the disposition of the judicial system" was not disclosed. But after a decade of war that had seen the loss of 75,000 lives, more than half of them civilians, Colonel Benavides was the first officer of his rank ever to be held for a crime against human rights.

CHAPTER FOUR

WITH AN EXEMPLARY ARCHBISHOP IN THE NATION'S CRISIS

Christ invites us not to be afraid of persecution because, believe me, my brothers, he who commits himself to the poor must share their destiny. And in El Salvador we already know what is the destiny of the poor: to be abducted, tortured, captured, and to turn up as corpses at the roadside. . . . I am happy that our Church is persecuted precisely because of its preferential option for the poor and for trying to incarnate itself in the interests of the poor. . . . It would be sad if in a country where they are killing so terribly, we did not count priests among the victims. They are the testimony of a Church that is incarnate among the problems of its people.[1]

Monsignor Oscar Arnulfo Romero, 1979–1980

FOR many Jesuits the events of November 1989 recalled those of March 1977. Back then the assassination of Rutilio Grande had seemed like the culmination of the persecution of the Jesuits and the Church that was steadily rising over the preceding months. By 1989 that distant crime—for which no investigation was even undertaken—appeared more a beginning than an end.

Late in the evening of March 12, 1977, Jesuits, other priests and nuns, and hundreds of *campesinos* gathered in the convent in Aguilares. Many were crying. They were waiting for the new archbishop, Monsignor Oscar Arnulfo Romero. That afternoon Rutilio Grande, an old man, and a 15-year-old boy traveling with him on their way to mass in El Paisnal, the small town where Grande had been born forty-nine years earlier, had been waylaid, shot, and killed. Three children riding in the back of the priest's white jeep had been able to escape unharmed. They ran as fast as they could to El Paisnal where they told neighbors and friends how Rutilio had quietly said, "We must do as God wills" as they saw the armed men waiting for them on either side of the road.[2]

Jesuit Provincial César Jerez decided to begin the mass without the archbishop and the whole crowd of people moved into the church. The three bodies were laid out under sheets on tables from the parish house. One Jesuit,

Jon Sobrino, stayed behind. He was standing on his own when he heard a knocking at the convent door. He opened it to Archbishop Romero and his auxiliary Rivera, greeted them, and led them into the church.

THE campaign against the work of the Jesuits in Aguilares had been brought to the boil by events on December 5, 1976. Eduardo Orellana, owner of one of the three sugar plantations in the parish, was killed outside his home during a small demonstration of 250 *campesinos* from FECCAS.[3] Coincidentally, on this same day a large crowd of people, including Archbishop Chávez, some 40 Jesuits, and almost 2,000 *campesinos* had gathered in Aguilares to celebrate the ordination of three young Jesuits. While the two events were unrelated, the death of Orellana triggered virulent denunciations of those allegedly responsible as "hordes of assassins organized by third-world priests" amongst whom the Jesuits— "marxist leaders protected by official tolerance, bloodying our soil"—were preeminent.[4]

Over the New Year, with the campaign for the presidential election of Defense Minister Carlos Humberto Romero at the end of February well under way, the situation only got worse. Archbishop Chávez, old and frail and increasingly alarmed by what was happening, had spoken out on the Jesuits' behalf, but his voice was drowned out by the clamoring of the private sector and organizations such as the "Committee for the Defense of the Fatherland" or the "Catholic Association of Mothers." The Jesuits of UCAII watched television in amazement one night as Molina made a campaign broadcast on behalf of the PCN "candidate" General Romero. The president stood before a large blackboard with a piece of chalk in his hand. Then he slowly drew a line down the middle and announced that on one side of the line were to be found the enemies of El Salvador, and on the other, the friends. "Starting with the enemies," he went on, "number one: liberation theology."[5]

In January and February 1977, the threats of the previous months began to be realized. On January 5 Antonio Cardenal and Fernando Ascoli who, with Enríquez, were already in the process of leaving the Jesuits, were expelled from the country. The Jesuits did not protest the expulsion publicly, because the two were already on their way out of the Society, and because in this case they *had* been actively involved with the leadership of the popular organizations. Such reticence was not maintained by the organizations themselves: FECCAS and the Union of Rural Workers, UTC,[6] played up the expulsion as an attack on the Church in a manner that only confirmed the worst fears of the Jesuits' critics. The expulsion itself did not achieve its ends—if anything it hastened full incorporation into the FPL as they secretly returned to El Salvador. Cardenal told his family that he was going to continue his studies in Eastern Europe and wrote them long letters describing the cold and the snow; many months later the letters would reach Nicaragua, duly postmarked from East Germany or the Soviet Union.[7]

At the end of January the tension increased when the ERP's kidnapping of industrialist Roberto Poma was rapidly followed by the abduction and expulsion of Mario Bernal, a Colombian priest working in the neighboring parish to Aguilares. Juan José Ramirez, an ex-Jesuit, was detained by government forces in early February, and treated "like a priest and a Jesuit"[8]—his whereabouts unknown, he was interrogated, beaten, and tortured with electric shocks before materializing in a Guatemalan jail. On February 22 seven priests, including Ignacio Ellacuría, Luis de Sebastián, and Benigno Fernández (one of the three Jesuits working in Aguilares with Grande), were refused re-entry to the country and effectively exiled.[9] Four days earlier two American missionaries working in San Salvador, and a Belgian who had been tied to bedsprings while interrogated for twenty hours, had also been expelled.

In Apopa on February 13, Rutilio Grande had preached for the exiled Mario Bernal: "I greatly fear, my brothers, that very soon the Bible and the Gospel will not be allowed within our country. We'll get the covers and nothing more, because all its pages are subversive. . . . And I fear, my brothers, that if Jesus of Nazareth returned . . . they would arrest him. They would take him to the courts and accuse him of being unconstitutional and subversive."[10] Many thought the words sealed Grande's end.

General Romero's candidacy had marked a clear move to the right even by the standards of the Salvadoran military. The intensity of the repression mounted in the days before his election on February 20, 1977. Rumors were circulating that afterward the zone of Aguilares and its villages would be swept clean of all priests; the general had been heard to promise that there would be no Jesuits left in El Salvador within three months of his reaching office.[11] Election day itself brought a well-coordinated fraud: ballot boxes were stuffed, the voters' register inflated, the voters themselves and representatives of the UNO opposition intimidated and harassed. Mobile radio units crackling messages about "sugar," "tamales," and "little birds" traveled around the country to ensure that a proper manipulation of votes, fraudulent ballots, and opposition poll watchers was effected.[12]

By the end of the week, peaceful demonstrations in the Plaza Libertad in downtown San Salvador called by defeated UNO candidate Colonel Ernesto Claramount had been violently interrupted. At 12:30 A.M. on the morning of February 28 the 6,000 or so demonstrators camped out in the Plaza after the celebration of a mass were given ten minutes to disperse. Many of them left, but when the ten minutes were up the security forces opened fire, driving Claramount and up to 2,000 men, women, and children with him to take refuge in the Church situated on one side of the Plaza. Tear gas followed them in. While a truce was finally arranged through the intercession of Monsignor Rivera, demonstrations, arrests, casualties, and deaths (the government figure was 8, other sources cited up to 200) continued throughout the day and a state of siege was imposed. Claramount joined the growing ranks of Salvadoran politicians whose democratic pretensions led to exile, and another mass organization—named LP-28 ("February 28" Popular Leagues) in commemoration of the massacre—came into being.

ON February 22, 1977, in the midst of this crisis, Oscar Romero assumed responsibility for the archdiocese of San Salvador. For the majority of the clergy and members of the base communities it was not an occasion for celebration. They knew Oscar Romero, bishop of Santiago de María, as a timid and conservative man, a follower of *Opus Dei* whom the Papal Nuncio reportedly had recommended for the archdiocese after consultation with businessmen, government officials, military officers, and women of the upper reaches of Salvadoran society.[13] At this difficult moment the clergy had little confidence that Romero would defend the pastoral directions taken, under the guidance of Medellín, throughout the archdiocese. It had been no secret they and their lay collaborators alike would have preferred Chávez's auxiliary, Monsignor Arturo Rivera Damas. Pepe Simán, who held a post within the UCA as well as serving as president of the archdiocese's Justice and Peace Commission, spoke for many as he remembered that his "world caved in when I heard the news of Romero's nomination."[14]

The Jesuits were no exception. Over the years they had had a number of direct confrontations with Romero. He had been one of those behind the decision to have them removed from the seminary and had been an instigator of the public uproar over the *Externado* scandal in 1973. In Rome in 1975, as an adviser for the Pontifical Commission on Latin America, he had presented a "very confidential" memorandum entitled "Three Factors in the Priests' Political Movement in El Salvador" in which factor number one had been the Jesuits.[15] Romero had told his brother bishops of the influence exercised by the Jesuits on Salvadoran society through their work in the UCA, the Externado, and in the parish of Aguilares. Criticism of the UCA singled out *ECA, Año Político,* and the theology taught by Ellacuría and others in the CRT. Repeating the arguments and opinions of the Molina government, Romero was, as his biographer James Brockman has pointed out, "blind to his own political stance in support of the government while worrying about the 'politiciza-tion' of those who dared to question those in power."[16]

As speculation about the new archbishop mounted, the Jesuits had not hesitated to make their preferences known. Luis de Sebastían had joined Nicolás Mariscal in paying a visit on President Molina. The argument they presented was that Romero was so conservative that, should he become archbishop, he could only exacerbate the divisions already present within the clergy.[17] An *ECA* article written by Sobrino at the request of Ellacuría asked the question "Who will be the new archbishop?" In answer it listed a series of qualities the Jesuits deemed necessary for the job that led off with "a fundamental sympathy for the direction opened up by Medellín."[18] The Jesuits had been particularly impressed by the fact that the outgoing Archbishop Chávez had telephoned Jerez to say that it was his opinion that the next archbishop should be Rivera. "I've had them all here with me (as auxiliaries)," he said, "and he is the best of the lot."[19]

The night before Romero's appointment became public, Jerez received another telephone call. This time it was the Papal Nuncio, well aware that he was not the bearer of good news. "I am calling to ask for your support of the new archbishop of San Salvador." "Who is it?" "It is Monsignor Romero, tomorrow it'll be public." "Well," answered Jerez as he reminded the Nuncio of the Jesuits' past relationship with Romero, "I cannot guarantee you support. The most I can promise is that these Jesuits won't attack him, although it will depend on how he acts."[20] But the resentment ran deep. One Jesuit, on hearing the news of Romero's appointment, sent the new archbishop a three-word telegram. The last of the words was his own name, Ibáñez. It followed "*Lo lamento*"—"I'm sorry."[21]

PACO Estrada, still smarting from the differences he had had with Romero during his years as vice-provincial, saw the archbishop come in to the Aguilares church through one door and headed straight out through another, muttering to those around him that he was going to see about the coffins. He didn't stop to acknowledge Romero's presence and as he left he thought to himself, "these are the consequences of your calumnies. You said we were Marxists and now they are killing us."[22]

Romero agreed to concelebrate the mass for the dead with Jerez and the other dozen or so priests who had gathered in Aguilares. It was midnight before it was over and Romero asked for the priests and nuns to meet briefly as they tried to decide what the proper reaction of the Church should be. Despite the threats, despite the expulsions, no one had believed that the violence would come to the coldblooded assassination of a priest. And this had been not any priest, but Rutilio Grande, master of ceremonies at Romero's own episcopal ordination in 1970 and "a priest," as Ellacuría would write from Spain, "to the very marrow of his bones."[23] The telephone lines were down and a makeshift autopsy after the mass revealed that the wounds in the three bodies had been inflicted by a type of weapon only available to the government forces. Shock was mixed with fear in the people of Aguilares; Rutilio had been the first to be killed and with the murder of a priest it appeared that anything was possible.

To the Jesuits, Monsignor Romero seemed nervous, weighed down by the enormity of what he was facing. But while he appeared unsure of what should be done, they were impressed by the sincerity with which he asked for their help. "An archbishop was truly asking for our help. And he was asking for help from those he had held as suspicious, as Marxists, only weeks before," remembered Sobrino. "I felt a great tenderness for this humble bishop who was asking, almost begging, us for help in carrying the heavy load that was falling upon him, far heavier than any load his shoulders or anyone else's could bear."[24]

RUTILIO Grande's death was to prove a defining event for the Jesuits of Central America and for the Salvadoran Church under the leadership of Monsignor Romero. For the Jesuits, the internal disputes that had so characterized the painful years since the meeting in December 1969 were silenced by a unity born of persecution. For his part, Monsignor Romero emerged from his past to lead a Church under siege, but a Church that was unified by what many began to speak of as "the miracle of Rutilio."

In a matter of days Romero began displaying a strength founded on the twin pillars of genuine consultation of those around him and the taking of decisions from a Christian understanding of the extraordinary circumstances of the moment. He did not like people to talk about his "conversion," but it was hard for those around him to explain the change he experienced in other terms. As the weeks and months went by and the persecution of the Church and the people continued, opposition to the successive governments of Presidents Molina and Romero only intensified in reaction to a downward spiral into violence. Archbishop Romero responded with an orthodoxy grounded in the most fundamental of all commandments, "Thou shalt not kill," but with a conviction, courage, and prophetic power that were truly revolutionary. Monsignor Ricardo Urioste, Romero's vicar general, has often compared the archbishop to the blind man given his sight by Jesus in the Gospel of St. Mark. Until that moment the blind man had seen people, but people who were "as trees walking."[25] The change in Romero was a turning toward men and women, the people of El Salvador, *as people*—and a people suffering hunger and disease, repression and fear. "Facing this iniquity," Romero would explain to his critics in Rome, "all the more scandalous for occurring in a country whose rulers pride themselves on being Catholics, I could not remain silent."[26]

"Everyone is now having second thoughts about the archbishop," read the concluding section of a cable of March 16 from the U.S. embassy in San Salvador to the State Department.[27] The change in Monsignor Romero transformed his relationships to the Church he had served for the greater part of his life and to the more conservative elements of Salvadoran society that had supported his naming to the archdiocese. Throughout his three years as archbishop he would suffer not just the slander and abuse of the right-wing press, but also—and much more painful to him—the "systematic and incomprehensible opposition" of the Papal Nuncio and the majority of the Salvadoran bishops. This opposition poisoned not only the internal workings of the Bishops' Conference, but also much of the archdiocese's relationship with Rome.[28] No less tangible a result of his change was that those who had welcomed him to the archdiocese with reluctance offered support when he most needed them.

The Jesuits responded eagerly to this unlikely leader of men. Small and shy behind his thick glasses, he had been humble enough to seek their help, yet strong enough to do what needed to be done. Moreover he had become archbishop at a time when the Jesuits were at the epicenter of the attacks against the Church. In this hour of truth—and partly as a result of the leadership exercised by the Jesuits in the meetings at the time of Rutilio Grande's death—some Jesuits came to play key roles within the running of the archdiocese. To his great surprise Paco Estrada was not just named to the "senate" body governing the daily running of the archdiocese, but was asked to be its president. César Jerez offered himself as provincial and the Jesuits under his jurisdiction to the service of the archdiocese for consultation, research, and theological analysis. Whenever he was in El Salvador (the provincial's job involves constant travel) Jerez attended the Tuesday morning breakfast of Romero's closest advisers, sometimes bringing another Jesuit with him. Rafael Moreno became press secretary and a permanent member of the team providing information and ideas before Romero would sit down to write the homily for each Sunday mass.

In April 1977, Jerez brought Rogelio Pedraz, a Spanish-born Jesuit passing through El Salvador for a few days, to meet Romero, who was concerned about the state of the archdiocese's radio station YSAX. Realizing that Pedraz had six years experience of working in radio in the Dominican Republic, Romero made an impassioned appeal: "I beg you to help me save the radio, and if it is necessary I will go down on my knees." Pedraz was so taken aback that an archbishop should speak to him this way that he agreed to stay in the country for six months. It was a decision that he would remember, thirteen years later, as having changed his life.[29] As Pedraz threw his considerable energies into the technical reorganization of the station, it came to assume a role of the greatest importance within the country. Most popular among its programs were the weekly homilies of Monsignor Romero. To listeners hungry for information, consolation, guidance, and hope the ringing truths of these homilies came as "the voice of this people . . . the voice of the voiceless."[30]

One of the first tasks performed for Romero by the Jesuits of the UCA was the compilation of a "Dossier on the Persecution of the Church" for him to take on a somewhat impromptu trip to Rome made at the end of March. In Rome on this visit, as on others, Romero would find a friendly reception, support for the difficult task he had undertaken in El Salvador, and guidance through the myriad paths and quicksands of Vatican politics from Arrupe and the Jesuit headquarters. For a diocesan bishop without the extended family and political contacts enjoyed by religious orders, this assistance was invaluable. Of a later visit to Arrupe, Romero would write in his diary, "He has a lot of experience of false interpretations of the work of the Jesuits—experience that has helped me to keep a serenity in the moments of incomprehension and difficulty. He is a very saintly man."[31]

Back in El Salvador, a new crisis was precipitated by the kidnapping of Minister of Foreign Affairs Mauricio Borgonovo Pohl on April 19. While the FPL trumpeted its responsibility and demanded the freedom of a number of political prisoners in return, the UGB—the White Warriors' Union that had claimed responsibility for the bombing of the UCA in

1976—publicly declared that "Jesuits and other communist priests" would be held responsible for his life. In the event of his death vengeance would be extracted, "eye for eye, tooth for tooth."[32] At the end of the month Rubén Zamora—who served on the archdiocese's Justice and Peace Commission in addition to his job at the UCA and his political work—was captured with his wife and Eduardo Colindres, an UCA colleague and fellow Christian Democrat, as the three were walking home from the university. Detained on the charge of being "drunk without identity papers and suspicious," Zamora was held for six days by the National Police in a windowless cell infested with rats and cockroaches, drugged, and interrogated. The line of questioning told a familiar story—"all the time they were trying to make me link the work of the Church and priests with guerrillas."[33]

Despite the archdiocese's protests, there was no news of Zamora (who would eventually be released on condition he left the country), when on May 1 Jorge Sarsanedas, a young Panamanian Jesuit, was captured on his way back from saying mass in a small community of the parish of Nejapa. It was not until five days later that Romero and Jerez, accompanied by another Jesuit, were allowed to see him inside the National Guard barracks. When Sarsanedas appeared, looking thin, pale, and tired, Romero handed him the cup of coffee he had just been given and asked how he was. He told them he had generally been treated well, but that he had been held blindfolded for five days, had eaten only twice, and had been kicked around and insulted for being a "son-of-a-bitch of a priest." Romero was asked to sign a release form with a totally false time and place of capture that also maintained Sarsanedas had been well treated. National Guard Director Colonel Alvarenga was obsequious throughout the meeting, but his protestations that "in the Guard there is only very simple food and not a lot of it," did not get past Romero. He read the release out loud and refused to sign.

Romero and Jerez drove to the airport behind the vehicle taking Sarsanedas out to his deportation. As they saw him on to the airplane, Carlos Cabarrús, a friend and contemporary of Sarsanedas, stopped beside Romero. " 'Thank you for helping Jorge, Monsignor,' 'I wasn't always like this.' Romero replied. 'No, Monsignor, you weren't.' 'This is the fruit of the blood of Father Grande.' "[34]

IT was perhaps on June 19, 1977 that the Jesuits began to realize the full significance that Monsignor Romero would have for many of them personally and for the Salvadoran Church as a whole. It was on that day that Romero "re-took" Aguilares in the name of its suffering people and their God and showed that he had a quality and power of leadership that was quite out of the ordinary. Put at its simplest he had the ability to do what Gustavo Guitiérrez identified as the primary task of liberation theology: to tell the poor that God loves them.[35] A fundamental mission and a fundamentally difficult one. But Romero could do it, and as archbishop he could do it as the representative of a Church that with him became fully Salvadoran in its incarnation in the lives and suffering of its people.

May 1977 had continued badly. After weeks of appeals to the FPL for compassion in its treatment of Borgonovo and to the government to negotiate his release, his body was found on the morning of May 10. The following day Romero said the funeral mass, but as he entered the Church of San José de la Montaña, he was greeted by a hostile murmuring that seemed to imply responsibility on his part.[36] That afternoon the UGB fulfilled its threats and killed the young diocesan priest, Alfonso Navarro, who had said the mass in the Plaza Libertad after the protest against the electoral fraud. A young boy who had opened the door to the murderers was killed with him. Leaflets were distributed throughout San Salvador urging: "Be a patriot, kill a priest!" As after the death of Rutilio Grande, President Molina was among the first to call Romero to offer his condolences and promise an "exhaustive investigation."[37] To an old friend who would complain about Romero's refusal to speak with the government, Romero would answer testily: "I am metropolitan archbishop and they're killing my priests. How am I going to be pleased with these people if, on top of it all, they are cynical enough to be the first to give their condolences? I am the spiritual father of my priests, and if they kill them, how can I be pleased, if they're my sons?"[38]

A few days later, the army launched the long-threatened "Operation Rutilio," with a full-scale military siege of Aguilares. Three Jesuits and three *campesinos* took refuge in the church. With an army tank at the church door they were nervously ringing the bells when soldiers burst through the door and shot the young boy on the bell ropes. As bullets sprayed the altar the priests were tied up and bundled into waiting vehicles. They were deported later that day, but nothing more was heard of them until they reappeared in a Guatemalan jail.[39] The town was left under military control. *Campesinos* were assassinated with impunity and no representative of the Church—not even the Nuncio—was allowed in to reclaim the violated church until the morning of June 19.

Romero came to Aguilares from San Salvador to install a new parish priest and pastoral team. Jesuits and other priests and nuns from the archdiocese accompanied him on a day that none would forget. *Campesinos* thronged around their archbishop in the hot sun. Many had traveled from afar. These were the people who suffered the persecution of the Church on a daily basis: delegates of the Word, catechists, and lay men and women, terrorized by the operations of the military and paramilitary forces. "It is my lot to go around gathering up the trampled and the dead and all that the persecution of the Church leaves behind it," said Romero, beginning his sermon with a startling definition of the work of a bishop. "We are with you," was what had come to tell the suffering people of Aguilares. "We suffer with those who have suffered so much, we are truly with you, and we want to tell you, my brothers, that your pain is the pain of the Church." He had come to tell the people of Aguilares that, in their suffering, they were the image of Christ crucified on the cross, "singing the precious music of liberation" for their very identity with the suffering Christ.[40]

Jon Sobrino and the Jesuits with him listened from amid the crowds and were profoundly moved by what they heard. "To tell some grieving *campesinos* that they are today Christ present in history," Sobrino would write years later, "and to say so with sincerity, is the most radical form a Christian has to return them their dignity and maintain them in hope . . . And the people of Aguilares believed him. That miracle does not happen all the time, but it was true. Those *campesinos* from Aguilares brought Monsignor Romero into their hearts and he stayed there forever."[41] Romero continued his sermon with a public thanks to the Jesuits for their work in Aguilares. But from this moment on, the Jesuits who had so gladly offered their help—pleased that the new archbishop was willing to accept it, but perhaps inclined to believe that it was they who had the skills, training, and intellect to illuminate his pastoral leadership—would be conscious that Romero's time in the archdiocese of San Salvador was something that the country, and indeed the continent, was fortunate to be witnessing. "With Monsignor Romero," Ellacuría would say a few days after Romero's death, "God passed through El Salvador."[42]

In late June, the Jesuits' publication in the national press of a full explanation of their work and its relationship to the political turmoil of the country, "The Jesuits before the Salvadoran People,"[43] was interrupted. On June 21, 1977 the UGB released a communiqué demanding that all Jesuits should leave the country within thirty days. "The wretched instigators of the FPL assassins have no reason to remain poisoning our

people," the communiqué declared, "our struggle is not against the
Church but against Jesuit guerrillaism." Should the Jesuits not leave, the
UGB warned that they would proceed to the "immediate and systematic
execution of all those Jesuits who stay in the country."[44] The Jesuits did
not waver. "We shall continue to be faithful to our mission and stay here
until we fulfill the work that is needed or they liquidate us," was the
assurance offered by the provincial César Jerez.[45] But the recent actions of
the UGB made it clear that the threat was to be taken seriously. While the
clock was ticking, the Jesuits had thirty days in which to mobilize
international pressure, establish clear lines of communication with the
Salvadoran government—General Romero was due to take Molina's place
as president on July 1—and take precautions.

The situation was as dramatic as it was alarming. It also came at a
moment when the outside world was just beginning to notice that things
were very badly wrong in El Salvador. In the United States, President
Carter had publicly pledged his administration's commitment to human
rights, and congressional hearings—the first to be exclusively devoted to
El Salvador—had been held in March on the fraud surrounding General
Romero's election. The Salvadoran government had objected to what they
believed to be infringement on their sovereignty by rejecting further U.S.
military aid, while the human rights violations escalated. But as President
Ford's outgoing ambassador to El Salvador, Ignacio Lozano, would
complain in July, where El Salvador was concerned, the provision of teeth
to the fine sentiments emanating from Washington was not readily
achieved: "Given the fact that the United States really has no vital interest
in the country, it is pretty difficult to get anybody to pay attention to
us."[46]

On his way back from Rome a few months before the UGB threat,
César Jerez paused in Washington to explain things to the Jesuit
Conference. Among those most impressed with what Jerez had had to say
had been Fathers James Connor, president of the conference, and Simon
Smith, an old friend from Jerez's days at the University of Chicago. They
had offered "all possible support and promised to 'move' if and when
César gave a clear signal."[47] Armed with an updated version of the Dossier
on Persecution that had gone to Rome, the U.S. Jesuits now got to work.
Requesting a meeting with Secretary of State Cyrus Vance to discuss the
situation in El Salvador, they also set about galvanizing the nationwide
contacts of Jesuits and other religious orders in a campaign of congressional lobbying, an unusual precedent for the little known region of
Central America. A third tier to the strategy was initiated by William

Rogers—a powerful ally as he had formerly been both under secretary of state and assistant secretary of state for interamerican affairs—who contacted the House Committee on International Relations and suggested that they should reopen the hearings on El Salvador to take a look at religious persecution. The new hearings held on July 21, 1977 included testimony by Paco Estrada, who was dispatched to Washington at the last minute with news of the measures being taken to protect Jesuits as the White Warriors Union's deadline expired.

In El Salvador, a series of rather uneasy meetings between the Jesuits and the government, whose general tone was described as "intimate cordiality in open warfare," had begun at the end of May before the UGB threat was issued.[48] The Jesuits had intended to protest the expulsion of three of their number during the siege of Aguilares and argue the case for the return of Ellacuría and de Sebastián. At the time, Molina had shown himself still resentful of the wounds inflicted by the *ECA* editorial "At your orders, Capital!" and had warned that their safety in El Salvador could not be guaranteed. In June discussions about the government's provision of security for the forty-nine resident Jesuits were complicated by the suspicion that not only was the UGB made up of members of the security forces, but also that there were close links between the new president of the country and these same forces.

It was clear that the governments of Molina and Romero were surprised by the international pressure that gathered behind the Jesuits. With a $90 million loan from the IADB for a new hydroelectric dam pending, the congressional hearings at hand, and letters, telegrams, and diplomatic protests arriving on a daily basis, curiosity finally got the better of General Romero. "How much is this international campaign costing you, Father?" he asked Jerez in one of their meetings. "It hasn't cost a thing," came the answer. "What it is is that we are an institution that for some is one of respect and dignity—perhaps not for you—and as an institution we are considerably older than any of these countries."[49]

As the deadline approached the Jesuits moved out of their more vulnerable residences and into the larger communities of Santa Tecla and the *Externado*. Even so there was something unnerving about needing to comply with requests from the security forces for a list of exactly who was living at which address. Inside the National Guard the word went around that the Jesuits were "off limits;" outside the Jesuit houses police and guardsmen kept vigilant watch.[50] "Nothing happened to us because the president said it wouldn't," was how Estrada remembered the episode, "and he had direct control over those behind the threat."[51]

THE Jesuits were often accused of manipulating Monsignor Romero. For many this was the most simple explanation of his behavior as archbishop. "The Jesuits did a form of psychoanalysis and discovered that his great failing was personal insecurity," was the view of Monsignor Freddy Delgado, in Romero's day secretary of the Bishops' Conference. "They drove the archdiocese as easily as a car, making it seem that he was in control."[52] Delgado's opinions were shared by Monsignor Romeo Továr Astorga, until early 1992 president of the Bishops' Conference, and by Monsignor René Revelo, bishop of Santa Ana and formerly an auxiliary bishop to Romero. According to Astorga, "The third-world clergy manipulated Monsignor Romero and of course that meant the Jesuits." Revelo commented, "Unfortunately Romero had no character. He let himself be dominated, and the brains behind all this were the Jesuits."[53] The Jesuits were perceived as having several centuries of Machiavellian experience behind them; they had no trouble at all running rings around this simple Salvadoran bishop. And inevitably, and despite the fact that he was out of the country until August 1978, the archmanipulator of them all was Ignacio Ellacuría. The charge was repeated in Rome, with Cardinal Sebastiano Baggio on one occasion upbraiding Romero as he pointed to a cover of a book authored by Romero, Rivera, Ellacuría, Sobrino, and one Tomás R. Campos (a pseudonym for Ellacuría, although it is unlikely the cardinal would have known) telling him, "You are in very bad company, Monsignor."[54]

During the intensely lived years of Romero's tenure, the Jesuits were much more intimately involved in the running of the archdiocese than they had been before or would be in the future. Educated and trained as theologians, philosophers, political analysts, and social scientists, and forming part of a well-informed international network, they were a resource that it would have been difficult to forego. But the point of connection for Romero went deeper than that. In the 1930s Romero had studied with Jesuits in the San Salvador seminary and at the Gregorian University in Rome. In the mid-1950s he spent a month in Santa Tecla in Spiritual Exercises given by Miguel Elizondo and he would return to them, to the rigor and consolation of Ignatian spirituality, throughout his life. It was a phrase of St. Ignatius, *"Sentir con la Iglesia"*—"to be of one heart and mind with the Church"—that he had taken for his standard when he became a bishop, and it was a Jesuit, Father Azcue, whom he would choose as his confessor.[55] As archbishop, Romero had also seen in the Jesuits a tranquility in the face of persecution that profoundly impressed him. "In these critical circumstances," he had written to Jerez of the UGB threat, "the Ignatian community has done none other than accept with the strength of the Lord His difficult will. This is confirmed by the words of Father Arrupe, general of the order, 'they have done no more than they should have done:' stayed with the utmost of apostolic generosity, even at the risk of suffering the supreme immolation."[56]

Romero knew himself to be easily influenced and his ministry was characterized by the enormous quantity of people he spoke and consulted with on both regular and irregular bases. In the context of a rapidly increasing political polarization of the country that had at its center the complex dilemma of the role of the Church in a prerevolutionary situation, tensions and disagreements were inevitable. The Jesuits represented a powerful force within the archdiocese both in their numbers and their combined strength of character and intellect. Humility has never been the most salient of Jesuit qualities and there were understandable conflicts, particularly with some of the diocesan priests.

Within the daily administration of the archdiocese, the most controversial figure was Rafael Moreno, whose objectivity, some believed, was called into question by the close connections he had established with FECCAS and the *Bloque* during his years in Aguilares. Romero, however, had need of advisers representing a wide range of sectors of society and did not doubt that he was faithfully served by Moreno. Other difficulties had as much to do with personality as politics. On their return to El Salvador Ellacuría and Luis de Sebastián threw themselves, with all the thirst of exiles, into full participation in the pressing events of the day.[57] At one point Urioste was to take César Jerez to one side and explain that while he could more or less tolerate his bringing one or the other of these brilliant and domineering Jesuits to the archdiocese's meetings, the combination of the two was "unbearable."[58] It was a view affectionately shared by some of their closest friends.

One of the most direct forms of the Jesuits' collaboration came in the preparation of Romero's annual Pastoral Letters, the major doctrinal works of his years as archbishop. The nature of the collaboration varied with the material to be covered in the letter: thus the Second Pastoral Letter, "The Church, the Body of Christ in History," more strictly theological in nature than the others, was drafted by Jon Sobrino who "tried to put [himself] in Romero's mind," after discussing the directions the Letter should take.[59] The third and fourth Letters published in 1978 and 1979—"The Church and Popular Political Organizations" and "The Church's Mission amid the National Crisis," respectively—were written by a very different process. Both responded to concrete problems in the life of the Church and the country; as attacks against the Church for its involvement in politics continued, and as it also became clear that priests within the archdiocese were being drawn into more direct political participation than the archdiocese could sanction, the need for orientation was pressing. As many as twenty-five people were involved in the preparation of "The Church and Popular Political Organizations," and there were a whole series of meetings held both at the archdiocese offices and in the UCA. Romero provided the general guidelines of what the Letter should contain and oversaw the evolution of three or four keenly discussed drafts. Notes taken from the meetings reveal the extent to which all involved were striving to respond to "the personal interest of Monsignor."[60]

The Letter itself addressed the challenge presented to the Church and to society in general by the rapid proliferation of *campesino* organizations, whose ranks were only swelled by the repression at the hands of government forces. Reaffirming the right to organize in the pursuit of an integral liberation, the Letter insisted that "faith and politics ought to be united in a Christian who has a political vocation, but they are not to be identified." As every month made clear that for many of those pursuing social, political, and economic change, paths forward other than that of violence were growing more scarce, the Letter was founded on an unequivocal commitment of the Church to a peace that is based in justice. While admitting the existence of legitimate instances for the use of violence as a last resort and in self-defense, the Letter reminded the people of El Salvador of the power of nonviolence—the Christian "can fight, but prefers peace to war"—and urged, "We are living in explosive times, and there is great need for wisdom and serenity."[61]

Every Saturday evening Romero held a meeting of a select group of advisers for the preparation of his Sunday homilies. Among the regulars at these sessions were Urioste; Roberto Cuellár, who collected data covering individual cases of disappearances, murders, and abuses of human rights from the legal aid office *Socorro Jurídico;* and Rafael Moreno, who gave an analysis of political developments and brought Romero up to the minute on the complex ebb and flow of the popular organizations. Romero would listen carefully and take copious notes as the advisers spoke. When disagreements arose among them he would want them argued out—"Go on, discuss it." The advisers would be invited to dine with him after each session and then would leave him at about 8:00 P.M. as he retired to write in the small room he lived in at a cancer hospital run by nuns. At eight o'clock the next morning the homily would be ready.[62] As Héctor Dada, a friend and regular adviser of Romero's, remembered, "sometimes on Sundays I'd be with Jesuits of whom it was said that they had written the homilies and we would be wondering what he was going to say. He gathered up the opinions of half the world and so, yes, often he did say things that one of the Jesuits might have written for him. But at other times he'd say the opposite of what I or any Jesuit had advised him."[63]

None of those closest to Romero believe him to have been manipulated—except perhaps by God. "Monsignor," Pepe Simán put it, "showed us all that God is greater than human beings."[64] Lay Christians, nuns, and priests, each of whom struggled privately with their own faith, witnessed in Romero an extraordinary ability to pray—sometimes he would even leave a meeting or hold up an appointment to do so. "Thanks be to God, I see that when I put myself to it seriously I achieve concentration and the elevation of prayer," Romero confided in one of his notebooks. "God is good and I find him easily."[65] It is with this capacity for direct communication with God that Monsignor Urioste laid the debate still raging around Romero's "manipulation" to rest: "Monsignor Romero never said anything or did anything about which he had not previously consulted God. . . . It didn't matter to him what people said to him afterwards, the accusations and the threats. He was certain, sure and convinced about what he said because he had talked it over with God."[66]

ROMERO had set forth on a path along which the Jesuits, as other members of his Church, were glad to follow. The situation was an unusual one. Historically somewhat detached from the Church hierarchy by virtue of their identity as members of the Society of Jesus, and prone to an arrogance born of an awareness of their own abilities, the Jesuits of El Salvador found in Romero a quite unexpected source of inspiration. As the crisis in the country worsened, so this inspiration extended beyond the actions of the Church itself and into the university. In 1985, as the UCA awarded Romero a posthumous doctorate in theology, Ellacuría would acknowledge that "It was with the arrival of Monsignor [Romero] in the archdiocese that the university gained a greater consciousness of its mission."[67]

In the Romero years, the UCA combined its identity as a Christian university enhanced by what was happening within the Salvadoran Church with a growing sense of urgency that something must be done to bring a halt to the country's downward slide into tragedy. The extent of the intellectual talent and the deep-seated knowledge of the country of those teaching, writing, and publishing at the UCA in the late 1970s created an atmosphere that was stimulating even in moments of disagreement. It was a rich, productive time in which formal meetings spilled over into meals and discussions far into the night, often accompanied by the guitar playing of Nacho Martín-Baró or Eddy Stein, director of communications. With the traditional political parties of the opposition necessarily somewhat dormant and the broad front organizations of the *Bloque,* FAPU, and the LP-28, aligned with the FPL, RN, and ERP respectively, gathering strength, political positions, and affiliations were fluid and highly complex.

Among the ideas with which Ellacuría had returned from his exile, few concerned him as much as the need to extend the UCA's "social projection" beyond its regular publications. From late 1978 the views and opinions of a wide range of the UCA's most able thinkers became—anonymously—available to a public hungry for the kind of analysis they would search for in vain in the national newspapers (if literate and solvent enough to buy them) as the UCA began a daily broadcast on the archdiocese's radio YSAX. Short commentaries "written with the hurry and heat of daily events," as Italo López Vallecillos, director of the university press and frequent contributor would write, went out at midday.[68] News, opinion or denunciation, the commentaries reached out into homes and communities throughout the country to do far more to mend "the divorce between the press and the oppressed people" than could ever be achieved by the printed word.

Much though some of the lay staff might grumble behind their backs, the Jesuits—and obviously Mayorga, who was seen as being part of the Jesuitical "block" within the UCA—ran a very tight ship; real power in the university was concentrated in the board of directors, where the Jesuits insisted on maintaining a four-to-one majority. Among the arguments the Jesuits used to quell dissent was that the university needed politically unaligned celibates at its head: their primary responsibility would always be to the university and not to the demands of a family or political organization. Constantly aware of the dangers of manipulation of an institution that prided itself on its freedom from ideological influence, the Jesuits' relationships with the popular organizations were ambiguous and ambivalent. "There were certain rules of the game," remembered one politically active faculty member, "and it was Ellacuría above all who insisted that they should be kept."[69] A FECCAS meeting within the UCA, for example, might be sanctioned, but it would always be on the basis that it was a loan of physical space and nothing more.

But there were cases where a growing commitment to the popular demand for change came with a seriousness that the Jesuits might not agree with, but could not deny. Such was Ellacuría's position with respect to one of his most brilliant philosophy students, Salvador Samayoa, who by the mid-1970s was a professor within the philosophy department and on the editorial board of *ECA*. Although Samayoa was not formally integrated into any organization, Ellacuría knew that his ties to the *Bloque* were close and appreciated what his knowledge and connections could bring to the UCA. But that was it. "My relationship with him was very warm," Samayoa explained, "in terms of friendship and intellectual companionship, but politically it was much less so. He knew that I was heading in a different direction—he might not have liked it, but he was respectful." Ellacuría never moved on to support armed struggle; in Samayoa's words "he accommodated himself to it as a reality."[70] As some students shifted toward the revolutionary left individual relations inevitably grew strained.

While sympathetic to the goal of social change, the Jesuits were intellectually critical of the sectarianism they perceived within the revolutionary organizations and morally critical of the methods—especially the targeted assassinations—these organizations pursued. Contact between the Jesuits of the UCA and the three ex-Jesuit scholastics within the FPL was avoided by both organizations during these years. Under the direction of Cayetano Carpio, whose ascetic, orthodox marxism took a very dim view of Jesuits to begin with, the FPL was as anxious to refute the charges it was facing from the ERP that it was "half-Jesuit and run by priests" as were the Jesuits to try and live down the same accusations coming from elsewhere.[71]

What the UCA did seek was the development of a civilized and rational political pluralism, and there was no more striking platform for this rapidly receding ideal than a masters program in political science taught between 1975 and 1979. The program was directed by Nicolás Mariscal, but its staff and students were aware of how much it meant to Ellacuría. "He saw it as a way to civilize individuals from the army, businessmen, politicians, and union workers and also those on the left," remembered one professor.[72] The program was taught by a wide range of the UCA's academics—among them Ellacuría, Martín-Baró, Dada, Héctor Oquelí, and Rubén Zamora—but it was clear from its much-publicized beginnings that it was really about who the students were, what they could learn from the UCA and from each other, and how the whole experience could help form a political class equipped to guide El Salvador through its crisis.[73]

With a couple of exceptions, the program was only open to those with political experience, whether as a party politician, a leader in a popular organization or as a member of the armed forces. Within each of the two years to take the program there was an extraordinary cross-section of people: a former minister of defense, the current army chief of staff and other officers; landowners, assemblymen of the ruling PCN, members of the MNR, PDC, and UDN; and militants with the popular organizations. Several of these students would be killed in the war, while others would rise to hold prominent political positions.[74] Among the latter were Hugo Carrillo, in the 1980s general secretary of the PCN; Mario Aguiñada Carranza, a member of the FDR-FMLN's Political Diplomatic Commission and then general secretary of the UDN; René Roldán, general secretary of the Social Democratic Party (PSD); and María Julia Hernández, director of archdiocese's legal aid office for Monsignor Rivera. While classes, understandably, sometimes generated heated debates, students and staff alike remember—almost with nostalgia—the "strange atmosphere" that surrounded the experiment as they were brought into contact with people far outside their usual circle of acquaintances. But by 1979, when the courses closed, El Salvador was well down the road toward a polarization so extreme that those classroom debates were already something of an anachronism. It appeared to be the last possible moment when the enlightenment of Salvadoran political culture could be imagined in such a form.

OUTSIDE the relative tranquility of the university, the events of May 8, 1979 were indicative of the brewing storm of violence, soon to engulf the country. The day began quietly enough, with 300 members of the *Bloque* peacefully demonstrating on the steps of San Salvador's cathedral against the "disappearance" of five of their leaders. The *Bloque* was by now some 60,000 to 80,000 strong, with the majority of its membership drawn from FECCAS and the UTC. A hated Law of Public Order[75] had been rescinded in February after the government suffered a highly critical report on its violations of human rights from the Organization of American States. Between January and June, however, there would be 406 people killed by the army, the security forces, and the paramilitary ORDEN (now a force of between 50,000 and 100,000 people) and 307 captured for political reasons.[76]

The OAS report had been but one of three—the others issued by the Department of State and a delegation from the British Parliament—that had helped focus attention on the escalating abuses within El Salvador.

But as the *Diario de Hoy* dismissed all critics as part of an international conspiracy controlled "like an electric circuit, with on and off switches in London, Washington, Havana, Moscow, and San Salvador,"[77] the abuses continued unabated. On January 20, 1979, a few days before Monsignor Romero was due to leave for the Third Conference of Latin American Bishops in Puebla (Mexico), the National Guard drove tanks straight through the closed gateway of a retreat house in San Antonio Abad, killing the young priest leading the retreat, Octavio Ortiz, and four of the teenage participants. Ortiz had been the first priest that Romero had ordained and was the fourth of the eleven priests to be killed between 1977 and 1980. Government accounts—immediately refuted by witnesses—found proof of "subversion" in photographs of Rutilio Grande, copies of *Orientación*, and the bodies of the victims themselves: laid out face up on the roof, guns had been placed in their hands, with their fingers crudely curled around the triggers.[78]

And now in May, as the *Bloque* protesters sang songs and carried placards, the security forces were at it again. Trucks rolled into the cathedral square and disgorged police and guardsmen. Before the demonstrators had time to register their presence, they had opened fire. The demonstrators dived and fell for cover, clambering over each other as they tried to get inside the cathedral. But the security forces were shooting to kill and the dead and wounded quickly accumulated on the steps. The whole thing was filmed by a cameraman from CBS television. As protests flooded in, the seriousness of the mistake became clear even to General Romero: the systematic slaughter of twenty-three people and the wounding of many more while they are demonstrating peacefully outside a church does not look good on network television. Members of the *Bloque* occupied the Venezuelan Embassy in protest at the cathedral massacre, but there too the security forces could find no other way to counter the situation than that of violence, and fourteen people were killed. A state of siege was imposed the same day. The FPL reacted quickly and decisively to the two massacres with the assassination of the minister of education. El Salvador was becoming ungovernable.

President Romero invited political parties, the universities, churches, business representatives, and "other legally recognized organizations" to join together in a National Forum. He went to particular lengths to secure the presence of the UCA, sending telegrams and on one occasion a minister to convince the university to take part. But after discussion in the Upper Council, the UCA said no. "We could not go and talk to the president because of the circumstances of the political climate," Vice-

Rector Luis de Sebastián told a Salvadoran journalist later in the year, "besides the Forum did not strike us as the best method of stimulating a dialogue."[79] The UCA's official statement explained that cooperation with the government would legitimize its repression not only of armed terrorism, but also of popular organizations and legally recognized unions. Instead the UCA undertook the preparation of a document that would, "propose the economic, social and political measures most suited to the present moment" and "a sequence of steps to bring those measures into practice."[80]

ON July 19, 1979 several hundred miles to the south, the streets of Managua, Nicaragua, were filled with exhausted, flag-waving, and triumphant Nicaraguans as the combined forces of the Sandinista Front for National Liberation (FSLN) celebrated their victory over the dictator Anastasio Somoza. The first successful revolution in Latin America in two decades sent shock waves, colored with hope by some and fear by others, throughout the continent. In El Salvador hopeful and fearful alike believed they would be next. In Washington Republican voices blamed President Carter and his human rights policy for "losing" Nicaragua. Over the next couple of months Cyrus Vance would dispatch both Assistant Secretary of State Viron Vaky and special emissary William Bowdler to San Salvador. Each was to reinforce the efforts of U.S. Ambassador Frank Devine and urge President Romero to make moderate reforms, bring elections forward, and release political prisoners. But not even dire predictions of "the next Nicaragua" could budge the general.[81] "Those imperialists want me to resign," he grumbled to his fellow officers, "when I have been elected by the Salvadoran people."[82]

But among those same officers there were more than a few who knew that this was not true. "We spent a night stuffing voting urns in 1977," remembered Colonel Román Barrera, at the time a young captain. He had been summoned by his senior officer to do a "special job" and felt proud to have been singled out for it, "but you can imagine my shock when I discovered what it was. There was I, a young officer, wanting to serve my country and my people. I obeyed the order of course—I was a soldier and a soldier obeys his orders."[83] Since then Barrera and others like him had come to think that President Romero was "a big mistake." And for many of the officers who had entered the military academy as conservative Christian youths with vague patriotic ideas about doing good for their country while they earned themselves some power and influence, the campaign against the Church was a key factor in their disillusion. "While the senior officers," Colonel Adolfo Majano, a national chess champion and deputy director of the military academy would write, "believed that the Church could be intimidated . . . it wasn't well thought of by the junior officers—rather it opened their eyes, it made them think that they were being badly led by their superiors."[84]

A graduate of a masters program at Ohio State University and of further studies in Japan, Lieutenant Colonel René Guerra y Guerra was unusually well educated for a Salvadoran officer. In 1978 he had spotted Barrera as someone who might be likely to share the ideas about long-term social change in El Salvador that he had nurtured since the early 1970s.[85] Both had priests as cousins; Barrera's cousin Neto had been one of the archdiocese's priests most intimately caught up in the popular movement. He had been killed in November 1978 in a confrontation between the National Police and the FPL and after his death—to the surprise of Monsignor Romero, and the delight of the Church's critics—it had transpired that he had been an active member of the FPL. Barrera became Guerra y Guerra's first collaborator in the preparation of a coup against the government of General Romero and the corrupt officers ensconced at the head of the armed forces. As discreet conversations began with officers throughout the country, another captain, Francisco Mena Sandoval, and an air force major, Alvaro Salazar Brenes, were added to the coordinating committee.

During the early months of 1979, the coup-plotters found that there were many among the junior officers whose fear of revolution and disenchantment with the institution they served was so great that they were seriously contemplating resigning. Such an attitude was defeatist, it was argued, and in the worst interest of the country and the army itself. "If I am irresponsible to want to leave the armed forces," an officer told Mena Sandoval, "then I'll stay. But if I stay it is to do something, and that something must be done quickly because I don't think we've got much time."[86] The sense of urgency was increased by the sight of Somoza's National Guard in flight from Nicaragua and arriving by the boatload on the shores of El Salvador's Gulf of Fonseca; here was a warning that the army's worst nightmare was becoming more possible by the day. But some of the colonels were still blind to what was happening. "Colonel, things are getting complicated," one captain ventured to say to his commanding officer over lunch one day in July. "I think we should be getting ready for a war of counterinsurgency." "Don't worry," the colonel had answered, "there'll never be guerrillas here—there aren't any mountains."[87]

The extent of the Jesuits' involvement in the coup depends—like much to do with October 15, 1979—on the person consulted. Never, obviously, direct instigators of the young officers' movement, the Jesuits' personal relationship with some of those involved meant that they were, from an early stage, well informed. At the same time the body of the UCA's research and analysis of the problems besetting the country was an obvious source of information for those seeking a change and, for the most part, seeking that change without a clear economic, political or social framework.

Mena Sandoval had been a regular visitor to the Jesuits of UCAII since 1977, and Alvaro Salazar Brenes—originally introduced to Ellacuría through a cousin who taught at the UCA—a student of the UCA's political science program. While Salazar Brenes was somewhat reserved and formal in his consultations with the Jesuits, Mena was warm-hearted, impetuous and politically rather naive. Through family connections Mena had come to know Paco Estrada, and through him the Jesuits of the UCA, especially Luis de Sebastián and Ellacuría. He was pleased to receive an annual subscription to *ECA* on his birthdays and "liked what they had to say about social justice." Flattered by the seriousness with which the Jesuits treated him on his visits—"hold on, we'll gather the High Command for you," they'd say on his arrival as three or four Jesuits cleared busy schedules to make time for him—Mena came to trust them "more than all the senior officers I had." As a result he provided the Jesuits with "Category A" information about the inner workings of the National Guard, where death squads ran wild and one Roberto D'Aubuisson, an expert in "political warfare" and head of ANSESAL, the feared army intelligence agency, was a frequent visitor. Although he was transferred to a desk job at the end of 1978, Mena's visits continued—supplemented by visits from Salazar Brenes and a small group of other officers—throughout the frenzied months of 1979.[88]

The Jesuits first learned of the plans for a coup in August 1979, when Salazar Brenes came to see Ellacuría. "I'm thinking of doing a doctorate," he began. "Well—good," Ellacuría answered. "But it's a practical doctorate, not a theoretical one." Ellacuría remained perplexed until Salazar explained that the subject of this "doctorate" was "changing the country."[89] The question the plotters brought to the Jesuits was a simple one, "What can be done?" "Our answer was quite easy to formulate," de Sebastián would say. "We told the young officers that our path was clearly defined and if they wanted to follow it, if they accepted our principles of Christian ethics and a realistic analysis of the national problem, we could walk together."[90] As a contribution to this process the Jesuits passed them a copy of the document that had been drawn up in response to the proposed National Forum, "A Democratic Solution to the Salvadoran Crisis." The document was completed in September 1979, but after a heated discussion it had been rejected by the UCA's Upper Council, which considered that it paid too little attention to agrarian reform, the popular organizations, and the political aspects of violence. Only thirty copies were produced, each bound in a yellow cover that earned the document the title "The Yellow Book." Explained to some of the less well educated officers by Salazar Brenes and Guerra y Guerra, it influenced the various drafts of the young officers' Proclamation that would be prepared in the following weeks.

The Jesuits were among those who had introduced various members of the army to Monsignor Romero. Always open to the opinions of different sectors within the country, Romero's diary shows that he was in constant communication with officers concerned about the directions in which the country was heading. The officers plotting the coup knew that his support was vital to their credibility with the people of El Salvador and had first contacted Romero after the cathedral massacre in May.[91] As his Fourth Pastoral Letter, released in September 1979, made clear, Romero's view of the Church's proper contribution to the process of liberation of the people of El Salvador was rooted not in politics but in the Gospel and the "preferential option for the poor."[92] While the Letter outlined the importance of a pastoral policy of "accompaniment" of those who had taken radical political options, it also, in a section largely written by Ellacuría, warned against the idolatry of a particular organization or ideology—as well as the more obvious idolatries of wealth or a doctrine of national security—to the exclusion of Christian values. The Church would look favorably on that which favored the people of El Salvador. It was from this position that Romero, advised of the imminence of the coup on the evening of October 7, promised "my prayers and all the moral collaboration that the Church can offer in these delicate circumstances."[93]

As plans for the coup advanced, relations among the officers involved had deteriorated, principally through the addition to the coordinating group of Abdul Gutiérrez, a colonel believed deeply suspect by Guerra y Guerra for his connections to some of the hard-line officers the coup was intended to oust. One of them was Colonel José Guillermo García, the former president of the state-run telephone company ANTEL—a post that offered potential for lucrative pickings and first-rate access to intelligence—and a close associate of Molina. Gutiérrez learned about the coup from Mena Sandoval in August and persuaded him that he and

Colonel García were well advanced in their own plans for a coup and should be included on the coordinating committee. Gutiérrez had lobbied Monsignor Romero through shared acquaintances and was thus able to ensure his own place on the committee, but, to Mena Sandoval's initial fury, Romero threatened to withdraw his support of the movement if it included García. ("Who is Monsignor Romero to give us orders?" Mena had raged at the Jesuits as soon as he heard. "Listen Francisco," they told him, "if President Romero came to place himself at the service of the people, Monsignor Romero would support him. He's not trying to give any orders."[94])

Divisions only increased as the committee attempted to name the five-man Junta that was to govern the country: three of the five were to be civilians, one representing the private sector; the remaining two would be military officers. Votes were cast and Colonel Majano, who was highly thought of by the young officers, was agreed on unanimously. But voting for the second position did not achieve an absolute majority. In a move he would live to regret, Mena Sandoval maneuvered adroitly to have Gutiérrez, his commanding officer at the time, given the job.[95]

There was a consciousness throughout the UCA of a terrible crisis preceding a bloody civil war. Many staff members were aligned with the "Popular Forum" of opposition political parties and organizations that had grown up in reaction to the idea of a National Forum, and rumors of what might happen next were rife. Román Mayorga was first told that there was going to be a military coup and that he would be asked to join the Junta by Italo López Vallecillos, within the UCA a man of legendarily good military contacts. He then heard no more until Mena appeared in his office one day, disguised as a bookseller from the Hispanoamerican bookstore, to sound him out as a possible Junta member. Mayorga had never met Mena before, but Mena struck him as sincere. He told him that his reaction was "cautiously positive;" they should press ahead and would talk if the coup became a real possibility. The feeling in the university, as Mayorga remembered it, was that "people wanted to do something, the politicians for understandable reasons, the rest of us because we felt we had to. When the coup came we saw it as a bad option, but one that was preferable to worse ones."[96]

On October 10, Monsignor Romero called a meeting to discuss the position the Church should assume in the event of a coup's success. His advisers, who included Mayorga, Héctor Dada, Ellacuría, Estrada, and Urioste, recommended that Romero should wait and see what sort of platform a post-coup government would present.[97] Worries shared by all—whether the country was not already too polarized and whether it was not too late to try and make a bridge between the two forces—were perhaps most acutely felt by Mayorga, who was not a professional politician and knew that he would be called upon to assume a position of daunting responsibility. Welcome, if not reassuring, advice came from Ellacuría: "It's possible you'll be burned by this, or worse," he told him, "but in the circumstances I don't think you have a choice. It is the only way, if there is one, to avoid bloodshed while at the same time searching for a positive change for the country."[98]

Two days later, Mayorga was summoned to a meeting at which he met the coup-plotters. He was favorably impressed by Guerra y Guerra, whose family he knew; and by Barrera, Salazar Brenes, and Mena, although he thought they seemed "a bit innocent and naive." "My great mistake was Majano," he would remember later. "The others spoke well of him, I liked him and thought he must be a fine officer if he was their leader. I thought we could work together." When formally asked if he would join the Junta, Mayorga laid down three conditions: he wanted to select the proclamation—and therefore the political platform—from the three he had been shown; he wanted there to be a cleansing of corrupt and brutal officers from the army after the coup; and he insisted that someone from the Popular Forum should be named to one of the civilian posts on the Junta.[99]

By the afternoon of October 15, 1979, General Romero had left the country for Guatemala after a military operation so bloodless that it had taken all involved by surprise. That evening Mayorga was in the San Carlos barracks, still uncommitted to a final "yes" as the finishing touches were put to the proclamation. The Popular Forum was initially split over their representative on the Junta, with the PDC wanting their candidate, José Antonio Morales Erlich, and the MNR pushing—in the end successfully—for Guillermo Ungo. While the Jesuits of UCAII had been told the night before, as Mena Sandoval, his pockets bulging with grenades, paid a lightening visit to Calle Mediterráneo, on the morning of the 15th the news was slow to filter around the city. Luis de Sebastián—who had left the UCAII community prepared for any eventuality with his radio, his passport, and $300—was with Segundo Montes when Ungo appeared. He began telling them, in a conspiratorial whisper he reserved for political discussions, about a meeting in Mexico he had just returned from. "Never mind that, Memo," the Jesuits interrupted, "two and a half hours ago there was a coup." Incredulous at first, Ungo put in a quick telephone call to his MNR deputy, Héctor Oquelí, and then hurried off muttering, "around here the priests know more than the politicians, dammit." The next day he was on the Junta.[100]

The proclamation eventually released was one of the three presented to Mayorga. It had been written by a group of civilians, some of them members of the MNR, working with Guerra y Guerra in the preparation of the coup. Its final version would be lightly altered by Mayorga and by some of the young officers who were loath for the civilians to have the last word on a document that was a "Proclamation of the Armed Forces of El Salvador." The platform it presented was one of far-reaching change, from the abolition of the hated ORDEN to a total restructuring of the social, political, and economic landscape of the country. The proclamation called for a transitional period in which the country would move toward "authentically free elections:" political parties of all ideologies would be allowed, the right to organize respected, measures leading to the "equitable distribution of the national wealth" would be introduced, and an agrarian reform begun, as El Salvador moved forward into a "new epoch, defined within the principles of peace and effective respect of the human rights of all its citizens."[101]

The promises of the proclamation did much to encourage those harboring doubts about entering the new government. The first few days were filled with a flurry of activity as cabinet and ministerial posts were filled. Seeking as many allies he could get, Mayorga had proposed the architect Alberto Hart Déneke, who worked with a Jesuit-run housing program, for the fifth position in the Junta. He had refused, but agreed to serve in the government as minister of planning. Mayorga than sought out Enrique Alvarez, an oligarch by birth and former minister of agriculture with ties to the left, who first refused, then consulted with others, and finally agreed to do it. But by then the post had gone to Mario Andino, a businessman proposed by the Chamber of Commerce. For Mayorga himself indecision had been quenched by a visit he paid to Monsignor Romero on October 17. He told Romero of his doubts and warned him that, in spite of the proclamation, it could all go terribly wrong. "Even if there were only one chance in a thousand of success," Romero had told him, "a Christian must try to do everything possible to avoid bloodshed for the country." In a gesture of humility that moved Romero, Mayorga went down on his knees and asked for the archbishop's blessing.[102]

SO MANY of the new government's ministers and officials had ties to the UCA and the Jesuits that critics began to talk of the *GolpUCA* or

UCACoup. "People say the Jesuits have taken power in our country," one headline announced.[103] But while the new government represented an extraordinary drain of nineteen highly qualified UCA staff members, many of them left for reasons more to do with political commitments than personal ties to Mayorga and the UCA. Thus Ungo was on the Junta as the leader of the MNR; Héctor Dada, who became foreign minister, and Rubén Zamora, minister of planning, went as recognized members of the PDC, and Héctor Oquelí from the MNR became Dada's deputy. Others, it was true, joined the government as a result of their confidence in Mayorga and because of the more generally shared feeling within UCA circles that all possible efforts were needed to make this rather perilous venture a success.

The Jesuits were well aware of how exposed the composition of the new government left them, but were careful to keep out of political positions themselves (Paco Estrada had been asked to be minister of education and there was a move to have Luis de Sebastián appointed to run the Central Bank). Much as they tried to maintain their independence, a confidential Jesuit memo admitted that they could not avoid the image of participation: "if this new attempt fails we shall not escape the hatred and criticism of the extreme right and the extreme left, with the danger of ending up like a sandwich."[104] But for the moment it appeared that it was a "thinking man's government" of enormous breadth, the like of which El Salvador had never seen before, with the military on one end of the spectrum, a minister of labor who was a Communist party member at the other, and a mix of individuals such as Alvarez and Salvador Samayoa (ministers of agriculture and education, respectively) whom Ungo and Mayorga valued for their clear channels of communication with the organized left. The trouble was, as Mayorga remembered twelve years later and with pain in his voice, "we were forgetting the little detail of military power, and the impossibility that human qualities alone can triumph."[105]

One member of the UCA—and the MNR—who had not joined the government was Italo López Vallecillos. On October 16 he had been in the barracks of San Carlos with Román Mayorga and had seen that Gutiérrez had already prevailed over Majano to place his friend García in the key position of minister of defense. Guerra y Guerra would be relegated to vice-minister of the interior, and the idealistic young officers around him were scarcely to be seen. García had done what Monsignor Romero had feared of him and brought in the old guard: Eugenio Vides Casanova as director of the National Guard, Reynaldo López Nuila to run the National Police and, worst of all, the extreme-right Nicolás Carranza as vice-minister of defense, all of them officers fully implicated in the repression of the years El Salvador was struggling to leave behind. "*Nació muerto,*" López Vallecillos would say of the coup to his friend Mayorga, "It was born dead."[106]

CHAPTER FIVE

IN THE KINGDOM
OF TERROR AND LIES

We are not for one government or another; we are only for good government. Our commitment is to the whole country and, given its internal division, it is a commitment that must be to the poor majorities in their struggle for liberation. We shall be with power when power truly favors the majorities and we shall be against it when it does not, or when it betrays the cause of justice and the common good. Nobody should think that we are about to lose our independence or our spirit of criticism. We shall continue to offer our resources to the study of the national reality, the preparation of projects, the formation of the young, in the service of the collective conscience and in vigilant preoccupation for the rights of the poor. As Christians we believe that the truth will make us free, but it will not be surprising if the freedom of that truth continues to cost us much sacrifice.[1]

The UCA, after October 15, 1979

IN November 1979, Ellacuría became the rector of the UCA. It was a time of cautious hope and institutional sacrifice, with the UCA left weakened by the mass exodus of so many of its best and brightest but, as the new rector would assure his audience in his first public address, still "full of strength and dynamism."[2]

Together with Monsignor Romero, whom César Jerez had respectfully advised to assume the role of "humble arbiter supported by the power of God,"[3] the Jesuits gave their critical support to the new government. That support was based on a tenuous web of trust in the quality of individuals—among the civilians in the Junta and in the young officers' movement—an understanding of the urgency with which El Salvador needed a bloodless revolution if it was ever to stave off a bloody one, and the hope that the interests of the majority of Salvadorans could win out against the priorities of entrenched political positions. The Jesuits, however, were careful to place themselves as no more than commentators on the dramatic events of the moment. After the first few days their energies were channeled into the UCA's daily YSAX broadcast where they found themselves confronted by a series of editorial decisions of extreme delicacy. With regret Luis de Sebastián would remember one commentary

129

prepared with the help of Mena Sandoval: in the early days of the Junta it was to describe how Colonel García was emasculating the original young officers' movement. The piece was never broadcast. In what de Sebastián described as a "betrayal" of the movement he had helped to form, Salazar Brenes deemed it too destabilizing to air.[4]

In his homily at the end of the first week of the new regime, Monsignor Romero reminded the government that the people and Church of El Salvador would expect "deeds" and not just the "beautiful promises" of the proclamation. Sadly, the deeds he had to report did not augur well for the future: striking workers had been evicted from their factory; in Soyapango on the edges of San Salvador security forces had overrun the church and convent and abducted the sacristan; the National Guard had attacked the town of Arcatao in northern Chalatenango. No less troubling had been the "precipitate and irresponsible" call for insurrection on the Tuesday and Wednesday following the coup by the ERP and its mass organization the LP-28. Although still poorly prepared militarily, ERP guerrillas had handed out weapons to their followers, and the resulting conflict had left at least thirty-one dead and more than eighty wounded.[5] In a hurriedly convened meeting in the seminary, Guerra y Guerra and Salazar Brenes appealed to the Jesuits to intervene and "stop" the guerrillas. But the appeal itself was assuming too much of Jesuit influence: at this point they had no direct contacts with the ERP leadership and had to explain that there was nothing they could do.[6]

Romero called for the Junta to produce the 176 people whose disappearance the archdiocese had documented. Over the following weeks the demand would be repeated as the fate of the disappeared persons and political prisoners became a symbol of the Junta's inefficacy. Majano had promised that "the gates of the country's jail will be open for them to look where they want to,"[7] but by the time a commission was appointed and the gates opened, there was very little to see. The army had made sure of that. Román Mayorga would be near tears as he faced grieving and angry families, unable to tell them what had happened to their sons and daughters, husbands and wives. The discovery of clandestine prisons and the testimony given by one of their survivors, an ERP leader named Ana Guadalupe Martínez, made sad speculation easy.[8]

The ten short weeks of the first Junta's government passed in almost constant crisis as each sector of Salvadoran society responded to the change with its own interests foremost. Gutiérrez and García prevented the institutional transformation of the army that had been a purpose of the coup in the first place and thus guaranteed a military veto of the promises contained in the proclamation. ("My mission," García would remember of his time in this Junta, "was to defend the armed institution in order to avoid its collapse."[9]) The more reactionary sectors of the army were ably aided by their land-owning and business counterparts. By early December new and anonymous front groups were appearing daily in a flurry of activity reminiscent of the clamor of the private sector that had prevailed against Molina's Agrarian Transformation in 1976. On the left the coup revealed disunity and indecision, underlined by the fear that the success of the new government would steal its revolutionary thunder: the ERP's call for insurrection was retracted as it aligned itself with the Popular Forum, but FAPU would stay outside, and the *Bloque*—still the most powerful of the popular organizations—denounced the Junta as a brainchild of the United States and seized and occupied the ministries of labor and economy. Dialogue with the Junta was limited to the negotiations necessary to bring an end to these occupations and never addressed the organizations' wider concerns.[10]

Within the highly polarized environment, those who backed the coup were seen by some as communist subversives of the worse sort and by others as traitors to the popular cause. Among the most painful of the divisions was that between the priests, seminarians, and lay workers active within the base ecclesiastic communities and the position adopted by Monsignor Romero and the Jesuits of the UCA. Confrontation spilled over from private meetings, where Romero faced opposition from some of those with whom he had worked most closely in the preceding years, to a public statement condemning the Junta issued by the coordinating body of the base communities in November.[11] Everyone listened to what the UCA had to say, but its radio broadcasts too became a focus of criticism from all sides. In response the anonymous broadcasters testified repeatedly to their independence of spirit and criticism. "We speak because we believe in the effectiveness of the word . . . our word is not pro-Junta or pro-*Bloque,* pro-capitalism or pro-socialism, but it is pro-justice and pro-reason."[12]

Conspicuously absent from the scene was effective U.S. support of the Junta and its political program. Informed of the coup's imminence by Gutiérrez a few days earlier, the U.S. embassy had not played an active part in its planning, but had welcomed its smooth execution. The perception that Román Mayorga was in some sense the president of the Junta was also deemed positive by Ambassador Devine: "Mayorga is a highly respected moderate leader well known to the embassy," he cabled to Washington. But despite a pre-emptive distancing between Mayorga and the Jesuits

within the first few days, Devine would remember that Mayorga "soon
came to be criticized in some quarters for having unduly close relations
with the Jesuits."[13] Certainly the embassy itself maintained closer relations with Majano and Gutiérrez than with the civilians. Cable traffic
referred to Mayorga, Ungo, and others in the government as "leftists,"
which was more than enough to ensure the less than 100 percent support
of a State Department alarmed by the inclination of the new regime in
Managua.[14]

By December, the civilians in the government who were on the
center and left of the political spectrum had realized that they were
powerless to implement the reforms they had pledged to introduce.
Thirty-three ministers, deputy ministers, magistrates, and officials—
including Guerra y Guerra—sent an ultimatum to the armed forces.
Among their demands was a return of the political representation of the
army to COPEFA, the "Permanent Council" established by the original
young officers' movement; the subordination of the armed forces to the
ruling Junta; an end to military intervention in labor disputes and
demonstrations; and the opening of dialogue with the popular organizations.[15] On December 26, a few days before the ultimatum was due to
expire, the military High Command summoned the Junta and cabinet
and in a stormy session made it clear to them that they were in government
at the army's sufferance. It was a question of orders, and "Colonel García
gives the orders, not the Junta," as Colonel Vides Casanova put it.[16]

Out of San Salvador for a few days, the Jesuits of UCAII received a
message that things were bad, that the collapse of the Junta they had feared
for weeks was imminent, and that they should be especially careful. On
December 27, 1979, three bombs exploded in the UCA's computer
center. "Never again will we go in with the army," Ellacuría would say
later. "No more alliances with the army. The left us *enganchados*—
dangling on a hook." "The mistake," de Sebastián remembered him
saying, "was not to insist on the reform of the army as a prerequisite to
anything else."[17]

In a last effort to salvage the situation, Romero arranged to mediate
a meeting between the military and civilians held at the seminary on
January 2. He believed he could hear "pathways of solution" amidst the
problems, but too many minds were already made up. The military was
not about to turn its back on its previous fifty years of power and had, in
any case, already opened negotiations—with the blessing of the U.S.
embassy—with the Christian Democrats. Those on the left of the Junta,
disillusioned by the failure of the government to respond to the interests of

the popular organizations, were turning toward them and their revolutionary demands, while independents believed that the time had come when honest men could stay on longer. Over the next two days the resignations of Mayorga, Ungo, and all those who had signed the ultimatum were presented to the Salvadoran people. Andino's was to follow. Majano and Gutiérrez stayed on, and so did Colonel García.[18]

"THIS was perhaps the last attempt at a peaceful solution to the problems El Salvador has experienced in recent years," stated an *ECA* editorial of unprecedented somberness. "God willing, may 1980 be truly the year of liberation for El Salvador, and may that liberation be realized without the excessive spilling of blood and without fighting among brothers."[19]

But 1980 was to confirm the fears and not the hope contained within these words, as political violence claimed more than 10,000 lives. It was the year in which the opposing forces gathered for the outbreak of open civil war at the beginning of 1981; the year in which the United States became fully engaged in the Salvadoran crisis; and the year in which political and military organizations of the left found the unity necessary to launch a revolutionary front. It was the year in which the Jesuits of the UCA came closest to believing in the triumph of the left and political liberation of the people of El Salvador. It was, above all, the year in which the Jesuits would find "the criterion of truth" in the repression that was more extensive and more profound than at any other time in El Salvador's history. With its thousands of victims, the repression exposed "the true nature of the regime and the achievements of its proposals."[20]

The unlikely marriage between the Christian Democrats and the army was slow to reach consummation in the second Junta, even with the brokerage of the acting U.S. Ambassador James Cheek, who had replaced Devine as the gravity of the situation in El Salvador became clear. The PDC laid out conditions for the partnership consistent with the goals of October 15: they wanted García and Carranza out of the ministry of defense; the opening of a dialogue with the popular organizations; a program of agrarian, banking, and foreign trade reforms; and an end to repression. But the second Junta, eventually formed with Colonels Majano and Gutiérrez, Héctor Dada, José Antonio Morales Erlich, and an independent, José Ramón Avalos, would find that such reforms as they were able to get off the ground were accompanied by intensified repression. In January alone there were between 300 and 500 politically motivated killings, more than in any month of the Molina or even General Romero years. The army would honor none of its other promises and yet received in exchange what one Salvadoran would call at the time, "a respectable mask, the moderate, democratic, American-supported PDC."[21]

Yet in El Salvador in 1980 there was not much evidence of "moderation" and little that was "democratic" in the PDC's power base. What the Second Junta had was the support of the United States and of a sector of the army astute enough to appreciate the value of legitimacy and the promise of future aid. The broad range of political interests represented in the first Junta had moved into the opposition and, with a speed that spoke of the urgency of the moment and a genuine response to the popular will, toward the formation of the Democratic Revolutionary Front (FDR). This alliance of political parties and popular organizations, with Enrique Alvarez at its head, presented its program for a "new, just and humane society" at a meeting in the UCA in mid-April. With an ever watchful eye to its institutional and political autonomy, the UCA would publicly welcome FDR's launch, dedicate a double issue of *ECA* to the search for this "national project," and align itself with the FDR with the status of "observer."[22]

Impelled by the events of the recent months to bury, or at least lay to one side, sectarian divisions of the past, the guerrilla organizations too were moving toward unity. The FPL and RN joined with the Communist party, now also committed to armed revolution, to issue a manifesto calling for "Armed struggle today, socialism tomorrow!"[23] Differences between the RN and ERP, however, still precluded a full integration of the revolutionary forces. A powerful symbol of the increased breadth of the sectors calling for revolution had been a televised press conference given by Salvador Samayoa on January 8. Twenty-nine years old and minister of education the week before, Samayoa was known as a brilliant, soft spoken philosophy teacher from one of the "better" families of Salvadoran society. In a dramatic farewell to his family, friends, and colleagues, Samayoa announced that he was joining the FPL. The press conference ended as he raised a gun and, surrounded by masked and armed *compañeros,* disappeared from the television screen and into hiding.

The public celebration of the new "Revolutionary Coordinator of the Masses" (CRM), the union of the popular organizations of the *Bloque,* FAPU, LP-28, and the political party UDN that would later affiliate with the FDR, was to be a peaceful demonstration held in San Salvador on January 22, 1980, the forty-eighth anniversary of the uprising in 1932. Despite a virulent campaign in opposition spearheaded by the television messages of ex-Major Roberto D'Aubuisson—whom the October coup had banished from the army if not from public view—the demonstration brought more people onto Salvadoran streets than at any other moment in the country's history. Francisco Andrés Escobar, an UCA professor and poet, spent the hours of the morning and the early afternoon of the demonstration on the streets of San Salvador. More than 100,000 people waved flags and banners of red, yellow, and black, brilliant against the clear blue sky. People sang and chanted slogans as they slowly marched through the city in their well-ordered columns, until the bullets started.

Unprovoked firing by the security forces left over twenty dead, two hundred wounded, and thousands cowering for protection in the National University. Escobar ended his account citing the words of another poet: "The pain of those below / sustains the ones above / and those above have forgotten / that the debt is owing."[24] Shed the rings from your fingers, Monsignor Romero had warned the rich just two weeks earlier in words of terrible prophecy, before they come and cut off your hands.[25]

IN mid-February the newspapers began reporting that the U.S. government had made a request to send military assistance to the governing Junta. Romero wrote to President Carter and appealed to him as a Christian and as a defender of human rights to forbid the release of military aid and guarantee that the government of the United States would not intervene in "determining the destiny of the Salvadoran people."[26] The request presented a challenge to the United States' commitment to human rights as a policy, from one who held, as a Christian, human rights to be an absolute and nonnegotiable principle.

On the evening of February 18 Romero had been surprised by a visit from Fathers Ellacuría and Estrada. It was the day after the Sunday homily in which he had read his letter to Carter out loud, to the enthusiastic response of the people packed inside the church. The two Jesuits had come to tell him that the letter had already caused something of an uproar in Rome and that Arrupe had sent for César Jerez to explain to the Vatican the exceptional circumstances that had led to its writing. Jerez had been in Panama, on his way to a conference in Brazil, when he received the message. Abandoning these plans he went straight to Rome to be "interrogated" by the Vatican's secretary of state who warned him that it might be necessary for him to present his defense of Romero's action to the Pope himself.[27]

A few hours after Ellacuría and Estrada left Romero powerful bombs all but destroyed the YSAX radio station and part of the UCA's library. "Evidently," Romero would dictate calmly into the tape recorder he used for his diary, "these are the maneuvers of the extreme right against the voice of the Church and the demands for social justice."[28] The bombs came three days after the UCAII residence in Calle Mediterráneo had been sprayed with gunfire in the middle of the night. The attack, like so many at the time, followed threats made by D'Aubuisson: less than forty-eight hours earlier he had announced on television that the Jesuits were responsible for the violence in the country and that blood would flow.[29]

In Washington Romero's letter was welcomed by the staff of President Carter's human rights bureau, but discounted by the White House and ranking State Department officials. One former U.S. ambassador to El Salvador noted Romero's objections to military aid as he prepared to testify against the administrations' request. He pointed out these objections to Robert Pastor, National Security Council adviser for Latin America, who had shocked him by telephoning his home to request that he not testify. "Archbishop Romero is naive," had been Pastor's comment.[30] "Romero defended fundamental values," was how Ellacuría remembered the archbishop's actions during these months. "He was not a politician who has to look after his power; he was a priest who had to look after the Kingdom of God, and so he could be prophetic and he could be utopian, and much less pragmatic. But at that time, it was he who saw things most clearly."[31] The reply to Romero's letter from Secretary of State Cyrus Vance—promising to "use our influence to avert any misuse of our assistance in ways that injure the human rights of the people of El Salvador"[32]—was hand delivered by the new U.S. ambassador, Robert White. Outspoken and with a track record that included standing up to Paraguay's General Stroessner, White had arrived in early March. Romero was impressed by his meeting with White, and White by the archbishop: his presence at Romero's Sunday mass over the following two weeks was a gesture that did not go unnoticed by any political sector.

White had known the Central American Jesuits and "where they were coming from" since his days in the U.S. embassy in Nicaragua in the early 1970s. He remembered Paco Estrada, provincial at the time, from then and had renewed his acquaintance with him at the meeting with Romero. Within a few weeks White had the first of two dinners with Estrada, Ellacuría, and Segundo Montes. The Jesuits had asked that the dinner be "off the record," but Ellacuría's carelessness on a trip to Spain in early May breached their own request. Warming to the Jesuits' company, White told them that if he were Salvadoran he would be aligned with the guerrillas. No doubt delighted by this admission, Ellacuría repeated the remark, adding "he talks too much for an ambassador," in the presence of one Emilio Zuñeda, who subsequently wrote up an "Interview with the Rector of the UCA" for the Spanish magazine *Ecclesia*. The piece was reprinted in the Salvadoran newspaper *Prensa Gráfica* and White had to answer to his bosses in the State Department.[33]

WASHINGTON'S attention would be focused on the issue of military aid to El Salvador on Tuesday, March 25, 1980. That morning hearings before the House Foreign Operations Subcommittee were scheduled to consider the administration's request to reprogram $5.7 million for "nonlethal" aid to El Salvador. Just a few hours before the hearings were due to begin, congressmen, their staff, and witnesses learned that on the previous evening, March 24, 1980, Archbishop Romero had been shot and killed while saying mass in the chapel of the hospital where he lived.[34]

As colleagues paid tribute to "one of the true saints walking on this earth" and urged the subcommittee members "to honor the last request of Archbishop Romero" rather than that of their president, legislators were faced with a dilemma that went to the heart of the uncertainties surrounding Carter's policy toward El Salvador.[35] The aid being requested was a small amount, yet its significance was great. Those in favor of its release would argue that Romero's death had been an example of exactly the type of violence the aid was intended to reduce. But Romero himself, in his letter to Carter, repeatedly referred to in the hearings and in the voluble protest from the churches, had pointed out that the $200,000 of nonlethal aid provided to the security forces the previous November had been anything but nonlethal in its effect. No one present at the hearings could ignore the thousands of civilian casualties—including Dr. Mario Zamora, Rubén's brother and the PDC attorney general—there had been since then. But what to do?

On the previous day in San Salvador, Jon Sobrino had been alone in the house on Calle Mediterráneo when the telephone rang shortly after 6:30 P.M. A woman in tears was asking for a priest. "They've shot Monsignor," she sobbed. "Monsignor is bleeding." Sobrino left the house immediately and found César Jerez in his office up the road. The put the radio on and a few minutes later heard "Monsignor Romero is dead." The news preceded them to the UCA. Inside the rectory, the heart of the university, Jesuits, staff, and secretaries stood in blank, stunned silence. Then, prompted by the fear of a spontaneous uprising in protest, they interrupted classes to tell teachers and students what had happened and send them hurrying home.[36]

It was not exactly a surprise. "They kill those who get in the way," Romero had said, and he had certainly done that. Ellacuría and Estrada had been with Romero on the evening of March 22 to help in the preparation of his homily for the following day. Rafael Moreno was out of the country and Ellacuría had been taking his place as political consultant for the last two homilies and at the press conferences that followed the Sunday mass. That Saturday he arrived full of outrage: earlier in the afternoon the UCA had been overrun by a large contingent from the National Police. Worse still, a student leaving the UCA through its back entrance had been struck down by random bullets and killed. The troops had claimed to have entered the UCA in pursuit of a group who had attacked a nearby supermarket, but this was not the case.[37] The attack on the UCA came at the end of a long list of denunciations of the week's obuses, gathered and checked, as usual, by the legal aid office *Socorro Jurídico* and headed by the 50 to 140 people killed the previous Monday as the CRM called a strike to protest the repression. Romero worked through the list—a massacre of nine *campesinos* here, twenty-five somewhere else, a grueling account of torture, unclaimed bodies found beside the roadside at different points in the country—and then turned to his advisors: "Can I tell the soldiers that they do not have to obey orders if they're being ordered to kill without reason?" Yes, you can, the advisers replied, confident of the absolute authority of the fifth commandment. "Make it dramatic, Monsignor," Ellacuría added.[38]

The next morning Romero ended his homily with a special appeal to the men enlisted in the army, in the National Guard, and the police: "Brothers, you are part of the same people and you kill your brother *campesinos*. Before an order to kill given by a man, the law of God must prevail that says, 'Thou shalt not kill.' No soldier is obliged to obey an order that is against the law of God." Applause interrupted him as he spoke. "In the name of God, and in the name of this suffering people whose cries rise up to the heavens every day more tumultuously, I beg you, I beseech you, I order you in the name of God: Stop the repression!"[39]

Within a few days Romero's funeral was disrupted by military violence that left forty people dead, crushed and suffocated as thousands pressed into the cathedral to avoid bombs and shooting in the square outside. In Washington a vote already delayed until the archbishop was buried went 6 to 3 in favor of the aid, but it was a vote backed only by the hope, and certainly not the conviction, that the funds might help turn the tide in an increasingly violent El Salvador. Carter officials claimed that the aid would "help strengthen the army's key role in reforms," but their protestations carried less weight than a paradoxical kind of credibility won by the transparency of the administration's doubts. In private, there was an awareness that the armed forces were the "greatest offenders" when it came to repression; in public, cables presented to the subcommittee acknowledged that the embassy saw "acts of violence from the right as more of a threat than those of the left." White had been quick to attribute the murder of Romero to the right and was noticeably "queasy" when it came to military aid: he expressed his support for its release even as he agreed that "there is no military solution to the problems of El Salvador." Congress was prepared to give the administration the benefit of the doubt, but the doubt itself suggested that attempts to steer El Salvador toward reform by now had about as much chance of success as the harnessing of a runaway train.[40]

HÉCTOR Dada's departure from the Junta in early March ("We haven't been able to stop the repression," he wrote in his letter of resignation[41]) was indicative of the crisis within the Christian Democrats. A few days later Rubén Zamora and a group of PDC leaders would leave the party that had promised so much in the 1960s and early 1970s to form the Popular Social Christian Movement (MPSC). Faithful to the old ideals in the new political circumstances, the MPSC moved quickly into the opposition within the FDR. Dada was replaced by Napoleón Duarte, the party leader who had returned from his exile the previous November. Enormously popular when he left the country after "winning" the elections of 1972, Duarte was considered by some to be out of touch with the political evolution of his people. He brought to the Junta a rhetoric of self-justification—things were bad, but would be worse without the Christian Democrats—that was anathema to the Jesuits' view of the fundamentals of Christian commitment.

A direct confrontation between Ellacuría and Duarte came quickly. Ellacuría and representatives of the UCA went to the Junta to protest the government version of the National Police's operation in the university. That version had maintained that the assassinated student had been injured in crossfire as he took part in the fictitious attack on the supermarket. Colonel Gutiérrez heard Ellacuría out, and then left the room as Duarte conceded, "I admit that there was an assassination, but, for reasons of State, I cannot admit it." "Can you, a Christian Democrat," shot back Ellacuría, "a humanist, and a Christian, sit there and tell me that for reasons of State this boy will remain an assassin and a thief?" The government version was never retracted nor the incident forgotten by

Ellacuría.[42] "In El Salvador today," read an *ECA* editorial in May, "the lie is the queen consort of terror."[43]

This Third Junta began the agrarian and banking reforms that would be the mainstay of United States and Christian Democratic policy. Rejected by sectors of the right and lacking in credibility with the left, the reforms came with a state of siege under which to implement them and a strict censoring of the press to quell the expected opposition. The agrarian reform was to have three stages: the purchase of large properties—over 1,250 acres—for redistribution as peasant cooperatives; the purchase and redistribution of properties between 250 and 1,250 acres; and the final "land-to-the-tiller," or Phase III, in which *campesinos* would be assisted in the purchase of the small plots of land they worked as tenants. The basic outline of the reforms had been drafted by Enrique Alvarez during the first Junta, and, on paper, they amounted to what successive government spokesmen and U.S. officials would claim to be among the most revolutionary land reform programs in Latin America. But in practice the achievements of the agrarian reform program, which was overseen by the overtly anticommunist American Institute for Free Labor Development (AIFLD),[44] were severely limited by the conditions of its implementation by the armed forces. "The agrarian reform," *ECA* would explain at the end of the year, "was a mechanism that made possible the militarization of the Salvadoran countryside and the systematic elimination of any potential enemy."[45]

The Jesuits did not lose touch with the young officers who had been behind the October coup, even as these same officers were excluded from power and influence.[46] And now, much more than before the coup, there developed a particularly close relationship with Colonel Majano, who was perceived as the leader of the progressive elements within the armed forces, consistently supported by White and the U.S. embassy, yet losing ground within the Junta throughout the year. White would remember that "Majano was honest but naive at the time. The Jesuits gave him their course 1A in politics, and I was giving him another course—they coincided in a large part."[47] A particular blow to Majano's authority was suffered in May after the backfiring of an operation that led to the capture of D'Aubuisson and a group of right-wing coup-plotters with documents so incriminating in their connection of some of those present to the murder of Romero that D'Aubuisson reportedly tried to eat them.[48] Gutiérrez emerged from internal elections as the commanding officer of the armed forces as Majano's fortunes went steadily down hill.

Captain Alejandro Ricardo Fiallos was in many ways an exemplary officer. The son of a colonel, he had graduated from the military academy first in his *tanda* in 1968, studied medicine, and become a military doctor. Intelligent, responsible, and concerned for the future of his country, he had served nearly sixteen years in the Salvadoran army when he first made his way to the UCA in early 1980. He was one of a number of officers who came in search of Ellacuría and later came to know and respect Montes and Martín-Baró. These officers appreciated the respect with which Ellacuría received them as "citizens who had chosen to enter an army where, unfortunately, the training fell a long way short of answering the needs of the country."[49] Through them the UCA would encourage Majano to explore the possibilities of a second uprising of the more progressive young officers in September 1980. "But this would have meant combat within the barracks and then between them," was how Ellacuría remembered these discussions, and Majano "in the end decided, in a chess-player's calculation, that they were not going to win and that a colonel should not send his troops into a battle they cannot win."[50]

A younger, more radical staff at the UCA and a series of meetings with mid- and low-level members of the revolutionary organizations contributed to the Jesuits' belief that a triumph of the left was a definite possibility. Some of these meetings gave rise to an informal "pact" that was an obvious extension of the "rules of the game" in evidence before the young officers' coup: the UCA was a place in which high-level contacts could be made, but it was not to be used for "agitation." In May, members of the RN came to give the Jesuits "security instructions." As they explained what to do if under gunfire, how to change their appearances, and the need to vary the routes by which they traveled around the capital, the young guerrillas appeared fully assured that victory would be theirs. For Ellacuría and Luis de Sebastián the climax of their clandestine contacts came in October, the month that would see the guerrilla organizations finally united in the Farabundo Martí National Liberation Front (FMLN).[51] In safe houses in San Salvador they met both "Marcial," the legendary Cayetano Carpio of the FPL, and a young Joaquín Villalobos, leader of the ERP. More than eleven years later Luis de Sebastián would remember, "They told us they had 10,000 men armed to the teeth. We asked, 'what, more than the army?' and they said, 'well, almost.' " With a laugh, de Sebastián summed up the meetings by saying, "They lied to us. They exaggerated enormously and we believed them." But he could not deny that both Jesuits had been profoundly moved by the *abrazo* (embrace) given them by "Marcial" as they left. "In the UCA," he told them, "you are doing a great good for the Salvadoran people."[52]

More than ever, 1980 had been a good time to have "well-placed sources." During that year, in addition to their residence being sprayed with gunfire, the Jesuits denounced six separate bombings of the UCA or their home, the invasion of the university, the harassment and shooting at students and staff on various occasions, and the assassination of three of the Externado's teachers.[53] The officers who came through the UCA told them that the majority of these attacks were planned and executed by members of the security forces. So widespread was the violence that the Jesuits would surprise themselves by their own acceptance of this level of persecution. On October 24, two high-powered bombs exploded at 2:00 A.M. in the Calle Mediterráneo house, the first of them leaving a meterwide hole at the foot of Segundo Montes' bed. It did not even occur to them, despite their discovery of ten more small but unexploded bombs in their garden, to move out of their residence. Three nights later the house was bombed again and partially destroyed. Then the Jesuits moved to Santa Tecla.[54]

But when the message came for Ellacuría at the end of November, the Jesuits knew it was the real thing. Mena Sandoval had been at an officers' meeting of the Second Brigade in Santa Ana when it was announced that the High Command had given the order that they should begin to kill the intellectuals "controlling the subversion," particularly the Jesuits, and that the first of them should be Ellacuría. Mena left the meeting and went straight to his friend and fellow *tanda* member Fiallos. They contacted Majano to find out if he—a Junta member after all—knew anything of this order (he didn't) and then made sure a message got to Ellacuría that same day. On the telephone "Dr." Fiallos told one of Ellacuría's colleagues that "the patient is in grave danger." "Can the patient wait?" came the question. All concern, the doctor explained that something might happen to the patient at any moment and that his advice was that he should be taken to a clinic in the United States as soon as possible. Ellacuría went straight to the Spanish Embassy and the next day left the country. His ticket was issued in the name of one I. Beascoechea—the second surname he never used.[55]

NOVEMBER 4, 1980 was an exciting day for the Salvadoran right wing. Parties rocked the exclusive neighborhoods of Escalón and San Benito as residents celebrated the triumph of Ronald Reagan in the U.S. presidential elections. The Carter administration had been considered liberal and ineffective even by those who did not, like D'Aubuisson and his followers, believe it a force behind the "marxist strategy" to take over El Salvador.[56]

Shades of Nicaragua's victorious FSLN in the Salvadoran revolutionaries' new FMLN only underlined the need for a strong hand. Candidate Reagan had made it very clear that when it came to Central America, he was there to provide one: "Must we let Grenada, Nicaragua, El Salvador, all become additional Cubas, new outposts for Soviet combat brigades?" he had asked his audience at the Chicago Council on Foreign Relations. "Will the next push of the Moscow-Havana axis be northward to Guatemala and hence to Mexico and south to Costa Rica and Panama?"[57]

By the beginning of December the number of civilians killed in 1980 was approximately 9,000. These included an archbishop, four priests, the rector of the National University, political leaders, numerous catechists and teachers, and thousands of *campesinos,* old and young, men, women, and children. The latest atrocity had been one that illustrated most clearly the intransigence of the Salvadoran right in the weeks before Reagan assumed the presidency. On November 27 five members of the Executive Council of the FDR, including its president, Enrique Alvarez, were abducted from a press conference in the Externado by over a hundred heavily armed men and murdered. Few in San Salvador doubted the responsibility of the security forces.[58]

But for many in the United States, repression in El Salvador became real on December 4, 1980, as they heard and saw how four North American missionaries, three of them nuns, were dug from an unmarked grave. Two days earlier they had been followed from the airport in their white Toyota van by national guardsmen, detained, raped, and killed near the roadside. Sisters Maura Clarke, Ita Ford, and Dorothy Kazel and lay missionary Jean Donovan were murdered for working with the Salvadoran Church, the Church of Monsignor Romero. In La Libertad outside San Salvador and in Chalatenango they had dedicated themselves to the accompaniment of people whose lives and deaths they helped to make a little bit less unbearable. To do so they relied on the protection from the security forces they believed was given them by their nationality to travel to communities suffering the worst of the repression in the countryside. They had been threatened, they were frightened, but they would not leave. They were the first North Americans to be killed by forces of the Salvadoran government in the newly escalated conflict.[59]

Salvadoran in their death—no longer the untouchable blond *gringas* beyond the reach of history—the very fact of the four women's North American birth was of enormous importance. As Ambassador White, his face twisted in anguish and anger, stood above the makeshift grave, he was heard to mutter, "This time they won't get away with it. They just won't."[60] American public opinion erupted in protest and the Carter administration reacted immediately and emotionally, interrupting national television programs and suspending economic and military assistance to El Salvador, pending a "thorough, professional and exhaustive investigation." This was something that touched America. These women, their families, and friends were represented by Congress. The churches, by far the most organized sector when it came to lobbying against U.S. policy in El Salvador, threw themselves into action as never before. Representatives and senators vied with each other in their condemnation of the crime and in the steeliness of their demands for justice. "How many more such incidents must take place before the U.S. policy toward El Salvador will change?" asked one congressman of his colleagues.[61] Progress in the "nuns' case," as it became known, would become a litmus test for public and congressional opinion of United States' action in El Salvador.

A high-level commission led by former and current Assistant Secretaries of State William Rogers and William Bowdler went to San Salvador to report on the four women's death and—less publicly—to assist in a restructuring of the Salvadoran government that would see the final demise of Majano and assure the restoration of economic aid. Duarte pushed hard to become the new Junta's president, but it was a purely cosmetic position: García remained minister of defense and Gutiérrez— not the president—was named commander in chief of the armed forces. And as the dust from this latest upheaval settled, it became gradually clearer that a new crisis was looming: the FMLN was preparing for a concerted military effort to overthrow the government. Although not to the extent that the Jesuits had been led to believe in October, during the course of 1980 the number of armed guerrilla combatants had indeed swelled from 500 to around 5,000. Encouraged by Fidel Castro and judging the attention and power of the Carter administration to be failing, the FMLN was ready to make a move. Rumors of a military offensive were confirmed by Fermán Cienfuegos, the senior *comandante* of the RN, on December 26. The "final offensive" was imminent, he told journalists in Mexico City. "Mr. Reagan will find an irreversible situation in El Salvador by the time he reaches the presidency."[62]

"More than 10,000 political assassinations," began *ECA's* summation of the year, "an economy destroyed to a tragic degree and artificially maintained by ambiguous North American aid and galloping inflation; social order adrift; thousands of refugees dragging their grief through mountains or into camps; a population pale and terrified; a corrupt and demoralized state apparatus with its controlling strings leading straight to

Washington; a silent and bloody civil war with a formal and more bloody civil war at the gates—this is the truly terrifying legacy that 1980 leaves El Salvador, a legacy whose pain cannot be assuaged by the hope of liberation."[63]

RONALD Reagan would like to remind his critics that El Salvador was a problem he inherited, not created. What he inherited, however, by the time he took his presidential oath on January 20, 1981, was not an irreversible situation, but a brief and perhaps unrepeatable opportunity.

The FMLN had miscalculated: the people of El Salvador did not rise up in insurrection—the moment of mass popular protest and political effervescence had already been missed—and nor did the outgoing Carter administration abandon what was seen as a sinking ship. On January 14 military aid to El Salvador was resumed amid a flurry of statements, which later turned out to be grossly exaggerated, claiming the discovery of extensive arms shipments to the FMLN from Nicaragua. The decision was reached, according to the State Department spokesman, "taking full account of the progress in areas of concern to us, especially the investigation of the murders of the four American churchwomen."[64] This view of the investigation was in direct contradiction to the assessment of Ambassador White: "It is amazing to me," he complained in a cable a few days later, "that the Department can state publicly that the investigation of the nuns' deaths is proceeding satisfactorily. This is not backed up by any report from this embassy. I reiterate for the record that in my judgement there is no sign of any sincere attempt to locate and punish those responsible for this atrocity."[65] Within days a further $5 million was approved in an emergency procedure that bypassed Congress. For the first time since 1977 the package of military advisers and training facilities included lethal weapons.

The FMLN's "final offensive" was quickly beaten back, although the insurgents established pockets of control in distinct areas of the country. Among the most dramatic of military operations had been an uprising planned and led from within the Santa Ana barracks by Mena Sandoval in coordination with the forces of the ERP he subsequently joined. The crisis and initial possibility of a triumph of the left made way for the introduction of martial law, a curfew, and intensified repression that included the military occupation of the UCA. But with revolutionary victory anything but imminent—the offensive and the armed forces' reaction had resulted in "both sides fighting to a draw," one embassy cable would explain in February[66]—a rare moment emerged in which all political forces were prepared to talk. "The message from every Salvadoran leader is the same—" White described as the situation of January 20. "Please, no more military assistance. What we need is economic help and a political solution."[67] But the time for talking was over.

Reagan arrived in the White House in an aggressive mood, surrounded by foreign policy advisers committed to the restoration of the damage they felt had been done to the United States' place in the world by the "loss" of Nicaragua and Iran and by the persistent memory of Vietnam. El Salvador seemed like a good place to start. "Mr. President, this is one you can win," the new secretary of state, Alexander Haig, insisted in the first two meetings of the National Security Council.[68] El Salvador, as Haig saw it, was the place to "draw the line" against communism: a small country, with only a few thousand meagerly armed and recently suppressed guerrilla combatants, in which success seemed readily assured. Within the first two months of office, the Reagan administration launched a political campaign that had El Salvador firmly planted in the East-West conflict of the Cold War and more than doubled military aid with a March 2 announcement of an additional $25 million.

A radical shift in U.S. foreign policy was obvious to Washington insiders from a mere perusal of the hard-line conservatives on board the Reagan machine as campaign advisers. Leaked reports from the transition team told of a purge within the State Department of career ambassadors considered "social reformers." At the top of the list was White, who was removed from his post in San Salvador before Reagan had been in power for two weeks. For the American public nothing could have been clearer than the message given at Haig's first press conference. Signaling a "change in priorities," Haig announced the move away from a concentration on human rights that characterized the Carter years to the area he considered "the greatest problem . . . rampant international terrorism."[69] The use of the word "terrorism" as the focus of broad policy directives would be a hallmark of the next eight years of U.S. foreign policy. It would deny political and revolutionary movements their legitimacy and seek to portray the Soviet Union if not as the "evil empire" referred to by Reagan at the beginning of his presidency, then at least as the mastermind of an international terrorist conspiracy. When it came to El Salvador, Haig's understanding of the situation was straightforward: "Our problem with El Salvador is external intervention in the internal affairs of a sovereign nation in this hemisphere—nothing more, nothing less."[70]

There was much in the language of this "Reagan offensive" that was consistent with that used by the forces aligned with the government of El

Salvador. "It was a real advantage that they placed us within the East-West conflict," one colonel fully aware of the Salvadoran origins of the civil war would remember.[71] A list of names of "those delinquent bandits and terrorists . . . pro-Soviet and Cuban extremists responsible for the terrorism in El Salvador and the shame of our fatherland in the international community," produced by the armed forces in March 1981, showed just how dangerous such rhetoric could become when translated from Washington to San Salvador. With no attempt to distinguish between genuine members of the FMLN, the politicians of the FDR or individuals associated more generally with the opposition—human rights workers with *Socorro Jurídico,* Ellacuría, and Román Mayorga— the army assured the public that it would "persecute the traitors of the fatherland without ceasing."[72]

A white paper released by the State Department on February 23 to show the world that El Salvador presented "a textbook case of indirect armed aggression by Communist powers" was central to the political offensive. Carefully tailored for its sensationalist value, the white paper presented a highly unbalanced view of the political and revolutionary forces in El Salvador. The FDR, for example, with its ex-ministers, Social and Christian Democrats, was "a front organization . . . created to disseminate propaganda abroad." Out of sensitivity to potential criticism from the vocal U.S. churches, the paper conveniently neglected to mention the extensive Christian base to the political and military opposition; the persecution of the Church; the murdered archbishop, priests, catechists, and so forth. Instead it boasted "definitive evidence . . . drawn from captured guerrilla documents and war matériel and intelligence reports" for a "strikingly familiar case of Soviet, Cuba and other communist involvement" in the "imposition of a communist regime in defiance of the will of the Salvadoran people."[73] Unfortunately the white paper did not bear the close scrutiny to which it was subjected by journalists from the *Los Angeles Times,* the *Nation,* the *Washington Post,* and the *Wall Street Journal.* They found that the "captured" documents on which it had been based, conveniently handed to a U.S. official by a member of the National Guard, were not only neither as fully authenticated nor as conclusive as the white paper had maintained, but had also been subjected to further manipulation and mistranslation by the State Department.[74]

Prominent among the ideologues of the new administration was Jeanne Kirkpatrick, a professor at Georgetown University and political analyst with the American Enterprise Institute, who had gained Reagan's attention with a justification of U.S. support for "traditional autocrats," exemplified by Somoza and the Shah of Iran, for the purpose of staving off the totalitarianism of "revolutionary communist regimes."[75] Kirkpatrick had swung into action well before she assumed her post as U.S. ambassador to the United Nations with a couple of statements supporting the new political direction. "People who choose to live by the sword can expect to die by it," she remarked of the murder of the FDR's civilian leadership. The following week she "explained" to another journalist that the four U.S. churchwomen were "political activists," who had been murdered for that activism. Within a couple of months Haig too would be blundering into unfounded allegations that the women had been killed running a roadblock, "and there may have been an exchange of fire."[76]

Such remarks reflected an intensified suspicion of what Kirkpatrick had referred to as "the affinity of liberalism, Christianity, and marxist socialism"[77] that found, for the Reagan right, its most dangerous manifestation in liberation theology. "Modern communications and increasing education have brought about a stirring among the people that has had a tremendous impact on the Church," Governor Nelson Rockefeller had warned the president of the United States in a report prepared in 1969, "making it a force dedicated to change—revolutionary change if necessary."[78] Since then, Rockefeller's suspicions that for all the Church's "profound idealism" it would be "vulnerable to subversive penetration" had been, in the eyes of many of those moving into key policy-making positions, amply confirmed. A foreign policy paper presenting candidate Reagan with "A New Inter-American Policy for the Eighties" (better known as the "Santa Fé Document"), addressed the subject directly, warning that U.S. policy should begin to counter liberation theology as it is "utilized" in Latin America: "Unfortunately, Marxist-Leninist forces have utilized the church as a political weapon against private property and productive capitalism by infiltrating the religious community with ideas that are less Christian than Communist."[79]

In 1981, ideology led the way for State Department officials notably lacking in expertise in the region. Congressmen on the key subcommittees had been grappling, in one form or another, with human rights in Central America and elsewhere throughout the 1970s. Visits to the region and congressional hearings produced witness after witness—among them Captain Ricardo Fiallos, who had left the army, and the country, in January—to internal problems besetting El Salvador and to the true origin of the greatest share of the violence. "The simple truth of the matter," Fiallos testified in April, "is that *los escuadrones de la muerte* [death squads] are made up of members of the security forces and acts of terrorism credited to these squads such as political assassinations, kidnappings and indiscriminate murders are, in fact, planned by high-ranking military officers and carried out by members of the security forces. I do not make this statement lightly, but with the full knowledge of the role which the military High Command and the directors of the security forces have played in the murders of countless numbers of innocent people in my country."[80] For those who were prepared to look and wanted to see, it was clear that the Reagan rhetoric had overstepped the mark.

Congress countered the vehemence of the new policies with a mechanism that tied the release of military aid to a presidential "certification" that, once every six months, there was progress in the following areas: human rights, the conduct of the security forces, economic reform, elections, negotiations toward a political settlement, and the investigations into the murders of six U.S. citizens (the four churchwomen and two AIFLD workers who, together with the Salvadoran president of the Agrarian Transformation Institute—ISTA—were assassinated in the El Salvador Sheraton in early January 1981). Important for its focus on the internal affairs of El Salvador, the certification process would dominate the release of aid to El Salvador over the next few years. But it was an indication of the bottom-line consensus in Washington—the left must not be allowed to take power—that, while the certification had to be presented to Congress, and Congress could kick and scream for a while, it was the administration that did the certifying. And El Salvador would get that aid.

FROM El Salvador or from the exile into which many Salvadorans were forced in 1981, it was difficult not to find the Reagan administration insulting. It was not just a question of political disagreement, nor even the fact of external intervention. More, for those who had experienced the last ten, fifteen, or twenty years of Salvadoran history, it was the ignorance of the analysis, the cavalier lack of attention to facts in the construction of a policy of enormous and immediate repercussion that was so hard to bear.

Ellacuría had flown to Spain in November 1980, and over the next year and a half would travel between Spain and Nicaragua, although his heart and head remained firmly planted in El Salvador. In Managua in early 1981, he found several of the Jesuits normally based in San Salvador (among them Jon Sobrino and Rogelio Pedraz), whom César Jerez had thought safest outside the country for a while, and Nicaraguan contemporaries caught up in the heady events of the early years of Sandinista rule.

Amando López had left El Salvador in 1975 to head the *Colegio Centro América;* with the triumph of the revolution he had moved over to assume the post of rector of Managua's UCA. As such he was playing a key role in the nationwide literacy campaign led by the Jesuit Fernando Cardenal. A recent arrival—together with the Ignatian Center, its magazine *Diakonía,* and its library, all of which he had founded in Panama—was Juan Ramón Moreno. On the board of the UCA and the coordinator of the literacy campaign in a village called Santa Lucía, Moreno's sphere of activity in Nicaragua, as it had been in Panama and would be again in El Salvador, was that of the religious orders. Through them and through the Spiritual Exercises he gave throughout Central America, he came to be known by an enormous number of people.[81]

But not even Nicaragua provided distraction from El Salvador and concern for a depleted UCA left under the care of interim-Rector Axel Soderburgh, the Jesuits Francisco Javier Ibisate, Montes, and Martín-Baró (who in 1981 assumed the position of academic vice-rector vacated by Luis de Sebastián[82]) and key members of the lay faculty such as Christa Beneke. Sobrino would be back in San Salvador by March; for Ellacuría return was quite clearly out of the question. Instead, and throughout his exile, he strove to maintain his presence in the orientation, if not the day-to-day business of the university. On three occasions UCA board meetings would be held in Costa Rica. These allowed not just Ellacuría, but others closely associated with the UCA and now scattered throughout Central America, to discuss the situation in El Salvador, and assess how and what they could and should be doing to improve it. Articles were written in *ECA,* new publications—such as the weekly news magazine *Proceso*—were founded, and the spirit of the UCA, thanks in no small measure to the courage and tenacity of the Jesuits and staff who stayed behind, remained intact.

These were months in which Ellacuría maintained frank conversations in Managua, Madrid, and occasionally in Mexico with members of the FDR-FMLN's newly formed Political–Diplomatic Commission and with leaders of the FMLN not actively engaged in combat in El Salvador. When in Spain, Ellacuría returned to his work with Zubiri, but also seized any and every possibility to talk, lecture or write about what was happening in El Salvador as accounts of massacres in the countryside of unbelievable brutality mounted and the civilian casualties rose to more than 20,000 in the two years since October 15, 1979. Yet the lectures, interviews, and articles, for all their value, could not sate a restless, driving energy that took reluctantly to the role of exile. "Here I am doing this,"

Ellacuría would grumble to one magazine journalist, "giving interviews and talks, taking part in forums . . . I arrive, I speak and people think: 'How brave he is, how sincere, how entertaining.' It is all applause. But this is not for me. My destiny is back there in El Salvador."[83]

At a meeting of the leadership of the Central American Province held in Managua in February 1981, Ellacuría surprised his fellow Jesuits by his conclusion that the Salvadoran conflict "hasn't got a military solution. Nobody is going to win this war."[84] In the germ of a thesis that the UCA would raise sooner, and then argue more coherently and more flexibly at every possible juncture over the next decade than any other body in Salvadoran life, an editorial of the January–February *ECA* would recognize that the "new phase" of the Salvadoran process "appears to be demanding an attempt at mediation and negotiation."[85] Over the years the arguments in favor of negotiation would vary with the vicissitudes of the political process, but never depart from a recognition of the initial legitimacy of the Salvadoran revolution, the conviction that a negotiated solution was in the best and most urgent interest of the Salvadoran people, and the insistence that, in its power and proximity, the United States was an unavoidable reality in the present and future of Central America.

A few months later, Ellacuría published an article titled "Political or Military Solution for El Salvador?" as part of a special edition of *ECA* calling for "reflection, peace, and a global solution to the conflict." The central thesis—that only a solution that is both political *and* military could be both realistically achieved and provide a "real" solution—was derived from an analysis of a moment at which the war in El Salvador was open, as it had not been until 1981, but also stalled, and in danger of an escalation whose only sure outcome would be further suffering. Finding the idea of a purely political solution "utopian" and without internal support, Ellacuría dismissed a military solution as "inadequate" to the needs of El Salvador. He argued that it was unlikely that the Salvadoran armed forces, even massively supported by the United States, could defeat the type of opposition presented them by the FMLN—a guerrilla army supported by a wide spectrum of political organizations—without a slaughter of such magnitude that it would preclude guarantees of democratization of the country or the resolution of the structural problems that lay at the root of the war. Victory for the FMLN was improbable, and even if it were to be achieved, could "lead to important deviations on the way to victory and in the manner in which it was administered."[86]

Ellacuría concluded his article by arguing that a political and military solution "implied some form of negotiated end to the conflict." Realistic in his assessment of the forces involved and the "complexity and arduousness" of any such solution, Ellacuría acknowledged the seriousness of the problems to be encountered before it would be possible for the two sides to harness the correlation of military forces and allow for reasoned discussion to win the day. It would not be realistic to ask the left to lay their weapons aside before entering into dialogue because "the reason of the left without arms is a reason without weight." At the same time the army and Christian Democrats feared that any kind of mediation would somehow favor the guerrillas. An even greater obstacle than these was the suspicion that the axis of power represented by the United States, the army, and the Junta would not be prepared to consider talking until it had witnessed the success or failure of its military aspirations.

Clearly enshrined in the doctrine of the Reagan administration and eagerly seconded by the Junta in San Salvador was the notion that one does not negotiate with terrorists. It was for this reason understandable that Duarte should have remembered the granting of diplomatic recognition of the FDR-FMLN as a "representative political force" by the governments of Mexico and France in August 1981 as "the lowest point" for the Junta.[87] At the time he dismissed the Mexican and French Declaration (welcomed, incidentally, in a long analytical article by Ellacuría[88]) as "an interference in the internal affairs of our country." Duarte assured his people that El Salvador was embarked on a path toward a political solution of the conflict that would include dialogue with all those who accepted the "rules of the democratic game." Unfortunately, this precondition inevitably excluded the FDR-FMLN. Duarte discounted this alliance as being of "terrorist organizations with minority political sectors" operating within El Salvador as part of "the international conspiracy against our fatherland."[89]

ELLACURÍA returned to El Salvador in April 1982 to a country in the grip of a devastating civil war and to a people enduring, suffering, and resisting a living nightmare. Besides the tens of thousands dead, the two and a half years since the October 1979 coup had seen half a million people driven from their homes. Abandoning land, livelihood, and the scant possessions amassed over a lifetime, those with the resources to do so had made for the United States; others had fled their homes for makeshift shelters in the capital or refugee camps in neighboring Honduras. El Salvador had hit and held the international headlines as a Central American hell hole where death squads ran riot, unarmed *campesinos* were slaughtered by the score, and unidentified bodies, or parts of them, turned up on the roadside each morning.

The war in El Salvador was far removed from Al Haig's gung-ho characterization of "one we can win." Colonel John Waghelstein took up his post as U.S. MilGroup commander early in the year and found that "guerrillas were at the gate."[90] Two years of ferocious repression had proved remarkably effective in the destruction of the popular organizations, but it had also fostered the militarization of the conflict as the bereaved and angry members of communities decimated by violence joined the ranks of the FMLN. Determination, ingenuity, intensive combat experience, and a bedrock of civilian support without which no guerrilla army would have been able to survive in the cramped and inhospitable terrain of El Salvador had helped to forge a fighting force that was more than a match for the badly led, poorly motivated, and popularly feared Salvadoran army. As the FMLN gradually expanded the territory under its control through the northern and eastern regions of the country—with the FPL most active in the province of Chalatenango and the ERP in Morazán—and showed itself capable of launching sporadic, but spectacular, attacks throughout the country, a professionalization of the armed forces became a primary goal for U.S. policy.

The Reagan administration's approval of an extra $25 million in military aid had placed a strong emphasis on the training of Salvadoran troops in counterinsurgency and combat-related skills, but results were slow. As the months went by and the possibilities of an easy military victory receded, the idea of elections as the political component to the military solution being sought by Washington became more and more attractive. At home, where public opposition to increasing U.S. involvement in the war was growing, the promise of elections offered a welcome alternative to the ugly specter of "another Vietnam." But it was a difficult tag to shake off. By June 1981 one of the four U.S. mobile training teams in the country was hard at work in a converted teacher's training school some twenty miles outside San Salvador. The Green Berets were assigned to a new kind of unit in the Salvadoran army, a Rapid Reaction Battalion named "Atlacatl" after a legendary hero of the Pipil Indians. Simultaneously, to get around a fifty-five man limit on the U.S. trainers in the country at any one time, Salvadoran cadets were enrolled in the School of the Americas in Panama. "We teach them that there is no need to bomb a village, sort through the bodies and find that they have killed innocent women and children and that the guerrillas have escaped," explained an instructor to a visiting journalist.[91]

In January 1982, President Reagan rode roughshod over congressional qualms and the 13,000 victims of political violence in the previous year to certify that "the Government of El Salvador is making a concerted and significant effort to comply with internationally recognized human rights."[92] The day before the certification was announced the *Washington Post* and the *New York Times* carried reports of the most extensive of the large scale civilian massacres that had so characterized 1981: an army operation had swept through the communities around the village of El Mozote in Morazán, killing anywhere up to 1,000 men, women, and children. Their bodies, charred and decomposing, had been left to litter the ground and fill the air with stench. Relatives of the victims told the *New York Times* that the Atlacatl Battalion, not six months out from their Special Forces' training, had been responsible. The existence of the massacre was denied by the U.S. government.[93] "The President has just certified that up is down and in is out and black is white," was the comment of Democrat Gerry Studds. "I anticipate his telling us that war is peace at any moment."[94]

The cornerstone of U.S. policy had been that the elections would produce a victory for Duarte and the Christian Democrats, endorse the U.S.-backed reforms, and smooth the way for Congress to approve the dollars so necessary for the "strategic victory" in the war recommended in a late 1981 Pentagon report by Brigadier General Fred F. Woerner.[95] It is not surprising that it was difficult for those inside El Salvador to see how the elections held on March 28, boycotted and sabotaged by the FMLN, conducted during a civil war and under a two-year-old state of siege, could contribute much to "democracy" in El Salvador. "The key point is not to pass from 'apparent' to 'formal' democracy," Segundo Montes wrote in *ECA* a couple of months before election day, "but to install 'real' democracy. However clean and honest the coming elections may be, they cannot resolve the fundamental problems of El Salvador."[96]

When election day came, congressional leaders and administration spokesmen waxed lyrical about the "hundreds and thousands of Salvadorans" who "braved gunfire and threats of violent death . . . to demonstrate their thirst for liberty."[97] The problem for the United States was that a majority of Salvadorans voted for right-wing parties now forming an alliance behind Roberto D'Aubuisson and his newly founded National Republican Alliance party, ARENA. A combination of careful footwork and heavy pressure was exerted to ensure that an interim president, acceptable to the United States, the political right, and the army, was installed in the place of the unacceptable D'Aubuisson. The new president of El Salvador would be Dr. Alvaro Magaña, a shrewd lawyer without a political party behind him, but with close ties to the army gained from years spent as president of the Mortgage Bank, where he facilitated many army officers' loans.

The FDR-FMLN were offered the chance to lay down their arms and enter the election under Duarte's "rules of the democratic game," but there had been no possibility of them doing so. This was the army that had stolen the elections of 1972 and 1977 and the same army that, although charged with guaranteeing impartiality and electoral integrity, had declared that alliance members were "traitors" and therefore legitimate military targets. As the advertising campaigns saturated radio and television programs and papered the country with posters and leaflets, the issue of voting—in defiance of the "terrorists"—took center stage. "If someone says they prefer not to vote, they are favoring dictatorship, totalitarianism, and terrorism," ran an advertisement by the ruling Junta in Duarte's name.[98] That they were also liable to run afoul of the Salvadoran authorities was well known: a voter's identification card would be stamped with invisible ink and records kept of his signature or fingerprints. Those not on any electoral list would be known to have opted for dictatorship, totalitarianism, and terrorism and could expect to suffer the consequences.

On election day, the massive turnout "surpassed all predictions made in the final days preceding the elections," the official U.S. observer team noted, and raised suspicions that the count had been artificially inflated in order to repudiate the FMLN.[99] At the forefront of those making the charges was the UCA, whose researchers challenged the official count in two articles published in the April and the May–June issues of *ECA*.[100] Their findings were to bring the university into a head-on collision within the combative new U.S. ambassador, Deane Hinton, for whom the elections had been "extraordinarily successful" and "a turning point in history."[101] "Bullshit!" was the response he gave the *New York Times* correspondent's mention of the UCA's conclusions. "It would take a professor in an ivory tower who didn't go out to vote because the guerrillas told him not to to come up with a theory like that."[102]

Hinton had arrived in El Salvador with a clearly defined mission: "to make sure that the guerrillas and communists don't take over El Salvador."[103] He had kept his distance from the Jesuits of the UCA, but would meet Ellacuría and three others at a lunch in June which, judging by the account of the meeting left by Ellacuría, was not characterized by cordiality on either side.[104] Declassified cables belittling the charges against the election reveal that the embassy's antipathy to the UCA, unsurprisingly, ran deeper than the issue of vote counting: "*ECA* is a regular publication of the Jesuit run university . . . It is the most important

of the very few nonclandestine pro-FMLN/FDR publications available in
El Salvador. The editorial is a leftist critique of the current political process
consistent with this perspective."[105] As reports in the international press
used the UCA's research to back up the charges of electoral fraud
circulating San Salvador, an internal State Department memo recast the
UCA's accusations as an exercise in damage control. The "strongly leftist
university . . . has sympathized with the armed left from the beginning of
the conflict. . . . The attempt to discredit the Salvadoran elections
indicates the UCA is striving to limit the damage from what remains a
severe blow to the leftist cause."[106]

AMBASSADOR Hinton would startle his audience with a speech he gave to
the American Chamber of Commerce in San Salvador the following
October. His subject was the criminal justice system, or the lack of it, and
his starting points were facts that no Reagan administration official had
yet confronted so directly or so publicly: "Neither internal confidence nor
external support can long survive here in the absence of an effective system
of criminal justice. . . . If you are not convinced that I am talking about a
fundamental and critical problem, consider these facts. Since 1979
perhaps as many as 30,000 Salvadorans have been MURDERED—not killed
in battle, MURDERED." While, for the record, the State Department
would soften these words to "killed illegally, that is, not in battle," there
was no escaping their truth, nor the lack of progress in the key cases
identified by the United States as yardsticks for the six monthly certifica-
tions prior to release of further aid.[107]

　　　Six national guardsmen had, indeed, been arrested for the killing of
the U.S. churchwomen in May 1981. Two days before the first certification in January 1982, Colonel García had promised a trial "within a very
few days." Since then progress toward a trial had been minimal.[108]
Meanwhile in September the National Guard lieutenant held for the
murder of the two AIFLD officials and the president of ISTA in the
Sheraton Hotel had been released. The presiding judge claimed, in a flat
contradiction of the findings of the AIFLD and the U.S. embassy, that
there was too little evidence to warrant further detention. The embassy
expressed itself as "dismayed and incredulous" at the judge's decision.[109]
The response contained in Hinton's speech had been simple, but sounded
tough: there must be progress in bringing those responsible for the murder
of U.S. citizens to justice, including those who gave the orders; there must
be progress in respect for human rights and in control of the security forces
or else "the United States, despite our other interests and our commitment

to the struggle against communism, could be forced to deny assistance to El Salvador."

A senior Reagan official, later identified as Judge William Clark, director of the National Security Council, expressed to the *New York Times* the administration's "surprise" at the speech. The piece would run under the headline "U.S. Envoy to Salvador Ordered to Stop Criticizing Rights Abuses."[110] Underneath the worries about justice, the revulsion at the trampling of human rights, the anger of U.S. officials at their inability to get through to their clients an understanding of the terms under which the giving of aid was palatable to the American public, and the warning that the "survival" of the government of El Salvador depended on the curbing of the "gorillas" of the right, lay the war. And as the FMLN appeared to be gaining strength throughout the second half of 1982 and 1983, the war was going badly from a U.S. point of view.

Early in 1983, President Reagan himself would take center stage in the struggle for El Salvador. At the height of his popularity, he was the administration's greatest asset. In an unusual joint session of Congress he appealed for support to prevent a crisis in Central America that might "directly affect the security and well-being of our people." The communists were at the gates: "El Salvador is nearer to Texas than Texas is to Massachusetts. Nicaragua is just as close to Miami, San Antonio, San Diego, and Tucson as those cities are to Washington." It was time for the people and Congress of the United States to stand up and be counted in their opposition to "totalitarianism." The president was asking for "the foundation of a bipartisan approach" toward Central America in the release of greatly increased amounts of aid. The package included $110 million in military aid for El Salvador. "The national security of all the Americas is at stake in Central America," Reagan concluded. "We have a vital interest, a moral duty, and a solemn responsibility."[111]

CHAPTER SIX

CONGRESS COMES TO TOWN

I am a bread and butter politician from South Boston—not a foreign policy expert. This is my first foray into the world of international politics. But when it comes to the issues of life and death, justice and injustice, dignity and inhumanity—you do not need a Ph.D. in foreign policy to take a stand. I am taking a stand today. Enough is enough. The time to act has come. They killed six priests in cold blood. I stood on the ground where my friends were blown away by men to whom the sanctity of life means nothing—and men who will probably never be brought to justice. Mr. Chairman, it is time to act."[1]

Congressman Joe Moakley, 1990

"CONGRESS is a funny place," mused one senior foreign policy aide in 1991. "People go on for years, tacitly agreeing to ignore certain realities—in this case the realities of the Salvadoran military—and then something like the Jesuit case happens that makes it impossible to ignore them any longer. It seems to cause a sea-change in what people know, but it isn't really, it is more a sea-change in the politics of that knowledge. Unlike the intelligence community with its 'need-to-know,' Congress works on a 'need-not-to-know' basis. It was politically useful for a variety of reasons to have El Salvador under Duarte as a democracy. You operate as if this is realistic and you are unaware of what is happening until something happens that brings you face to face with what you knew all the time."[2]

BY January 1990 Deane Hinton's speech seemed long ago. While President Reagan's appeals in early 1983 had met with a mixed reception in Congress, by the summer of 1984 the election of Napoleón Duarte as president of El Salvador and the conviction of a handful of national guardsmen for the murders of the U.S. churchwomen had reinforced the recommendations for an increase in military aid made by the bipartisan Kissinger Commission at the beginning of that year.[3] During the 1980s direct military assistance had totaled more than $1 billion out of an aid package of over $4 billion.[4] El Salvador had become the sixth highest recipient of U.S. aid in the world, and on a per capita basis only Israel could top it. But as the violent and dramatic events of the previous few months were absorbed it became clear to policy makers and legislators alike that the country was facing a crossroads.

The lessons of the 1989 offensive had been many.[5] On a purely military level the FMLN was a stronger and more effective force after nearly a decade of war than either the Salvadoran army or the United States had imagined. While calls for insurrection had been rejected, the relative ease with which several thousand combatants had moved down from the traditional FMLN strongholds of Guazapa, Chalatenango, and Morazán and into the city of San Salvador bespoke an important level of underground support among the civilian population. Revulsion at the murder of the Jesuits undoubtedly deflected some of the international condemnation of the rebels' launching of the offensive in the first place, but the offensive highlighted intelligence and operational weaknesses in the army that went beyond the premeditated murder of unarmed priests. In its wake both sides faced military stalemate. Those in the FMLN who had believed that the conditions for an insurrection existed in El Salvador had been shown to be wrong; those in the armed forces who had followed the United States in their advocacy of a long-term counterinsurgency strategy saw the possibilities of success severely diminished. Differences between hard-line officers in favor of an all-out "total war," and more moderate officers prepared to consider an end to the war through negotiations became more defined. Not for nothing, however, had the army as an institution historically opposed negotiations: from a negotiated settlement it could only stand to lose in size and influence within the country, while the very process of reduction would create serious internal divisions.

Central American and international pressure for negotiated solutions to regional conflicts had been mounting since the 1987 initiatives of the president of Costa Rica, Oscar Arias. The so-called Arias Plan was presented in February 1987, approved by Western European governments and Democrats in the U.S. Congress, and adopted in a modified form in the August 1987 agreements known as "Esquipulas II."[6] The five Central American presidents had called on the United Nations to verify aspects of the agreements, beginning with the February 1990 elections in Nicaragua, which became the first major U.N. operation in the Western Hemisphere.[7] The 1989 government of Cristiani was publicly committed to "dialogue," and two rounds of negotiations between representatives of the Salvadoran government and FMLN, observed by the U.N. and Salvadoran Church, had preceded the violence of November. While the offensive had responded, in part, to the breakdown of the negotiating process, in early December Salvador Samayoa and Ana Guadalupe Martínez of the FMLN's Political-Diplomatic Commission had sought out Alvaro de Soto, the special assistant to the secretary general of the United Nations, to request a more active role for the U.N. in the peace process.[8] Later in the month the five presidents of Central America met in Costa Rica and made a direct appeal to Secretary General Javier Pérez de Cuéllar to use his good offices to "reinitiate the dialogue between the government of El Salvador and the FMLN."[9]

A need to address U.S. policy toward El Salvador was also evident in Washington. There was praise for President Cristiani's announcement of the detention of Colonel Benavides, the lieutenants, and the enlisted men for their alleged responsibility in the murder of the Jesuits, but the mood was one of frustration. "El Salvador underscores the limits of American policy and the inability of the United States to impose its preferences to produce our stated policy goals," Gus Yatron, chairman of the Subcommittee on Human Rights and International Organizations, stated in his opening remarks at hearings on January 24 dedicated to the situation in El Salvador. "All the military assistance we send will not defeat the guerrillas and all the human rights conditions we attach to our aid programs will not result in a just society."[10]

In August 1984, the commanding officer of the U.S. Southern Command, General Paul Gorman, had told Congress that it was his estimation that within two years the Salvadoran army would "have 80 to 90 percent of the country under control and the guerrillas' ability to resurge would be severely attenuated."[11] The estimation came in the context of effusive praise for the "institutional transformation" of the Salvadoran military in a "remarkable advance toward apolitical profession-alism." Nearly six years later, in February 1990, General Maxwell Thurman, one of Gorman's successors at SouthCom, had a very different assessment of the military situation in a country where a constabulary force of 12,000 men, swollen by U.S. aid and assistance to a standing army of 55,000, was held at bay by a guerrilla insurgency of approximately 7,000 combatants: "I think they are ultimately going to have to go to the table and negotiate."[12] With Secretary of State James Baker also telling the Senate "this is the year to end the war through a negotiated settlement,"[13] the question that remained was what the government of the United States was prepared to do about it.

A major impediment was endemic military corruption. In an article published in the *New York Times* in December 1989, freelance journalist

Joel Millman reported on a year's worth of research on the financial practices of the Salvadoran military.[14] The picture he painted of an officer corps more concerned with looking after its own interests than in the prosecution of the war was a grim one indeed for legislators. Bolstered by U.S. aid, the "fourteen warlords" at the top of the military hierarchy had come to replace the so-called "fourteen families" of the Salvadoran oligarchy as the leaders of the most powerful economic force in the country. Contributing to the structural shift that had entrenched the military as "the final power broker in the country, for now and in the indefinite future,"[15] as one U.S. colonel described it in 1986, had been the flight of capital (and indeed capitalists) induced by the kidnapping and extortions of the late 1970s and the reforms of the early 1980s. From the relatively petty levels of corruption involved in the financial abuse of enlisted men and the payment of whole companies of nonexistent "ghost soldiers," to the development of assets held in the army social security fund IPSFA from $2 million in 1980 to more than $100 million by the end of 1988, Millman concluded that "Instead of fostering reform, the American money has been absorbed into a network of corruption and patronage that has made the Salvadoran military an empire unto itself."[16]

On February 8, 1990, Assistant Secretary Aronson reminded the Senate Foreign Operations Subcommittee of how, the day after Ellacuría's death, he had told Congress that the only fitting memorial to him would be "renewed commitment . . . to mobilize whatever resources and pressures that can be brought to bear to negotiate an end to the conflict in El Salvador." But the subcommittee chair, Senator Leahy, cut Aronson short: "Mr. Aronson, I could not disagree with you more. 'The only fitting memorial is to keep on saying, well, we would like to bring the parties together.' Baloney. I think a fitting memorial would be finally, once and for all, to say—having made a threat every year that next year we are going to cut you off if this goes on—that we actually mean it. We should actually do it, and actually bring the pressure so that those who might want to stop the killing down there have some leverage. *That* would be a fitting memorial."[17]

LEAHY'S Massachusetts neighbor in the House of Representatives, Joe Moakley, had been surprised to be named chairman of the Speaker's Special Task Force on El Salvador. "Why me?" he asked Speaker Thomas Foley. "If you put out a list you might have 434 guys put their names on it. Not me." "I know, that's why I'm calling you," Foley had replied.[18]

Moakley was South Boston Irish born and bred and an ultimate congressional insider. His father was a truck driver and ran a bar, while young Joe was a tough street-fighting kid who lied about his age and, at 15, ran away to join the navy and fight in the South Pacific. Back in the United States he won a boxing scholarship to study law at Miami University, but then returned to Massachusetts to join the state legislature at 25 and finish his law studies in evening class. He entered Congress in 1973, but had not been known for his leadership on foreign policy issues. With a position on the House Rules Committee, his legislative focus had been on issues raised by his largely Irish and Italian constituents: housing, labor rights, and the environment among them.

One of the problems that walked in off the streets of South Boston in 1983 was that of Salvadoran refugees. After listening to the grueling descriptions of tens of thousands of people killed and displaced by a U.S.-backed war, Moakley set an aide, Jim McGovern, to research their situation. He took up the issue with the administration in an attempt to get the Salvadoran refugees in the United States "extended voluntary departure" visas that would allow them to stay in the country until the war abated. But the administration was not interested. Moakley began filing legislation, and kept filing it in various different forms until an extension of the departure of Salvadoran refugees finally cleared Congress in 1990. Not a man to stray far from a well-beaten path between South Boston and Capitol Hill, Moakley had not been to El Salvador before the Jesuits were killed, although he had met both Ignacio Ellacuría and Segundo Montes in Washington.

"It is an honor just to be appointed to the Rules Committee," explained one congressional aide, in an attempt to conjure up a picture of the respect due to Moakley's power as chairman of the House Rules Committee. "Traffic cop" for the daily business on the floor of the House of Representatives, the Rules Committee has a power unlike that of any other committee within Congress. It reviews all legislation produced by other committees and decides which bills will proceed for House action and when, what amendments may be attached to them, and how much time should be allowed for debates. The House of Representatives acts under a constitutional mandate by which it writes its own laws; if need be, House Rules take precedence over the law and the Constitution itself. Within the House, the Rules Committee therefore has "an unparalled ability to screw things up for others if they want to," the aide continued. "If Rules tells you 'later' that's like 'see you in ten years.' "[19]

You do not get to be the chairman of the Rules Committee without the proven ability to hold a consensus together. Moakley's appointment to chair the Speaker's Special Task Force reflected a real fear that the Jesuit case would prove a catalyst for potential polarization. No issue had been more hotly debated over the last ten years than Central America; it was felt that the kind of intense partisanship that would have been exacerbated by the appointment of one of those most active in the battles of the past would only prove counterproductive. Moakley is an imposing man with a fleshy, wide-mouthed face, whose years as one of Congress' "old-bull powerhouses" have failed to smooth away the rough edges and have left a disarming charm and straight, no-nonsense manner. "Until I got involved I thought El Salvador was an amusement park in Texas," Moakley would freely admit. "What do I know about El Salvador? But I do know that people are people no matter where they come from and I know what moves people and I know what you have to do to get to the bottom of things—you have to go out there, and you have to play hardball."[20]

AMBASSADOR Walker led the caravan out to San Salvador's Ilopango air base to meet the Moakley task force on February 11, 1990. Never before had Congress sent a delegation of such size to El Salvador. Never before had one delegation concentrated so exclusively on a particular case.

While the task force appointed by the Speaker had been Democratic, the delegation of fifteen congressmen included five Republicans and combined congressional stature with political diversity. Surveying the Democrats on the delegation, a Defense Department official concluded, in an internal memorandum, "this group could cause a lot of trouble."[21] The range was from liberals such as Gerry Studds and George Miller— who had been vocal critics of U.S. policy in Central America for many years—to Dave McCurdy, seen as a key "swing" figure on Central America for his mid-1980s leadership of a group of "moderates" who had held the balance in the closely contested votes on *contra* aid, and John Murtha, a "hawk" with a history of siding with the administration when it came to El Salvador. Equally imposing were the Republicans behind the conservative Bud Shuster—among them Bob Dornan, a former pilot who had become known to some as "B-1 Bob" for his affinity for all things military.

A staff delegation had traveled to El Salvador the previous month to prepare for this visit. They had flown down on the morning of January 8 and as they opened their newspapers in the airplane, the headlines greeting them told of Cristiani's announcement that there had been "some involvement of the military" in the killing of the Jesuits. Embassy officials brought them up to speed on the Buckland-Avilés revelations, which had yet to hit the press, and told them they had run into trouble with polygraphs. The January 2 meeting in Colonel Ponce's office had created a standoff between an American major saying one thing and a Salvadoran colonel saying another. Under FBI supervision, both were asked to submit to lie detector tests, but the results of both sets of tests had been inconclusive. Buckland had seemed under great strain and, at the FBI's suggestion, had left the country on January 6 to complete the tests in a less stressful environment. Days later Cristiani had announced the names of the four officers and five enlisted men to be detained.

Setting up the staff interviews, or at least the most sensitive among them (breakfast with D'Aubuisson, for example), was Leonel Gómez, a Salvadoran who would come to play a crucial role in the task force's work. Formally outside any institution, Gómez was, nevertheless, something of an institution himself when it came to Washington's perception of El Salvador. From a wealthy background in coffee-growing Santa Ana, Gómez had been the deputy director of ISTA when its director, Rodolfo Viera, was assassinated in San Salvador's Sheraton Hotel with the AIFLD officials in January 1981. Under threat himself, Gómez had left El Salvador and sought asylum in the United States. Once there he had shocked and impressed those who had heard him denounce the corruption and brutality of the Salvadoran armed forces in congressional hearings. "The Salvadoran army is held together by a vast network of corruption," he had said ten long years ago. "The fundamental problem in my country is the army, an army that presides over a military dictatorship."[22]

Although he did not return to his country until 1989, Gómez had long been one of the prime sources for Washington's many Salvador watchers. In a political culture where distrust and fear have a pervasive and often tangible presence, he had done what was almost impossible and maintained contact with a range of Salvadorans across the political—and military—spectrum. Through him, staffers and journalists had access to Salvadorans—be they military officers, bankers, judges or FMLN *comandantes*—and the Salvadorans access to the Americans, unimaginable either through official embassy channels or the international human rights organizations. But all this had won him a strange and complicated profile: while sectors of the political center and left believed he worked for the CIA, others on the right had him down as a member of the FMLN. Still others had appreciated—even as they admitted never being *quite* sure where he was coming from—that the role that Gómez filled as a back-channel bridge builder and conduit of information, was as useful to all concerned as it was unique. A close personal friend of Bill Walker's since the 1970s, Gómez was under the intermittent protection of the U.S. embassy, as he was well aware that San Salvador contained a good number of people who would not have been unhappy to see him dead.

On the plane to El Salvador, congressmen and their staff found themselves drawn into the case by the graphic details of the extrajudicial confessions of the lieutenants and enlisted men that had led to formal charges being brought against them by Judge Ricardo Zamora on January 19, 1980. "This is a situation where it is them or us," they read in Espinoza's account of the orders received from Colonel Benavides. "We are going to begin with the leaders. Inside the sector of ours we have the university and there is Ellacuría."[23]

They arrived in El Salvador with a clear agenda. Beside an extended visit to the UCA, congressional attention at this stage was focused on three areas: Buckland and Avilés, a meeting of the High Command and other senior officers on the evening of November 15, reported in the *Washington Post* and *Baltimore Sun* the previous week, and the conduct of their own embassy in the investigation of the case.[24] Individual congressmen had other concerns, but for the most part the delegation acted as one, surprised by a cohesion that had its source in a shared sense of outrage at the murder of the Jesuits. Although it was difficult to escape the "circus" aspects of such a large group—convoys of cars with bulletproof windows, guards with rifles sweeping at every halt at a traffic light—the three-day visit was one that even veterans of such hit-and-run assaults on the complexities of Central American politics were to find productive. And throughout it was Joe Moakley's party, whether defusing the tension with the Salvadoran military, sliding out for a late-night rendezvous with a nervous source in a parking lot, or regaling his audience in the hotel bar with jokes as he rested his feet, clad in ruby-red patent leather slippers.

THE visit to the UCA on the morning of February 12 had considerable impact. The tour began at the UCA chapel where the six Jesuits were buried, and followed the footsteps of their killers down the covered passageway at the back of the Monsignor Romero Pastoral Center. The delegation could not but be shocked by the dried blood still evident on the floor of the room in which Elba and Celina Ramos had been killed, the trail on the ground where the body of Juan Ramón Moreno had been dragged inside the residence—traces of violence in stark contrast to the hot sunny morning and peaceful garden setting. The congressmen were shown around the site by Fathers Tojeira and Estrada. Assured, attentive, and well informed on the progress in the investigation, the Jesuits expressed their appreciation for the measures already taken by Cristiani and their conviction that the responsibility for the murder of their brothers did not stop with one colonel, Benavides, not known for his extremism or driving leadership. The "intellectual authors" of the crime must be found and brought to justice.

Something of a fixation for many of the congressmen was the need to persuade Lieutenant Colonel Rivas to submit to a lie detector test. According to Buckland, Rivas had been informed by Benavides of his responsibility for the killing of the Jesuits in early December. In a meeting at the U.S. embassy on the morning of February 12, Rivas came under heavy fire from several congressmen, with Miller and Shuster as the front-runners. He did not take it well, pleading that "my honor is at stake," and the meeting had ended so badly that Moakley returned to see him on his own. Rivas assured him "I was thinking of resigning," but Moakley consoled him: "You've just been balled out by a bunch of congressmen—you should try my meetings in South Boston." They parted amicably, with Rivas even supplying Moakley with copies of Buckland's affidavit and his letter to his sister Carol which the congressman had been able to get out of his own embassy.[25]

For the old Salvador hands on the delegation the official meetings with Colonels Ponce, Zepeda, and Elena Fuentes brought few surprises. But to Moakley the experience was new. Ponce and Zepeda received them in a darkened lecture room where congressmen, some of them big men by any standards and probably twice the size of the average Salvadoran officer, squeezed themselves into school desks. "I just couldn't believe it," was how Moakley remembered this meeting. "I mean they open up with talking about how much they're interested in human rights, in how much they pray before every meeting. I just thought some of the things they said were right out of Hollywood." Unable to remember whether the Jesuits or the UCA had been mentioned at all during the November 15 meeting, the colonels had been at pains to tell the congressmen how they had been so worried by the military situation that they had joined hands and prayed together for "divine intervention." At that moment the lights went out, leaving Moakley to crack, "I wish you'd put your hands together and pray for light from above right now."[26] The delegation left unimpressed. "Pat answers," a staffer wrote in his notebook. "Insulting."[27]

"Moakley could have fried the embassy after that trip if he had wanted to," was how one aide expressed a common opinion.[28] The delegation had arrived with serious concerns about Ambassador Walker's apparent assumption of the role of public relations officer for the

Salvadoran government during and after the offensive, the embassy's handling of Lucía Cerna, and what some perceived as its "burning" of Colonel Avilés. While Walker would defend him loyally, criticism was also mounting—fueled by the indignation of the Jesuits—for the role played by Legal Officer Rick Chidester. In two long meetings at the beginning and end of the trip, Walker was apologetic and defensive. Congressmen were concerned that however valid the excuses being offered by Walker and his embassy, however genuine the protestations of a commitment to the unraveling of the Jesuit case, whatever the technical collaboration of the FBI, or a senior DEA agent brought down from Mexico to assist in the investigation, the impression given was that the U.S. embassy was doing everything in its power to obstruct and not further the truth. "Every time he rolls his eyes and waves his arms," one congressman remarked to another about Walker's responses as they left the second meeting, "he is lying."[29]

The embassy's life was further complicated by the presence in the country of a delegation of U.S. Jesuits led by Paul Tipton. Both the Salvadoran government and the State Department were coming to appreciate that the Jesuits in the United States were anything but the "bunch of leftists" it was relatively easy to dismiss in El Salvador. In December the Jesuits had coordinated letters of condemnation of the murder to presidents Cristiani and Bush signed by the representatives of 4,000 American colleges and universities: this represented a cross-section of the educational establishment of the entire nation. In early February Tipton had led a two-hour meeting between seven presidents of Jesuit universities and President Cristiani in the Marriott Hotel in Washington. Commending Cristiani for his "forthright and courageous efforts" to date, the Jesuits had insisted that the naming of Benavides as the sole intellectual author of the crime was "unacceptable" to them.[30] Men of the stature and influence of those now accompanying Tipton—Father Leo Donovan, president of Washington's Georgetown University, and the presidents of Fordham University, Boston and Loyola colleges, and St. Joseph's and Loyola universities[31]—were no more inclined than the congressmen to swallow the protestations of the U.S. embassy.

"I think there were a lot of members on this trip, particularly on the Republican side, who went down expecting one thing and were shocked to find another," was the verdict of one aide with over twelve years' experience on Central America.[32] Shortly before they left El Salvador, Moakley read out a statement on behalf of the entire delegation: it included praise for the SIU's "good police work," but expressed concern that the investigation of the intellectual authors of the crime was not over and that the available evidence might not be sufficient to bring all those charged with the crime to justice. More serious was the raising of the question of whether the human rights problems on the government's side, including the Jesuit killings, "are the actions of a few renegade military figures or whether, in fact, they stem from attitudes and actions that go to the very heart of the armed forces and other major institutions in the country."[33]

THE sign above the entrance read "Welcome to camp Hell." Beneath it an obstacle like a giant tiger trap spanned a ditch. No one, it was explained by the captain conducting a tour of the Atlacatl's base at Sitio del Niño, could enter the camp of the elite of the elites, the Atlacatl's own commando unit, without overcoming this imposing contraption.[34]

The history and identity of the Atlacatl Battalion raises serious questions of the U.S. influence on the Salvadoran armed forces. It is true that by 1989 there remained few soldiers from the original Atlacatl Battalion that was created by U.S. Special Forces in 1981 and led by the legendary Lieutenant Colonel Domingo Monterrosa. Most men in the ranks of the Atlacatl in 1989 were *campesino* forced recruits serving a compulsory two-year term in the army. They received thirteen weeks of intensive instruction from the training center, CEBRI, located in Sitio del Niño and under the authority of the Atlacatl's commanding officer. Emphasis within the training was placed on the "mystique" of being part of the BIRIs (Immediate Reaction Infantry Battalions)[35], among which the Atlacatl—which fought *"Por la Patria y con Dios"* (For the Fatherland and with God)—was regarded as *"lo mejor de El Salvador"* (El Salvador's best). In mid-1990 an Atlacatl officer would explain that this mystique was best expressed by the Atlacatl insignia: a skull pierced through by an arrow and a ray of lightning. "The arrow is the symbol of the legendary silence and stealth of our weapons, the lightning of our speed and the skull of our total destruction of the enemy."[36]

Since 1981 the Atlacatl was reliably reported to have carried out a series of massacres and human rights abuses: El Mozote in 1981, the murder of 100 civilians near Lake Suchitlán in 1983, the massacres of Los Llanitos and Gualsinga River in July and August 1984, the torture and killing of captured combatants in 1985 and 1987, the rape and beating of a civilian woman in January 1989, the rape and execution of FMLN medical personnel and their wounded in February 1989, and the murder of the six priests and two women the following November.[37] Yet as late as

1987 the Atlacatl was described by Colonel Waghelstein as being "still the best unit in the country."[38] Throughout the war, army officers, U.S. officials, and FMLN combatants would confirm that the Atlacatl was, if not the "best," then certainly the most efficient killing machine that the Salvadoran army had to offer. Eric Buckland described them as, "the equivalent, essentially, to the 75th Rangers."[39]

"Remember guerrillas, you don't play with the Atlacatl Battalion," the *Miami Herald* reported loudspeakers blaring in 1984 after civilians encouraged to come forward and surrender to the Atlacatl had been peremptorily slaughtered in Los Llanitos.[40] Their boast would be echoed nearly seven years later as Antonio Cardenal, *Comandante* "Jesús Rojas" of the FPL, remarked, holed up in a guerrilla camp until the Atlacatl gunfire from across the Chalatenango hills died down, "you don't mess with the Atlacatl."[41] A month later he was killed in an ambush, for the army one of the most valued scalps of the war. Who killed him and the thirteen who died with him? The Atlacatl.

The problem for the United States was that the two aspects of the Atlacatl—aggressive combat force and brutal and recurrent violations of basic human rights—had gone together and over the years the former had been supported at the very great cost of the lack of reform of the latter. One U.S. officer would look back on his time in Salvador and remember Monterrosa as "one of the finest combat officers I had ever seen." But he was shaking his head in puzzlement as he continued, "then you look at the human rights type things they did. I just didn't like to think about some of the things that went on that I wasn't supposed to hear about."[42]

An exchange between Assistant Secretary of State Elliot Abrams and Areyeh Neier, director of Human Rights Watch, on ABC Television's "Nightline" in February 1985, made the point succinctly. The discussion turned to the massacres at Los Llanitos and Gualsinga River. They had been widely reported in the U.S. press and well documented by human rights organizations. Yet they did not appear in the State Department's country report on El Salvador. When challenged by ABC's Ted Koppel, Abrams had explained their absence as being, "Because neither of them happened. Because it is a tactic of the guerrillas every time there is a battle and a significant number of people killed to say that they're all victims of human rights abuses." "That's why the *New York Times,*" Neier countered, "and the *Boston Globe* and the *Miami Herald* and the *Christian Science Monitor* and Reuters and all the other reporters who went to the scene and looked at what took place, they were simply being propagandists for the guerrillas? Is that right?" But 1984 was, for U.S. policy, a turning point in the war. It was Duarte's year and these massacres did not fit in with the political needs of the moment. "I'm telling you," Abrams insisted, "that there were no significant—there were no massacres in El Salvador in 1984."[43]

Moakley had to push hard to extricate background material on the members of the Atlacatl responsible for the murder of the Jesuits. When it finally came, the Pentagon's assessment that "the very presence of U.S. military advisers is a reminder to the Salvadoran armed forces of the U.S. government's commitment and insistence on human rights" sounded somewhat naive.[45] According to answers given to the FBI by U.S. Major Samuel Ramírez, resident with the CEBRI from October 1989 to October 1990, the commando unit that murdered the Jesuits was considered to be the "best" of the units in the Atlacatl—tougher, more experienced, and more motivated than any other.[46] Its leader, Lieutenant Espinoza, came across as a model young officer: a product of cadet training in Fort Benning, instruction as a pilot on San Antonio Texas' air base, and a veteran of a Special Forces course in Fort Bragg. His unit, it also emerged, had undergone intensive training by Green Berets not forty-eight hours before they forced unarmed priests to lie face down in the grass and then shot them in the back of the head. To what end, task force members wondered, the Pentagon's calm assurance: "human rights issues have been and continue to be a central issue in the U.S. military effort in El Salvador"?[47]

"OUR relationship with Moakley was always reactive," was how a State Department official characterized the uneasy tension between branches of the U.S. government supposedly at one in their desire for justice to be done in the Jesuit case. "At times we felt we were walking around wondering when the next bag of sand was going to fall on our heads."[48] In part a function of on-going executive-legislative conflict in matters relating to foreign policy, the tension was exacerbated when the task force's "Interim Report," released on April 30, jolted the investigation it condemned as having come to a "virtual standstill" into a semblance of activity.

At the time of the report's release no progress had been made in gathering evidence to strengthen the case against Benavides and the others already charged, and the future was not encouraging. Speculation that the planning of the crime involved officers senior to Benavides was widespread, yet the task force found "a series of questions" about such involvement "unanswered and, as far as can be determined, unasked."

Although both raw intelligence and the suspicions of the U.S. officials closest to the case were indicating that Benavides had not acted on his own, the possibility was not one that any officials had been prepared to discuss. Congressmen and staff had been shocked to ear the murder described to them by Salvadoran military officers as "stupid," "self-defeating," and "dumb" while no senior officer with whom they spoke "said it was wrong."[49]

There was no surer indication of this lack of moral condemnation than the treatment given to Benavides. As reported in the *Washington Post*, Benavides was living in a "luxury apartment in the National Police headquarters," where he received regular visits from his colleagues from the *tandona*. And Benavides had found, on at least one occasion, relief even from this gilded confinement, being spotted in a beach hotel owned by the military on the Pacific coast.[50] To those appreciative of the depth of the wound inflicted to the military's sense of its own impunity by the unprecedented detention of a colonel, this display of military gall was not surprising. Benavides was thought—by President Cristiani himself, within the army, and beyond it—likely to get off the charges, while few had any doubts that the younger officers would be served up for the obeying of their seniors' orders.[51]

Benavides's life of luxury provoked a barrage of complaints from the U.S. embassy and the Salvadoran government, reinforced by a telephone call from Secretary of State Baker to President Cristiani. More worrying for congressional staff who visited El Salvador in mid-April were their doubts about the commitment, competence, and honesty of the SIU. "Rivas is ours," Rick Chidester had told visitors to the U.S. embassy in the first weeks of the investigation.[52] So it had certainly seemed as the tall figure of Chidester trailed Rivas on his rounds. Yet with the official record of the SIU's investigation now available, the congressional staff had been disturbed to find that Rivas was either unable or unwilling to answer their questions. The precise function of the military Honor Commission, in particular, seemed shrouded in mystery. Appointed by President Cristiani on January 6 to review the available evidence, no one could explain what it had actually done to produce the names of the men to be charged.

One congressional aide had been pleased to be introduced to the Honor Commission's senior officer, General Rafael Villamariona, at a reception held in Ambassador Walker's residence. Villamariona had been the hand-picked successor to the long-time head of the air force, the hard-line rightist General Juan Rafael Bustillo. "I'm glad to see you General," the aide began. "I wanted to talk to you about the Honor

Commission." "Who told you I was on it?" came the reply, to the aide's surprise. "Well, President Cristiani actually. We were interested in asking you exactly how you came up with the names?" Chidester had been standing beside the aid during this exchange. The shock on his face as Villamariona explained that they had been given the names by Rivas and had just "exhorted" them to tell the truth was palpable. Rivas had always told *him* that the SIU had provided the commission with general information and they had taken it from there. Questioned later about the role they had played, Villamariona would explain, "We told them it was a question of military honor. That was why it was called the Honor Commission."[53]

One of the most disturbing conclusions of the Moakley task force was that those charged with the crime might never have been arrested if Major Buckland had not come forward and named Benavides in early January. The staff delegation met Colonel Avilés for the first time on April 20. They were struck by how "Americanized" he seemed, with his never *quite* accurate colloquialisms, but this did not go very far in persuading them to believe what he had to say. Avilés described the entire incident as a "nightmare" that had had a serious effect on his family and career. He said he was shocked that Buckland had made the allegations and that all he had told him was that the focus of the investigation was divided between the FMLN, the army, and a right-wing death squad. Asked why Buckland might have made up his story he had answered, "I wish I had a crystal ball that would help me learn the answer."[54] An interview with Buckland in Washington became possible only after Moakley countered intense resistance from the Defense Department with a threat to have the Rules Committee issue a subpoena.[55] Those task force members who eventually met him, however, believed that he had been telling the truth. The implications of that truth were very serious. Not least among them was the inference that Lieutenant Colonel Rivas, director of the SIU and the investigation and a man enjoying the full confidence of the U.S. embassy, had been aware from early on that Benavides and the Atlacatl were involved in the murder of the Jesuits. Such knowledge would put subsequent "good police work" in a very different light.

MAY 1, 1990 was probably the single day on which Secretary of State James Baker devoted most attention to El Salvador. In the morning he testified before Senator Leahy's subcommittee, where senators, primed by that morning's front page story in the *New York Times* on the Moakley report, if not by the report itself, plied him with questions on the progress—or lack of it—in the Jesuit case.[56] Remarkably, it had become clear that as far as Congress was concerned, this one case could provide grounds for a cut in military aid. Baker was back on Capitol Hill that afternoon, this time for separate meetings with House Democrats and Republicans about the possibility of forging a bipartisan policy to hasten an end to the war in El Salvador.

Much store was set by what was seen as the policy success in Nicaragua ("The country's a disaster," a State Department official explained in 1991, "but the *policy* was a resounding success"[57]). The crowning glory on the previous March's bipartisan accord had been the defeat of the Sandinistas in the elections of February 1990. It was time to clean up the mess in El Salvador. Baker had opened discussions with House Democrats on April 3, just one day before the signing in Geneva of an historic agreement between representatives of the Salvadoran government and FMLN. After a meeting presided over by U.N. Secretary-General Javier Pérez de Cuéllar, and following months of behind-the-scenes diplomacy, the two sides agreed to embark on a "continuing and ongoing process" of negotiations whose purpose would be "to end the armed conflict through political means as speedily as possible, promote the democratization of the country, guarantee unrestricted respect for human rights, and reunify Salvadoran society."[58] Reinforced by the provision that allowed for the U.N. secretary-general to maintain contact with other interested governments during the negotiating process, the Geneva Accord represented the strongest prospect for peace in El Salvador in ten years of civil war.[59] From April 1990 on, no political decision in or about El Salvador could be made without reference to the status of the negotiating process to which all political sectors were publicly committed.

Within Congress the position evolving around a bill introduced by Senator Christopher Dodd on February 8 reinforced the terms of the Geneva Accord. Dodd had been in El Salvador in January in order to assess for himself the aftermath of the offensive and the killing of the Jesuits. His bill sought to condition all U.S. military aid to El Salvador on the willingness of the Salvadoran government to stay at the negotiating table, besides introducing an immediate cut of 50 percent "in an effort to convince the FMLN forces of our determination to support a political settlement." But, just as the government would be bound by the initial condition, so the FMLN would be required—at a risk of the reinstatement of the 50 percent in cut aid to the Salvadoran army—to stay at the negotiating table, accept the involvement of the U.N. secretary-general, and hold back from military operations that might threaten the survival of the Salvadoran government.[60]

In the talks held on Capitol Hill on May 1, Baker appeared to accept the idea of witholding at least some of the aid as part of a "carrot-and-stick" approach to policy toward El Salvador suggested by Dodd and in a similar amendment to the House foreign affairs bill put forward by Gerry Studds. But he criticized their proposals as too "one-sided" in punishing the government and rejected out of hand the 50 percent cut being advocated by Democrats. As trading of percentages began, there were complaints from Republicans that the Jesuit case was nothing but a "tool" being used by liberal Democrats to strengthen the hand of those who "for ten years have been trying to pull the plug on El Salvador."[61]

ON May 1 Ambassador Walker went on Salvadoran television to say that more investigation was needed in the Jesuit case.[62] It had suddenly become clear that the cut in military aid being demanded by congressional Democrats might be for real. The ambassador's statements were part of the flurry of activity with which San Salvador greeted the release of the Moakley report. The charges that the case was stalled had been rejected out of hand by the president of the Salvadoran Supreme Court, Dr. Mauricio Gutiérrez Castro, as "flippant and irresponsible." It was as a direct result of the release of the task force's report, however, that the judge was calling new witnesses and President Cristiani was saying that the case "could be raised to the plenary or trial stage within 90 days."[63]

Walker's was a move that marked a fundamental change in his public statements on the case. Only the week before, CBS's *60 Minutes* had carried an interview in which Walker had welcomed the detention of a colonel as "historic:" "I'm saying all the indications we have are that the people responsible for solving the crime have been working very diligently, very professionally, and have in fact solved it." The twenty-minute report presented a picture of an embassy blocking the investigation at every turn, reluctant, as Congressman Miller put it on the program, to "turn in its own client . . . the Salvadoran government and Salvadoran military."[64] If it were not bad enough to have the treatment of Lucía Cerna and the burning of Carlos Avilés brought to the attention of the American public, it had emerged that the embassy had forwarded a copy of their audiotape of Walker's interview with CBS's Ed Bradley to Colonel Ponce to help him prepare for his own interview. "Watching the ambassador prevaricate, hearing him praise the 'diligent' investigation of the murders," commented *New York Times* columnist Anthony Lewis, "I thought he had really become the ambassador of the Salvadoran military to us."[65] "This is a system that we've poured $5 billion into," Congressman Miller had complained in his interview, "that has slaughtered and murdered people with impunity. And now we're supposed to shout, 'Hallelujah, they've got a colonel'?"

The CBS broadcast raised the issue of higher orders through an interview with retired Colonel Sigifredo Ochoa, a close associate of Roberto D'Aubuisson, who in the early 1980s had enjoyed a reputation as one of the most effective combat commanders in the army. Politically ambitious, yet with no firm allegiance to a particular position other than the pursuit of power, Ochoa was now a member of ARENA and the head of the state electricity company. Interviewed as one in a position "to know about the inner workings of the Salvadoran army"—and in part because the CBS team, like everybody else working on the case, had been met by a wall of silence from within the High Command itself—Ochoa turned in a performance befitting a veteran ham that nevertheless proved useful in the channeling of "informed gossip" into the public arena. He charged that the order to kill the Jesuits had come from a meeting of a small group of officers who had stayed behind after the larger meeting on the evening of November 15. Benavides, he maintained, "is a man who could never take or even conceive of making a move as big as assassinating the Jesuits. Benavides acted under orders. He didn't act alone."

Support for Ochoa's position came in early May in an anonymous open letter from a group of young officers calling themselves "Domingo Monterrosa Lives!" The letter suggested that Ochoa stated what many officers believed, but were unable to express through fear of punishment. Junior officers, it claimed, had learned about the murder of the Jesuits a few hours after it had happened. They had not expected repercussions from the case because of the "priests' militancy with the FMLN," but had thought it a "senseless and irrational act all the same." Within the letter the officers charged that the High Command deliberately withheld information from the nominal commander-in-chief of the armed forces, President Cristiani, and supported speculations made by CBS about the involvement of Colonel Zepeda, who had accused the UCA of FMLN involvement only months before the crime.[66]

The Moakley report was entered into the official record of Judge Zamora's Fourth Criminal Court and provided the basis for the pursuit of a number of leads. The judge himself came under heavy criticism from the U.S. administration,[67] but the problems he faced were largely structural: a Salvadoran investigation depends almost entirely on the initiative, persistence—and given a history of bribery, intimidation, and murder of those working on sensitive cases—courage of the individual judge. On the Jesuit case Judge Zamora felt very alone, walking a "razor's edge" between those who wanted him to speed up the process so that he either made a major mistake leading to the case's dismissal or failed to gather evidence against Benavides, and those who wanted him to slow down so that the case would be forgotten. His reluctance to ask things of the army beyond those questions for which he could cite a source undoubtedly slowed the process. But he would later say that in the first months of the investigating process he felt he was "investigating in the dark"; the U.S. embassy, for example, while criticizing him constantly on and off the record, had not provided him with any material concerning the allegations made by Buckland.[68]

As Judge Zamora moved to dispel the impression of his own inactivity, the Salvadoran Supreme Court began to release press releases on the "progress" being made in the investigation. The May 4 press release was able to report that the logbook containing details of all those who entered or left the military academy on the night of November 15 to 16 had been "mislaid"; two of the members of the Honor Commission who had been subpoenaed to appear in court had failed to materialize and four cadets who were on guard duty at the military academy on the night of the crime were out of the country and subsequently unavailable to present their declarations. Over the following weeks, as it emerged that Benavides's diary had also "disappeared"; as military witnesses failed to answer the judge's summons, or left their barracks to present themselves before him, but found their way to a bar before they got there; as those who did arrive didn't know, couldn't remember, or just plain wouldn't respond to questions about the Jesuit murders, there could be no doubt that the Salvadoran army was making sure that the investigation made little headway.[69]

TALK about U.S. bipartisan policy on El Salvador broke down in mid-May, the victim of what the *Congressional Quarterly* would call "partisan politics, procedural arguments, and differences over substance."[70] No less a factor was a lack of personal interest on the part of the secretary of state, who was otherwise engaged in preparation for a summit meeting between presidents Bush and Gorbachev.

Moakley had gone through a series of meetings with Dave McCurdy in an attempt to bring him on as cosponsor of an amendment that followed the outline of the Dodd bill. Their discussions finally fell apart on the day before Moakley's Rules Committee needed to move the legislation forward, so Moakley appealed to his good friend John Murtha.

Not a Central American activist, Murtha was a sizeable ex-marine wielding—as chairman of the Appropriations Subcommittee on Defense—power to the tune of some $300 billion. Like Moakley a long-term insider, he had a history of involvement with El Salvador. Speaker Tip O'Neill had trusted Murtha as a hard-nosed, straight-talking emissary and had sent him to observe the Salvadoran elections in both 1982 and 1984. In 1984 he had not only voted with the Reagan administration, but had been a cosponsor, with Republican William Broomfield, of the amendment that, by a painfully close 212 to 208 margin, had paved the way for a massively increased aid package for the government of Napoleón Duarte. Murtha's decision to join Moakley in 1990 was an indication of the shift in Congress' attitude toward El Salvador. As the two of them circulated a "Dear Colleague" letter asking for congressional votes, a ripple of surprise went through those closest to Central American policy in Washington. Aronson called him up, but no sooner had he put the telephone down than Murtha called Moakley: "Bernie says I'm being used." "Tell Bernie to get lost," came the answer, with a laugh.[71]

The debate was preceded by intense lobbying. Within Congress, a bipartisan caucus's release of an extensive report profiling the leaders of the Salvadoran military as "Barriers to Reform" served as a timely reminder of exactly who had been at the receiving end of all those tax payers' dollars for all those years. The report reviewed the records of the fifteen most senior officers in the army, twelve of them members of the *tandona*. It found that fourteen of them had risen to their positions despite being guilty of abuses of human rights carried out under their command and that in none of the over fifty cases considered had even junior officers been brought to trial. Military accountability was as glaring in its absence as was military impunity in its pervasive presence.[72]

But Congress is a very personal place, and probably nothing made quite as much difference as the imposing presence of Murtha ("good for 40 votes," in one senior aide's assessment[73]) and the two days Moakley spent working his Rolodex to put in direct calls to colleagues throughout the House. The timing was good too, as the debate in the House took place on May 22, one day after the close of the first meeting between the FMLN and Salvadoran government under the terms of the Geneva Accord. In Caracas, and with the mediation of de Soto, the two sides had agreed on an agenda and schedule for the negotiation process: their objective was to reach the political agreements necessary as a prerequisite for a cease-fire by mid-September. In this first stage they would discuss the armed forces, human rights, the judicial system, the electoral system, constitutional reform, the social and economic problems faced by the country, and the verification of the agreements by the United Nations. Only after the achievement of a cease-fire would they move on to discuss the incorporation of the FMLN in the political process.[74]

During the debate, Moakley presented to his colleagues an opportunity to help make the cease-fire discussed in Caracas a reality. Democrats supporting the amendment believed that the complicated set of conditions it contained providing for when and how either side might trigger the reintroduction or termination of all military aid had, at last, provided Congress with a formula through which it could express its displeasure to the Salvadoran military without unduly rewarding the FMLN. "We are not playing games here," one congressman would tell the House. "We are trying to get both sides to the negotiation table." To Republican arguments that the proposed leverage was indicative of a "moral symmetry" between the "freely elected government" and the guerrillas, congressmen responded, as they had done for years, that one side in the war had received millions and millions of dollars in U.S. aid, the other had not. The point was to bring the suffering to an end. "Let us finally stand up for the majority of Salvadorans who have said over and over again that they want peace now," Moakley urged colleagues. "Support the Moakley-Murtha substitute and support the peace process."[75]

The voting went in favor of the Moakley-Murtha amendment 250 to 163; the margin of victory was the largest the Democrats had achieved on any Central American vote in the previous decade. While the moment of glory was temporarily deflated by the defeat shortly afterward of the foreign aid bill of which it formed a part, the Speaker himself would hail the Moakley-Murtha effort as "a watershed amendment in the House with respect to military aid in El Salvador."[76] A month later the amendment would be inserted into the Foreign Aid Appropriations Bill for 1991. With a Senate vote looming in the autumn, for the first time ever it appeared that the Salvadoran military might suffer a substantial cut in their aid. And Moakley's explanation? "I think what happens is that people who for years sent money down there to defeat communists, finally have come to the realization that these people who are supposed to be trained in human rights are shooting priests."[77]

THOSE tempted to suspect that Moakley might drop the baton on the Jesuit case after the vote in the House were startled by the force of a statement he released in August 1990 after a staff trip to El Salvador. "I believe the High Command of the Salvadoran armed forces is engaged in a conspiracy to obstruct justice in the Jesuits' case," the statement began. "Salvadoran military officers have withheld evidence, destroyed evidence, falsified evidence and repeatedly perjured themselves in testimony before the judge. I do not believe this could be done without at least the tacit consent of the High Command."[78]

For the Salvadoran army, which was already suffering under the strain of negotiations, this was a severe blow indeed. At the end of July a round of talks in San José, Costa Rica, had ended in a deadlock over a government proposal on the armed forces, but produced a two-part human rights accord "pulled out of a hat" by de Soto at the last minute.[79] Both sides agreed to take immediate measures to protect individual rights and gave their approval for the establishment of a U.N. mission to monitor and promote human rights within the country. In El Salvador congressional aides had found a good many of the people they met with in an official capacity considerably more wary since the publication of Moakley's April report. Colonel Ponce, who was expected to ascend to the post of minister of defense in September, had thought it, as he told the aides, "one of the best things he had ever seen, given that it was inspired by FMLN propaganda."[80] But beyond direct rejection of the report's conclusions was the realization that while the ongoing negotiations were damaging enough, military aid might be cut because of the actions of the High Command. The *tandona* had never lacked for critics among the officers in the years below them and there were plenty who thought the leadership they were being given on the Jesuit case brought with it too heavy a price for the institution to bear. People were beginning to talk, to each other, and—some—to the Moakley task force. Some of them knew things and some just said they did, but on August 11 two aides, Jim McGovern and Bill Woodward, had a meeting with a senior military source that they considered a breakthrough. Given the information provided by this source they believed to be "credible," the statement drafted for Moakley three days later was moderate indeed.[81]

Military "cooperation" was in the court record for all to see. The fact that the cadets on guard duty at the military academy had been posted abroad was widely commented on in the Salvadoran and U.S. press. When they were eventually made available to the judge it was discovered that, through an "involuntary error," they were the cadets who had been on duty on December 16 and not November 16. More than two months after Zamora had first sought to question them, the right cadets were brought forward to give their declarations. On guard duty, on November 16, they had all passed a peaceful night in the military academy: they didn't see anybody leave the academy, couldn't remember, didn't write anything down, or had been asleep throughout—a familiar litany. Considerable court time had also been dedicated to the missing logbooks. It emerged that all of the logbooks for 1989 had been burned in early December on the orders of then Major Camilo Hernández, Benavides's deputy in the military academy. The act itself had been carried out by the military academy lieutenant already charged for the murder of the Jesuits, Yussi Mendoza. He maintained that the burning of the sixty-odd books was standard practice since the academy had bought a computer in 1987. The civilian academy archivist testified otherwise and Camilo Hernández was charged with his part in the coverup.[82]

Some members of the army would prove less adept at lying than others. On August 24 two Atlacatl sergeants who had participated in the search of the UCA residence on November 13, the operation on the night of the November 15–16, and a reconstruction of the crime run by the SIU at the end of December, were brought before Judge Zamora. One of the sergeants, Molina Aguilar, denied any physical knowledge of the UCA and was so nervous he had to excuse himself to be sick. The other one, Solorzano Esquivel, had featured prominently in the defendants' extrajudicial testimonies. He too claimed never to have been to the UCA. When he was shown a series of photographs of himself within the UCA, taking part in the reconstruction, he was forced to admit that maybe the person in the photograph "did look a bit like him."[83] Zamora ordered that he should be detained for giving false testimony, but while the detention order was being written out, Solorzano fled from the court into an Atlacatl-manned car waiting outside with its engine running. The whole episode was recorded by television cameras, and an embarrassed sergeant was returned to the court a few days later.

All five military and the two civilian members of the Honor Commission had either submitted written testimony or given declarations before the judge, yet the sum total of what had been learned was remarkably little. There was still no adequate explanation of where the names of the nine men charged had come from, why the SIU's investigation had flagrantly ignored the obvious chain of command and had never, for example, questioned Camilo Hernández, the acting head of the military academy in Benavides's absence, or whose had been the idea to include the military academy's Lieutenant Yusshy Mendoza. Moakley concluded: "I believe that the High Command's goal, from the beginning, has been to control the investigation and to limit the number and rank of the officers who will be held responsible for the crimes."[84]

One of the most immediate results of Moakley's August 15 statement was an angry telephone call from Salvadoran Ambassador Miguel
Salaverría. He countered the accusations made by the chairman and
charged that their timing (two days before the fourth round of talks
between the Salvadoran government and the FMLN) was to the benefit of
the guerrillas. In El Salvador the two aides had relayed the contents of
their August 11 meeting to Ambassador Walker, prompting a flurry of
cables and renewed diplomatic pressure on the military. On August 20
Walker delivered a strong démarche to the High Command demanding
action on the Jesuit case (the third in six weeks presented by either himself
or his deputy, Jeff Dietrich) and then held a private meeting with Colonel
Ponce. The future minister of defense, Walker cabled to Washington,
assured him "he planned to make changes in the ESAF leadership and was
considering how best to handle the problem posed by the Jesuit case."
Earlier that day an unusual meeting had been held between the High
Command, President Cristiani, the president of the Salvadoran Supreme
Court, and Judge Zamora. Although Walker would report to Washington
that the meeting was "a PR effort, still essentially throwing words at the
problem," it was publicly represented as a commitment on the part of the
military to collaborate in Judge Zamora's investigation of the Jesuit
murders.[85]

A few weeks later Cristiani, president of the republic and commander in chief of the armed forces, laid aside the privileges that would
allow him to reply to the court's questions in writing and presented
himself, unannounced, before the judge. His personal involvement in the
case since January had not lived up to expectations: he had waited five
months before providing the court with the written report prepared for
him by the Honor Commission and until a press conference in July to
reveal publicly what he had told the U.S. Jesuits in February—that he had
authorized the search of the Jesuit residence, albeit two hours after it had
taken place. In the same press conference he had repeated unfounded
charges that that search had yielded a haul of guerrilla weapons from inside
the Jesuit residence.[86] Now, on September 7, nearly ten months after the
murder, he told the court that he had been inside the High Command
headquarters from 11:00 P.M. to 2:00 A.M. on November 15 to 16 during
the time of the operation against the Jesuits.

In the circumstances, there was nothing remarkable about Cristiani's
presence inside the High Command: he had been summoned in order to
authorize the use of tanks and heavy artillery in the north of the city.

Moreover his declaration to the judge set a good—if tardy—example to those colonels who shared with him the privilege of being able to choose how to respond to the court's inquiries. Out of the August 20 meeting came the possibility for the court to question the senior officers present at the meeting in the *estado mayor* on the evening of November 15. Over the following weeks, as Cristiani's attention turned to Washington and the upcoming vote in the Senate, five colonels—Vice-Minister of Defense Zepeda among them—followed the example set by Cristiani and put in unprecedented personal appearances. Others emulated the conspicuous absence of Ponce and replied to the court on paper.

By the time Cristiani visited Washington at the end of September, the tide was strongly against him. With the names of both Senators Dodd and Leahy on the proposed legislation, those pursuing a change in the policy toward El Salvador were in a position to overcome the traditional fracturing of the more liberal wing of the Senate that had, in the past, allowed for easy wins by conservatives. Cristiani was personally popular— "President Cristiani makes a good impression with his integrity" one Democratic senator would tell the *New York Times*[87]—but he could do little to sway the prevailing hostility to the Salvadoran military. The Jesuit case had caused even Republicans traditionally attentive to their wishes to undergo a reassessment of their views of El Salvador. Although in many cases this did not extend to a switch in voting, there was a new wariness in the air. The previous December, shortly after the Jesuits were killed, Colonel Zepeda had formed part of a Salvadoran delegation to Washington that had stated in no uncertain terms that the FMLN had been responsible for the killing of the Jesuits. It now appeared that he had not been merely wrong, but in all probability deliberately lying. After Moakley's August statement a Republican aide who had worked closely with the task force circulated a confidential memo that was seen by Republicans of both House and Senate. Its message had been that "Republicans might want to exercise extreme caution on this issue—when Moakley says the army is covering up, the army is covering up."[88]

Cristiani had occasion to see Moakley three times, yet all he had to offer on the Jesuit case was the suggestion that "noted jurists" from the United States should be asked to assist with the investigation. The idea was dismissed out of hand: a layer of legal overseers could do nothing to address the Salvadoran army's resistance to uncovering the truth. One of the three occasions was a private meeting in Moakley's office. Moakley took the opportunity to explain to Cristiani that the strength of his August statement was reinforced by a conviction he now had that the Jesuits' murder had been ordered by the High Command. Moreover the August 11 source had told his aides that he had taken his information to Cristiani himself. "I know who did it and you know who did it," he had said to Critiani. "So what are you going to do about it?" The president said not a word.[89]

IN the interest of ensuring that the task force's monitoring of the Jesuit case would remain wholly relevant to the development of U.S. policy toward El Salvador, Moakley had worked hard to keep the channels of communication with the State Department and U.S. embassy in El Salvador open. While the motives and competence of a number of his staff were questioned, the task force held the view that "Bill Walker is basically a decent guy." And this is why Moakley "went ballistic" when in mid-October it was brought to his attention that at one point during his January interrogations by the FBI, Major Eric Buckland had claimed to have prior knowledge of a plot to kill the Jesuits.[90]

On September 28, Buckland had testified before Judge Zamora in San Salvador. His declaration had followed months of debate amongst U.S. officials before a decision was reached to waive Buckland's diplomatic immunity. Appreciative of the exception being made, Zamora had allowed the declaration in rather unusual circumstances: for reasons of security Buckland spoke from within the home of an embassy official and then left the country that same day. Unusually for a mere witness, he was accompanied by *two* lawyers—one of them the Pentagon's Chief Counsel. It was understood, although the court was not told why, that no questions could be asked concerning anything that had happened after January 6, the day on which Buckland left El Salvador. In all other respects the judge found Buckland "a cooperative, plausible and relaxed" witness, who ratified everything he had said when he came forward in January with the information that Avilés had told him that Benavides was responsible for ordering the murder of the Jesuits.[91]

As soon as he was told of the possibility of Buckland's prior knowledge, Moakley had telephoned Bernie Aronson. During their February visit to El Salvador members of his task force had specifically asked the embassy whether Buckland had had prior knowledge of the Jesuits' murder. The answer they had received had been an unequivocal "No." "I'm pissed off," he had fumed on the telephone. "It has come to my attention that Buckland at one point said he had prior knowledge . . . I'm pissed off because I have been lied to and jerked around by the State Department. Does such a statement exist, yes or no?" "Let me look into it," had been the assistant secretary of state's reply.[92]

Moakley's information referred to affidavits signed by Buckland after interrogation by the FBI on his return to the United States in January 1990. One of them, he believed, related an incident that had happened some ten days before November 16, 1989, in which Buckland had become aware that Benavides was planning to kill the Jesuits. Moakley also understood that Buckland had recanted this information in a signed affidavit, but he believed it of the utmost importance that it should be provided to the Salvadoran court to assess for itself. But the State Department was holding out on him. Increasingly frustrated, he called again to demand access to Buckland's original affidavit, "I want to see it and I want the judge to have it immediately," he insisted. Moakley was told that the judge would get it on the following day, but it had not been decided whether he would be given access to the document. Inquiries of the judge in San Salvador were met with the answer "No," he had received nothing, and when a Justice Department official telephoned to say, "No, you cannot see it, Congressman," Moakley's patience snapped. On October 18, he released a statement berating the fact that "American officials withheld from Salvadoran authorities for more than ten months a statement that I believe is of obvious relevance to the investigation into the Jesuit murders."[93]

The embassy was full of excuses. In mid-September a junior officer had been preparing for Buckland's September 28 declaration in Chidester's absence when he stumbled across the January affidavits in the files. Realizing their importance he had taken them to Deputy Chief of Mission Jeff Dietrich, who at first "forgot" ever knowing anything about the prior knowledge claim, despite having been briefed by the FBI in January along with Walker, Chidester, and Colonel Menjívar. Aronson's office in the State Department had also been supplied with a summary of Buckland's statements on January 13. Signed affidavits—claiming prior knowledge on January 11, retracting it on January 18—together with a videotape shot of a Buckland interrogation on January 12 that amplified what he had said on the day before, had subsequently been provided to both the embassy and State Department. At the time, embassy officials would claim, they had been told by the FBI that Buckland was "not a credible witness" and instructed not to share the affidavits or video with anybody. To Moakley, however, the FBI denied such a characterization, maintaining they had sent a cable to the embassy, dated January 24, recommending that Buckland's statements should be investigated further. The embassy claimed never to have received the cable.

In late January or early February portions of the video were shown to President Cristiani who, perhaps surprisingly, did not recommend that it or the accompanying affidavits be presented to the judge. Believing their responsibilities to the Salvadoran president, if not to the Salvadoran justice system, thus completed, embassy officials consigned the whole issue of Buckland's claim of prior knowledge to "file and forget," and continued in their public criticisms of the failings of the Salvadoran justice system. According to Rick Chidester, however, his assistant's stumbling across those same files in mid-September had resurrected the whole issue. The embassy now felt that "not credible" was "perhaps an oversimplification" and that if they were "not absolutely certain that this was not true," then they should tell the Salvadorans. Chidester had been "just about" to write a cable to Washington recommending this course of action when the embassy had learned that Moakley was on to the whole business.[94] Documents declassified in November 1993, however, revealed that State and Defense Department concern that "Moakley may know about the tape" dated back to February 1990 and was considered "a potentially very serious problem." The ensuing coverup was intentional, with officials "confident" that the issue of prior knowledge would not come up in Buckland's September testimony and then forced into action by Moakley. "One important consideration in suppressing even false information," Walker cabled "Eyes Only" to Aronson on October 12, 1990, "is that it may surface from other sources. If it is clear that the information will likely surface, the embassy should anticipate leaks from other sources by sharing it with our GOES [Government of El Salvador] interlocutors, particularly Judge Zamora."[95]

At 1:30 P.M. on the afternoon of October 22, Judge Zamora received "a series of photocopies" including the affidavits of January 11 and 18.[96] They revealed that Buckland had declared that at some time at the end of October or early November 1989, he had accompanied Colonel Avilés on a visit he made to the military academy. The January 11 affidavit had been handwritten by FBI Agent Paul Cully and initialled by Buckland in six places. Avilés, Buckland had explained, had been sent by Ponce to "sort out a problem" with Benavides. Avilés appeared "very uncomfortable" and had explained to Buckland that Benavides had told him that "Ella

Coria [sic] was a problem." "Avilés told me they wanted to handle it in the old way by killing some of the priests," the affidavit had continued. "Avilés told me that Benavides was old school and was still the 'rammer.' "[97] The second affidavit described the same visit to the military academy, now dated at the end of October, but claimed no knowledge of what the two colonels' conversation might have been about. Any prior knowledge was categorically denied in precise and distant legal language very different from the rambling statements of the January 11 affidavit.[98] Buckland blamed his interrogator Cully for forcing him to believe that he must have had prior knowledge and "suppressed" it. But neither his references to how he had "broken down and cried" on several occasions during the interview, nor some of the details he recanted coincided with the three-page affidavit of January 11. It was obvious that the videotape, held back by the State Department and embassy, had more of the story to tell.

"They certainly unearthed things that we wished they hadn't unearthed." a State Department official would say of Moakley's role in uncovering the issue of Buckland's prior knowledge. "There was no question but that it wouldn't have come out otherwise."[99] FBI agents, asked confidentially by congressional aides whether, if they had been investigating the case, they would not have considered it important enough, retraction and all, to warrant immediate attention, had answered "absolutely." Despite all its protestations of commitment to the pursuit of truth in the Jesuit case, the U.S. government had implicated itself in the coverup.

MOAKLEY'S statement on the Buckland debacle was made the day before the Senate met to debate the Dodd-Leahy bill's proposal to cut military aid to El Salvador. The October 19 debate focussed on two amendments, the one a minor change introduced by Leahy himself including reference to the Geneva Accord in the new legislation and the other, sponsored by Senators Graham and McCain, proposing that the 50 percent cut be maintained with one extra—and colossal—"tripwire," as Dodd called it: the conditioning of the 50 percent to both sides' agreement to a cease-fire within sixty days.

The Graham-McCain amendment had been the basis of Cristiani's lobbying in September and was strongly backed by the State Department. As the vote approached, Assistant Secretary Aronson offered reassurance on the Jesuit case as he wrote in the *Washington Post* that "either justice will be done or military aid will be cut."[100] In a flurry of eleventh-hour lobbying, phone calls, and letters from Baker, his deputy, Lawrence Eagleberger, and Aronson rained down on senators thought still to be undecided. For many the Graham-McCain amendment must have appeared attractive: it proposed a cease-fire within two months. Who could vote against a cease-fire in El Salvador? Yet full of praise as it was for the negotiations, the amendment, as Dodd and Leahy pointed out in a "Dear Colleague" letter circulated to other senators, would quite clearly undermine the commitment to a two-stage process of negotiation made by the Salvadoran government and FMLN negotiators at their May meeting in Caracas.[101]

In the end the margins—74 to 24 in favor of Leahy's amendment and 39 to 58 against Graham-McCain—left the administration very little room to maneuver at the all-night conference session that followed. On November 5 a 50 percent cut in military aid was signed into United States law. The president would have to report to Congress on a complex series of conditions applicable to both sides in the conflict, but would retain the right to decide when and if they were infringed. The Salvadoran government would lose all the military aid if they left the negotiating table or negotiated in "bad faith," rejected the mediation of the United Nations, failed to conduct a "thorough and professional investigation into and prosecution of" those responsible for the UCA murders, or allowed for military violence against civilians. The cut 50 percent would be restored if the FMLN failed to comply with similar conditions in the negotiations, threatened the survival of the Salvadoran government with its military actions, continued to receive "significant" military assistance from outside El Salvador, or again, committed acts of violence against civilians.[102]

The year 1990 had been one of real change in U.S. policy toward El Salvador. For the first time Congress did more than offer outrage, pass toothless resolutions condemning atrocities, and throw up its metaphorical hands in horror at the plethora of problems besetting El Salvador. It passed legislation publicly committed to a process of negotiation. Despite the tens of thousands of civilian causalities claimed by Salvadoran conflict over the previous decade, this legislation had resulted from the murder of six Jesuits and two women in the depths of one November night. The act itself had shocked the world, but the shock would have receded had not, as Joe Moakley said in an address given on the anniversary of the murders, the investigation into that act "provided a litmus test of Salvadoran pretensions to democracy, to justice, and to any claim on U.S. aid."[103]

"You know what really bothers me?" he had remarked to the *New York Times* a few months earlier. "If some speaker had organized a task force when Archbishop Romero was killed to challenge the administration, the aid could have been cut a long time ago."[104]

Ignacio Ellacuría (second from front) arrives in San Salvador, March 22, 1949.

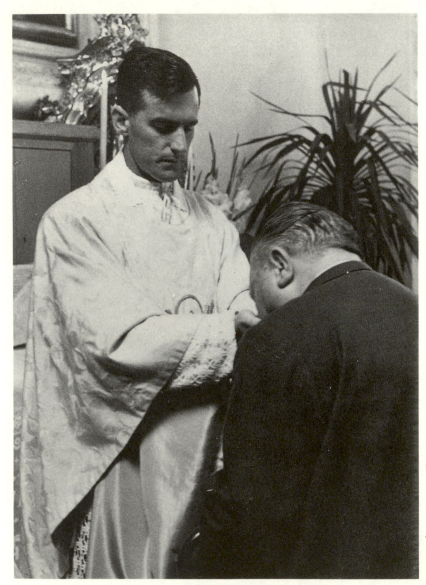

Ignacio Ellacuría's first mass. Innsbruck, September, 1961.

Ignacio Ellacuría,
Rector of the UCA

Ignacio Martín-Baró in the parish of Jayaque

Fifth Anniversary of the
death of Monsignor Romero,
March 24, 1985

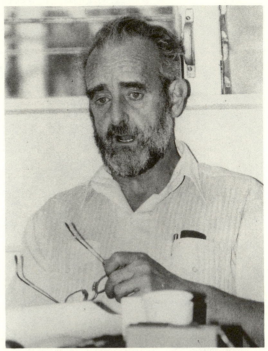

Segundo Montes

Ignacio Ellacuría with President Alfredo Cristiani, September 1989

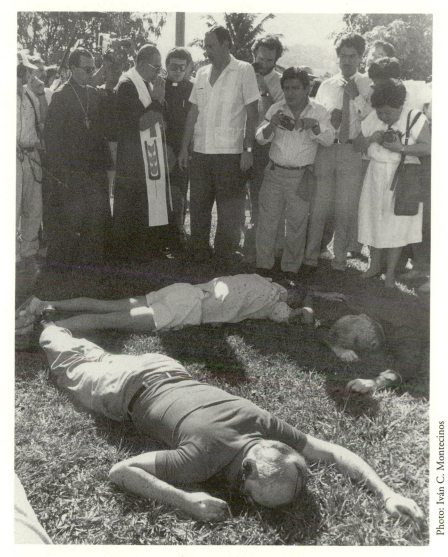

November 16, 1989. Jesuit Provincial Jose Maria Tojeira (center),
Archbishop Arturo Rivera Damas, Mons. Gregorio Rosa Chávez
(both left) and María Julia Hernández (far right)
survey the bodies of the murdered Jesuits

Photo: Iván C. Montecinos

November 16, 1989. Rogelio Pedraz with a portrait (left) of
Monsignor Romero in the ruins of the Pastoral Center

From top left: Gen. Juan Rafael Bustillo, Gen. René Emilio Ponce, Col. Francisco Elena Fuentes, Gen. Juan Orlando Zepeda

Plaza Cívica, San Salvador, January 16, 1992

Photo: Iván C. Montecinos

Obdulio Ramos in the rose garden at the UCA, March, 1994

CHAPTER SEVEN

A Utopian Rector

You served in the UCA, but not ultimately in the UCA. You served in the Church, but not ultimately the Church. You served in the Society of Jesus, but not ultimately the Society of Jesus. The more I came to know you, the more I came to be convinced that you served the poor of this country and of the entire third world and that this service is what gave an ultimate sense to your life. You were a faithful disciple of Zubiri, a theoretician of popular political movements, but you did not fight for these theories as if they were 'dogma.' No, rather you changed your points of view—you, so inflexible—and when you did it one thing alone was what made you change: the tragedy of the poor. And so I believe that if you did have any immoveable 'dogma' it was this, and this alone: the pain of the crucified peoples.[1]

Jon Sobrino to Ignacio Ellacuría, November 1990

IN 1986 Victor Codina, a theologian from the Catholic University in Bolivia who had known Ignacio Ellacuría on and off for twenty-five years, spent four months at the UCA in San Salvador. He later described the exhausting timetable followed by the university's rector:

> One day he was giving a conference in the UCA's Forum on National Reality on the participation of the government of El Salvador in the Iran-*contra* affair, on another he was lunching with the foreign ministers of the EEC; he was called to the U.S. embassy, received some Italian union leaders, or was interviewed by Austrian television. He traveled to Berlin for a scientific conference, to Madrid to speak about utopia and prophecy, to Córdoba to address the issue of liberation in the Abrahamic religions and to California to receive an honorary doctorate. Then he'd have a meeting with some of his colleagues to structure a dictionary on fundamental concepts of liberation theology. He was on television debating with Major D'Aubuisson, of the far right, or off for an interview with *Comandante* Joaquín Villalobos of the FMLN.[2]

All these activities had their origin in Ellacuría's dedication to the pursuit of a just peace in El Salvador, to doing, in an oft-repeated phrase, "everything possible within the realm of the possible."

"ELLACURÍA was a philosopher in the full sense of the word," wrote Antonio González, a student and philosophical disciple, "although per-

203

haps not in the usual sense."[3] A theologian too, Ellacuría could have dedicated himself to either or both and secured the reputation he enjoyed in the relatively enclosed circles of Spanish philosophers or Latin American theologians on a wider level. But his understanding of what it meant to be a philosopher and a theologian, an intellectual in El Salvador, relegated the pursuit of academic honors to a low priority.

Although Philip Berryman would write that Ellacuría "can be regarded as one of the founders and more important producers of liberation theology,"[4] he was the author of no book-length theological works. The two volumes of theology published during his lifetime were both collections of articles first published elsewhere.[5] At the time of his death only the first, and more abstruse, volume had been translated into English, and that was long since out of print. Like the handful of key articles on philosophy, published over the years in *ECA* and elsewhere, his theological work could appear buried in the midst of a vast bibliography of editorials, political analyses or theoretical essays on the role of the university, much of it bearing the mark of being written in hurried response to the events of the day. In the years of his first exile from El Salvador Ellacuría did write the greater part of a major philosophical treatise; on his return to El Salvador its content would be incorporated into the classes he taught, yet he never found time to finish it. González would edit a posthumous edition because this philosopher, "in the full sense of the word," had found better things to do with his time.[6]

Ellacuría was fond of quoting Plato's observation in *The Republic* that "until philosophers are kings, or the kings and princes of this world have the spirit and power of philosophy . . . cities will never have rest from their evils—no, nor the human race."[7] But it was in the figure of Socrates himself, that "inconvenient philosopher who paid with his life for the absolute necessity to philosophize," that Ellacuría found a model of what a philosopher should be. Socrates' identity as a philosopher was defined by his being a member of the *polis* of Athens in the fifth century B.C.: "He was a philosopher because he was a citizen, that is because he was political, because he was profoundly interested in the problems of his city, his state." His life and death set an example that all those who followed him in seeing a need for philosophy could only hope to emulate: "To want to know, to want to possess true knowledge about man and his city, about, in short, himself; to understand this knowledge as critical and operative; to do so with a desire for service, with detachment and liberty; to dedicate his life to this to the ultimate consequences . . . these are some of the characteristics of this man who was the critical conscience of his city."[8]

Deriving much of the structural and scientific basis of his thought from Zubiri, Ellacuría held that the object of philosophy was *la realidad histórica*, "historic reality." More than just "history," "historic reality" was understood to embrace all other types of reality—material, biological, personal, and social.[9] While Ellacuría's philosophical work is largely autonomous from a specifically Christian orientation, when considered as a whole his writing on the "historic reality," be it in strictly philosophical terms or in the analysis of events in El Salvador, is given a further dimension by an openness to the presence of God in history that is unsurprising in a philosopher who was also a priest. Necessarily political for its public and social nature, history can only be fully realized by this divine presence just as, as St. Augustine maintained, it was only by being more than man through the gift of God that man could be *fully* man.

In Ellacuría's profoundly theological political philosophy and profoundly philosophical political theology, the historic reality open to the presence of God is mediated by an understanding of intelligence that is truly Ignatian in its synthesis of contemplation in action. In 1975, in the keynote article of the edition of *ECA* that was dedicated to liberation theology and thought to have been the cause of the first of the bombs placed against the UCA, Ellacuría outlined his assessment of a "rightful conception of human intelligence" as he wrote of the philosophical basis of a proposed methodology of Latin American theology.[10] Insisting that "the formal structure of intelligence and its differentiating function . . . is not that of an understanding of being or of sense, but that of apprehending and confronting reality," Ellacuría elaborated a triple dimension to that confrontation. In a play of words that is wholly typical of his written or spoken discourse, and wholly untranslatable, Ellacuría distinguished between the need to *hacerse cargo de la realidad, cargar con la realidad,* and *encargarse de la realidad.*

The three phrases play on the noun *cargo,* in Spanish a physical load, a duty, burden, or accusation, and its related verbs *cargar* and *encargarse,* to develop distinctions in the different forms in which the human intelligence should apprehend reality if it is to be fully human in that apprehension. *Hacerse cargo de la realidad* is to acquire a profound knowledge of reality—a task for which Ellacuría's long years of formation had well prepared him. When used with the conjunction *con,* the verb *cargar* implies an assumption of responsibility indicating "the fundamentally ethical characteristic of intelligence, which has not been given to man so that he might evade his responsibilities, but rather that he might take on what things really are and what they demand of him." The final element of these interactive strands of intelligence is contained in *encargarse de la realidad*—an expression that brings the human intelligence from recognition of the ethical burden laid upon it by knowledge of reality, to an appreciation of what Ellacuría calls "the practical characteristic of intelligence, which only reaches its fulfillment, when it assumes for itself a real task."[11]

From the particulars of one or other reality it becomes the duty and task of the philosopher to produce a philosophy both of and for that reality, a philosophy that can only be measured by its effectiveness within it. From this position Ellacuría would argue from his lecture hall or office in El Salvador for the need for a philosophy that was truly Latin American, produced from the reality of Latin America and for the reality of Latin America. As such it should both join the successful production already present in other areas—literature, fine art, or theology, for example—and answer a real need for a philosophical contribution to the solution of the structural problems besetting the continent. Within his classes, Ellacuría would give himself as an example—in all his myriad activities—of what a philosopher should be in his commitment to what he termed "the Liberating Function of Philosophy."[12] Unrelentingly demanding of his students, Ellacuría drew on the critical and creative functions of philosophy to outline a philosophical vision that "without ceasing to be philosophy . . . could be really effective at the hour of bringing liberation not to a few educated elites, but to the totality of culture and the totality of social structures."[13]

The demands made by Ellacuría's view of intelligence and interpretation of reality are for a dialectic of theory and action, or *praxis*. Central to the contribution of philosophy to the historical process was its strength as a tool for the freeing of political discourse from ideological excess. The danger of ideology, in Ellacuría's opinion, was that it "confronts us with the nothing given the appearance of reality, with lies given the appearance of truth, and with the non-being given the appearance of being."[14] Here the firm scientific grounding of Zubirian thought, and the very great realism his scientific knowledge ensured, was of preeminent importance. Philosophy students in the UCA studied one branch of the natural sciences and would become used to being told "there can be no philosophy without science."[15] They were brought into contact with an enormous range of texts—where possible, in their original form, as Ellacuría had little time for commentaries—but encouraged never to succumb to the primacy of the text over the ability to think critically and creatively. And, most importantly, they were taught to relate and return their philosophical endeavors to the "historic reality" within which they lived.

The fulfillment of the demands for *praxis* is something that underpinned Ellacuría's life, from his calls for change within the Society of Jesus in the late 1960s to his increasing impact in and on the reality of El Salvador. A fully realized *praxis* of a fully human intelligence is what González found characteristic of his former teacher's intellectual labor: "not so much having put the historical *praxis* of liberation in the center of his philosophical reflections, as in having made of philosophy a constitutive element of an existence dedicated to liberation."[16]

"BEFORE all else they were human beings," Jon Sobrino would write of his murdered brothers, "Salvadorans, who tried to live honestly and responsibly in the midst of the tragedy and hope of El Salvador."[17] Their living honestly and responsibly led to such conflict that another of their Jesuit contemporaries, Juan Hernández Pico, would comment, "they could have joined the prophet Jeremiah in crying, 'A disaster for me, mother, that you bore me to be a man of strife and dissension for the whole country' (Jer. 15:10)."[18] Of none would it have been more true than of Ignacio Ellacuría. As a Jesuit, a theologian, a philosopher, and as rector of the UCA, Ellacuría lived, worked, and died within conflict. He responded to that conflict honestly and responsibly and with great personal valor. He was greatly admired and greatly reviled—even by some of his admirers— yet a man whom none could lightly dismiss.

Ellacuría placed great faith in what could be achieved by talking. In El Salvador the limitations and restrictions of the press and extreme polarization (never mind the exiled or clandestine status of so many of the major political actors) placed a consummate importance on direct personal contact as a means of gathering information and participating in political debate. Ensconced in San Salvador during periods in which many others were absent, Ellacuría's information was second to none. Three spiral-bound notebooks left among his papers document 273 meetings he held with leading figures of El Salvador's political life between 1984 and 1989.[19] Each entry is a meticulously structured record of what the respective politician, bishop, ambassador, FMLN *comandante,* leader of a popular organization, Salvadoran colonel or State Department official said and when and where he or she said it. As a whole the notebooks, even with Ellacuría's own part in each exchange unrecorded, are testament to a unique mediation within the unfolding history of the country.

Ellacuría would answer criticisms—and they were frequent—that he was a foreigner meddling in the internal affairs of El Salvador by reminding his critics that not only had he been the holder of Salvadoran nationality for many years, but that he had first arrived in the country as a boy of nineteen. By the late 1980s forty years of dedication to the people of El Salvador, twenty of them in the face of revolution and war, gave him, as it gave his generation of Jesuits, both the historical credibility and the moral authority necessary for their voices to be heard, if not always heeded. The position Ellacuría assumed, consistent with the "socratic existence" he recommended for philosophers, was one of "critical distance," colored by a realism that appreciated the difference between the understanding of the world and its ills by a philosopher—or university rector—and the transformation of that reality by its leaders. In this context a critical distance was "only the confirmation that not even the best of actions attain their own *telos* [end] all at once; it is probable that they get stuck or go off course long before they come close to it; political vanguards are not adequate to the needs of the people any more than political platforms are to the fullness of reality; still less is the need to maintain power able to avoid the practice of wrong."[20]

An intellectual impatience, accentuated by his authoritative manner and unwavering self-assurance, led to repeated charges of arrogance. Combative in his presentation of his ideas, Ellacuría was fully in command of an awesome dialectic, founded on an apparently implacable reason and a formidable intellectual armory sharpened by the tools of the sophists. While his opinions would change over time and he could admit to errors of the past, within an argument Ellacuría was virtually unassailable, as daunting an "adversary" within the UCA or in political discussion as he had been in the early 1970s in the battles for change within the Central American Jesuits. Other Jesuits would summarize the difficulties of trying to take him on with the phrase: "Ellacu conquers but he doesn't convince."[21] Yet the politicians, rebel leaders and diplomats who sought him out so regularly did so for an honesty, an ability to listen and a challenge to their own ideas which could not be found elsewhere. Above all, perhaps, he made them think.

The strength of Ellacuría's character and his own imperviousness to criticism both enforced his qualities as a leader and polarized the differences that the force of his leadership created. Yet he was emotionally reticent and gave himself with difficulty to intimacy. Although fellow Jesuits, close friends, and favored students found him infinitely generous and tender in advice or spiritual guidance at moments of crisis, they were aware that he covered himself with layers of protection, most evident in his obvious brilliance and ironic wit. Cerebral, cool and critical, Ellacu's guard rarely came down, but when it did it was to show the passion and commitment that lay beneath the rational constructions of his intellect and fueled his extraordinary capacity to keep on going, to live in El Salvador creatively, constructively, and with Christian hope.

César Jerez, one of those whose close relationship to Ellacuría stretched back to the 1950s, remembered how moved he had been by an incident in 1976. Jerez was in his first months as provincial when a Salvadoran Jesuit who subsequently left the Society expressed the opinions of many of those opposed to and alarmed by Ellacuría by warning him, "watch out for Ellacuría, because he'll get you into a whole lot of trouble, and when you're in the trouble, he'll up and off to Spain." Jerez, who had no doubts of Ellacuría's loyalty to the province and to Central America, told him what was being said about him, more for his own information than anything else. He had been expecting a light-hearted dismissal of the accusations and was surprised when Ellacuría put his hand on his shoulder and said, "*Gordito*"—using the affectionate diminutive of the nickname *Gordo* by which Jerez was known— "*Gordito,* the only thing I can say is that I am with you to the death."[22]

A younger Jesuit remembered with similar emotion the moment in the early seventies when he suddenly realized what lay behind the controlled exterior of Ellacuría. One of those whose formation was under Ellacuría's charge, Napoleón Alvarado enjoyed an almost filial relationship with Ellacuría (that included being taught to swim by him). Nevertheless he remembered a single moment as being what most impressed him in five years of study and in all the years that followed. Ellacuría was lecturing on the historical Jesus when, "something, in all the rational structure he used even for teaching theology, just went. . . . He was going along, saying that Jesus embodied justice and so forth, and that at the same time he embodied mercy, and had the eyes and heart of mercy to understand sin and to understand human beings, and he could do both things, and unite the dialectic of the two and so on . . . and then he just stopped. And his voice went very quiet, and then, overflowing with emotion, he said, 'because he was a great man.' And I thought, 'Ay, Ellacu!' "[23]

Few who were not close to Ellacuría, or who had not studied his theological writings, would cite "mercy" as a word that came to mind in a description of the rector of the UCA. He could "seem only head, only justice without mercy," one Jesuit put it. [24] And yet it was in Ellacuría's "mercy" that Sobrino found one of the sources of his friend's humanity. "Perhaps the most important thing I learned from him," he would acknowledge modestly, "as a human being, a Christian, and a Jesuit, was how to look at the reality of the third world through God, and how to act on this reality with the mercy—justice in structural language—of the heart of God."[25] Not outwardly given to expressions of faith, frequent masses and the like, and deeply involved in the secular life of his adopted country, Ellacuría's life's work, it is important to remember, was a university of Christian inspiration confronted by the tragedy of El Salvador. It was faith, understood from and for El Salvador and Latin America as a whole, that underlay Ellacuría's intellectual, ethical, and political relationship to his historical reality. Actions undertaken and positions assumed in consonance with that faith would provoke his death.

ALTHOUGH the philosophical structure of Ellacuría's thought is present in all of his work, he had long held that when it came to the concrete reality of Latin America, it was theology that was of more immediate use. While on a practical level this had to do with the deeply Christian character of the continent, intellectually the reason is to be found in what Ellacuría saw as a necessary relationship between the history of salvation and the salvation in and of history. This vast subject was concisely defined in the theme of his first collection of theological writings, *Freedom Made Flesh:* "salvation history is a salvation in history."[26] Ellacuría addressed himself to his theology prompted by "a real-life situation and a real-life necessity" and in response to an understanding of the historical nature of Jesus' life and death as essential to any understanding or practice of faith in the world. "Christianity must take seriously the thrust and import of the Word made flesh in history," he insisted. "God revealed himself in history, not directly but in a sign: humanity in history. There is no access to God except through this sign in history."[27]

The return to the words, deeds, and historical context of Jesus' life on earth is central to liberation theology. In the early 1970s—like the Brazilians Clodovis and Leonardo Boff and then Jon Sobrino a few years later—Ellacuría was consciously forging a "new Christology" that must give "the history of the flesh-and-blood Jesus its full weight as revelation."[28] Most startling in the clarity of its implications for the salvation of history is a short article, embracing much of what had gone before in *Freedom Made Flesh,* explaining "Why Jesus Died and Why They Killed Him."[29] Read "from below,"from the words and actions of Jesus' life, the Gospels present the life of Jesus as one of increasing opposition between him and those who will eventually cause his death. As an enemy of the power and social structures of his day, Jesus was persecuted and eventually captured, brought before Pontius Pilate, and condemned to death. Little imagination is needed to realize that Jews and Romans were "not confused" in killing Jesus: his annunciation of the Kingdom of God was clearly a direct and revolutionary threat to the established social order. Arguing that the redemptive qualities of that death cannot be isolated from its causes, Ellacuría concluded: "They killed Jesus for the life he lived and the mission he fulfilled . . . The history of salvation is never separate from salvation in history. It was not by chance that the life of Jesus was as it was; nor was it by chance that his life led him to the death it did. The struggle for the Kingdom of God necessarily supposes a struggle in favor of the unjustly oppressed; this struggle led him into confrontation with those responsible for that oppression. For this he died, and in this death he overcame them."[30]

The consequences, for the Christian living in history, of the demands exerted by the history of salvation are profound. Christian history takes place between the annunciation and realization of the Kingdom of God, but the Kingdom of God that Christ preaches was something grounded in his historical moment, with work for the Kingdom grounded in historical actions. The Kingdom of God, where truth and justice, peace and love reign supreme, may be unrealizable in history—liberation theology maintains—but it is announced within history so that Christians may work for a future that will be a closer approximation to the Kingdom than is their present existence. The struggle for freedom from the wrongs of the present toward the ideal held out by the Kingdom is the ongoing and active process of liberation. "Action in and on history, the salvation of social man in history is the real pathway where God will ultimately deify man," is how Ellacuría summarized it. "It is not just that salvation history entails salvation in history as a corollary. Rather the salvation of man in history is the one and only way in which salvation history can reach its culmination."[31]

A characteristic of the Kingdom of God is that it is *of* the poor and oppressed, *of* those who suffer persecution. In demanding an "option for the poor," liberation theology returns the poor to their central, privileged position in Christianity and returns to Christianity the poor as they are represented in the life and actions of Jesus. Over the centuries, accepted references to the importance of "poverty of the spirit" (as opposed to the poverty of the poor) had, for much of Christendom, dulled the radical edge of Jesus' message. The very existence of the poor of the third world, as recognized by liberation theology, precludes the lethargy of the past. Jesus' citation of Isaiah as he announces his mission gains a new and revolutionary strength when understood, as it is all over Latin America, in its most literal sense: "The spirit of the Lord is upon me, for he has anointed me to bring the good news to the poor. He has sent me to proclaim liberty to captives, sight to the blind, to let the oppressed go free, to proclaim a year of favor from the Lord" (Lk. 4:18). The established social order, like that of Jesus' own day, was right to be alarmed by what the "good news" brought to the poor by Christ and reinterpreted from and for Latin America might mean. "Yes it is socially dangerous," Ellacuría would say of liberation theology, "but one must ask for whom and what."[32]

The title of Ellacuría's second book of theological writings, *Conversion of the Church to the Kingdom of God: To Announce the Kingdom and to Realize It in History,* is long and unwieldy. It also embraces the major themes of his theological thought, founded as it is on the relationship between Christian faith, the Church, and history, with the Kingdom of God firmly implanted on the horizon. Essential to the Church's conversion to the Kingdom was its becoming a Church of the poor. Ellacuría held that the Beatitudes, the series of blessings given as part of the Sermon on the Mount in the Gospels of Matthew and Luke, occupied a central place in any understanding of what this Church of the poor must look like. In a careful analysis of the two versions he argued that the poor held to be "blessed"—and around whom the Church should be constructed—are especially "blessed" for actively overcoming the limitations imposed on them by their poverty in the construction of the Kingdom. These are the poor who have "hunger and thirst for justice," who are "merciful," "peacemakers," and "persecuted." These are the poor whom Ellacuría described as being "poor with spirit," *pobres con espíritu.*[33]

In order to be fully a Church of the poor, the Church must be what Ellacuría calls, in a rephrasing of Vatican II, "an *historic* sacrament of salvation." Obvious as its incarnation in history had been, this incarnation had been, over a period of centuries, one that had exposed the Church as an institution to the risks of secularization. In Latin America, as elsewhere, its institutional identity had at times represented and reflected worldly structures of injustice more akin to the prevailing "anti-Kingdom"—of lies, injustice, oppression, and death—than to the Kingdom of God. In this anti-Kingdom, or Kingdom of sin, as Ellacuría sometimes referred to it, idols hold sway, predominantly those of wealth and national security. As Sobrino has described them, these idols "claim to be the ultimate reality, self-justifying, untouchable, offering salvation to their worshippers even though they dehumanize them."[34]

In the developed world it is harder to talk of idols than in an El Salvador where Catholics murder priests and civil war is waged under the banner of "God, Union, and Liberty" and in the interest of the "national security" of the United States. But in that developed world, as Ellacuría would tell a Spanish audience in the mid-1980s, Christian faith itself had become "a conservative element, an element in support of the established order." Those who read the Gospel clearly, he continued, would find that the countries of the first world had transformed, "not water into wine, but wine into water."[35] Proposing a freedom from its own worldliness, Ellacuría argued consistently for a "re-turning," a "con-version" of all of the Church to the Kingdom: "The Church should have a center outside of itself, a horizon that lies beyond its institutional frontiers, in order to orientate its mission and even direct its structural configuration. And this center and this horizon cannot be other than those of the evangelization of Jesus: the Kingdom of God."[36]

THE poor themselves had long been present as the theological and political referent of Ellacuría's work. Their needs had been held up as the ultimate end of the university he and others struggled to create. Yet an undoubted change in his understanding of the denunciation and hope presented by the poor or "popular majorities" (to use the political rather than theological term) can be detected after the intensely lived years in which Monsignor Romero occupied the archdiocese of San Salvador. Monsignor Romero was the last of the five men to exert a major influence on Ellacuría's life, and in many ways the most surprising. That his years as archbishop coincided with the rise of the popular movement had immeasurable consequences for the entire country that were inevitably reflected in Ellacuría's thought.

Unlike other Jesuits of his community, whose university work was supplemented and lives and faith enriched by weekend visits to parishes and work with base communities or refugees, Ellacuría was not a man much given to direct and relaxed contact with the poorer communities of El Salvador. Over the years this lack of direct contact provoked bitter criticism of his being "out of touch" with the poor he spoke for. "Ellacu was something else," remembered one Jesuit with affection. "He was capable of winning any argument, of forcing you to accept that night was day. He'd tell you that in order to defend the struggle of the poor one didn't actually have to spend time *with* the poor. In his case it was probably so, but his was a very special case. The rest of us mortals are not like that."[37] "Your best argument now is your blood," another Jesuit would write with startling directness after his death. "Before, some of us didn't believe you much. We used to say that you spoke from within the UCA's air conditioning. Now you've got your hands dirty, you've humbled yourself like your master and emptied your strengths and the remains of your pride in the earth that's the same for all of us. Now your Father will hear your priestly prayer."[38]

In the first half of the seventies, as Ellacuría expressed reluctance to let some of his most promising young Jesuits complement their university studies with the practical experience offered by the parish in Aguilares, he had worried that their time could have been better spent in pursuit of academic excellence. For their part they had grumbled that the philosophy classes they attended at the UCA in the evenings were of little relevance to the needs of the people in Aguilares. Amid insistence that his students would, in time, come to see the point of their grounding in philosophy, Ellacuría's enthusiasm for their work in Aguilares grew rapidly as it became clear both what a "sign of conflict" it was presenting in the Salvadoran countryside, and how much the experience was contributing to the production of theology in the CRT. Yet he still doubted the political efficacy of *campesino* organizations such as FECCAS and questioned the speed with which they had emerged. But the widespread persecution of those years, and the UCA's active collaboration with the archdiocese in the development of the proper relationship for the Church with the popular organizations, particularly in the preparation of Romero's Third and Fourth Pastoral Letters, contributed to a profound change, and a profoundly human presence of the popular sectors in Ellacuría's subsequent writing.

Of all those who influenced Ellacuría, Romero was the one who most obviously had qualities that Ellacuría did not possess. Elizondo had been a defining presence in all the Jesuits of his generation. If Ellacuría often referred, over the years, to his more specific intellectual and human debts to Espinoza Pólit, to Rahner, and to Zubiri, these were men, *maestros,* in the humanities, theology, and philosophy, whom he felt open to and able to criticize, with respect and affection, but with his characteristic intellectual acuity. But Romero meant something else to him; his influence was not that of the great intellectual (and Ellacuría was not one to feel intellectually inferior to anyone), but that of what Sobrino would characterize as "an older brother in faith." With the sole exception of wondering whether Romero might not be "getting himself into trouble" by his decision to preside over the funeral mass for Neto Barrera, openly acknowledged by the FPL as one of their militants, Sobrino never heard Ellacuría offer any criticism of Romero at all.[39]

In Romero, the Jesuits saw not just a human being of great faith, but a human being who made present in this world an historic transcendence. He was fully realized as a man because there was in him something that was more than what he was as a man. "I believe that for them, and for me and so many others," Sobrino would write of the UCA Jesuits, "Archbishop Romero was a Christ for our time and, like Christ, a sacrament of God."[40] It is in his writing and public speeches on Romero, as well as his essays on the poor with eyes in some way opened by Romero, that Ellacuría's own faith, and with it even a humility, is most evident. Five years after Romero's death, as the UCA awarded Romero an honorary doctorate, Ellacuría would speak with immense tenderness, and immense gratitude, of the relationship between the university and the archbishop: "in all our collaborations there was no doubt of who was the master and who the assistant, of who was the pastor who laid out the directions to be followed and who was the executor of those directions, of who was the prophet who unraveled the mystery and who was the follower, of who was the animator and who the animated, of who was the voice and who the echo. . . . Completing his words that, 'with this people how easy it is to be a good shepherd,' one can say, 'with this shepherd, how easy it is to be people of God.' "[41]

Through the life, preaching, and martyrdom of Monsignor Romero, Ellacuría could write "of what the people of God must be and of what the Church must be if it wishes to be an effective sign of total salvation." In "The True People of God According to Monsignor Romero,"[42] he analyzed the gradual recognition by Romero and his Church that the people of God cannot be understood except from their own efforts to attain "their full historic dimension and their theological transcendence." As a basic element of the people of God, Ellacuría included among "the poor" the popular majorities living in inhuman conditions of poverty, exploitation, and oppression; the popular organizations; and all those who in some way identified with the just causes of the people and worked in their favor. The poor had thus two characteristics, the most important of them *being* the poor, the dispossessed, and the marginalized, but at the same time complementing this state—in the past perceived from the outside as being accepted with Christian resignation and the confidence of better things to come in the next world—with a contribution, as "poor with spirit," to its end through a process of liberation.

Romero was both an exemplary figure of the way to unite the interests of the people with the interests of God and one whose very grandeur and saintliness came from the people he led. Physically with the poor in the austerity of the small annex of the cancer hospital he chose to live in, Romero's relations with the people were founded on a great compassion for their sufferings. "Their sufferings grieved him," wrote Ellacuría, "their tortures and their deaths grieved him, the prolongation of their days of struggle and of persecution grieved him. And none of this was abstract for him, but all who suffered these things had their own names, their own faces." ("We are with you," Romero had told the people of Aguilares, and they had heard him.) Through the figure of Monsignor Romero, Ellacuría gave mercy, which responds more to people of flesh and blood than to members of a social class, a preeminent place as a necessary ingredient for struggles for liberation. As a quality, mercy may be present in all dimensions of human endeavor. "It is not against struggle, the passion for justice or even the use of violence"—any more than it is alien from the exercise of the intelligence—"what it does is make more human the justice, struggle, and violence." What it also does is inform the view, held by Romero and shared by the Jesuits of the UCA all their lives, that each and every political decision or action should be measured against the interests of the majority of the people and not the demands of ideology or political dogma.

Mercy understood in these terms suffused Ellacuría's understanding of "the crucified people." The phrase derives from the German theologian Jürgen Moltmann's work on *The Crucified God* and was used as the title of an article first published in 1978.[43] Ellacuría insisted that reference to the crucifixion purely through the mystery of "the cross" is overly abstract in its divorce of the act of crucifixion from its proper historical context. Instead he directed attention to Jesus as "the crucified one," with the use of the past participle implying that someone, or something, did the crucifying: the political, economic, and religious powers of the day. Christian faith in the universality of Christ in "the least of my brethren" equates the original act of crucifixion with all those through the centuries suffering a daily "crucifixion" in poverty and repression, torture, imprisonment, and death. Whether they be the Romans and pharisees of Jesus' own day, or the structure and individuals behind the slaughter in the third world today, those responsible for the crucifixion pertain to the very antithesis of the Kingdom of God preached and prefigured by Christ.

Since the meeting of Central American Jesuits in 1969, Ellacuría had encouraged his brothers to follow a crucified Jesus resurrected within the third world in Isaiah's suffering servant of Yahweh, disfigured and rejected by man yet chosen by God as a redemptive figure whose suffering was for the salvation of mankind. Use of the servant in the understanding of the death of Christ goes back to the early Christians. Ellacuría extended this to find in the servant "all those crucified unjustly by the sins of man," and in the crucified people of the historical moment in which his faith was grounded, incarnation of the servant and of the crucified Christ. "The crucified people thus have a double significance," he concluded toward the end of the article. "They are the victims of the sin of the world and at the same time the bearers of salvation to the world." The daily sufferings of the poor in a country such as El Salvador are therefore integral to the relationship between salvation history and the salvation of history.

St. Ignatius had determined that his Jesuits be "contemplatives in action." In light of the thirty-second General Congregation's call for "a service of faith and promotion of justice," Ellacuría rephrased the formula to express the need for Jesuits who were "contemplatives in action for justice."[44] It was a sense of urgency for the need for justice that lay behind his recasting of a Spiritual Exercise to frame in Ignatian terms the most fundamental endeavor of all those embarked on the struggle for Christian liberation. The Exercise calls for the practicant to meditate on his sins in the presence of the crucified Christ and ask himself three questions: "What have I done for Christ? What am I doing for Christ? and What should I be doing for Christ?" Ellacuría related these three questions to the third world and its crucified people to ask, What have we, as a world, done that all these people should be crucified? What are we doing about their daily crucifixions? and What can we do to bring the crucified people down from the cross?[45]

THE classic criticism of liberation theology, whether at the level of the Vatican's Congregation on the Doctrine of Faith or El Salvador's *Diario de Hoy,* has been that it is based on "concepts uncritically borrowed from marxist ideology."[46] And among the most common of the accusations leveled against Ellacuría was the charge that he was a Marxist. Never one to shy away from the relationship between contemporary Christianity and marxism in Latin America, Ellacuría readily dismissed the criticisms, not least because of his well-founded confidence that he knew what he was talking about while those who criticized him did not. "They can accuse me of being a communist," he would say to a Spanish interviewer during his exile in the early 1980s, "and I'm not one. They can accuse me of being a Marxist—I know Marx, as I know Hegel, Aristotle, or Zubiri. Yet I am not a Marxist. When they accuse me, I reply 'I am a Christian.' And a Christian is much more radical than any communist. Christianity understood in its purity is so radical that it is almost impracticable."[47]

Ellacuría held that the influence of Christianity on Marxism in Latin America was at least as strong as that of Marxism on Christianity. In such an overtly Christian continent, any revolutionary movement that maintained a dogmatic belief in the incompatibility of faith and revolution would be doomed to extinction. And nowhere had there been less room for this view than in El Salvador, where the greater part of the revolutionary masses were brought to the point of revolution from a clamor for justice awakened and encouraged by the changes in the role of the Church and demands of faith in their lives. "A committed Christian faith," Ellacuría pointed out, "not only did not brake the revolutionary movement, but actually impelled it forward. The living *praxis* overcame clear prejudices of theory."[48]

This was an issue that would recur in discussions Ellacuría held with various members of the FMLN at different stages of the war. In a meeting with senior members of the FPL in October 1985, for example, Ellacuría charged that the practical realities of the revolutionary movement were, when it came to its relationship with Christianity, in advance of some of its theory. On those practical realities, as the FPL's Gersón Martinez would stress in an interview in 1991, there was coincidence in the opinion that: "There could never be a Salvadoran revolution without the Christians. You cannot separate them. To build a guerilla movement, a movement for change, a revolutionary movement without counting on the Christians just is not possible."[49] But Ellacuría wanted more, encouraging the *comandantes* to be creative in a Latin American rereading of Marxism just as, in liberation theology, Christians reread the Christian tradition from the experience of Latin America. This rereading would open up their revolutionary theory to Christianity and supersede the Leninism that Ellacuría always considered to have very little place in a truly Latin American revolution.[50]

In 1988 the discussion would continue, this time with the ERP's leader Joaquín Villalobos. Villalobos told him how the *campesinos* of Morazán, attended since the beginning of the war by priests with whom they had experienced the revolutionary upheaval of the 1970s, rejected the atheism of classical Marxism. "The people are religious and need their faith," is how Ellacuría cited Villalobos in his notebook.[51] With the memory of the meeting still fresh in his mind he would elaborate on this, writing that Villalobos "maintains that Latin America is at the same time a continent that is profoundly Christian in its popular masses and profoundly revolutionary. The present moment of faith is the patrimony of Christianity as the moment of revolution is the patrimony of Marxism.

But they [the FMLN] try to combine the two in their respect for the people."[52]

Liberation theology and marxism were, for Ellacuría as for other theologians, neither interchangeable nor incapable of coexistence.[53] While the biblical poor to which liberation theology responded shared, for example, many characteristics with Marx's proletariat, they were not synonymous: they were poor imbued with Christian spirit and, as such, could never remain solely a social class. Denunciation of existing structures of injustice from apparently similar analyses, shared opposition to the capitalism and imperialism that lay behind these structures, and a common goal of liberation could not detract from the central—and tautologous—fact that liberation theology is, first and foremost, theology, with its horizon the Kingdom of God. The identification of an option for the poor with an option for revolution is therefore, quite simply, "not acceptable."[54] Inherently critical and anti-ideological in its comparison of the actual state of affairs with the Kingdom announced by Jesus, it was the task of liberation theology to offer to Marxism the same kind of criticism and orientation that the social doctrine of the Church had offered capitalism.[55]

The case of Nicaragua had been particularly interesting. While Ellacuría would praise the extent to which the presence of Sandinistas, Marxists, and Christians within the revolution had led to a Nicaraguan *perestroika* in the rethinking of Marxism and, especially, Leninism,[56] he criticized the Jesuits of Managua endlessly for being too supportive of the Sandinista government. "Liberation theology should never ally itself with power," he told a conference in Spain in 1987. "It should always be in opposition, even in countries like Nicaragua."[57] Ellacuría was, understandably, broadly in support of the Sandinistas. He had, in particular, been deeply moved on his arrival in Managua shortly after the triumph of the revolution in 1979 to find that the Sandinistas were exercising a degree of mercy in the pardoning of some of their Somocista captors and torturers. Yet he also believed that the Sandinistas should be publicly held to account for their failings in, for example, the handling of the economy or in the area of human rights. When the Jesuits of Nicaragua assured him that they had provided the Sandinistas with "critical support," Ellacuría was apt to grumble that it was "more support than criticism." His own idea of what "critical support" should be would be expressed in an *ECA* editorial written on the sixth anniversary of the Sandinistas' triumph. He observed that, even taking into account the intervention of the United States, the Sandinista revolution was "still very inferior" to its own ideals.[58]

César Jerez, rector of Managua's UCA since 1985, would take pains to explain the criticism that went on behind the scenes and the dilemma the Jesuits were presented by not wanting to supply ammunition for the constant barrage of criticism raining down on Managua from Washington. "I'd just like to see what you do," he was reduced to countering at one point, "on the day of triumph of the revolution in El Salvador." But Jerez would have been no more surprised than the FMLN themselves to find in Ellacuría, in that hypothetical future, an implacable—if constructive—critic.[59]

THE theoretical issues raised by the relationship between the popular struggles in Nicaragua and El Salvador were discussed in an article written by Ellacuría in 1987, "Liberation Theology and Socio-Historic Change in Latin America."[60] The argument was launched with the hypothesis that "liberation theology is not on its own sufficient to bring to the people an effective liberation and the [political] liberation movements are not sufficient on their own to give people an integral liberation."[61] Consequently the desire to make liberation theology effective within history leads to a variety of decisions, both for the individual Christian and in a correct assessment of the proper relationship for the Church with the social, political, and revolutionary organizations of the moment. Ellacuría offered three models for liberation theology's relationship to political and social organizations. Insisting that the proper approach for liberation theology was "realism"—and a realism of permanent discernment that held the greatest good for the popular majorities to be the ultimate arbiter of any political process—the preferred model was that of "social collaboration."[62]

Back in the 1970s, Ellacuría had responded with alacrity to the charges that the Church led by Monsignor Romero was "politicized": "If by politics one understands the incarnation of the gospel message in historical processes and the impulsion of the popular struggle in all that it undertakes justly, the Church in El Salvador has gotten involved in politics; if by politics one understands the denunciation of the oppressors and violators of the people, the calling of sin what is sin and grace what is grace, then the Church has interfered in politics." All these actions had been proper to a social force that had offered its services in "collaboration," without either dominating political forces or putting itself at their service. All these actions had brought persecution upon the Church, persecution for "the incarnation of heroically Christian virtues and, especially, for being with the poor and persecuted."[63] Such a Church had been an example of how the renunciation of a strictly political role had not led to a renunciation of an effectiveness based on a critical autonomy and expressed through "social pressure, the word and the gesture and not the wielding of power."[64]

The schematic division into "models" is one that to a certain extent masked Ellacuría's openness to the "humanizing" work of the Church even in the midst of the violence. An example of this is provided by Rogelio Poncele, a Belgian priest who arrived in El Salvador in 1970 to work in the parish of Zacamil on the outskirts of San Salvador. The parish was one whose movement—from the priests' pioneering work of "conscientization," through base communities to an explosion of organized protest—paralleled the experience of Aguilares. Targeted by the persecution of the late 1970s, Rogelio had been faced with a three-way decision: to stay in San Salvador and, in all likelihood, be killed, to abandon El Salvador and head into exile or to follow the members of his parish into hiding and minister to them in their revolutionary struggle. It is the "Priestly Presence with the Guerrillas" that emerged from the third option that Ellacuría wrote of in an introduction to a German edition of the book, *Death and Life in Morazán*, that is Rogelio's testimony, description, and justification of "a very precise *praxis* maintained over ten years."[65]

During the 1970s Ellacuría had spoken in Rogelio's community in Zacamil and, during moments of increasing political tension, loaned the parish of Zacamil space for a meeting at the UCA on the condition that its political content did not exclude or obscure its Christian orientation. He had been fully aware of the closing of the political space for Rogelio's ideal of nonviolent action and had no doubt of the Christian necessity to which he had been answering as he took to the hills. His introduction to Rogelio's testimony is full of respect for the discernment that led to Rogelio's decision and for the symbol he represents: a pastor who left everything behind to tend to his flock and a priest whose accompaniment has led him to undertake all the risks of armed conflict without himself ever carrying a weapon. More important in Rogelio's decision than the possible legitimacy given to armed insurrection by Pope Paul VI or Medellín (as justified in exceptional circumstances) had been "the necessity of accompanying some Christians whom the sociopolitical context and their Christian vocation had brought to risk their lives for others."[66]

Ellacuría was still being accused of advocating violence—even in the *New York Times*—well after his death.[67] Yet his position on violence and the one he advocated for liberation theology was characteristically both critical and realistic. Its clearest explanation was in an article, "Nonviolent Work for Peace and Liberating Violence," published in the magazine *Concilium*.[68] "If by violence one understands the unjust use of force, violence is always unacceptable," Ellacuría stated at the outset. "If by violence one understands no more than the use of force, then at least one would have to affirm that there are some violences worse than others—and with that statement we enter fully into the theory of the lesser evil."[69] In common with other liberation theologians, Ellacuría insisted that liberation theology could not be considered to advocate violence, not least because one of its fundamental goals was to liberate *from* violence. The principal violence denounced by liberation theology, however, the structural violence underlying the injustice of the third world, was one that engendered other violences that could in turn lead to a reluctant and pained endorsement of a liberating violence as the "lesser evil." El Salvador was a case in point: popular protest against the injustices of its society had been met with a repressive violence that had closed all forms of expression or protest other than that of revolutionary violence.

Ellacuría was much criticized by the FMLN for what was seen as the undue haste with which he qualified his support of their armed struggle. Yet he held that support for violence, even when it is as a last resort, must have possibilities of success as the basis for its justification: "Being in itself an evil, its exercise can only be justified if it will achieve either a good or the lessening of that evil."[70] On this principle had been founded the conviction with which Ellacuría first called for negotiation in the Salvadoran conflict in 1981, his incessant demands for its peaceful resolution throughout the decade, his arguments for the need of a "third force" between the two extremes to pressure for peace, and his condemnation of the United States' backing of a military solution that only served to raise the level of the violence suffered by the Salvadoran people. Before, during, and after the rare moments in which it can be justified, violence in its direct negation of the original gift of God to man—life—is a negation of God in his relation to man. "When *Radio Venceremos* and COPREFA announce the number of deaths each side have caused"—Ellacuría used to say of the FMLN radio and army press office—"they should be doing so in tears and not in triumph."[71]

"NO historical process can fulfill the utopia of the Kingdom of God on earth," Ellacuría declared categorically. "Nothing realized in history can attain the ideal that the Kingdom of God demands for men and for peoples. Yet the full announcement of the Kingdom serves to indicate limits and to animate struggles; it serves above all, to contribute specific directions and values that purely terrestrial processes cannot supply."[72]

The struggle for liberation, whether understood in a Christian sense or not, is necessarily utopian. In Latin America, as elsewhere, revolutionary movements and upheaval within the Church revived, and perhaps rescued, the term "utopia" from the degeneration into which it had fallen. Far from the vision outlined by Thomas More, "utopian" had become a pejorative adjective to be applied to a vision unrealizable in history and easily dismissed for its illusory nature. In a discussion of utopia's relationship to faith and political action, Gustavo Gutiérrez restored to the term the quality of being "subversive to and a driving force in history," meaningless except in its "relationship to present historical reality."[73] More's Utopia was only "Noplace" to the extent that it was a negation of Tudor England; the vision it held out cannot be understood in a vacuum. More's Utopia might seem today less than "utopian" in its organization of society—with capital punishment for repeated adultery, for example—but More's work was produced from and for his own time. None of its elegance or wit can disguise the denunciation in which the vision of Utopia is rooted. The point is clearly made by More through his fictional narrator Raphael: "Now, will anyone venture to compare these fair arrangements of Utopia with the so-called justice of other countries?—in which I am damned if I can see the slightest trace of justice or fairness. For what sort of justice do you call this?"[74]

Gutiérrez's analysis had followed that of Paulo Freire in seeing utopia as both a denunciation of the wrongs of the existing order and an annunciation of a new and better order to be attained in the future.[75] Between the two was the time for historical *praxis,* within which "authentic utopian thought" must be verified as it "postulates, enriches and supplies new goals for political action." Its beginning in denunciation is one that confirms its rational nature and informs Gutiérrez's conclusion that "Utopia leads to an authentic and scientific knowledge of reality and to a *praxis* which transforms what exists."[76] Writing some twenty years later—and twenty years that had tested to the limit the strengths and limitations of utopian thought and action—in his last published theological work Ellacuría would redefine the relationship between denunciation and annunciation in terms specifically relevant to the historical context of Latin America. In doing so he established the "privileged position" of Latin America as a place for "prophecy as a method and utopia as an horizon." While taking pains to point out how far from being satisfied is the continent's potential for the liberation that is a synthesis of the two, the article, "Utopia and Prophecy from Latin America," provides a theological framework for much of Ellacuría's own life.[77]

For Ellacuría, prophecy and utopia by definition sustain a dialectical relationship. A Christian utopia, understood as a "permanent process of approximation," could only be constructed from a prophecy that was "the critical contrasting of the annunciation of the fullness of the Kingdom of God with a determined historical situation." Both prophecy and utopia respond to this historical situation and need to remain with their feet firmly planted within it if they are not to lose their force. What is denounced by the prophecy is precisely that which makes necessary the utopia. Prophecy impels the force of history that the utopia attracts and ensures that the utopia does not become an evasion of reality. There is nothing abstract or elusive about Ellacuría's understanding of these concepts. They are grounded in the historic reality of Latin America, with the beginning of all utopian *praxis* in the prophetic denunciation of a continent that had come to assume the characteristics of Yahweh's servant: "It is a region maltreated since the armed Conquest made by Spanish Christendom, a region that, without losing its human heart, has a face that is disfigured and hardly recognizable as human if it is not in what it holds of pain and tragedy."[78]

Beyond Latin America, the condition of "the servant" is shared with all the other regions of the third world, whose very existence, as Ellacuría had pointed out to his brother Jesuits all those years ago in 1969, is a denunciation of the supposed "world order" that maintains it. Yet even within the developed world, this "order" cannot be considered as a desired utopia. It is enough to look at the increasing distances between the rich and poor within the countries of the first world and the dehumanization of those who live for the accumulation of wealth and power to realize that they fall far short of anything approaching an ideal. From El Salvador, and a belief that capital itself represents the first and greatest of the idols of the anti-Kingdom, the ascetic Ellacuría finds little to be envied in a "lifestyle governed by fear and insecurity, by interior emptiness and the need to dominate in order not to be dominated, by the urgency to exhibit what one has, no longer able to communicate what one is."[79]

Considered on an international level, the "civilization of capital," as Ellacuría dubs it, is only worse, not only because of the progressive exploitation represented by something like the Latin American debt crisis and the burden its servicing places on the poor, but also, and most importantly, because the capitalist system offered as a model for "humanization and freedom" by a country such as the United States is neither economically nor ecologically sustainable at a universal level. And being, in good Kantian terms, even potentially unrealizable for all humankind it is, in itself, less than human, even for those who propose it. "From my point of view," Ellacuría told an audience gathered to hear him talk on the fifth centenary of the "Discovery or Conquest" of Latin America, "the United States is much worse off than Latin America. The United States has a solution, but in my opinion it is a bad solution both for them and for the world in general. In Latin America, on the other hand, there are no solutions, only problems; but, painful as this may be, it is better to have problems than to have the wrong solution for the future of history."[80]

If Latin America is paradoxically privileged in the clarity of the prophetic denunciation it offers, it is also privileged in its potential for affirmations of utopia, whether expressed through revolutionary or Christian movements. In both political and Christian terms these utopias have been fueled by the very patent contrast between the natural wealth of resources the "new world" has always offered and the actual state of poverty in which the majority of its people live. For the Christians, whether revolutionary or not, who make up the vast majority of the continent's population, "the No of prophecy . . . generates the Yes of utopia in virtue of the promise that it is the Kingdom of God already present among men in the life, death and resurrection of Jesus."[81] Among these people progress toward the vision of utopia is fueled by hope, given a new primacy within liberation theology because of its openness to the God of the future even in circumstances of injustice and repression that are truly "against all hope." "Beyond all rhetoric and in spite of all difficulties the continent flows with rivers of hope," Ellacuría remarked with the wonder of one who, like so many others, found his own hope fueled by that of the "poor with spirit." In these people, their hope both a grace and something that can grow through the process of liberation or from the presence and inspiration of a prophet such as Monsignor Romero, Ellacuría finds "a real and valid sign that there are in the world tasks full of sense and significance."[82]

In response to his own denunciation of the international world order, Ellacuría outlines a Christian utopia he describes as a "historicized ideal"; not intended as a realizable future, but as a "focus of attraction" in opposition to the United States—the dominant "attraction" presented to millions of Latin Americans eager for emigration to or emulation of the superpower to the north. In place of the "civilization of capital and wealth"—in Ellacuría's view neither a valid response to reality nor Christian—he proposes "a civilization of work and of poverty." Such a civilization would be founded in what he calls "materialist humanism." In its Christian inspiration it would reject the accumulation of capital as the moving force of history and the possession of wealth as a principal of humanization and replace them with the dignity of work—with the perfection of man rather than the production of capital as its goal—its moving force; the universal satisfaction of basic needs its principle of development; and a shared solidarity its foundation for humanization.

Ellacuría cited Pope John Paul II's encyclical On Social Concern, *Sollicitudo Rei Socialis,* to denounce the "tendency toward imperialism" evident in both great power blocks engaged in the East-West struggle.[83] Ellacuría's utopia clearly draws on the economic and social ideal held out by socialism, yet the "necessary revolution" that he proposes, with its accent on the social rather than the political, and a priority given to the people of God rather than institutional structures, is markedly different. Held as a vision on the horizon, his utopia is seen as providing a "permanent opening" for all those advancing through history. Although the liberty of the "new" and promised land may still be distant—and will in all likelihood remain so—that liberty is one which can only be sought through concrete achievements in a process of liberation. It is the task of the "new man," historically realizable through active protest and constant struggle and the very center of an utopia based on humanization, to give all that he has to liberation. In words that echo Monsignor Romero's description of his last retreat and that have struck readers as presenting a synthesis of Ellacuría's own life, the "new man" is described as one for whom "the spirit breathes in many ways, supreme among them being the disposition to give one's life for others, whether by tireless daily commitment or by the sacrifice of a violent death."[84]

TWENTY years before writing these words, Ellacuría had proposed a renewal of the Central American Jesuit vice-province through "effective action in the third world." The call for action, shared by so many throughout the Latin American Church in the 1960s and 1970s, was one that rose from the problems besetting the continent. Even then the utopian strain had been qualified by a call for its "effectiveness" *(eficacia)* in what two of his students would describe as Ellacuría's "idea of history as a process of realizing possibilities *(posibilitación).* '[85] "Ellacu was a man who was convinced that there must be effective solutions within history," Sobrino would remember. "If they were not effective, they were not solutions." "Intentions and proposals are worth little in history," Ellacuría wrote in 1978. "The truth of what is intended and proposed is in the results obtained, the historical works."[86]

Articles of political analysis in *ECA,* as much as the theological and philosophical work they complement, all pay tribute to a realism that insisted on this tension between the utopia on the horizon and the *eficacia* of the means to get there. Its clearest expression, however, was in the most durable of Ellacuría's and the Salvadoran Jesuits' "historical works": the UCA itself. From a belief that within history the "permanent process of approximation" to the Kingdom of God demanded real—and realizable—solutions to real problems, came the conviction that the effectiveness could best be achieved by the harnessing of an institution that could obtain an authority and a voice within the society it was trying to change. The UCA could be the "critical conscience of the national reality" because, as a university, it had an autonomy, an audience, and a social weight. Yet its very nature as a university would force it to confront, in a body of theoretical work developed over the years and in practice, the Christian dilemma that Ellacuría had presented his fellow Jesuits as a challenge back in 1969: how to live in the world without necessarily being part of it.

The tension was only complicated by the tremendous force of Ellacuría's own character, inevitably accentuated by the platform the university gave him. During the 1980s, as the extraordinary circumstances of the war raised him, as the UCA's rector, to national and international prominence, his strengths and defects heightened and were reflected in the contradictions of the university he led. His critics would charge that he put his own influence and that of the UCA before the interests of the Salvadoran society as a whole. He would counter that from a position of critical distance he was not looking for "power" but "effectiveness": it was, he claimed, to this end that he sought access to the U.S. ambassador, rather than some junior political officer, an FMLN *comandante* rather than his messenger, and, when conditions allowed it, the president of the republic himself. More important than the question of influence (whose existence no argument of Ellacuría's could deny) was that of for whom or what that influence was exercised.

Within the Central American Province, the same tension lay behind a long-running discussion between the two distinct centers of the most progressive and intellectually powerful of the Jesuits: the San Salvador UCA and the more mobile team of Jesuits working within the Center of Social Investigation and Action (CIAS). The two had been founded in the same year—1965—and had been led, over the years, by Jesuits key to the transformation of the province in the early 1970s and the incarnation of its mission from then on. While the Jesuits of each remained respectful of the others' abilities and Christian commitment to the struggle for justice for the people of Central America—and in many cases true "companions of Jesus" in friendships that stretched back to the novitiate in Santa Tecla—over the years the differences between them had been not inconsiderable.

Formed by a highly qualified and cohesive group of social scientists, the CIAS had first been based in a community in Guatemala. From there its sociologists, anthropologists, and economists had embarked on a process of accompaniment of the Guatemalan people and their organizations, many of them indigenous, in the spirit of "critical support" they would bring to Nicaragua when forced to abandon Guatemala by the genocide of the early 1980s. César Jerez remembered how, right from the beginning of this experiment, Ellacuría had criticized them for not believing in institutions. But it had been a criticism tempered by the admission, "listen, what you want to do is more Christian, but what I want to do is more effective." Jerez had laughed and asked him what he meant. "The testimony of poverty given by your community—" he had explained, "the living in a poor neighborhood and the working in the countryside and all that you want to do—that is more Christian. But over the long run, what we want to do with the UCA will be more effective."[87]

Criticisms of the UCA's ability to combine its institutional place in society with its prophetic denunciation, its effectiveness with its utopian vision, were silenced by the starkness of the truth that it was in fulfillment of their mission, the synthesis of their prophecy and their utopia, that Ellacuría and his "companions of Jesus" were killed. Ricardo Falla, one of the most influential of the CIAS Jesuits, would write of the light thrown upon the life of "Ellacu" by the darkness of his death in a "Prayer to Ignacio Ellacuría":

They left you face down, Ellacu. Are you despairing? Will you look no more at the November stars? You were, in truth, utopian. Your thoughts were of a 'third force,' you wanted negotiation, you tried too hard to be a mediator, you looked for peace in this storm of hatred. From the university you wanted to open up a new path, and for this you listened to politicians of every shade, you scrutinized ambassadors, you traveled to distant meetings. You were, in truth, utopian, but a utopian who never crossed his arms. We see you now, face down. Did you despair? Did you throw in the towel? We are beginning to understand that the 'third force' was not a third way, that negotiation was not prevarication, that criticism of revolutionaries was not an obstacle to liberation, that your talking to the president was not betrayal of the poor. Now the utopia you did not reach is beginning to light up our way.[88]

CHAPTER EIGHT

THE UCA IN A TIME OF WAR

A Christian university must take into account the gospel preference for the poor. This does not mean that only the poor study at the university; it does not mean that the university should abdicate its mission of academic excellence—excellence needed in order to solve complex social problems. It does mean that the university should be present intellectually where it is needed: to provide science for those who have no science; to provide skills for the unskilled; to be a voice for those who have no voice; to give intellectual support for those who do not possess the academic qualifications to promote and legitimate their rights.[1]

Ignacio Ellacuría, 1982

THERE is an understandable note of pride in the documents and speeches with which, in 1985, the UCA celebrated the first twenty years of its existence. Yet the pride in those years was presented as something dynamic, a pride directly challenged by the depth of the crisis undermining every area of life in El Salvador. The anniversary, Ellacuría told the assembled university community, was therefore "an exceptionally auspicious occasion on which to reestablish what has to be done as we look to the future."[2]

Ten years earlier Ellacuría had asked, "Is a different kind of university possible?"[3] The question had come at a moment of great hope and great change for the UCA: the tenth anniversary celebrations were the culmination of the long struggle for power that brought Román Mayorga to the rectory and the UCAII Jesuits, led by Ellacuría, into a majority position on the UCA board of directors. If the first five years of the UCA's existence had been necessary to establish its institutional identity and to begin the shift away from "development" and toward "liberation" expressed in the 1970 IADB speech, the intense debates of the second five years had led to the formation of an infrastructure within which the university's principles could begin to be realized. Yet despite the body of theoretical work produced by Ellacuría, Mayorga, Martín-Baró, and others and a number of isolated achievements (such as the publishing of *Año Político*), at the beginning of Mayorga's rectorate what the university actually *was* was still very far from what it should be.

Somewhere between effectiveness and utopia, Ellacuría's idea of a "different kind of university" was one that—like his philosophy and theology—had to be measured "from the criterion of its impact on the historic reality within which it exists and which it serves." The demands of the reality of El Salvador on the UCA were, as Ellacuría held the demands of reality always to be, both ethical and practical. They were also, obviously, political, and it was here that he saw the definition of difference as being most important: "the distinct character of the university will not be in fulfilling its political mission, but in fulfilling it in a different way."[4] Universities in Latin America, and Catholic universities not least among them, had tended to one or other of two models of "political" identity that were consistently rejected by the UCA. If not contributing to the strengthening of the existing system through a professed apoliticism that, nevertheless, frequented the world of economic, political or ecclesiastic power, universities, particularly in the late 1960s and early 1970s, had become overrun by a militant left holding as its principal objective the gaining of power for itself.

The UCA derived its strength and autonomy relative to any external authority from the "Christian inspiration" upon which it had been founded. While commonly referred to as the "Catholic University," the UCA always rejected absorption into a formal Church hierarchy. Within the university, as Ellacuría insisted repeatedly and Sobrino made explicit in a speech given in 1987, "Christianity" could no more be measured by these formal relations than it could by insistence on religious education of its students or religious practice by its staff. These elements had little relevance to the Jesuits' understanding of a Christian university as "one which puts itself at the service of the Kingdom of God from an option for the poor."[5] As the university grew to maturity in the second half of the 1970s and early 1980s, so it became, in theory and practice, a different kind of Christian university, comparable to that outlined by John Newman in the nineteenth century in the consciousness and coherence of its mission, but wholly different in the specific conditions within which it functioned.

In both political and Christian terms, the UCA directed itself toward the "national reality" of El Salvador. This was the reality the university had to know in all its profundity and respond to with its full weight and influence. From within a reality as polarized as that of El Salvador there could be no doubt where a university of Christian inspiration should stand. "People tend to say a university should be impartial," Ellacuría would tell an audience in Barcelona just ten days before his death, "but we think not. A university should try to be free and objective, but objectivity and freedom can demand one to be partial. And we are freely in favor of the popular majorities because they are unjustly oppressed and because in them, negatively and positively, is the truth of our reality."[6]

In the first ten years of its existence, internal divisions had combined with structural problems to prevent the UCA's conversion to the "different" kind of university Mayorga, his board of directors, and a majority of the members of the UCA's Upper Council were pursuing in 1975. As the political and economic situation of the country deteriorated, the UCA had evolved against a background of economic dependence on sources that could be shut off at will. Social and political resistance to change in the university was exacerbated by the perception by some that the Jesuits had "betrayed" their former allegiance to the country's elite. Paradoxically the UCA also had an image problem among those to whose interests it was ostensibly directed: it was perceived as a "private" and therefore lucrative institution, its students were members of the upper echelons of Salvadoran society, and its campus and physical structure were, in Ellacuría's words, "proper to a bourgeois mentality at the service of bourgeois mentalities."[7] The UCA had not resolved its Catch-22: how to provide the professionals and technicians necessary to elevate the country from underdevelopment without deepening the marginalization of the poor, unskilled majority. In the second decade of its life, the UCA and its commitment to real change would be tested to their limits by the terrible demands of historical circumstances still unimaginable in 1975.

THE abrupt halt to the UCA's relationship with Molina and state power brought about by the president's about-face on Agrarian Transformation in 1976 was a watershed for the entire institution. As the murder of Rutilio Grande in 1977 was followed by widespread persecution of the Church and mounting violence, the relatively abstract theories and ideals of the UCA came under new scrutiny. A second loan from the IADB involved consultations throughout the university in order to structure future developments around the UCA's desired impact in and on the country. A document finally presented to the UCA community by the board of directors in May 1979 was the result of more than five months of discussions. The identity, function, and workings of the UCA were carefully laid out in a blueprint of the "different" kind of university now in the process of realization.

"The UCA tries to be an answer, as an institution and a university, to the historic reality of the country, considered from an ethical perspective to be an unjust and irrational reality that must be changed," the document began. "As such, it has one end in sight: the contribution to social change within the country. This it undertakes in a way that befits a university and in a way that is typified by its Christian inspiration."[8] The three elements of the UCA's identity—for social change, as a university, and with Christian inspiration—were mutual both in their support and in their tension. If social change was to determine the manner in which the UCA must be a university, it was its existence as a university that defined its activity in pursuit of that change. The Christian inspiration both underlined the need to seek social change—in a permanent approximation to the Kingdom of God—and invited the university to work from the perspective of Christian values toward a more humane configuration of society. Only when the three were evenly balanced could a "different" kind of university be possible. Such a university would be an institution of undeniable power in Salvadoran society—a power founded on knowledge and communication of the truth of the national reality—yet a power given credibility by its effectiveness in serving interests beyond those of the university itself. "The UCA is not *for* itself or its members," the document stated. "It is an institution for the Salvadoran people, and they should be the center and ultimate end of its activity."[9]

Since 1970, the UCA had described itself as the "critical and creative conscience of the Salvadoran reality," understanding "conscience" both as a moral watchdog and to mean *"con-sciencia,"* "with" a scientific knowledge of that same reality. In the fulfillment of its mission in El Salvador the UCA developed a concept of three functions: "social projection,"[10] research, and teaching. While the three were connected, with teaching the foundation for the UCA's existence and research the guarantor of the scientific rigor of the other two functions, it was the social projection that formed, shaped, and gave sense to the teaching and research as the ultimate arbiter of the UCA's impact in El Salvador. The fusion of the three branches of the university's activity were seen as the result of the rational, ethical, and Christian responsibility of *being* a university *in* El Salvador. It was, quite simply, not possible to live in a situation as desperate as that of El Salvador without wishing to change it. The research and projection of the truth had to be a fundamental task of a Christian university committed to social change, but would always be a task laden with risks the UCA fully assumed. Nobody expected a president to be pleased to be told he is the illegitimate holder of power; a governing Junta to welcome the news that it is murderously repressive; a foreign superpower to agree that it is misguided, interventionist, and war-mongering.

Most radical of its departures from the accepted image of an university was the UCA's position that teaching was "the most necessary element" of the university's life, but "not the most important."[11] A shift toward a university committed to liberation implied a shift away from the insistence on education for development toward a liberating education, that, while not belittling the country's need for skilled technicians, did not hold that the responsibilities of a university stopped at the classroom door any more than the responsibilities of one possessing a university education stopped with the receipt of a degree or diploma. Rather than forego academic exigence by adopting an "open door" policy toward student admissions, the UCA's attitude to its students sprang from a recognition that—even with a means-adjusted sliding scale of admission fees—only the elite 1 percent of the Salvadoran population could obtain access to a university education. What was important in the pursuit of social change was not where the students came from, but where they were heading when they left.

It was only half in jest that Ellacuría would refer to the students of the UCA as the "lesser evil." The vast majority of them studied at the university for the same reasons students from middle and upper class homes attend universities all over the world—be they social or professional—and were largely oblivious to the wider preoccupations of the university and those who ran it. In itself, this was and remains a tribute to the respect due the UCA as a "center of excellence" even for those to whom many of its public statements are anathema. The document distributed to the UCA community in 1979 made no attempt to disguise that the desired "impact" of the UCA on the transformation of the country would be "less immediate" through teaching than through its other activities and "much more ambiguous through its students." Teaching was a necessary backbone to the university's life and would always occupy the greater part of its human and material resources. Quite apart from providing for the formation of the relatively small proportion of students (among them young Jesuits) believed likely to contribute positively to the future of the country, teaching guaranteed the UCA's very existence. If, on one level, the students' fees helped keep the always precariously funded university afloat, so, on another—and particularly given the difficult circumstances of the National University—the UCA's training of professionals justified the university in the eyes of those who largely determined its continuing operation.[12]

The balance was always going to be delicate. The UCA maintained that it was *from* the Salvadoran people yet not *of* the Salvadoran people. Its pursuit of social change and real and realizable solutions to the problems facing the country would take it into the world of the powerful as it championed the needs of the poor. With the same kind of critical distance and realism that Ellacuría deemed proper to the existence of a philosopher, the UCA aimed "to make concrete its ideal aspirations within the real possibilities of the country in each and every historical moment." Never accepting political developments that would "make impossible its utopian project for society," the UCA could support—and had supported—others that, while less than perfect, it judged likely to help the process advance.[13] Yet stretched as the UCA was by the difficulty of maintaining tensions between what should be and what can be, it gained an unparalleled credibility in the country and abroad as an obligatory point of reference for all seeking information on El Salvador. Its arguments were enforced by the rigor of its research and the ethical interpretation of that research projected into society by means of that most powerful of arms, the "effective word." It had remained fully Christian as it had become truly a different kind of university.

BY 1985, the war in El Salvador was in its fifth year. Napoleón Duarte was firmly ensconced in the presidency with the full backing of the United States. His victory in the 1984 elections, heavily endorsed by the U.S. government and covertly supported by the CIA, had effectively silenced congressional reservations about aid to El Salvador. Duarte had been welcomed by the effusive U.S. press as leading a long-sought-after democratic center, a "fragile democracy" struggling to hold its own amid violent extremes of the right and left.[14] With a background that included a Notre Dame education and an election victory denied by the military in 1972, he was regarded as heroic for having suffered torture at the hands of the right and reassuring in his antagonism to communism. The heated debates over aid that had characterized the early part of the decade evaporated into the consensus that Duarte was U.S. policy *in situ.* "Today, the debates in Washington are simpler," the NACLA *Report on the Americas* would write. "Would the Reagan administration prefer its blank check for aid to El Salvador to be served on a china plate or a silver platter?"[15]

Throughout his presidency, Duarte's hold over the mainstream of U.S. political opinion and the access to funding that this brought him would remain his strongest political card. Yet his election represented something of a contradiction: necessary to the Reagan administration for the continued waging of the war, Duarte had campaigned on a platform that promised peace. In Washington to agree to a "pact" with President Reagan the week before he assumed power in El Salvador, Duarte put his name to a joint communiqué which underlined the incompatible aspirations of his presidency. The presidents agreed that in El Salvador they should be pursuing a strengthening of the democratic institutions, improvements in the quality of life, and economic development. Undercutting these objectives was the stated need to achieve a higher level of aid from the United States in order to sustain the peace *and* continue to wage the war.[16]

Between 1980 and the end of 1984, U.S. funding for El Salvador had increased nearly tenfold in response to the manifest failure of the U.S.–backed government to win the war. In 1983 a number of key developments had contributed to the smoothing of the way to the consensus achieved in the following year. President Reagan's direct appeal for substantially increased levels of aid had been greeted by congressional queries about the legitimacy of the Magaña government and renewed complaints that over two and a half years after the murder of the U.S. churchwomen, a date had still not been set for the trial. Congressional concern over the case would be expressed through a 30 percent cap on military aid devised by Republican Senator Arlen Specter as a mechanism to encourage the Salvadorans to bring the national guardsmen charged with the crime to trial, if only for reasons of self-interest. Such was the rapid increase in the volume of aid being requested by the Reagan administration that, even with the cap, the military aid released in 1983 was more than double that of 1982. Five men would be convicted of the churchwomen's murder on May 24, 1984, a fitting postscript to the victory of Duarte a few short weeks before.

In El Salvador it had become clear that the dirty war waged since 1979 by incompetent and repressive armed forces would not succeed. A military notorious for fighting a 9–to–5, five-day-a-week war, sweeping the countryside in large units easily avoided by the FMLN, had to be converted into an aggressive fighting force, capable of combating guerrilla warfare on its own terms and more sophisticated in its understanding that continued abuses of human rights only contributed to the legitimacy of their enemy's struggle. In 1983, despite the presence of a new Salvadoran defense minister, Eugenio Vides Casanova, more amenable to the U.S. position than his predecessor García, and the introduction of a "National Plan" of coordinated military activities and civilian pacification campaigns that was indicative of the strategy of counterinsurgency now advocated by the U.S., progress was still slow. During the course of the year the U.S. embassy became increasingly alarmed by a resurgence of death squad activity and a rise in the number of death threats against Ambassador

Thomas Pickering. This was no way to loosen the congressional purse strings and no way to win the war.

Vice-President George Bush, accompanied by National Security Adviser Colonel Oliver North, was dispatched to San Salvador in December 1983 to deliver a message of unprecedented clarity and directness. He had brought with him a list of military officers and civilians involved with the death squads. In confidential meetings he warned that future U.S. aid would be dependent on action being taken against these individuals and, at a dinner hosted by President Magaña, he made public the U.S. concerns. "Your cause is being undermined by the murderous violence of reactionary minorities," he told Magaña and his assembled guests. "If these death squad murders continue you will lose the support of the American people, and that would indeed be a tragedy."[17] It was a message that received at least as much attention on Capitol Hill as it did in San Salvador. The Bush visit was publicly represented, at the time and for the next ten years, as the single most successful assault on extremist right-wing violence made by the U.S. government. A CIA memorandum prepared in January 1984, however, tells a different story. "We believe efforts by the civilian government and the military High Command to crack down on right-wing violence have made little progress and have been aimed almost exclusively at placating Washington," read the summary.[18]

Published in the same month as this memorandum was written, the Report of the President's National Bipartisan Commission on Central America, or Kissinger Commission, helped Washington on its way to a consensus in its recommendations for the application of counterinsurgency principles to the war in El Salvador through enhanced levels of aid *and* more attention to human rights. Duarte's election, and the green light it provided for the approval of over half a million dollars of economic and military U.S. aid that year, was all the commission could have hoped for. Together, these milestones in the evolution of U.S. policy endorsed a recognition of the legitimacy of at least some of the grounds for revolution in the first place. Such a recognition transformed the Salvadoran conflict into a battle for the "hearts and minds" of the civilian population and led to the adoption of "low-intensity conflict" (LIC) strategy as the basis for the conduct of the war. LIC strategy held, as Colonel John D. Waghelstein would write in a paper drawing on his experience as MilGroup commander, "that simply killing guerrillas will not solve El Salvador's problems."[19] Yet the Duarte government, like the Kissinger Commission before it, remained clear that whatever the policies necessary to address those problems, they had to be subordinated to a concentration on the war.[20]

Direct U.S. military aid increased the size of the Salvadoran armed forces from 12,000 in 1980 to 42,000 in 1984; forced the FMLN into a new phase of more purely "guerrilla" warfare—with an emphasis on, for example, the use of mines and economic sabotage; and encouraged the government to depend more on aerial bombardment and mobile air attacks. Defeat had been averted, but victory was as elusive as it always had been and, according to a textbook application of LIC, complicated by its dependence on the transformation of the army, the introduction of economic reforms, and the encouragement of wider political participation. Through its determination to justify—and fund—the counterinsurgency effort in El Salvador, the United States had, in the words of one study commissioned by the Pentagon and released to the public in early 1992, "assumed responsibility for ameliorating the pathology produced by centuries of abuse perpetrated by the very armed forces and governing elite that its policy now supported."[21] A difficult task was made harder still by the fact that Duarte, as the instrument of this policy, not only did not represent the consensus he stood for in the United States, but did not even exercise the full power represented by his presidency. Considered to be a dangerous communist by political forces on his right and a powerless tool of U.S. interests by those on the left, Duarte was able to hold on to what power he did have only because the army knew that in his personal popularity abroad lay the key to military aid.

SINCE 1979, when the UCA had responded to the exceptional circumstances presented by the October coup, the university had been assailed by the persecution and repression common to the Salvadoran people as a whole—poised, to use a phrase common to the Jesuits of the UCA, in a *situación límite* or "limit-situation."[22] Writing the prologue to his textbook of social psychology in April 1983, Martín-Baró vividly recreated both the hardship and the privilege of academic work undertaken in such a time and place. These, he explains, are pages "written in the heat of events, in the midst of a police search of one's own home, after the assassination of a colleague or suffering from the physical and moral impact of a bomb that has destroyed one's office. These are the experiences that allow one to enter into the world of the oppressed, to feel a little bit closer to those who bear on the shoulders of their social class centuries of oppression, those who are today trying to emerge into a new history.

There are some truths that can only be discovered through suffering or from the critical vantage point of limit situations."[23]

Although the exodus of lay staff and Jesuits in 1979, 1980, and early 1981 constituted a terrible drain on the university, the UCA as an institution was, by then, sure enough of its own identity within the country to react to the national crisis with integrity and efficacy. Indicative of the institution's commitment to the service of a wider public was the mushrooming of its publications. By the middle of the decade the UCA had seven magazines, in addition to the long-established *ECA*, and a growing list of volumes published under the label of *UCA Editores*. Over the years the UCA's printing operation, founded in the early 1970s and upgraded in 1978, 1979, and 1982, had grown into the largest publishing entity in the country and, under the skilled management of Rogelio Pedraz, undoubtedly the most efficient.

Answering the needs and concerns of the particular academic departments, the majority of the magazines first appeared at the beginning of the 1980s. Like the Center for Information, Documentation, and Support for Research (CIDAI), founded in May 1980 under the direction of Ricardo Stein, the magazines responded to an increasing sense of urgency. The university was conscious that the new political process under way must be documented and analyzed. Moreover, this process was beginning at a moment in which not only were the last vestiges of El Salvador's independent media disappearing, but thousands of Salvadorans were being forced into exile. From outside, the exiles would be doubly isolated from authoritative and independent news of the country they had left behind. As a university, the UCA should be preparing the resources for the writing of history in the future and doing so with what one staff member would describe as the "very Jesuit" determination that no matter how the UCA rated as an authority on engineering, the pure sciences, or the humanities, there should be one subject on which it was better informed, more authoritative, and more frequently consulted than any other educational center in the world—El Salvador itself.

But it was not easy. The UCA and the Jesuits' residences were bombed regularly until 1983. As the conflict claimed between 45,000 and 50,000 casualties by 1984, the university had to tread a difficult path between self-preservation and self-immolation as it pursued its goals with intellectual honesty, but with an appropriate realism. "A permanent self-censorship has been forced upon us," Ellacuría told a visiting journalist in September 1983. "Circumstances do not allow us to do as much for this country as we could."[24] While the academic nature of *ECA* articles precluded them from presenting a threat to the government, its pages were carefully scanned by a small but influential number of civilian and military leaders across the political spectrum. The UCA's position was consistent. "We do not envisage a military victory on either side," Ellacuría had continued. "We are trying to show that negotiations are the best road to a solution. We are pushing for negotiations in our publications, in our personal contacts with officials, and in our conversations with foreign diplomats." At this point the UCA, and Ellacuría in particular, was daring to say things from inside the country, as Rubén Zamora (who would not be able to return to El Salvador until the end of 1987) would remember, "that nobody else would say and precious few wanted to hear."[25]

Across San Salvador the empty shell of the National University, closed since military intervention in June 1980, presented an eloquent reminder of the price that would be paid if the UCA stumbled from its narrow path. "The kind of things that used to go on at the National University were going on at the UCA last year," President Alvaro Magaña claimed in 1983. "They have printing presses and they have used them to publish subversive propaganda. I passed the word to the university officials that they should think very carefully about what they are doing there, and since then I have not had any more complaints from other members of the government. And I am glad about that. . . . I don't want to be remembered for closing down the Catholic University."[26] Inside the UCA, the university authorities kept a tight rein on the political activities of individuals and student organizations in order to guarantee a margin of political space within which the university as a whole could act. Demonstrations were not allowed and late-night meetings of any kind were avoided; graffiti was erased or covered up as soon as it appeared and the campus as a whole preserved a sense of ordered calm.

As Ellacuría outlined for the university community the challenges it faced on its twentieth anniversary, the picture he drew of El Salvador was a grim one. The social and economic situation in 1985 was worse than it had been in 1965: twenty years of work and suffering by the Salvadoran people had only led to a worsening of the poverty within the country. The population had grown considerably as the per capita income had diminished. By Ellacuría's calculation, 3.5 million people, more than two-thirds of El Salvador's population, were living at inhuman levels of poverty. Although the barbarous repression of 1980 to 1982 had receded, it had been replaced by a conflict in which two armies faced each other in interminable civil war. The combined effects of the economic crisis and the war had wrought havoc on the social structure of the country, most visible not just in the 80,000 Ellacuría estimated to be in arms, but also in the hundreds of thousands displaced from their homes by the conflict and forced to take refuge in camps or shantytowns in the cities. And pervading it all was a national identity torn asunder by the trauma of a civil war pitting Salvadorans against Salvadorans, brothers against brothers, absorbed by dizzying logic into the East-West conflict.[27]

The university Ellacuría now led was, while still young, infinitely older and wiser than it had been ten long years before. As Ellacuría appealed to his fellow Jesuits, lay colleagues, students, and staff for further effort in the fields of research and analysis, a constant improvement in the professionals trained by the university, and a renewed attention to communication with El Salvador's popular majorities, he was addressing a university fully immersed in the national reality it was there to serve. This was a university held together by something fostered by Román Mayorga, Ellacuría and their supporters in the quest for a "university for social change" in the early 1970s—something that Ellacuría would call "university mystique." Tremendously demanding in its union of the classical vocation of a university with a commitment to the most needy sectors of the population, the university mystique, as Ellacuría understood it, included a call for the members of the university community to give all their professional energies to the UCA.

The university mystique was a hard and insatiable master, but also a force for inspiration as Ellacuría brought his anniversary speech to a close: "On this our twentieth birthday we have much to thank many for, but we must also ask more from all. One can always give more, particularly if the cause for which one is working is noble. And there are few more noble causes than that on which our university has embarked: the creation of a new earth, plowed and cultivated with the best of human intelligence as we keep before our eyes [the fact] that those who have most right to enjoy it are those who have been most marginalized by history. . . . To work together in this, to contribute as members of a university to the solution of the great national crisis—this is the challenge we have before us as we leave behind us twenty rich years of history."[28]

FOR those opposed to the counterinsurgency strategy represented by the alliance of the Duarte government, the army, and the United States, the doctrine of low-intensity conflict brought a paradoxical—if slim— opening through which opposition could be expressed. Between 1983 and 1986, unions, popular organizations, and social forces tentatively re-emerged from the silence and fear of the early years of the war and first filled and then pushed beyond the narrow margin of legality granted them by a U.S.-driven policy committed to "democratization" in the midst of war. The gradual formation of a popular movement comparable in size and influence to that of the 1970s, but qualitatively different in its own structure and in relation to the changing social, economic, and political circumstances, was a complex phenomenon that rapidly escaped what some had envisaged as a possible cooption by the U.S.-backed Christian Democrats.[29]

As a university, the UCA was in a position both to benefit from and contribute to a shift in the political conditions. Although the change in the space in which it was possible to operate was as impossible to quantify as its limits were to determine, the UCA extended its social projection with the founding both of a new Human Rights Institute (IDHUCA), headed by Segundo Montes, and the "Forum on National Reality" *(Cátedra de la Realidad Nacional)*. In 1985 IDHUCA added its presence to the small but extraordinarily brave nongovernmental human rights community (whose most redoubtable figure was the archdiocese's María Julia Hernández). The Forum presented a series of open symposiums and discussions in which leading political, social or religious figures were invited to express their views on the most pressing issues of the day. At a moment when space for the proposition, commentary or analysis of ideas held by vast sectors of the population was lacking in the Salvadoran media, the UCA's Forum rapidly attracted capacity audiences. Publicized by paid advertisements in the press, those with no formal connection to the UCA joined in with students, staff members, and journalists to partake of a form of education and communication unavailable anywhere else in El Salvador at the time.

But both IDHUCA and the Forum represented additions and not changes to the UCA's presence in the country. Throughout the 1980s, as the 1970s, it was into the pages of *ECA* that the university poured the best of its research and analysis of the Salvadoran reality. Over the years the names on the masthead of the magazine's editorial board changed— Román Mayorga, Luis de Sebastián, and Salvador Samayoa among them—but *ECA* always remained the intellectual core of the university. Individual issues were planned with a consciousness that the issue was not only a document of record, but also, and more importantly, a magazine whose editorials and articles were inserted within the reality they commented upon. When its pages were, for example, opened to an examination of "The State of the War and Its Perspectives" by Joaquín Villalobos, the magazine's introduction made clear that the views expressed within "do not necessarily reflect the opinions of its editors," even as it argued for "difference and dialogue" being essential to intellectual life.[30] Under Ellacuría's editorship from 1976, *ECA* was the UCA activity to which he devoted most time, care, and attention. He was an editor whom, as Mayorga remembered, one had to see in action in the editorial meetings to appreciate fully: "He was a torrent of ideas, and used to unfurl with the full breadth of his virtues of limitless creativity and total dedication to intellectual production. He would propose subjects, write editorials, prepare his own articles, solicit contributions, invent new sections, comment on completed work and stimulate all of us to produce always more and always better."[31]

The *ECA* editorial board met regularly to analyze the political situation and establish the position the UCA should be disseminating through the pages of the magazine. In addition to his editorial skills, Ellacuría brought to these meetings a wealth of information gleaned from his regular contacts with journalists and diplomats and politicians from the ruling PDC to the PCN, ARENA, and the FMLN. While little escaped his attention, editorials would sometimes be written by others once their ideas had been accepted by the board as a whole. Not even Ellacuría could challenge the depth of learning and fine-tuned prose of Ignacio Martín-Baró. Another who weighed heavily in the magazine, if not as a writer of editorials, was Italo López Vallecillos, who returned from a second exile in Costa Rica to fill the position of director of *UCA Editores*. Once the editorial was written it would be distributed to the board and they would meet again to discuss it, presenting their comments and criticisms. "You had to be brave to take on Ellacuría," remembered one former board member, "for if you criticized him at all he always demanded that you produce something better than what he had written. But if you could do it, he respected the challenge."[32]

Characteristic of the *ECA* editorial, although much more marked on some occasions than others, was its clear sense of direction, the product of a decision as to which political actors should be given what message and when. While the circulation of *ECA* was small—around 3,000 in the mid–1980s—its audience was both potent and attentive. Over the years it could be seen on the shelves of offices that ranged from the U.S. Embassy to popular organizations, from government ministers to opposition politicians, from right-wing "think tanks" who published their opposition to the UCA in the pages of the *Diario de Hoy* to the political offices of the FMLN in Managua and Mexico. "I am going to tell the government this

. . . ," Ellacuría would begin, or, "let's say this to the U.S. embassy . . . or this to the army . . . or such and such to the FMLN."[33] It was clear that *ECA's* message got across. In 1987, for example, an urgent message arrived from César Jerez in Managua, saying that the FMLN were so incensed with *ECA's* analysis of "The Question of the Masses" in the July editorial that they wanted to see him at once.[34]

MUCH as the lay staff objected to the Jesuits' hold on the reins of power at the UCA in the late 1970s, the onset of civil war tended to prove the priests right. As more than a third of the faculty members left the university at the beginning of the 1980s, it was the Jesuits who had remained. But the quality of the people the UCA lost to the Junta in October 1979 and then into exile was irreplaceable. During the following decade, the university, caught in the focus of attention on the Salvadoran conflict, gained international stature as a reasoned voice of opposition to the governing forces. While within the UCA a pluralism of opinions and positions coexisted—as they always had—from outside it could appear monolithic. It was a university in which individuals, particularly individual Jesuits and particularly Ellacuría, loomed large in the public consciousness, and this did not always make for an easy internal dynamic.

The quality of his leadership was something that characterized Ellacuría throughout his life. But his exercise of authority over the UCA was something that could appear to his critics as being at odds with the radical nature of his theological, social, and political ideas. "It's just as well he was a priest," Guillermo Ungo, a friend of many years, would remark with a typically enigmatic smile, "otherwise he'd have wanted a political party and he'd have gotten in a terrible muddle. He was obviously progressive but the only structure he'd have wanted would have been monarchic."[35] Pouring his extraordinarily creative capacities into the founding of institutes and individual projects throughout the UCA, once he saw they were up and running Ellacuría would turn his attention to something else. Individuals and entire departments were granted a certain autonomy, yet Ellacuría held the strings of all and did not hesitate to pull on them when necessary. "You are all free to do exactly what I want," he would tell the staff of *Proceso,* the weekly news magazine produced by CIDAI, his irony doing little to obscure what they knew to be the truth. "The ideal model of government," was an often repeated phrase, "is that of God."

There were times, however, when the predominance of the figure of

Ellacuría obscured the extent to which even he formed part of a team without which the multidisciplinary endeavor of the UCA would have been impossible. If the university as a whole took as its beginning and end the "national reality," then the national reality had also to be the beginning and end of the study not just of philosophy or theology, but also of economics and sociology, engineering and literature, architecture and business administration. There were, of course, some areas directed to the more "professional" of academic studies (the Law Faculty was an obvious example) in which the UCA's attempt at a "different kind of university" proved much more difficult than others, and was never fully realized. But among the Jesuits and key lay staff the vision of what the university could and should be within Salvadoran society was a shared goal, evolved over many years, to which they were completely dedicated.

Besides Ellacuría, Segundo Montes and Ignacio Martín-Baró were preeminent figures within this intellectual community, not least because of the sheer number of academic and administrative tasks they performed. With seats on the UCA board of directors throughout the decade, these three occupied the rectorate, the academic vice-rectorate, and the director-ship of three departments and two institutes. On a daily basis the three ran their departments of philosophy, sociology, and psychology with a dedication to the importance of their own field within the life of the university as a whole. Each formed close and somewhat paternal relation-ships with their most gifted students, the majority of whom would, quite naturally, be channeled back into the UCA as teachers or researchers. The centers of research and social projection that each oversaw—CIDAI, IDHUCA, and the Institute of Public Opinion (IUDOP), respectively—readily became extensions of these departments and reflected their personal loyalties. Ellacuría, for example, was neither the director of CIDAI nor the editor of *Proceso,* but both were so unmistakably "his" that by the second half of the decade almost all of the center's researchers and writers were former students in philosophy.

Within the UCA, however, a commitment to all that was "different" about the university and expressed by the Jesuits' leadership was accompa-nied by a constant rumbling of discontent. The primary and most recurrent source of complaint was financial. The UCA's finances—in no small part due to the servicing of the IADB loans—were always perilously tight. In the mid–1970s a sliding salary scale had been devised to respond "to the demands of justice and the needs of the members of the university and their families,"[36] but the problem of low salaries remained. As Ellacuría acknowledged in 1985, it was in part thanks to the "mystique" of the UCA that a good number of people had chosen "to earn less in order to serve better" the people of El Salvador.[37] Many staff members, however, perceived the issue differently: they knew that "mystique" alone did not feed, clothe, and educate their families and they felt that the Jesuits had little sense of the economic and domestic realities of life outside the material security of a religious order. "Sometimes they forget that *we* never took their vows," one staff member would remark, "and yet have lives and problems outside this university."[38]

A related source of disagreement, and one that would cause several highly able faculty members to leave during the 1980s, was the perception by the lay staff that the "Jesuitical" structure of the UCA allowed little room for dissent. It was felt that the Jesuits' concern to preserve the integrity of "their UCA" led to their own domination of positions of responsibility within the university that not only forced the individual Jesuit to overwork to a ridiculous degree, but also blocked advancement to such positions by anyone else. Efforts to form some kind of staff union were not encouraged and, finding this difficult to square with the UCA's public commitment to the people's right to organize, dissenters resented being unable to have their own rights balanced with the university's wider goals within Salvadoran society. While some of these concerns had been around since the 1970s, they would flair up again toward the end of the 1980s, particularly in the annual "retreats" in which the entire university community would attempt a frank and critical assessment of their concerns and preoccupations. Irritating for those seeking outlet for their discontent was the attitude communicated by some of the Jesuits: they held the reins of power within the university because they were the best qualified to do so.

SYNTHESIZING arguments put forward by the UCA over the better part of two decades, in 1987 Jon Sobrino proposed that a university of Christian inspiration could overcome its inbuilt contradictions through its option for the poor: "It is unrealistic to think that a university could be physically in the world of the poor but it is necessary that it sees the world from the perspective of the poor, and that this world enters into its mind and its heart."[39] This was the way, he argued, to avoid the "worldliness" that the institutional nature of the university presented as a constant temptation. It was to the advantage of the university that it could equip itself with the tools with which to make concrete its "option." And among the tools with which to "see the world from the perspective of the poor" the social sciences were primary, as liberation theology had suggested. "If"—as

Sobrino wrote elsewhere of theology—"the concern is to liberate the real world from its wretched state, [the university] will turn spontaneously to the social sciences. For they analyze the concrete misery of the world, the mechanisms that create it, and consider possible models of liberation from it."[40]

Within the UCA social sciences were used as the basis for analysis of the reality of El Salvador and of the university's insertion into that reality in a manner complementary to the philosophical and theological principles upon which it was founded. In Ignacio Martín-Baró and Segundo Montes (as in others at the UCA and in the Jesuits of CIAS) there was a synthesis of social scientist and priest, with their vocations for "the service of faith" lived out through a "promotion of justice" in a reality subjected to rigorously empirical analysis. Rarely given to overtly theological writings, the Christian inspiration of the university as a whole was, nevertheless, in all that they did as fully realized men of the Church, of the university, and of El Salvador.

Ignacio Martín-Baró was the youngest of the original UCAII Jesuits and among the most obviously talented. "A Cervantes with his pen or at the computer, as an orator he could have captivated an auditorium of the deaf," was how his friend Mayorga described him.[41] Since his early years, Martín-Baró had written in the pages of *ECA* on a broad and eclectic range of subjects—from the latest Nobel Prize for literature to James Bond, from *machismo* to marijuana.[42] While studying humanities in Bogotá in the early 1960s, he became particularly fascinated by psychology, devouring every book he could get his hands on. Back in San Salvador in the 1970s, he taught psychology, was briefly editor of *ECA,* and became a popular dean of students. In 1977 he left again, this time to spend three years completing first a master's degree and then his Ph.D. in social psychology at the University of Chicago, where other students remembered him as being buried in his thesis on population density in El Salvador and anxious for news from a country in turmoil that had yet to make the U.S. headlines.[43]

During the 1980s, Martín-Baró combined his key administrative and academic posts in the UCA with extensive and innovative production in social psychology. A visiting professor in a number of Central and South American universities, he became vice-president for Mexico, Central America, and the Caribbean of the Inter-American Society of Psychology. One North American colleague, Adrianne Aron, would describe him as "perhaps the most important psychological theorist of our day."[44] Academically fêted abroad, Martín-Baró was one on whom the tragedy of the Salvadoran conflict weighed heavily. Within the UCA he worked a truly punishing schedule—arriving at his desk at 5:30 A.M. and, apart from a brief break for lunch, working through until 8:00 P.M. Although Martín-Baró was infinitely attentive to the problems of the students and secretaries closest to him, those who had known him from the 1970s were struck by the cost to his health and mood. A different Martín-Baró, or so it could appear to those who did not know him well, was the *"Padre Nacho"* of his weekend visits to the parish he tended in the coffee-growing region of Jayaque, 30 kilometers west of the capital. "His face would light up as he got in the car to go out there," remembered one student. "It was as if he left the cerebral Nacho behind in the UCA. Out there he was all love, all joy."[45]

Another former student remembers how impressed he had been by seeing Martín-Baró, whom he had yet to know personally, telling an audience seeking some kind of statement on armed conflict in the heated days of 1980 that, "there are different types of arms—and reason is among them."[46] There were different ways to live the Salvadoran conflict, and, as Martín-Baró lived it, being a social scientist was one of them. From the level of commitment that he assumed, the full realization of a social scientist within a process as convulsive as that of El Salvador demanded a position that bordered on the prophetic. "It is not easy," he would write of his professional vocation, "for many reasons, some of them extrinsic and others intrinsic. The most obvious difficulty comes from the risks run by the lives of those who try to illuminate the problems that are at the root of the conflict or contribute to the search for its solution. It is not in your interest to know what the reality is when the reality is so expressive, so clear in what it means, that the mere fact of calling it by its truthful name constitutes something 'subversive.'"[47]

A less obvious difficulty was one intrinsic to the social sciences themselves, and particularly the "young science" of psychology that was Martín-Baró's own. The theoretical and technical baggage it brought with it could be an obstruction, rather than a help, in a situation as particular and extreme as that of El Salvador. The University of Chicago had provided Martín-Baró with an excellent training in social psychology, but it had been a training in a discipline formed and practiced in a world very different from that in which he lived. And in 1980, as El Salvador plunged into war, it became clear to him that his training was inadequate to the task with which he was confronted.[48] Martín-Baró would describe psychology as "enslaved" to the influences of "big brother" to the north, where the subject had already won social and scientific respectability.[49]

Lacking its own vocabulary, Latin American psychology had followed in the footsteps of a science that, in its individualistic and historical preoccupations, was unable to respond to the psychological needs of the Salvadoran people.

Wholly consistent with the multidisciplinary focus of the UCA and its overall orientation, Martín-Baró rewrote the role of psychologist in a Central American context. He proposed a "psychology of liberation" that presupposed a "liberation from psychology," a reorientation of psychology's priorities away from a concentration on itself, on its scientific and social status, and toward "an effective service of the needs of popular majorities."[50] If the psychologist was not to serve the interests of the established social order, then he or she had to move away from a consideration of the social context as "a sort of natural background, an accepted given before whose 'objective' demands the individual should seek individually and even 'subjectively' the resolution of his problems."[51] The psychologist, like other social scientists, had to take into account his or her historical circumstances even when, as in El Salvador, this meant "starting to look for solutions almost from zero, without models or orientation" and the assumption of the real risks that in the early 1980s led some psychologists to fall victim to the death squads and others to flee into exile.[52]

Returning to the historical roots of psychology, Martín-Baró argued that the human consciousness is "not simply the individual's private ambit of knowledge and subjective feeling, but that ambit where each person encounters the reflected impact of his being and action within society, where he assumes and elaborates a knowledge of himself and of his reality that allows him to be someone, to have a personal and social identity."[53] Understood in this way, the human consciousness is essentially psychosocial, unintelligible without reference to its surrounding and—at least partially—defining reality. To the psychologist befalls the task of helping this human consciousness move toward a greater understanding of its personal and social identity. Martín-Baró returned to the phrase and concept coined by Paulo Freire—"conscientization"—to describe this task more adequately. Freire used "conscientization" to characterize the experience by which the oppressed of Latin America become literate through a dialectical engagement with their surrounding world. "Becoming literate," as Martín-Baró explained, "is above all learning to read the surrounding reality and to write one's own history."[54] For the oppressed of Latin America it is a process that implies a personal and social transformation embraced by the word "liberation."

The service of the needs of the popular majorities began with a psychosocial diagnosis of the war itself, which was suffered most directly by the poor, whether in the ranks of either of the two armies, as civilian casualties or as individuals and entire communities forced to abandon their homes for exile or internal displacement within El Salvador. Martín-Baró found the war to be characterized by violence, polarization, and the institutionalized lie. The best that either side had to offer had been absorbed by the attempted destruction of their respective enemies and in each "reason had been displaced by aggression, considered analysis by military operations." Society itself had been pulled apart by the "ethical mirror" that had the two sides contemplating each other as "them" and "us," "the good" and "the bad," across an unfathomable gulf in which common sense had no place. And all of it was clouded by a climate of lies that came to reinforce the idea that more violence was the only solution to the violence itself: "Almost without realizing it we have become accustomed to thinking that institutions are precisely the opposite of what they are supposed to be: those who should be assuring our security are the principal source of insecurity; those responsible for justice defend abuses and injustice, those called upon to give orientation and direction are the first to deceive and manipulate."[55]

ELLACURÍA liked to tease Martín-Baró by saying that an Institute of Public Opinion had been *his* idea. He would claim that he had been sitting on an airplane, wondering what was lacking in the armory of the UCA, when it occurred to him that everybody talks in the name of the people—the political parties, the army, the FMLN, and indeed the UCA itself—but nobody asks the people what they think. The UCA should use its resources to go out to the people of El Salvador and ask them. But whether the original idea had in fact been his or Martín-Baró's (as *he* remembered), there can be no doubt as to IUDOP's success.[56]

By the middle of the decade, the change in the nature of the war was inescapable. Martín-Baró would write of the shift from the "dirty war" waged until 1983 to what he termed the "psychological war" of the low-intensity conflict in the years following, but would find that there was not a major difference.[57] The three elements—of violence, polarization, and the institutionalized lie—remained, even as, during the years of Duarte's government, the profile of the violence changed, the level of polarization decreased (largely through exhaustion and disillusion with the positions of the extremes), and the systematic masking of reality underwent an obvious transformation. Under Duarte there were "two images of El Salvador." The image projected by the U.S. government was that El

Salvador was the "best of the new Latin American democracies": there had been free elections, there was increasing respect for human rights, the Salvadoran army was more professional, more obedient to civil power, and, while the country still suffered some economic problems and an ineffective justice system, these could, in general terms, be laid at the door of the Marxist-Leninist purveyors of violent terrorism supported by Cuba and Nicaragua.[58]

For Martín-Baró, this image represented "an ideological elaboration specific to the government of Reagan with little or nothing to do with the real situation of El Salvador."[59] From the UCA it was clear that the truth was otherwise—a truth of increasing poverty, the functioning of an authority that was above the law, and a continuing civil war. This, certainly, was what emerged from the pages of *ECA, Proceso,* and the university's other magazines, and in the classrooms and auditoriums dedicated to the analysis of the national reality. The problem, and this was clearly pointed out by Ellacuría in his 1985 speech on the occasion of the UCA's twentieth anniversary, was how to counter the ideology trumpeted by the Salvadoran media through communication with the popular majorities. "If we are really thinking about solutions from the popular majorities, for the popular majorities and also—through the means proper to the university—with the popular majorities," he had insisted, "it is only just that we should communicate with them as directly as possible and in the most suitable language that, without abandoning its essential rigor, can readily be assimilated and become an active part of the popular consciousness."[60]

Here lay the effectiveness of public opinion polls against excessive ideological posturing, both in the nature of the information the polls made available to the public and in the ease with which it could be understood. Under Martín-Baró's direction, from its founding in July 1986 until September 1989, IUDOP conducted twenty-three separate surveys among metropolitan, urban, and rural populations on subjects that ranged from dialogue and negotiations to health, religion, and upcoming elections. Supervised by a former student of Martín-Baró, Arely Hernández—whom Ellacuría would liken to a "troop commander"—IUDOP's interviewers traveled the country and, in Martín-Baró's words, "bore the heat of the sun and torrential downpours, answered cursory rejections and personal insults with a smile; they have crossed bridges held by the military and braved minefields; they have stood up to lengthy interrogations at military checkpoints and even suffered death threats from Civil Defense patrols."[61] Testament to IUDOP's objectivity was the fact that it was accused of being an instrument both of the FMLN guerrillas and of the right-wing ARENA party.[62] The institute was one of the most successful of all of the UCA's forms of social projection and, by the time of Martín-Baró's death, had been preparing to fill a five-minute daily slot on a national television station.

Rigorously conducted, IUDOP's polls provided the Salvadoran people with what Martín-Baró termed a "social mirror" in which to see an image of themselves as they moved forward in the construction of thei world.[63] The man or woman who, for example, hesitated through an understandable fear to agree that he or she backed a negotiated solution to the war in May 1988, could see that over 40 percent of the population felt as he or she did.[64] Martín-Baró would compare the effect that public opinion polls could have in times of social crisis to the impact caused by the homilies of Monsignor Romero. The two shared a starkness and authority with which they bared the most significant events in people's daily lives. Like Romero's homilies, "public opinion polls can be a way of returning their voice to the oppressed peoples, an instrument that, as it reflects the popular experience with truth and meaning, opens the consciousness to a sense of a new truth to be constructed in history."[65]

WRITING in 1984, Martín-Baró found the "prototype" of the civilian population affected by the war to be groups of old people, women, and children driven from their homes as refugees and displaced people.[66] Settled in camps or squatter communities, within El Salvador or in neighboring Honduras, these people were waiting out the war in conditions of great hardship and complete uncertainty. Most of those whom the violence pushed into the agonizing decision to leave their homes had lost family members to the conflict; some had sons and daughters still in arms. Many had arrived at their "refuge" only after bleak odysseys, or *guindas,* in which entire communities were forced to take to the hills. With what belongings they could carry piled on their backs, slowed by the old, the young, the sick, and the scared, thin lines of people walked a perilous course between military units on the ground and bomb-laden airplanes in the sky scouring the countryside for caravans like theirs. They traveled by night to avoid detection, holed up in cramped caves or shallow dug-out shelters during the day, sometimes for weeks on end. Behind them stretched a human trail of those who could not make it, those unlucky or unwary enough to be detained on the way and shot or tortured as a "delinquent terrorist" by an army unable or unwilling to distinguish between guerrillas and civilians.

By 1984, those forced from their homes by the war, scattered throughout El Salvador, Central America, and the United States, would number over a million: one in every four Salvadorans.[67] Their plight, the denunciation, challenge, and example of some of their communities came to be of particular and then—with characteristic intensity—burning interest to Segundo Montes. During the last six years of his life he would gain stature within El Salvador and in the United States as the leading researcher and analyst of the phenomenon of the displaced, the refugees, and the exiles. In El Salvador and Honduras he visited their communities, offering advice on development projects while appreciating what he could learn from the communities themselves. In the United States he became increasingly in demand for his expertise on the subject, co-authoring a study for Georgetown University;[68] serving on the advisory board of the Washington-based CARECEN, the Central American Refugee Center; and briefing congressmen—among them Joe Moakley—on the need to amend U.S. immigration laws for the protection of the Salvadorans who arrived in the United States with all other options exhausted.

Segundo Montes had not always been a social scientist. Drawn to more exact sciences, he had begun his time at the *Externado* (1957 to 1960, 1966 to 1976) teaching physics. While he would move on to sociology, and complete a doctorate in social anthropology in Madrid in the late 1970s, something of the physics teacher would always remain with him in his enjoyment of practical tasks about the UCAII community. Fiery, with an energy that spilled from his long frame, Montes expressed himself forcefully whether in the large classes he liked to give in the UCA's auditorium; at mass in the church of Quezaltepeque, Santa Tecla, where he served from 1984; or in interviews with visiting journalists. Despite his rather brusque manner, Segundo was a figure to whom people were instinctively drawn. Intense in his enthusiasm for what he considered important—from his own sociological research to the need to have fireworks on New Year's Eve or a garden in the new UCA residence—and teased by the other Jesuits for being "a child all of his life," Segundo was fiercely loyal to Ellacuría, whom he would tell one colleague he considered to be "the most extraordinary man I have ever met."[69]

Even among his fellow Jesuits, Segundo Montes was remarkable for the profound and direct knowledge he had of a range of different aspects of Salvadoran society. Years at the *Externado,* teaching physics and sociology, as prefect of discipline, and then as headmaster in the years following the "*Externado* affair," had left him with an enormous range of friends and contacts as *Externado* boys found their way into positions of influence in every possible political or business organization, the army, and the FMLN. Yet Montes's knowledge extended beyond this old boys' network. His tireless drive to understand better the social reality of the country led him to write on social stratification, the complex web of patronage that lies behind El Salvador's idea of *compadrazgo,* the pattern of land holding and, increasingly, the military, which was a subject on which he considered himself an expert.[70] It had been his sharp eye for a new and curious phenomenon in Salvadoran life—the "loss" of dollars sent in the mail by Salvadorans in the United States—that had first alerted him to the importance of Salvadoran emigration to the country's economy.

Montes was leaving the country for Christmas in 1982 when he asked his closest collaborator, Juan José García, to write a brief commentary for *ECA* on the missing dollars. They discussed the issue together and concluded that the money entering the country from the United States in small denomination dollar bills, checks, and money orders represented an important flow of funds and, it was not exaggerated to say, the possibility of survival both for the poor families receiving them and for the economy of El Salvador.[71] Montes had wanted to look further into the subject at the time, but it would be some years before he returned to it, and then via extensive research on the Salvadoran displaced and refugees begun, with the help of a grant from the Ford Foundation, in 1984. The research fell into two phases, first assessing the profundity of the problem presented by displaced and refugee populations, and then working out a possible solution.[72] But while this project concentrated on the phenomenon as it affected the Salvadoran population scattered through Central America, Montes did not lose his interest in the social and economic significance of Salvadorans living in the United States. In 1985 he returned to the concerns first raised by the theft of dollars at the end of 1982. By 1988 Montes's calculations had an estimated one million Salvadorans living in the United States sending monthly remittances to their families that totaled a staggering $1.3 billion a year.[73] Equivalent to the sum of U.S. aid plus all Salvadoran exports, and almost double the country's national budget, the remittances provided an informal connection to the United States that could not be written out of the consideration of El Salvador's economic and social future.

The gravity of the problem presented by the displaced persons and refugees offered not just an opportunity to assess the profundity of the crisis affecting El Salvador, but also, in its very annihilation of existing structures, the possibility for the restructuring of society along more just and humane lines. "If this problem is not handled properly," Segundo

Montes would write, "perhaps the war will end, but the conditions that caused it will last, and will return to a crisis point or an explosion at any moment."[74] In 1988 and 1989, Montes would find grounds for hope in visits he made to the community of Santa Marta, in Cabañas, one year after its repopulation from the refugee camp of Mesa Grande, and to the refugee communities still in the Honduran camps of Colomoncagua and San Antonio. He returned from these trips brimming with energy and optimism for the future of the country. These battered *campesinos* had left the bullets and bombs of El Salvador behind them for life in poorly situated camps that promised little. Yet in a few years they had experienced a profound transformation. They had made a qualitative leap, as Montes would write after his return from Colomoncagua in February 1989, "from individualism to the solidarity of a community, from illiteracy to enviable levels of education, from primitive manual labor to delicate and complex cultivation." In these communities forged from the hardship of the war Montes found that a "painful birth" had given way to "a strong offspring, a youth and a new promise that augur hope for El Salvador."[75]

THE phenomenon of the displaced persons and refugees had all the characteristics of the "limit-situation" first remarked upon by Ellacuría in El Salvador in 1981 and often referred to by Martín-Baró. Providing a "critical vantage point" for the university as a whole, the limit-situation was also something within which the university itself was immersed. For the UCA, as for the Salvadoran refugees, or for individuals such as Martín-Baró's parishioner in Jayaque who was captured and gang-raped by the Atlacatl Battalion yet had the courage to go before television cameras to tell her story, the limit-situation was something that brought to light human resources unimagined before each individual had been subjected to the unimaginable.

Two weeks after her rape, the young woman from Jayaque joined the relatives of a young man killed by a Civil Defense unit while trying to prevent the forced recruitment of his brother to speak out at a mass and encourage the other members of the congregation, "not to shut their eyes to injustice, not to be afraid of those who practice evil and not to fall silent before atrocities."[76] The UCA's Christian inspiration was one that placed it at the service of that woman, and of so many other men, women, and children throughout El Salvador suffering injustice, the practice of evil, and atrocities on a daily basis and down through the years. Science for the scienceless, skills for the unskilled, voice of the voiceless, it was a mark of its success that the UCA should not just represent, but also resemble these people. "If the university had not suffered," Ellacuría told an audience at the University of Santa Clara in California, "we would not have performed out duty. In a world where injustice reigns, a university that fights for justice must necessarily be persecuted. . . . Our history has been that of our nation."[77]

CHAPTER NINE

WHAT'S DONE HERE . . . STAYS HERE

From a current U.S. policy perspective, any discussion on respect for human rights in El Salvador begins with the Jesuit case. The importance of the case is the need for a clearly accountable military, one that obediently serves the ends of society rather than its own institutional ends or the ends of a particular coterie of officers such as the tandona. The credibility of the military and the integrity of the Salvadoran judicial system are on the line.[1]

Desk Officer, U.S. Department of State, 1991

"TO want to understand the Jesuit case as an institutional problem is wrong, it displays a lack of objectivity. I respect Moakley's position, but I don't share it, and, being in a democratic system I have the right to reject it. This is no den of assassins." The office of Colonel Mauricio Vargas, deputy chief of staff of the Salvadoran armed forces and its representative at the negotiations, was littered with soft toys. Amongst the assorted teddy bears, a rabbit in blue dungarees, and a china cat with pink ears, stood a tall, thin Madonna, her arms outstretched above the small bear at her feet. On the desk a glass mug from Fort Benning, where Vargas spent two years as an instructor at the School of the Americas, sat next to a grinning bulldog in a grubby turquoise T-shirt. Printed on its front were the three words, "Handsome, intelligent, and charming." It was January 1991, and Colonel Vargas appeared untroubled by the charges that the intellectual authors of the Jesuit murders had yet to be found, that the investigation had highlighted problems that went right to the heart of the Salvadoran armed forces. "We are passing through a terrible storm," he continued, "but I am not frightened because the ship I'm in has a sufficiently strong structure to survive the storm."[2]

BY the first anniversary of the Jesuits' death, the investigation had reached what Legal Officer Rick Chidester described as a "point of no return."[3] A year had passed and it was expected that the case would soon be raised to the "plenary" or trial stage. Although four hundred witnesses had

259

appeared before Judge Zamora, those four hundred had produced remarkably little in terms of admissible evidence. Instead, the thousands of pages of transcribed declarations revealed some two or three hundred inconsistencies and a pattern of forgetfulness, deception, and straightforward lying that was in itself an eloquent testimony of the nature of military "collaboration." Part of the purpose of a judicial investigation is to uncover new information and, if it is deemed appropriate, new defendants. In this case there had been both, but what new information that did emerge had done so only by seeping through the cracks in the coverup, and it was for the coverup itself that the only new defendants had been charged.

On November 16, 1990, the anniversary celebrations in the UCA culminated in an enormous outdoor mass, concelebrated by 27 bishops and 180 priests before the families of the six Jesuits and of Elba and Celina Ramos, and between six and eight thousand people. That same day additional charges against the defendants were lodged by Judge Zamora for acts "preparatory to terrorism" and acts of terrorism in their destruction of UCA property. The charges set a legal precedent: never before had members of the Salvadoran armed forces, most of whom understood their constitutional mission as the unceasing battle against the "terrorism" they saw in all the FMLN's actions, been accused of terrorism themselves.[4] "These types of crimes cannot be attributed to the armed forces," the defendants' lawyers objected, "the law establishes that acts preparatory to terrorism are those executed by clandestine organizations, and the army is not an institution that has been acting in secret."[5] "Terrorism," Ignacio Ellacuría would have countered, "is not what those who are previously labeled terrorists do, but rather they are terrorists who commit acts of terrorism."[6]

At the request of the attorney general, on December 6, 1990 the court's period of investigation was closed and, with the judge ruling that sufficient evidence existed against the charged men, the Jesuit case was elevated to its plenary stage. Ten days later the defense lawyers challenged Zamora's decision and the case was passed to San Salvador's First Appeals Court. Although the Salvadoran legal system allows for further evidence to be presented to the court only in the final eight-day evidentiary period that directly precedes the trial, the Jesuits insisted that the elevation of the case did not mean the end of its investigation: "We are confident that in the next phase new proof and documentation will bring us closer to the truth. The people of El Salvador deserve it and the cause of justice in this country deserves it."[7] But the cause of justice was up against considerable odds, odds favoring a military confident that it had weathered the worst of this particular storm.

THE peace negotiations entered a new phase at the end of October 1990 when it was agreed that Alvaro de Soto should take a more active role as mediator. For de Soto this marked the beginning of a period of intensive shuttling between the negotiating parties themselves and the wider circle of political and social forces not directly represented at the table. Formal talks would not be resumed until January, but during November and December, as the FMLN upped their military activity across El Salvador, both sides discussed a working paper on military reform proposed by de Soto. In the air was a new seriousness that owed much to the cut in military aid: officers of the Salvadoran army had seen that they could no longer count on the United States for the funding of their war. Moderate by comparison with the FMLN's demands for a total dissolution of the armed forces, yet strongly resisted by sectors of the military, the working paper's suggestions—among them the "purging" of the armed forces by an Ad Hoc Commission, the need to overcome military impunity, the abolishing of the Immediate Reaction Battalions (including the Atlacatl), and the restructuring of the security forces, with the National Guard and the Treasury Police to be dismantled and the National Police placed under civilian control—would provide a framework for all future discussions of the armed forces.[8]

The FMLN's successful use of surface-to-air missiles prompted a shift in the military balance, traditionally maintained by the government's monopoly of the skies. Between November 20 and November 30 the FMLN claimed two airplanes and two helicopters destroyed in the air, while an additional two planes were destroyed on the ground and seven helicopters damaged. But on January 2 this strategy was to have very negative consequences for the FMLN. A military helicopter carrying three U.S. advisers was brought down and the two North Americans who survived the crash summarily executed. The FMLN fudged and hedged for the first few days following the episode that one FMLN leader described as a "disaster."[9] The killings were a clear violation of the rules of war and they came just days before President Bush was due to determine whether to continue to hold back 50 percent of the aid cut for 1991.

Condemned as "absolutely-outrageous" by Secretary of State Baker, the killing of the advisers provoked heated criticism from all quarters in Washington.[10] Administration officials insisted that the executions justi- fied the immediate release of the aid. Congressional Democrats responded that the release of aid now would give a green light to the military and damage both the negotiations and progress in the Jesuit case. The administration was adamant: the FMLN had specifically infringed on two of the "tripwire" criteria established by Congress in the autumn—the rebels had "engaged in acts of violence directed at civilian targets" and, in using surface-to-air missiles traced to Nicaragua, they had acquired "significant shipments of lethal military assistance from outside El Salvador"—and the aid must be released. No doubt anxious to avoid a battle with Congress over El Salvador while the situation in the Persian Gulf deteriorated, President Bush was, however, prepared to suspend delivery of the aid for two months "in the interest of promoting a peaceful settlement to El Salvador's tragic conflict."[11] The end of the two months' grace would coincide with the March elections for the Salvadoran National Assembly. By then, it was hoped, the spectre of restored aid might prod the FMLN to agree to a United Nations' supervised cease-fire.

The restoration of aid sent mixed messages to El Salvador, where the impact of the two-month delay was somewhat muted. "We are satisfied," was the comment of the army's spokesman. "The vote of confidence the Congress had taken away from the armed forces has been restored."[12] The decision was represented by the U.S. government as favoring the negotiations, but this view was in direct contradiction to the assessment of their progress given the week before by the man best placed to know exactly what was going on, U.N. mediator Alvaro de Soto. Writing in the *Wall Street Journal,* de Soto had reiterated the difficulties of being "stuck with wartime negotiations" and warned that the negotiating agenda—as agreed upon in Caracas the previous year—ruled out the possibility of an immediate cease-fire. Nevertheless, he stated: "The talks are on track and proceeding apace—but quietly and out of the limelight, as befits serious negotiations. There is no doubt in my mind that this effort can lead to success."[13]

Many of those in Congress who had labored long and hard to forge a "carrot-and-stick" policy toward El Salvador believed that the president's decision was a one-sided application of a piece of legislation designed to be even-handed in its support of an end to a two-sided conflict. Among the conditions on the Salvadoran government which, if found to exist, should legally require a total cutoff of military aid, had been the failure to conduct "a thorough and professional investigation into, and prosecution of those responsible" for the eight UCA murders.[14] In the State Department's report on El Salvador required by Congress, it had been clearly stated that the army's cooperation "has not been satisfactory to date."[15] Yet in the document providing the "Justification for the Presidential Determination" no mention of the Jesuit case was made at all.

"IT is difficult to see how we could have kept good relations with the Jesuits unless we had turned around U.S. policy one hundred-eighty degrees," Ambassador Walker would say in an interview in early 1991.[16] Relations between the Jesuits monitoring the case and the U.S. embassy had gotten off to a bad start with the treatment meted out to Lucía Cerna, and they never recovered. Added to historical distrust on both sides was the profound conviction on the part of the Jesuits and their U.S. legal advisers, the Lawyers Committee for Human Rights, that the embassy's approach to the case was motivated by a desire for "damage control" rather than the truth. "They did not set out from the beginning to find the solution to the case," Tojeira insisted, "but rather studied the repercussions of the case and then tried to take steps to limit them. Their has been a highly politic game and, in some aspects, I would say a dirty one."[17]

The difficulty for Walker and his embassy officials, eager to defend themselves against the Jesuits' criticism, was that history had dealt them a very weak hand and the course of the investigation only made it weaker. The Salvadoran army was funded and assisted by U.S. dollars and U.S. advisers. Those same U.S. dollars and advisers had paid for the weapons and trained the men who killed the Jesuits. For years U.S. officials had criticized the Jesuits of the UCA for their "leftist" and "pro-FMLN" positions, while the UCA itself was viewed as "a center for intellectual opposition and a haven for revolutionaries."[18] One former defense attaché described how Ellacuría's "goal" was "simply to bring the present system tumbling down, and let the future take care of itself."[19] The repetition of such charges down through the years led to their ready absorption by U.S. officials new to El Salvador. After the Jesuits' deaths, the very existence of such charges provided ample fuel for those seeking to blame the United States for moral complicity in the murder.

To these considerations was added what is difficult to interpret as anything other than a deep insensitivity both to the particulars of the Jesuits' situation and, in a more general sense, to their identity as priests in El Salvador. An obvious example was the check for $1,000 the embassy sent to the UCA after the murder. The check was returned. Some Jesuits objected to the photograph of Ellacuría hung on the wall of Walker's office. "I think the U.S. government in general and the embassy in particular do not understand the role of the Catholic Church in El Salvador," one U.S. official formerly posted in San Salvador would confide, and certainly opinions expressed in interviews, as well the clumsiness of individual actions, would appear to bear this out. "I don't think I've ever met a man with so little sense of religion," another U.S. official would add, out of no desire to see Walker do anything except transfer this "sense" into his diplomatic actions, "with so many years in Latin America you'd think he would have realized something."[20] Chidester, as others in the embassy were fond of pointing out, was a Catholic convert, "so that should have been alright." Yet when he confessed surprise at the fact that the Miami Jesuits he had met while with Lucía Cerna had protested, "we're not like the Jesuits in El Salvador," he revealed a blithe ignorance of the complexities of Central American Church politics. "To me a Catholic priest is a Catholic priest," had been his comment.[21]

The aftermath of the assassinations had only confirmed the suspicion of the U.S. embassy's actions to which the Jesuits were predisposed by their aversion to the U.S. role in El Salvador. The embassy had not extricated itself from the accusations that it had deliberately discredited the first witness to come forward, Lucía Cerna, before it had burned the second, Colonel Avilés. Despite assurances that the embassy was in pursuit of the same "truth and justice" as the Jesuits and not engaged in a coverup, it was revealed to have withheld Buckland's affidavits claiming prior knowledge of the plot to kill the Jesuits. By the end of the investigation phase, there were nine U.S. names in the official court record, yet not one of them had come forward to volunteer information.[22] Nor did it appear that any members of the Green Beret unit training the Atlacatl just days before the Jesuits' killing had been questioned. Moreover, although two U.S. military advisers believed to have information of relevance to the Jesuit case were interviewed by the FBI in November 1990, the contents of those interviews were not shared with the Salvadoran authorities.[23] Silence only fed the suspicions of a conspiracy in conspiracy-hungry El Salvador.

Over the months, antipathy toward the Jesuits centered on the figure of Chema Tojeira. As provincial, Tojeira had been the source of almost all public statements on the progress of the case. His periodic appearances of Salvadoran television were front-page news for the sole opposition daily, *Diario Latino,* and the source of angry cables from the U.S. embassy. "Jesuit Provincial for Central America Slams U.S. Role in Jesuit Case" one cable was headed.[24] And there was no denying that he did. Outspoken and denunciatory in his style, Tojeira spoke his mind with an authority that grew with time, but did nothing to endear him to U.S. officials. While he used his interviews as forums from which to communicate specific pieces of information—Cristiani's having ordered the search of the UCA retrospectively, for example—to the court and the Salvadoran public, he also consistently maintained that the United States government knew more than was being revealed. Tojeira's anger was stoked by the Jesuit's attempt, through the Lawyers Committee and under the Freedom of Information Act, to secure all documents relevant to the Jesuit case from the various U.S. government agencies. Replies were slow in coming and when they came, unsatisfactory.

"They have a bully pulpit," Walker would complain. "The press wants to talk to them. They can say what they want and I cannot rebut them."[25] Embassy officials countered the sallies of the Jesuits with attacks directed to journalists in background briefings or visiting delegations. Since his role in the Lucía Cerna affair and stalwart defense of the actions of the SIU's Colonel Rivas, Rick Chidester had come in for searing criticism by the Jesuits. Although at times their animosity toward him appeared to overlook the fact that all of his actions had been endorsed by his superiors, Chidester did little to help himself. With a picture of Daniel Ortega, captioned "Take a shot at communism," on his office wall and an Uzi on the floor beside his desk, he drove around San Salvador in the kind of license-plate-less vehicle more suitable for those the U.S. government claimed to want to apprehend than for its legal officer. He explained that Tojeira signaled him out for criticism him "because I worked in Honduras with the *contras*," and followed that by a startling reference to the FMLN killing of a U.S. lieutenant commander, Albert Schaulfeburger, at the UCA in 1983. "The Jesuits are not clean—no Jesuit has been killed on embassy grounds. The Jesuits never did squat to help on that investigation."[26]

Tojeira fared little better with the State Department. Indeed his visit to Washington in early October 1990 appears to have instilled alarm in some of those he met. Part of the problem was the fear associated with Central American Jesuits as purveyors of liberation theology. Then again, articulate and forceful as he was, Tojeira was probably few Washington officials' idea of a Jesuit Father Provincial. But it was still surprising to hear one official describe Tojeira's meeting with Assistant Secretary of State Aronson as the worst of all the meetings there had been in the two years in which Aronson had held his post. "It was just terrible," he commented. "Tojeira is a guy who comes out of 1960s knee-jerk liberalism that sees the CIA behind everything."[27]

Both the Jesuit case and the negotiations, which were badly stalled at the time, had been on the agenda for discussion at this meeting, but in the end the subject of the case was hardly broached. Tojeira began by agreeing with the assistant secretary on the difficulties in moving the negotiations forward: the army was refusing to accept restructuring and the FMLN had hardened its position. He remarked that Ellacuría, if he had been alive, could have provided a bridge between the two. The point was taken up by Aronson, who reminded Tojeira and the Jesuits with him of his meeting with Ellacuría in April 1989 and asked Tojeira to commit the "moral influence" of the Jesuits to exerting pressure on the FMLN. This was the source of the meeting's tension. With the Senate debate pending, the administration was openly favoring the cut in aid being tied to a cease-fire, while Tojeira, following the Caracas agenda, insisted that if a cease-fire were to be acceptable to the FMLN, it had to be the result of a negotiated agreement. Aronson was, according to those present, "a bit testy" as he expressed surprise that a representative of the Church could be opposed to a cease-fire under any circumstances.[28]

The figure of Ellacuría loomed large at this meeting. Repeated references to what he had stood for eventually roused Tojeira into irritation. At one point, as he was explaining that neither he nor the Jesuits could assure the FMLN that the army could be trusted in regard to a cease-fire, he cited the congressional report, "Barriers to Reform," that had found all but one of the fifteen top colonels in the Salvadoran army to have had violations of human rights committed by soldiers under their authority. Aronson responded that this was "an interesting view of justice," like blaming Ellacuría for Villalobos's actions because he had been his teacher (he hadn't). The assistant secretary then returned to his central point: this was the moment for the Jesuits to achieve, through their good offices with the FMLN, the negotiated settlement that Ellacuría had always pursued. The observation provoked Tojeira into outlining, in no uncertain terms, what should have been obvious. Ellacuría and his colleagues had been pushing for negotiations for years and years in the face of widespread opposition in El Salvador and from the United States government. And now these men were dead. "That is why he was killed, for supporting negotiations," Tojeira insisted. To have the U.S. government asking the Jesuits to adopt a more public position on negotiations *now* was a little much.

"IT'S just plain hogwash that we don't want the truth to come out," Walker would insist with vehemence at the end of March 1991. "If I were to learn tomorrow that the entire High Command was involved and 172 officers all conspired to kill the Jesuits, I'd be on the roof shouting it out loud—it could not be as bad as this constant undermining of our policy and what the U.S. is trying to do down here." It was almost a year and a half since the Jesuits had been killed, yet despite the enormous resources available to the embassy in El Salvador, Walker was "somewhat embarrassed to have to say that at this point I don't know what happened."[29] If this was the case, then it raised questions about the kind of service he was receiving from his intelligence agencies.

Since publication of the Moakley task force's interim report the preceding April had pushed the embassy to take a more aggressive stance in pressuring the army on the Jesuit case, Walker had become clear that "convicting Benavides is not justice." Too much time had passed and too many questions had been asked. But the informal pitches, formal démarches, and general peptalks on the need for the army to come clean on the Jesuit case delivered by U.S. military personnel, political officers, the ambassador, and a range of heavy-weight visitors, from four-star generals to senators and the assistant secretary of state, had been to little effect. One U.S. military officer would complain of his Salvadoran counterparts, "they just don't get it—sometimes you read these things at them, you'll see the old head move up and then down, up and down again, but you wonder how much is getting through, how much good you're doing."[30]

Frustration with the ability of the U.S.-aided judicial system to deliver justice where the military was involved had grown in February 1990 as the embassy watched how an appeals court dropped charges against all but one of the officers held for the 1988 San Sebastián massacre. The case had been something of a personal crusade for Walker and a pet project of Vice-President Quayle, yet it had evaporated into thin air. Efforts to prosecute a kidnapping-for-profit ring run by civilian and military right-wingers had collapsed soon afterwards—again leaving just one defendant to face trial—as judges were pressured, bribed, shot at, and, in one case, killed.[31] In August the administration had expressed its disappointment by cutting the $2 million legal aid program. Unfortunately, the lack of teeth in the U.S. position was transparent. After the August 11 revelations to the Moakley task force were passed on to the embassy, $19 million in military aid was held back to protest the army's record in the Jesuit case. The move went unreported to Congress and was opposed by Defense Secretary Dick Cheney. It fell to Walker to deliver the bad news in meetings with Cristiani and the High Command. At each meeting the ambassador made it quite clear that the aid would be withheld until the U.S. government "was convinced of ESAF cooperation with the Jesuit investigation."[32] Yet these strong words proved to be as ephemeral as the threats that had gone before them; when the FMLN stepped up their military activity in November, the aid was promptly released, the lack of military cooperation in the Jesuit case notwithstanding.

An indication of Walker's personal frustration with the failure of the embassy's initiatives was his support of a memorandum prepared by Jim McGovern and Bill Woodward, the congressional aides to the task force, after a trip to El Salvador in December 1990. The keynote of the memorandum was given in a remark made to the staffers by a Salvadoran official: "The armed forces wrote the first act of the Jesuits' case by murdering the priests, now they are writing the final act in controlling the investigation."[33] Concentrating on two unresolved issues, the role of Salvadoran military intelligence and the apparent control of the investigation by the military hierarchy, the memorandum elaborated on the conviction of High Command involvement in the crime expressed six months earlier by Congressman Moakley. How it had been decided, and by whom, that Benavides and the lieutenants were to be questioned and charged for the Jesuit killings, while none of the officers between them on the chain of command were even investigated, was still unexplained. Speculation led the staffers to suggest "that the military hierarchy—not the investigating authorities—controlled who was questioned, who was detained and who was charged . . . that a deal may have been cut wherein a senior officer, Colonel Benavides, was required to take responsibility, while mid-level officers were shielded from prosecution . . . that the entire investigation may have been a charade calibrated to meet the minimum— and only the minimum—demands of meddlers from Congress and elsewhere."[34]

That Ambassador Walker could find nothing to object to in this memorandum confirmed the worst fears of every U.S. official following the Jesuit case, and left the embassy hamstrung, protesting its commitment to push forward toward the truth with what could only be assertions of its own impotence, yet suspecting that the revelation of that truth might involve the unmasking of some of the officers most trusted, supported, and praised by the United States as the cold-blooded murderers of priests. Over $1 billion to the Salvadoran military and an estimated CIA investment of over $500 million, all to be beaten by an institution among whose most proven sayings is the legend: "What's heard here, said here, done here, stays here."[35]

Central to this dilemma was the figure of the recently ascended

General René Emilio Ponce. Since 1966, when he graduated from the military academy first in the forty-seven-member *tandona,* Ponce had always been his *tanda*'s leader. One who had known him since he was a cadet described him as "the last officer fully prepared to be a future president of the country."[36] Surrounded by the *compadres,* the select and tightly knit group of eight to ten officers who had, over the years, looked after *tandona* interests (besides being genuine *compadres,* godfathers, of each other's children), Ponce's authority among his peers had grown as he moved up through the ranks. In accord with the collegiate nature of the Salvadoran military structure, his strengths lay in his ability to construct and maintain a consensus and his facility to shift with the mainstream as the mainstream shifted.

During the 1980s, the history of Ponce's relationship to the United States had been somewhat checkered. As executive officer (second in command) of the Treasury Police from 1980 to 1982 and then director of the Traffic Department at the National Police in 1983, the relationship had been less than cordial. These were the years of the worst human rights' abuses, the security forces were the worst abusers, and by 1983 the CIA had gathered information that branded Ponce as a death squad member.[37] With the embassy trying to "freeze them out," U.S. officials required the specific permission of Ambassador Deane Hinton before communicating with the Treasury Police at all. One U.S. adviser with a senior position at the time remembered of Ponce that, "he hated us."[38] Improvement began in 1984 when Ponce assumed the first of his key command positions, chief of operations on the Joint General Staff. From then on assiduously cultivated by military advisers and the embassy's political staff, Ponce was elevated to colonel in 1986 and rose to chief of staff in 1988 to preside over the consolidation of the *tandona*'s power. In 1989 he had been fully expected to succeed the outgoing General Vides Casanova as the new minister of defense when opposition to the plans of the army and the embassy emerged from the air force, strongly backed by COENA, the Executive Council of the ARENA party.[39]

As ARENA came to power and divided the key government posts between the hard-liners on the party's far right and the technocrats behind Cristiani, D'Aubuisson and COENA got Cristiani to promise the position of minister of defense to air force chief General Bustillo. At the time he was the senior officer serving in the Salvadoran armed forces and facing retirement if he did not ascend to the ministry. Bustillo was also a man with a past: in command of the air force since 1979, he had run the Ilopango air base as a fiefdom built on power and money from the U.S.

dollars pouring in to support the most expensive yet most vital area of the war. Over the years, as journalist Charles Lane documented in a portrait entitled "The Pilot Shark of El Salvador," Bustillo backed a mutiny that resulted in the firing of the defense minister in 1983; agreed not to destabilize the government of Duarte in return for U.S. funding of his private, murderous and drug-dealing "military dictatorship"; and by-passed his president and minister of defense to lend "his" air base to the CIA and Oliver North for the supply weapons to the *contras*. When that arrangement was blown apart by the Iran-*contra* revelations, Duarte contemplated firing Bustillo, but without the support of U.S. Ambassador Edwin Corr, he did not have the power to do so. He was only the president.[40]

Bustillo was the only Salvadoran officer invited to President Bush's inauguration, yet by 1989 he represented an aspect of the U.S. presence in Central America that the new spirit of pragmatism preferred to jettison. When it became known that Bustillo's choice for the two vice-ministers were officers in exile for their human rights' violations, U.S. officials made it clear to Cristiani that a change in his plans would be called for. But the air force was not happy. A week before Cristiani was sworn in as president, air force planes buzzed a ceremony being attended by the outgoing Defense Minister Vides Casanova, drowning out his speech, and Mil-Group commander Colonel Milton Menjívar had his life threatened by an air force officer. In the end a compromise was found in General Rafael Humberto Larios. Nearing the end of his career, Larios was acceptable to Ponce and the army because they knew that the younger Ponce could wait in the wings, and was tolerable to Bustillo because at least he wasn't Ponce. With Larios, as a U.S. officer described him, a "do-nothing" minister of defense, Ponce remained chief of staff and was effectively in control during the November 1989 offensive.[41]

"Colonel Ponce is a very respected senior leader of the High Command," Aronson had said in a congressional hearing in January 1990 in defense of Menjívar's delivering of Buckland and Avilés to the chief of staff. "And not somebody who one would not trust with information."[42] Yet as the investigation of the Jesuit case inched forward, some embassy officers became uneasy. Like others outside the armed forces they had always dealt with the *tandona* through Ponce, who had established particularly close relationships with Menjívar and the political-military officer Janice Elmore. The purging of corrupt, brutal or incompetent *tandona* officers was a long-term project, and one, like everything else, for which Ponce was the point man. While hopes of deeply rooted change had

been undercut in December 1989 when the *tandona* emerged with the
command positions in all three security forces and five of the country's six
brigades, the U.S. embassy believed that Ponce as minister of defense was
still the best option they had for cleaning out the armed forces and holding
them together through a difficult period of negotiations. There was only
one problem: the possible implication of the High Command, and within
them Ponce, in the Jesuit case.

Démarches, an aid cut and yet more words from the ambassador
preceded Ponce's eventual elevation to minister of defense on September
1, 1990. Walker would note that the new minister's first speech "fell short
of the proactive comments we had hoped for,"[43] and among the most
conspicuous of his early actions was his refusal to follow the example set by
Cristiani and present himself in person to testify before Judge Zamora. As
the months went by, the failure of the U.S. government to establish the
truth in the Jesuit case questioned the wisdom of having bought into the
army's own power structure. Ponce was the leader of the *tandona* long
before and would remain the leader of the *tandona* long after he was a
client and friend of the United States embassy. During 1991, while
embassy officials would go out of their way to praise Ponce for providing
"progressive" leadership through the negotiations, it was praise tempered
by the knowledge that when it came to the Jesuit case, the Salvadoran
military had run rings around them from start to finish. "I mean I see
Ponce and talk to him and we talk about the Jesuit case," Walker would
admit, "but it isn't as if he gives me direct answers."[44]

ONE Republican congressional aide who had worked for many years on
Central America described his shock at having his attempts to impress
upon a senior Salvadoran officer the political need to resolve the Jesuit case
brushed aside by the remark, "You don't understand—they were communists."[45] A Salvadoran colonel put the point more clearly by telling how
one of his majors presented himself in his office one day saying, "Colonel,
can you explain something to me?" The colonel had asked the major what
the problem was and the major had answered. "I don't understand why
those who killed the Jesuits have been detained. They are heroes of the
armed forces. We should be building statues to them, not locking them
up."[46] Within the armed forces this view was widely held. It would have
taken more than international outrage, more even than cuts in military aid
to alter views firmly held for years. In conversation with a visiting
American during the April 1990 military air show in Chile, air force
commander General Villamariona remarked that it was "stupid" for the

Salvadoran army to have killed the Jesuits, although, he added, "they needed killing."[47]

In public, Ponce and other senior officers would continue to promise collaboration, insist on the individual rather than institutional responsibility for the killing of the Jesuits, and blame the "enemies of El Salvador" working for the FMLN in the international community for their exploitation of the case. "I cannot possibly think who could have given that order," Ponce would affirm in January 1991. "I must assure you that this case has done more harm to the institution than has the FMLN in eleven years of war."[48] Yet in private, the terms for "collaboration" were clearly laid down. Officers were ordered not to discuss the case even among themselves and in February 1991, at a meeting of senior officers called to discuss the United Nations working paper on military reform and the document the armed forces had drawn up in reply, Ponce would make himself quite clear on the issue. "Someone has been talking to the Americans," he is reported to have said, "and it is not Colonel Avilés"—who was present at the meeting—"whoever it is is betraying the armed forces."[49] One officer briefing Ponce on the political mood in the United States had insisted, on a separate occasion during the same period, that the Jesuit case was "key" to relations between the two countries. Ponce fell silent and then answered only: "then we'll have to reach a negotiated settlement this year."[50]

Resistance to U.S. pressure ran deep. Much as Salvadoran officers acknowledged that without the United States they would have lost the war to the FMLN, nationalistic resentment of any foreigner coming into their country and telling them what to do was always present. "We're like a guardian elephant in the sitting room," one U.S. official would explain. "It might be a very nice elephant, but every time the son-of-a-bitch moves it breaks the furniture. Once a day it shits all over the place and you get to clear it up."[51] Complicating this relationship was the legacy of the Reagan rhetoric. The Salvadorans had been told that their country was on the front line for the fight against international communism and that the national security of the United States was at stake. Over the years many had, not surprisingly, come to believe that they were fighting and dying for the United States and that it was the United States that should be grateful to them. Pressure smacked of betrayal. And then again, the army had been threatened and pressured before, endlessly; experience had taught that there was nothing to fear, that fighting the war was the first priority and when necessary, the aid would flow.

Walker would cite one particular episode as an example of the problems he faced in trying to arrive at the truth. By October 1990, Colonel Menjívar, Janice Elmore, and Colonel Wayne Wheeler, the defense attaché—the three officials closest to the Salvadoran military—had left San Salvador. Worried about lack of communication while the new staff brought themselves up to speed, Walker brought down a U.S. military officer with previous experience of El Salvador and good contacts inside the Salvadoran military. After a few weeks the officer had reported to him that he thought he had a source who might be able to "turn" Lieutenant Espinzoa—what could he offer him? Walker had run through the available options, discussing the possibility of granting Espinzoa asylum in the United States if he "came clean" to the judge and reminding the officer that a reward of $250,000 had been offered by the Salvadoran government soon after the Jesuits were killed. The officer left, and Walker thought nothing more of it until he was visited by Arturo Tona, Cristiani's private secretary, a few weeks later. Tona told Walker that allegations had been brought to Cristiani that "a U.S. military officer had offered bribes to ESAF officers to induce testimony in the Jesuit case." As Walker would recall in an interview, Tona then explained that in a culture in which "the concept of a reward is unknown," the embassy was perceived to be "trying to bribe somebody to stand up and tell lies."[52]

The army's displeasure soon made itself felt in an anonymous telephone call telling the U.S. officer to get off the case. A few days later he was flown back to the United States. "Whatever you do or don't do," Walker would comment the following March, "you get misinterpreted. The bottom line is that we're always misinterpreted on all sides. Whatever you do people are going to see it either as interfering too much or not trying hard enough." "Given this turn of events," he had cabled to Washington on November 13, "embassy has reexamined its role in unilateral pursuit of further information relating to the Jesuit case."[53]

IN November 1990, and in response to a demand of Judge Zamora, the Salvadoran Supreme Court asked the foreign ministry to request that the videotape made of Major Eric Buckland on January 12, 1990 be provided to the court. A transcript and its Spanish translation were presented to the foreign ministry in January 1991 and forwarded to Zamora in March 1991.[54] When the transcript filtered out to the press it became clear why it had not been provided to the court in October along with Buckland's January 10 and 11 affidavits claiming prior knowledge of the Jesuit murders.

The January 12 interview with FBI Agent Paul Cully summarized

Buckland's interviews of the previous two days. Buckland provided a detailed description of his visit to the military academy with Colonel Avilés at the end of October 1989, in which—as Buckland remembered it—Avilés had told him that Benavides was "a rammer" of the "old school" and planning to kill Ellacuría. Buckland's interview also included the information that Avilés had told him on November 15 that there was an operation planned against the UCA that night.[55] But this was not all. What the transcript made clear was that Buckland's January 12 interview revealed so close an identification with the Salvadoran military on his part as to challenge his loyalty to the United States and an acquiescence to the killing of the Jesuits that questioned both the effectiveness and the will behind the U.S. commitment to improving the human rights record of the Salvadoran army.

Buckland had wanted to belong. In Carlos Avilés he believed he had found the best colonel he had ever worked with. He believed Avilés was destined to become the future commander of the First Brigade, then chief of staff and minister of defense, and Buckland had wanted to be part of it: a member of his staff, not an adviser. "I did not feel disloyal to the United States, but I felt for a long time that I loved the ideals of my country, but I don't much like the people . . . And I really loved the Salvadorans and I like their military." Thrown into a situation where his Special Forces training called for a building of "rapport" with his opposite number, Buckland had "got caught up in the country," high on the idea that "we're at war—who understands better than us? We're here, we're at the front, at the cutting edge." "I thought I could save the world," he had said at one point. "Thought I had all the answers. I was going to be Lawrence of Arabia, you know—Eric of El Salvador."

No doubt sensing the admiration of this newcomer to El Salvador, Avilés had paid Buckland a lot of attention and talked to him about a range of things, from "leisure shit and that kind of stuff" to the inside story of the Salvadoran military. Among the discussions had been an explanation of exactly what was meant by the phrase "old school," used to describe Benavides. "Before the civil war," Buckland explained to his interviewer, "when you got made colonel, you got a phone call from the oligarchy and somebody basically bought you. You made good bucks and you looked out for that guy, or whatever it was that was going on. And they also played pretty hard ball. Human rights was not a discussion." In the old days there had been "plenty for the liberals to grab onto" in "organized going around and killing people. There probably still is, obviously, but I mean organized every day." The abc's of military impunity, then and now, Buckland had learned from his driver: "When the police stop you, they don't ticket you. You carry a pistol wherever you want to, you can do pretty much whatever you want to, you're above prosecution. My bodyguard asked me, in the States could I run red lights? I said, no, I'd get a ticket. 'Well, you carry your pistol around with you?' I said no. 'Can you beat women up?' I said no."

In the old school, "the enemy is not necessarily the guy carrying the weapon, it's the mouthpiece too," which is where the Jesuits came in. Buckland described how he was told that, "some of the terrorist activities" had been coming out of the UCA, "rockets being fired, mortars and some of that stuff," and how action was going to be taken against Ellacuría and the university as a result. He understood this to mean that Ellacuría was to be killed, but had little problem with it. "I can honestly say that I had no love for any of the leftist people. Okay. I loved El Salvador, and I can honestly say I knew the ramifications of any of those kind of murders to the country, but I didn't think a whole lot about somebody getting killed." Buckland had not known about Ellacuría's contacts with Cristiani, but from what he had heard within the military—and, as he claimed elsewhere, from discussions of Ellacuría and his work in Fort Bragg[56]—he "just knew he was dirty." "And I struggled," was how he described his reaction to the possibility of the killing. "You know, I've been struggling with this for a while—how do you win these kinds of wars? If you're nice all the time you're going to get your butt kicked."

While Buckland believed that Avilés had "handled" the problem with Benavides, he also remembered a brief meeting on the afternoon of November 15 in which Avilés had told him that the military was going to "go in and clean out the UCA . . . to get the dirty people in there." His empathy for the Salvadoran army led him to lose all the perspective of an outsider and admit that he would have accepted the killings: "Again, I hadn't gone through ten years, but I mean they had. So all the pain and stuff and I know they're big on vengeance and I kind of understood . . . I understood the blood, the blood feeling, but it was their war and their country." Out of this confusion had come Buckland's decision to wait and see if the Salvadorans themselves would act on the information implicating Benavides that Avilés brought to him on December 20. Worrying about El Salvador, he had explained that he "didn't trust the American government. I thought they'd pull the rug out from El Salvador."

"I was broken like a prisoner of war," Buckland stated in a lengthy interview the following November with officials from the Justice and Defense departments.[57] The interview came after the story of his prior knowledge and subsequent retraction became public. He was granted immunity in an effort to clear up the facts once and for all and the account he gave of his treatment by Special Agent Cully does little for the image of the FBI. According to Buckland, Cully had pushed him, asking questions along the lines of "Are we talking murder? Did you do it? Did you plan it?" until, provided with the "out" that "prior knowledge was not bad," Buckland had dredged back to memory the visit he made to the military academy and suddenly thought, "Oh, my God, I did know, I did suppress it."

Although Buckland recanted his prior knowledge and forever stuck to his recantation, the damage of the January 12 interview had been done.[58] If Buckland had been—like Lucía Cerna—"broken" by his FBI interrogator and forced to give him what he wanted to hear, the substance of what he had said about his relationship with Avilés, his conflict of loyalties, and his take on what a U.S. adviser might consider acceptable within the Salvadoran conflict could not have come out of thin air. "Reprehensible!" was the reaction of Menijívar's successor as the head of MilGroup, Colonel Mark Hamilton, on whose watch the video transcript broke. "It's institutionally humiliating—I mean really—the idea that he wasn't sure where his loyalty lay. I'm sorry, but given the order I will take this place apart!"[59] While other U.S. officials would repeatedly refer to Buckland as "an emotional wreck" and "a screwup," Buckland had highlighted all that is most dangerous about an international alliance built on a foundation of personal relationships when, as another member of the U.S. military team in El Salvador would comment, with laconic under-statement, "we're still with guys that, all things being equal, I would not seek out as friends."[60]

The irony of the whole Buckland saga was that while it would seriously damage the relationship between U.S. advisers and the Salva-doran military, it had been—until Menjívar burned Avilés—an example of the "buddy" relationship actually working. Exactly what Avilés thought Buckland would do with the information he gave to him will probably never be known, but he did pass it to him, Buckland did (eventually) take it to his superiors, and it played a major role in the breaking of the case. Getting close to an army that, while a heavily funded ally, will always be a foreign force, has its risks, but they are multiplied inordinately if that army is as corrupt and abusive of human rights as is that of El Salvador. Advisers arrived in the country often with only a minimal knowledge of a complex situation, they spent most of their time with the Salvadoran military, and had their understanding of what was going on filtered through their military counterparts. They were fully aware that their effectiveness depended on their ability to be accepted, yet the gaining of acceptance always contained the risk of cooptation. Nor was it helpful that, as one official commented, there were "two ways of getting in with the High Command—drinking and whoring."[61] "The Salvadorans," former Mil-Group commander Colonel Waghelstein had told the *New York Times,* "are very adept at telling you what you want to hear." "As an attaché," one U.S. officer would put it, "you got treated like you were really somebody—you'd think you were Jesus Christ returned to earth."[62]

The phenomenon was not restricted to military advisers. Within the State Department El Salvador had a bad reputation for "clientitis," as U.S. officials across the spectrum were encouraged to "buddy up" to their opposite numbers. "You know Americans," an official remarked. "We like to be friends, we like to operate on a personal level, and this leads to over-identification."[63] Yet the "he's-my-friend" school of diplomacy cuts both ways. That clientitis was particularly bad in El Salvador reflected both the polarization of the country and the highly ideological presence of the United States within that polarization. For many it was the last battleground, somewhere an individual could get a real sense of being able to make a difference, of striking a blow—however metaphorical—for "freedom." "Eric of El Salvador" may be an extreme case, but the questions the episode raised are real. Such questions could only underline the United States' difficulty in extracting the truth from an institution with which it was so intimately involved. Buckland's assessment that "I was making foreign policy decisions on my own"[64] fueled speculation—among U.S. officials as well those on the outside—that there were others in the U.S. mission who had, like Buckland, mistaken loyalty for integrity and concealed information that could have helped the investigation into the Jesuit murders.

RESISTANCE to the direction in which Moakley was pushing the investigation, even as the case lay dormant in the courts, came not only from the military. A copy of the congressional staff memorandum had been delivered to President Cristiani by Congressman John Murtha while on a flying visit to El Salvador on January 13, 1991. Cristiani had not reacted well to the document and had commissioned his Washington based public relations firm, Hannan and O'Connor, to draft a reply. The first Moakley's office had learned of this had been via a late night call from Walker: the embassy had heard that the document was being prepared, suspected that it would be a hatchet job, and wanted the two aides responsible for the original memo, Jim McGovern and Bill Woodward, to be sure that the embassy had nothing to do with it. Shortly after that, Joe Blatchford, who headed the Cristiani account within Hannan and O'Connor, sent two lawyers to see McGovern and Woodward to "clarify the issues." At a Washington reception Moakley—who is fiercely protective of his staff—bumped into one of Hannan and O'Connor's senior partners. The firm is a big one, with a varied slate of clients, so Moakley's threat that if such a report came out, neither Hannan and O'Connor nor any of their clients would "ever get anything past the Rules Committee ever again" struck home.[65]

But work on the report went forward and a copy was eventually passed to the U.S. embassy in El Salvador and through them to the State Department, although not to Moakley. One State Department official found the document "inordinately shrill," but agreed with a lot of the points made within it, not least that the aides' memo had been "without appreciation of due process, the specifics of Salvadoran law or the minimum guarantees of U.S. law."[66] The central thesis of the document had been that the staff memo "attacks the integrity of the investigation and that of Salvadoran government officials, while ignoring the unprecedented progress that has been achieved in this case." Hannan and O'Connor echoed the Salvadoran army in finding "much evidence already on record demonstrating that the military High Command has cooperated in this investigation."[67]

As part of its defense of the role played by President Cristiani, the public relations document referred to what Moakley's aides had believed was a confidential lunch with Salvadoran Ambassador Salaverría. Back on August 11 they had been shocked to learn from their source that he had come forward to speak to the task force only after he had taken his information about the High Command's link to the murders to Cristiani. Cristiani, he claimed, had done nothing about it, and had appeared more interested in the source's motives than the implications of what he had to tell him. The aides had gone to the Ambassador Salaverría with discretion and yet here, amid denials that Cristiani had ever been given any such information, was their confidential material writ large. That elsewhere in the document Cristiani was quoted as claiming that when shown the Buckland videotape in Ambassador Walker's home he had recommended— in flat contradiction of the embassy version of the incident— "that the tape should either be given to the SIU, to some other judicial support body, or directly to the judge," was another example of the extent to which the public relations document, if allowed to become public, would have proved embarrassing for the Salvadoran government. The point was clearly made in a telephone call Assistant Secretary of State Aronson put in to Cristiani as he recommended the document should be squelched.[68]

Congressman Murtha's January 13 visit to El Salvador had been an unusual demonstration of freelance diplomacy. In his meetings with Cristiani, Defense Minister Ponce, and Lieutenant Colonel Rivas from the SIU, he had stressed that as the United States prepared for war in the Gulf, El Salvador was a low priority. Washington was rapidly losing patience with the Salvadoran army, which was in danger of losing military aid altogether if they did not make progress on the Jesuit case. General Ponce's response—"we have decided to cooperate with the investigation"—was one that left the congressman incensed.[69] It was more than a year after the murders and *now* the army was saying it was going to cooperate. Yet nothing appeared to be happening.

In early February, Walker took steps to increase direct pressure on Ponce: he arranged with General George Joulwan, the incoming chief of the U.S. Southern Command, to fly Ponce down to the farewell ceremony for Joulwan's predecessor, General Maxwell Thurman. Joulwan had met with Moakley in January and had asked the congressman if there was anything specific he could do on the Jesuit case. Moakley had asked him to try and get Ponce to testify in person, rather than continue to take refuge in his written replies to the court. On the way back from the ceremony, the minister of defense was temporarily trapped between the senior U.S. military officer in the region and the U.S. ambassador. "General Joulwan and I spent two and a half hours pounding poor Ponce on the Jesuit case," Walker remembered, "two and a half hours on that plane."[70]

Ten days later, Walker received a telephone call from Ponce: "Bring the general back, I've got something to tell you." Joulwan flew in for a meeting and the something turned out to be a letter from the High Command to the justice minister, dated February 22, 1991. "Given that the judicial process has not yet concluded," the letter read, "as members of the High Command of the armed forces, we consider it of urgent necessity that some complementary investigations should be undertaken that might help clear up the truth in this delicate case." Insisting there had been "no institutional responsibility in the planning or execution" of the operation against the Jesuits, the letter asked the SIU to investigate events previous to the crime, among them a meeting held by the officers of the newly created security zone that took place in the military academy on the night of November 15, 1989. The letter provided a list of the ten officers, with Lieutenant Colonel Camilo Hernández the most senior, present at this meeting and also recommended that the SIU should seek to amplify the declarations of the then–Director of Intelligence Colonel Guzmán Aguilar and of a DNI lieutenant, Hector Cuenca Ocampos, who had accompanied the Atlacatl in the November 13 search of the Jesuit residence.[71]

Within the U.S. embassy there were differences of opinion as to the real worth of this letter, but room for a measured response was denied by the enthusiastic welcome it was given in Washington. On March 13, as Walker drafted a cable bemoaning the travails of an embassy that had been "swiped at by the Jesuits, stonewalled by the military and put off by the government," Assistant Secretary Aronson told the *New York Times:* "There has been a breakthrough that I think is important. This action by the High Command is a serious development."[72] One positive indication, or so it was perceived, was that Ponce had telephoned Judge Zamora on his return from a trip to England and the United States and offered to testify in person. Although Walker would criticize the judge for not taking Ponce up on his offer, Zamora explained to Ponce that for the moment the case was on appeal and he was not in a position to do anything about it. But it appeared to Walker and to Joulwan—who wrote to Moakley with the good news of the success of his efforts—to be something of a breakthrough. "I think it is finally sinking in," Walker would comment of both the letter and telephone call. "Ponce and the High Command have finally understood that the world wants and needs to be told what happened."[73]

BY the time the eight-day evidentiary period in the Jesuit case opened in late May 1991, elections that had seen the left-wing coalition of the Democratic Convergence treble its vote since 1989,[74] and an extended period of negotiations in Mexico had created a climate in which real change seemed a possible, if still a distant, goal. Yet the mixed signals from the State Department had continued. On the eve of a new round of talks in early February, the *New York Times* made public U.S. officials' discontent with U.N. mediator de Soto. Believed to have emanated from sources such as Assistant Secretary Aronson himself and reinforced by a background briefing given to journalists in El Salvador the previous week by Walker, the apparently planned leak charged that de Soto was "less than energetic pursuing the peace process" and that he "accedes to the guerrillas' delaying tactics."[75] The article was subjected to the highest level of "spin control" as the U.S. ambassador to the United Nations (and former ambassador to San Salvador) Thomas Pickering called U.N. Secretary General Pérez de Cuéllar to assure him that the unnamed sources "did not reflect the U.S. position,"[76] but its charges could not be withdrawn. De Soto found his efforts "seriously undercut" as those in El Salvador with an interest in restricting the government's room for manuever encouraged the belief that a hardening of the position toward the United Nations would have U.S. support.[77]

In mid-February 1991, the FMLN had offered to sign a cease-fire in return for the military reforms proposed by the United Nations and a recognition of the areas of the country under their control. With the legislative elections looming in March, the Salvadoran government was unable to accept what became known as the "territoriality" of the FMLN and rejected the offer. Soon after the elections, the FMLN again took up the initiative, proposing to enter nonstop negotiations in April aimed at producing an agreement on constitutional reform before the disbanding of the current Legislative Assembly at the end of April and at achieving a cease-fire by May 30.[78] Talks began in Mexico on April 4 and ran through to a cliff-hanging conclusion on April 27. Accords were signed that, if less than the FMLN had hoped for, were more than it had appeared that the government would be able to accept.

Specific amendments to the 1983 Salvadoran constitution paved the way for a package of reforms that included "a clearer definition of the subordination of the armed forces to the civil authorities" and other reforms designed to improve the judicial system and establish safeguards for human rights.[79] The drama did not end with the signing of the accords: two days later the ARENA-dominated assembly rejected two of the provisions agreed to in Mexico. Only after vehement protest from the FMLN, pressure from the United Nations, the EEC, the governments of Colombia, Mexico, Venezuela, and Spain now gathered around the U.N. secretary-general as the "Group of Friends"[80] and—most importantly—some hectic working of the telephones by senior State Department officials, did the deputies reconvene for a special session and decide to change their minds.

These April talks proved a turning point in the negotiating process. One FMLN negotiator commented that "we would not have continued had this fallen through,"[81] while in El Salvador the entire right wing erupted in protest at the prospect of any kind of constitutional change. Paid advertisements assumed a new virulence, a wave of kidnappings of wealthy businessmen began, and there were constant rumblings from within the army. Accused of "betrayal," Cristiani's government had never looked more vulnerable. Rumors of a Bustillo-backed coup were rife and would eventually lead to the sudden resignation of Salvadoran air force chief General Villamariona. The news that D'Aubuisson was suffering from terminal cancer only increased the sense of instability. Within the army, opposition to the talks also came from lower ranking officers. Worried about their futures, they believed the *tandona* was prepared to go along with negotiations because its members had already ensured "their share of the pie."[82] Particularly unpopular was the agreement to form a "Truth Commission" to investigate the most serious acts of violence and human rights violations that had occurred since 1980. The army had wanted to maintain a military majority within the commission and was less than pleased with the accord's acceptance of three commissioners, none of them Salvadorans, to be designated by the secretary-general of the United Nations.

In the midst of the talks, the Jesuit case emerged from the appeals court and moved closer to its trial. As the officers indicated in the High Command's February letter—all but three of whom had already given testimony—were questioned by the SIU, it became clear that the initial enthusiasm of those who had believed the letter a "breakthrough" had been misplaced. The letter's most obvious effect had been to feed the discontent among junior officers. They resented that the High Command was "throwing a bone to the *gringos*," as one officer put it, at their or their *tanda*-mates' expense.[83] Some officers had spoken to the detained lieutenants and had been alarmed by what they were saying. The lieutenants were angry. They considered they had been set up by their own institution. They had been told that they could talk to the Honor Commission in all confidence and that their testimonies would remain a military affair. Then those same testimonies had been altered, presented to the court, and ratified by SIU witnesses. Although all the defendants had denied the veracity of these extrajudicial confessions, they were still the most damning of all the evidence against them. So now they were talking. Not to a lot of people. But talking. Names were being mentioned—names of officers above Benavides.

The officers named in the February letter had been in the military academy on the night of November 15 to 16, 1989. They all had either participated in or knew details of the operation against the UCA. They had lied in their testimony because they had been told to. Their understanding from Benavides had been that the order had come from officers within the High Command. Some of these former military officers had been planning to take their information to the U.S. embassy—to Walker himself, not the military advisers. But in the end it wasn't necessary: the pressure eased up after one of their number was summoned before the High Command. "What do you know about the killing of the

Jesuits?" he had been asked. "Nothing," he answered. "You must know more about it than that," the generals insisted. The young officer made a decision and decided to speak: "I know this is being recorded, but I don't care. Why are you asking me when you know all about it—you ordered it, you, you, and you [pointing with his finger]. From now on, I'll hold you responsible for my life. It's sad, but from today on, I'm going to be more frightened of my own army than of the guerrillas."[84]

ON May 6, 1991, two young lawyers presented themselves to the Salvadoran court as private prosecutors acting on behalf of the families of the murdered Jesuits and of Elba and Celina Ramos. Sidney Blanco and Henry Campos had been the most active of the public prosecutors working on the Jesuit case throughout 1990. On January 8, 1991, they had resigned in protest against the extent to which their own role had been limited by the reluctance of the Salvadoran attorney general's office to pursue the investigation fully. In a press conference, the two prosecutors described how they were illegally restricted from initiating charges against some of the "long list" of witnesses who had committed perjury. They had been prevented from questioning an SIU lieutenant and from being present at all at the declaration of Lieutenant Colonel Rivas. They had been forbidden from talking to the press after they made comments about the army's role in the investigation and believed that, in its indifference to these issues, the attorney general's office was conforming with restrictions imposed by the military.[85]

The document Blanco and Campos delivered to the court enraged the army and elicited a threat to sue from General Ponce. It argued that the murder of the Jesuits had either had the authorization of the High Command or was the product of a "criminal conspiracy" of individuals present within the armed forces. Their thesis was rooted within a consideration not only of who the Jesuits were, and what that might have to do with why they were killed, but also of what this case must mean for El Salvador as a whole: "If the murder of these individuals, of such moral standing, with such international support, with so much evidence of its authorship, remains unpunished, the repercussions will be terrible not just for the judicial system but for the entire country. For many the logical conclusion will be that it is possible to kill the best of Salvadoran society without that same society being capable of confronting and finding a solution to the problem. And this conclusion would to a certain extent destroy the hopes of a future that is not only peaceful, but also rational and humane."[86]

The final obstacle to the opening of the eight-day evidentiary period had been a plan to present successive writs of *habeas corpus* coordinated by the defendants' families. All writs were rejected by the Salvadoran Supreme Court and the evidentiary period was opened on May 23, 1991. The private prosecutors submitted an extensive brief to Judge Zamora, requesting further information, testimony, and four "confrontations" between witnesses whose declarations had contradicted each other. An extra three months were added by Zamora's acceptance of the petition for interviews with ten U.S. citizens, under a process known as Letters Rogatory allowing for the collection of evidence from a foreign court, but otherwise the prosecutors were disappointed. Despite a flurry of activity that included the appearances in court of Colonel Benavides and Lieutenant Espinoza, vying with each other in their protestations of innocence and faith that God the Almighty would let the operation of justice of El Salvador prove truth to be on their side,[87] the new evidence revealed in this period was as scant as it had been throughout the judicial process.

The judge refused to cite six senior officers—including General Ponce—on the grounds that they were legally exempt from appearing in court and also rejected the confrontations.[88] The long investigation phase had shown, more clearly than anything else, where the limits of legal action lay. A face-to-face confrontation between Generals Ponce and Zepeda, minister and deputy-minister of defense, was clearly beyond them.

IN Washington, the Democratic leadership had been working hard to collaborate with the State Department in forging a responsible reaction to the delicate negotiations in El Salvador. In early March representatives and senators asked the administration to maintain the spirit of the "Moakley-Murtha" and "Dodd-Leahy" legislation and extend the two-month delay in the "released" aid announced in January. With the April negotiations looming, State kept the money on ice and, hopeful for a cease-fire by May 30, requested that for its part Congress should withhold from any legislative action on El Salvador before that date. In early June, with a cease-fire still a distant prospect as the negotiations faltered once more, U.N. mediator Alvaro de Soto appealed directly to the House leadership, asking for them to hold off on any action on El Salvador until September. Congressmen appreciated de Soto's concern to keep both sides in the talks guessing as to future action on El Salvador and wrote to President Bush to explain that they were, for the moment, postponing a debate on El Salvador. At the same time they put in a strong request that the withheld aid should continue on hold. The unfreezing of this aid, it was argued, "would take the pressure off the government with respect to the negotiations and the Jesuit case and with respect to human rights in general."[89]

All this explains why Moakley would grumble to his aide Jim McGovern that the release of aid announced at the end of June 1991 was "the stupidest thing this administration has done."[90] Continued attacks by the FMLN were cited as having triggered the release, but the real reason was just business as usual: there was a six-month pipeline in the delivery of aid to El Salvador and the possibility that, by December, the armed forces might be feeling the pinch. For Moakley himself the timing could not have been worse. On June 28 he was due in El Salvador for a previously scheduled visit in which he would be trying to exert one last push on the Jesuit case before it came to trial. He had met with Assistant Secretary Aronson on June 26 and had been told that the aid release was imminent; he had assumed that meant sometime the following week, which would inevitably weaken the impact of what he would be saying to those he met in El Salvador. But the announcement came the following day. "It almost looked like they wanted to put it on my schedule," Moakley would say at the end of a visit in which he had found himself having to criticize his own government at every turn.[91]

When it came to the Jesuit case Moakley was, if anything, more determined than ever. "I feel like Alec Guinness in the *Bridge Over the River Kwai* on this thing," he said in May. "I never wanted to build the bridge in the first place. But I am sure as hell not going to let them blow it up on me."[92] The aid release highlighted a fundamental difference between his position on the relationship of the Jesuit case to negotiations and that of the administration. In a carefully pitched piece of diplomacy he contributed to House Foreign Affairs Committee hearings in April, Moakley had placed on the record his "great admiration" for Secretary of State Baker and Assistant Secretary Aronson and his "special respect and friendship" for Ambassador Walker. "One of the reasons why this case is so important," Moakley continued, "is because it tests the Salvadoran government's commitment to tackle the sensitive issue of military impunity. And I believe, if these current negotiations between the Salvadoran Government and FMLN are to succeed, this issue must be resolved."[93]

Moakley had no doubt about where to begin: Ponce had had operational responsibility as chief of staff at the time of the Jesuit murders and he had institutional responsibility now as minister of defense. Even if the task forces's sources suggesting that Ponce had been involved in the decision to kill the Jesuits proved to be false, Ponce had quite clearly lied to every branch of the U.S. government for a year and a half and overseen an institutional coverup of an immense scale. He should either come clean or go. This kind of talk made the State Department very nervous. "The administration thinks peace means a cease-fire," McGovern would complain.[94] Ponce was, after all, a general and minister of defense. To the suggestion that it might not be for the best interests of El Salvador to seek to enter a negotiated settlement guaranteed by a High Command that administration officials knew had done nothing but lie to them and even, privately, would admit probably ordered the Jesuits' murder, one State Department official would only reply. "We might prefer George Washington to head up the Salvadoran armed forces. We have to try to deal with what there is, to do the right thing, and support the civilian president."[95]

As Moakley and two aides flew down to El Salvador they were conscious of the strong nationalistic sentiments running against the work of the task force. It seemed obvious, also, that the army believed that as far as the Jesuit case was concerned, it was more or less home and clear. Leonel Gómez had been in El Salvador for extensive periods of time and Moakley and his aides believed they knew where responsibility for the killing of the Jesuits lay. But it was difficult to know what to do about it. They had nothing that was legally solid and no one to come forward on the record. They could not burn sources and they suspected that within the military either a threat or some kind of deal was ensuring that the defendants kept their mouths shut.

That the United States government might not be too disturbed that the heat was off the Salvadoran High Command had been suggested by a meeting with General Joulwan the week before Moakley arrived in San Salvador. Joulwan had congratulated the congressman on all he had achieved and had seemed totally taken aback when Moakley countered by asking exactly what he was referring to. Heads had not rolled, nor did their rolling appear imminent. The difference between Moakley and the official line was now evident in Walker too: he appeared to have let his fine sentiments about justice take refuge in State Department *realpolitik*. Straddled between his friendship with Gómez, whose work on the Jesuit case was coming to represent the antithesis of official policy considerations, and his bosses in Washington, Walker would never suggest that Moakley was exactly wrong. Rather he believed that the congressman had to be brought to realize that the Jesuit case "is not an Agatha Christie book, where you just have to solve it and everything is OK." The danger presented by Moakley, Walker would protest, was that the officers he believed to be implicated were at the highest level and "some of the officers thought to be most supportive to the president in the negotiations." If Moakley should be successful in cleaning them out, "it would create a hole that is very detrimental to the peace process."[96]

Moakley's relations with the U.S. embassy were shaken by the knowledge that the embassy had burned another source. A couple of months before Moakley's visit, a junior officer had come forward to an official within the embassy with information that, while not of the order of a "smoking gun," had been solid and useful information nonetheless. The embassy official had gone to Walker, and Walker had gone to Cristiani. The next thing that had happened was that the Salvadoran officer had been invited to a meeting at which those present had been Walker, President Cristiani, his wife—and General Ponce. Cristiani had asked," Now what exactly did you tell the embassy?" And the officer had answered, "Nothing." Moakley brought up the incident at one of his two meetings with Cristiani. "Why did you do it?" he had asked, as he suggested that if the officer had thought he could go and talk to Ponce he probably would have done so in the first place. "Are you suggesting General Ponce is involved in the Jesuit case?" had been the answer.[97]

Although this trip was to contain an expedition, with Walker, to the repopulated community in Santa Marta, Cabañas—marking a U.S. ambassador's first-ever venture into guerrilla-controlled territory[98]—the majority of Moakley's meetings were dedicated to discussions of the upcoming trial and the measures to be taken to ensure its fairness. Among the most delicate of all the encounters was an afternoon spent inside the Treasury Police headquarters with Lieutenant Espinoza, his deputy Guevara, their families, lawyers, and attendant military officers. The two lieutenants had assured Moakley of their innocence and asked him whether they believed him. Realizing that this might be their only opportunity to reach the lieutenants directly, and suspecting that it was Espinoza who, of all the junior officers, had the most to tell and was most likely to tell it, Moakley presented a carefully worded scenario that, without mentioning names, described the circumstances in which he believed the order to kill the Jesuits had been given. The two young officers listened in stone-faced silence. "You've given me a lot to think about," had been Espinoza's sole comment.[99]

"GENERAL Ponce, you have an institutional problem," was a refrain that ran through Congressman Moakley's public address at the UCA on the evening of July 1, 1991.[100] Moakley had held one meeting with Ponce on this trip, but it was not a success. He had wanted to pin him down, and had offered Ponce a second shot at answers to questions he had first posed him almost a year and a half ago, in February 1990. When had the general first known of Benavides's involvement in the killing of the Jesuits? In January 1990, came the answer, nearly two months after the crime and only a few days before Cristiani announced it on television. Ponce was sticking to his story and Moakley got almost nowhere. Less than helpful was the presence of the embassy official accompanying Moakley's party: he was as condescending toward the congressman as he was defensive of the general. Every time Ponce said something, it was improved and polished by the official's translation on its way back to Moakley. Moakley had torn a shred off the official on the way back to the car, but was left wondering, "Whose side are they [the embassy] on?"[101]

There was little doubt about whose side the audience packed into the UCA auditorium was on. Only the contingent from the U.S. embassy looked a little apprehensive. While the nature of Moakley's sources prohibited him from advancing any new facts into the public forum, his speech was a clear denunciation of the army's role in the Jesuit killings and in the subsequent investigation. Rhetorically directing his remarks to General Ponce, he reminded him, "You have an institutional problem when it is the institution that instills fear in potential witnesses; when it is the institution that teaches its officers to be silent, to be forgetful, to be evasive, to lie; when it is the institution that demands loyalty to the armed forces above loyalty to the truth or to honor or to country."[102]

Delighted by the tributes Moakley paid to what the Jesuits had achieved in their lives and to the sufferings of the poor El Salvador, Jon Sobrino gave the formal reply on the university's behalf. "I do not remember when I have ever heard such true words spoken by a U.S. politician on Salvadoran soil," he told the congressman.[103] The truth was that Moakley spoke words that insisted on the importance that the Jesuit case had at this key moment of El Salvador's history: "I want the truth because I believe the Salvadoran people deserve the truth. The whole truth. There is no such thing as half justice. You either have justice or you don't. There is no such thing as half a democracy. You either have a democracy in which everyone—including the powerful—is subject to the law or you don't. That's why I believe it is so important that the truth emerge in this case. Truth is not the enemy. Without the truth the armed forces will never be cleansed of the responsibility of this crime, and for shielding those involved in it. Without the truth, this government cannot lay claim to truly democratic institutions. Without the truth, the argument that those in opposition to the government should lay down their arms is undermined. Without the truth, the path towards peace in El Salvador will grow steeper still."[104]

CHAPTER TEN

DIALOGUE WAS A CRIME

Neither side in the war appears to doubt that it can remain in it for a long time and even that it could triumph when conditions are more favorable; neither side, and the United States least of all, is inclined to bring to the fore the interests of the majority of the Salvadoran people. Both sides defend models of society very distant from each other and both think that it is only from a position of power that they can guarantee their own model. Bearing in mind the principal actors who would take part in negotiations and the problems that must be resolved within them, one must speak of difficult negotiations. But this does not mean that they should be impossible.[1]

Ignacio Ellacuría, 1983

IN nothing was the UCA more consistent than in its arguments for the need and demand for a negotiated settlement to the war. And nothing could have been more controversial in a political context in which, for a long time, to talk of dialogue was a crime. Grounded in its analysis of the national reality at any given moment and with the greatest good of the popular majorities on the horizon, the UCA's voice was never still. Rather, as the war dragged on, counting among its casualties not only the tens of thousands of dead and wounded, or even the hundreds of thousands of exiles and refugees, but damage to the physical infrastructure of the country and to the economic, social, and psychological welfare of its people, the UCA insisted that the need for a lasting peace was ever more pressing, the continuation of the conflict ever more irrational and unjustifiable. It was to be an ironic twist of history that it was only with the dramatic events of 1989—and the murder of the Jesuits among these events—that the conditions for the real and substantive negotiations that would bring an end to the war were finally present.

The UCA argued for negotiation, worked to open political space for others to urge negotiation, and gave its critical support to any local or regional development that could favor negotiation. Out of public sight, although well known within political and diplomatic circles, was the intense activity of Ellacuría, whose contacts and credibility among individuals across the political spectrum were unrivaled. "He spoke with vigor and critical independence to both sides in the conflict," Salvador Samayoa remembered, "and really in this sense he filled an important vacuum. Nobody dared to speak to the government or to the military or the U.S. embassy in that way. And probably nobody spoke directly to the FMLN as he did."[2]

A review of the *ECA* articles authored by Ellacuría down through the years reveals a flexibility built on the foundations of positions firmly held since the failure of the FMLN's "final offensive" in January 1981.[3] While the specifics of the political moment would change with the fortunes of each side in the civil war, electoral politics, the pressures from the United States, and the dawn of *perestroika,* the principles from which Ellacuría argued in a favor of negotiation never shifted. These principles, as Ellacuría explained in an article written in mid-1986, were both ethical and political.[4] They were based on his belief that dialogue was not just the most effective way to bring an end to the war in El Salvador, but also the way to address the structural injustice that lay behind the armed conflict. Without such dialogue the FMLN presented Duarte's government with an "insuperable limit": El Salvador was ungovernable without the resolution of its revolution and war.[5]

Until 1984, the subject of dialogue was all but taboo. "Dialogue is treason to the fatherland," the Secret Anti-Communist Army (ESA), a death squad described by the CIA as being the ARENA party's "paramilitary organization," announced in September 1983, "and so we warn all the parties, political and military forces interested in negotiating the future of the country, that the eyes and the guns of the true patriots of El Salvador are on them."[6] Within days bombs had exploded in the UCAII residence in Calle Mediterráneo and in the home of Italo López Vallecillos. Fliers left littered on the ground claimed responsibility for ESA as a communiqué explained that "it is only those who want to follow the path of the FMLN who will dialogue."[7]

Although the Salvadoran Catholic Church had called for national reconciliation and offered itself as a mediator in October 1980, during the early years of the war its success in pursuing these ends was limited. A shift from the prophetic role of Monsignor Romero to the understandably more cautious leadership of Monsignor Rivera Damas contributed to a moderation in official pronouncements and actions. Working from within a conservative Bishops' Conference, Rivera was not helped by the lack of confidence in his own authority indicated by the Vatican's initially naming him merely apostolic administrator. It was only shortly before Pope John Paul II visited El Salvador in March 1983 that Rivera would be elevated to archbishop of San Salvador. By then his first personal contribution to dialogue—the hand delivery in October 1982 of a proposal from the FDR-FMLN to the Salvadoran government—had set a precedent for the role of official mediator he would come to fill in years to come, even as the proposal itself was rejected outright.

The possibility of "talking about talks" changed dramatically in 1984 when, on October 8 and to the surprise of all but the closest of his advisers, Duarte announced in the United Nations that he was inviting the FDR-FMLN to take part in direct talks in La Palma in just one week's time. The offer came, in part, in response to pressure from the Christian Democrats' political bases, gathered in the U.S.-backed organization Popular Democratic Unity (UDP), for Duarte to fulfill the promises of peace and reconciliation on which he had been elected, but it was certainly an audacious one. Duarte governed under the constant threat of a military coup and therefore had only the narrowest of margins for movement when it came to negotiations.[8] He had informed both Defense Minister Colonel Vides Casanova and the U.S. Ambassador Thomas Pickering of his intentions just days before he spoke in the United Nations. Both had responded with caution. Vides Casanova pledged his personal loyalty, but warned that he did not know how the army would react. "I'll come with you when they kick us out of here," he remarked, only half in jest. Pickering had thought the initiative a good one, but warned that the United States did not view its timing as "prudent."[9]

The FDR-FMLN accepted the invitation promptly. Both the leaders of the FDR, Guillermo Ungo and Rubén Zamora, and FMLN *Comandantes* Fermán Cienfuegos and Facundo Guardado, traveled to La Palma for the meeting on October 15, the fifth anniversary of the young officers' coup. Popular expectation of what could be gained there was high. Crowds of people accompanied Duarte and his caravan along the road to Chalatenango and the atmosphere, as thousands stood in the sun outside La Palma's church, was one of celebration. Ellacuría was gratified to learn that an *ECA* editorial he had written on "The Military and Social Peace" had been read aloud to Vides Casanova on the journey up to La Palma and used constructively within the talks themselves.[10] A carefully pitched appeal to the military to seek "a greater dose of national pride" in their conduct of the war, the editorial maintained that it was duty of the Salvadoran military, as Salvadorans, "to explore through dialogue with the opposite side the possibility of a rational, just and worthy end to the horror of war through negotiation."[11]

Duarte and Vides Casanova, Ungo and Cienfuegos, all were greeted by bursts of applause as they came out onto the church steps to read a moderate concluding statement. Most important was the commitment of both sides to continue the dialogue. But for many, as an *ECA* commentary would note, "the day was an illusion that became a deception with the setting of the sun."[12] If La Palma happened it was because El Salvador was in the midst of a war whose origins were deeply embedded in the social and economic structures of the country. As both sides withdrew to prepare for a second encounter, profound differences obscured the hope held out by this one day's meeting.

Between La Palma and the talks held in Ayagualo at the end of the November 1984, Duarte came under intense pressure from the business sector and from the army, while the FMLN had time to prepare its own proposal. Ayagualo made clear just how difficult dialogue—rather than just talking about it—would be. For the first time the two sides in the conflict placed their positions on the table. With each maintaining a wary eye on the forces behind them that were in most vehement opposition to the talks, political tactics, such as they were, appeared to be designed to reinforce confidence that neither side would sell out to the other rather than to foster a new faith in the effectiveness of dialogue between the two. As the meeting ended, a mood of pessimism descended. The weakness of the government, the complexity of the situation, and the intransigence of some sectors of the FMLN made dialogue difficult in the extreme. "But if the opportunity for dialogue is lost," Ellacuría would insist in a long article he wrote [under his pseudonym, Tomás R. Campos] analyzing the proposals presented at Ayagualo, "then once more a solid hope for the greater part of the Salvadoran people is squandered and destroyed. The responsibility will be of those who have made it impossible, or simply not given it the encouragement it was due."[13] It would be three years before the government of El Salvador and the FDR-FMLN would once again sit down in direct talks.

"THE contribution of Ellacuría," one FMLN *comandante* explained in 1991, "was that he understood that this country is sadly polarized, and that the positions of the two sides, the two poles, have radicalized. But between one camp and the other there are an enormous number of people who are not expressing themselves politically, people who want to see a solution to the problems of the country without being connected either to the FMLN or the government. Ellacuría insisted on the need for these forces to express themselves and play a real role in society."[14]

In Managua in 1981, Ellacuría had addressed a meeting of the leaders of the FDR-FMLN on the need to pay attention to the "third forces" within El Salvador. It was a brave thing to do at a crucial moment in the development of the Salvadoran revolution. Predominant within the meeting was Salvador Cayetano Carpio, who had met Ellacuría a couple of times before, but was unsure what to make of him. He saw him as a representative of the Church, and was therefore surprised and not a little alarmed by the force and political acuity with which he spoke. "Who does he represent?" he had asked an adviser as the meeting ended.[15] The point, Ellacuría explained, was that the Salvadoran people the revolution claimed to represent were badly served by the FMLN's internal wrangling over which group, or which faction within which group, embodied the true revolutionary vanguard. The violence of the polarization had sent one in ten Salvadorans into exile and cost the lives of one in a hundred. The last thing the FDR-FMLN should be doing was alienating its popular base with excessive ideologizing.

In an *ECA* editorial written at much the same time, Ellacuría had maintained that while each of the opposing forces believed it could triumph over the other, it was clear that such triumph could not come soon and that, even then, it would not be "acceptable" to the broad mass of Salvadoran people unless new elements came into play. While some, among them new organizations such as the UPD, demanded the formation of a political center from a broad sector of people united in the pursuit of economic and social development, Ellacuría argued that it was the responsibility of the popular and democratic revolution of the FDR-FMLN to respond to the needs of the populace. One of the things that the FDR-FMLN should do most urgently was confront the Salvadoran reality with "less dogmatism" and open up its democratic base to include the "third forces." "He who really trusts in the people," he insisted, "should have no reason to fear divergences nor reason to consider himself the sole possessor of truth and justice."[16]

Ellacuría's position was founded on the conviction that the popular majorities were not the same as the politically conscious minority that made up the bases of the FDR-FMLN. But what could be recognized in 1991, within an FMLN of a flexibility and realism beyond all comparison with the early years of the revolution, as a "contribution" of great value, had been a source of disagreement between Ellacuría and the revolutionary left for much of the preceding decade. Over the years Ellacuría maintained regular contacts with the FDR-FMLN both inside and outside the country, with conversations with mid-level individuals in San Salvador supplemented by meetings with members of the General Command in Managua, or the Political–Diplomatic Commission in Mexico. Those within the FDR-FMLN who knew or came to know Ellacuría well did not doubt the honesty of his positions or his fundamental commitment to the interests of the people of El Salvador, but many of the meetings were characterized by difficult and even confrontational discussions.[17] While Ellacuría "certainly made sure he was listened to," as Samayoa would remember, he himself was known to grumble to the Jesuits back in San Salvador, "they listen to what I say, but they do not hear me." "The dominant note in those meetings," Samayoa concluded, "was one of apprehension. In this respect the military were complete idiots. Ellacuría never endorsed the FMLN."[18]

In retrospect, it is possible to see that underlying the specific and variable points of disagreement was a yawning gulf between Ellacuría's reasoned and principled argument for negotiation and the political will and objective conditions governing the positions and actions of both sides in the conflict. Although Ellacuría exerted some influence on the FMLN in his criticism of some of their methods (the use of explosives in urban guerrilla warfare, for example), there were other areas in which the UCA's "social" reading of the war and its effects was one with which the FMLN could only disagree most energetically. A constant argument, for example, was Ellacuría's insistence that he and the UCA spoke with the authority of those who lived—even within the exceptional circumstances of a university—within the reality shared by the majority of the Salvadoran people. Weariness, skepticism, and longing for an end to the conflict were widespread. Living and fighting among the sectors of the population with whom they worked and whose support they undoubtedly enjoyed, the FMLN paid too little attention to the unrepresentative nature of the base from which it operated.[19]

Ana Guadalupe Martínez first met Ellacuría in Mexico in 1981. Her work in the Political–Diplomatic Commission would bring her to see him with relative frequency. Over the years they developed a relationship of real warmth and affection, even amid differences that extended from thinking that Ellacuría's talk of negotiation in the early months of the war was "a little out of place" to the extreme tension prevalent in a last meeting Ellacuría would have with the FMLN leadership in late September 1989. The period when she came to know him best, a period she would describe as being one of "interminable discussions" with Ellacuría, was the one immediately following the 1984 elections. While the FDR-FMLN boycott dismissed the elections as an instrument of the U.S.-backed war of counterinsurgency, a special issue of *ECA* devoted to analysis of the election results insisted that the massive electoral turnout that had produced a victory for the Christian Democrats, could not, on this basis alone, be discarded as meaningless.[20] The option for Duarte had reflected a reaction against the polarization expressed by the war and had responded to real aspirations that the elections might bring some improvement to the situation.

Martínez remembers Ellacuría "trying to convince us that we had to insert ourselves within the democratic society that was beginning to be constructed under Duarte."[21] With time, and the dissipation of the hope held out by La Palma, the analyses emanating from the UCA hardened in their criticism of the Christian Democrats' loss of autonomy within a conflict whose prime movers operated from Washington and the *estado mayor*. Martínez believed that with this change came a greater respect for the FMLN's position from Ellacuría, and on their part a greater respect for the good intentions of one whose relative optimism in the early days of Duarte's government, as much as his subsequent criticism, was true to his "really wanting to achieve peace in this country." While alarm at the position of Ellacuría would resurface in 1986 as he returned to some of the ideas he had first floated in 1981 in a fully worked thesis of a "third force," Martínez for one had come to see that in a man from whom she learned so much, "there was never the desire to disarm us, to disarticulate us or to make us disappear as a political force—rather he wanted to use what he saw us to be in order to change the country."[22]

IN September 1985, the kidnapping of Duarte's daughter would bring Ellacuría in from the role he had carved out for himself as unofficial mediator and theorist of dialogue to playing an active part within negotiations that, although conducted at the margin of the war itself, held the attention of the country. The kidnapping came at a time at which "global" dialogue toward the resolution of the war was badly stalled, if not definitively abandoned. Legislative elections in March 1985 saw the Christian Democrats win control of the assembly from ARENA at the high tide of their popularity. Since then Duarte had come to appreciate the limits of his power as pressures from the right kept the door on dialogue firmly closed. He would talk of a lack of "political space," but negotiations themselves only diminished in their appeal to his government, the armed forces, and the United States as the massive influxes of U.S. military aid made a real impression on the war.

Within this unprepossessing landscape, the sole initiative in the furthering of dialogue had come from the archdiocese of San Salvador in a public commitment to the negotiation of accords for the repopulation of Tenancingo. A municipality of the department of Cuscatlán, Tenancingo had seen nearly ten years of social conflict culminate in a September 1983 attack by the air force that had killed approximately 100 civilians and driven the town's remaining families from their homes. By the time its repopulation was announced in July 1985, Archbishop Rivera Damas had already obtained initial agreement to the project from both the FMLN and the armed forces. Confidential negotiations, brokered by the archdiocese and the development agency FUNDASAL, continued over the following months. Statements on their progress drew public attention to the opportunity presented by Tenancingo to further the process of a wider dialogue. Under the scrutiny of the international community and the mediation of the Church, neither side could afford to sacrifice the appearance of its seriousness and in the end the repopulation of Tenancingo would begin in January 1986.[23]

More immediately destablizing for the government than the emergence of the Tenancingo accords was the crisis into which it was thrown by the capture on September 10 of Inés Guadalupe Duarte, together with her friend Ana Cecilia Villeda. Although the kidnapping had occurred in the midst of a series of FMLN kidnappings of mayors, the responsibility of the FMLN was initially denied. The kidnappers called themselves the "Pedro Pablo Castillo" commandos, demanded total confidentiality, and insisted that they would communicate only in radio conversations with Duarte himself, who was given the code name "Jupiter." The vulnerability of the president was there for all to see as he came close to breaking down in tears during an Independence Day speech devoted almost exclusively to the subject of Inés Guadalupe. As the daily business of government went on hold, Duarte made his son Alejandro, Defense Minister Vides Casanova, and Abraham Rodríguez, a PDC lawyer who had been among the founders of the party, responsible for the safe return of his daughter. Also working closely on the kidnapping were Julio Rey Prendes, minister of communications, Planning Minister Fidel Chávez Mena, and Colonel Reynaldo López Nuila, the deputy defense minister who took charge of the investigation.

The first demands made by "Pedro Pablo Castillo" were for the exchange of the two women for twenty-two political prisoners, including two senior leaders of the Communist party and *Commandante* Nidia Díaz of the PRTC. The list would be extended to include nine others, until then "disappeared," of whom it was demanded that they should either be produced or accounted for. But as the negotiations with Duarte dragged on and Inés Guadalupe's kidnappers realized the strength of their hand, they would become entangled with a parallel negotiation being conducted for the freedom of twenty-three PDC mayors kidnapped by the FMLN over the preceding months. The FMLN had been demanding that ninety-six of their wounded should be given safe conduct out of the country and twenty-nine union workers, imprisoned for FMLN sympathies, should be released. Until now the government had shown little interest. As it became clear that it was probably the FMLN who held the two women, a desire to negotiate dwindled among all except those closest to Duarte himself. It was the FMLN that would suffer the political consequences if the women came to any harm, and opposition to "negotiating with terrorists" came not only from the army and right wing, but also from the U.S. Embassy and even from Duarte's own party.

An appeal for help from Archbishop Rivera Damas, who had been a close personal friend of Duarte's since their youth, was an obvious beginning, but the situation was complicated by the recent differences between the FDR-FMLN and the Bishops' Conference over a Pastoral Letter on "Reconciliation and Peace." The FDR-FMLN had found in this letter a clear partiality toward the government position and had criticized it strongly.[24] In the wake of the letter the FMLN had explicitly rejected Rivera Damas's role as mediator. In these difficult and delicate circumstances it occurred to Chávez Mena and Rodríguez that Ellacuría might be able to help.

Duarte took some persuading. He was hugely suspicious of the Jesuits as a group—in 1983 he described them (and in Rome, of all places) as "the intellectual authors of the violent revolution"[25]—and the personal antipathy between himself and Ellacuría was well known. Both Chávez Mena and Rodríguez had known Ellacuría for years and, despite political differences, liked and respected him. Their insistence that they needed Ellacuría eventually overcame Duarte's reluctance. At a first meeting Ellacuría appeared sure that the FMLN could not be responsible for the kidnapping. "It would," he reasoned, "cause them too much harm internationally." He promised to see what he could find out from the FPL. "Talk to the FPL!" Colonel López Nuila scoffed when the news came back to him. "If Ellacuría wants to talk to the FPL all he has to do is go into his bedroom, shut the door, talk to the mirror, turn round and come out again. And then he will tell you that he has talked to the FPL!"[26]

A couple of days later Ellacuría looked worried. He had been in touch with his regular, midlevel contact in the FPL who, while not absolutely positive, had told him that he considered that it had been the FMLN, or at least a part of it, that had undertaken Inés Guadalupe's kidnapping.[27] Following up a suggestion made at this meeting, the FPL offered to act as intermediaries for the political prisoners' front group, the

"Pedro Pablo Castillo" commandos. They invited Ellacuría and Rivera Damas to Chalatenango to open direct discussions with their senior *comandantes,* among them the FPL's leader Leonel González, and Antonio Cardenal and Fernando Ascoli (now known by their *noms de guerre* Jesús Rojas and Ricardo Gutiérrez).[28] At that meeting the FPL *comandantes* explained that they could not speak or act on behalf of the entire FMLN and invited Rivera and Ellacuría to a meeting with representatives of all five FMLN organizations. Only then, in Aguacayo on the Guazapa volcano, would be become clear that behind "Pedro Pablo Castillo" lay the armed forces of Schafik Handal's Communist party, the FAL.

The visits to El Zapotal in Chalatenango on October 12 and 13 and to Aguacayo two days later were opportunities for more than just the negotiation of the freedom of Inés Guadalupe. The need for the Church's presence within FMLN controlled territory allowed both Monsignor Rivera and Ellacuría (in the company of their "chauffeur," Jon Cortina) to see at first hand the "other" reality of El Salvador. The areas visited were within the archdiocese, yet populated by Christians, whether civilians or combatants, who suffered the effects of the war to an extent that was almost unimaginable from San Salvador. In both Chalatenango and, especially, Guazapa—where the two of them joined Rogelio Poncele in a celebration of the word before the negotiations began—Rivera's small party was welcomed by people who had walked for miles to see their archbishop and tell him of all that they had suffered since 1980. Among the combatants Ellacuría was delighted to find a number of familiar faces: students he had lost sight of as their revolutionary commitment took them into hiding in the late 1970s.[29]

Although the negotiations were complex, they were notable for the respect and courtesy with which they were conducted. While Rivera was there as the guarantor of the interests of the government, from the beginning he made it clear that it would be Ellacuría who would be doing the talking. A proposal brought from the FMLN to Ellacuría in the interval between the two meetings by Hans Wichsnewski, a prominent German from the Socialist International, would become the basis for their negotiating position: the case of Inés Guadalupe was combined with that of the mayors, but combined in such a way that the exchange of the mayors for the wounded moved up to take priority over what the FMLN knew to be their trump card—the freedom of Inés Guadalupe in exchange for their political prisoners. In addition, they demanded the freedom of the union workers and Duarte's promise to investigate what had happened to the nine "disappeared."[30]

Wichsnewski's visit was followed by one from Chávez Mena and Rodríguez. Duarte was in trouble. The army wanted the two women to be negotiated against the political prisoners, and the mayors to be freed without meeting the conditions set by the FMLN. To get the army to accept even this much had taken Colonel Vides Casanova an eight-hour meeting in which the right-wing maverick Colonel Sigifredo Ochoa and his supporters had gone so far as to demand Duarte's resignation. They charged that he had put his own interests before those of his country. Things were little better within the PDC's own political committee, where there were calls for Duarte to be replaced by one of his ministers. But Duarte was not moving.[31]

Up in Aguacayo, the negotiations revolved around the importance given to the fate of the wounded, and ended in confusion. While the government was ready not to introduce the issue of the mayors into the exchange of the political prisoners for the two kidnapped women, the FMLN was not willing to hand over Duarte's daughter without the resolution of the problem of the wounded. Matters would become still more complicated in the following days as, on October 18, a radio communication revealed an understanding of the negotiation's status different from what had actually been agreed on within the meeting. Claiming that the government had accepted their latest offer, those still calling themselves the "Pedro Pablo Castillo" commandos proposed a direct meeting to put the agreement into operation.

With the disingenuous understatement of an article authored under a pseudonym, Ellacuría would write that "the negotiations in Panama cannot have been easy as they lasted three days."[32] Inside the FMLN the confusion had almost equalled that within the government: conscious that time was running out, and that if agreements were not reached soon they might end up with nothing at all, the General Command designated Mario Aguiñada Carranza (political representative of the FAL) and Salvador Samayoa to undertake direct and final negotiations on their behalf. Rivera Damas, Ellacuría, Aguiñada, Samayoa, Rodríguez, and Rey Prendes sat around a table in a room in Panama's Canal Zone almost continuously from Sunday October 20 to late on the following Tuesday afternoon.

All present remember Ellacuría's creativity, flexibility, and powers of persuasion as being absolutely crucial to the successful resolution of the kidnappings, with which the three-day session ended. Particularly important was his proposal that, in order to unblock a seemingly insurmountable sticking point, the FMLN should offer something new in exchange for the safe conduct granted to their wounded. Although formally a commitment of the FMLN alone, as the government could not be seen to "give" anything more, it was established that each side should undertake to respect the lives and rights of all the family members of the other. Kidnapping and the targeted assassination of children, spouses, or parents of the FMLN or of government and military officials was to be declared off limits. The common sense of this was underlined by Rodríguez's timely reminder to Aguiñada that his brother worked for him—did he want him to take him a message? A curious addition to the process was the diminutive figure of General Manuel Noriega. "Everything alright, *señores*?" he asked as he appeared for an informal meeting on the final day.[33]

The negotiations were complicated by the tensions within the Duarte government.[34] The team in Panama tried to equate what they believed desirable with what Vides Casanova in El Salvador was telling them would be acceptable to the armed forces. What they ended up with was a precarious balance between the two, positive for Duarte the father, but clearly negative for the president of the republic and roundly condemned by the army. It was agreed that on October 24 there would be a simultaneous exchange of Inés Guadalupe and Ana Cecilia for the twenty-two political prisoners, and that the captured mayors would be freed in exchange for the safe conduct out of the country for the FMLN wounded. The army would measure the 27 individuals released to the government against the 123 members of the FMLN who benefited directly from the arrangement and blame Duarte for allowing the FMLN to convert what could have been a political disaster into a significant political victory.[35]

The drama of the kidnapping of the president's daughter and Ellacuría's role in its resolution had postscripts that said much about the wider Salvadoran process and his part within it. The week after Inés Guadalupe's release, Duarte took her to Washington where she was photographed collapsing elegantly into the arms of President Reagan. In a gesture Ellacuría would characterize as being of political submission rather human thanks, Duarte stated publicly that Nicaragua had been the principal instigator of the kidnapping. Duarte "knew or should know that this is a lie," Ellacuría would write with scorn. It had been a lie of obvious utility in its bolstering of the Reagan administration's need to maintain the thesis of Nicaraguan terrorism, and Duarte "abased himself before this need."[36] In El Salvador Duarte's advisers had reported back to him how important had been the role played by Ellacuría within the negotiations. They had never doubted his objectivity and they really did not know what they would have done without him. Shouldn't the president invite him for lunch to thank him? Write him a formal letter? Duarte never did thank Ellacuría for the role he played in securing the safe release of his daughter.

Ellacuría himself saw the outcome of the kidnapping as a victory not so much for the FMLN as for negotiations themselves and for all those in favor of a humane response to the war: "The fact was that there was an effective dialogue between the FMLN and the government in the presence of the Church and this dialogue came to negotiated conclusions of almost immediate execution."[37] For his part he had emerged from the whole episode with an enhanced prestige that could be understood as something of a mixed blessing. Within a couple of months, one of his contacts in the private sector would pay him an unexpected visit. He had heard on the grapevine that word had gone out that "Ellacuría should be liquidated." While he believed that the threat was meant to frighten and not to be acted on, he had thought it only proper that the rector of the UCA be informed.[38]

BY the end of 1985, it would be clear that what scant room Duarte had been allowed for dialogue in the early months of his presidency had been mortgaged to the hilt by the concessions wrested from him for the return of his kidnapped daughter. Since the failure to achieve a third meeting after La Palma and Ayagualo, Duarte himself had been remarkably silent on the subject of dialogue, despite repeated proposals from the FDR-FMLN. It had fallen to Ambassador Pickering to keep the idea alive, but his was a "dialogue" adroitly addressed only to the humanizing of the war, and not to the war itself. Ellacuría had taken Pickering's proposal to the FDR-FMLN in Mexico in May, but it had been brusquely dismissed as being a "façade" that would only obscure the real issues.[39] The readiness of the United States to talk to the FMLN at all was given a violent setback only three weeks later when, on June 19, FMLN urban commandos attacked a group of off-duty U.S. marines in a restaurant in the Zona Rosa, killing four of them amid a total of nine civilians. Condemned by all political sectors including the FDR (and on television with notable severity by Ellacuría), the organizations of the right saw in the Zona Rosa killings sufficient reason to call for the definitive suspension of all dialogue with the FDR-FMLN. In November, Ungo and Zamora tried without success to meet with Duarte in Madrid. In El Salvador the following week, Ellacuría launched his thesis for the solution of the conflict through negotiations encouraged by pressure exerted on both sides in the civil war by a "third force."[40]

Ellacuría would argue for his third force in the face of opposition from all sides throughout 1986 and into the beginning of 1987. The thesis itself was straightforward. Ellacuría maintained that both sides in the conflict had been forced to adopt new frameworks for their political and military action. The FMLN had achieved greater unity among its five organizations than had been possible in the early years of the war and had realized the heavy cost of the neglect of its civilian base in 1980 and 1981. In response to the improvements in the army in its shift to "low-intensity conflict" fostered by the massive involvement of the United States, the FMLN had changed its military tactics from those of open confrontation to a true guerrilla war. The government had acknowledged the structural injustice facing El Salvador and had introduced political, economic, and social reforms in pursuit of the "hearts and minds" of the population. But neither side was succeeding in its object of weakening the other; on the contrary, each appeared stronger than ever.

"If this is so," Ellacuría reasoned, "it is necessary to do something that is qualitatively new and is not just in the mold of strengthening one of the sides in conflict. It is not a question of creating utopian solutions. It is a question of attending to the real fact that the greater part of the population and a sizeable group of more or less organized social forces want a solution different to that of war."[41] Insisting that he was *not* suggesting a political party of the center, Ellacuría outlined how a third force could be consolidated from social forces as diverse as existing unions, the Church, the educational sector, small- and medium-scale businesses, and those popular organizations not specifically aligned with the FMLN. On the way to a negotiated settlement, such a force could exert pressure for limitation of the armed conflict, defense of the economic interests of the popular majorities, and democratization of the country. Once a settlement was achieved, it could work toward the extraction of El Salvador from the East-West conflict and the implementation of reforms that would attack the structural injustice that had given rise to the war in the first place.

At the time, the "third force" was criticized for proposing a "third way" that played into the hands of the government, for being an idealized abstraction that did not respond to the reality of the political and social conditions of the time, and for being a vehicle for the power and influence of Ellacuría and the UCA within El Salvador.[42] Those who did support the thesis—like Hugo Carillo, secretary general of the PCN and a veteran of the UCA's Political Science program—were accused either of being overly influenced by Ellacuría or of "lining up with groups of the left to gain more political space."[43] At a more serious level were the criticisms that questioned whether the proposal of a third force really responded to what was happening in El Salvador, where an agent capable of uniting diverse and fragile new organizations behind a common program was clearly missing.

Responding to the changes in both the government and the FMLN was the resurgence of what can be broadly labeled as the popular movement. This had begun with the UPD, which was funded by AIFLD as part of counterinsurgency strategy and worked in support of the Christian Democrats. But in a much more discreet process trade union and *campesino* organizations also emerged to fill and then test to the limits what political space became available to them under the Duarte government. By the end of 1985, the UPD itself faced internal crisis as one part of it realized that the priorities of the government did not respond to those of the majority of the people. This more critical sector of the UPD moved away and joined a range of *campesino* and trade union organizations to form the UNTS (National Union of Salvadoran Workers), the new backbone of the popular movement.[44] Over the following years, the FMLN would work assiduously in the establishment of what it would term "double power": structures of government and organization rooted in the mass movement and alternative, whether clandestine or not, to those provided by the state.

It was precisely because all this activity represented a development of individual groups suitable to what Ellacuría appeared to be proposing that his thesis of a third force caused such a sense of panic within the FMLN. In mid-1986, the army had launched a major counterinsurgency campaign, "United for Reconstruction," heavily funded by AID and seeking to include every sector of Salvadoran society within its pacification. The FMLN feared that the Duarte government and the Reagan administration would latch on to the potential for cooption they saw within the idea of the third force and so read or heard Ellacuría's arguments from within the same wartime polarization that he was attempting to counter. From Morazán, Joaquín Villalobos wrote editorials on *Radio Venceremos* specifically directed to the ears of Ellacuría. Other rebel leaders were able to voice their objections in person: Ana Guadalupe Martínez remembered objecting that Ellacuría "wanted to bring sectors of ours into this third force, which would have weakened us. For the level of the war we were waging it was impossible for us to assume his position as a correct one, because it would have been taking our very lifeblood away."[45]

Intellectually closer to Ellacuría than his *compañeros,* Salvador

Samayoa would agree with his former teacher's assessment that his idea of the third force was "misunderstood" by the FMLN as a whole, but find in it, nevertheless, something of "desperation." "Ignacio wanted society to grow in its own consciousness and possibilities of expression in order to be able to tell those fighting the war 'Enough!'," he explained, "because he could see no real possibility of understanding between the two sides."[46] If there was a streak of the utopian in this position, it was a streak that would have Ellacuría assume, by default and for himself, the role of critical conscience of Salvadoran society he could but dream of for a broad-based social force.

The popular movement would accelerate and become more radical and complicated at such a rate that talk of a third force dwindled even from the UCA's vocabulary. "The Question of the Masses," as Ellacuría titled the *ECA* editorial of July 1987, became instead a search for the proper role of the "mass" organizations across the political board. Ellacuría dismissed both the government's assertion that all those popular organizations not within its sphere of influence formed part of the broad "front" of the FMLN, and the FDR's claim that these organizations represented the political and democratic arm of the revolution, as "partial and wrong."[47] The FMLN, he reminded the *comandantes* he knew would be reading his words, should look to the past and learn from what he saw to be the "substantial errors" committed in the 1970s as the "conscientization" of the Church rushed precipitately into social, then political, and finally military organization. If they did not want to repeat the repression of the early 1980s, the FDR-FMLN should support a new relationship with the popular movement in which the masses "should not only be autonomous and so construct their own organizations, but also decide autonomously on their own strategy, tactics and alliances."[48]

By 1990 and 1991, as both sides in the conflict came to appreciate not just the military stalemate but also the overwhelming pressure from the Salvadoran people for a negotiated settlement, the third force proposed just five years earlier seemed not so untenable after all. Rubén Zamora would recognize that the Jesuits of the UCA had been the first to appreciate the importance of the social phenomenon—the resurgence of the popular movement—that would characterize the transition from the period of the war defined by polarization to that in which a political solution began to appear more feasible.[49] As political leaders of the left and right admitted the much-reviled "third force" to have been "before its time," one FMLN *comandante* would exclaim, "we certainly miss the voice of Ellacuría" and then, after a pause: "The son of a bitch was right."[50]

ELLACURÍA'S introduction of the thesis of the third force in an UCA Forum was reported in characteristic fashion by the *Diario de Hoy* as being based on his "Marxist interpretation" of "the terrorism imported by the communists."[51] Files of newspaper clippings Ellacuría kept in an archive in the UCA rectory are testimony to a level of political suspicion and primitive hatred that can only be described as obsessive. The UCA and the Jesuits had never been forgiven for their betrayal of the social and economic classes with which the Society of Jesus was so long associated. The university itself was seen as a bastion of subversives, the "principle source of guerrillas," directed by a Jesuit who was not only a "Basque agitator" and communist—"the agent who directs all Marxist-Leninist strategy in Central America"—but "nefarious," "satanic," and "the anti-Christ."[52]

The obsession went beyond the historical role of the Jesuits in Aguilares, in the "manipulation of Romero," in the 1979 coup or as the "poisoners" of the minds of the young El Salvador. One contributory element was the almost pathological fear of liberation theology as a fermentor of revolution that was, of course, by no means restricted to El Salvador. In 1987, for example, at the XVII Intelligence Conference of the American Armies, liberation theology featured strongly in a working paper prepared by the section of the conference devoted to "the strategy of the international communist movement in Latin America" (El Salvador was represented by Colonel Orlando Zepeda). One of those theologians deemed to have ended up outside the Catholic Church through his union of "marxist methods and philosophy . . . and subversive praxis" was Ellacuría.[53] More basic than this was a nationalist resentment of "foreign" priests, and a personal antipathy to Ellacuría that had almost as much to do with the form with which he presented his opinions as the opinions themselves. "You have to understand," explained one political figure of the right, "that his whole way of being was difficult for Salvadorans to take. The way he spoke was elevated, arrogant, blatantly intellectual, very Spanish. He made no effort to accommodate his manner to what in a country like this might be more tolerable to people."[54]

The political discourse of the Salvadoran far right was glaring in its crudity. In 1988, one member of a "think tank" called the Institute of International Relations (IRI) criticized Ellacuría's support for negotiations by telling a visiting Mexican journalist that "the strategic conspiracy known as dialogue-negotiation is nothing other than yet another manoeuver of the Popular Church to disguise its support for the subversive plan to take power."[55] Yet on Ellacuría's occasional visits to Washington, those who set up meetings or translated for him would find that officials reacted to him with an ambivalence about Jesuits and a suspicion of liberation theology not inconsistent with the more viscerally expressed opinions of his opponents in El Salvador. "People found it hard to believe that this *priest* could have his finger on the pulse of what was going on in El Salvador," remembered one experienced lobbyist who worked with Ellacuría in Washington, "and still harder to realize that he could have a role in promoting political pluralism."[56]

Within the Reagan administration, suspicion of liberation theology and "meddlesome priests" in general was widespread. The doubts sown by the Santa Fé document had been amply fanned by the public nature of the political commitment of some sectors of the Nicaragua Church and the vocal campaigning of a wide range of churches in the United States against their country's policy in Central America. In early 1983, newly appointed Secretary of State George Shultz, locked in a battle with Congress for increased military aid, had lashed out against the pressure for negotiations coming from church-led opposition to U.S. policy in El Salvador by denouncing "churchmen who want to see Soviet influence in El Salvador improved." The remark was widely reported and described as "outrageous" in a letter to President Reagan from a prominent congressman. It would be deleted from the Hearings' record, yet it represented a very real sentiment.[57] Particular suspicion of Jesuits and Maryknoll missionaries emerged clearly from a 1988 CIA report on "The Political Role of the Catholic Church in Central America." A contrast was drawn between the "turbulence" in Nicaragua, Guatemala and El Salvador in the 1970s and "the relative calm in those Central American countries where the Jesuit and Maryknoll orders failed to gain a foothold."[58]

Ellacuría's first meeting with William Walker, during a visit to Washington in May 1986, was exemplary of the kind of obstacles created by the "baggage" that Ellacuría brought with him. Walker was at the time deputy assistant secretary of state to Elliot Abrams. Ellacuría had arrived wanting to talk about the need for dialogue and negotiation in El Salvador. Nicaragua was uppermost in State Department concerns at the time and Walker, pleased to have the opportunity to meet someone from the Central American Church, had wanted to know what he thought of Managua's Archbishop Obando y Bravo, who had just been made a cardinal. It is unlikely that Ellacuría was at all polite about Obando y Bravo ("I'm not accusing Cardenal Obando y Bravo of moral weakness," he had said in an interview given on the same trip, "but I believe he is not the right man in the right place"[59]) and Walker was left with the impression that he was "just an arrogant Spanish priest." The two would not meet again until 1989.[60]

"Ellacuría is almost always news" the archdiocese's magazine *Orientación* had remarked rather dryly on the UCA rector's return from the United States. Highlights of the trip had included participation in a conference at Georgetown University alongside the Peruvian novelist Mario Vargas Llosa, a chance to meet Jeanne Kirpatrick that Ellacuría would relish[61] and the receipt of an honorary doctorate from Loyola University in Chicago. Yet in El Salvador nothing received so much attention as Ellacuría's remarks on the FMLN's use of land mines and his admission that, when it came to promises of dialogue and negotiation, he had more confidence in the FMLN than in the government. With him to his death ("Mines which the priest defends mutilate more *campesinos*"[62]) was a "justification" of the mines that came from a somewhat imprudent fidelity to the truth. Under pressure from a journalist, he had pointed out that Elliot Abrams was wrong to claim that the mines were a purely terrorist weapon that killed civilians. As used by the FMLN, he believed, they were a weapon of war primarily directed against the army and they tended to mutilate horribly rather than kill. Any civilian casualty, however, as any act of terrorism, would always elicit his strongest condemnation.[63]

Duarte returned to the subject of dialogue in a speech on June 1 marking the end of his first two years in office. In the next few months, his government and the FDR-FMLN exchanged proposals, counterproposals, and more counterproposals for a renewal of the dialogue that had been suspended since Ayagualo. But as Ellacuría repeated in interviews, the government, weak as it was with respect to domestic support and subordinate to the exigencies of U.S. policy, had "less margin than the guerrillas with which to seek a political solution to the armed conflict."[64] Duarte responded by accusing Ellacuría of being a spokesman for the FMLN and the "creator of the theory and conception of the guerrillas' rebellion."[65] A place and a date for talks, September 19 in Sesori, was proposed by the FDR-FMLN and accepted by the government, yet as the day approached it appeared more and more unlikely that the conditions would be conducive for the FDR-FMLN to appear. Duarte's assessment of the moment was one that only revealed how distant the prospect of valid negotiations remained: "There are two scenarios: either [the FDR-FMLN] reincorporate into the democratic process and form political, social and economic forces from which they can influence and participate in this process or they decide for the road of arms and violence and the taking of power by force—and what Ellacuría is proposing is the second scenario."[66] The story was the same: if they give up their weapons, they can be part of my democracy.

This interview contained the veiled threat that a nationalized foreigner—like Ellacuría—may "lose his nationality or be detained, because he has insulted the executive, the government, the president, and the people." As Ellacuría became embroiled in a public row with Foreign Minister Rodolfo Castillo Claramount, who charged that Ellacuría was an "apostle of violence," ARENA deputies joined battle and presented a motion in the assembly to appoint a commission to investigate Ellacuría's "activities."[67] "Our only objective," explained Armando Calderón Sol, the future mayor of San Salvador, "is to clarify if the priest Ellacuría, being a foreigner, is interfering in Salvadoran politics; if that is so, he would be an undesirable alien."[68] No longer the party's general secretary but still its guiding light, D'Aubuisson was quoted as finding confirmation "of what has always been said: the true masterminds of subversive movements like the BPR and the FPL are not in the mountains, but close to the UCA." A headline in the same edition of the *Diario de Hoy* was a word-for-word repetition of one the newspaper had first printed nine years before: "Dr. Ignacio Ellacuría, SJ—Go, Please Go."[69]

IN a contribution to a conference in Miami that he would not live to attend, Ignacio Martín-Baró wrote of the "paradoxical space for communication" offered by the installation of the counterinsurgency project in 1983.[70] The most remarkable of its manifestations was the change in the nature of the information available on television to viewers throughout the country. Pioneers of this change had been the two independent news programs, *Al Día* on Channel 12 and *El Noticiero* on Channel 6, which first appeared in 1985 and 1986, respectively. Individual strands offering forums for discussion and debate soon followed. Not surprisingly, Ellacuría and the Jesuits of the UCA were much in demand as commentators. Their appearances, together with those of a gradually broadening range of political and social figures, would play a significant role in the encouragement of what Ellacuría in 1986 called a "state of dialogue" within El Salvador.[71]

Producers and television journalists remember there being no interviewee in San Salvador who displayed fewer signs of nervousness in front of a camera than Ignacio Ellacuría. His contributions to the public debate were quite unlike those anyone else in the country could offer; his great rationality, mastery of dialectic, and supreme confidence in the quality of the information that lay behind his analysis were aided by a fearlessness that let ethics win out over caution with a calm that was truly impressive. From within the university, his appearances were viewed with a mixture of pride and apprehension: although Ellacuría spoke for himself he was always perceived as "the UCA." The teaching staff had families to return to at night and were well aware that in his television interventions, their rector pushed the possibility of expression, so suddenly and surprisingly available, to its limit. Asked once by an UCA colleague whether he was never frightened, Ellacuría had answered, "No, I have never been afraid, but there is no merit in it because that's just how I am."[72]

The two-hour special of "Point of View" broadcast in September 1987 provided a notable example of Ellacuría's television style.[73] Its subject was "Esquipulas II and Dialogue" and participating, first in discussion with each other and then in response to questions telephoned in by members of the public, were Ellacuría, Rey Prendes, and D'Aubuisson. Seated between the seasoned politician and the charismatic ex-major, most notorious of all the death squad leaders, Ellacuría was relaxed and confident, fully aware that in political debate the advantage was his—even as caller after caller charged that he was a marxist-leninist or member of the FMLN. "The media," Ellacuría explained at one point, "is making an enormous contribution to dialogue, because it is showing people talking and understanding each other. I don't think the three of us agree about much"—with a laugh at the other two—"but we haven't shown our teeth yet."[74]

Criticized by some for not accommodating himself to what was "acceptable," Ellacuría's contributions to public debate were relentlessly honest. "Don't say I'm a communist because I am not one," he replied to one of his questioners. "And I don't go in for deception. I say what I think, I have absolutely no need to hide my relationship with people, or with whom I meet, or what I say—no need whatsoever." With D'Aubuisson fidgeting at his side, Ellacuría spoke of his meetings with Sandinsta officials, of the "great ignorance and prejudice" of those who denied that marxism did not have a lot to contribute to socioeconomic analysis, and confided that, while it was difficult to argue with the *comandantes* of the FMLN because of the conviction with which they held their positions, they were people of "good will, idealism, and 'Salvadoraneity.'" As he joked that he did not, of course, speak as one whom the FMLN obeyed ("What more could I want? If they obeyed me, the dialogue would be tomorrow and we'd reach some agreements") he was on the perilous boundaries of what was and what should be tolerable within political discourse in El Salvador.

This discussion was held at the moment of surprising optimism that followed the signing of the Central American peace plan in Guatemala on August 7, 1987. Esquipulas II, as the plan was most commonly called, had been a long time coming. In El Salvador, nineteen months separated the meeting between the government and the FDR-FMLN in Ayagualo from their failure to meet again in Sesori. The month after that, on October 10, 1986, even the war was reduced to a secondary place in the national consciousness as El Salvador suffered the most devastating earthquake of its history. Between 1,200 and 1,300 people were killed, more than 10,000 injured, and some 200,000 lost their homes.[75] By the end of the year, the economic damage had amounted to more than two years of El Salvador's national budget, and a peace based on social and economic justice seemed ever more remote.

Temporarily obscured by the earthquake was the importance of the downing of a small C-123 airplane on October 5 in the south of Nicaragua. The capture of the sole surviving passenger, the U.S. citizen Eugene Hasenfus, and his revelations of the *contra* supply network being run out of San Salvador's Ilopango airport, would be a key catalyst in the unfolding of the Iran-*contra* scandal over the following months. For those in El Salvador most critical of U.S. policy toward the region, there was almost something inevitable about the whole affair. At the beginning of the war, much of the rhetoric justifying U.S. involvement in the conflict had centered on the communist aggression from Nicaragua. Although small amounts of arms would continue to be discovered, the course of the war had made it quite clear that the continued existence and obvious strength of the FMLN depended on more than a few mules' worth of AK47s. By the mid-1980s, the patent lack of large-scale armament by the Sandinistas would be admitted even by the U.S. embassy. Ellacuría would maintain that over breakfast with Edwin Corr, who had replaced Pickering as the U.S. ambassador in mid-1985, he had persuaded him to accept that the Nicaraguans had been responsible for at most 5 percent of the FMLN's arms since 1983.[76] And now it turned out that it was the other way around after all. El Salvador had been used to supply arms to the *contras*. And El Salvador's president had known nothing about it.

As the Reagan administration struggled to hold its own amid a regional policy ever more clearly revealed to be, in Ellacuría's words, "politically inadequate and ethically immoral,"[77] new possibilities of a Central American approach to the region's problems emerged in a proposal that Oscar Arias of Costa Rica presented to the Central American presidents, the countries of Contadora, and their support group. The

"Arias Plan" was publicly revealed in February 1987. It was an extension of the positions put forward by Contadora since 1983, calling for "national reconciliation" with each country on the basis of amnesty and internal dialogue, cease-fires and the pursuit of a pluralist democratic process based on free elections. Individual countries were to reiterate their commitment not to let their own territories be used for the military or logistical support of those working to "destabilize" other governments and, in an essential feature of the plan—and one that was unsurprisingly unpopular in Washington—governments outside the region who "openly or clandestinely supply military aid to the insurgent or irregular forces" were asked to stop it.[78] Months later, after a Latin American diplomatic offensive made possible by the relative weakness of U.S. standing in the region, the central tenets of the Arias Plan were accepted as Esquipulas II and signed by the presidents of Costa Rica, Nicaragua, Honduras, El Salvador, and Guatemala.

Duarte's characteristic fondness for the word "I" ("*yo*") resulted in the coined word "*yoismo*" to describe his style of presidency. He tried to take credit for Esquipulas II and publicly committed his government to fulfill its terms even though for months El Salvador had opposed the initiative in the interests of continued favors from the North. In June, for example, while maintaining a lofty silence on the FDR-FMLN's latest proposal of eighteen points for the "humanization" of the war,[79] Duarte had sought to postpone the Central American presidents' summit until September. By then it was hoped that the Reagan administration would have won Congress' support for renewed aid to the *contras*. Now that September had come and the agreement was signed, Rey Prendes would repeat on television the promises of his president to fulfill the terms of Esquipulas II. But as he did so there were indications that the dialogue that underlay all of its proposals was no nearer to being a priority for the Duarte government and its backers than it ever had been.

The terms of Esquipulas II were perhaps less favorable to the FMLN—in the structural parallel they created with the other "irregular" forces, the *contras*—than to any other actor in the region. The FMLN, however, had responded positively with the statement that "Esquipulas II establishes a general framework favorable to the search for political solutions to the internal conflicts in each country." Ellacuría read this aloud to Rey Prendes and asked, with the emphasis of exasperation, "What more does the president want?" The answer that came back was unequivocal in its repetition of the view that anything the FDR-FMLN should propose was subordinate to their pursuit of power and that the terms on which dialogue would be acceptable still involved the laying down of arms before negotiation could begin. "Those of us who have no desire for power," Ellcuría countered [as Rey Prendes suppressed a smirk], "can see things in another way from those who do. I don't believe one can attribute this wanting of power to the FMLN more or less than to either of you . . . What I am afraid of is that neither for them, nor for you is a negotiated peace the principal policy, while for the Salvadoran people this is a priority—a negotiated peace whoever ends up with the power."[80]

An interview with Ambassador Corr recorded in the same month underlined exactly how far the "reconciliation" called for by Esquipulas II would be able to go: "I use the word reconciliation and not the words dialogue or negotiation because I believe that the government and the armed forces have been seeking to reconcile the armed opposition from the level of single individuals in groups to the entire FDR-FMLN, and to bring them into the mainstream, into the political process within the constitutional framework." Corr foresaw this "reconciliation" through the "grinding down," "marginalization," and "elimination" of the FMLN. And a continuation of the war for another five or six years.[81]

By the end of 1987, it would be clear that the Duarte government had neither the political will nor the autonomy to achieve anything but the most peremptory compliance with the letter of Esquipulas II. The spirit of the regional initiative was quite another matter: its very existence and inevitable discussion contributed to the quiet currents of change that would make the following year, 1988, one that *ECA* would greet as "a year of transition." Moreover, the initial flurry of activity following the signing of the accords had been in noted contrast to the stagnation that had preceded it. An amnesty, dialogue, a cease-fire, democratization, and an end to aid to the irregular forces and insurrectional movements all within ninety days had been a lot to expect from a seven-year-old war. But after the mediation of Oscar Arias, the first round of high-level dialogue between government and FDR-FMLN since Ayagualo was convened in San Salvador's Nunciature on October 4 to 5. Once again the results of the meeting fell far short of the expectations of the Salvadoran people—over 80 percent of whom, according to an IUDOP survey, favored dialogue at the time.[82] Three weeks later, the assassination of Herbert Anaya Sanabria, the coordinator of the Nongovernmental Human Rights Commission, caused the FMLN to call off further talks.[83]

Most scandalous of all the measures taken by Duarte's government as a result of Esquipulas II was, paradoxically, the one in which he most exactly fulfilled the formal requirements of the agreement: the signing of a Law of Amnesty as part of national reconciliation. As Colonel López Nuila, the government official responsible for the implementation of the law explained, "all the famous cases of abuses of human rights could be suppressed with Esquipulas II and the amnesty."[84] In accordance with the agreement Duarte had signed, the army was bound to release over four hundred members of the FMLN. The prospect of letting all these "subversives" walk free—and no doubt rejoin the rebel forces—was something senior officers were quite unprepared to accept. They put the pressure on and the government ceded. At one stroke Duarte "forgave and forgot" ("*perdón*" and "*olvido*" were the words he used to describe the law) all those responsible for the worst genocide in El Salvador's history. Tens of thousands of murders (with the sole and symbolic exception of Monsignor Romero), perpetrated by members of El Salvador's security forces and army, were wiped clean away. "The amnesty comes," an *ECA* commentator remarked succinctly, "to legalize impunity in our country."[85]

Whatever breathing space Duarte's government had been given by Esquipulas II was exhausted by the beginning of 1988. In Washington, signs that not all was well with the "success story" of Central America were brought to the attention of Congress by the Arms Control and Foreign Policy Caucus' publication of a report whose title said it all: "Bankrolling Failure."[86] In 1987, for the first time in the history of U.S. foreign aid, El Salvador was a country that received more than it had contributed to its own budget. Of the $608 million of U.S. taxpayers' money, three dollars were spent on the war and its effects for every dollar spent to address its causes. And yet the war showed no sign of ending. The caucus estimated that 2,700 combatants (of both sides) had been killed in 1986 and rebel attacks on the economy had increased by 29 percent. The counterinsurgency campaign had failed to erode the base of the support for the FMLN and evidence of corruption and "serious misuse" of U.S. funds was mounting. The per capita income had declined by 38 percent since the beginning of the war. Half the population was under- or unemployed, infant mortality had jumped 36 percent in 1986, and one in every four children was malnourished. Judicial reform was stalled. Although attention was concentrated on Nicaragua, "Congress and the administration should recognize," the report concluded, "that the pursuit of a military solution to the conflict of the war in El Salvador has produced a complete standstill. Major changes in the nature of United States policy are needed."[87]

In El Salvador as much as in the United States, major changes were ruled out by the domination of the political scene by upcoming elections. While nothing could be expected from Washington in the final months of the Reagan era, legislative elections in March provided an opportunity for Salvadorans to express their opinion of the Duarte mandate while indicating that what might be expected from the presidential elections that would follow in 1989. Victory for ARENA came both as a rejection of the Christian Democrats and a reflection of a profound shift in the political structure of the country. The combination of the two would pave the way for the future government of a party that had built on a past of death squads, disenchanted oligarchs, and renegade military officers to become a direct representation of the most powerful economic interests in the country. ARENA's ascendancy was in obvious contrast to the crisis into which the PDC was plunged by its loss of the legislature. Compounding the inefficacy in the execution of its own promises and programs was an abundance of well-founded allegations of corruption. In the culmination of months of internal wrangling, a final split between factions headed by Chávez Mena and Rey Prendes in the run-up to the presidential elections appeared inevitable. When Duarte was told he was suffering from terminal liver and stomach cancer, it was a diagnosis that many believed extended to the U.S.-backed counterinsurgency project he had come to represent.

ARENA had learned a lot from its electoral defeats in the middle of the decade. In September 1985, D'Aubuisson relinquished the post of general secretary to a little known businessman from a wealthy coffee-growing family: Alfredo Cristiani. The move was a tacit acknowledgement of D'Aubuisson's own unacceptability to the United States and had marked the beginning of ARENA's steady progress to power. Since 1983, when the ARENA-led assembly had presided over the demise of the ambitious land reform program introduced in 1980,[88] AID had turned its attention to the modernization of the business sector through the streamlining and funding of private enterprise through organizations such as FUSADES (the Salvadoran Development Fund). While D'Aubuisson would always remain the most popular and powerful individual within the party he founded, during the second half of the 1980s FUSADES-trained technocrats gradually came to join the more traditional ARENA business-men gathered in organizations such as ANEP. Besides providing the sheen of respectability all-important for future relations with the United States, this new dimension to ARENA would be crucial to its successful metamorphosis into a political party that maintained elements of extreme ideological conviction alongside a more classical neo-liberal economic policy.[89]

Only the FMLN believed that 1988 would be a year of decision. Ungo and Zamora of the FDR had first returned to the country at the end of 1987. With their respective parties, the MNR and the MPSC, the two had joined with the Social Democratic Party (PSD) to form the Democratic Convergence. The year 1988 saw the Convergence's gradual reintegration into Salvadoran society as a nationally recognized entity dedicated to arriving at the end of the war through a negotiated political solution and providing the popular movement with the means for legal political activity. Yet as their former allies prepared the way for their participation within the elections of March 1989, the efforts of the FMLN were clearly directed elsewhere. Documents captured by the army representing communications between *comandantes* Villalobos and Cienfuegos indicated the hope that there would be a qualitative advance in the mass revolutionary movement in preparation for the armed revolution's final triumph.

As critical as ever both of the FMLN's reading of the situation and its potential for insurrection, Ellacuría had insisted back in January that there was no "objective basis" for the FMLN's view of the year as "decisive": "1988 is a year of indefinition, a year of transition to who knows what, a year lost for grand solutions. But this presents us with the question of what to do during a year whose potential and possibilities are from the beginning so negative, the question of how to extract from the negative a positive dynamism in favor of a truly liberating process."[90]

THE archdiocese of San Salvador had been talking about convoking some kind of "national dialogue" for at least two years. But little appeared to be happening. While Monsignor Rivera was respected for the moral authority with which he carried out his role as mediator, many sectors believed that the labor of the archdiocese was characterized by its caution, sloth, and lack of initiative in moving forward what was, admittedly, a painstakingly difficult process. At the beginning of December 1987, Rivera had been one of a number of individuals representative of the major political and social forces to make a presentation in a series of UCA forums proposing solutions for the problems facing the country after Esquipulas II. Ellacuría had met with Rivera at the end of November and they had discussed the possibility that the UCA might help initiate a dialogue or debate among all the social forces in the country.[91] Still in the vaguest of forms, the idea lay behind Rivera's contribution to the UCA's forum. He ended his detailed narration of how the attempts to maintain the dialogue after Esquipulas II had come to naught by suggesting that this was the moment to return to the proposal for a public debate. "I think that the UCA can help us to implement it," he added.[92]

Ellacuría immediately offered the UCA's technical help in the preparation of a national debate. Over the next few months, as suggestions for the form, content, and participants in the debate went back and forth, the possibilities, limitations, and practicalities of what the debate could be slowly evolved into a concrete shape. Throughout this phase, the relationship between the UCA and the archdiocese—historically respectful on either side, but never uncomplicated by the shadows of criticism—was a matter of some delicacy. In this year of "transition," Ellacuría and the UCA saw in the national debate a unique opportunity to bring the social forces together around fundamental agreements in a manner that was wholly in line with positions they had sustained throughout the years of the war. Yet they were actuely aware that it was the archdiocese that had the authority to convoke such a debate and that it was only proper that the technical expertise of the university should be put at its service for the benefit of the country as a whole. The Bishops' Conference had approved the archdiocese's launching of the debate, but had warned of the risk involved in the UCA's participation in its planning. It had been no surprise when Monsignor Rivera requested that the controversial (and incontestably domineering) figure of Ellacuría should not form part of the organizing committee.

The national debate responded to the concern, shared by the archdiocese and the UCA, that the problems facing the country should be addressed not only by the political parties, but by the widest range of social forces it was possible to assemble. While the activity of the mass organizations dismissed by the government as FMLN "front groups"— among them the organizations grouped together in the UNTS—was ever more evident on the streets of San Salvador, social forces were otherwise isolated from discussion at a national level. It was wholly appropriate that it was the Church, whose magisterium places the social above the political, that should have decided to organize "a broad and free national debate," as Rivera put it in the letter of invitation sent out to 102 different organizations on June 20. Once points of consensus had been achieved, he continued, "these can help the government, the armed forces and the political parties, on the one hand, and the FDR-FMLN, on the other, to bring the conflict to an end through dialogue and negotiation."[93] But it was also wholly unsurprising that the initiative should be greeted by headlines screaming, "The ecclesiastic hierarchy involved in politics again" and "Debate favors dialogue as a Marxist strategy."[94]

For the months of July and August 1988, the national debate became, as Ellacuría would write in an *ECA* editorial (not without a note of pride) "the newest and most dynamic factor in the socio-political process."[95] Even ARENA gave the debate its support until the organizations of the far right—IRI, the Crusade for Peace and Work, and the Salvadoran Institute of Political, Economic, and Social Studies (ISEPES)—got to work in the pages of *Diario de Hoy*. The debate must have caused "great satisfaction to the traditional bastions of the left—the Zamoras, Ellacurías, Rosas Chávez, Handals, Ungos and other representatives of armed violence in El Salvador," they claimed, "the national debate of the archdiocese serves the conspiratorial strategy of dialogue-negotiation of the FDR-FMLN."[96] Gradually, the organizing committee began to receive letters of refusal from a large number of the private sector forces originally invited. The fundamental reason for their rejection remained the same as the private sector's rejection of any new initiative (Agrarian Reform and Transformation in 1970 and 1976, for example) had always been: it might not favor their economic and social interests.

By September 3, when delegates from sixty "vital forces" met in the buildings of the girls' school La Sagrada Familia for the national debate's two-day public assembly, the UCA's technical team had reduced the results of questionnaires they had distributed to all invited to 164 theses on which the various delegates could vote. Their work had been accompanied by Monsignor Rivera's public updates on the progress being made and an opinion poll conducted by IUDOP on the fundamental points being covered by the debate. More than 50 percent of the participants found that they were in agreement on 147 proposals to be included in a final document. The debate called for the government and the FDR-FMLN to attend to its conclusions "with responsibility" by agreeing to a cease-fire and a reactivation of the process of dialogue, charged the new Permanent Committee of the National Debate (CPDN) to oversee the fulfillment of its accords, and appealed to the political parties to include the points on which consensus had been obtained in their electoral platforms. One of those points read: "Dialogue constitutes the most rational, just and Christian method for the solution of the conflict. It is the most viable method and it is the one that is in the majority supported by popular demand."[97]

IT fell to the UCA to invite the presidential candidates of the four major parties to present their positions on the results of the national debate. With dialogue all but dead in El Salvador, despite the continuing efforts of Oscar Arias from outside, candidate after candidate spoke out in favor of a peace achieved through political means. Among those candidates was Alfredo Cristiani, the first ARENA politician ever to accept an invitation to the UCA. Impressing his audience with his "moderation, flexibility, and openness," Cristiani acknowledged that he agreed with 85 percent of the conclusions of the national debate and even went so far as to commit an ARENA government to a process of "permanent dialogue" with the FMLN.[98] If only at the level of campaign promises, things were on the move in El Salvador.

CHAPTER ELEVEN

Never So Close, Never So Far

One can see the difficult position of the ARENA government. It might be able to do things, but not want to do them, might want to do them and not be able, and in the worst instance might neither be able nor want to do them. The most likely scenario, however, is that it will attempt to follow a new path, in line with what was offered in the campaign and has been confirmed after its electoral victory. For the moment there have been no signs of arrogance or violence. The night of the long knives is not upon us. Only if the way of negotiation should fail, only if the situation hardens, will the temptation of the way of violence and terrorism return.[1]

Ignacio Ellacuría, 1989

"WE have never been so close to peace. We cannot let this opportunity escape us," Ellacuría told the crowd gathered before him on March 4, 1989 in the Plaza Libertad in San Salvador. As he spoke, his right hand underlined the emphasis in his voice with the precision of gesture of a conductor. Between 12,000 and 20,000 people, assembled in representation of the organizations of the National Debate for Peace and hot and dusty after their march through the streets of San Salvador, listened quietly. "The peace process," he continued, "comes fundamentally from the Salvadoran people. It comes from the 60,000, the 80,000 martyrs of the people, it comes from the murdered union workers and *campesinos,* from the murdered students and professionals, from the murdered priests, bishops and nuns. This message of death is today being transformed into a message of life. And if the entire people demand peace with social justice, that peace will come."[2]

Ellacuría founded his optimism on the consideration that the transitional year of 1988 had given way to a "new phase" in the Salvadoran process, qualitatively different from anything that had gone before it and much more conducive to the resolution of the civil war through political means. The end of the Reagan era and the rise of *perestroika* had helped to create a climate favorable to the predominance of reason over violence in the settlement of conflicts emerging out of the Cold War. As the summits between the superpowers produced treaties contributing to the slowing of the arms race, so examples of a new realism were given by the Soviet withdrawal from Afghanistan and the departure of the Cubans from Angola. Another element within the shifting balance of international affairs was the United Nations, which appeared to be acting with a new strength and authority on the world stage. It was still too soon to tell how the pragmatism of the Bush administration would make itself felt in Central America, but that the failure of Reagan's policy toward the region had been openly admitted even by the outgoing Secretary of State George Shultz struck Ellacuría as an enormous step forward.[3]

Within El Salvador, these new international circumstances complemented the regional impetus provided by Esquipulas II. For the first time since the war began in 1981, Ellacuría detected a real change, expressed through the individual political and military forces, but more far reaching than a dependence on any one of them would imply. Pre-electoral polls conducted by IUDOP suggested that the ARENA victory in the legislative elections of 1988 would be followed by a victory for Alfredo Cristiani in the presidential elections of March 19, 1989. Such a victory, coupled with a patent failure to defeat an FMLN that independent analysis could only find stronger than ever, would signify a moment of reassessment for the counterinsurgency project backed for so long and at such cost by the United States. In the pages of *ECA,* on the makeshift platform in the Plaza Libertad, in meetings with journalists, politicians, and diplomats, including the still to be confirmed Assistant Secretary of State Bernard Aronson and—at the end of May—the executive director of the cabinet of the United Nations, Alvaro de Soto, Ellacuría lost no opportunity to hail the importance of this "new phase" to the future of El Salvador.[4]

Seizing the initiative had been a proposal presented by the FMLN on January 23 "to convert the elections into a contribution to peace."[5] The product of a long period of reflection by the FMLN's General Command, the proposal was timed to coincide with the arrival of Bush in the White House as surely as the "final offensive" of 1981 had been designed to greet President Reagan. An indication of how far the FMLN had come since then was that what it was now proposing was, in its essence, what Duarte and the U.S. had been pursuing for years: the recognition of elections that "would make possible an irreversible political solution to the conflict." There were, of course, conditions—principally that the elections should be suspended until September 15, 1989 in order for there to be time for a number of electoral reforms. Come September, the FMLN would not itself participate in elections, but would, in the context of a military truce, encourage all its base to vote in favor of the Democratic Convergence and then accept the legitimacy of the final result.

Ellacuría would liken the process by which the FMLN arrived at this proposal, begun in May 1988, when Joaquín Villalobos left the hills of Morazán for the first time in six years, to that of Vatican II. The "council" had involved all five of the rebels' senior *comandantes* being out of the country for months on end and an intensive period of diplomacy. Villalobos and Leonel González had visited various presidents and senior statesmen within different Latin American countries while Schafik Handal, Fermán Cienfuegos, and Roberto Roca traveled to the Soviet Union and the countries of the socialist bloc. "They are attempting a fundamental *aggiornamiento,*" Ellacuría would write in March 1989, "an updating of their strategy, their attitudes and tactics, which, as in the case of the Vatican Council, does not suppose a break with what is essential to their inspiration and proposals, but does mean a profound change in reply to a situation that is profoundly different."[6]

Ellacuría had been able to follow the progress of the FMLN's strategic reassessment in high-level meetings held in Managua in May and November 1988. A few days before he left for the May meetings, he had received an upbeat briefing from his regular contact in San Salvador. The legislative elections and the subsequent division in the PDC were evidence that Duarte and the counterinsurgency project had been defeated, he was told; the greater degree of polarization that would come with an ARENA triumph would favor the FMLN.[7] Only in Managua, first in a meeting with six *comandantes* and then in a lengthy discussion with Villalobos the following day, would the seriousness with which the FMLN was prepared to address the new political circumstances become clear. Villalobos explained that the FMLN had had three successive military strategies: the 1981 offensive with its inauguration of the widespread use of armed force, the major operations and construction of the revolutionary army from 1982 to 1983, and the entrenched guerrilla warfare starting in 1984. It was time to seek a fourth strategy that was a synthesis of the earlier three at the same time as it was necessary to seek a "political and negotiated solution that would allow for a transition to democratic socialism."[8]

It had been by chance that Ellacuría's meeting with the *comandantes* occurred just the day after Villalobos first emerged from the far reaches of Morazán. Ana Guadalupe Martínez had been among those meeting with Ellacuría on May 20 and had suggested to him that the two men should talk on the following day. When reached on the telephone, Villalobos responded enthusiastically. As far as he could remember, the two of them had never met.[9] Ellacuría's own eagerness was understandable: in the decade of war, and particularly since the rupture at the top of the FPL, the *comandante* had obtained a legendary status within the FMLN. The youngest member of the General Command and, in the ERP, leader of one of the two largest of the five organizations, Villalobos was reputedly the most brilliant military strategist in either army. Yet with his reputation scarred by his involvement in the murder of Roqué Dalton in 1975, he had been labeled as the most hard-line of all the FMLN's ideologues. He denied this charge to Ellacuría and claimed that "people have tried to pass him the Cayetano Carpio role . . . he is not against dialogue nor is he dogmatically doctrinaire." As in subsequent meetings Ellacuría was struck by Villalobos's ability to argue and by a flexibility that would only increase over the coming months. "Talking with Ellacuría," Martínez commented on the conversation she witnessed, "really helped Joaquín to begin to understand that the *Frente* itself was a very narrow world and that it was necessary to think in a more integral way."[10]

By the time of his November visit to Managua, Ellacuría had witnessed the disintegration of the PDC (with Fidel Chávez Mena providing first hand accounts of his progression to presidential candidate) and met the man most likely to play a leading role in any new developments in El Salvador—Alfredo Cristiani. On August 30, Ellacuría, Segundo Montes, and Francisco Javier Ibisate were invited to the home of Alejandro Samayoa to meet "the candidate," San Salvador's new mayor Armando Calderón Sol and a selection of the technocrats from the wing of the party that represented the interests of "modernized" capital. "Do you know what they call us?" one of them joked. "The ARENA communists."[11] The three Jesuits were struck by their genuine wish for dialogue and the informality of the atmosphere (helped by the fact that "the majority of them were pupils of the *Externado* or the UCA," Ellacuría would note[12]) and listened attentively while Cristiani and his advisers explained their plans to address the extreme poverty they admitted was at the root of all the country's problems. Ellacuría secured Cristiani's acceptance to speak at the UCA and promised the university's support "in anything that goes in favor of the people." As the three Jesuits left, he assured Cristiani that he would have a good reception at the UCA—"according to our polls 40 percent of our students will be voting for you."[13]

In Nicaragua on November 2—after Cristiani's commitment in the UCA Forum to a process of "permanent dialogue" with the FMLN—Ellacuría found that the *comandantes'* diplomatic travels and a month-long meeting of the General Command in Managua were bearing fruit. Their assessment both of the new international climate and of the consistency with which they had been promised support for dialogue rather than insurrection had led them to revaluate their political and military strategy. They could not accept the UCA's view that an insurrection leading to a military victory was not possible, but serious negotiation was now seen as a necessity and a priority. That they had realized that a marxist-leninist regime was no more desirable than it was likely did not mean that the FMLN faced defeat. The FMLN was confident of its own strength as never before. Revolutionary victory, as Villalobos also explained in a long article published in *ECA* at the beginning of 1989, would now be open, pluralist and democratic.[14]

The day before he spoke in the Plaza Libertad, Ellacuría received a message that the FMLN would like to see him in Managua that weekend. As they explained on his arrival, they had been surprised by the reception the January proposal had been given. They had really expected it to be rejected out of hand. Instead, although it was by now obvious that the elections on March 19 would go ahead, it continued to provoke intense debate within the government, among the political parties, and in Washington. In a meeting headed once again by Villalobos, the *comandantes* warned Ellacuría that while they were so convinced of their political potential that they had been prepared to risk their entire strategy of insurrectional warfare in their January proposal, if the road of elections and negotiations were to be closed off to them, the one of armed violence would always remain. "This is not a threat but something inevitable," Ellacuría would write in his notebook. "The FMLN's social and/or political bomb could explode at any moment. . . . The FMLN sees a risk in the atmosphere of peace becoming a harmful pacifism. [They believe] a false peace could have a higher cost than a brief explosion of violence that would lead to a true peace."[15]

ARENA won the elections on March 19 with a comfortable margin of 54 percent of the vote. Their campaign had promised "a change for the better," while the Christian Democrats had never looked like a winning team. Not even a costly advertising campaign masterminded by Washington consultants[16] could invest Fidel Chávez Mena with the charisma of leadership or wipe clean the Salvadoran people's memory of five years of government that had brought not peace and stability, but more war, corruption, and economic hardship. But a turnout of scarcely 37 percent of the population of voting age—in part attributable to the FMLN's call for a boycott—and the violence surrounding the elections themselves were symptomatic of the fragility of the situation.[17]

Ellacuría saw an ultraconservative party in power, more closely representing real forces within Salvadoran society than the Christian Democrats ever did, avowedly committed to dialogue with the FMLN and pressured by an opposition strengthened in its unity to the left of the government as contributing positively toward the "new phase."[18] ARENA's murky past was a secret to none, but Ellacuría believed that the changes within the party were more than cosmetic. The emergence of the politic, pro-dialogue stance of Cristiani from the more militaristic and violent line of D'Aubuisson was underpinned by the logic of economic interests and by the pragmatism of a government that needed to maintain the support of the United States. The visit of Vice-President Dan Quayle prior to the elections, with its concentration on human rights issues in general and the San Sebastián case in particular, left no doubt on this point. As President Bush's first message to the new president-elect emphasized: "there must be no turning back to the dark and terrible past."[19]

But there were elements within ARENA too closely related to that past to expect that a more moderate line could prevail without what Ellacuría would describe as "turbulence." Much of ARENA's base was characterized by violent and primitive anticommunism and the identification of nationalism with the interests of class and party. These elements made no secret of their view that the more moderate wing of the party gathered behind Cristiani had sold out. This was the party whose television commercials claimed "happiness is coming" while its rallies were brought alive by an anthem promising: "El Salvador will be the tomb where the reds are buried."[20] D'Aubuisson himself, drunk at the time according to Ellacuría's source, had named one of his closest cronies, Francisco "Chico" Merino, a man widely believed to have overseen the operation of the death squads in the provincial capital San Miguel, as vice-president without consultation with anyone. The source also told Ellacuría that he had warned Cristiani that "they" would kill him when they could in order to leave Merino in the presidency.[21]

The one force that Ellacuría would single out as having given few signs of entering into a new phase was the military. As the delicate situation arising out of the naming of a new minister of defense would show, the "more moderate" face of the army, represented by Colonel Ponce, the United States, and some sectors of ARENA, could prevail over the extremes represented by figures such as the air force's General Bustillo or, within ARENA, retired Colonel Ochoa, but only just. And with the *tandona* firmly ensconced in power, the corporate interests of the armed forces, which were to a considerable extent dependent on the continuation of the conflict, were better safeguarded than ever. "There will be no democracy without the democratization of the armed forces," Ellacuría stated bluntly. "There will be no peace without the pacification of the armed forces and no pacification without a conversion to an ideological position that is more modern and less militaristic."[22]

Ellacuría predicted that the "turbulence" surrounding the elections could last a number of months. The FMLN was increasing the pressure for negotiations by showing that without them the country was ungovernable; elements to the right of Cristiani achieved the same effect in their pursuit of a military solution through "total war." The escalation of violence and violations of human rights had begun after the legislative elections in March 1988 and increased most notably in March and April 1989. And in February, there began a series of targeted assassinations, several eventually attributable to the FAL, if not to overall FMLN strategy, and a level of persecution of the Church that had not been seen for years.[23]

The publication in 1988 and 1989 of *The Popular Church Is Born in El Salvador* and *Marxist Infiltration in the Church,* by Monsignor Freddy Delgado and (director of IRI) Alvaro Jerez Magaña gave new life to the accusations leveled against the Jesuits in the 1970s.[24] Delgado's book "confirmed" for the *Diario de Hoy* that "all those groups at the service of international communism were planned and organized in the installations of the UCA with the active participation of its Jesuit leaders, beginning with the sadly famous Ignacio Ellacuría, the most nefarious individual ever to set foot on Salvadoran soil."[25] Although both authors were known for their advocacy of extremist positions, in the mounting tension of the political situation such charges increased existing dangers. The Jesuits wisely declined to make any public comment on the two publications' fiction and ignorance. They knew they were on firm ground and within the Church hierarchy they received support not only from Monsignor Rivera, but also from the nuncio, Monsignor de Nittis, who would assure Ellacuría, on a visit to the UCA for the inauguration of the new Monsignor Romero Pastoral Center, that he had written to Rome to set the record straight. Over the following months, however, politically motivated assassinations would introduce a new level of violence into the ideological battlefield.

In Washington on April 10, Ellacuría encouraged Bernard Aronson not only to back negotiations but also to enter into direct conversations with the FMLN. Aronson had been briefed by a memo from Walker describing a meeting Walker had with Ellacuría three weeks earlier and had responded positively, if with caution, to the idea that the United States and the rebels should talk. Recent events however—and here Aronson referred to the February assassination of FMLN dissident Miguel Castellanos and the violence surrounding the elections—did not favor improvements in the relationship between the two. Ellacuría should let it be known to the FMLN that as far as the United States was concerned, increased violence weakened rather than enforced the credibility of their proposals for negotiation.[26] Ellacuría challenged the example Aronson had made of Castellanos: was he aware (he was) that Castellanos was an army informer and had interrogated some of his former *compañeros* from the FPL on their behalf? While he deplored Castellanos's assassination, Ellacuría could not accept a portrayal of him as only a dissident intellectual. (A detail Ellacuría did not add in the interview, but recounted to his translator as their taxi wove its way through the Washington traffic, was that one of the subjects on which Castellanos's interrogations had dwelled was the prisoner's knowledge of Ellacuría himself.[27])

Much more disturbing, and greeted by the "absolute condemnation" of the UCA, was the assassination on March 15 of Dr. Francisco Peccorini. Peccorini had been a Jesuit and had coincided with Ellacuría, some fifteen years his junior, in the San Salvador seminary at the end of the 1950s. He had left the Society to marry and since then had spent twenty-five years in the United States as a professor of philosophy. On his return to El Salvador, he had become a severe critic of liberation theology and had debated against Ellacuría on television. That he had founded some of his political arguments on "facts" he had read in the *Diario de Hoy* drove the usually unrufflable Ellacuría to an unprecedented display of irritation.[28] The supposed enmity of the two men would be used to insinuate that the UCA had a role in the assassination. It also lay behind the rumors flying around the capital on the morning of March 16 alleging Ellacuría had been "executed."[29]

In April, attacks against the Church intensified. A development that reflected the new balance of power within the country was the proliferation of accusations, and threats—against the archdiocese's legal aid office as well as individual priests—proceeding not from the usual shady front groups and think tanks, but from the armed forces and ARENA. For the Jesuits it was also unusual that it should be Segundo Montes who was accused in paid advertisements taken out by ARENA and the army High Command of being "inhuman and immoral" for his "justification of the terrorist acts" of the FMLN in a television interview.[30] In a letter addressed to ARENA, Montes explained that he had been giving an overview of the situation of the country after the March elections and a new proposal for negotiations presented by the FMLN on April 6. More detailed than the January proposal in its requirements for future negotiations, the proposal was almost guaranteed rejection for its suggestion that the Cristiani government should be one of "transition" with new elections to be held in six months' time under conditions produced by "real negotiations." Rather than justify any violence, Montes had observed that as both sides attempted to arrive at negotiations from a position of strength, the probability was that "acts of violence will continue and possibly increase."[31]

The letter was published on April 14, 1989, and the events of that and the following few days only proved its assumptions to be right. In the early hours of April 14 the residence of Vice-President-Elect Francisco Merino was badly damaged by the explosion of a charge of dynamite. Then, on April 19, Attorney General Roberto García Alvarado was assassinated by a bomb placed above his head on the roof of his jeep. Official identification of sectors of the Church with supposed guerrilla attacks was never clearer than in the reactions to these two episodes. Merino wasted no time in holding a television conference in which he laid blame on the FPL, and, in a list of commandos alleged to have been directly involved, Daniel Sánchez, a parish priest in one of the poorest of San Salvador's neighborhoods. Five days later, Colonel Zepeda, standing at the scene of the attorney general's assassination, charged that the operation had been carried out by the FMLN, but planned within the UCA. The university, he maintained, "is serving as a refuge for leaders who go there to plan the terrorist strategy the FMLN is carrying out in El Salvador."[32] The following week the UCA would suffer its first physical attack since 1983 as three bombs exploded outside the printing plant.

IN an *ECA* editorial written in the period before Cristiani's inauguration, Ellacuría asked: "are these violent eves going to lead into a new period of total violence or are they only tactical attempts to consolidate positions?"[33] In private he extended his concept of "turbulence" to explain that the Salvadoran process was like an airplane buffeted by the elements, but surely bound, sooner or later, for its final destination. The second scenario was thus more probable than the first.

Ellacuría and Montes met with Cristiani in late April. Once again, their impressions of Cristiani as an individual conscious of the difficulties he was facing were good. "He seems honest and to want to resolve things," Ellacuría would be quoted as saying of the president-to-be, "but one can see a lack of political instinct and weight to manage a difficult situation."[34] Worried by the possibility that the FMLN might be attempting to provoke a violent response from his government, Cristiani had also shown himself well aware that there might be forces within the right interested in destabilizing the situation. An obvious example was Zepeda's attempt to form new units of "patriotic civil defense" at a moment when political repression was already escalating alarmingly. That the deputy defense minister's paramilitary force should number among its seventy-two members ideologues of the extreme right best known for their pathological anticommunism led many to believe that the new structure was nothing more than a legal cover for organized death squads. So widespread was this view that the "civil defense" was dissolved only a week after its foundation.[35]

In the weeks preceding Cristiani's inauguration on June 1, 1989, the upsurge in political violence was complemented by renewed military activity on the part of the FMLN. "The FMLN is acting on the hypothesis that the governments of El Salvador and of the United States will only give the green light to serious negotiations when they are forced to it," Ellacuría wrote in mid-May. "This thesis is pretty well established." The danger was that the destabilization of the government and the consolidation of a negotiating process, while not necessarily mutually exclusive, were difficult to reconcile. Reason, as well as past experience, might be on the side of the argument that negotiations would not be handed to the FMLN on a plate, and therefore that reason underlined their use of force, but there was a risk that "reason and force might come to contradict each other."[36] The contradictions were particularly clear when it came to targeted assassinations, which were greeted with widespread condemnation. In a series of internal meetings the FMLN as a whole had come to consider that the murders such as those of Peccorini and the attorney general were a political mistake and should be publicly admitted.[37]

All the more disconcerting, then, was the assassination of the new minister of the presidency, José Antonio Rodríguez Porth, only nine days into Cristiani's government. Ellacuría happened to see the leadership of the Democratic Convergence—Ungo, Zamora, and Reni Roldán—just hours after the assassination. They too were concerned and confused. They assured Ellacuría that in conversations they had had with the FMLN just ten days ago, they had understood that the rebels had categorically decided not to continue with actions of this type. Rodríguez Porth was a founder of ARENA and one of the key figures in the new government; with more political experience than most incoming ministers, he was known to have favored Ponce over Bustillo as minister of defense and to back dialogue with the FMLN. (He had been a frequent visitor to the UCA's bookstore as he didn't trust the Salvadoran mail to get his monthly copy of *ECA* to him with any regularity.) The Convergence leaders knew that there was a possibility that his murder had come from the right, and whatever its origin they would condemn it "publicly and emphatically."[38] The loss of one of his closest advisers was a bitter blow to the new president and a telling indicator of quite how precarious his government was to be.

"My theory is that bombs don't kill," Ellacuría had remarked in April of the attack on Merino's home to an audience of foreign journalists. "And I am an expert in bombs because they have left me ten of them. They don't kill, but they frighten."[39] A week later his words had been put to the test when the UCA too was bombed. The *Diario de Hoy* answered the UCA's observation that the articles carried by the newspaper contributed to the climate that made such attacks possible by insisting that "minor bombs" such as the ones that had exploded at the UCA "do no substantial damage . . . but can be used to 'fabricate martyrs' and justify later acts of terrorism."[40]

The bombs that exploded in the UCA's printing plant in the early hours of July 22 would be quite another matter. As Jesuits, workers, and journalists joined Rogelio Pedraz to survey the damage caused by four of the seven large bombs left within the plant itself, beneath the computer system, and underneath the university bus parked outside, it was clear that this time the purpose had been destruction. Partly through the good fortune that three bombs did not explode, the damage inflicted was not worse than the $70,000 worth caused by the other four. Drawing sharply on a cigarette as he supervised the National Police's extrication of the three unexploded bombs, the wiry, agitated figure of Rogelio Pedraz was too furious to talk to the press. It was left to Nacho Martín-Baró to comment calmly, "these kinds of events come after a continuous campaign of defamation, blaming the university and the Jesuit priests who work here for the evils that happen in the country."[41]

After the murder of Rodríguez Porth, ideologues had continued to fall among the victims of the targeted killings. At the end of June it was IRI's Edgar Chacón, one of those sworn into Zepeda's "civil defense" units and one of the two or three individuals in the country most consumed by an obsession with the Jesuits. On July 19 his associate Gabriel Payes would also be struck down, fatally wounded. The Jesuits were, once again, in the crossfire as, apparently in reaction to Chacón's slaying, the shadowy "Crusade for Peace and Work" published a paid advertisement attributing the "brutal wave of violence and cowardly assassinations" to the "terrorist hordes." *First* among a list of names that included actual guerrilla *comandantes* (Villalobos and Handal among others) and the political leaders of the Convergence and UDN, had been those of Ignacio Ellacuría and Segundo Montes. The advertisement was addressed to the president and demanded a state of siege, the introduction of the death penalty, and the capture and application of "justice" to all those it named.[42]

A well-placed regular among Ellacuría's visitors hurried over to the UCA as soon as he heard about the bombs left in the printing plant. He believed that the attack had probably come from within the Treasury Police. On one of the most recent occasions when the two men had met, soon after ARENA's electoral victory, he had argued long and hard against Ellacuría's interpretation of D'Aubuisson and the "pragmatism" of the extreme right. The fact that a desire for power had led D'Aubuisson to moderate his stated views could not be relied on in such fragile circumstances. Thinking to himself that it was perhaps Ellacuría's religious formation that led him to believe too much in the human potential for change, he had argued that "they have changed for political convenience. If things change again, they'll kill you." On this occasion he found Ellacuría as calm as ever. "Freddy called me immediately," he said of Cristiani. "He guaranteed that the government had nothing to do with it. And Ponce called. He says it wasn't the army." "Look, Ignacio," the visitor insisted. "This is a warning."[43]

Ellacuría flew to Spain within a few days of the bombing. He had been invited to speak at the prestigious summer school held by Madrid's Complutense University at El Escorial. From the lecture podium, in private meetings, and with journalists he tried to make intelligible the urgency of the search for peace in El Salvador. Under Cristiani, he assured *El País*, there were more possibilities for negotiations than there had ever been under Duarte. "Aren't you afraid that you might end up like Monsignor Romero?" had been the journalist's final question. "For me the danger would be in death squads," Ellacuría answered. "But they don't have the same support as before. They could kill me. But I am not worried."[44]

NEVER so close, yet still so far. In private, Ellacuría was not quite so sanguine. "Now it could happen," he told Jon Sobrino in July in an admission that, for the first time since his return to the country in 1982, his own assassination was a possibility.[45] Negotiation had never been closer and Ellacuría himself had never been more obviously a bridge across the gulf still separating the two sides in the war. And bridges, in wartime, are vulnerable and strategic targets.

Such bridge-building as the Jesuits undertook with the army was handled for the most part by Segundo Montes. Throughout the 1980s, Montes maintained a relationship with officers he had come to know at the end of the 1970s. Among them was the *tandona* officer Mauricio Vargas, who enjoyed the chance to discuss politics and sociology with Montes and was pleased to receive from him the occasional academic paper. In return, on several occasions Vargas had helped Montes obtain the necessary safe-conduct passes to travel into the conflictive zones of the country. Perturbed by the precedent set by the army's paid advertisement against him, Montes had contacted Colonel Galileo Torres—head of the army's press office COPREFA and an officer who had taught a few courses at the UCA in the 1970s and even in the early 1980s—to try and get some sense of what was going on. Over dinner at Torres's home he was told that yes, there were "strong interests" inside the armed forces in opposition to the Jesuits and that they should be careful. Although in itself this hardly constituted a novelty, the warning came to reinforce a rumor that arrived at the UCA through one of the members of staff with contacts inside the army. There was a plan, the rumor went, for the elimination of the entire directorate of the UCA. Montes's reaction had been characteristic: "what am I going to do?—if they kill me, they kill me."[46]

More serious was an incident with Major Mauricio Chávez Caceres, who as a young lieutenant had been a student on the UCA's Political Science program. Montes and his assistants used to drop in to see him in the military barracks in Sensuntepeque, where he was stationed, on their way to the repatriated community of Santa Marta, Cabañas. The major prided himself on his progressive outlook, yet had become implicated in the coverup of the August 1988 capture, torture, and murder of a Swedish theologian, Jürg Weiss, by a patrol that came under his responsibility. An *ECA* commentary on the detailed report of a delegation from the European Parliament had, like the report itself, singled out Chávez Caceres's attempt to placate the delegation with a whitewash.[47] When Chávez Caceres saw the *ECA* commentary he had stormed across to the UCA where, unable to find Montes, he confronted one of his former teachers. "How can you do this?" he asked. "This war is going to end in negotiation and you are going to need people inside the army. Please don't burn the only people who could help you."[48] Undoubtedly he had a point. A future edition of *ECA* would carry the High Command's response to the European report, distancing the Sensuntepeque barracks—and Chávez

Caceres in particular—from the events, and a carefully worded commentary, this time by Montes himself.[49] The matter would be brought up again, just to make sure that it would not be the cause of future resentment, at a meeting Montes would have with Colonel Ponce in September.[50]

As far back as February, Martín-Baró had spoken of an environment in which there prevailed "the possibility of being killed any moment of the day, and the possibility of being involved in a violent clash at every moment."[51] The tension of living in such conditions—even when the worst of it was not, of course, suffered at first hand—and working maybe fourteen or fifteen hours a day, day after day, year after year, was one that was taking a very real toll. Hours of insomnia could be filled by reading or listening to the radio, but they contributed to a notable deterioration in the health of the majority of the UCA Jesuits. Martín-Baró suffered a bad back brought on by days spent over his beloved computer and Ellacuría suffered from trouble with his liver that increased as he redoubled his efforts on behalf of negotiations. But over and above particular medical complaints, colleagues and other Jesuits noticed that *los viejos*, as they were referred to (although old they were not), seemed worn down by their experience of the past ten or fifteen years. Ellacuría, in particular, was withdrawn and somber and somewhat liable to snap. Any suggestion that he should rest was abruptly dismissed with the argument that the people of El Salvador had no rest from the war and the economic crisis, so why should he?

The core of the UCA II community—Ellacuría, Montes, Sobrino, Martín-Baró, Jon Cortina, and Rodolfo Cardenal—had remained intact since the early 1980s, but 1989 saw a long awaited move into a new residence above the Romero Center. The new building, with its austere study-bedrooms along a corridor that led out into a large garden, had been carefully designed to combine the convenience of living within the UCA grounds with the autonomy and privacy proper to a Jesuit residence. Martín-Baró had worried that is physical isolation from all but the UCA itself would only exacerbate the distance between this rather intimidating group of Jesuits and other communities. He had hesitated to move, but loyalty to his household had prevailed. Among the changes that did come with the new residence, however, was the departure of Jon Cortina to work among repopulated communities in Chalatenango and the addition of both Amando López, who had returned to El Salvador in 1984, and Joaquín López y López, tireless and silent as ever in his dedication to *Fe y Alegría* despite the knowledge that he had been diagnosed with cancer.

The move itself was gradual, with Jon Sobrino and Juan Ramón Moreno—back since 1985 to teach theology and tend the library in the old Center for Theological Reflection—among the first to sleep above their new offices. While work on the building had progressed, the Jesuits had taken an obvious delight in showing friends around and wrangling over who would get which of the nearly identical rooms. Off the covered passageway, at right-angles to the corridor of bedrooms, were a kitchen, a dining area, and a guest room with a pair of divan beds. As the Jesuits moved their possessions—scant apart from a quantity of books, the odd radio and computer terminal—across from Calle Cantábrico, the stark and functional residence gradually began to take the shape of a home. Montes and Amando López spent hours in the planning of the new garden. The family of Elba Ramos, for many years cook, cleaning woman, and friend to the Jesuits, had moved into the small house near the gate onto the Avenida Einstein in June. Once they were installed in the residence, her husband, Don Obdulio, would take Montes or Amando López, or sometimes both, on a morning round to inspect the progress of the mango trees, the papayas, and the carefully ordered vegetable garden he planted and tended during the day. The idea, he would remember later, had been to supply the Jesuits and the UCA with all the fruit and vegetables they would need.[52]

FOR the August–September 1989 edition of *ECA,* the UCA pulled out all stops in an analysis of "The First Hundred Days of ARENA."[53] In his inaugural speech, Cristiani had presented the search for a solution to the armed conflict as the first of the challenges with which his government was faced. Almost at the limit of the hundred days under discussion, on September 13, 14, and 15, talks were held in Mexico between delegations of the government and the FMLN. The talks ended with the signing of a preliminary accord agreeing to the reinitiation of the process of dialogue-negotiation stalled since the meeting in the Nunciature in October 1987. This achievement, reinforced by Cristiani's ratification of the principles of Esquipulas II in the meeting of the Central American presidents at Tela in Honduras in early August, weighed strongly in the government's favor.

Ellacuría had been to see Cristiani in the middle of August. The official reason for the visit had to been to ask whether the ARENA government would be disposed to continue the arrangement established under Duarte by which the state cofinanced the UCA's debt to the IADB. Cristiani saw no problem at all with this, and even remarked that "the subsidy seemed small compared with what the UCA is."[54] Dismissing the matter as something that they could leave to others to arrange, he made it clear that what he really wanted was to talk politics to Ellacuría. From the beginning, Cristiani had proposed a new formula for talking to the FMLN, in which a commission of "democratic personalities of broad national recognition" would replace the presidential delegations that had taken part in the three formal meetings achieved during the Duarte years.[55] Although it was still proving difficult to get an acceptable commission together, he did not appear discouraged. Rather he wanted to know how Ellacuría assessed the FMLN's disposition to accept a procedure that would lead to an end to hostilities.

There is no doubt that Cristiani came to power inexperienced. In the FMLN he was up against leaders who had been politically active for the better part of twenty years. Over the last nine years, some of them had had extensive experience in international diplomacy. As he felt his way into government, he was bombarded by proposal after proposal underwritten by increased military pressure. It was not easy, particularly as many of those closest to the president could stomach the concept of "dialogue" only if they could be assured that nothing would be conceded to the FMLN. One political figure involved in the discussions in the early days of the ARENA government remembered how little Cristiani seemed to know: "He believed that the guerrillas would give up in three months, his people were saying that it would be possible to become independent from the *gringos* and give the guerrillas the opportunity to surrender with honor."[56] Ellacuría sensed Cristiani's lack of historical background, particularly where it came to the FMLN, and believed that he and the UCA could be useful. What mattered was the encouragement of everything that could contribute to a negotiated peace. And within what it was possible for the UCA and its rector to do, the ear of the president was not a bad thing to have.

Ellacuría left the August meeting concluding that Cristiani "gave the impression that he was the president and that he would make decisions prudently but effectively."[57] This positive view of a man whose caution he believed to be rooted in pragmatism rather than reluctance was reflected in the edition of *ECA* devoted to the "hundred days" (Martín-Baró would grumble that it read like "an ode to Cristiani"[58]). In June Ungo, Zamora, and Roldán had complained to Ellacuría that the position on dialogue presented by Cristiani was "poor—the minimum necessary to please the United States and respond to his electoral promises and the maximum that the hard-line sector could tolerate."[59] In September, with the benefit of hindsight provided by the success of the Mexico meeting, Ellacuría considered that Cristiani's original commitment had been "solemn and risk taking."[60] Such support did not go unnoticed. Coupled as it was with censure of some of the actions of the FMLN, it constituted headline news: "Ellacuría praises the sanity and serenity of Cristiani"; "Ellacuría changes his opinion and condemns barbarity of the FMLN."[61] Although there would be criticisms from the left, and, indeed, from some inside the UCA, that Ellacuría was separating the individual, Cristiani, from his social class, his party, and the political situation, Ellacuría did not doubt that while the nature of Cristiani made his support possible, what he was actually supporting was the process toward negotiations and not just the person of the president.

Ellacuría's idea to invite D'Aubuisson himself to take part in an UCA Forum and have him publicly commit his support to dialogue did not get past a consultation with the members of his own community. It was, however, in support of the process toward negotiations that Ellacuría would invite Cristiani to the UCA's award of an honorary doctorate to President Oscar Arias for his contribution to peace in Central America. It was also in support of the process that Ellacuría met regularly with David Escobar Galindo, the one constant component in the nebulous makeup of the government's dialogue commission. Escobar Galindo was a well-known poet and a close friend of Cristiani. He had known the Jesuits for about twenty years and had several volumes of his work published by *UCA Editores*. He was not a member of ARENA, nor a man with wide-ranging political experience. As his very presence on the commission had come under attack from the left, it had been, he remarked, "natural" for him to seek advice from Ellacuría. In their five meetings between July and October, Escobar Galindo drew support from Ellacuría's "faith that the process would bear fruit."[62]

After their initial rejection of Cristiani's commission, the political parties of the opposition—with the PDC, PCN, and Convergence working together on this issue—played a positive role in bringing the government and the FMLN together. They met with the FMLN in Mexico and responded to the rebels' request for them to help achieve an early meeting with the government, and then pressured the government into including the Church at any dialogue session. Among the opposition's leaders were those whose personal knowledge of Ellacuría allowed for a broad understanding of the UCA's relationship to Cristiani. Rubén Zamora, for example, considered the relationship to be indicative of how far the Jesuits had come since the days of Molina when, from inside the UCA, he had felt their dealings with the president had been a somewhat naive attempt to win influence that had been doomed to failure. As the basis for Ellacuría's attitude toward Cristiani, Zamora saw the coincidence of the realism of Ellacuría's recognition of a right wing-government "with some abilities" and his unswerving commitment to contributing to a necessary change in the country with "what there was."[63]

Increasingly tired and even morose ("It's easy to be in a good mood if you have nothing to do"[64]), Ellacuría responded sharply to criticisms of his relationship with Cristiani. "If you say things in favor of Cristiani," he complained three days before the president's visit to the UCA for the Arias award, "you have gone over to his side; if you say things in favor of the FMLN it's because you're always defending the FMLN."[65] But he was torn between this kind of curt dismissal and a knowledge that, while he knew perfectly well what he was doing, perhaps others were confused by what appeared to be a shift to the right. Guillermo Ungo had paid him a visit after a trip to Managua before the Mexico meeting and had told Ellacuría that he was perceived as having "saved" Cristiani too often. "He said it as a joke," Ellacuría would write in his notebook in deference to the well-known difficulty of "reading" Ungo's irony, "but he was obviously worried."[66] In an unusual gesture, Jon Sobrino made a formal appointment to see the rector and suggest that perhaps he *appeared* to be going a little far. In early October, Ellacuría would address some of these worries in a television broadcast, hoping to establish, once and for all, the rectitude of his position. As he returned from the studio he asked Rolando Alvarado, the young Jesuit who worked as his assistant, whether people really thought he was on Cristiani's "side." But he gave him little time to answer: "What do I care what they think? If the devil would bring me peace, I'd negotiate with the devil himself."[67]

The message left on Ellacuría's car one night in October as it stood parked outside the residence of the Costa Rican ambassador was less sophisticated than the concerns that he was overly favoring Cristiani. Ellacuría and Segundo Montes emerged from dinner to find the small white car covered in red-painted slogans and swastikas. "Death to the communists of the UCA!" read the words roughly daubed along its side.[68]

NO small factor in the bleakness of Ellacuría's mood was a meeting he had with the FMLN in Managua on September 29. Until the FMLN had shown itself willing to sit down to talk to the government in Mexico, Ellacuría had been increasingly worried by the delicacy of the situation within the *Frente*. These worries, which were the subject of a conversation he had with Rubén Zamora in July, centered on the preparations for a general offensive that had run parallel to the evolution of an FMLN strategy on negotiation. Many combatants and *comandantes* still believed in the possibility of military victory and longed for the opportunity to prove such a victory to be within their grasp. They had been prepared to launch an offensive at the end of 1988, on March 19 and on June 1, 1989, and were now worried that the FMLN was presenting too "political" an image. Suspicious of the government's intentions, at the very least they wanted to use military pressure to secure better conditions within which to talk.[69] Ellacuría had agreed with Zamora that it was important to get the FMLN and the government to meet as soon as possible. The Mexico talks had appeared to achieve this end and reconciled Ellacuría to the rebels' seriousness of purpose.

In Mexico the FMLN delegation, led by Villalobos and Handal, was larger and of higher ranking members than the one eventually assembled by the government. The lack of balance was perceived by the FMLN as a lack of commitment on the government's part. Certainly the imbalance was reflected in the documents that each side presented: while the FMLN wanted to discuss fundamental structural issues, the government preferred to concentrate on matters of procedure. That a compromise was reached, and a further meeting in Costa Rica agreed upon in which to discuss an end to hostilities seemed almost too good to be true. In his analysis of the fortunes of "dialogue" in ARENA's first hundred days, Ellacuría concluded that, in Mexico, "things could hardly have turned out better."[70] But only two weeks later, as he met with Villalobos and Ana Guadalupe Martínez from the ERP, Fermán Cienfuegos of the RN, Antonio Cardenal from the FPL, Nidia Díaz from the PRTC, and Marroquín of the FAL, Ellacuría was brought face to face with the likelihood that force would once more come into play before the promise held out by the Mexico talks could be realized.

Ellacuría made the short flight to Nicaragua on the morning of September 29 and returned to San Salvador at the end of the day. Not even César Jerez, at Managua's UCA, was aware he was in the country. He had come to gauge the depth of FMLN's genuine commitment to negotiations and to try and persuade them not to dismiss Cristiani out of hand, but the meeting was charged with tension. To the *comandantes'* insistence that Cristiani was, if not "the enemy" then at least their "immediate oppressor," Ellacuría countered that they should make the most of the fact that the "immediate oppressor" was someone with whom it was possible to talk. He praised Cristiani for his efforts to isolate the extremists who were opposed to dialogue in any form. Joaquín Villalobos responded that he was fundamentally wrong in his understanding of Cristiani's intentions with respect to the negotiation of the structural issues that were of concern to them and "too optimistic" about the "murderers" with whom he was surrounded. "Joaquín, let's not talk about murderers!" Ellacuría fired back in a remark laden with reference to the past that few others would have dared to touch upon.[71]

Ana Guadalupe Martínez and Toño Cardenal stayed behind with Ellacuría after the meeting ended, vying with each other for the opportunity to continue the discussion by driving him to the airport. Cardenal secured the job of chauffeur, but as Ellacuría waited with Martínez before they left, he took advantage of the few moments on their own to float an idea it would have been impossible to raise in front of the others. He suggested that they should attempt to bring Villalobos and Cristiani together in a direct meeting. He believed it would be productive because, "they are both practical people . . . I know them both, and Joaquín and Cristiani would get on well." "Where on earth did you invent all this?" was Ana Guadalupe's astounded reply. "After hearing what you were saying inside, and now this, I can see you're totally in love with Cristiani. Who knows what he's done to you, what he's put in your food, to make you come out with all this propaganda." "No, no," Ellacuría replied. "Tell Joaquín that it's not propaganda—rather I think it's a practical mission. The two of them are the men who can find a solution for the country."[72]

Impractical and even unrealistic as it was, the suggestion came too late. As Ellacuría argued, valiantly but in vain, for the need and point of continuing with the process of dialogue initiated in Mexico, it became increasingly clear that a decision had been made and that on the basis of that decision a major military offensive was imminent. "The Salvadoran people want an insurrection," Villalobos had declared. "What the Salvadoran people want is to go to the United States," was Ellacuría's searing reply. Never, in the long years of his confrontations with the FMLN had he received such a buffeting. On their way to the airport, Cardenal remembered Ellacuría sitting, tense and furious, beside him in his car. "They didn't understand me, they didn't understand me," he repeated. "They didn't want to understand."[73]

The list of the names of the *comandantes* present at this meeting, its date, and place, were entered into Ellacuría's third notebook. The rest of the page is blank. It was the last of 273 entries. In the days that followed his return from Managua, the political situation deteriorated sharply as the FMLN announced the end of the suspension of sabotage that they had introduced after the meeting in Mexico and an intensification of direct attacks on the armed forces. Ellacuría's meetings with politicians, diplomats, and Church leaders anxious to keep the negotiation process on the rails continued, but either a lack of time or the anger and foreboding with which the Managua meeting had left him prevented him from filling his notebook's pages.

ELLACURÍA wrote one last editorial for the weekly *Proceso* before leaving on October 21 for a three-week trip to Europe. Few others could find that there was "still basis and reason for hope" after the meeting between the government and the FMLN in Costa Rica.[74] In the presence of the Church, the OAS, and the U.N. and with members of the army as additional observers, the fundamental differences in the two sides' negotiating positions emerged when the talks began on October 15. The government demanded a cessation of all hostilities from October 18 and then the beginning of negotiation; the FMLN insisted that a cease-fire could only emerge from the talks themselves. But as the *comandantes* dismissed the government's proposal out of hand, so they presented a list of demands that threatened to force the dialogue to breaking point. Worse even than the appeal for constitutional reform or the insistence that those responsible for the murder of Monsignor Romero be brought to justice before a cease-fire could be agreed upon, was a blueprint for the reform of the army. While claiming that they were calling for the armed forces' *self*-cleansing, the FMLN demanded restructuring of the army and the retirement of Minister of Defense Larios, General Bustillo, and all sixteen officers of the *tandona* on active service. If this was negotiation, the army was not going to like it one little bit. Only the intervention of Oscar Arias allowed for an agreement to resume discussion in Caracas on November 20 to be reached.

An internal memo issued from Ellacuría's office would express the hope that his European trip "would be of enormous benefit for the university and the country." He would be giving conferences in universities across Germany and addressing the parliament in Bonn, seeking financing from Spanish universities for a variety of masters' degree courses the UCA hoped to start, receiving the prize awarded to the UCA by the Comín Foundation in Barcelona, attending the inauguration of the Xavier Zubiri Foundation in Madrid, and participating in a meeting of the rectors of Spanish, Portuguese, and Latin American universities in Salamanca.[75] But while he lectured on utopia and reality, on marxism and christianity, and on the advantages of a civilization of work over a civilization of capital in Hamburg, Basel, and Frankfurt, back home in El Salvador the precarious achievements of San José were unraveling under the pressure of the differences exposed on the way to them and a tit-for-tat exchange of violence that threatened to spiral out of all control.

Ellacuría had counseled that after San José there should be a return "to a process that is gradual on each side—gradual, uninterrupted, and objectively in search of a negotiated agreement."[76] Nothing could have been further from what actually happened in the days that followed. The army was hopping mad. Not only were the demands of the FMLN an affront to its dignity and integrity, but on October 17, hours before the talks ended, the daughter of Colonel Edgardo Casanova Vejar was brutally murdered outside her home. The army was convinced the FMLN was responsible. Two days later the homes of Rubén Zamora and his sister-in-law, Aronette Díaz, were bombed. The FMLN and the political opposition were convinced that the army was responsible. The next day Larios declared that the FMLN's demands for change within the armed forces were "absurd, ridiculous, and impossible." On October 22, Cristiani reinforced the words of his minister of defense by saying that he would never allow "a minority group to give orders to change the Supreme Court of Justice and restructure the armed forces. All these absurd ideas have to come off the FMLN's agenda if they really want peace." The FMLN responded that they understood the tone of these statements as a "virtual declaration of war." On October 30, they launched a military attack on the *estado mayor,* firing missiles (somewhat inaccurately) from mobile platforms constructed in nearby streets.[77]

But these and other individual incidents of violence—an attack on a demonstration inside the National University, the assassination of the president of the Mortgage Bank—dwindled into insignificance alongside what happened on October 31. The explosions that rocked central San Salvador that lunchtime were the second of the day. In the morning it had been the offices of COMADRES, the organization of the mothers and wives of the political prisoners, the assassinated, and the "disappeared." One hundred and nine people had been inside the building when an explosion occurred; only four of them had been wounded. But the lunchtime bombing was different. News spread quickly across the city, and when viewers turned on their television sets that evening they could see the carnage for themselves. Large quantities of explosives had been left in the central office of the labor federation FENASTRAS at one of the busiest times of the day. As the force of the bombs ripped through the offices, ten prominent unionists were killed and thirty-five people were wounded. Watching in horror as Febé Elizabeth Velázquez, one of the most important of all the leaders of the popular movement, ran out of the wreckage, the back of her head quite visibly blown right off, a sickening fear descended on the country. This massacre was on quite a different scale from anything that had preceded it. In the minds of the people of El Salvador there could be little doubt that it had come from the right. What would happen now?

CRISTIANI held a crisis meeting the next morning. He was visibly shaken by the FENASTRAS bombing and concerned about what to do next. There was a lot of talk about the seriousness of the investigation that must take place, a lot of guarantees from General Larios and Colonel Ponce that, of course, it had been nothing to do with the armed forces. One adviser warned that it was not enough to promise an investigation: the credibility of the government and of the president himself was on the line. Why not establish an independent investigative commission? What about asking the dialogue's observers—the Church, the U.N., and the OAS—to take part? Cristiani promptly gave the idea his support. Then Oscar Santamaría, minister of justice and senior government representative at the talks, spoke up. "I agree completely," he told the president, "but, listen, people say you consult with Father Ellacuría. He is respected internationally—why don't we put him on the commission?" Cristiani asked others for their opinions, but the question was deflected with an understated reminder from one of those present that the greater part of the army thought that Ellacuría favored the left. What did the minister of defense and the army chief of staff have to say? Larios and Ponce repeated that it was important that the bombing should be fully investigated, and Cristiani ordered that the Church, the OAS, the United Nations, and Ellacuría should be contacted as soon as possible.[78]

Ellacuría was moving rapidly through Europe. He was in Frankfurt on October 31 and then traveled to the Basque country to pay visits to two universities and to his 93-year-old father in his home town of Portugalete. The old man lived with his brother Jesús (one of the two other priests in the family) and his health was increasingly frail. A visit from his son from El Salvador (another son, José, was a Jesuit in Taiwan) was a source of real pleasure, however brief. And then he was off again, this time to Barcelona, to catch up on old friends—among them Luis de Sebastián; to visit yet another university in search of support for the UCA's postgraduate program; and, on November 6, to offer the UCA's thanks for the Alfonso Comín Prize awarded for its commitment to justice for the oppressed of El

Salvador and Central America. Ellacuría spoke of the university and its objective partiality in favor of the poor majorities, of the relationship between utopia and prophecy, and of the need to work toward a new historical model, different from those presented by the decadent capitalism of the West or the decaying socialism of the East. "There is a lot that remains to be done," he told the upturned faces in front of him, so distant from the crisis being experienced in El Salvador. "Only utopically and full of hope can one believe and have spirit enough to join with all the poor and oppressed of the world and try to revert history, to subvert it and to launch it in a different direction."[79]

In Ellacuría's absence, the telephone calls from the presidential residence were coming thick and fast. Colonel Juan Antonio Martínez Varela, Cristiani's minister of the presidency, was anxious that Ellacuría should respond to the invitation to take part in the commission to investigate the FENASTRAS bombing. In regular communication with his assistant Alvarado, Ellacuría learned of the invitation and asked that not only the formal letter from the president, but also the counsel of Provincial Chema Tojeira, and of his own Jesuit community be relayed to him by fax.[80] The Jesuits cautioned Ellacuría against "burning" himself from outside the country. The situation was changing more quickly than he could tell from Europe: in reaction to the bombings of COMADRES and FENASTRAS, the FMLN had called off further dialogue with the government until there were guarantees for the security of the popular movement. On November 6, Assistant Secretary Aronson had paid an unscheduled visit to the country to plead for calm and prudence in what was clearly an incendiary situation. The next day, two members of Rubén Zamora's MPSC were captured by the army in Sonsonate and assassinated. Rumors of an FMLN offensive were a daily occurrence and the whole country was on tenterhooks. And the FMLN, Ellacuría should know, were looking for him everywhere. They wanted him to stop in and see them in Managua before he returned to El Salvador.

Ellacuría was not that surprised to be hearing from the FMLN. They had asked him to see them in Nicaragua on his way to Europe, but he had not been interested. After the last meeting he felt they had little to talk about; he was going to be away long enough as it was and a ticket had already been bought for him to travel to Madrid via Guatemala. And now, during his brief stay in de Sebastián's Barcelona home, César Jerez was on the telephone from Managua. "Who wants to talk to me, you or the others?" Ellacuría asked. "The others," came the answer, "and they say its important." Ellacuría held firm. He would return to El Salvador as planned and from there go and see them in Managua. Jerez called again, "but what they want to say to you is really *very* important." As Ellacuría put the telephone down, still adamant, he turned to de Sebastián and grumbled, "the trouble with them is they always think that what *they* have to say is very important."[81]

The business of the FENASTRAS commission was a different matter. The members of FENASTRAS themselves had refused Cristiani's invitation for their organization to be represented within the commission, though they had said that they would respect any position adopted by the OAS and the United Nations on the matter. Either way, Ellacuría's decision would have enormous significance. On November 9—his fifty-ninth birthday—Ellacuría replied to the letter from Martínez Varela that had reached him in Salamanca. "I am stunned by this act of terrorism," he wrote, "I am ready to work for the promotion of human rights, I am convinced that President Cristiani rejects these types of actions and that he has proposed this commission with good will, I would like to support any reasonable effort that may help negotiation advance in the most effective way possible." But he asked, most politely, whether he might postpone his decision until after his return to the country on November 13.[82]

A few hours later, at the oldest of all of Spain's universities, Ellacuría was unanimously chosen to be president of the Upper Council of the Iberoamerican Postgraduate University, the coordinating body of universities offering postgraduate studies throughout Spain, Portugal, and Latin America. As he ended his contribution to the meeting, he turned to his colleagues and reminded them that, in accordance with the Council's statutes, he would be the host the next time they met: "You are all invited to the next meeting of our Council, which we shall hold in El Salvador. If I am still alive, I shall welcome you there in two years time. Let's hope that it will serve as a contribution to the peace we so long for."[83]

THE FMLN launched the largest offensive of the war at 8:00 P.M. on Saturday November 11. "Out with the fascists! Long live Febé Elizabeth!" was its name. In San Salvador simultaneous attacks were mounted on the presidential residence and Cristiani's private home and on the homes of the president and vice-president of the assembly. Among the military targets were the National Police barracks in Zacamil, their training installations in Santa Tecla, and the San Carlos barracks of the army's First Brigade. Within an hour, the entire city was under fire and within three, all radio stations had been ordered to participate in a national network broadcast from the army's *Radio Cuscatlán*. Machine guns, mortars, bombs, and the distinctive rattle of helicopter Gatling guns could be heard all night.

The offensive had been more than a year in the planning and months in preparation. Thousands of guerrilla combatants were brought down from the hills of Chalatenango and Morazán into a city many of them had never seen before. Stockpiles of arms, far in excess of those of the existing military force, were prepared for the insurrection expected by so many of the FMLN's leaders. In late October and early November, the possibility of a guerrilla offensive of some kind had been discussed at every level of political, diplomatic, and military life. During the week preceding its launch, quiet messages had been passed to prominent figures of the political opposition—including the Jesuits of the UCA—warning them that they should be prepared to leave their homes and seek refuge elsewhere. Yet the strength and scale of what was launched on November 11 took almost everyone by surprise. Only the night before, for example, the U.S. embassy's regional security officer concluded that the threat of an offensive was not great enough to warrant canceling the annual Marine Ball. Colonel Menjívar, the senior U.S. military officer in the country, with access to both U.S. and Salvadoran information, would later remember that it had been at about three o'clock in the afternoon of November 11, just five hours before it began, that he had "come to the conclusion that the offensive was about to start."[84]

The Jesuit communities of the UCA and Calle Mediterráneo had been thrown as quickly as anyone into the thick of the offensive. Shortly after 8:00 P.M. on the Saturday night, they were shaken by a series of loud explosions. The whole neighborhood was plunged into darkness and a bullet ricocheted through an upstairs window of the Mediterráneo house. Bombs went off beside the supermarket not thirty yards away and fighting broke out around Democracy Tower on the corner of Avenida Einstein and the Southern Highway to the UCA's immediate north. Shortly afterward, a group of FMLN combatants blew open the Einstein gate beside the Ramos's house and fled through the new residence. Ten minutes later members of the army arrived on the scene; after a few rounds of gunfire outside the gate, the situation appeared to be under control.[85] The episode left Elba Ramos and her daughter Celina frightened and unable to sleep, anxious about who or what might come through the damaged gate. Another night of this and they would be asking the Jesuits whether they could not come in to sleep in the peace and quiet of their residence.

By the next day, the only source of news for the majority of the population was the FMLN's *Radio Venceremos*. At 6:00 A.M. the guerrillas reported attacks on the National Police, National Guard, Treasury Police, the Belloso Battalion, and the air force, and combat in twenty zones of the city. There was no word from Cristiani until a national broadcast at 10:30 A.M. in which he assured his people that "the army will triumph." At the end of the day he returned to the airwaves to announce the suspension of all constitutional guarantees, the introduction of a state of siege, and a 6:00 P.M. to 6:00 A.M. curfew. Promises that the scattered groups of "terrorists" responsible for the violence would soon be under control were sounding increasingly hollow. Interspersed with the official announcements and easy-listening music playing on *Radio Cuscatlán* were a series of telephone calls denouncing leaders of the political opposition, of the labor movement, and of the Church. Hardened as they were to vitriol, the Jesuits listened in horror to the attacks on Rivera, Ungo, and Zamora; to the demands for Ellacuría's head and for him to be "spit to death"; and to charges offered by no less a figure than Vice-President Merino that the Jesuits had "poisoned the minds of the Salvadoran youth."[86]

Poised on the edge of the city, the UCA and its neighborhood were a natural corridor for guerrilla and army forces alike. On the morning of November 12, a sergeant presented himself to the UCA Jesuits and asked permission for his patrol to inspect the route taken by the guerrillas the night before. Segundo Montes showed them around and handed over an unexploded device that had been found near the gate. The soldiers, as he told the others, were from the Belloso Battalion. A few hours later, Fermín Saínz, director of the Loyola Center and a member of the Meditérraneo community, received an urgent telephone call from the Center's housekeeper. "Come quickly Father, they've found some weapons," she told him. Seriously worried by what this could mean at such a delicate time, Saínz jumped in his car and drove the kilometer and a half up the hill to the retreat center isolated above the city in its own ample grounds. There, at the far edge of the terrain, he found a number of agents from the Treasury Police standing beside a young man with his thumbs tied together behind the his back. Under a pile of ash were the small backpacks and weapons of a unit of four guerrillas. "Don't worry Father," Saínz was told. "We're finding them all over the place."[87]

ELLACURÍA left Salamanca on the afternoon of November 10. On the Saturday, he spent a quiet day in Madrid, saying mass in the home of his youngest brother, Juan Antonio, and his wife, and following the afternoon's soccer on television. As he had so often over the years, he lunched with Zubiri's widow Carmen Castro. Like the doting mother she had become to him, she listened appreciatively to his account of this most successful of European trips.[88] Worried by the news from El Salvador that had reached him during the week, his concern deepened when on the Sunday morning he heard the first reports of the offensive broadcast over the radio. It was difficult to judge the scale of things from the news bulletin, but that it had been launched at night, he explained to his brother and sister-in-law as they drove him to the airport, was an important indicator of its seriousness. The normal practice of the FMLN, he told them, was to time their actions to leave themselves enough daylight to make their getaway. Launched at night and on such a scale—this must be the general offensive so long threatened for the time when the FMLN considered that the way of negotiations had failed.[89]

Ellacuría dismissed suggestions that maybe he shouldn't return to El Salvador with the reminder that the president of the republic had asked him to take part in the FENASTRAS commission. Whatever his decision on the matter, the fact that he had been asked was a sign of the respect with which he was considered and an indication that he could count on Cristiani's support. If anything, the news of the offensive only made him more anxious to get back to where he belonged. Only a few days earlier he had been interviewed by the Catalan newspaper *Avui*. Wasn't he afraid of the threats he received, the journalist had asked in a piece that would run on November 15. "Never. I'm not afraid," had been the answer. "Fear is not a feeling which normally overcomes me. It would be too irrational to kill me. I've done nothing wrong."[90]

But in El Salvador things were increasingly fraught. The university, like the rest of the city, was closed. Since the Belloso Battalion's visit on Sunday morning, there had been a group of soldiers guarding the UCA's main entrance. Starting Monday, they prevented anyone from entering or leaving the campus. While the Jesuits could always slip in through the house on Calle Cantábrico, Antiguo Cuscatlán was so heavily militarized that from within the UCA the sensation was of being under siege. Early on Monday morning, Segundo Montes appeared in Rolando Alvarado's office on the third floor of the unusually empty rectory. Ellacu had spent the night in Miami, hadn't he? Was there any way he could get in touch with him and tell him not to come back? But Rolando had no idea where to reach him. Quite apart from other concerns, collecting Ellacuría from the airport was not going to be easy. His flight from Miami was due at 4:30 P.M., it took three-quarters of an hour to drive back from the airport, and the curfew began at 6:00 P.M. The airport itself was isolated from everything except the Bracamonte Battalion, which had its base nearby, and a couple of hotels on the coast a few miles away. If the plane was late, it might be necessary to spend the night down there. And a night in the airport was dangerous enough at any time.[91]

On Ellacuría's flight from Miami were two friends and UCA staff members, returning from a conference in Uruguay. Although their safe delivery home would add precious minutes to the drive back to the UCA, they were squeezed into the car that Paco Estrada and Amando López had driven out to meet Ellacuría. He had appeared pleased to be back in El Salvador, but the underlying tension showed through when it became clear that he was going to have to leave the airport without his luggage. The handlers had left early to get back to San Salvador and only one wealthy-looking passenger had managed to extract his suitcase. "Why did they give him his suitcase and not me mine?" Ellacuría grumbled. He drove quickly and in a silence that made the others nervous. Estrada and Amando López told him about the offensive, about the guerrillas who had come through the UCA, and the telephone callers who had attacked him so bitterly, but he hardly said a word. His anger with the FMLN hung like a heavy cloud over all of them. One of the few questions he asked was about the aerial bombardments of the residential areas under guerrilla occupation—had there been a public protest? Yes, he was assured, Rivera had already condemned them.

After dropping the other two off at one of their homes, the three Jesuits reached the main gate of the UCA at about twenty to six. A young officer appeared and, without introducing himself or asking any questions, addressed Ellacuría: "Ah, Father—you're back." "Yes, I'm back," said Ellacuría. "Let them through," came the order.[92]

Ellacuría had been home less than an hour when the soldiers arrived. He was telling the other members of the community about his trip when they heard people below them in the Romero Center, kicking down doors and working their way through the offices. There appeared to be about two patrols—certainly no fewer than twenty men—involved in a search. Ellacuría introduced himself and asked for the officer in charge to do the same and explain this intrusion. But the officer—who also addressed Montes and Martín-Baró by their names—refused to identify himself or his unit. When Ellacuría challenged the army's right to search their private residence and demanded that the minister of defense be called, the officer explained that they had orders to search the entire campus and, given the state of siege imposed the day before, they could do anything they liked.

According to an account written by Martín-Baró, the search was conducted in an orderly fashion. Soldiers worked through the offices of the Romero Center and—at the officer's insistence—the bedrooms of the residence, but found nothing they could qualify as incriminating. They left and Martín-Baró made a quick telephone call to the Mediterráneo community to warn them that the soldiers might be heading their way. Segundo Montes, priding himself on a knowledge of the military he knew to be superior to that of the others, told him he believed it had been the Atlacatl Battalion. But whoever it had been, it seemed surprising that, although Ellacuría invited them to return the following morning and search the entire university, they never did. And indeed daylight revealed that, for the thorough campus search they claimed they had been ordered to conduct, it had been remarkably superficial. The padlock on the pedestrian gate into Jardines de Guadalupe was broken, there was damage in the Romero Center and to some of the doors into some of the laboratories, but that was about it. Ellacuría would try in vain to get through to the *estado mayor* for an explanation.[93]

Rolando Alvarado remembered that he had never seen Ellacuría so annoyed as he was on that Tuesday morning. The offensive, Ellacuría maintained, "would do the FMLN more harm than good." While they were saying that they wanted to put more pressure on the negotiations, he knew that a great number of them still sought military victory. This offensive was not going to lead to victory, of that he was quite sure. It would put the process of negotiations back who knew how far and could only bring yet more suffering to the civilian population. After nearly ten years, he complained, "we're returning to 1980." Rolando turned the conversation to the search on the night before. "It's called reconnaissance," Rolando suggested, his own mind going back to his teens in Somoza's Nicaragua, "shouldn't you go somewhere else?" "Don't be paranoid," snapped Ellacuría. "They've already been here and they have seen that we haven't got anything. And, in the last instance, where do you want us to go, the U.S. embassy? We have fought from here and here we will stay."[94]

Ellacuría repeated this argument to anyone who raised the subject of the Jesuits' security. It was a rational argument. It made sense. The Jesuits had done nothing wrong. Their residence had been searched and nothing had been found. Guarding the UCA as they were, the army must know that they had no cache of weapons, no guerrillas hidden inside the university campus. And if the FMLN themselves had suggested that they should seek refuge elsewhere—as had the leaders of the political opposition (to Ellacuría's disapproval: they too had done nothing "wrong," so why hide?)—then who were the FMLN to give them orders? Rather, as Ellacuría explained to Tojeira over lunch on Wednesday, it was a shame he had never been able to ask, as he had meant to in a meeting he had pending with Colonel Zepeda, for the UCA to be declared neutral territory, off limits to either side in the war while it worked for a peaceful resolution. No, rather than leave, it was important to show that there was nothing wrong with what the UCA did by carrying on, as much as possible, as before.

THE place was thick with soldiers. Fermín Saínz had been roused from his customary nap on Wednesday afternoon by another telephone call from the Loyola Center. "You'd better come, Father," the housekeeper had said, and he could see why. As he drove his car up to the entrance, the soldiers had to move out of his way. There must have been 120 or 130 of them, sitting where they could or sprawled across the grass; some were drinking coffee and eating cake the Center staff had given them. They had carried out a quick search of the inside of the Center—one soldier asking, "This is the UCA's too, isn't it? Here they are planning the offensive"— but otherwise did not appear to be doing anything at all. A young sergeant took Saínz up the hill to meet the lieutenant under whose command these men from the Atlacatl Battalion appeared to be. They did not seem to be in a hurry to go anywhere and Saínz stayed most of the afternoon with them, reassuring the staff by his presence and chatting in general terms with some of soldiers. "You can talk to this priest," the lieutenant remarked. "The ones down below just get angry." At one point a captain appeared in a jeep. The men jumped rapidly to attention, the officers and sergeants clustering around as he spread out what looked like a map and gave some kind of orders about their troop displacement in the city below.

Only the next day would some of those present understand what the soldiers had said to them that afternoon: "There'll be a lot of noise around here tonight, so stay inside and don't come out"; "Now we're going to find those Jesuits. We don't want foreigners—this has got to end"; "We're going to look for Ellacuría, and if we find him, we're going to give him a prize!" At about 6:30 P.M., an officer ordered the soldiers to move out and they began to make their way slowly down the hill toward the UCA.[95]

ONE of the telephone calls the Jesuits managed to make that night was from Nacho Martín-Baró, who spoke to his sister Alicia in Valladolid, Spain. He sounded distant and composed, but scared. However, she was much relieved to hear his voice, and would tell her colleagues at work the next morning how glad she was to have been able to talk to him, to hear for herself that he was alright. He told her that they were surrounded, that they were virtually besieged by the army. "Listen, listen—wait—can you hear the bombs?" he asked as, at his end of the telephone, her voice was drowned out. "Oh, Nacho and when is this going to end?" she asked. "A lot more people will have to die yet," he answered. "A lot more people will have to die."[96]

CHAPTER TWELVE

DEAD WITH SPIRIT

Our dead are dead "with spirit." They are not dead that destroy, that kill, or that are easily forgotten, but dead who have continued to be profoundly active and alive in the society to which they belonged, generating human spirit, generating human dignity, generating the capacity for dialogue and humane rationality, generating a critical capacity, a constructive capacity, and generating imagination. And these "dead with spirit," as we have seen throughout these two years, have gradually been vanquishing—and with them all El Salvador's "dead with spirit"—those who murdered them.[1]

José María Tojeira, November 1991

THE defense would claim that it was the trial of "national dignity." Brought before the Salvadoran people by continuous television coverage and before the international community by the presence of numerous observers, the trial of nine members of the Salvadoran military for the murder of the six Jesuits and of Elba and Celina Ramos opened in San Salvador on the morning of September 26, 1991. Only the day before, the government and the FMLN had signed agreements in New York preparing the way for an end to the war and a fundamental restructuring of Salvadoran society. And now, in an improvised courtroom erected among the fourth-floor offices of the Salvadoran Supreme Court, Colonel Guillermo Benavides, three lieutenants, and four soldiers from the Atlacatl sat side by side before Judge Ricardo Zamora.[2] This was a case that had taken almost two years of judicial activity and international pressure to bring to trial, even as the evasion and resistance with which both had been met had set the limit on exactly who was being tried for what.

THE latest round of negotiations had concluded in New York after months of deadlock and a final ten days of intense and difficult discussions. The agreements on political and constitutional reform signed in Mexico at the end of April seemed far away. They had been followed by an optimism that soon dissolved under the pressures of the agreements' own limitations and a hardening of the position of the Salvadoran right.[3] Military actions increased and were matched by rhetorical *machismo* until, in August, General Ponce had boasted that military victory was still a possibility and the FMLN had launched a campaign under the slogan "if the armed forces want our weapons, they'll have to win the war."[4]

As bad as things seemed as the rounds of talks followed hard upon each other without any tangible results, the process of negotiation itself was too far advanced to be stemmed. The United Nations installed its Observers' Mission, ONUSAL, in El Salvador on July 26—the first anniversary of the agreements in San José that had led to its founding. Predictable hostility toward U.N. officials dubbed, "communist bureaucrats" by the *Diario de Hoy,* had been easily overridden by the cordiality of the mission's official reception by the two sides in the conflict and by the warm welcome offered by the social and political forces active within the country.[5] The continuing presence of the war rendered ONUSAL's mission more delicate even than its architects had imagined, yet its very existence—its patrol vehicles and staff soon seen throughout the country—was to the broad mass of Salvadorans a concrete sign that the talks that had faded into the background of their daily lives might now be real.

The Mexico agreement would be remembered by U.S. State Department officials as being "key . . . the first time that we in Washington saw an FMLN that was committed to ending the war."[6] Over the following months, all involved in the negotiations felt the effects of a new-found engagement on the part of the United States. From Congress the message to the administration had been clear. When the House Democrats' decision to defer consideration of military aid until September was dismissed by the announcement of the aid release at the end of June, attention passed to the Senate. On July 25, Senators Dodd and Leahy introduced an amendment to the 1992 Foreign Aid bill to strengthen restrictions on military aid. Although they would be forced to bow before a Republican filibuster, it was not before the senators had inflicted a solid defeat on an attempt to have the amendment "tabled" and barred from further debate.[7] Renewed action in both branches of Congress would have to wait, but with the votes stacked up behind the leadership in each body, the administration was left with little room to maneuver.

No less important was the support to the peace process given by the increased activity of the countries grouped together as the "Friends" of the U.N. secretary-general: Colombia, Mexico, Spain, and Venezuela. Like the United States, the "Friends" were worried not only by the lack of progress since the beginning of May, but also by the knowledge that the clock was ticking on the final months of Pérez de Cuéllar's term at the United Nations. While hands-on mediation had been the province of Alvaro de Soto, he was seen as de Cuéllar's protégé and a negotiated peace in El Salvador as a project that had flourished due in no small part to the secretary general's personal concern for the undertaking. No one knew who his successor might be, but another Latin American was out of the question. Then there were the rumors—fed by steady criticism "on background" that would continue to emanate from U.S. officials in Washington and San Salvador—that de Soto himself might not continue as mediator under a new regime in the United Nations.[8]

A measure of the change in the international climate was a letter, sent to the U.N. secretary-general in early August, jointly signed by the U.S. Secretary of State James Baker and the Soviet Foreign Minister Aleksandr Bessmertnykh. The letter came after Pérez de Cuéllar had given the governments of these two countries a list of ideas suggesting how they might help revitalize talks, the latest round of which stood postponed as the letter was dispatched. Bouncing the ball straight back to the United Nations, the letter both distanced the Cold War adversaries from past rivalries in Central America and provided the impetus for Pérez de Cuéllar to convene an extraordinary session of talks in New York on September 16 and 17, 1991. "Your own role in this process is critical," Baker and Bessmertnykh had written. "The sense of urgency and high priority which your personal and direct leadership of a new negotiating round will send are essential for its success."[9]

Pérez de Cuéllar invited President Cristiani to attend the make-or-break session in New York in person. Cristiani would later refer to "coming to New York" as the greatest of all the concessions he would make to the FMLN.[10] Besides what Pérez de Cuéllar called the "Gordian knot" of the negotiations—the future of the armed forces—the central question under discussion would be the FMLN's reintegration into the political life of the country.[11] Over the last few months the FMLN had repeated, with increasing insistency, that the two-stage Caracas agenda established the year before could no longer respond to the complexities of the situation. Their demands for the guarantee of conditions within which they could reincorporate into civilian society ruled out the concession of a cease-fire before all other elements of the settlement were in place. It was a position reinforced by common sense. Anything else, as de Soto would remark, was equivalent to asking the FMLN, "to dive into a swimming pool without water."[12]

Cristiani had told congressmen in Washington that he would be finished with the United Nations by the second day of the meeting; but it was only after two days had extended into ten that, on September 25, agreements were reached. While the government came under intense pressure from the United States, the FMLN was persuaded to withdraw its demand for fusion with the armed forces in exchange for participation in the new National Civilian Police (PNC). The two sides signed documents establishing a new National Commission for the Consolidation of Peace, COPAZ, providing for the subordination of the army to the constitutional authorities and addressing the underlying causes of the war in a series of preliminary resolutions on the fundamental issue of land.[13] Two documents accompanied and expanded upon the accords themselves. For the public record, there was a "compressed agenda" responding to the FMLN's demands for all substantive issues to be negotiated and agreed upon before a cease-fire. Of a supposedly confidential nature was a document of "understandings" that clarified the role to be played by COPAZ in the structuring of the PNC and that fleshed out skeletal agreements on the reform of the military academy and the "purging" of the armed forces by an Ad Hoc Commission. On Salvadoran television, the accords would be hailed by a government negotiator as a cause for "great jubilation by the Salvadoran people" and by a member of the FMLN delegation as "the beginning of the end of the war."[14]

The accords as a whole had an end more ambitious than a cessation of hostilities and the reduction and redefinition of the armed forces. In COPAZ and the promise of a Forum of economic and social consensus (*concertación*), the accords gave implicit acknowledgment to the social and political forces active in the country that had not been represented on either side of the negotiating table. As a mechanism of control and participation in the changes that would result from eventual peace accords, COPAZ would be composed of all political parties within the legislative assembly.[15] Opened still further to the inclusion of the much maligned "third forces" in the labor and business sectors, the Forum projected a climate of political pluralism that had been unimaginable up to that time. Not since the proclamation of the young officers behind the military coup of October 15, 1979, had a document held out so much hope to the people of El Salvador.

"THERE isn't a person in this room who wouldn't like to put me up there." Ambassador Walker was joking, but as he joined a diplomatic corps swelled by a high-level delegation from the Spanish parliament, observers, and human rights lawyers waiting for Judge Zamora to admit them to the trial, he sounded edgy. While the accords signed the night before generated a widespread sense of relief among those working closely with El Salvador, all eyes were now on this hastily modified Supreme

Court building. The atmosphere was one that shifted between cynicism and bemused expectation. Confusion colored the face of a tall monsignor, the Secretary of the Papal Nuncio, taken to one side by a youthful court secretary and asked to remove his clerical collar. "Please—no uniforms inside the court," she explained.[16]

The trial was being heard some months ahead of its natural timetable. This haste responded in no small measure to the political need to "clear" the army's name—ironically with a conviction—before judgment was meted out by a U.S. congressional vote on military aid. What would happen next was quite a different matter. The Jesuits' intention to press for further investigation of the intellectual authors still at large was well known, but it was going to be a lonely crusade. Although the public position was more carefully tempered, in August one U.S. official had admitted that the administration "wants this case over and done with. They want Benavides convicted as soon as possible and then that will be that and no one will have to mention the word Jesuit ever again."[17]

In this context, the existence and, above all, the persistence of Moakley was becoming awkward. His visit to El Salvador at the end of June had ended with a distinct cooling of relations with the U.S. embassy, and the presence of Moakley's aide Jim McGovern among the trial observers would only add to the prevailing mood of flustered self-defense. Put out by the fact that he had not been given an advance copy of Moakley's July 1 speech at the UCA—while the Jesuits had been given one for translation and for Jon Sobrino's preparation of a formal reply—Ambassador Walker had told Moakley afterward that he found the congressman's insistence that "General Ponce, you have an institutional problem," "unnecessarily sarcastic." Although Moakley, somewhat to the disappointment of his audience at the UCA, had been effusive in his praise of Walker and had scrupulously refused to offer anything remotely quotable at a breakfast with the international press the following morning, Walker had clearly been unsettled by the whole episode.[18]

In the days that followed Moakley's departure from the country Walker let his personal sensitivity to all things Jesuitical lead him, once again, by the nose. Less than diplomatic were the complaints the ambassador presented to both a prominent U.S. Jesuit and a Senate delegation that Moakley's nice remarks about himself had been "mistranslated" in the UCA. Walker also maintained that Moakley was deeply unhappy at having been "manipulated" by the Jesuits as Sobrino twisted his response into an unguarded attack on the United States.[19] These comments, not surprisingly, found their way back to Moakley within days;

as he had believed the event at the UCA to have gone excellently, he was not impressed. A public letter from Moakley thanking the Jesuits for their hospitality attempted to patch over the damage, but expectations of cooperation from the State Department were low.

One of the requests submitted to Judge Zamora in May by the private prosecution had been for the questioning of ten United States citizens under the Letters Rogatory process. With the exception of Eric Buckland's sister Carol, the others—including Buckland himself, Rick Chidester, and Colonel Milton Menjívar—all had been serving in El Salvador, in either a political or military capacity, at the time of the Jesuits' murders. That none of the ten, other than Buckland, had come forward before with information for the court was indicative of the nature of U.S. collaboration with Judge Zamora's efforts. Now they were to answer questions prepared for them by the private prosecution, but delivered by an official of the U.S. Justice Department whose lack of knowledge of the case made it likely that there would be no awkward follow-up questions. The Jesuits complained that the State Department was "seriously slowing down the investigation of the case" by preventing their representatives in the United States, the Lawyers Committee for Human Rights, from conducting the interrogations, but their protests went unheeded.[20] The ten individuals were to be questioned as cooperating witnesses; only a subpoena would have called them to face the grilling they could have expected to receive from Lawyers Committee counsel.

In the end, the testimonies given in the Justice Department and delivered to Judge Zamora in late August added little to the sum total of knowledge of the events surrounding the Jesuits' murder. This was hardly surprising. After nearly two years, it was not just a question of the memories fading. Any U.S. officials with substantive information who came forward *now* would hardly be serving their own best interests. Although others in the U.S. embassy and State Department would speculate on what the witnesses knew, no hint of that knowledge was likely to enter the public record. The responses of Political/Military Officer Janice Elmore were a case in point. A veteran of four years of service in San Salvador, she was considered by her colleagues to have unparalled access to a wide range of military officers. Members of the High Command were frequent visitors to her home on a social as well as formal basis. Describing "part of my job" being "to discuss these murders with any and all members of the Salvadoran military with whom I had contact," she had spoken to approximately 300 people over a period of time. "The officers with whom I talked assured me that the Salvadoran military would cooperate fully with the investigation," she remembered; "at no time was I given any direct answer as to who did the murders."[21] One former colleague remarked that "whatever she knows she is taking to the grave."[22]

Besides speculation about the verdict, the months leading up to the trial had been dominated by discussion of two issues upon which that verdict would obviously depend: the possibility of any defendants found guilty being granted an amnesty and the court's ability to seat and protect a jury. During his brief visit to San Salvador, Moakley had met twice with Cristiani. On both occasions he had brought up the subject of an amnesty and his concern at reports that the defendants had been promised that, even if convicted, they might either never reach a jail cell or receive an amnesty—so long as they kept to themselves any information implicating others in the crime. Cristiani had replied that any decision about amnesty fell under the province of the legislative, and not the executive branch of government. Given the particular importance of this case in the peace process, Moakley had insisted, might it not be possible for the president to say that he was personally against an amnesty? Not a chance. And in Argentina in early September, Cristiani was reported as stating that his government "was studying the possibility of granting an amnesty" to those accused of murdering the Jesuits.[23]

For the moment, however, Benavides and the others were to be tried in the midst of a war, and by a judicial system that had as its weakest link the five-person jury or "Tribune of Conscience." In El Salvador's civil law system, the jury becomes involved in a case only after its investigation has been completed. A list of twelve potential jurors is chosen by lot in the presence of both the defense and the prosecution. Although the names are theoretically kept secret from all but the judge and the court official responsible for their summons, in the past Salvadoran juries had repeatedly been subjected to threats and bribes. And this was always assuming they got as far as the trial itself. Jury lists were drawn up from records that were way behind the mobility and displacement of the population. Fines for those whom the court official *had* been able to find, but who preferred, for whatever reason, not to present themselves to the court on the appointed day, were staggered between the equivalent of $12.50 and $62.50. Many would contend that as a way out of handing down a verdict on Colonel Benavides, three lieutenants, and five members of the Atlacatl, it was cheap at the price.[24]

Behind the scenes, at least one leading political figure had suggested to both President Cristiani and General Ponce that they should make public statements guaranteeing the jury's safety and encouraging those who might be summoned to come forward. Yet none had been forthcoming. Instead, the personal involvement of the Supreme Court president, Dr. Mauricio Gutiérrez Castro, became increasingly evident. He gave a public endorsement of the Jesuits' right to demand indemnification from the state and made careful preparations for the jury's concealment and sequestering during the trial. Visited some weeks before the jury's installation by a respected Salvadoran businessman, Gutiérrez Castro had asked him what he thought would be the outcome of the Jesuit trial. "If everything is the same as normal," had been the businessman's answer, "everyone will get off and it will be a disaster. There'll be a great international outcry, they'll cut off the aid, and everyone will blame the judicial system." "You're right," Gutiérrez Castro had replied in an admission not only of the state of the courts over which he presided but also of the kind of "justice" being sought of this trial; "for my part I am going to do everything possible to guarantee the security of the jury—and if that jury acquits Benavides, I'll resign as president of the Supreme Court."[25]

Only later would a small detail emerge that questioned quite how far the political urgency of the moment had led Gutiérrez Castro to go in "doing everything" to guarantee the operation of Salvadoran justice: one of the five members of the jury was an employee of the Supreme Court. Confirmed by sources within the Salvadoran judicial system (one of whom would respond by saying, "but she was only a secretary—it's quite legal"[26]), the occupation of this juror was never placed on the public record for fear of undoing all that the trial, whatever its imperfections, had achieved.

READING of the *minuta*—the summary of the court record prepared by the judge for the jury's benefit—had just begun when the international observers emerged from the elevator to receive their first view of the courtroom. Presiding over the scene was Judge Zamora, flanked by his secretary and assistants. Beside him, and to the other side of an ineffectual electric fan, were the lawyers of the Salvadoran attorney general's office. They would be splitting the prosecution with the two private prosecutors. The team of lawyers for the defense, led by General Ponce's *compadre* Carlos Méndez Flores, were seated behind tables lining the right-hand side of the room. The observers filed quickly into the middle of the three public sections facing Zamora and sat down.

To their right were the families of the accused, with Colonel León

Linares, commanding officer of the Atlacatl Battalion at the time of the
Jesuits' murder, buried among them by the public dress code that had so
startled the Nuncio's Secretary. The families of the enlisted men were
campesinos in the main. Seven of the eight defendants in court were
evangelical Christians and, as the trial wore on, the parents of Espinoza
(long since disillusioned with the shift in the Catholic Church they had
perceived through the education of their sons at the *Externado San José*)
led the others in prayer. Beside the sleek, confident foreigners, the poverty
of some of the families, the fear in their eyes, bespoke a war that had for
years changed boys like their sons into hardened men. Over to the left of
the observers, and beside the ceiling-high partition obscuring the jury
from view, sat the Jesuits and their supporters. At the front left was
Tojeira, with Paco Estrada at his side and María Julia Hernández beyond
him at front right. Behind them were relatives of Elba and Celina Ramos
and Joaquín López y López, members of the Lawyers Committee, staff of
the UCA, and a delegation of Jesuits from the United States: the president
of Boston College, a representative of the Association of Jesuit Colleges
and Universities, and Father Vincent O'Keefe, for many years assistant to
the general of the Society.

Yet all these people, listening to the monotonous drone of the
documents being read by Zamora's assistants, faded into insignificance
beside the courtroom's dominating feature: the eight members of El
Salvador's army ranged across the public areas on the far side of a flimsy
formica partition. Staring out at the bank of cameras and lights glaring
down upon them, they presented an image that none would forget. A
capitulation to political necessity it may have been, but a colonel and his
officers and men were standing trial. And not just this courtroom, but all
of El Salvador could see this.

It would take until lunchtime the following day to complete the
minuta. Its 200 pages had been selected from the 5,600 pages in the full
court record to establish that the crimes with which the defendants were
charged had taken place, and then to present the evidence of the
defendants' participation. Painfully repetitious and indigestible in its bulk,
in the heat of the courtroom the *minuta* was something of an ordeal even
for those observers fully versed in the details of the case. A difficult and
incomprehensible introduction for the jury, the *minuta* illustrated, more
graphically than any of the warnings that had gone before, how little hope
there was that any legal process whose phase of judicial investigation had
been so deficient could result in anything other than a flawed trial and
highly questionable justice. After nearly two years the evidence against the

defendants was minimal, with the notable exception of the confessions provided in January 1990 to the SIU under circumstances never fully explained. Their pivotal nature to the prosecution's case was emphasized as, over a five-hour period, the court and jury were read each extrajudicial confession and then the near verbatim ratifications signed by the requisite SIU witnesses.

The observers scoured the faces exhibited before them. All men were charged with murder of the eight victims and with terrorism.[27] If found guilty, they could expect sentences of thirty years. On the far left, Tomás Zarpate Castillo, "Samson," sat with his head tilted back and his eyelids heavy over half-closed eyes; in his confession he had admitted killing the two women. At his side was Angel Pérez Vásquez, responsible for "finishing off" López y López, an elderly man who had reached out and clutched his foot as he walked down the corridor of the Jesuit residence. Like Ramiro Avalos Vargas, he was a veteran of a 1987 Small Unit Training Management Course in the United States; like Avalos Vargas, his face remained unmoved, his eyes locked still as if he were in another place altogether.[28] Yusshy Mendoza, his lieutenant's stripes on his shirt collar, came next. Unflinching, he listened to his own confession. Neither his name nor that of his commanding officer Benavides had appeared in the SIU's record of its own investigation. No one had ever known who had provided the information that linked him to the crime.

Beside him, and exercising a mesmerizing hold on the attention of the courtroom, sat Amaya Grimaldi, or Pilijay—the "hangman" in the indigenous language Nahautl and the "key man" in the operation against the UCA, as he himself had affirmed. Handy with an AK47, he had confessed to the killing of Ellacuría, of Montes, and of Nacho Martín-Baró. Although he too sat hostage to the military discipline protecting all eight defendants from the indignity of their ordeal, there was something deeply wrong with the emotions playing across his face. When still, he had the wide-eyed face of a baby. With his mouth moving to the persistent rhythm of chewing-gum, a cold hint of menace spread into his eyes, and then, intermittently, as when he listened to the most graphic of his own words read back to him, his whole face lit up with a smile. This was the man who had helped himself to a beer when the night's job was done.

Espinoza's sublieutenant, Guevara Cerritos—"Lynx"—looked young and frightened. His eyes twitched in his small face perched on top of a long thin neck, in obvious contrast to the stolid gaze of Avalos Vargas (responsible for Amando López and Moreno) at his side. At the far end of the line, nearest their families and in front of their lawyers, were Colonel

Benavides and the Jesuit-educated Lieutenant José Ricardo Espinoza. A couple of times the colonel bent over to whisper in the ear of the younger man. Pale and bespectacled, he lacked the imposing presence of his heavy-jowled *tanda*-mates in the High Command. Shifting about in his chair, holding his chin in his hand, and shaking his head when his name was mentioned, Espinoza was the only one of the eight who looked visibly relaxed, even cocky. At a break in the first day of the trial he confidently predicted to a local television station that "Justice will prevail."[29] During the second day he made a beeline for Tojeira. The other two lieutenants clustered around as Espinoza explained: "Inside this uniform there's an innocent human being, believe me."[30]

It was a trial so weighted by its political context that seasoned observers were thrown into something of a quandary by worries about whether, as one U.S. lawyer put it, "these murderers are getting a fair trial." In part this was a reflection of the idiosyncrasies of a legal system that retains the investigating judge for the supervision of the trial and the imposition of the sentence. In this case, the jury had every reason to believe that the proof against these men was, in the eyes of the Salvadoran legal establishment, solid: Judge Zamora had considered it so in his original decision to order detention and press charges; those charges had withstood rulings by both the Appeals and Supreme Courts. Served up to the legal system by the Honor Commission and their own confessions, it was difficult to believe that the junior officers and material authors of the crime would not be found guilty. The question was whether the jury would reach up and extend that verdict to Benavides too.

In the rounds that followed the *minuta*, prosecution and defense presented their cases. Although Henry Campos, Sidney Blanco, and the lead public prosecutor, Eduardo Pineda Valenzuela, gave cogent enough arguments for the defendants' guilt, their speeches were not distinguished for the help they gave the jury in understanding the great mass of material they had just had read to them. From the defense came florid expositions that made much of exhortations to God the All Powerful, but contributed little to the assembling of a coherent case and not at all to the "national dignity" the lawyers were so anxious to uphold. The "law student" Eulogio Barahona had the bearing of a sleazy buffoon in a third-rate operetta. He argued for Benavides' innocence, for example, by describing the recovery of a sick and hospitalized son. Such a "miracle," ran his reasoning, could only befall an innocent man—"Blessed be the Lord!" Abuse was scattered liberally about the courtroom as personal insults were leveled at Tojeira, Estrada, María Julia Hernández, and even Obdulio

Ramos. More general references to U.S. intervention in the country and this case ("let them pay the *mariachi,* but we'll pick the tune" ran a Méndez Flores plea for independence) were supplemented, for the benefit of the Spanish parliamentarians, by a reminder of the need to free El Salvador, once again, from the "Spanish yoke."

The vision of the army that emerged from the three-day trial served as a rapid reminder of the urgency of the reforms so recently agreed upon in New York. Inside the courtroom, the defense never tried to argue that their clients did not commit the crimes with which they had been accused. "What a crime of yours," Eulogio Barahona remarked with a flourish, "Amaya Grimaldi, to have defended the glorious fatherland!" How could members of the armed forces be terrorists when the armed forces represent the legal, constitutional defense against terrorism? It was a line of argument that represented a defense of nothing so much as military impunity itself, a justification, as Campos pointed out, that "winds up concluding that as long as there is a war, the army has a license to kill." At one point, Méndez Flores went through a list of all those connected with the case who had since lost their lives, in combat or elsewhere. "This is a country where people die all the time," he told the jury. "Who knows what will happen when you leave this courtroom and go out into the street. Let's hope you all reach home safely." The sharp intake of breath from the entire courtroom made it quite clear that his point was taken.

From outside the court there was intimidation of another kind when, on the morning of September 28, 1991, the sound of the national anthem and military "taps" came blaring up from the Supreme Court parking lot, supplemented by the repeated noise of some kind of aircraft. Disturbing enough for observers concerned by what the jury must be thinking, those who left the court to go downstairs for a better look discovered that, as a C37 airplane buzzed around the building, a crowd of about 200 demonstrators, officially organized by officers' wives, but using loudspeakers on loan from the High Command and accompanied through the Supreme Court's security by hard-line Colonel René Majano, had gathered in the parking lot to demand "justice for all."[31] Interviewed by local journalists, the women explained that the Jesuits were killed "for many reasons." "There was a lot of talk of hatred and class struggle inside the UCA," said one, while another mentioned "terrorists with guns and terrorist ideologues."[32] Placards and banners read "The army will live as long as the republic lives" and—with scant appreciation of the irony— "We reject foreign intervention."

Although the U.S. embassy would play down the protest, when

Walker's deputy, Jeff Dietrich, put in a call to the *Estado Mayor* to find out what on earth was going on and why, he did not find Chief of Staff Colonel Rubio all that responsive. "And the plane?" he had asked, "What about the plane?" "Don't worry," had come the answer. "It isn't armed."[33]

JUDGE Zamora had already begun reading out the jury's verdict when the public, press, and observers returned to the courtroom late in the evening of Saturday September 28, 1991. The jury had been out for five and a half hours considering their responses, yes or no, to a list of eighty questions. The questions listed each of the charges—for the murder of the eight individuals, as well as for acts of terrorism and acts preparatory to terrorism—for each of the defendants. Within the jury a simple majority, three against two, would be enough for a conviction. Tense and crowded on the stairs, the observers heard the steady voice of Judge Zamora. "With respect to the accused Guillermo Alfredo Benavides Moreno and the crime of murder of the Jesuit priest Ignacio Ellacuría Beascoechea: is the jury personally convinced that the accused Guillermo Alfredo Benavides Moreno is guilty?" "Yes." For the first time in the history of El Salvador a ranking military officer had been found guilty of murder. "With respect to the accused Guillermo Alfredo Benavides Moreno and the crime of murder of the Jesuit priest Ignacio Martín-Baró?" "Yes." "Segundo Montes Mozo?" "Yes." "Juan Ramón Moreno Pardo?" "Yes." "José Joaquín López y López?" "Yes." "Amando López Quintana?" "Yes." "The woman Julia Elba Ramos?" "Yes." "The minor Celina Mariceth Ramos?" "Yes."[34]

But that was almost it. With the sole and, it appeared, inexplicable exception of Lieutenant Yusshy Mendoza, who was found guilty of the murder of Celina Ramos, all the other answers had been "No." No to the terrorism across the board. No to the lieutenants for the operation they had led. No to the self-confessed killers of priests. No to each and every member of the Atlacatl Battalion. Shock, disbelief, confusion, and anger vied with one another in the reactions of the observers as they left the court. Behind them, the defendants' families gathered around the families of Benavides and Mendoza with comfort, tears, and prayer ("This is my God," the mother of Espinoza would say as she brandished her bible in vindication of her son's acquittal). The final image of this strange courtroom, source of a stranger justice, was almost the same as the first. The eight men sat in silence. Only their hands, now clasped tightly with those who sat at either side, had moved.

Downstairs Chema Tojeira responded calmly to a hail of questions. As observers from the Spanish delegation, visibly shaken, muttered comments about "Macondo," "a farce," and "banana republic," Tojeira admitted that what had just happened was "a little surprising." Salvadoran law does not ask the jurors how they arrive at a decision. Article 363 of the Criminal Procedure Code stipulates that each juror must consider whether, after hearing the evidence, he or she has *una íntima convicción*—are they personally, internally convinced of the guilt or innocence of the defendant? To convict Benavides, the only defendant not thought to have been present at the scene of the crime, they must have believed the confessions of the others. Yet with one exception, they had found them not guilty. While it could be presumed that the jurors had brought some kind of "due obedience" criterion into play, this could not explain the single guilty verdict for Yusshy Mendoza. Not only was a direct connection between Yusshy Mendoza and Celina Ramos impossible to extract from the evidence, but anyone who had seen even a photograph of the two women's bodies, entwined together as mother embraced daughter in a final act of protection, would know that their murders were the result of a single act.

"It is difficult to think that one person could be responsible for these murders," Tojeira had continued, "and if the jury has decided that those below Benavides are innocent then it is those above him that should continue to be investigated."[35] The view was not one echoed by the U.S. State Department. Walker and his staff in San Salvador had been put on a tight rein when it came to immediate comment on the outcome of the trial, with all questions from journalists being referred to Washington. From there came the lauding of the conviction of Benavides as "an historic achievement" and an attempt to counteract the opinions of Moakley and McGovern flooding the U.S. press. In a *Washington Post* piece that had cited McGovern denouncing the army demonstration outside the court as "a blatant attempt at intimidation" and included a remark from an openly combative Moakley—"Some people may be stroked by the conviction of a colonel. But if they're talking about the intellectual authors, let's go for the real ones higher up in the ranks"—the senior administration official sounded decidedly lame: "You can't keep moving the goalposts for El Salvador and trivialize what happened here. Benavides was the only colonel on trial. The fact that he was convicted is very significant."[36]

International observers would be accused by U.S. officials of "ethnocentricity" in their criticism of the Salvadoran justice system.[37] It was an argument much favored by Gutiérrez Castro. In an interview with the *Diario de Hoy* he described some of the observers as "petulant and ignorant," the makers of "light-weight" judgments born of an arrogance about the supposed superiority of their own justice systems to that of El Salvador.[38] On a separate occasion, the Supreme Court president insisted on the "salvadoraneity" of the verdict and explained the importance of understanding what it is to administer justice in the context of a war. Thus the jury had understood that within the armed forces a subordinate has, whatever the law might say, no other alternative than to obey an order. As a lieutenant from the military academy, he believed Yusshy Mendoza had been perceived as being Benavides's direct subordinate and thus somehow more responsible than Espinoza. Mendoza's conviction for the murder of Celina alone, within this same "wartime" mentality, responded to a desire to "give the Jesuits a message." Celina was somehow more "innocent" than the Jesuits, a true noncombatant in a war in which the Jesuits were popularly perceived to be combatants of a kind.[39]

With admirable presidential ambiguity, Cristiani took time out from ARENA's tenth National Congress to comment that the convictions of Benavides and Mendoza in the Jesuit trial provided "an example of what it is to administer justice" in El Salvador.[40]

MOAKLEY'S concern not to be "stroked" into submission was stimulated by a piece of information that had come his way just days before the trial began. A State Department cable, with a "show Moakley" addendum attached, told how a Salvadoran military officer had approached the U.S. MilGroup to say that Espinoza had sent a letter to a friend in the United States to be opened in the event of his conviction, and that this letter contained details about the ordering of the murder of Jesuits by officers senior to Benavides. It was no secret either to the Moakley task force or to the embassy staff most closely following the case that Espinoza had talked "all over the place" within the military and had threatened to talk publicly. News of a letter in the United States was entirely consistent with rumors percolating the army and its closest observers even before the Salvadoran officer approached the U.S. embassy.[41] Colonel Hamilton, the MilGroup commander to whom the Salvadoran officer had turned, assured him that there was nothing the embassy could do except let justice run its course. In a later discussion of the matter, Hamilton dismissed the information as just one among a myriad of unsubstantiated reports surrounding the Jesuit case ("my reaction was 'ho, hum,'" he remembered[42]). But Moakley believed that the fact that Espinoza had indeed been found not guilty added fuel to the rumors already—and inevitably—circulating San Salvador that the fix was in.

From the army there were mixed reactions. While there was partying in the Atlacatl Battalion to celebrate the acquittal of all their men, there could be no doubt that the verdict against Benavides and the public humiliation of the trial reinforced a sense of insecurity prevalent in the days following the New York accords. But although the outspoken Colonel Elena Fuentes would tell the press that he did not agree with the conviction of Benavides, his more pragmatic colleagues knew that, for them, the verdict had been a good one. "For us," one colonel would explain, the Jesuit trial had produced "the best result possible." Not only did the verdict, with its introduction of the idea of due obedience, respect the military hierarchy (and this when it was well known that the lieutenants had not wanted to obey the orders they received), but it also responded to both the external and internal needs of the army. Had it been the other way around—acquittal for Benavides and conviction for the junior officers and men—it would have been "disastrous." In addition to a loss of military aid, the army, this colonel believed, would have run into "serious problems" with lieutenants and captains outraged by the perceived sacrifice of the junior officers and, in the wake of the agreements signed in New York, increasingly worried about their own futures.[43]

"Where is the outrage?" Joe Moakley would ask in an article published in the *Washington Post* two weeks after the trial; "Where is the leadership?"[44] A vent for worries about the possibility of military intervention in the trial, his "grave disappointment" at its outcome, his "anger" at the attempt to intimidate the jury, and his criticism of the silence of both the State Department and President Cristiani in the face of the "terrible injustice" that had it that the murderers of the Jesuits should now walk free, Moakley asked that a number of concrete steps should be taken. Among them was a request, couched in vague terms, for a full investigation of the alleged Espinoza letter, the urging of Cristiani to dismiss all the defendants from the armed forces and of the State Department to make sure that none of them would ever be granted U.S. visas. Another individual—and this was the article's real surprise—that Moakley wanted to see denied entrance to the United States was retired General Juan Rafael Bustillo "until a full investigation has been conducted into his possible involvement in instigating the murders."[45]

Perceived in Washington as a "political cheap shot" or product of the "culture shock" induced in Jim McGovern by the trial, in El Salvador the *Washington Post* article received surprisingly little play. "The Jesuit case is all over as far as the embassy is concerned," one official would explain just a few days after the article's publication; "nobody is doing anything or wants to do anything." Publicly at least, the embassy, like the army, was home and dry. In private, the quiet voice of the official would add, "the trouble is that Moakley is right."[46]

"You do not use a word like 'instigating' unless you know," was the comment of one veteran Salvadoran political figure with close ties to the military, "and I think Moakley knows what happened."[47] Moakley and his task force had believed they knew "what happened" for over a year. They believed that the murder of the Jesuits had been decided on at a small meeting on Wednesday, November 15, 1989. Among those present, and the "instigator" of the crime, had been General Juan Rafael Bustillo. He had been strongly backed up by Colonel Orlando Zepeda. Chief of Staff Ponce had been present and had agreed to the decision. Benavides had initially expressed reluctance. Unlike Bustillo and Zepeda, Benavides had no history of far-right fanaticism, of covert operations and death squads run from under his command. But Bustillo and Zepeda had found support in Colonel Elena Fuentes, who had helped convince Benavides to take command of the action against the UCA.[48] Although speculation on the exact location and time of the meeting had continued within the task force, information they had obtained from one eyewitness and confirmation by another individual had them place the meeting within the military academy on the afternoon of November 15.[49]

From sources that Moakley would describe as "experienced, respected and serious," the task force had received information that they believed credible.[50] But it was not evidence, and it was information provided only on the basis of the very strictest confidentiality. From these sources, the task force had learned how Benavides had told officers gathered in the military academy on the night of November 15 that he had received "the green light" to act against the Jesuits. This had been understood to imply that the decision was not his alone. One of those present at this meeting had been the officer who, goaded by the High Command's letter of February 1991 to the justice minister, directly accused Ponce and the High Command of being responsible for the ordering of the murders.[51] From the air force came a report that Bustillo had told senior officers, also on the night of November 15, 1989, that a decision had been made to kill the Jesuits (Elena Fuentes had told a similar gathering in the First Brigade that "Ellacuría will not see the light of day"[52]).

Although Moakley had consistently encouraged these sources and others with details of the coverup to come forward and present their testimony to the judge, they had refused to do so, giving reasons no visiting congressman could lightly brush aside: "All cited the risk of retribution against themselves or their families by extreme right wing elements of the armed forces," ran the litany. "Some said they had already been warned not to talk. Some said they would violate the confidence of others if they were to speak openly. None expressed faith in the protective capabilities of the United States. None wanted to leave El Salvador. And none expressed faith in the ability of the judicial system to convict high-ranking officers even with the evidence they could provide."[53] Contributing to this reticence was the belief widely held among mid- and lower-level officers that too much knowledge of the Jesuit case had cost the lives of at least two of their number.[54] "No one wanted to come forward," Moakley explained in an interview, "because they were afraid they would be on somebody's menu the next day."[55]

Over the months since the breakthrough meeting on August 11, 1990, Moakley had built on what he already knew with information gleaned from other sources. Although what he had would not stand up in court, he was determined not to let it lie dormant, out of the public domain. Back in August 1990, it had been this concern that had led his aides to relay their belief of High Command responsibility for the Jesuit murders to Ambassador Walker. They had found him, as one of them put it, somewhat "cranky," and critical of their lack of hard proof. Yet what they told him can have come as no surprise. The embassy had first heard of Bustillo's possible involvement in the crime in December 1989.[56] Moreover, the eyewitness with whom part of the information had originated was a source officials shared with the task force. He had spoken to someone on the CIA payroll and the agency had reported to the embassy.[57] In July 1990 the embassy, in the person of Deputy Chief of Mission Jeff Dietrich, had cited information gathered from "various sources" to present the High Command with a "non-paper" describing a meeting within the military academy at 2:00 P.M. on November 15, 1989.[58]

Task force and embassy alike had heard more than enough of Espinoza. Both knew that he first confessed his involvement in the murders in December 1989, as the SIU were just beginning their investigation of the Atlacatl. The information had been relayed to Espinoza's commanding officer, Colonel León Linares, and then to Colonel Ponce, but nothing had been done. Since then, as Chidester would remember, "Espinoza had every opportunity in the world to talk. People were ready for him. We were going through sources who were talking to him. Some of them got messed up by us. We offered him everything."[59] One such attempt, and perhaps the high-water mark of the embassy's efforts to get to the bottom of the Jesuit murders, involved not only Walker himself, but also President Cristiani and a senior, although not *tandona,* officer, Colonel Roberto Pineda Guerra, at the time in command of the Treasury Police. The episode was one that revealed much about the balance of power between the U.S. embassy, the civilian authorities, and the Salvadoran army High Command. Not for nothing would Walker describe it as "very disappointing."[60]

Walker had met Pineda Guerra on several occasions before the colonel told him, in April 1991, that he believed that the lieutenants, who were at the time being held under his authority within the Treasury Police barracks, would be willing to talk if approached in the right way. He suggested that Walker should go back to the embassy and think about it. After dismissing a series of ideas that included trying to work through their families, it was decided that an attempt should be made to get Pineda Guerra authorized by Cristiani "to examine the lieutenants and get the truth out," as Walker put it. Before going back to Pineda Guerra, however, Walker proposed to President Cristiani that a three-person civilian-military commission should be appointed under his auspices. Cristiani wanted no part in it, but suggested that if the embassy could pull it off without a presidential endorsement, then he would have no objection.[61]

Over a long three hours in Pineda Guerra's home, Walker tried every form of persuasion. He argued that this was Pineda Guerra's chance to get a factual basis to what he had been telling him. He reminded him that as a known critic of the *tandona,* he would gain credibility for breaking the Jesuit case. Appealing to his ambition, Walker suggested that "you don't want to lead an army still under the shadow of the Jesuit case and the *tandona*" and even that "President Cristiani would be grateful to have it taken off his plate." Pineda Guerra insisted that he could only collaborate if he had the president on his side, and asked that he have a few days to think about it. Three or four days later, there was still no news from him when Walker met Cristiani at a reception. The president pulled the ambassador to one side and got straight to the point, "I understand you've talked to the colonel." "He told me he'd think about it," came the answer. "The very next day the army High Command came to me and told me that the U.S. ambassador and the embassy had come up with this crazy idea." Pineda Guerra had gone directly from his meeting with Walker to Ponce, leaving Walker high and dry. A disillusioned ambassador would complain that the colonel's "institutional loyalty weighed against any desire to work with me or the embassy in getting the truth out." But from the army, as one Salvadoran officer put it, "it just looked like the embassy was meddling again."[62]

Cristiani had quite obviously not done all that he could on the Jesuit case. The negotiations had put his government under enormous pressure even without this case complicating an already complicated relationship with the armed forces. While all who dealt with the army during the negotiations would agree that they had been "softened" at the table by the Jesuit case and its consequences for military aid, that "softening" had clearly defined limits. Moakley had information from "a reliable Salvadoran source" that Cristiani had been among those to receive threats against speaking out on the Jesuit case.[63] As president, he had no more desire or self-interest in siding with the U.S. embassy in an attempt to penetrate the silence of the High Command than had Colonel Pineda Guerra. Although Walker fully believed that Pineda Guerra would have cooperated if he had Cristiani's backing, on another occasion he would admit that, "It is easy for me as the U.S. ambassador to say what Cristiani should have done. It is his country and he has got to live in it."[64] After this rather chastening experience the embassy's attempts at extracting the truth subsided. There was a bitter note in Walker's voice as he remarked of Pineda Guerra, "if he was so unwilling to put his money where his mouth was, what credence can you give to what he was telling Moakley?"

Long held back by a reluctance to disrupt the peace process that had been encouraged by the dire predictions of the State Department, Moakley's last hope had been that the pressure of the forthcoming trial in the fall of 1991, combined with the persistence with which the United States opposed talk of an amnesty, might, finally, have persuaded Espinoza to come forward. But with the trial over and the administration ready to lay the Jesuit case to rest, Moakley was left believing not only that he knew what happened, but that the various agencies of the U.S. government had a pretty good idea themselves. That knowledge may have come from confidential sources, and individually the scraps of information those sources had produced could not stand up, but there were seven or eight sources leading in one direction, and it was not within the mandate or character of the task force's work to file and forget them as unsubstantiated rumor. Rather, Moakley would remember that Speaker Foley had charged the task force "with sharing what we learned with the Members of the House and the American people."[65] The weekend of November 16, 1991 seemed a good time to do so.

"IF we look back on these last two years," Tojeira remarked in a conference given at the UCA during the commemoration of the second anniversary of the murders, "we must be profoundly pleased." Right at the beginning, Tojeira reminded his audience, there had been a desire to "bury" the dead of the UCA among the 75,000 dead of El Salvador. However, the continued sense of outrage at the murder itself and then the military's handling of all that had followed had made this impossible. "They said: 'all this fuss for eight people when 75,000 have died. Why such uproar for them when no one says anything about the others?' And what did they achieve by this? They breathed new life into the 75,000."[66]

No small part of the satisfaction with the last two years came from the most recent developments in the negotiations. After ten years it really did appear that, as the UCA would say in its second anniversary communiqué, "reality has come to confirm the prophetic vision of Ignacio Ellacuría."[67] Back in 1981, Ellacuría had surveyed a war only two months old. "History is irreversible," he had written. "The war that yesterday seemed sadly inevitable is today part of the problem to be solved." Difficult and distant had seemed a solution at the time; more difficult and more distant and infinitely more costly than could be imagined in the early months of 1981 it had proved. "Mediated negotiation," Ellacuría had written then, "is a historical necessity and an ethical demand."[68] As impossible to short-cut as it is to reverse, the history of the intervening decade had been one in which substantial changes—institutional, political, economic, and social—had been required, within El Salvador and outside it, before that "mediated negotiation" could at last succeed.

After New York, the peace process entered into a phase of feverish activity. A new round of negotiations opened in Mexico on October 12, 1991, just two days after the initiation of COPAZ. Work began on the "compressed agenda" with attention, once again, focused on reform of the armed forces. Although the talks soon ran into trouble over the details determining how the Ad Hoc Commission would go about its business of clearing out the army's officer corps, the agenda's division into well-defined areas for discussion allowed the negotiations to move on to other issues while leaving the most intransigent points for later. By October 22, agreements had been reached in seven out of fourteen areas. Progress had been made in four more, allowing for partial agreements on eleven to be placed "in the freezer" to be added to future accords. Still pending were the not inconsiderable obstacles of the new police force, the reduction of the army and its subordination to civilian authority. When Alvaro de Soto spoke to the press near the end of the meeting, however, he was decidedly optimistic: "we have never before advanced as rapidly, but the rule is nothing is agreed until all is agreed."[69]

After a brief recess, the negotiations resumed at the beginning of

November. Speculation was mounting that a cease-fire might be possible before Christmas; this session of talks was unrestricted and could be moved to New York at any time. But it was a supremely delicate moment and de Soto urged restraint from both sides in their dealings with the press. Events in Washington reflected a similar caution. Action on the Foreign Aid Bill for 1992 had been deferred as part of an agreement made by Congress with the White House to hold back consideration of Israel's request for $10 billion in loan guarantees. Instead of the long-threatened House debate on Salvadoran military aid, on October 24 Congress passed, as a stopgap measure, a Continuing Resolution that would extend for a further six months the restrictions established in the legislation of the previous year. Congressional leaders, including Senator Dodd and Congressman Moakley, were both unwilling to jeopardize the peace talks with further cuts in military aid and were hopeful that when they addressed the issue again the following March, it would be possible to discuss sending U.S. dollars for the funding of reconstruction and not war.[70]

Adding to the difficulties inherent in what still remained to be negotiated was a sudden upsurge in the military activity of the FMLN and, in particular, an increase in their sabotage of the electrical system. While the government lashed out at ONUSAL—ARENA president Calderón Sol accused the U.N. mission of being "ineffective" and of "intervening in internal politics" while its members disported themselves on the country's many beaches[71]—ARENA itself came under attack from organizations of the far right, which accused the country's leaders of being "traitors" who had "conceded everything" to the FMLN.[72] Although the extremists appeared increasingly isolated, government difficulty with the negotiations was real. On the morning of November 11, 1991, the second anniversary of the FMLN's 1989 offensive, Cristiani took to the television to announce that the FMLN's heightened military actions were really a "third offensive, launched by the FMLN on November 8." In response, he revealed at a press conference afterward, the government was considering retiring from the current round of talks.[73]

How far the FMLN's actions were from a full-scale offensive was shown a few days later as the FMLN declared a unilateral truce until a final cease-fire agreement could be reached. In a mark of respect to the murdered Jesuits, as well as astute recognition of the political worth of the anniversary, the truce was to begin at midnight on November 16. Responding to a desire expressed by the FMLN's *Radio Venceremos* that "not one more Salvadoran should die in this war,"[74] the truce was clearly designed to isolate the extremist sectors opposed to negotiations and to pressure the military to concede on the remaining issues. Although its announcement left the government off-balance, Cristiani was prompt to recognize it as a "signal of goodwill" and one that would speed the end of the war. In El Salvador, where a poll conducted by the UCA's IUDOP had revealed that only 32 percent of Salvadorans had believed that "peace was really close" after the New York accords, the mood was of somewhat incredulous amazement.[75]

Hundreds gathered in the grounds of the UCA, as they had the year before, for an anniversary mass held beneath the shade of the campus trees. Less solemn than the first ceremony, less overrun by visitors from outside, the mass was centered around the ordination of two young Jesuits. As they lay face down on the altar before Archbishop Rivera, their bodies were for many a visual reminder of the bodies of those other Jesuits, forced to lie face down in the grass just a few hundred meters away, but in circumstances so different, exactly two years ago. "Make me an instrument of your peace," sang the choir as the ordination was completed, using words that had taken new life in El Salvador.

THE army was still disconcerted by the news of the FMLN's truce when it was hit by a bombshell contained in a November 17 article in the *New York Times*.[76] Moakley had gone public and had named generals Bustillo, Ponce, and Zepeda and Colonel Elena Fuentes as those he believed responsible for ordering the Jesuits' murder. His statement played a typically politic hand. Suspecting the uproar that he would cause with his detailing of the "direct and circumstantial evidence" provided by the unnamed sources, Moakley went out of his way to praise the U.S. embassy, the limited progress in the judicial system that had succeeded in convicting Benavides, and the work of Judge Zamora, Gutiérrez Castro, and even President Cristiani. But the congressman was blunt in his assessment of the possibilities offered by further recourse to the Salvadoran authorities: "I am under no illusion that the Government of El Salvador is likely to take further steps to investigate the case or to examine seriously the possibility that top military officers ordered the crimes." The statement contained information he believed to be true, and that truth had a certain point. "I do recommend very strongly," he concluded, "that Congress and the administration bear this information in mind when making further decisions with respect to U.S. policy in El Salvador."[77]

General Ponce was "absolutely furious," according to MilGroup commander Colonel Hamilton, who saw him within hours of his telephone call from the *New York Times*.[78] Ponce, Cristiani, and "many,

many others" had been informed of what Moakley believed "had happened" soon after the task force aides told the embassy. They had said that no such meeting took place.[79] In the days following the release of the statement, those directly implicated by Moakley's charges vied with each other in their protestations of innocence and denunciations of Moakley like so many angry hornets reacting to the lobbing of a brick into their carefully guarded nest. The government statement was the first to come out and was relatively restrained in its reference to "political manipulation and attacks on individual members of the armed forces" as it reiterated that "the Salvadoran courts are open to those who have evidence in this case."[80] There followed something of a free-for-all as Bustillo called Moakley "a liar . . . a politician without scruples or professional ethics," and Elena Fuentes remarked that "there are obvious coincidences between the statements of the terrorist leader Joaquín Villalobos and Moakley."[81]

At a press conference given with Zepeda on November 19, Ponce was sweating profusely. Rejecting "emphatically" Moakley's "irresponsible accusations" made without any concern for the "moral and professional damage" the congressman might have caused to themselves as individuals and to the institution to which they so proudly belonged, the two generals released a communiqué that denied everything.[82] The suspicions of those who still tended toward the belief that a meeting of such senior officers must have taken place within the *estado mayor* were raised by the reply given a journalist who asked if Ponce denied that it took place in the military academy. "I deny it categorically," had been his answer, "because I was not at the military academy. I was here at my command post in the *estado mayor*."[83]

"The congressman's report contains charges but no direct evidence." The State Department's official reaction sounded remarkably like that of the Salvadoran government: "We urge him or anyone else who may have evidence related to this crime to present it to the Salvadoran authorities."[84] In the days following the release of Moakley's statement, a silence fell on Washington. There were no official rebuttals, no sign of Republican congressmen or senators crowding Congress to attack Moakley, no reaction at all. There were cries of "terrible timing" that raised specters of one man sabotaging the entire negotiation process, and the inevitable accusations that Moakley's need to go public responded to domestic political interests, but there was no one who would say he was wrong. Within the inside channels of Congress, word soon spread that in private officials of both State and Defense departments "had no problem" with the general outline of what had been said, although could not corroborate all the details. Even the CIA sent its people to pay a quick visit to the Intelligence Committees to caution representatives and senators that they might be best advised to let this one go.[85]

Within the U.S. embassy in San Salvador, officials got a little tangled in mutually exclusive arguments. One ran "we have all that stuff anyway . . . have had it for years" and "much of it we developed or helped Joe Moakley obtain"; and the other went "there is nothing there anyway." "We have tracked down literally dozens of rumors," said Ambassador Walker in an interview, "and they all evaporate. Every one of them. Every one of them has turned out to be a mirage out there."[86] Yet long gone were the days when an official could, with a straight face, suggest that Benavides might have ordered the murders on his own. Like others in the embassy, Walker was prepared to admit that "anyone who knows Bustillo can believe it of him" and did not appear too troubled by talk about Zepeda and Elena Fuentes.[87] Colonel Hamilton was a little more specific in presenting a thesis by which Bustillo, who was seated beside Benavides during the large meeting in the *estado mayor* on the evening of November 15, 1989, had been provided with several hours and a golden opportunity to "whisper in the ear" of the weaker man.[88] Only Rick Chidester, out of the State Department at the time, but still smarting from the criticism heaped upon him for his role in the case, would say of Moakley's statement: "I don't disagree with anything in there. As far as I am concerned they are right on track."[89]

The sticking point, of course, was Ponce. Never more adamantly defended than in these final stages of the negotiations, he was portrayed as the mainstay and guarantor of the army's continuing presence at the table. Whether real or imaginary—and the political cohesion of an army without Ponce at its head could only be speculated upon—the dependence on Ponce rendered an admission that he could have agreed to the murder of the Jesuits and then strung them all along so effectively all this time more than most officials could stomach. Hamilton had taken up his post as MilGroup commander in September 1990 with no previous experience of El Salvador. He had found Ponce "a very progressive guy" and would defend him in the strongest possible terms: "I absolutely, absolutely do not believe that Ponce knew beforehand, I am convinced." "It's just hard for me to believe that Ponce could have believed that it would be beneficial," explained another official. Even Chidester would join in the chorus: "I want not to believe that Ponce was involved in the decision to kill the Jesuits."[90] Tired by two years of work alongside officials whose relationship with the High Command he would describe as being "like enablers for alcoholics," Jim McGovern had a rather bleaker assessment: "I wouldn't trust Ponce to tell me the time of day."[91]

And then there was the Salvadoran through whom Ponce had good reason to believe that information would filter back to Washington. He would remember a short meeting with the general weeks after Moakley's statement came out. "I want you to know," Ponce had said, "I didn't want it."[92]

CROWDS had been gathering in San Salvador since first light on the morning of January 16, 1992. Expectation crackled in the air. Faces were split wide by smiles as buses, trucks, and pickups brought *campesinos* from all parts of the country to join in the celebration to be held in the Plaza Cívica. Today, in the Castle of Chapultepec in Mexico City and in the presence of the new secretary general of the United Nations, Boutros Boutros-Ghali, of the heads of state of Colombia, Mexico, Spain, and Venezuela, of Costa Rica, Guatemala, Honduras, Panama, and Nicaragua and U.S. Secretary of State James Baker and other dignitaries, the government of El Salvador and the FMLN were signing definitive agreements that both marked the end of the war and laid the foundations for the evolution of a new society. While no piece of paper could guarantee the transformation of the social and economic conditions under which Salvadorans would live, the parameters for future political action were clear. Besides the subordination of military power, the two sides had reached agreements on the reform, strengthening, and separation from political interests of both the judicial and the electoral systems and on the principles along which economic and social problems, including the redistribution of land, should be settled. These were agreements that reflected, in the words of Alvaro de Soto, no less than a "negotiated revolution."[93]

It had been close, but in the end the impending departure of Pérez de Cuéllar had proven providential. Throughout December, and despite a final spasm of protest by the Salvadoran right, with death threats sent to journalists and ONUSAL observers and a massive demonstration organized nominally "for Peace and Unity," but actually in order to express support for the military, pressure on the negotiations had mounted. The United States and former Soviet Union issued a joint statement calling for a cease-fire by the end of the year and on December 6, after meeting with the ambassadors of the four friendly countries, Pérez de Cuéllar suggested that the talks that had bogged down in Mexico should be moved to New York, where they resumed on December 16, 1991.

With the clock ticking ever louder in the background, the U.N. secretary-general telephoned Cristiani on December 26 to invite him to make, in political terms, the very long trip north. Amid protests from some in his party, he arrived in New York two days later with both Calderón Sol and General Ponce in tow. Even then, it had taken the hand-holding, cajoling, and persuasion of the government by a high-level contingent from the United States (Assistant Secretary Aronson, Ambassadors Pickering and Walker, and Colonel Hamilton among them) and all the skill of the U.N. officials and the "Friends" to bring the two sides to sign the hurriedly written New York Act in the last few minutes of Pérez de Cuéllar's term of office. Remaining issues, including a calendar for the agreements' implementation, were to be negotiated from January 5, with the signing of final agreements set for January 16, 1992. A nine-month cease-fire would begin on February 1, 1992. Twenty months after the signing of the Geneva Accord, negotiations mediated by the United Nations had brought an end to one of the hemisphere's bitterest conflicts.

By noon the Plaza was packed. Only a few blocks away, the Plaza Libertad too was swarming with activity as loyal *areneros* prepared to greet their president on his return from Mexico that night. The center of the city was jammed solid with traffic, the pavements overflowing with people crowding into the two plazas and vendors of food, soft drinks, ice-cream, and a form of merchandise new to the streets of San Salvador: FMLN souvenirs. As the revolutionary songs rose up into the burning blue skies, an enormous portrait of Farabundo Martí himself looked down on it all from the cathedral's facade. With the terrible polarization of the past obscured for a day as the curious passed between the rival *fiestas*, Martí hung amid a sea of banners in the red and black of a revolution triumphant in this negotiated settlement: "We Won the Peace!" "New York Agreements: Popular Triumph!" "Peace Accords: Victory of the Salvadoran People!"[94]

Throughout El Salvador radios and televisions were tuned to the ceremony in Mexico. Formal as it was, in the presence of so many presidents and grey-suited politicians, the gravity of the commitments and compromises agreed to by both sides, and its transcendent importance for the history of El Salvador, the ceremony was charged with emotion. During the beginning of January, debate had raged within the government and among sectors of the right as to whether Cristiani should sign the peace agreement himself or, in strict obedience to the protocol of negotiations (and the wishes of the hard-liners of his party), leave that formality to his negotiators. Cristiani not only signed, but then, in breach of all that had been planned or foreseen, followed his own speech by crossing over to the FMLN delegation and greeting each member warmly. His gesture prompted a standing ovation. On the streets of San Salvador, with tears flowing freely in recognition of the end of the war, the crowds in the two Plazas settled in to celebrations that would last until dawn.

"The long night of El Salvador is coming to its end," proclaimed Secretary-General Boutros-Ghali. Taken in conjunction with the agreements of San José, Mexico, and New York, the documents signed in Mexico prepared for "a new and much better El Salvador," an El Salvador that had to overcome not just the war, but the flagrant injustices that lay behind it. Speaking as the FMLN's elder statesman, Schafik Handal singled out "the principal achievement" of the agreements as being: "the end of military hegemony over the civilian nation, the end of a long, long period in which the liberal ideals of the fathers of our independence were suffocated for the benefit of an opulent minority." In a speech of moderation and measured responsibility, Cristiani too told his people that their war had "profound social, political, economic, and cultural roots . . . in synthesis, the absence of a truly democratic form of life." It was to this "truly democratic form of life" that the accords now paved what all who had signed them knew must be a very difficult way.[95]

THERE could be no doubt but that Ellacuría would have been pleased by the peace agreement signed in Chapultepec. During his life he had been a champion of negotiations even in their darkest hour. His death and the deaths of his brother Jesuits and the two women had catalyzed the reinitiation of negotiations, and in the following two years the progress of the Jesuit case, as Alvaro de Soto remembered, had been "a determining factor" in their successful outcome.[96] The case had kept the army on the defensive and had consistently contributed to the change in U.S. policy that allowed negotiations to prosper. In a climate of full endorsement of the settlement, most dramatically expressed by a lightning visit paid to El Salvador by Secretary of State James Baker, few U.S. officials like to remember how faint had been U.S. support for negotiations until the offensive of 1989. Only then, with military stalemate compounded by revulsion at the killing of the Jesuits, had a change been triggered.

Yet just as the progress of the Jesuit case had illuminated the institutional problems of the army and the weaknesses of the justice system, so the questions still remaining presented a vital test of how the people of El Salvador, collectively, moved forward from the past. Behind the fine speeches of either side lay not just followers and subordinates brought along this far, in some cases, only by a combination of silk-thread guidance and capitulation to the ultimate inevitability of the process, but men and women who had suffered real and terrible losses in the last fifteen years of their lives. Reconciliation of some kind had to be fundamental to the advance of the agreements outlined in the documents of Chapultepec.

Since before the trial, Tojeira had stressed the need to temper justice with mercy. But rather than a blanket amnesty, the Jesuits favored—in their own case as in others—a pardon based on knowledge of the truth of who was to be pardoned for what. In this the Jesuits were entirely consistent with what had been established within the April 1991 Mexico agreement as the purpose of the Truth Commission: the investigation of "grave incidents of violence which have occurred since 1980, which have left a mark on society that demands as a matter of the greatest urgency that the public should know the truth." The commission's recommendations were to foster "national reconciliation" as they helped prevent the repetition of the violence of the past.[97] The three commissioners had been named by the outgoing U.N. secretary-general in December 1991 as Belisario Betancur, former president of Colombia; Reinaldo Figueredo, former foreign minister of Venezuela and Thomas Buergenthal, former president of the OAS Inter-American Court for Human Rights. As 1992 began, the Jesuits, like others in El Salvador, anticipated the Truth Commission's installation later in the year, if with some trepidation as to how much of its mandate the commission would be able to fulfill.

Before then, however, as February 1 and the cease-fire to be supervised by up to 1,000 U.N. civilians, troops, and police advisers approached, an amnesty of some kind was needed with urgency. Without one, the leaders of the FMLN, eager to return to their country to begin their political lives, remained terrorists and outlaws in the eyes of the Salvadoran state. ARENA lost no time in calling for a sweeping general amnesty, but this was met with protest from broad sections of the political opposition, the FMLN, and from Washington. In the end the Law of National Reconciliation emerged from within COPAZ in time for its approval by the National Assembly on January 23 as a testament to a new style of consensus decision making. FMLN leaders would be allowed to return to El Salvador as the cease-fire began on February 1; combatants would be given amnesty as they disarmed in accordance with the cease-fire's calendar. The Law of National Reconciliation allowed the Truth Commission the authority accorded in the Mexico agreement and—in response to what was a desire for some, and a political need for others, to keep the officers convicted for the murder of the Jesuits behind bars—exempted from the amnesty anyone tried and convicted by a jury.[98]

"There will be no democratization without the democratization of the armed forces," Ellacuría had said on many occasions. As the army began its long, slow process of transformation, there were many who were incredulous that such a democratization could ever take place. With the final figure of the army's reduction fixed at a little over 50 percent, there was a concern that, thus reduced, the army would still be three times the size it was at the beginning of the war.[99] But with the dissolution of the hated security forces, the "purging" of army officers by the Ad Hoc Commission, and the dismantling of the Atlacatl and the other four Immediate Reaction Battalions still to come, external doubts were equaled by insecurity within. "It's difficult," one Salvadoran officer explained in February 1992. "Before we always believed we were right. We were told we were right and that we were fighting the enemy. And now it looks like we were the problem all along."[100]

AFTERWORD

APRIL 1994

Successive Salvadoran governments (the Junta, those of Magaña, Duarte, and Cristiani) and their ministers of defense (García, Vides Casanova, Larios, and Ponce), the presidents of the Supreme Court of Justice, and also the U.S. ambassadors (Hinton, Pickering, Corr, and Walker), their secretaries of state (Haig, Shultz, Baker), and their presidents (Reagan and Bush) knew all about what was happening. They tolerated it, they financed it, and they hid it. For the majority of them it was also legitimate. They took the name of "democracy" in vain in order to justify the physical elimination of their political enemies.[1]

ECA Editorial on the Report of the Truth Commission, April 1993

THE boom in El Salvador's construction industry was among the most visible of changes. In March 1994, days before Salvadorans voted for a new president, a new assembly, and new local authorities, much of San Salvador resembled a building site. Spanning the busy traffic circle where the Boulevard de los Héroes becomes the road leading out to the airport, the defiant arch of an overpass was a cause of admiration and apprehension alike. Built within six weeks upon pillars appropriated from the old guerrilla target of the Puente de Oro, the overpass brought immediate relief to an intersection made almost impassable by the enormous increase in traffic the capital had seen in the two years since the signing of the peace agreements. However, its opening had not been without speculation as to what might happen to those taxis, trucks, and overladen buses caught unawares by a sudden *temblor,* or earth tremor.

Other changes were mixed in with the vestiges of the past like the conduct and content of the election campaigns themselves. While the presidential frontrunner was ARENA's Armando Calderón Sol, whose campaign song still looked towards the day when El Salvador would "be the tomb where the reds are buried," his main rival, and candidate of an FMLN and Democratic Convergence coalition, was Rubén Zamora. As ARENA rallies across the country resounded to the cry; *¡Patria sí, communismo no!* ("Fatherland yes, communism no!"), in San Salvador the former communist Schafik Handal was running for mayor in the first elections of his life in which he had taken part.

The euphoria of the first few weeks of 1992 had long since been replaced by the difficulty of realizing the "negotiated revolution" they promised, but at no stage had fighting between the two sides looked likely to recur.[2] This in itself was an achievement that distinguished El Salvador from other countries struggling to emerge from conflicts of the past into the complicated waters of a post–Cold War world. Even so, transition had been anything but easy. The reappearance of death squad–type killings in the months before the elections was a chilling reminder that the country had yet to put behind it its terrible past.[3] Meanwhile the alarming escalation of common crime—which rose by 300 percent during a nine-month period in 1993[4]—indicated not just the inordinately high level of violence fostered by the militarization of the previous decade, but also the economic hardship that the majority of the population was experiencing during this most extraordinary period of their country's history.

Although the agreements signed at Chapultepec had included a calendar synchronizing completion of the various stages of reform and demobilization agreed to by the former civil war adversaries, it was held up by innumerable delays. Public criticism of the sloth, incompetence, or lack of good will of the other side provided a constant chorus to the perhaps inevitable spectacle of each side attempting to extract what it could from the bargained accords while blocking the efforts of the other. Throughout this process, which culminated in a ceremony presided over by the United Nations secretary-general, the U.N. observer mission ONUSAL operated as arbiter. Moments of crisis called for flying visits from New York by de Soto, now serving as senior political adviser to the U.N. secretary-general, and by Under Secretary-General Marrack Goulding. By December 15, 1992, however, Boutros Boutros-Ghali was able to declare that "the armed conflict in El Salvador has come to its end." Far from triumphant, his speech also warned that "there are still Salvadorans who continue to wage war within their hearts."[5]

Iqbal Riza, who served as ONUSAL's chief of mission throughout this first period of transition, would describe the areas of the peace agreements that lay beyond his remit as being "the two great unknowns."[6] Faced with the task of military reform through the "purging" of officers from the armed forces and the investigation of the war's most notorious cases of violence, the work of the Ad Hoc and Truth Commissions was bound to be controversial. In the end, the labors of both commissions far exceeded public expectation and provoked deep crises in the peace process.

The Ad Hoc Commission was installed on May 1992 and led by three prominent Salvadorans.[7] After a review of each officer's respect for human rights, professionalism, and democratic commitment, the commission delivered its report to the U.N. secretary-general and President Cristiani on September 23, 1992. It called for the dismissal or transfer of 103 officers. In the early weeks of September, as it became known that Minister of Defense Ponce and his deputy, General Zepeda, headed the list, pressure of all kinds and from all quarters was brought to bear on the commissioners. President Cristiani, who was bound to implement the commission's recommendations within sixty days, telephoned to warn that he felt himself "unable" to dismiss the numbers of colonels and generals he had learned the list contained. The generals themselves offered vague and not so vague threats as to what the commissioners might expect if they proceeded as planned.[8] Washington also weighed in, with an hour-and-a-half telephone call from Assistant Secretary Bernie Aronson, who argued the case for keeping Ponce on from every conceivable angle. The commissioners were not budging.[9]

The repercussions of the Ad Hoc Commission's recommendations were far reaching. As the High Command dug in its heels, the months of October, November, and December, 1992, were rife with rumors of impending military coups. But the tide for the *tandona* had turned. While compliance with the commission's recommendations became linked to the continuing demobilization of the FMLN, from inside the armed forces large groups of captains and majors made sure their desire to see the *tandona* go was communicated to the High Command.[10] The deadline for the Ad Hoc purge slipped back until, on December 31, 1992, Cristiani informed the U.N. secretary-general of the measures taken to transfer or dismiss ninety-four officers. That seven of these officers had been named as military attachés and a further eight—including Ponce and Zepeda—still remained on active service was in clear violation of the Ad Hoc Commission's recommendations. On January 7, 1993, Boutros-Ghali informed Cristiani that his proposals were "not in compliance with the Peace Accords."[11] International pressure for Cristiani to "regularize" the positions of these fifteen officers mounted, and the incoming Clinton administration froze $11 million in military aid to that end. The country waited on tenterhooks for the forthcoming report of the Truth Commission.

"THE publication of the report of the Truth Commission has thrown Salvadoran society into commotion," began an *ECA* editorial of April 1993, "and this when until now it had seemed that almost nothing was capable of surprising it. . . . What is surprising is not the contents of the report, but that those who accepted the Truth Commission and gave it its mandate should be surprised."[12]

Inaugurated in July 1992, the Truth Commission had been faced with a daunting task: to investigate within a period of six months the grave acts of violence that occurred during a twelve-year war. A staff consisting of around twenty lawyers and human rights professionals from North and South America took testimony from a remarkable 2,000 Salvadorans. Although the three commissioners came under pressure to limit the scope of the eventual report and not name those they found responsible for particular abuses, they did not cede before it.[13] Instead, on March 15, 1993, after a two-month extension, the Truth Commission delivered a document, "From Madness to Hope: The Twelve Year War in El Salvador," of lasting importance for the precedent it set for the international community's pursuit of accountability for human rights' abuses and in the official recognition it gave to the dark truth of El Salvador's recent history.

Unmasking the "institutionalized lie" denounced by Ignacio Martín-Baró, the Truth Commission exposed the incontrovertible responsibility of the Salvadoran state—and by implication those who had supported it—for the carnage of the past. The Truth Commission found that while the FMLN was responsible for a mere 5 percent of the cases for which it received denunciations, no less than 85 percent could be attributed to state agents, paramilitary groups or death squads aligned with them. This level of violence had originated in "a political mindset that rendered the concept of political opponent, subversive and enemy synonymous."[14]

While the commission brought new and significant details of many of its "exemplary" cases into the public arena, most importantly it confirmed information that had long been "known" at a general level, although never officially accepted or acted upon.[15] Into the historical record went the fact that Roberto D'Aubuisson had ordered the murder of Monsignor Romero in March 1980; that in December of that year security forces were responsible for the abduction and execution of the leaders of the FDR; that two senior officers covered up the murder of four U.S. churchwomen a few days later; that more than 500 civilians were "deliberately and systematically" executed by the Atlacatl Battalion in El Mozote and its surrounding villages in December 1981; that, eight years later, Colonel René Emilio Ponce, in the presence of General Juan Rafael Bustillo and Colonels Juan Orlando Zepeda, Inocente Montano, and Francisco Elena Fuentes, gave Colonel Guillermo Alfredo Benavides the order to kill Ignacio Ellacuría and leave no witnesses.[16]

An early analysis of the report cabled to the State Department from the U.S. embassy in San Salvador found the detailed description of the ordering of the murder of the Jesuits "perhaps [its] most damaging aspect."[17] Certainly it cannot have been unexpected. Ponce had believed that he had been included on the Ad Hoc list "because of the Jesuits."[18] He had been aware of the military officers interviewed by the Truth Commission, as all requests went through his office, and must have been aware of the extent to which they were talking. Days before the report was published, in a gesture that smacked more of political expediency than substance, Ponce had submitted his resignation as minister of defense to the president.[19] Although the denials came thick and fast—including one from a U.S. embassy official who obstinately maintained that "I shall not believe that General Ponce gave the order to kill the Jesuits unless he tells me so himself"—the arguments were over.[20] As chief of staff, and in the presence of other members of the military High Command, Ponce had ordered the murder of the Jesuits. He and they had lied about it and instructed others to lie about it on their behalf for three and a half years.

The Truth Commission's investigation of the murder of the Jesuits was facilitated by the work of those who had gone before them, particularly the Moakley task force. However, the Truth Commission's account of the planning, operation, and coverup of the crime provided substantial amplification of existing information. Laying to rest the debate about the location of the small meeting where the murder was ordered, the Truth Commission described how, after the large meeting of military commanders in the *estado mayor* on the evening of November 15, 1989—at which Colonel Ponce authorized "the elimination of ringleaders, unionists, and known members of the FMLN leadership"—officers remained behind talking in groups. It was to one of these groups—composed of Ponce, Bustillo, Zepeda, Montano, and Elena Fuentes—that Benavides was summoned. After receiving his order, Benavides returned to the military academy and convened a meeting of the officers under his command. He told them what they had to do and asked that any man who opposed the order raise his hand. None did so. Relaying the orders he had received from his superiors, Benavides instructed that the Atlacatl unit that had searched the UCA two days earlier should carry out the operation, and that Major Camilo Hernández should organize it.[21]

Hernández, it emerged, had been no less pivotal to the execution of the crime than he was to its coverup. It had been Hernández who gave the orders to Lieutenants Espinoza, Mendoza, and Guevara Cerritos; Hernández who provided the AK47—his own—with which Ellacuría, Martín-Baró, and Montes would be killed; and Hernández, together with a military academy lieutenant, who reported the night's events to Ponce early in the morning of November 16. The two officers brought with them the small brown case taken from the Jesuits the night before, which still contained photographs and personal documents. Ponce ordered that it be destroyed. A well-placed Salvadoran officer interviewed after the publication of the Truth Commission report explained that it was at this morning meeting that Ponce told Hernández—whom he described as a "favorite son" of the chief of staff—not to worry *("no te preoccupes")*, he would be protected.[22]

Hernández's connections did not stop with Ponce. His relationship with Rodolfo Parker Soto, legal adviser to the *estado mayor,* was described by the same officer as being that of *compadres,* "like brothers." Parker Soto had been a civilian member of the military Honor Commission. He had ensured that any mention of higher orders, including those of Camilo Hernández, be deleted from the extrajudicial confessions of the junior officers and men of the Atlacatl. The action was consistent with the wider pattern of the coverup which began with the entity supposedly charged with the murder's investigation—the Special Investigative Unit.

As the Buckland-Avilés version of events had indicated so long ago, a nervous Benavides went straight to the SIU's commanding officer, Lieutenant Colonel Manuel Rivas, and asked for help. Rivas, whom Ponce ordered should be aided by Colonel Iván López y López, advised Benavides to destroy the barrels of the weapons used in the operation against the UCA, because the SIU would need to run ballistics tests on them. He also suggested checking the logbooks at the military academy for incriminating evidence of exits and entrances on the night of the Jesuit murders. Benavides would be helped in the destruction of the weapons by Lieutenant Colonel Oscar León Linares, the commanding officer to whom Espinoza reported as soon as he returned to the Atlacatl. Together with Hernández, Benavides would also subsequently order the destruction of the logbooks.

The Truth Commission recommended that those individuals mentioned by name, in this as in other cases, be removed from their positions of authority and that COPAZ draft a law banning them from public office for at least ten years.[23] Other recommendations included a call for the full implementation of those elements of the peace agreements addressing military and judicial reform and, in consideration of the "enormous responsibility" born by the judicial system for the impunity within which the abuses they documented occurred, the resignation of all members of the Supreme Court.[24]

Notably absent from the Truth Commission's recommendations was a demand for the individuals it named to be prosecuted or—perhaps the more realistic aspiration—a warning against the imposition of an amnesty. In the days of frenetic activity that followed the report's release, the wisdom of this second decision was called into question by the manifest refusal of the country's authorities to accept either the report or the spirit in which it had been delivered. In a televised press conference that conjured up memories of the military rule of the 1970s, a stone-faced General Ponce sat flanked by other members of the High Command. Thumping the table in front of him, he declared the report "unjust, incomplete, illegal, unethical, biased, and insolent."[25] While Supreme Court President Gutiérrez Castro fulminated that "only God" could remove him from his post, President Cristiani produced a more nuanced reaction, but one scarcely in tune with the agreement with which his government had signed the Truth Commission into existence. The report, he claimed, did not "respond to the desire of the majority of Salvadorans, which is to forgive and forget all about our painful past."[26]

A sweeping general amnesty was rushed through the assembly only five days after the report's release. A last minute amendment including acts of judicial misconduct within the amnesty was greeted as a new low in the Salvadoran establishment's esteem for the rule of law. "When in the history of the world," one opposition lawyer was left to ask, "has it been necessary for a country to grant amnesty to its entire judicial system?"[27] Among the recommendations of the Truth Commission had been that a request for the pardon of Colonel Benavides and Lieutenant Mendoza already submitted by the Jesuits should be upheld. That this recommendation received immediate attention was, in such a climate, unsurprising. The two were released from jail on April 1, 1993, having served a little over a year of their thirty-year terms.

THE findings of the Truth Commission prompted a flurry of activity in the United States. The report had carefully avoided direct comment on the role played by the United States in the Salvadoran conflict, but as an indictment of that role it proved devastating. Pointedly delivering the challenge of past policy to its source in Washington, the three commissioners kindled a bitter return to the battles of the past with an appearance before a duly appalled House Western Hemisphere Subcommittee. Yet given congressional complicity in the ready flow of U.S. dollars to El Salvador throughout the 1980s, the spectacle presented by newly outraged Democrats, such as Chairman Robert Torricelli, who vowed to review "every word uttered by every Reagan administration official" in search of perjury in congressional testimony, was less than edifying. More predictable was the response of unrepentant Reaganites like Elliot Abrams. Dismissing Torricelli's threat as "McCarthyite crap," Abrams hailed the administration's record in El Salvador as one of "fabulous achievement."[28]

The liberal Democrats who had long opposed the Reagan and Bush policy towards El Salvador knew themselves to be vindicated, but it was a hollow victory indeed. In El Salvador the ends had justified the means, but those means had contributed to the deaths of tens of thousands and the devastation of a country. Obsessed with the threat of the "red scare," as Senator Mark Hatfield, a longtime critic of U.S. involvement in El Salvador put it, "neither Congress or the administration was willing to shut off the pipeline of support to the crippled Salvadoran government and the corrupt Salvadoran military."[29] In a *Washington Post* Op-Ed titled, "Of Course We Knew," Rand corporation analyst Benjamin Schwarz gave protestations of aggrieved ignorance an elegant dismissal: "In El Salvador, we filled our dance card long ago. It would be dishonest now to express surprise at the character of our partner."[30]

Beyond these heated discussions, the Truth Commission report had two direct consequences. "Deeply shocked" by the report, Secretary of State Warren Christopher appointed a small panel to "examine the activities and conduct" of the State Department, with particular attention to its handling of human rights, during the period covered by the Truth Commission.[31] A wider review of the operations of U.S. agencies was envisaged by the request forwarded to President Clinton by a group of congressional leaders coordinated by Joe Moakley. They asked that the president authorize the declassification of all U.S. documents pertaining to the thirty-two cases investigated by the Truth Commission.[32] Taken together, "The Report of the Secretary of State's Panel on El Salvador," which was released in mid-July, and the 12,000 documents declassified in November 1993 as a result of the congressional petition, were to provide a telling epilogue to the U.S. presence in El Salvador during the twelve-year civil war.

The report commissioned by the secretary of state was a disappointing response to the atrocities chronicled by the Truth Commission. Written by retired career ambassadors George S. Vest and Richard W. Murphy, the report found that while "mistakes were made"—most notably in the handling of the December 1981 massacre at El Mozote—State Department personnel "performed creditably and occasionally with personal bravery in advancing human rights in El Salvador." It painted a picture of an embassy staffed with diligent ambassadors pushing officials to prepare "honest, detailed human rights reports" and exerting "enormous effort" to develop El Salvador's "institutional capacity to deter and punish human rights abusers."[33] Where it failed, however, was in its refusal to address the connection between the "modest" success of these efforts with what it admits to have been a "positive gloss" put on the department's public statements on human rights.[34]

"Pulling the punches to support the policy" when it came to the reporting of human rights' abuses attributable to the military and rightist sectors had a direct consequence on the ability of the United States to exert its influence on human rights issues. Throughout the 1980s, the signal given to the perpetrators of abuses was that the State Department would oblige with a positive spin in order to guarantee a flow of military aid. By treading lightly over this difficult terrain, the report never addressed the central dilemma posed by the United States' stated pursuit of human rights within a context in which it was dancing, if not with the devil, then with government forces the Truth Commission had found to be responsible for 85 percent of twelve years' worth of abuses.

The Panel's praise of the U.S. embassy for working "closely with the SIU" in its investigation of the Jesuit murders, and of the SIU itself for its "technical work,"[35] suggested a less than attentive reading of the Truth Commission's narration of how the military High Command had controlled the Jesuit case from beginning to end. For a full account of the extent to which this case had destroyed what the Panel described as State's attempt to pursue simultaneously the goals of human rights and the prosecution of the war, it was necessary to wait until November, when the Clinton administration declassified a large part of the record on El Salvador.[36] In these documents, and especially in the anguished deliberations of Ambassador William Walker, is a dramatic and, in many respects, pitiful account of the end of an era of a particular kind of U.S. presence in Central America. The dilemma faced, as Walker would put it in a somewhat desperate cable of February 1991 titled "The ESAF and the Jesuit Case: Reaching the End of the Rope," was that "of pursuing two objectives while . . . they are essentially incompatible."[37]

Besides confirming the extent to which the U.S. government mistreated the witness, Lucía Cerna, and withheld the testimony of Major Buckland claiming prior knowledge until forced to deliver it to the proper judicial authorities by the actions of Congressman Moakley, the declassified documents illustrated how consistent had been the "positive gloss" put on the conduct of the Salvadoran government and military in the Jesuit case. They also gave a historical perspective to the murder of the Jesuits that rendered the subsequent defense of Salvadoran military officials, particularly the key figure of Ponce, unconscionable. Extending from Assistant Secretary Aronson's January 1990 description of Ponce as "very respected" to the State Department's 1992 suppression of a document, drafted for the Truth Commission by one of its own officials, suggesting Ponce's responsibility for the Jesuit murders, this defense emerged as the gravest error in the handling of the Jesuit case by all agencies of the U.S. government.[38]

A "Briefing Paper on Right-Wing Terrorism in El Salvador," prepared in October 1983 by CIA and State Department desk officers, described Ponce as "supportive of ARENA death squad activities and himself a member of the National Police paramilitary squad." Director of the National Police traffic department at the time, Ponce was listed among individuals representing "major elements of the country's right-wing terrorist subculture." More specifically, he was said to have "provided assistance" to Hector Regalado, the dentist and ARENA security chief who was among the most powerful of El Salvador's death squad leaders.[39] A few months later, in the CIA report to Vice-President Bush outlining the "little progress" made by the military High Command in the crackdown on right-wing violence promised after his much-vaunted visit in December 1983, Ponce was named as one of the "notorious right-wing extremists" recently posted to prestigious commands. The lieutenant colonels—with Zepeda among them—were described as "all close associates of ultrarightist standard-bearer Roberto D'Aubuisson."[40]

"When scholars have the ability to open the files," Ambassador Walker had said in an interview in March 1991, "I think they'll be surprised by the efforts to try and force, cajole, and rationally discuss with the armed forces what they should try and do about this case."[41] A reading of the declassified documents, however, lends more credence to the view expressed by Joe Moakley: U.S. officials and intelligence agencies must have been "deaf, dumb, and blind" not to have solved the Jesuit case themselves, "and that's putting a good face on it."[42] What the files reveal is an accumulation of reported intelligence indicating High Command responsibility for the Jesuit murders in one of a number of scenarios. Although isolated sources presented conflicting theories (in a couple of cases explanations of how Benavides came to act on his own), a clear pattern emerges in which sources indicate that the decision to kill the Jesuits was taken on November 15, 1989, either in an afternoon meeting at the military academy, or at the small meeting later in the evening at the *estado mayor*. While some of the sources were traceable to Espinoza, others reported on the participation of Major Camilo Hernández and on his protection by Ponce, and others again on the readiness of Benavides to "name Ponce as the authority who ordered the Jesuit murders."[43]

Individually these reports were dismissed on the basis that they originated in sources whose reasons for coming forward—self-interest and/or a desire to do the *tandona* down—were suspect. That this critique could be extended to any member of the Salvadoran armed forces lends a disquieting air to the reading of the cables in a collective form. Who or what would it have taken to convince the U.S. government of the High Command's guilt? The suggestion is that that conviction would come only with "incontrovertible" evidence, and the armed forces, under Ponce's leadership, made sure they could not get it. Seen in this context, the fact that the pressure point for the numerous representations, démarches, threats, and pleas the U.S. government in general and Walker in particular undoubtedly made was Ponce himself only adds to the surreality of the United States' position.

Although information on the High Command's possible responsibility for the Jesuit murders had been available since June 1990,[44] things came to a head in the weeks before Colonel Ponce became minister of defense at the beginning of that September. The debriefing given to Walker by the two aides to the Moakley task force on August 11, after one of the armed forces' "most senior and respected officers" implicated Ponce and the High Command, proved the catalyst. "If basic story is true or if Congress believes it to be our policy is at peril," Walker cabled "Eyes Only" to Bernie Aronson on August 13. Underlying this statement was not just the implied guilt of Ponce and the High Command, but the "desperate silence" maintained by "possibly hundreds of officers," and the inaction of President Cristiani.[45] In a more reflective cable of the following day, Walker listed mutually unsustainable "concerns" that succinctly illustrated the maze into which U.S. policy had been plunged the Jesuit case: "1) that we do not act precipitously and irretrievably burn our relationship with Ponce at this critical stage; 2) that we do not imperil ESAF cooperation on the peace process through unreasonable pressing for action on the Jesuit case; 3) but at the same time that we do not let the ESAF get the impression that it can continue to stonewall on its involvement in the Jesuit case."[46]

"Near total frustration" for Walker was to come in the early months of 1991. In a "Note to SouthCom" on February 10, 1991, MilGroup Commander Mark Hamilton described the "very somber tone" evident in what he referred to as "the Washington side of the house." Reporting a telephone call between Aronson and Walker in which the assistant secretary let it be known that both "had their personal reputations on the line in the Jesuit case," Hamilton described an embassy meeting in which Walker had discussed "asking State to direct him to tell Christiani [sic] that all funds should be cut off if the entire Tandona did not resign within 30 days."[47] Hamilton was evidently among those who dissuaded Walker from such a move, but the cable the ambassador did write on February 19—"Reaching the End of the Rope"—was stronger than anything to come out of the embassy so far. "USG pleas, threats, turning on and off the military assistance spigot, and appeals to institutional honor have all had the same results—zilch," was the blunt assessment of the attempt to coerce cooperation from the armed forces. Recognizing Ponce as "a fatally flawed leader," Walker claimed to "see only two choices—admit defeat and attempt to move on to other matters, or pull the plug, i.e., demand a new leadership with a clear understanding of what they, and we face. I opt for the second option."[48]

Given the combative tone of this cable—which, as the product of discussions with the country team was no doubt relayed to General Ponce even before Walker got a chance to "pound him" on the Jesuit case in person—it is not surprising that Ponce and the High Command saw this as the opportune moment to throw their "bone to the *gringos*" in the form of the letter of February 22 recommending "complementary investigations" in the Jesuit case.[49] As they had been since the night of November 16, 1989, the Salvadoran armed forces were one step ahead of the United States. The "damage control" of the early months of the investigation, built as it was on a policy of accommodation to the Salvadoran military that long preceded the Jesuit murders, meant it was far too late to reach the conclusion, as Walker did, that Ponce's "style of leadership, developed over twenty-five years at the helm of the Tandona . . . makes for a leader who is not leading, a consensus follower in a group whose only consensus is to protect its narrow interests."[50]

Although Ponce and the *tandona* rode out Ambassador Walker with little difficulty, the complicated manner in which the Jesuit case contributed to negotiations, and within them to the acknowledgment of a need to address the military impunity of the past, was still to prove their nemesis. On his eventual retirement on July 1, 1993, under pressure from the U.N. and the international community, Ponce laid the blame for his departure, and that of the generals who accompanied him, on the "evil intent" of the Ad Hoc and Truth Commissions. Presiding over the formal ceremony in which they handed over their commands was Cristiani, a president widely praised for allowing the peace process to reach fruition, but one who had proven unequal to his military officers when it came to the Jesuit case. As the generals prepared to exchange their military careers for lucrative positions in public life, Cristiani paid tribute to their having "fulfilled their time in the institution with honor, efficiency and loyalty."[51]

WHILE Washington's researchers, journalists, human rights advocates, and historians began a meticulous raking over of the United States' less than "fabulous achievement" in El Salvador, El Salvador showed the world that the goals laid out by the Chapultepec agreements—the reconciliation, respect for human rights, and democratization that were to follow the end of the armed conflict—lay beyond the "culmination of the peace process" that some chose to see in the elections. Certainly the country had changed, and changed inordinately for the better, since 1989. Even in early 1992 the sight of an FMLN "official" on early morning television had seemed extraordinary. But the resurgence of the death squads, the vitriol employed by the ARENA party and its more extremist fringes, and the shadow thrown over the left by personal and ideological differences still as deeply felt as in the past, all warned of a long, hard struggle toward full and representative democracy. The year since the publication of the Truth Commission report had seen some important changes, but it had also seen the majority of the Truth Commission's own recommendations ignored, and the peace accords, as a whole, pushed somewhat rudely aside by the fevered preparations for the March elections.[52]

Election day itself, March 20, 1994, presented the Salvadoran people with an array of obstacles. Despite an intensive campaign to amend the electoral register, there were still an estimated 350,000 men and women of voting age without the necessary voter card, while the register (of 2.7 million) remained swollen by as many as 400,000 dead or otherwise departed Salvadorans.[53] Three thousand international observers fanned out across the country to respond with mixed reactions to a process that, while in all respects a great improvement on the blatantly fraudulent or wartime elections of the past, still left much to be desired. Polling stations opened late, and were often far from residential areas. Long lines in the boiling heat were exacerbated by the complexities of voting and anomalies that meant that at least 25,000 of those in possession of voter cards still could not find their names on the lists.[54] As the polls closed, the leaders of the FMLN gave a bitter and emotional press conference challenging the credibility of the low voter turnout (an estimated 54 percent) and charging that the elections had been deeply flawed.[55]

International observers offered carefully measured assessments that took note of what British academic David Browning called "fumbling ineptitude," but stopped short of accusations of fraud. Avoiding the glowing rhetoric with which he had anticipated the vote, the outgoing head of ONUSAL, Augusto Ramírez Ocampos, judged that "despite serious deficiencies in organization and transparency . . . these elections can be considered acceptable."[56]

Tempers on the left cooled as it emerged that, as expected, Armando Calderón Sol had defeated Rubén Zamora by a wide margin (obtaining 49 percent of the vote to Zamora's 25 percent), but without the overall majority needed to avoid a second round. Similar levels of voting in the elections for the National Assembly left ARENA, with 39 of a total of 84 deputies, able to commandeer a majority in partnership with the PCN, but faced by 21 deputies of the FMLN in opposition. Most disturbing for the left was its showing in the local elections, where the voting "irregularities" weighed heavily and no doubt contributed to the FMLN's winning in just 16 out of 262 municipalities.[57] But as Zamora began his campaign for the second round and Salvadorans of all political persuasions digested the lessons for the future, it was difficult to deny the elections their preeminent achievement: although they had brought the continuing existence of El Salvador's polarization to the fore, they had done so peaceably and allowed a former guerrilla organization to establish itself as the second political force in the country.

The second round of the presidential elections, held on April 24, 1994, was emphatically won by Armando Calderón Sol with 68 percent of the vote. That it merited a smaller international presence and press coverage than the first was not surprising. As the international community struggled with the latest crisis in the former Yugoslavia and contemplated the epoch-making elections in South Africa, the fortunes of this diminutive Central American country were understandably low on the political agenda. The task faced in El Salvador, however, was a heavy one. The country looked forward to difficulties in the full implementation of the peace accords under the government of Calderón Sol at a time of diminishing international support and increasing disunity with the opposition parties. While to have come this far so quickly was remarkable, there was no need to look beyond the person of the incoming president—to whose unswerving allegiance to D'Aubuisson declassified documents had added the taint of association with death squad operations—to see that the past was ever-present.[58] The "prophetic denunciation" and the "utopian horizon" offered by Ignacio Ellacuría as the model for a life lived "full of hope" were as necessary now as they ever had been.

IN the five years since the elections that brought Alfredo Cristiani to the presidency, the UCA had faced tragedy and overcome it as that tragedy contributed so notably to the country's search for peace. Back in 1989, the UCA had been tense amid the blackouts that had characterized the violence surrounding the elections; the UCA of 1994, like its city San Salvador, resounded to the noise of construction work. At one end of the Monsignor Romero Pastoral Center, an extension designed to accommodate increased numbers of students studying for theology degrees grew by the day. It was to stretch out from the balcony where, in the early hours of November 16, 1989, Ignacio Ellacuría had stood beside a hammock and requested the soldiers of the Atlacatl Battalion to "stop making such a racket" while he opened the door and let them in.

Outside, Obdulio Ramos watched quietly as a swathe of his vegetable patch was swallowed by the new foundations. Since the loss of his wife and daughter, he had tended the garden he had planned with the Jesuits with care and devotion. A special attention was reserved for the small patch of ground that lay to the right of the door to the upstairs corridor. On this ground, in early 1990, Obdulio had planted a circle of six red rose bushes in memory of six men who lived and died honorably and responsibly in El Salvador. At the center stood two yellow rose bushes, for the two women who accompanied them and the thousands of Salvadorans who preceded them in their deaths. Over the years the pattern had lost some of its ordered symmetricality, but there always seemed to be flowers.

CHRONOLOGY

EL SALVADOR	JESUITS	OTHER
1864	Jesuits arrive in El Salvador	
1872	June. Jesuits expelled from El Salvador	
1914	August 18. Jesuits return to El Salvador	
1930	November 9. Ignacio Ellacuría (I.E.) born in Portugalete, Bilbao, Spain	
1932 January. 30,000 killed when Gen. Maximiliano Hernández Martínez suppresses uprising in *matanza*		
1937	February 7. Jesuit Vice-Province of Central America founded	
1944 May. Hernández Martínez ousted after national strike and military revolt.		
1947	September 14. I.E. enters Jesuit novitiate in Loyola	
1948 December. Military junta led by Col. Oscar Osorio comes to power after coup		

	EL SALVADOR	JESUITS	OTHER
1949		March 22. Miguel Elizondo, I.E., and novices arrive in Santa Tecla	
1950	Col. Osorio named president	Segundo Montes arrives in Santa Tecla	
		to 1955. I.E. studies in Quito, Ecuador	
1951		Amando López arrives in Santa Tecla	
1953		Juan Ramón Moreno arrives in Santa Tecla	
1955		to 1958. I.E. teaches in San Salvador seminary	
1956	September. Col. José María Lemus elected president		
1958		to 1962. I.E. studies theology in Innsbruck	
1959			January. Triumph of Cuban Revolution
1960	October. Civilian-military junta brought to power by coup	Ignacio Martín-Baró arrives in Santa Tecla	
1961	January. Countercoup brings Col. Julio Rivera to power	July 26. I.E. ordained a priest	March. President Kennedy launches Alliance for Progress
1962	July. Col. Rivera elected president	to 1967. I.E. studies philosophy in Madrid with Xavier Zubiri	October. Second Vatican Council begins

	EL SALVADOR	JESUITS	OTHER
1965	September 15. University of Central America (UCA) founded	May. Pedro Arrupe becomes father general of the Society of Jesus	December. Second Vatican Council ends
1967	July. Col. Fidel Sánchez Hernández elected president	I.E. returns to El Salvador and begins work at the UCA	
1968		May. Arrupe visits Latin America for Jesuit meeting in Rio	August-September. Second Conference of Latin American Bishops in Medellín, Colombia
1969	July. Five-day war with Honduras leaves 2,000 dead	Joaquín López y López founds *Fe y Alegría* December 24 to 31. Vice-provincial meeting in San Salvador	
1970	January. Congress on Agrarian Reform April. Dissident cell leaves Communist party to found FPL June. Salvadoran priests meet for Pastoral Week	April. Miguel Francisco Estrada becomes vice-provincial September. Vice-province decides for future structured around "liberation"	
1971		April. Immigration authorities threaten I.E. with expulsion	

EL SALVADOR	JESUITS	OTHER
1972 February. Col. Arturo Molina becomes president after elections won by UNO opposition leader Napoleón Duarte September. ERP founded	September. Jesuits dismissed from seminary September. Rutilio Grande arrives in Aguilares	
1973	Publication of *El Salvador: Año Político 1971–1972* April-July. Externado Affair	
1974	I.E. founds Center for Theological Reflection (CRT) April. Vice-Provincial Congregation ends in discord. I.E. removed from vice-provincial government December-March 1975. General Congregation XXIII commits Jesuits to "the service of faith and promotion of justice" December. Román Mayorga becomes rector of the UCA	
1975 July 30. Massacre of students leads to occupation of cathedral and formation of BPR		

EL SALVADOR	JESUITS	OTHER
1976 July-December. Violence increases following President Molina's failed attempt at Agrarian Transformation. The UCA is bombed repeatedly.	Vice-province ascended to province; César Jerez new provincial December 6. Death of Aguilares landowner blamed on Jesuits	November. Jimmy Carter elected U.S. president
1977 February 20. Gen. Carlos Umberto Romero becomes president in fraudulent elections February 22. Msgr. Oscar A. Romero becomes archbishop of San Salvador	February 22. Amid mounting repression of Church, I.E. and Luis de Sebastián refused entry to El Salvador March 12. Rutilio Grande assassinated June 21. UGB issue threat demanding all Jesuits leave El Salvador within 30 days	March. In Washington, U.S. Congress holds hearings on El Salvador July. Hearings in Washington reopened to examine religious persecution
1978 August. In response to rise in popular movement, Msgr. Romero publishes "The Church and Popular Political Organizations"	Montes returns to El Salvador having completed doctorate in Madrid August. I.E. and de Sebastián reenter El Salvador UCA begins radio broadcasts on YSAX	

EL SALVADOR	JESUITS	OTHER
1979 May 8. Security forces kill twenty-three on steps of cathedral October 15. Young Officers' coup brings in military-civilian junta	Martín Baró returns to El Salvador having completed doctorate in Chicago October–November. UCA loses Mayorga and other staff to new government; I.E. becomes rector of UCA December 27. Three bombs explode in the UCA	January–February. Third Conference of Latin American Bishops in Puebla, Mexico July 19. Triumph of Sandinistas in Nicaraguan revolution Amando López becomes rector of Managua UCA
1980 January 3. Civilians resign from government, led by junta members Mayorga and Ungo; PDC and military join forces in new junta January 22. 20 killed and 200 wounded in largest demonstration in Salvadoran history March 24. Msgr. Romero assassinated April. FDR founded in meeting at the UCA October. FMLN formed by coalition of five armed revolutionary organizations November 27. Six leaders of FDR abducted from Externado and killed December 2. Four U.S. churchwomen abducted, abused, and murdered	March 22. National Police invade UCA campus; student killed October 24 and 27. UCAII residence bombed twice within a week; UCA bombed six times within year Late November. I.E. begins exile after death threat from army	March 25. In Washington, debate in congressional committee on military aid to El Salvador November 4. Ronald Reagan elected U.S. president

	EL SALVADOR	**JESUITS**	**OTHER**
1981	January 3. President of ISTA and two AIFLD officials assassinated January 10. FMLN launch "final offensive" December 11. Up to 1,000 villagers massacred by army in and around village of El Mozote, Morazán	January 17. Military occupy UCA campus February. In Managua, I.E. begins to talk of need for "mediation and negotiation" of conflict	January 17. President Carter sends emergency $5 million in military aid to El Salvador February. State Department white paper describes conflict as "textbook case of armed aggression by communist powers"
1982	March 28. Alvaro Magaña emerges as caretaker president after legislative elections	April. I.E. returns to El Salvador	January 28. President Reagan certifies that El Salvador has complied with human rights conditions for receiving aid
1983	Conflict shifts from dirty war to a war waged under counterinsurgency strategy of LIC	September 6. Secret Anticommunist Army bombs Jesuit residence and home of UCA professor	April 27. President Reagan appeals to Congress for increased aid to El Salvador
1984	May 6. Napoleón Duarte (PDC) elected president May 24. Five national guardsmen convicted of murder of U.S. churchwomen October 15. Government and FDR-FMLN meet for talks in La Palma November 30. Second round of talks held in Ayagualo	Amando López returns to El Salvador	January. Kissinger Commission calls for increased military aid and attention to human rights in El Salvador

	EL SALVADOR	JESUITS	OTHER
1985	March 31. PDC win control of assembly from ARENA in elections	Montes founds IDHUCA, the UCA's Human Rights Institute; UCA begins to hold regular Forum for public discussion	
	September 10. Inés Guadalupe Duarte and friend kidnapped by FMLN	November. In UCA Forum, I.E. introduces thesis of "third force"	
	October 24. I.E. and Msgr. Rivera negotiate exchange of kidnapped women for FMLN political prisoners	Juan Ramón Moreno returns to El Salvador July. Martín-Baró founds IUDOP, the UCA's Institute of Public Opinion	
1986	September 19. Government and FDR-FMLN fail to meet for talks in Sesori	September. ARENA launches campaign to strip I.E. of Salvadoran citizenship	October 5. Downing of Eugene Hasenfus's plane in Nicaragua triggers Iran-*contra* revelations
	October 10. Earthquake in El Salvador kills more than 1,200		
1987	October 4 to 5. Government and FDR-FMLN meet for talks in San Salvador		August 7. Central American presidents sign Esquipulas II agreements
	October 22. Duarte passes law of general amnesty		U.S. aid exceeds El Salvador's own contribution to its budget
	November. FDR leaders Ungo and Zamora return from exile		

	EL SALVADOR	**JESUITS**	**OTHER**
1988	March. ARENA trounces PDC in legislative elections September 3. National Debate holds assembly in San Salvador	May 20 to 21. I.E. meets FMLN *comandantes* in Managua at the beginning of their strategic reassessment August 30. I.E., Montes, and Ibisate meet Alfredo Cristiani for the first time	*Perestroika* gathers pace in USSR November 8. George Bush elected U.S. president
1989	January 23. FMLN propose to "convert elections into a contribution for peace" March 19. Alfredo Cristiani (ARENA) elected president April 19. Attorney General Roberto García Alvarado assassinated. Colonel Zepeda claims assassination planned at the UCA. June 9. Minister of the Presidency José Antonio Rodríguez Porth assassinated September 13 to 15. Talks in Mexico between government and FMLN October 15 to 17. Talks between government and FMLN resume in San José, Costa Rica	I.E. outlines his idea of a "new phase in the Salvadoran process" April 13 and 16. ARENA and High Command accuse Montes of justifying terrorist acts April 24. Three bombs explode outside the UCA printing plant July 22. Large bombs explode inside UCA printing plant September 29. I.E. meets FMLN *comandantes* in Managua for last time	February 3. U.S. Vice-President Dan Quayle visits El Salvador and delivers warning on human rights March 24. Bipartisan Accord on Nicaragua signed in Washington August 7. Central American presidents ratify accords of Esquipulas II at Tela, Honduras

EL SALVADOR	JESUITS	OTHER
October 17. Daughter of Colonel Edgardo Casanova Vejar assassinated	October 21. I.E. travels to Europe	November. Berlin Wall comes down
October 31. Offices of FENASTRAS bombed	November 13. I.E. returns from Europe; Jesuit residence searched by Atlacatl Battalion	December 6. Congressman Joe Moakley appointed chairman of Speaker's Special Task Force on El Salvador
November 11. FMLN launch general offensive	November 16. Six Jesuits and two women murdered by Atlacatl Battalion	
November 15. Senior officers of Salvadoran army give orders to kill I.E. and leave no witnesses		

	EL SALVADOR	JESUITS	OTHER
1990	April 4. Under U.N. auspices, government and FMLN sign Geneva Accord agreeing to end conflict "through political means"	January 2. Colonel Ponce told that U.S. Maj. Buckland implicated Col. Benavides in the Jesuit murders	February 25. Sandinistas lose elections in Nicaragua
	May 21. Government and FMLN agree on negotiating agenda in Caracas	January 10 to 12. In Washington, Buckland tells FBI he may have had prior knowledge of murders	May 22. In Washington, House passes amendment to cut fifty percent of military aid
	July 26. Talks in Costa Rica deadlock on military reform, but both sides agree to San José Accord on human rights	January 13. Cristiani announces detention of Col. Benavides, junior officers, and enlisted men	August 2. Iraq invades Kuwait
		April 30. Moakley task force releases "Interim Report"	
		August 11. Task force staff have breakthrough meeting with senior military source in San Salvador	

EL SALVADOR	JESUITS	OTHER
September 1. Col. Ponce named minister of defense	August 15. Moakley releases statement accusing army High Command of "obstructing justice" in the Jesuit case	October 19. U.S. Senate passes bill cutting military aid
Late October. Alvaro de Soto assumes more active role as U.N. mediator		November 5. 50 percent cut in military aid to El Salvador signed into U.S. law
	October 18. Moakley makes public Buckland's onetime claim of prior knowledge	
	December 6. Judge raises case to the trial stage	
1991 January 1. Ponce, Zepeda, and Rubio become generals	January 7. Moakley task force staff report on trip to El Salvador and charge that "the armed forces are controlling the investigation"	January 16. U.S. launches Desert Storm in Gulf War
January 2. FMLN executes two U.S. military advisers		January 16. Cut of 50 percent of military aid to El Salvador reinstated, but delayed two months
March 10. Legislative elections	February 22. Letter from army High Command to justice minister. Hailed by U.S. officials as breakthrough in case in early March	
April 27. Talks between government and FMLN in Mexico conclude with agreement on constitutional reform		June 5. House leadership asks administration to keep delay on military aid
	July 1. At the UCA, Moakley charges that the Jesuit case shows Ponce that he has "institutional problem"	June 27. Bush administration announce release of delayed military aid
July 26. ONUSAL installed in El Salvador		
September 16 to 25. Lengthy negotiations conclude with the signing of the New York Accords		August. Failed coup in Moscow hastens disintegration of USSR

EL SALVADOR	JESUITS	OTHER
November 16. FMLN declares unilateral truce until a final cease-fire can be agreed upon	September 26 to 28. Trial of Jesuit case ends with Col. Benavides found guilty of the murder of all eight victims and Lt. Mendoza guilty on one charge	
December 31. Government and FMLN sign agreements in New York preparing the way for an end to civil war	November 18. Moakley issues statement: the Jesuit murder was planned at a meeting of senior officers including Gen. Bustillo and then Cols. Ponce, Zepeda, and Elena Fuentes	

	EL SALVADOR	JESUITS	OTHER
1992	January 16. Peace accords signed in Chapultepec, Mexico	January 10. Assembly rejects a December 1991 request by Jesuits to appoint a commission to investigate UCA murders	November 3. Bill Clinton elected U.S. president
	January 23. Law of National Rec-onciliation approved		
	February 1. Cease-fire begins with installation of COPAZ in San Salvador attended by FMLN General Command	August 12. Tojeira announces that Jesuits are considering requesting a pardon for Benavides and Mendoza	
	February 13. ONUSAL begins verification of Peace Accords	December 16. Tojeira requests pardon for convicted officers from National Assembly	
	May 15. Ad Hoc Commission begins review of army officers		

	EL SALVADOR	**JESUITS**	**OTHER**
	July 13. Truth Commission begins examination of acts of violence committed during the war		
	September 23. Ad Hoc Commission presents lists of names of army officers to be purged to U.N. and Cristiani		
	December 15. Day of National Reconciliation marks end of armed conflict in El Salvador		
1993	January 7. U.N. secretary-general states government "not in compliance" with peace accords for not removing 15 officers indicated by Ad Hoc Commission	April 1. Col. Benavides and Lt. Mendoza, convicted of the UCA murders, released from prison.	March 24. U.S. Secretary of State Warren Christopher forms panel to investigate conduct of State Department during period covered by Truth Commission
			July 15. Secretary of State's Panel on El Salvador releases its report
			November 5. Clinton administration declassifies 12,000 documents relating to the thirty-two cases investigated by Truth Commission

EL SALVADOR   **JESUITS**   **OTHER**

March 15. Truth
Commission releases
its report, "From
Madness to Hope: the
twelve-year war in El
Salvador." It finds that
"on the night of 15
November 1989, then
Colonel René Emilio
Ponce, in the presence
of and in collusion
with General Juan
Rafael Bustillo, then
Colonel Juan Orlando
Zepeda, Colonel Ino-
cente Orlando
Montano and Colonel
Francisco Elena
Fuentes, gave the order
to kill Father Ignacio
Ellacuría and leave no
witnesses"

March 20. An
immediate and general
amnesty is pushed
through the Assembly
by ARENA deputies

July 1. Defense
Minister General
Ponce and military
High Command resign

EL SALVADOR   **JESUITS**   **OTHER**

1994 March 20. Presidential,
legislative, and
municipal elections in
El Salvador. ARENA
presidential candidate,
Armando Calderón
Sol, wins 49 percent of
the vote against 25
percent won by left
wing coalition
candidate Rubén
Zamora, but fails to
achieve the overall
majority necessary to
prevent a second
round. In the
legislative elections the
FMLN emerges as the
country's second
political force.

April 24. In a second
round of elections
Calderón Sol wins a
comfortable 68% of
the vote.

June 1. Armando
Calderón Sol
inaugurated president
of El Salvador.

ACRONYMS

AID: Agency for International Development
AIFLD: American Institute for Free Labor Development
ANEP: National Association of Private Enterprise
ANSESAL: Salvadoran National Security Agency
ANTEL: Salvadoran National Telecommunications Company
ARENA: Nationalist Republican Alliance
BIRI: Immediate Reaction Infantry Battalion
BPR: Popular Revolutionary Block
CACM: Central American Common Market
CAFOD: Catholic Fund for Overseas Development
CARECEN: Central American Refugee Center
CEAT: Special Antiterrorist Command
CEBRI: Immediate Reaction Battalion Training Center
CIA: Central Intelligence Agency
CIAS: Center of Investigation and Social Action
CIDAI: Center for Information, Documentation, and Support for
Research
COCFA: Armed Forces' Joint Command Operations Center
COENA: Executive Council of ARENA
COMADRES: Committee of Mothers of the Detained, Disappeared, and
Assassinated
COPAZ: National Commission for the Consolidation of Peace
COPEFA: Permanent Council of the Armed Forces
COPREFA: Armed Forces Press Office
CPDN: Permanent Committee of the National Debate
CRM: Revolutionary Coordinator of the Masses
CRT: Center for Theological Reflection
DIA: Defense Intelligence Agency
DNI: National Intelligence Directorate
ECA: *Central American Studies*
ECLA: Economic Commission on Latin America
ERP: People's Revolutionary Army
ESAF: El Salvadoran Armed Forces
FAL: Armed Forces of Liberation
FAPU: Front for Unified Popular Action
FARN: Armed Forces of National Resistance (or RN)
FARO: Agricultural Front of the Eastern Region
FBI: Federal Bureau of Investigation
FDR: Democratic Revolutionary Front
FECCAS: Christian Federation of Salvadoran Peasants

FENASTRAS: National Trade Union Federation of Salvadoran Workers
FMLN: Farabundo Martí National Liberation Front
FPL: Popular Liberation Forces
FSLN: Sandinista National Liberation Front
FUNDASAL: Salvadoran Foundation for Development and Basic Housing
FUSADES: Salvadoran Development Fund
GOES: Government of El Salvador
IADB: Inter-American Development Bank
IDHUCA: Human Rights Institute of the University of Central America
IPSFA: Armed Forces' Social Security Fund
IRI: Institute of International Relations
ISEPES: Salvadoran Institute of Political, Economic and Social Studies
ISTA: Salvadoran Institute of Agrarian Transformation
IUDOP: University Institute of Public Opinion
LIC: Low-Intensity Conflict
LP-28:   "February 28" Popular Leagues
MAC: Authentic Christian Movement
MNR: National Revolutionary Movement
MPSC: Popular Social Christian Movement
ONUSAL: United Nations Mission to El Salvador
ORDEN: Democratic Nationalist Organization
PCN: National Conciliation Party
PCS: Salvadoran Communist Party
PDC: Christian Democratic Party
PNC: National Civilian Police
PRTC: Central American Workers' Revolutionary Party
PSD: Social Democratic Party
RN: National Resistance
SIU: Special Investigative Unit
UCA: University of Central America "José Simeón Cañas"
UCS: Salvadoran Communal Union
UDN: Nationalist Democratic Union
UGB: White Warriors Union
UN: United Nations
UNO: National Opposition Union
UNOC: Union of Christian Workers
UNTS: National Union of Salvadoran Workers
UPD: Popular Democratic Unity
USG: United States Government
UTC: Union of Rural Workers

NOTES

Unless otherwise indicated, all translations are by the author.

EPIGRAPH

Ignacio Ellacuría, "El segundo general de los jesuitas vasco," (manuscript, Archive of Ignacio Ellacuría [AIE], UCA, San Salvador), p. 3.

INTRODUCTION

1. Ignacio Ellacuría, "Quinto centenario de América Latina: ¿Descubrimiento o encubrimiento?" Lecture given in Barcelona in January 1989, reprinted in *Revista Latinoamericana de Teologia (RLT)* no. 21 (September–December 1990), (Centro de Reflexión Teológica, UCA, San Salvador), p. 281. For full bibliographies of the works of Ignacio Ellacuría, Ignacio Martín-Baró, and Segundo Montes, see those provided in John Hassett and Hugh Lacey, eds., *Towards a Society that Serves Its People: The Intellectual Contribution of El Salvador's Murdered Jesuits* (Washington, D.C.: Georgetown University Press, 1991), pp. 373–94.

2. Primary sources for the opening section of the Introduction are interviews with Jesuits present in the UCA on November 15, 1989: Rodolfo Cardenal, April 10, 1991; Miguel Francisco Estrada, February 6, 1991; Francisco Javier Ibisate, June 26, 1990; and Rogelio Pedraz, June 21, 1990. All were interviewed by the author in San Salvador.

3. Ignacio Ellacuría, interview by Televisión Española, c. March 1985. included in television documentary "A Question of Conscience," (New York: Icarus/Tamouz Media, 1990)

4. Ignacio Martín-Baró, interview by Tom Gibb and Joyce Hackel, San Salvador, November 8, 1989.

5. Ibisate, interview, June 26, 1990; Lawyers Committee for Human Rights, "The Jesuit Murders: Report on the Testimony of a Witness" (New York: Lawyers Committee for Human Rights, December 15, 1989), p. 7. The Lawyers Committee published regular reports on the progress of Jesuit case from 1989 on; the culmination of their labors can be found in Martha Doggett, *Death Foretold: The Jesuit Murders in El Salvador* (Washington, D.C.: Lawyers Committee for Human Rights and Georgetown University Press, 1993).

6. "El asesinato de los jesuitas (1)," *Proceso* (Centro Universitario de Documentación e Información, UCA, San Salvador) no. 409 (November 29, 1989), p. 8.

7. The primary sources for the second section of the Introduction are the transcriptions of the extrajudicial declarations of the officers and men charged with the killing of the Jesuits in January 1990, reproduced as "El caso de la masacre de la UCA: Sentencia interlocutona para detención provisional," *ECA* nos 393–394 (November–December 1989), pp. 1155–68. Additional information on the military academy and the Atlacatl Battalion was gained from visits by the author to both during 1990.

8. Copies of the military records of all those accused of the murdering the Jesuits are held in the *Court Record,* Fourth Criminal Court, San Salvador. A Defense Intelligence Agency (DIA) cable of February 1, 1990 stated that Espinoza "did not pass flight training in the U.S., and was subsequently discharged from the air force as an example to other aspiring pilots." U.S. document declassified November 1993, Washington, D.C.

9. *Pilijay* is the word for "hangman" in the indigenous Nahautl language.

10. Lawyers Committee, "Report on the Testimony of a Witness," p. 7.

Chapter 1

1. Alberto de Mestas, "Cómo es El Salvador," *ECA* no. 29 (April 1949), p. 919.

2. Fabián Zarrabe, interview with author, San Salvador, June 27, 1990. According to the prevailing rules of the Society of Jesus, the novices expected never to see their families again.

3. Jon Sobrino, interview with author, San Salvador, June 22, 1990.

4. José Ellacuría, in a talk given at the UCA, San Salvador, November 15, 1990.

5. Zarrabe, interview, June 27, 1990.

6. "El volcán jesuita: Entrevista con el padre Ellacuría, rector de la Universidad Centroamericana," *ABC,* Madrid, March 28, 1982.

7. James Dunkerley, *Power in the Isthmus: A Political History of Modern Central America* (London: Verso, 1988), p. 172. El Salvador is the same size as the state of Massachusetts.

8. Dirección General de Estadística, *Anuario estadístico de la República de El Salvador 1949* (San Salvador, 1949) pp. 196 & 22.

9. De Mestas, "Cómo es El Salvador," p. 921.

10. David Browning, *El Salvador: Land and Society* (London: Oxford University Press, 1971), pp. 222–23.

11. Roqué Dalton, "Todos," *Las historias prohibidas del pulgarcito* (San Salvador: UCA Editores, 1988), p. 124.

12. Albert F. Nufer to Robert A. Lovett, November 17, 1948, cited in Walter LaFeber, *Inevitable Revolutions* (New York: W.W. Norton & Co., 1984), p. 131.

13. *Anuario estadístico, 1949,* p. 33.

14. Jon Cortina, interview with author, San Salvador, April 3, 1991.

15. Judex, "Cincuentenario de la llegada de los jesuitas a El Salvador," *ECA* no. 198 (October 1964), pp. 289–91; Cesareo García del Cerro SJ, "Aportación de los jesuitas españoles a Iberoamérica," *ECA* no. 214 (April 1966), pp. 64–68.

16. Alain Woodrow, *Los jesuitas: Historia de un dramático conflicto* (Barcelona: Planeta, 1985), p. 54.

17. Ibid., p. 55.

18. Honduras would be included within the full province of Central America in 1979. Until then it had been dependent on the Jesuit province of Missouri, U.S.A.

19. Rodolfo Cardenal, "La Provincia de Centro América en sus diez últimos años, 1969–79," (manuscript, Archives of the Central American Province of the Society of Jesus [ACAPSJ], San Salvador), p. 72.

20. Salvador Carranza, interview with author, Santa Tecla, El Salvador, January 25, 1991.

21. Miguel Elizondo, interview with author, Guadalajara, Mexico, December 31, 1990.

22. César Jerez, interview with author, Managua, Nicaragua, February 18, 1991.

23. Estrada, interview with author, February 6, 1991.

24. Among Jon Sobrino's most treasured newspaper cuttings is an article published on the sports pages of *El País* on February 18, 1985. Under the title, "The Athlétic and Liberation Theology," Patzo Unzueta discusses the passion for Athlétic Bilbao shared by Ellacuría and Sobrino throughout the years of their friendship.

25. Estrada, interview February 6, 1991; Jon Sobrino, interview with author, San Salvador, March 7, 1991.

26. Elizondo, interview, December 31, 1990.

27. The phrase was first used by St. Ignatius in a letter to Juan de Verdolay, July 24, 1537, *Cartas de San Ignacio de Loyola,* Vol. I (Madrid: V. E. Hijo de D. E. Aguado, 1874), p. 53.

28. Peter H. Kolvenbach, interviewed by Renzo Giacomelli, *Men of God: Men for Others* (Slough, England: St. Paul Publications, 1990), p. 28.

29. Cited by Jon Sobrino, "El mayor servicio, carisma de la Compañía de Jesús," *Diakonía* (Boletín de CICA, Managua), no. 22 (July 1982), p. 24.

30. Elizondo, interview, December 31, 1990.

31. Jerez, interview, February 18, 1991.

32. Alocución del Santo Padre a los participantes en la Congregación General XXXII, *Congregación General XXXII de la Compañía de Jesús* (Madrid: 1975) Razón y Fe, p. 248.

33. Fernando Cardenal, interview with author, Managua, February 15, 1991.

34. Salvador Carranza, "Dejenme vivir memorias" (manuscript, Honduras, December 1989), p. 5.

35. "Ignacio Ellacuría SJ, *Noticias SJ* (Noticias de la Provincia Centroamericana, San Salvador), no. 159 (December 1989), p. 6, ACAPSJ.

36. Ignaccio Ellacuría, "El P. Aurelio Espinoza Pólit SJ," *ECA* no. 178 (January–February 1963), p. 21.

37. Ibid., p. 23.

38. Estrada, interview, February 6, 1991.

39. His first articles, published in three issues of *ECA* in 1956, were on the Spanish philosopher José Ortega y Gasset.

40. Pepe Simán, interview with author, San José, February 24, 1991; Rubén Zamora, interview with author, San Salvador, April 12, 1991.

41. Aurelio Espinoza Pólit to Ignacio Ellacuría, October 2, 1959, AIE.

42. Víctor Codina, "Ignacio Ellacuría, teólogo y mártir," *RLT* no. 21 (September–December 1990), p. 263.

43. Report on Theological Studies of Ignacio Ellacuría, 1962, ACAPSJ.

44. Juan Bautista Arríen, interview with author, Managua, February 18, 1991.

45. Jon Sobrino, "Karl Rahner y la teología de la liberación," *ECA* no. 431 (September 1984), p. 699.

46. Arríen, interview, February 18, 1991.

47. Jon Sobrino, "Querido Ellacu," letter read at the anniversary mass for Ignacio Ellacuría in the UCA Chapel, November 10, 1990. *Carta a las Iglesias* no. 223 (December 1–15, 1990) (Centro Pastoral, UCA, San Salvador), p. 12.

48. C. A., "Ha desaparecido el último gran metafísico: Xavier Zubiri," *ECA* no. 420 (October 1983), pp. 891–94; Ignacio Ellacuría, "Zubiri en El Salvador," *ECA* nos. 361–62 (November–December 1978), pp. 949–50.

49. Ignacio Ellacuría to Luis Achaerandio, October 3, 1963, describing meeting on September 8, 1961, AIE.

50. Carmen Castro, in a talk given at the UCA, November 15, 1990.

51. Ignacio Ellacuría to Luis Achaerandio, March 22, 1963, AIE.

52. "Zubiri sigue vivo," *ECA* no. 420 (October 1983), p. 896.

53. Ignacio Ellacuría to Xavier Zubiri, February 23, 1963, AIE.

54. "Zubiri sigue vivo," p. 896.

55. C. A., "Ha desaparecido el último gran metafísico," p. 894.

56. Cited by Cynthia Arnson, *El Salvador: A Revolution Confronts the United States* (Washington, D.C.: Institute for Policy Studies, 1982), p. 19.

57. Survey of Latin America, April 1, 1964, cited by LaFeber, *Inevitable Revolutions,* p. 172; 12 percent growth rate is also in LaFeber, p. 174.

58. "De cara al futuro de la Vice-Provincia," Survey de la Vice-Provincia de Centroamérica, vol. XI, pp. 52–61, ACAPSJ.

59. Santiago de Anitua, "Universidad—Gobierno—Política," *ECA* no. 197 (September 1964), p. 241.

60. Fabio Castillo, interview with author, San José, Costa Rica, February 26, 1991 and "La crisis de la educación en El Salvador en las postrimerias del Siglo XX" (Cartas Salvadoreñas, Costa Rica, March 1985)

61. "Universidades privadas en Centro América," Editorial, *ECA* no. 203 (April 1965), p. 92.

62. Cited by Ignacio Ellacuría, "Sobre la fundación de la Universidad José Simeón Cañas," September 30, 1982, AIE.

63. Survey de la Vice-Provincia, vol. XI, p. 53.

64. "Discurso del Rector de la Universidad Centroamericana José Simeón Cañas, Florentino Idoate, con motivo de la inauguración de la universidad," *Planteamiento Universitario 1989* (San Salvador: UCA Editores, 1989), pp. 135–38.

65. Penny Lernoux, *Cry of the People* (Harmondsworth, England: Penguin Books, 1982), p. 33.

66. Stephen Webre, *José Napoleón Duarte and the Christian Democratic Party in El Salvador* (Baton Rouge: Louisiana State University Press, 1979), p. 72.

67. Jenny Pearce, *Under the Eagle: U.S. Intervention in Central America and the Caribbean* (Boston: South End Press, 1982), p. 209.

68. "Pobreza de la Iglesia," 1, 1, *Los Textos de Medellín* (San Salvador: UCA Editores, 1977), p. 103.

69. Pablo Richard, "La Conferencia de Medellín: Contexto histórico de su nacimiento, difusión e interpretación," in *La Iglesia Latinoamericana entre el temor y la esperanza* (San José, Costa Rica: DEI, 1980), p. 49.

70. "Christianity and Social Progress," May 15, 1961; "Peace on Earth," April 11, 1963.

71. "Consciousness raising" is a thin paraphrase of this method, which is most fully described in Paolo Freire, *The Pedagogy of the Oppressed* (New York: Seabury, 1973).

72. "Justicia," 1, 2, *Los Textos de Medellín,* p. 25.

73. Cited in Woodrow, *Los Jesuitas,* p. 135.

74. Ellacuría, "Pedro Arrupe, renovador de la vida religiosa," *RLT* no. 22 (January–April 1991), p. 12.

75. "Carta del Apostolado Social," December 12, 1966, in Pedro Arrupe, S.I., *La Iglesia de hoy y del futuro* (Santander, Spain: Sal Terrae, 1982), pp. 286–87.

76. Ellacuría, "El CIAS, nuevo tipo de communidad religiosa," AIE.

77. Provincials of the Society of Jesus, "The Jesuits in Latin America," May 1968, in Alfred T. Hennelly, ed., *Liberation Theology: A Documentary History,* (Maryknoll, N.Y.: Orbis Books, 1990), p. 77.

78. Matt. 25:40.

79. "Justicia," 2, 3, *Los Textos de Medellín,* p. 26.

80. Hennelly, *Liberation Theology: A Documentary History,* p. 62.

81. Gustavo Gutiérrez, "Introduction to the Revised Edition: Expanding the View," *A Theology of Liberation* (Maryknoll, N.Y.: Orbis Books, 1988), p. xxxiv.

82. Hennelly, *Liberation Theology: A Documentary History,* p. 78.

CHAPTER 2

1. Ellacuría, "Ponencia sobre vida religiosa y tercer mundo," in "Reunión de Madrid: Primera reunión de los Jesuitas Centroamericanos en Europa," Madrid, June 26–30, 1969, p. 14, ACAPSJ.

2. Román Mayorga, interview with author, Washington, D.C., May 1, 1991.

3. Gaudium et Spes, 4a.

4. Ignacio Ellacuría to Xavier Zubiri, April 30, 1968, AIE.

5. Paolo Dezza to Segundo Azcue, April 23, 1968, ACAPSJ.

6. Juan Hernández Pico, interview with author, San Salvador, June 15, 1991.

7. Cited in *Noticias SJ* (March 1970), ACAPSJ.

8. Ellacuría, "Ponencia sobre vida religiosa y tercer mundo," p. 12.

9. Letter of Pedro Arrupe introducing the conclusions of GCXXXI, 1967, cited in "Reunión de Madrid," p. 1, ACAPSJ.

10. Ellacuría, "Reflexión teológico-espiritual de la VP Jesuítica de Centroamérica," in "Reunión de Ejercicios," San Salvador, December 24–31, 1969, Survey vol. II, Dia 29–1, pp. 1–12, ACAPSJ.

11. Napoleón Alvarado, interview with author, Managua, Nicaragua, February 15, 1991.

12. Segundo Azcue to Pedro Arrupe, December 31, 1969, cited in Cardenal, "La Provincia de Centro América," p. 92, ACAPSJ.

13. Pedro Arrupe to Segundo Azcue, March 23, 1970, ibid., p. 93.

14. Cited in "Reflexiones en torno a la situación en Guatemala, El Salvador, Nicaragua, Panama El Salvador," Survey vol. IX, p. 9, ACAPSJ.

15. Unemployment and casualty figures from Robert Armstrong and Janet Shenk, *El Salvador: The Face of Revolution* (Boston: South End Press, 1982), p. 57. Col. Sánchez Hernández had been elected in 1967.

16. Cardenal, "La Provincia de Centro América," pp. 72–73, ACAPSJ. Besides the Externado San José in San Salvador, the high schools were the Liceo Javier in Guatemala City and Colegio Centro América in Managua.

17. "De cara al futuro de la Vice-Provincia," Survey vol. XI, p. 65, ACAPSJ.

18. Cardenal, "La Provincia de Centro América," p. 148, ACAPSJ.

19. Román Mayorga, "Breve reseña histórica de la Universidad Centroamericana José Simeón Cañas," *ECA* nos. 324–25 (October–November 1975), p. 593.

20. Ellacuría, "Algunas notas sobre el resumen del Survey de la Universidad J. S. Cañas," Survey vol. VII, UJSC, p. 22, ACAPSJ.

21. Román Mayorga, "Recuerdo de diez Quijotes" (manuscript, Montevideo and Washington, D.C., March 1991), p. 10.

22. "Discurso de la Universidad Centroamericana José Simeón Cañas en la firma del contrato con el BID," *Planteamiento Universitario,* p. 12.

23. Mayorga, interview, May 1, 1991.

24. "Reunión V. Provincial," September 10–20, 1970, Survey vol. XII, p. 137, ACAPSJ.

25. For histories of the Central American Church, see Philip Berryman, *The Religious Roots of Rebellion* (Maryknoll, N.Y.: Orbis Books: 1986) and Guillermo Menéndez and Pablo Richard, eds., *La iglesia de los pobres en América Central* (San José, Costa Rica: DEI, 1982).

26. Monsignor Oscar Romero to Miguel Francisco Estrada, October 13, 1972, cited in, "Apuntes ante la salida de la Compañía de Jesús del Seminario Central de San José de la Montaña de San Salvador," p. 5, ACAPSJ.

27. "Contrato entre la Conferencia Episcopal de El Salvador y el Superior Mayor de la Compañía de Jesús en El Salvador," ibid., p. 87.

28. Estrada, interview, February 6, 1991.

29. "Apuntes ante la salida," p. 20.

30. "Mensaje del Señor Presidente de la República Coronel Arturo Armando Molina," cited in *La investigación y la docencia en la educación*

universitaria de El Salvador (San Salvador: Proyecto UCA/PREDE-OEA, 1990), p. 144.

31. The title of the study was "Análisis de una experiencia nacional." Mayorga, "Breve Reseña Histórica," p. 593.

32. Cardenal, "La Provincia de Centro América," p. 144.

33. "Síntesis Final: Educación Media y Primaria," Survey vol. XI, p. 65, ACAPSJ.

34. "Carta del Apostolado Social," in Arrupe, *La Iglesia de hoy,* p. 288.

35. "Charla del P. General en Medellín sobre los Colegios," *Noticias SJ* (October 1968), p. 5, ACAPSJ.

36. Woodrow, *Los Jesuitas,* p. 80.

37. Asociación de Padres de Familia del "Externado San José" to Rev. Padre Francisco Javier Colino SJ, April 27, 1973, ACAPSJ.

38. Biographical portrait in Rodolfo Cardenal, "Ser jesuita hoy en El Salvador," *ECA* nos. 493–94 (November–December 1989), p. 1033.

39. *Prensa Gráfica,* June 16, 1973.

40. *Orientación,* May 27, 1973.

41. *Diario Latino,* June 8 and 26, 1973.

42. "El Arzobispo se pronuncia en caso del Externado San José," June 25, 1973, ACAPSJ.

43. Estrada, interview, February 6, 1991.

44. Transcript provided by Carmen Alvarez.

45. "El Externado piensa así," *ECA* no. 296 (June 1973), p. 422.

46. These meetings are described in Cardenal, "La Provincia de Centro América," p. 128.

47. Enrique Mayorga Rivas.

48. Accounts of the meetings on May 14 and June 18, 1974 are in *Noticias SJ* (May and June 1974, p. 53 & pp. 69–71), ACAPSJ.

49. President Molina, as reported in *Noticias SJ* (May 1974), p. 53 ACAPSJ.

50. Ungo had been private secretary to Fabio Castillo, the rector of the National University; Zamora a student; Dada active in Catholic University Action (ACUS).

51. Guillermo Ungo, interview with author, San Salvador, December 15, 1990; Héctor Dada, interview with author, Mexico City, January 9, 1991; and Rubén Zamora, interview, April 12, 1991.

52. Vincent O'Keefe, interview with author, New York, May 27, 1991.

53. Estrada, interview, February 6, 1991.

54. "Thirty-Second General Congregation of the Society of Jesus 1974–1975," *The Way,* Supplement 29/30 (London, Spring 1977), p. 12.

55. Cardenal, "La Provincia de Centro América," p. 151.

56. *Noticias SJ* (December 1989), p. 8, ACAPSJ; Hernández Pico, interview, June 15, 1991.

57. Cardenal, "La Provincia de Centro América," p. 227.

58. Pedro Arrupe, "A los padres y hermanos de la nueva Provincia Centroamericana," Guatemala, August 5, 1976. *Noticias SJ* (August 1976), pp. 2–5. The second remark was made at the reception following the ceremony, Ibid., p. 7, ACAPSJ.

59. Ellacuría, "Pedro Arrupe, Renovador de la vida religiosa," p. 7.

60. "El Salvador se conmueve," Editorial, *ECA* no. 321 (July 1975), p. 328.

61. For English-language accounts of the origins of the Salvadoran revolution, see Armstrong and Shenk, *El Salvador: The Face of Revolution;* Tommie Sue Montgomery, *Revolution in El Salvador: Origins and Evolution* (Boulder, Colo.: Westview Press, 1982); and Jenny Pearce, *Promised Land: Peasant Rebellion in Chalatenango El Salvador* (London: Latin America Bureau, 1986).

62. For a history of the FPL, see Marta Harneker, ed., *Con la mirada en alta: Historia de las FPL–Farabundo Martí a través de sus dirigentes* (San Salvador: UCA Editores, 1993).

63. The taking of the cathedral is described in Rodolfo Cardenal, *Historia de una esperanza: Vida de Rutilio Grande* (San Salvador: UCA Editores, 1985), p. 450.

64. In gratitude for Mayorga's mediation, Molina asked him if there was any favor he could do him in return. "Yes there is, as a matter of fact," Mayorga remembered replying, "could you give Ignacio Ellacuría and Luis de Sebastián Salvadoran nationality?" Mayorga, interview, May 1, 1991.

65. *Rutilio Grande: Mártir de la evangelización rural* (San Salvador: UCA Editores, 1978), p. 64.

66. Ibid., p. 67.

67. Carranza, interview, January 25, 1991.

68. Alberto Enríquez, interview with author, San Salvador, June 4, 1991.

69. Carlos Cabarrús, *Genésis de una revolución: Análisis del surgimiento y desarrollo de la organización campesina en El Salvador* (Mexico City: Ediciones de la Casa Chata, 1983), p. 150.

70. "Paz," n. 27, *Los Textos de Medellín,* p. 39.

71. ORDEN was founded in the mid-1960s by Colonel José Alberto Medrano, allegedly as part of U.S. security assistance. Michael McClintock, *The American Connection, Volume One: State Terror and Popular Resistance in El Salvador* (London: Zed Books Ltd., 1985), pp. 204ff.

72. Cabarrús, *Genésis de una revolución,* p. 157.

73. Antonio Cardenal, interview with author, Chalatenango, March 12, 1991.

74. Ibid.

75. Rutilio Grande, "La dinámica de una nueva acción pastoral," and a letter dated January 11, 1976, both ACAPSJ.

76. A companion of these three was Emilio Baltodano, a Nicaraguan Jesuit scholastic whose intellectual brilliance fostered a particularly close relationship with Ellacuría. He left the Jesuits in 1974 to enter the revolutionary struggle in Nicaragua. He would later serve as minister of industry and deputy minister of agriculture in the Sandinista government. Interview with author, Managua, Nicaragua, February 20, 1991.

77. Juan Hernández Pico, "El testamento—para mí—de Ignacio Ellacuría" (manuscript, San Salvador, May 1991), p. 42.

78. Hernández Pico, interview, June 15, 1991.

79. Sobrino, interview, March 7, 1991.

80. "Una bomba contra *ECA*," Editorial, *ECA* nos. 327–28 (January–February 1976), p. 5.

81. Luis de Sebastián, interview with author, Barcelona, Spain, January 21, 1992. A detailed account of Alas's experience is given in Montgomery, *Revolution in El Salvador,* p. 97.

82. Melvin Burke, "El sistema de plantación y la proletariación del trabajo agrícola en El Salvador" and Eduardo Colindres, "La tenencia de la tierra en El Salvador," *ECA* nos. 335–36 (September–October 1976), p. 476 and p. 467 respectively.

83. Cited in Armstrong and Shenk, *El Salvador: The Face of Revolution,* p. 83.

84. Ellacuría, "La historización del concepto de propiedad como principio de desideoligazación," *ECA* nos. 335–36 (September–October 1976), p. 431.

85. Cited by Rubén Zamora, "¿Seguro de vida o despojo? Análisis político de la Transformación Agraria," ibid., p. 523.

86. See declarations of Christian Democrats, the BPR, FAPU, et al. in ibid., pp. 622–33.

87. Ungo, interview, December 15, 1990.

88. "Pronunciamiento del Consejo Superior de la Universidad Centroamericana José Simeón Cañas," *ECA* nos. 335–36 (September–October 1976), p. 419.

89. Ellacuría, "La historización del concepto de propiedad," p. 428

90. September 15, 1976, cited by Ellacuría in "¡A sus órdenes, mi Capital!" Editorial, *ECA* no. 337 (November 1976), p. 640

91. Ibid., p. 641.

92. Zamora, interview, April 12, 1991.

93. Ellacuría, "¡A sus órdenes, mi Capital!" p. 641.

94. "¿Porqué nos ponen bombas?" Editorial, *ECA* no. 338 (December 1976), p. 733.

95. Pedro Arrupe to César Jerez, February 5, 1977, ACAPSJ.

CHAPTER 3

1. Sen. Mark Hatfield, *Congressional Record,* November 20, 1989, p. S16339.

2. "*Hártenselo!*" *Court Record,* Fourth Criminal Court, San Salvador, Declaration made to the Special Investigative Unit (SIU) on December 4, 1989.

3. José María Tojeira, "Días de muerte," Salvador Carranza, ed., *Mártires de la UCA* (San Salvador: UCA Editores, 1990), pp. 15ff.

4. Obdulio Ramos, interviews with author, San Salvador, June 26 and November 20, 1990. Description of the site from "Informe de la Oficina de Tutela Legal del Arzobispado de San Salvador," November 28, 1989.

5. Transcript of Lucía Barrera de Cerna's interview with members of the Moakley task force, February 25, 1990.

6. Ibisate, interview, June 26, 1990.

7. Salvadoran officer, interview with author, San Salvador, November 21, 1991.

8. Capt. Luis Alberto Parada Fuentes testified to the SIU on March 20 and May 13, 1991 and to the court on May 28, 1991, *Court Record.*

9. Ibid., Phil Bronstein, "The story behind the murder of the Jesuits," *San Francisco Examiner,* February 5, 1990; Salvadoran officer and source close to military, interviews with author, San Salvador, March 15 and 23, 1991. For more on this meeting see Lawyers Committee for Human Rights, "The Jesuit Case a Year Later: An Interim Report" (New York, November 13, 1990), p. 21.

10. Cited by Philip Bennet, "Burying the Jesuits," *Vanity Fair,* November 1990.

11. Cited in chronology contained in Instituto de Estudios Centroamericanos (IEC) and El Rescate, *The Jesuit Assassinations* (Kansas City, Sheed and Ward, 1990), p. 33.

12. William Walker, interview with author, San Salvador, February 5, 1991.

13. Lee Hockstader, "Our Man in El Salvador, Upbeat amid the Crisis," *Washington Post,* December 19, 1989.

14. U.S. official, interview with author, August 12, 1991.

15. Charles Lane, "Bloodbath in El Salvador," *Newsweek*, November 27, 1989.

16. Walker, interview, February 5, 1991.

17. Lawyers Committee, "The Jesuit Case A Year Later," pp. 23ff. and *Underwriting Injustice: AID and El Salvador's Judicial Reform Program* (New York, 1989), pp. 41–54.

18. The three security forces—National Guard, National Police, and Treasury Police—came under the direct command of the Salvadoran army.

19. Tojeira, "Días de muerte," p. 16.

20. "Informe de la Oficina de Tutela Legal," pp. 8–9 and Jesuit communiqué, "Cronología del asesinato de los jesuitas en El Salvador," in *Carta a las Iglesias* (November 16 to December 31, 1989), p. 26.

21. Channel 12 television archives, San Salvador.

22. María Julia Hernández, interview with author, San Salvador, June 23, 1990.

23. Channel 12, television archives, San Salvador.

24. Jon Sobrino, "Companions of Jesus," in Jon Sobrino, Ignacio Ellacuría et al., *Companions of Jesus: The Jesuit Martyrs of El Salvador* (Maryknoll, N.Y.: Orbis Books, 1990) pp. 4–5. Julian Filochowski, interview with author, London, October 29, 1990; and Sobrino, interview, June 22, 1990.

25. "Ambassador Walker's statement on the death of the Jesuits," November 16, 1989, U.S. embassy, San Salvador.

26. Richard Boudreaux and Marjorie Miller, "Six Jesuit Priests Slain in El Salvador," *Los Angeles Times*, November 17, 1989.

27. Tojeira, "Días de muerte," p. 19.

28. U.S. embassy/State Department cable "Ambassador's November 18 meeting with Cristiani," November 27, 1989, cable released to Americas Watch.

29. Moakley task force, "Interim Report of the Speaker's Special Task Force on El Salvador," April 30, 1990, p. 43.

30. Ricardo Valdivieso outlined his theory to several Jesuits, it was repeated in the *Prensa Gráfica*, November 18, 1989. Pacas Castro was interviewed on the "MacNeil-Lehrer Newshour," PBS, November 17, 1989 and "Face the Nation," CBS, November 26, 1989.

31. *Prensa Gráfica*, November 17, 1989.

32. "El asesinato de los jesuitas (1)," *Proceso* no. 409 (November 29, 1989), p. 9.

33. "El asesinato de los jesuitas (1)," p. 9; Rogelio Pedraz, interview with author, San Salvador, December 17, 1990.

34. "Remarks at a fundraising luncheon for Senatorial candidate Lynn Martin in Chicago, Illinois," November 20, 1989, *Public Papers of the Presidents:*

George Bush, 1989, (Washington, D.C.: U.S. Government Printing Office, 1990) p. 1555. For the record the word "priests" was altered to "people."

35. A CIA report on ARENA prior to the elections concluded that "D'Aubuisson's public deference to Cristiani is largely cosmetic." Directorate of Intelligence, "El Salvador: Rightist ARENA Party Election Frontrunners," March 14, 1989, U.S. document declassified November 1993, Washington, D.C.

36. CIA, Memo requested by the National Security Adviser to the President, March 4, 1981. U.S. document declassified November 1993. Washington, D.C.; Robert White in U.S. Congress, House Committee on Appropriations, Subcommittee on Foreign Operations, *Foreign Assistance and Related Programs Appropriations for 1982,* Part I, February 1981 (Washington, D.C.: U.S. Government Printing Office, 1981), p. 16. James Cheek was acting ambassador in early 1980 when D'Aubuisson slid a finger across his throat while warning that Cheek would "get what he deserved" for "leading El Salvador to communism." Raymond Bonner, *Witness and Deceit* (New York: Times Books, 1984), pp. 308–9. Plots against Ambassador Thomas Pickering were discovered in 1984 after ARENA lost elections heavily weighted toward the Christian Democrats by U.S. aid.

37. Statement by Press Secretary Marlin Fitzwalter on President Bush's meeting with President-Elect Alfredo Cristiani of El Salvador, April 7, 1989, *Public Papers of the Presidents,* p. 388.

38. "Bipartisan Accord on Latin America," *1989 Congressional Quarterly Almanac,* p. 14-C.

39. Whether the government deserved a final $34 million installment of military aid would then be decided. The amendment was proposed by Matthew McHugh (D., N.Y.) and defeated 185 to 233 on June 28, 1989.

40. Sen. Christopher Dodd, *Congressional Record,* September 20, 1989, p. S11455.

41. Sen. Patrick Leahy, ibid., p. S11474.

42. Rep. David McCurdy, *Congressional Record,* November 14, 1989, p. H8525; Sen. John Kerry, *Congressional Record,* November 15, 1989, p. S15369.

43. Sen. Patrick Leahy, *Congressional Record,* November 16, 1989, p. S15841.

44. U.S. congressional aide, interview with author, Washington, D.C., May 2, 1991.

45. U.S. Congress, Senate Committee on Foreign Relations, Subcommittee on Western Hemispheric and Peace Corps Affairs, *A Hearing on the Current Political Situation in El Salvador,* November 17, 1989 (microfiche, Washington, D.C.).

46. Aryeh Neier and Juan Méndez to Secretary of State James Baker, November 16, 1989. Letter released to public by Human Rights Watch.

47. Sen. Mark Hatfield, Rep. David Dreier, *Congressional Record,* November 20, 1989, p. S16338, p. H9194 and H.Con.Res.236, n4, p. H9186.

48. The House rejected 194 to 215 a motion that would have allowed a vote on an amendment to delay releasing 30 percent of military aid until after April 1, 1990. The Senate rejected a similar amendment 39 to 58.

49. Speaker Thomas S. Foley to the Hon. John Joseph Moakley, December 5, 1989, Appendix A, Moakley task force, "Interim Report." The idea had originally been that of Rep. Gerry Studds's aide Bill Woodward and Studds had proposed it to the Speaker.

50. This account is based on the Lawyers Committee's "A Report on the Testimony of a Witness"; the Moakley task force's "Interim Report"; the transcript of the task force's interview with Lucía Cerna on February 25, 1990; Tojeira's "Días de muerte"; press reports; and interviews.

51. Transcript, Lucía Cerna interviewed by Moakley task force, February 25, 1990.

52. Walker, interview, February 5, 1991.

53. Richard Chidester, interview with author, San Salvador, February 8, 1991. A CIA memo, written four months before the murders, described the UCA as "a think tank for radical leftists in El Salvador" which "has consistently lent political support to that country's Marxist insurgents," "Explosions at the Central American University," July 24, 1989. U.S. document declassified November 1993. Washington, D.C.

54. José María Tojeira, interview with author, San Salvador, June 6, 1991.

55. Chidester, interview, February 8, 1991.

56. Lawyers Committee, "A Report on the Testimony of a Witness," p. 1.

57. Ibid., p. 28.

58. Americas Watch, "Update on El Salvador: The Human Rights Crisis Continues in the Wake of the FMLN offensive" (December 16, 1989, New York: Americas Watch, 1989), p. 9.

59. Lindsey Gruson, "Dispute in Salvador on Witness in Jesuit Case," *New York Times,* December 11, 1989; Lee Hockstader, "U.S. Accused of Impugning Salvadoran," *Washington Post,* December 11, 1989.

60. Chidester, interview, February 8, 1991.

61. Patrick Burns, president, Jesuit Conference, interview with author, Washington, D.C., April 23, 1991. The Jesuit Conference is the Washing-

ton-based body overseeing the operations of all the Jesuits in the United States.

62. Letter of March 12, 1990, from FBI Director William Sessions to Father Patrick Burns, president, Jesuit Conference.

63. Paul S. Tipton SJ to the Secretary of State, December 10, 1989.

64. Paul Tipton, interview with author, Washington, D.C., May 6, 1991.

65. Chidester, interview, February 8, 1991.

66. International and Organized Crime Branch, Metropolitan Police, "Deaths of Six Jesuit Priests, a Lady and Her Daughter at San Salvador on 16 November 1989" (New Scotland Yard, London 1991).

67. Cited in Gruson, "Dispute in Salvador."

68. See Americas Watch, "Update on El Salvador," for a detailed account of persecution in this period.

69. Embassy official, interview with author, San Salvador, June 26, 1991.

70. Lee Hockstader, "Our Man in El Salvador," *Washington Post,* December 19, 1989.

71. Tojeira, interview with author, San Salvador, October 15, 1991.

72. Cited in Hockstader, "Our Man in El Salvador."

73. Walker, interview, February 5, 1991.

74. State Department to U.S. embassy, Madrid, "Jesuit Investigation in El Salvador," December 15, 1989. Cable released to Americas Watch.

75. "Killing of Jesuit Priests: Chronology of Events and Investigation," in K. Larry Storrs, "El Salvador—Legal System, Judicial Reform, and Major Human Rights Cases Involving the Military" (Congressional Research Service Report for Congress, March 23, 1990, Washington, D.C.), p. 15. For a detailed analysis of the SIU investigation, see Lawyers Committee, "The Jesuit Case a Year Later," pp. 23ff.

76. Germán Orellana Vásquez, SIU Report, November 17, 1989, *Court Record;* interviewed by the SIU on December 12, 1989, *Court Record.*

77. Henry Campos, prosecutor, interview with author, San Salvador, March 20, 1991. In the days following the crime, Attorney General Mauricio Colorado's contribution had been to write to the Pope and recommend that he should withdraw from the country those bishops (he was referring to Rivera Damas and Rosa Chávez) who had "insisted on keeping alive the questionable ideology of the 'Church of the Poor,' " suggesting that if they did not leave the country their lives would be in danger. "Carta del Fiscal al Papa," *Proceso* no. 411 (December 13, 1989), p. 14.

78. Fermín Saínz, November 28, 1989, *Court Record.*

79. December 11, 1989, *Court Record.*

80. Cited in Lawyers Committee, "The Jesuit Case a Year Later," p. 28.

81. Col. Carlos Avilés, interview with author, San Salvador, March 15, 1991.

82. Chidester, interview, February 8, 1991.

83. Moakley task force, "Interim Report," p. 27; Storrs, "Killing of Jesuit Priests: Chronology," p. 16.

84. Juan Antonio Gonzalez Torres, December 28, 1989, *Court Record.*

85. Transcript of the video declaration of Maj. Eric Warren Buckland, January 12, 1990, Washington, D.C. and Moakley task force, "Interim Report," p. 28ff.

86. Buckland, transcript of video declaration, January 12, 1990.

87. Letters Rogatory testimony of Col. Milton Menjívar, interviewed on August 7, 1991 by John Harris, U.S. Department of Justice, Washington, D.C., *Court Record,* p. 25.

88. Transcript of interview of Maj. Eric Buckland by officials of the Defense Department, FBI and Justice Department, in the U.S. Department of Justice, November 19, 1990, Washington, D.C., Court Record.

89. Letters Rogatory testimony of Col. Menjívar, p. 27.

90. Transcript of interview by CBS correspondent Ed Bradley with Ambassador William Walker, San Salvador, March 22, 1990, p. 15.

91. U.S. officials, interviews with author, San Salvador, February 8, and April 8, 1991.

92. Robert Pear, "Salvador Evidence Escaped U.S. Envoy," *New York Times,* January 15, 1990.

93. U.S. congressional aide, interview with author, Washington, D.C., April 26, 1991.

94. Chidester, interview, February 8, 1991.

95. Doug Farah, "Soldiers Killed Jesuits, El Salvador Says," *Washington Post,* January 8, 1990.

CHAPTER 4

1. Homilies of February 17, 1980; July 15, 1979; and June 24, 1979, cited in Ignacio Ellacuría, *Conversión de la Iglesia al reino de Dios* (San Salvador: UCA Editores, 1985), p. 113.

2. Jon Sobrino, "Mi recuerdo de Monseñor Romero," *Monseñor Romero* (San Salvador: UCA Editores, 1990), pp. 11ff. and Cardenal, *Historia de una esperanza,* pp. 572ff.

3. The *campesinos* maintained that Orellana and his brother had come

out of the house shooting, and that one of the bullets from his brother's gun had rebounded to kill him. Cardenal, *Historia de una esperanza,* p. 538.

4. *Diario de Hoy* and *Prensa Gráfica,* December 7, 1976.

5. Sobrino, interview, March 7, 1991.

6. The UTC had begun organizing in San Vicente, to the east of San Salvador, and established close ties to individual priests and base communities.

7. Antonio Cardenal, interview, March 12, 1991.

8. "Dossier sobre la persecución de la iglesia en El Salvador," pt. IV, p. 26, ACAPSJ.

9. Ellacuría had been working in Madrid with Zubiri at the time.

10. "Homilía del Padre Rutilio Grande en la misa del 13 de Febrero de 1977," in "La Voz de la Iglesia y los Mártires del Paisnal" (Publicaciones del Arzobispado de San Salvador, 1977).

11. "Dossier sobre la persecución," pt. IV, p. 26, ACAPSJ; Latin America Bureau, *Violence and Fraud in El Salvador* (London, 1978), p. 21.

12. U.S. Congress, House Committee on International Relations, Subcommittees on International Organizations and Inter-American Affairs, *The Recent Presidential Elections in El Salvador: Implications for U.S. Foreign Policy,* March 9 and 17, 1977 (Washington, D.C.: U.S. Government Printing Office, 1977), pp. 69–71.

13. Jesús Delgado, *Oscar A. Romero, Biografía* (San Salvador: UCA Editores, 1990), p. 69.

14. Simán, interview, February 24, 1991.

15. James R. Brockman, *Romero: A Life* (Maryknoll, N.Y.: Orbis Books, 1989), p. 56.

16. Ibid., p. 57.

17. de Sebastián, interview, January 21, 1992.

18. "¿Quién será el nuevo arzobispo?" Editorial, *ECA* no. 337 (November 1976), p. 644.

19. Jerez, interview, February 18, 1991.

20. Ibid.

21. Antonio Fernández Ibáñez recounted the anecdote in Managua, February 14, 1991.

22. Estrada, interview, February 6, 1991.

23. Ellacuría, "Un mártir en El Salvador," manuscript, AIE.

24. Sobrino, "Mi rescuerdo de Monseñor, Romero," p. 16.

25. Mark 8:24. Msgr. Ricardo Urioste made this point in an interview with author, San Salvador, February 4, 1991 and in "Monseñor Romero, auténtico mártir," *ECA* no. 497 (March 1990), p. 151.

26. Msgr. Oscar Romero to Cardinal Baggio, May 21, 1978, ACAPSJ.

27. U.S. embassy/State Department cable, "Church-State Tension Deepens," March 16, 1977. On file at the National Security Archive, Washington, D.C.

28. Romero to Pope John Paul II, cited in Brockman, *Romero: A Life*, p. 145.

29. Pedraz, interview, December 17, 1990.

30. Romero, Homily of July 29, 1979, *La voz de los sin voz: La palabra viva de Monseñor Romero*, introduction, commentaries, and selection of texts by J. Sobrino, I. Martín-Baró, and R. Cardenal (San Salvador: UCA Editores, 1980), p. 453.

31. Entry of June 25, 1978, *Monseñor Oscar Arnulfo Romero: Su Diario* (Arzobispado de San Salvador, 1990), p. 55.

32. Communiqué cited retrospectively in *Diario de Hoy*, May 13, 1977.

33. Account in Bonner, *Weakness and Deceit*, p. 103 and *Catholic Herald*, June 10, 1977.

34. "Narración de la visita del Señor Arzobispo y del Provincial SJ al cuartel de la Guardia Nacional," May 6, 1977, ACAPSJ; Carlos Cabarrús, interview with author, San Salvador, January 18, 1991; and Jerez, interview, February 18, 1991.

35. In the introduction to the revised edition of *A Theology of Liberation*, Gutiérrez poses "the great pastoral, and therefore theological, question: How is it possible to tell the poor, who are forced to live in conditions that embody a denial of love, that God loves them?" p. xxxiv.

36. Delgado, *Oscar A. Romero, Biografía*, p. 90.

37. Boletín no. 15, "Sobre el asesinato perpetrado en el Padre Alfonso Navarro O.," May 11, 1977, in *ECA* nos. 342–43 (April–May 1977), p. 339.

38. Delgado, *Oscar A. Romero, Biografía*, p. 77.

39. Salvador Carranza, account reproduced in Lernoux, *Cry of the People*, p. 61, Carranza, interview, January 25, 1991.

40. "Homilia de Monseñor Oscar A. Romero en Aguilares, 19 junio 1977," *ECA* no. 344 (June 1977), pp. 431–33.

41. Sobrino, "Mi recuerdo de Monseñor Romero" p. 35.

42. Cited in ibid., p. 64.

43. Reprinted as a single document, "Los jesuitas ante el pueblo salvadoreño," *ECA* no. 344 (June 1977), pp. 434–50.

44. Parte de Guerra, no. 5, Unión Guerrera Blanca, June 21, 1977, ACAPSJ.

45. Open letter from the Jesuit provincial, June 22, 1977, ACAPSJ.

46. U.S. Congress, House Committee on International Relations,

Subcommittee on International Organizations, *Religious Persecution in El Salvador,* July 21 and 29 1977, (Washington, D.C.: U.S. Government Printing Office, 1977) p. 17. The position of ambassador would be filled by Frank Devine.

47. Simon E. Smith, "From *Krisis* to *Kairos:* Anatomy of a Response," manuscript in ACAPSJ. This account also draws on James L. Connor, "El Salvador's Agony and U.S. Policies," *America,* April 26, 1980.

48. Meetings were held on May 23 and on June 24 and 27, ACAPSJ.

49. Jerez, interview, February 18, 1991.

50. Memo from Luis Achaerandio to Ignacio Martín-Baró, undated, ACAPSJ; former member of the Salvadoran National Guard, interview with author, Mexico City, January 5, 1991.

51. Miguel Francisco Estrada, interview with author, San Salvador, March 11, 1991. "Although it is impossible to say that the Government is behind the UGB," reads a U.S. embassy cable dated June 29, 1977, "it is hard not to see some connection, if only a mutuality of interests and enemies." On file at the National Security Archive, Washington, D.C.

52. Msgr. Freddy Delgado, interview with author, San Salvador, January 31, 1991. In 1988, Freddy Delgado published a pamphlet, *La Iglesia Popular nace en El Salvador* (no publisher indicated), that offers a wildly inaccurate account of the "Popular Church's" fomenting of the Salvadoran revolution. The Jesuits feature prominently.

53. Msgr. Romeo Továr Astorga, interview with author, Zacoteluca, April 12, 1991; Msgr. René Revelo Contreras, interview with author, Santa Ana, December 18, 1990.

54. The book was Mons. Oscar A. Romero, Mons. Arturo Rivera Damas, Ignacio Ellacuría, Jon Sobrino, Tomás R. Campos, *Iglesia de los pobres y organizaciones populares* (San Salvador: UCA Editores, 1978). The anecdote was related by Ellacuría in "La Iglesia y la UCA en el golpe del 15 de octubre de 1979," a talk given on October 15, 1989, transcript in *Presencia,* (San Salvador, January 1990), p. 133.

55. Azcue left a memoir of his relationship with Romero in *Noticias SJ* (April 1980), pp. v–vii, ACAPSJ.

56. Msgr. Romero to César Jerez, August 17, 1977, ACAPSJ.

57. A complicated operation, devised by Segundo Montes, brought them into El Salvador from Honduras through one of the quietest border posts, but at the busiest hour of a busy holiday in August 1978. Once back in the country the two Jesuits laid low for a while. Their first "public" appearance was at a reception at the U.S. embassy. General Romero's vice-president could barely conceal his surprise—"Good heavens, are you two here?" he asked. De Sebastián, interview, January 21, 1992.

58. Jerez, interview, February 18, 1991.

59. Sobrino, interview, March 7, 1991. The Pastoral Letters can be found in Romero, *La voz de los sin voz* and in English in Archbishop Romero, *Voice of the Voiceless,* Introductory Essays by Jon Sobrino and Ignacio Martín-Baró (Maryknoll, N.Y.: Orbis Books, 1985). The Second Pastoral Letter was the Romero's first as archbishop.

60. "Reunión del 29 de abril 1978 sobre la Carta Pastoral," ACAPSJ.

61. Romero, "The Church and Popular Political Organizations," *Voice of the Voiceless,* pp. 100, 109 & 110.

62. This description is derived from interviews with Urioste, Estrada, Sobrino, Héctor Dada, and Pepe Simán.

63. Dada, interview, January 9, 1991.

64. Simán, interview, February 24, 1991.

65. Cited by Brockman, *Romero: A Life,* p. 187.

66. Urioste, "Monseñor Romero, auténtico mártir," p. 150.

67. "La UCA ante el doctorado concedido a Monseñor Romero," *ECA* no. 437, March 1985, p. 168.

68. Italo López Vallecillos, under the pseudonym of Rodolfo R. Campos, as editor of the compilation of radio broadcasts made in 1979, *El Salvador: Entre el terror y la esperanza* (San Salvador: UCA Editores, 1982), p. 6.

69. UCA faculty member, interview with author, San José, Costa Rica, February 25, 1991.

70. Salvador Samayoa, interviews with author, Mexico and San Salvador, January 7, 1991 and April 3, 1992.

71. Fernando Ascoli, interview with author, San Salvador, April 4, 1991; Antonio Cardenal, interview, March 1991; and Enríquez, interview, June 4, 1991.

72. Mario Lungo, interview with author, San José, Costa Rica, February 24, 1991.

73. Dada, interview, January 9, 1991; Zamora, interview, April 12, 1991; Guillermo Galván, interview with author, San José, Costa Rica, February 27, 1991; Francisco Andrés Escobar, interview with author, San Salvador, April 3, 1991; Mario Aguiñada Carranza, interview with author, San Salvador, April 11, 1991.

74. César Valle and Salvador Viles were aligned with the FMLN and killed by the army; Lt. Col. Napoleón Lazo is believed to have fallen as a victim of internal corruption within the air force; PCN leader Rafael Rodríguez González was killed by death squads during the right-wing realignment around the formation of ARENA; Marianela García Villa, president of the nongovernmental Commission on Human Rights, was killed on Guazapa during an army ambush in 1983.

75. Introduced in November 1977, the law was framed within a doctrine of national security that effectively legalized repression of all those who raised their voices in criticism of the government.

76. Romero, "The Church's Mission amid the National Crisis," *Voice of the Voiceless,* p. 120.

77. Cited in "La OEA en la conspiración internacional," *El Salvador: Entre el terror y la esperanza,* p. 100.

78. "Terror en El Salvador," *ECA* nos. 363–64 (January–February 1979), p. 363.

79. Mario Rosenthal, "Vice-Rector de Sebastián Denies UCA Coup Involvement," *El Salvador News Gazette,* November 18–24, 1979.

80. "La UCA y el Diálogo Nacional," *ECA* no. 368 (June 1979), p. 381.

81. Arnson, *El Salvador: A Revolution confronts the United States,* p. 39.

82. Salvadoran colonel, interview with author, San Salvador, March 15, 1991.

83. Col. Román Barrera, interview with author, San Salvador, October 17, 1991.

84. Adolfo Arnoldo Majano Ramos, "El golpe de Estado de 1979; Una opportunidad perdida" (manuscript, Fundación Friedrich Ebert, San José, Costa Rica, May 18, 1989), p. 10.

85. For a detailed account of Guerra y Guerra's background and involvement in the coup, see Bonner, *Weakness and Deceit,* p. 148ff.

86. Capt. Francisco Emilio Mena Sandoval, *Del Ejército Nacional al Ejército Guerrillero* (Ediciones Arcoiris, 1991), p. 163.

87. Salvadoran officer, interview, March 15, 1991.

88. Francisco Mena Sandoval, interview with author, Mexico City, January 5, 1991.

89. De Sebastián, interview, January 21, 1992.

90. Interviewed by Rosenthal, "Vice-Rector de Sebastián Denies . . ." .

91. Ellacuría, "La iglesia y la UCA en el golpe," p. 133.

92. Romero, "The Church's Mission amid the National Crisis," *Voice of the Voiceless,* pp. 114–61.

93. Entry of October 7, 1979, *Monseñor Romero: Su diario,* p. 297.

94. Mena Sandoval, *Del Ejército Nacional al Ejército Guerrillero,* p. 178.

95. Mena Sandoval, interview, January 5, 1991.

96. Mayorga, interview, May 1, 1991.

97. Entry of October 10, 1979, *Monseñor Romero: Su diario,* p. 298.

98. Mayorga, "Recuerdo de diez Quijotes," p. 11.

99. Mayorga, interview, May 1, 1991.

100. De Sebastián, interview, January 21, 1992.

101. "Proclama de la Fuerza Armada de El Salvador," October 15, 1979, in *ECA* nos. 372–73 (October–November 1979), p. 1167.

102. Mayorga, interview, May 1, 1991; Entry of October 17, 1979, *Monseñor Romero: Su diario,* p. 305.

103. *Diario de Occidente,* October 27, 1979.

104. "Informe sobre los últimos acontecimientos de El Salvador," October 24, 1979, ACAPSJ.

105. Mayorga, interview, May 1, 1991.

106. Ibid.

CHAPTER 5

1. "Pronunciamiento del Consejo Superior Universitario de la Universidad Centroamericana José Simeón Cañas," November 14, 1979, *ECA* nos. 372–73 (October–November 1979), p. 862.

2. *Diario Latino,* November 5, 1979.

3. César Jerez, "Nota para Monseñor Romero," October 25, 1979, ACAPSJ.

4. De Sebastián, interview, January 21, 1992.

5. Romero, Homily of October 21, 1979, *La voz de los sin voz,* pp. 380–81.

6. De Sebastián, interview, January 21, 1992.

7. Cited in Bonner, *Weakness and Deceit,* p. 181.

8. In a press conference at the National University, reported in *El Salvador: entre el terror y la esperanza,* p. 680.

9. Gen. José Guillermo García, interviewed in Max G. Manwaring and Court Prisk, *El Salvador at War: An Oral History* (Washington, D.C.: National Defense University Press, 1988), p. 31.

10. Statements released by the different political organizations after October 15, 1979 reprinted in *ECA* nos. 372–73, October–November 1979, pp. 1022–30.

11. Accounts of some of these visits can be found in María López Vigil, *Piezas para un retrato* (San Salvador: UCA Editores, 1993), pp. 306ff. Among those who differed from Romero and the UCA Jesuits was César Jerez.

12. "El carácter de los comentarios de la 'AX,' " *El Salvador: Entre el terror y la esperanza,* November 23, 1979, p. 665.

13. U.S. embassy/State Department cable, October 15, 1979, no. 239 in the National Security Archives' *El Salvador: The Making of U.S. Policy,*

1977–1984 (Alexandria, Va.: Chadwyck Healey Inc., 1989); letter to the author from Ambassador Frank Devine, June 9, 1991.

14. Bonner, *Weakness and Deceit,* p. 164.

15. "El gabinete de gobierno . . . se dirigen a las Fuerzas Armadas por intermedio de COPEFA," December 7, 1979, in *ECA* nos. 375–76 (January–February 1980), p. 117.

16. Ungo, interview, December 15, 1990.

17. Rodolfo Cardenal, interview, April 10, 1991; de Sebastián, interview, January 21, 1992.

18. Entry of January 2, 1980, *Monseñor Romero: Su diario,* p. 373.

19. "1979: El fracaso de dos modelos," Editorial, *ECA* no. 374 (December 1979), pp. 1039, 1042.

20. "La represión, criterio de la verdad," Editorial, *ECA* no. 379 (May 1980), p. 415.

21. Cited in Carolyn Forché, "The Road to Reaction in El Salvador," *The Nation,* June 1980.

22. "En busca de un nuevo proyecto nacional," Editorial, *ECA* nos. 377–378 (March–April 1980), p. 155; FDR platform, ibid., p. 346. The FDR was a union of the CRM (discussed later in this chapter) and the short-lived Democratic Front, which was made up of former government officials, civilian political groups, trade unions, and professional organizations, and existed in its own right only for a week. De Sebastián was the Jesuit most closely involved with these developments.

23. "Manifiesto del Partido Comunista de El Salvador, de las FPL y de las FARN," *ECA* nos. 375–76 (January–February 1980), p. 133.

24. Francisco Andrés Escobar, "En la línea de la muerte," ibid., pp. 21ff.

25. Romero, Homily of January 13, 1980, *La voz de los sin voz,* p. 398.

26. The full English text of the letter is cited by James Brockman, "Archbishop Romero, the United States and El Salvador," *America,* March 24, 1990.

27. Jerez, interview, February 18, 1991.

28. Entry of February 19, 1980, *Monseñor Romero: Su diario,* p. 432.

29. "Ametrallan residencia de Jesuitas," February 16, 1980, ACAPSJ.

30. The ambassador was Murat Williams, the incident is reported in LaFeber, *Inevitable Revolutions,* p. 252.

31. Ellacuría, "La Iglesia y la UCA en el golpe," p. 135.

32. Cited in Brockman, "Archbishop Romero, the United States and El Salvador."

33. Robert White, interview with author, Washington, D.C., May 6,

1991; and "Rector de la UCA explica que preparó homilías," *Prensa Gráfica,* May 12, 1980. White laughed as he remembered how Ellacuría considered him, "quite well educated for an American."

34. U.S. Congress, House Committee on Appropriations, Subcommittee on Foreign Operations, *Foreign Assistance and Related Programs Appropriations for 1981,* March 25, 1980, (Washington, D.C.: U.S. Government Printing Office, 1980) pp. 323ff. See also account of these hearings in Cynthia J. Arnson, *Crossroads: Congress, the President and Central America* (University Press, Pennsylvania: Pennsylvania State University Press, 1993), pp. 41–44.

35. Senators Tom Harkin and Robert Drinan respectively, *Congressional Record,* March 25, 1980, p. S6391.

36. Sobrino, "Mi recuerdo de Monseñor Romero," p. 49; Sobrino, interview, March 7, 1991.

37. "Policia Nacional asalta recinto Universidad Católica y asesina estudiante en San Salvador," March 22, 1980, ACAPSJ.

38. Ellacuría's participation in the "writing" of this homily became a source of controversy through his indiscretion with the "journalist" from *Ecclesia* mentioned earlier in this chapter. Ellacuría would formally explain that there had been no interview in the *Prensa Gráfica* of May 13, 1980. He did not write the homily. Interviews, Estrada and Urioste, February 6 and 4, 1991.

39. Romero, Homily of March 23, 1980, *La voz de los sin voz,* p. 291.

40. Testimonies of John Bushnell, deputy assistant secretary of state for inter-American affairs and Franklin Kramer, deputy assistant secretary for defense, Cable from Ambassador White and Clerk's summary of Embassy cables all in *Foreign Assistance and Related Appropriations for 1981,* pp. 331, 339, 426, and 427, respectively. The private assessment of Bushnell is cited in Arnson, *Crossroads,* p. 43.

41. "Carta de renuncia de Héctor Dada Hirezi," in *ECA* nos. 377–378 (March–April 1980), p. 377.

42. Ellacuría, "La Iglesia y la UCA en el golpe," p. 138.

43. "La represión, criterio de la verdad," p. 416.

44. See "The American Institute for Free Labor Development as a CIA Front," Walter Poelchau, ed., *White Paper Whitewash: Interviews with Philip Agee on the CIA and El Salvador* (New York: Deep Cover Books, 1981), pp. 42ff.

45. "1980: Conflicto, agonia y esperanza," Editorial, *ECA* no. 386 (December 1980), p. 1126.

46. Some were sent out of the country to study; others were subjected to attacks. Mena Sandoval was almost killed in an assault on his car in April, a few days after a questionable accident befell an airplane in which Majano

was supposed to be traveling. Mena Sandoval, Interview, January 5, 1991 and "Crónica del mes de abril 1980," *ECA* no. 379 (May 1980), p. 507.

47. White, interview, May 6, 1991.

48. See the Lawyers Committee for Human Rights report, "A Decade of Failed Promises: The Investigation of Archbishop Romero's Murder" (New York, March 1990), p. 8. In March 1993 the United Nations–appointed Truth Commission confirmed that D'Aubuisson "gave the order to assassinate the archbishop." La Comisión de la verdad para El Salvador, "De la locura a la esperanza: La guerra de 12 años en El Salvador," (New York: United Nations, 1993), p. 132. Future references to "Truth Commission Report." The U.S. documents declassified in November 1993 contained many reports of D'Aubuisson's responsibility for the Romero assassination.

49. Ricardo Alejandro Fiallos, interview with author, Mexico City, January 7, 1991.

50. Ellacuría, "La Iglesia y la UCA en el golpe," p. 138.

51. The FPL, ERP, RN, PCS, and PRTC (the Central American Workers' Revolutionary Party, founded in 1976 as a splinter group from the ERP that was, in its regional ambitions, distinct from the RN) presented a united manifesto in October 1980.

52. De Sebastián, interview, January 21, 1991.

53. Files of the ACAPSJ.

54. Jesuit communiqué, October 24, 1980, ACAPSJ; *El Mundo,* October 27, 1980.

55. Mena Sandoval, interview, January 5, 1991; Fiallos, interview, January 7, 1991; Christa Beneke, interview with author, San Salvador, March 26, 1993.

56. See, for example, "Communicado del Mayor Roberto D'Aubuisson," in *ECA* no. 386 (December 1980), p. 1212.

57. Address by Ronald Reagan to the Chicago Council on Foreign Relations, March 17, 1990, from "Reagan for President" Press Pack.

58. "Aparece cadáver del señor Alvarez Córdova," *Prensa Gráfica,* November 29, 1980.

59. See Ana Carrigan, *Salvador Witness: The Life and Calling of Jean Donovan* (New York: Simon & Schuster, 1984) for a biography of Donovan and a detailed account of the circumstances surrounding the women's killing.

60. Christopher Dickey, "Four U.S. Catholics Killed in El Salvador," *Washington Post,* December 5, 1980.

61. Rep. William H. Brodhead, *Congressional Record,* December 5, 1980, p. H32830.

62. Cited in Bonner, *Weakness and Deceit,* p. 224.

63. "1980: Conflicto, agonia y esperanza," p. 1132.

64. Statement of January 14, 1981, *Department of State Bulletin* (Washington, D.C., February 1981), p. 69.

65. U.S. embassy/State Department cable, January 18, 1981, on file at the National Security Archive, Washington, D.C.

66. U.S. embassy/State Department cable, February 18, 1981, no. 1363, NSA's *El Salvador: The Making of U.S. Policy.*

67. Testimony of Hon. Robert E. White, U.S. Congress, House Committee on Foreign Affairs, Subcommittee on Inter-American Affairs, *U.S. Policy Toward El Salvador,* March 11, 1981 (Washington, D.C.: U.S. Government Printing Office, 1981), p. 133.

68. Cited by Lou Cannon, *President Reagan: The Role of a Lifetime* (New York: Simon & Schuster, 1991), p. 344.

69. News Conference of January 28, 1981, *Department of State Bulletin* (Washington, D.C., February 1981) p. 3.

70. Secretary Haig discusses Foreign Assistance, February 27, 1981, *Department of State Bulletin* (Washington, D.C., April 1981), p. 21.

71. Salvadoran colonel, interview, March 15, 1991.

72. *Prensa Gráfica,* March 30, 1981.

73. The white paper is reproduced in Poelchau, *White Paper Whitewash,* pp. A1–A87.

74. *Los Angeles Times,* March 17, 1981; *Nation,* March 28, 1991; *Washington Post,* June 9, 1981; and *Wall Street Journal,* June 8, 1991.

75. Jeanne Kirkpatrick, "Dictatorships and Double Standards," *Commentary* 68, no. 5 (November 1979), pp. 34–45.

76. In a discussion with James Cheek and Tom Quigley, "Cauldron in Central America: What Keeps the Fire Burning," *New York Times,* December 7, 1980. Kirkpatrick in the *Tampa Tribune,* December 25, 1980, and Haig's statement before the House Committee on Foreign Affairs, March 18, 1981, were cited in the Lawyers Committee for Human Rights, "Justice in El Salvador: A Case Study" (New York, July 1982), as reprinted in the *Congressional Record,* July 21, 1982, p. 17299.

77. Kirkpatrick, "Dictatorships and Double Standards," p. 40.

78. "Quality of Life in the Americas: Report of a U.S. Presidential Mission for the Western Hemisphere," *Department of State Bulletin* (Washington, D.C., December 8, 1969), p. 504.

79. Committee of Santa Fé, Lewis Tambs, ed., "A New Inter-American Policy for the Eighties" (Council for Inter-American Security, Inc., Washington, D.C., 1980), p. 20.

80. Testimony of Capt. Ricardo Fiallos. U.S. Congress, House Committee on Appropriations, Subcommittee on Foreign Operations. *Foreign*

Assistance and Related Programs Appropriations for F.Y. 1982 April 29, 1981 (Washington, D.C.: U.S. Government Printing Office, 1981), p. 361.

81. See biographical portraits of López and Moreno, in Cardenal, "Ser jesuita hoy en El Salvador," pp. 1030—35.

82. Luis de Sebastián left El Salvador in December 1980. From a base in Barcelona he would aid the FDR in its diplomatic contacts until 1983.

83. "El volcán jesuita," *ABC,* March 28, 1982.

84. Sobrino, interview, March 7, 1991.

85. "Un proceso de mediación para El Salvador," Editorial, *ECA* nos. 387–388 (January–February 1981), p. 3.

86. Ellacuría, "Solución política o solución militar para El Salvador?" *ECA* nos. 390–91, April–May 1981, pp. 295–324.

87. José Napoleón Duarte, *My Story* (New York: G.P. Putnam's Sons, 1986), p. 170.

88. "La declaración conjunta mexicano-francesa sobre El Salvador," *ECA* no. 395, September 1981, pp. 845–66.

89. "Texto de la declaración franco-mexicana" and "Discurso de rechazo del Ing. Duarte," ibid., p. 916.

90. Col. John Waghelstein, interviewed in Manwaring and Prisk, *El Salvador at War,* p. 170.

91. William Chislett, "Taming the Troops of El Salvador," *Financial Times,* June 13, 1981.

92. Cited in Arnson, *Crossroads,* p. 86.

93. See Americas Watch, "The Massacre at Mozote: The Need to Remember" (New York, March 4, 1992) and Mark Danner, "The Truth of El Mozote," *New Yorker,* December 6, 1993, for full accounts of the controversy.

94. U.S. Congress, House Committee on Foreign Affairs, Subcommittee on Inter-American Affairs, *Presidential Certification on El Salvador,* February 2, 23, and 25, March 2, 1982 (Washington, D.C.: U.S. Government Printing Office, 1982), p. 43.

95. Executive Summary, no. 7, "Report of the El Salvador Military Strategy Assistance Team," San Salvador, September 12 to November 8, 1981, p. iv. The "Woerner Report" documented a secret mission to study Salvadoran military capabilities and the future role for U.S. security assistance. Critical of the Salvadoran armed forces for their links to violence and death squads, the report had extremely limited distribution even within the Pentagon and was only (partially) declassified in early 1993. On file, National Security Archive, Washington, D.C.

96. Segundo Montes, "Las elecciones y el poder en El Salvador," *ECA* nos. 399–400 (January–February 1982), p. 63.

97. Rep. Jim Wright, *Congressional Record*, March 29, 1982, p. H5667.

98. Cited in Centro Universitario de Documentación e Información, "Las elecciones de 1982. Realidad detrás de las apariencias," *ECA* nos. 403–4 (May–June 1982), p. 579.

99. "Report of a delegation led by Senator Nancy Kassebaum," in Robert S. Leiken and Barry Rubin, eds., *The Central American Crisis Reader* (New York: Summit Books, 1987), p. 428.

100. The UCA's thesis combined three factors: the number of polling urns available, the hours they were open, and the time it took to vote. "Las elecciones y la unidad nacional: Diez tesis críticas," Editorial, *ECA* no. 402 (April 1982), p. 233ff.; "Las elecciones de 1982. Realidades detrás de las apariencias," pp. 573ff.

101. Deane Hinton, interviewed in Manwaring and Prisk, *El Salvador at War,* p. 183.

102. Bonner, *Weakness and Deceit*, p. 305.

103. Hinton, interviewed in Manwaring and Prisk, *El Salvador at War,* p. 111.

104. "Deane Hinton, San Salvador, 24 de junio 1982," AIE.

105. U.S. embassy/State Department cable, "Jesuit Publication Claims Electoral Fraud," June 9, 1982, no. 03215, NSA's *The Making of U.S. Policy.*

106. Hugh Montgomery to Ambassador Eagleberger, "Allegations of Election Irregularities in El Salvador," June 11, 1982, on file at the National Security Archive, Washington, D.C.

107. The original version is cited in Arnson, *Crossroads,* p. 104. For the record: "Address before the American Chamber of Commerce in San Salvador," October 29, 1982, *Department of State Bulletin* (Washington, D.C., December 1982), p. 68.

108. Lawyers Committee for Human Rights, "Chronology of the Investigation and Prosecution of those Responsible for Killing Four U.S. Churchwomen in El Salvador" (New York, January 1984) pp. 6–11.

109. Cited in Arnson, *Crossroads,* p. 103.

110. Bernard Weinraub, *New York Times,* November 10, 1982.

111. President Reagan, "Central America: Defending Our Vital Interests," address before a joint session of Congress, April 27, 1983, *Department of State Bulletin* (Washington, D.C., June 1983), pp. 1–5.

CHAPTER 6

1. Rep. Joe Moakley, *Congressional Record,* May 22, 1990, p. H2712.

2. Congressional aide, interview with author, Washington, D.C., April 24, 1991.

3. *The Report of the President's National Bipartisan Commission on Central America* (New York, 1984). The Commission took its name from its chairman, Henry Kissinger. See Chapter 8 for a more detailed account of these developments.

4. The figure of $1,019,850,000 includes the monies appropriated for Fiscal Year 1990. K. Larry Storrs, "El Salvador Highlights, 1960–1990" (CRS Report, Washington, D.C., March 13, 1990), p. 12.

5. See Tom Gibb and Frank Smyth, "El Salvador: Is Peace Possible?" Washington Office on Latin America (Washington, D.C., April 1991).

6. See Chapter 10 for a fuller account of the efforts made in favor of negotiation during the 1980s. The Esquipulas II agreements called for cease-fires, an end to outside support for regional insurgencies, democratization, and reconciliation.

7. ONUSAL, "The United Nations' Role in the Central American Peace Process," Fact Sheet No. 2 (New York: U.N. Department of Public Information, July 1991).

8. Not discussed with de Soto at this Montreal meeting was the FMLN's plan for a second wave of the offensive to be launched on December 11 in order to strengthen their position within the brief negotiations they then envisaged. Ana Guadalupe Martínez, interview with author, San Salvador April 4, 1992.

9. "Declaración de San Isidro Coronado," *ECA* nos. 495–96 (January–February 1990), p. 122. A full account of the negotiations is given by Terry Lynn Karl, "El Salvador's Negotiated Revolution," *Foreign Affairs,* Spring 1992, pp. 147–64.

10. U.S. Congress, House Committee on Foreign Affairs, Subcommittees on Human Rights and International Organizations and on Western Hemispheric Affairs, *El Salvador at the Crossroads: Peace or Another Decade of War,* January 24 and 31 and February 6, 1990 (Washington, D.C.: U.S. Government Printing Office) p. 2.

11. U.S. Congress, House Committee on Foreign Affairs, Hearing before the Subcommittee on Western Hemispheric Affairs, August 1, 1984 (Washington, D.C.: U.S. Government Printing Office, 1984), p. 23.

12. Before Senate Armed Services Committee c. Feb 1. Cited U.S. Congress, House Committee on Appropriations, Subcommittee on Foreign Operations, Export Financing and Related Operations, FY91 Hearings (Washington, D.C.: U.S. Government Printing Office, 1991), p. 424.

13. Cited in U.S. Congress, Senate Committee on Appropriations, Foreign Operations, Export Financing and Related Programs Appropriations, FY91 Hearings, February 8, 1990 (Washington, D.C.: U.S. Government Printing Office, 1990), p. 10.

14. Joel Millman, "El Salvador's Army: A Force unto Itself," *New York Times Magazine,* December 10, 1989.

15. Col. Lyman C. Duryea, transcript of interview with Lt. Col. Emil R. Bedard and Lt. Col. L. R. Vasquez on March 4, 1986, "Senior Officers Oral History Program" (Project 86–9, U.S. Army Military History Institute, Carlisle Barracks, Pa.), p. 99. "Can we, should we, are we trying to mitigate that corruption?" he was asked. His answer: "I think we can, I think we should, but we're not." p. 73.

16. Millman, "El Salvador's Army."

17. Hearings before the Senate Committee on Appropriations, FY91, p. 26. Cynthia Arnson has noted that Aronson's November 17 statement "marked the first time a U.S. official had explicitly gone on record favoring a settlement to the war through political negotiations." *Crossroads,* p. 248.

18. Joe Moakley, interview with author, Washington, D.C., February 6, 1992.

19. Congressional aide, interview, May 2, 1991; see also John M. Barry, *The Ambition and the Power: A True Story of Washington* (Harmondsworth, England: Penguin Books, 1989), pp. 75ff.

20. Moakley, interview, February 6, 1992.

21. Defense Department memorandum for Mr. Wolfowitz from Peter Fiory, February 9, 1990. U.S. document declassified November 1993, Washington, D.C. This account of the delegation's visit to El Salvador is based on interviews with Members and task force staff conducted in Washington, D.C., in April and May 1991.

22. U.S. Congress, House Committee on Foreign Affairs, Subcommittee on Inter-American Affairs, *U.S. Policy toward El Salvador,* March 5 and 11, 1981 (Washington, D.C.: U.S. Government Printing Office, 1981), pp. 191ff.

23. Extrajudicial confessions of Espinoza and Avalos Vargas, translation included as Appendix B in the task force's "Interim Report."

24. Ana Arana, "Salvador Officers Met just Before Jesuit Massacre," *Baltimore Sun,* February 4, 1990.

25. Joe Moakley, interview with author, Washington, D.C., May 8, 1991.

26. Ibid.

27. Congressional aide, interview with author, Washington, D.C., May 6, 1991.

28. Congressional aide, interview with author, Washington, D.C., May 6, 1991.

29. Congressional aide, interview with author, Washington, D.C., April 26, 1991.

30. Statement made by Rev. Paul S. Tipton SJ on meeting with President Alfredo Cristiani, J. W. Marriott Hotel, Washington, D.C., February 2, 1990.

31. The Reverends Joseph A. O'Hare, J. Donald Monan, Joseph A. Sellinger, Nicholas Rashford, James C. Carter, respectively.

32. Congressional aide, interview, May 6, 1991.

33. "Statement of the Honorable Joe Moakley on behalf of the U.S. Congressional Delegation," Camino Real Hotel, San Salvador, February 14, 1990.

34. Visits to the Atlacatl Battalion and interviews with its officers, Sitio del Niño, La Libertad, El Salvador, June 20, 1990 and February 5, 1991.

35. The other four Battalions were named Arce, Atonal, Belloso, and Bracamonte.

36. Presentation of Atlacatl to author and film crew, June 20, 1990.

37. See the U.S. Congress Arms Control and Foreign Policy Caucus staff memorandum, "The Atlacatl Battalion and Alleged Human Rights Abuses" (Washington, D.C., April 25, 1990).

38. Waghelstein, interviewed in Manwaring and Prisk, *El Salvador at War,* p. 235.

39. Buckland, transcript of U.S. Department of Justice interview, November 19, 1990.

40. Sam Dillon, "Troops Stall and Kill Rebels' Civilian Allies," *Miami Herald,* September 9, 1984.

41. Antonio Cardenal, interview, March 12, 1991; Cardenal was killed on April 11, 1991.

42. U.S. colonel, interview with author, Washington, D.C., February 11, 1992.

43. "Nightline," ABC Television, February 13, 1985, cited in Americas Watch, *Draining the Sea* (New York, March 1985), pp. 16–17.

44. The title of a handwritten Defense Department memo to the Deputy Assistant Secretary Nancy Dorn from "John" sets the tone with which Moakley's insistent requests were greeted: "Old Congressmen never die, they don't even fade away," March 1, 1990. U.S. document declassified November 1993, Washington, D.C.

45. Appendix A to the Moakley task force, "Interim Report," contains documents provided by the Pentagon in response to queries about U.S. training of the Atlacatl and the individuals implicated in the Jesuit killings.

46. Edited transcript of interview of Maj. Samuel Ramirez, 101st Airborne, Ft. Campbell, Kentucky by Special Agents Richard C. Staver and Paul Cully, December 20, 1990, p. 6.

47. Pentagon documents in Moakley task force, "Interim Report."

48. U.S. official, interview, August 12, 1991.

49. Moakley task force, "Interim Report," Executive Summary, pp. 6ff. Defense Department cables released to Americas Watch cite sources stating that Benavides "would have been the most unlikely person to have directed the murders. He is not an aggressive individual and no one would have thought that he would have been the intellectual author" and that "there is a belief in some quarters of the ESAF officer corps that Colonel [Benavides] is not the only high-ranking officer who should be implicated in the Jesuit killings . . . some officers believe someone in the ESAF High Command was involved." Parts 9 and 10 in "Jesuit Series," January 25 and 29, 1990. A memo on the "Jesuit Murder Investigation" to Richard Chidester from Arthur Sedillo, the DEA investigator brought down from Mexico to assist the embassy, dated February 28, 1990 and released to the Lawyers Committee, refers to the fact that while in El Salvador Sedillo "kept mentioning the possibility of a conspiracy beyond the indicted defendants."

50. Douglas Farah, "Colonel Charged in Jesuit Killing Lives in Luxury," *Washington Post,* February 22, 1990;

51. "I'm not confident that he's going to be convicted," Cristiani had said of Benavides; "I'd be sad if he was acquitted because I think he is guilty based on the investigation." Lee Hockstader, "Cristiani: Colonel May Be Acquitted," *Washington Post,* March 24, 1990.

52. Maggi Popkin, interview with author, San Salvador, January 10, 1991.

53. Congressional aide, interview with author, Washington, D.C., May 21, 1991; Gen. Rafael Villamariona, interview with author, Ilopango Air Base, April 3, 1991.

54. Moakley task force, "Interim Report," p. 31.

55. Defense Department memo, "Rep. Moakley legislative action." March 7, 1990, U.S. document declassified November 1993, Washington, D.C.

56. Hearings before the Senate Committee on Appropriations, FY91, May 1, 1990, pp. 351ff.

57. U.S. official, interview, August 12, 1991.

58. United Nations Press Release following Geneva meeting presided over by the secretary-general, New York April 4, 1990.

59. These governments, the Geneva Accord stated, were those "which may contribute to the success of the process through their advice and support." Gradually, as their role in the negotiating process developed, the governments of Colombia, Mexico, Venezuela, and Spain would become known as the "Group of Friends."

60. *Congressional Record,* February 8, 1990, p. S1159.

61. Rep. Bud Shuster, cited by John Felton, "Carrots-and-Sticks Policy Yields Possible Truce on the Hill," *Congressional Quarterly,* May 5, 1990, p. 1372.

62. Chris Norton, "Troublesome Priests," *Village Voice,* May 22, 1990.

63. Both remarks cited in Report from the Lawyers Committee for Human Rights to U.S. Jesuit Conference, et al., "Status of Jesuit Murder Investigation in El Salvador" (New York, July 27, 1990), p. 6.

64. Transcript of "The Jesuit Murders," CBS News "60 Minutes," April 22, 1990.

65. Anthony Lewis, "Paying for Murder," *New York Times,* April 24, 1990.

66. "Officiales jóvenes 'Domingo Monterrosa vive,' Pronunciamiento, May 3, 1990." *ECA* nos. 468–99 (April–May 1990), pp. 377–80. Monterrosa was killed in 1984 by the FMLN.

67. One official said that he illustrated "the fundamental weakness of the Salvadoran judicial system." Robert Pear, "Salvador Accused on Jesuit Inquiry," *New York Times,* May 1, 1991.

68. Judge Ricardo Zamora, interview with author, San Salvador, August 20, 1991.

69. Supreme Court Press Release, May 4, 1990; IEC and El Rescate, *The Jesuit Assassinations,* May–June 1990 chronology, pp. 79–109.

70. John Felton, "Collapse of Hill Negotiations Sets Stage for Aid Fight," *Congressional Quarterly,* May 19, 1990, p. 1571.

71. Moakley aide, interview with author, Washington, D.C., May 21, 1991.

72. U.S. Congress, Arms Control and Foreign Policy Caucus, "Barriers to Reform: A Profile of El Salvador's Military Leaders" (Washington, D.C., May 21, 1990).

73. Congressional aide, interview, April 26, 1991.

74. United Nations Press Release, "General Agenda and Schedule for Comprehensive Negotiation Process between Government of El Salvador and FMLN," May 21, 1990.

75. Debate in *Congressional Record* of May 22, 1990, pp. H2694ff.

76. Cited in John Felton, "House Fires a Warning Shot over El Salvador Policy," *Congressional Quarterly,* May 26, 1990, p. 1670.

77. Moakley, interview, May 8, 1991.

78. Statement by Congressman Joe Moakley on the Jesuits' case and the Salvadoran Negotiations, Washington, D.C., August 15, 1990.

79. Karl, "El Salvador's Negotiated Revolution," p. 156.

80. Congressional aide, interview, April 26, 1991.

81. U.S. embassy/State Department cables, August 13 & 14, 1990, U.S. documents declassified November 1993, Washington, D.C.

82. Lawyers Committee, "Status of the Jesuit Investigations," pp. 9–10.

83. Testimony, Sgt. Oscar Armando Solorzano Esquivel, August 24, 1990, *Court Record.*

84. Moakley statement, August 15, 1990.

85. U.S. embassy/State Department cable, August 21, 1990. The previous démarches had been made by Walker on July 6, and Dietrich on July 27. In between came a visit from Assistant Secretary Aronsen in which he had reiterated U.S. concern about lack of progress in the Jesuit case. U.S. documents declassified November 1993, Washington, D.C.

86. On November 12, 1989, Treasury Police had entered the Loyola Center, a Jesuit retreat house on the edge of a coffee plantation about a kilometer and a half above the UCA, with a young man in handcuffs who led them to a cache of arms left behind by the guerrillas. There was never any suggestion of the Jesuits' responsibility for the weapons, but U.S. officials had on several occasions (Walker to the task force in February 1990, for example) referred to their being "arms in the Jesuit residence," as if the Loyola Center were the UCA and the Jesuits responsible for them.

87. Senator Dennis DeConcini cited in Clifford Krauss, "Congress Resists El Salvador's Chief on Aid Cuts," *New York Times,* September 29, 1990.

88. Summary provided by author of memo during interview with author, Washington, D.C., May 5, 1991.

89. Jim McGovern, interview with author, Washington, D.C., November 8, 1990.

90. The account of this episode is based on interviews with Congressman Moakley, his aide Jim McGovern, and officials in the U.S. embassy in San Salvador, February, May, June, and August 1991; Memo to Hon. Joe Moakley from Jim McGovern, Bill Woodward, January 7, 1991; and Lawyers Committee, "The Jesuit Case a Year Later," pp. 2–5.

91. Judge Zamora, interview, August 20, 1991; declaration of Maj. Eric Buckland, September 28, 1990, *Court Record.*

92. Moakley aide, interview, November 8, 1990.

93. Statement of Rep. Joe Moakley, Washington, D.C., October 18, 1990.

94. Chidester, interview, February 8, 1991.

95. Defense Department memoranda for Mr. Wolfowitz, February 7 & 9, 1990; U.S. embassy/State Department cable, October 12, 1990. U.S.

documents declassified November 1993, Washington, D.C. The judge was actually given the relevant affidavits on October 16, two days before Moakley went public. Unfortunately for the embassy, he then denied having them because they had been given to him on a "confidential" basis and not entered in the court record.

96. Communicado Official, Juzgado Cuarto de lo Penal, San Salvador, October 22, 1990.

97. Maj. Eric Buckland, FBI Affidavit of January 11, *Court Record.* Interviewed by Judge Zamora in San Salvador in September, Buckland claimed that when he overheard Ellacuría's death being discussed by military officers on November 16, 1989, his poor Spanish led him to believe that, "God, we're at war with Korea." *Court Record.*

98. Maj. Eric Buckland, FBI affidavit of January 18, *Court Record.*

99. U.S. official, interview, August 12, 1991.

100. Bernard Aronson, "Peace in El Salvador," *Washington Post,* October 12, 1990.

101. Senators Christopher Dodd and Patrick Leahy, "Dear Colleague," Washington, D.C., October 17, 1990.

102. Public Law 101–513, November 5, 1990.

103. Remarks by Rep. Joe Moakley at Georgetown University, November 13, 1990.

104. Clifford Krauss, "Religion and Politics Become Fused in Congressman's District, and Heart," *New York Times,* August 23, 1990.

CHAPTER 7

1. Sobrino, "Querido Ellacu," p. 12.

2. Codina, "Ignacio Ellacuría: Teólogo y mártir," p. 265.

3. Antonio González, "Aproximación a la obra filosófica de Ignacio Ellacuría," *ECA* nos. 505–6 (November–December 1990), p. 981.

4. Philip Berryman, "Ignacio Ellacuría: An Appreciation," *America,* July 7, 1990.

5. Ellacuría, *Teología política* (San Salvador: Ediciones del Secretariado Social Interdiocesano, 1973), published in English as *Freedom Made Flesh: The Mission of Christ and His Church* (Maryknoll, N.Y.: Orbis Books, 1976); *Conversión de la Iglesia al Reino de Dios: Para anunciarlo y realizarlo en la historia* (San Salvador: UCA Editores, 1985).

6. Ellacuría, *Filosofía de la realidad histórica,* UCA Editores, 1990.

7. Plato, *The Republic and Other Works,* tr. B. Jowett (New York: Doubleday, 1989), bk. V, p. 166.

8. Ellacuría, "Filosofía, ¿para qué?" *ABRA,* no. 11, (1976), pp. 42–48.

9. Ellacuría, "El objeto de la filosofía," *ECA* nos. 396–97 (October–November 1981), p. 978.

10. Ellacuría, "Hacía una fundamentación filosófica del método teológico latinoamericano," *ECA* nos. 322–23 (August–September 1975), pp. 409–26.

11. Ibid., p. 419.

12. Ellacuría, "Función liberadora de la filosofía," *ECA* nos. 435–36 (January–February 1985), pp. 45–64.

13. Ibid., p. 46.

14. Ibid., p. 50.

15. Samayoa, interview, January 7, 1991.

16. González, "Aproximación a la obra filosófica," p. 980. González is paraphrasing Zubiri on Socrates.

17. Sobrino, "Companions of Jesus," p. 10.

18. Juan Hernández Pico, "Martirio en la UCA: Proceso al mundo," *RLT* no. 21 (September–December 1990), p. 241.

19. Ellacuría, *Notebooks,* June 5, 1984 to September 29, 1989, AIE. Earlier notebooks begun during Ellacuría's exile in 1981 appear to have been mislaid.

20. Ellacuría, "Función liberadora de la filosofía," p. 59.

21. The remark was originally made by José María Andrés; it was cited by Cabarrús and Estrada in their interviews, January 18 and February 6, 1991, respectively.

22. Jerez, interview, February 18, 1991.

23. Napoleón Alvarado, interview, February 15, 1991.

24. "Oración a Ignacio Ellacuría," *Noticias SJ,* December 1989, p. 90, ACAPSJ.

25. Jon Sobrino, "La comunión eclesial alrededor del pueblo crucificado," *RLT,* no. 20 (May–August 1990), p. 138.

26. Ellacuría, *Freedom Made Flesh,* p. 15.

27. Ibid., p. 18.

28. Ibid., p. 26.

29. Ellacuría, "Por qué muere Jesús y por qué lo matan," *Diakonía,* no. 8 (December 1978), pp. 65–75.

30. Ibid., pp. 73–74.

31. Ellacuría, *Freedom Made Flesh,* p. 18.

32. Ellacuría, "El desafío cristiano de la teología de la liberación," paper presented in the seminar "Lo temporal y lo religioso en el mundo actual," Madrid 1987. Photocopy from *Acontecimiento* in *AIE,* p. 83.

33. Ellacuría, "Las bienaventuranzas, carta fundacional de la Iglesia de los pobres," in *Conversión de la Iglesia,* p. 151.

34. Sobrino, "Companions of Jesus," p. 25.

35. Ellacuría, "El desafío cristiano de la teología de la liberación," p. 92.

36. Ellacuría, *Conversión de la Iglesia,* pp. 13–14.

37. Cabarrús, interview, January 18, 1991.

38. "Oración a Ignacio Ellacuría," p. 89.

39. Sobrino, interview, March 7, 1991.

40. Sobrino, "Companions of Jesus," p. 17.

41. Ellacuría, "La UCA ante el doctorado concedido a Monseñor Romero," *ECA,* no. 437 (March 1985), p. 168.

42. Ellacuría, "El verdadero pueblo de Dios, según Monseñor Romero," *Conversión de la Iglesia,* pp. 81–125. Citations in this and the following paragraph are from this article.

43. Ellacuría, "El pueblo crucificado, ensayo de soteriología histórica," in I. Ellacuría, et al., *Cruz y resurrección* (CTR, Mexico, 1978), pp. 49–82. Reprinted in *Conversión de la Iglesia,* pp. 25–63. Citations in this and the following paragraph are from this article.

44. The phrase "Contemplación en la acción de la justicia," is the title of an article Ellacuría published in *Diakonía* (April–June 1977), pp. 7–14.

45. Sobrino, "Companions of Jesus," p. 19.

46. Congregation for the Doctrine of the Faith, "Instruction on Certain Aspects of the 'Theology of Liberation,' " VI, 10, Vatican City, August 6, 1984, in Hennelly, *Liberation Theology: A Documentary History,* p. 401.

47. "El volcán jesuita," *ABC,* March 28, 1982.

48. Ellacuría, "Presencia sacerdotal en la guerrilla," written as the introduction to the German edition of María López Vigil's *Muerte y vida en Morazán* (manuscript, San Salvador, June 1988), p. 7, *AIE.*

49. Gersón Martínez, interview with author, San Salvador, March 18, 1991.

50. Ellacuría described this meeting, held with *comandantes* of the FPL during the negotiations over the kidnapping of President Duarte's daughter (see Chapter 10), in "Presencia sacerdotal," p. 8 and in a television appearance on Channel 6's "Punto de vista" in September 1987.

51. Ellacuría, *Notebooks,* no. 219, May 21, 1988.

52. Ellacuría, "Presencia sacerdotal en la guerilla," p. 8.

53. See Ellacuría, "Teología de la liberación y marxismo," reflections for a conference given in the UCA in 1985, *RLT* no. 20 (May–August 1990), pp. 109–35.

54. Ellacuría, "La teología de la liberación frente al cambio socio-histórico de América Latina," *RLT* no. 12 (September–December 1987), p. 252.

55. Ellacuría made this point in a televised debate with Dr. Francisco Peccorini, "Punto de vista," Channel 6 television, September 1988.

56. Ellacuría, "Presencia sacerdotal en la guerilla," p. 8.

57. Ellacuría, "El desafío cristiano de la teología de la liberación," p. 89.

58. "El ejemplo de Nicaragua en Centroamérica," Editorial, *ECA* nos. 441–42 (July–August 1985), pp. 475–94.

59. Jerez, interview, February 18, 1991.

60. Ellacuría, "La teología de la liberación frente al cambio socio-histórico," pp. 241–64.

61. Ibid., p. 243.

62. Ibid., p. 251. Alternate models led either to the loss of faith's autonomy through a process of "substitution or annulment" that placed a priority on liberation in the here and now, or to direct service of revolutionary movements through a declared "loaning or support" of individuals, communities or institutions of the Church.

63. Ellacuría, "El verdadero pueblo de Dios, según Monseñor Romero," p. 115.

64. Ellacuría, "La teología de la liberación frente al cambio socio-histórico," p. 252.

65. Ellacuría, "Presencia sacerdotal en la guerilla," p. 1.

66. Ibid., pp. 10–11.

67. In her review of Paul E. Sigmund's *Liberation Theology at the Crossroads* (New York: Oxford University Press, 1990), Miriam Davidson wrote that "Fr. Ellacuría was one of several Central American theologians who advocated revolutionary counter-violence to the poor and oppressed of El Salvador." *New York Times Book Review,* April 15, 1990.

68. Ellacuría, "Trabajo no violento por la paz y violencia liberadora," *Concilium* no. 215 (1988), pp. 85–94.

69. Ibid., p. 85.

70. Ibid., p. 93.

71. Sobrino, interview, March 7, 1991.

72. Ellacuría, "El verdadero pueblo de Dios, según Monseñor Romero," p. 100.

73. Gutiérrez, *A Theology of Liberation,* p. 135.

74. Thomas More, *Utopia* tr. Paul Torme (1516, reprint, Harmondsworth, England: Penguin Books, 1965), p. 129.

75. See, for example, "Conscientizing as a Way of Liberating" (1970), in Hennelly, *Liberation Theology: A Documentary History,* pp. 5–13.

76. Gutíerrez, *A Theology of Liberation,* pp. 136–37.

77. Ellacuría, "Utopía y profetismo desde América Latina: Un ensayo concreto de soteriología histórica," *RLT* no. 20 (May–August 1990), pp. 141–84.

78. Ibid., p. 147.

79. Ibid., p. 153.

80. Ellacuría, "Quinto centenario de América Latina: ¿Descubrimiento o encubrimiento?" p. 277.

81. Ellacuría, "Utopía y profetismo," p. 155.

82. Ibid., p. 158.

83. *Sollicitudo Rei Socialis,* 22, February 19, 1988.

84. Ellacuría, "Utopía y profetismo," p. 167. Alfred T. Hennelly cited these words at the beginning of a paper he presented on "The Political Theology of Ignacio Ellacuría" in a conference held at Swarthmore College on the first anniversary of the Jesuits' death, November 1990. Romero found "strength" in his last retreat from the old Jesuit Fr. Azcue, who told him "that my disposition should be to give my life for God, whatever might be the end of my life . . . More important than the moment of death is giving him all of life and living for him." Brockman, *Romero: A Life,* p. 234.

85. Francisco Morales and Allen Palacios in the thesis they prepared for the UCA's licentiate in philosophy: "La idea de liberación en Ignacio Ellacuría" (UCA, Facultad de Ciencias del Hombre y de la Naturaleza, January 1992), p. 5.

86. Sobrino, interview, March 7, 1991; Ellacuría, "Historización del bien común y de los derechos humanos en una sociedad dividida," in Elsa Tamez and Seul Trinidad (eds.), *Capitalismo: Violencia y anti-vida* (San José: EDUCA, 1978), pp. 81–94. Photocopy of article reprinted in *Christus* (October 1979), held in AIF, p. 47.

87. Jerez, interview, February 18, 1991.

88. "Oración a Ignacio Ellacuría," p. 89.

CHAPTER 8

1. Ellacuría, "The Task of a Christian University," speech given in Santa Clara University, California, in acceptance of honorary doctorate, June 1982, in Sobrino, Ellacuría, et al., *Companions of Jesus,* p. 150.

2. Ellacuría, "Los retos del país a la UCA en su vigésimo aniversario," Speech given in the UCA on September 17, 1985, *Planteamiento universitario,* p. 152.

3. Ellacuría, "Diez años después: ¿Es posible una universidad distinta?" *ECA* nos. 324–25 (October–November 1975), pp. 605–28.

4. Ibid., p. 606.

5. Jon Sobrino, "Inspiración cristiana de la universidad," *ECA* no. 468 (October 1987), p. 695. Originally delivered as a speech at the University of Bilbao on June 4, 1987.

6. Ellacuría, "El desafío de las mayorías populares," *ECA* nos. 493–94 (November–December 1989), p. 1079.

7. Ellacuría, "Diez años después: ¿Es posible una universidad distinta?" p. 617.

8. "Las funciones fundamentales de la universidad y su operativización," *Planteamiento universitario,* p. 47.

9. Ibid., p. 48.

10. "Proyección social": I have chosen the more literal translation than, for example, Hassett and Lacey's "social outreach," but neither phrase is altogether satisfactory.

11. "Las funciones fundamentales de la universidad," p. 89. So preeminent was the role assigned to teaching within Newman's *Idea of a University* (1873) that he questioned whether research should not be pursued in separate institutions.

12. "Las funciones fundamentales de una universidad," p. 89.

13. Ibid., pp. 58–59. "The philosopher," Ellacuría held, "can understand that it is necessary to tolerate certain wrongs and that the presence of something wrong does not make wrong either a political platform, or a vanguard or a state power . . . But he ought not to deceive himself to the point of calling the necessary evil a good that is justified for the end that is intended, but not yet realized." "Función liberadora de la filosofía," p. 59.

14. Marc Cooper, "Whitewashing Duarte: U.S. Reporting on El Salvador," *NACLA Report on the Americas,* January–March 1986, pp. 7–10.

15. "Duarte: Prisoner of War," *NACLA Report on the Americas,* January–March 1986, p. 13.

16. "Communicado conjunto del Presidente de los Estados Unidos y el Presidente Electo de El Salvador," May 21, 1984, *ECA* no. 428, June 1984, p. 466.

17. "Toast made by Vice-President Bush at a dinner hosted by President Alvaro Magaña in San Salvador," December 11, 1983, *State Department Bulletin* (Washington, D.C., February 1984), p. 9.

18. In a section called "Concrete Action, "the memorandum could only

report positively on the "reluctant" detention of one officer and the transfer of "two mid-level police intelligence officers" to diplomatic posts overseas. CIA Directorate of Intelligence, "Dealing with Death Squads," January 20, 1984, U.S. document declassified November 1993, Washington, D.C.

19. Col. John D. Waghelstein, "El Salvador: Observations and Experiences in Counterinsurgency" (U.S. Army War College, Carlisle Barracks, Pa., January 1, 1985), p. 60.

20. While a "mere" 37 percent of the aid was officially earmarked as directly war related, a report published by the bipartisan Arms Control and Foreign Policy Caucus would find that a further 40 percent could be classified as indirect war-related aid—aid that addressed "needs arising for the civil war" that "in some cases actually assists in the prosecution of the war." U.S. Congress, Arms Control and Foreign Policy Caucus, "U.S. Aid to El Salvador: An Evaluation of the Past, A Proposal for the Future" (Washington, D.C., February 1985), p. 16.

21. Benjamin C. Schwarz, "American Counterinsurgency Doctrine and El Salvador: The Frustrations of Reform and the Illusions of Nation Building" (Prepared for the under secretary of defense for policy, RAND, Santa Monica, 1991), p. 15.

22. See Hassett and Lacey, *Towards a Society that Serves Its People,* Introduction, p. 7 for a discussion of this concept Ellacuría borrowed from the German philosopher Karl Jaspers.

23. Ignacio Martín-Baró, *Acción y ideología: Psicología social desde centroamérica,* (San Salvador: UCA Editores, 1990), p. x.

24. Paul Desruisseaux, "Salvador's Jesuit University: A Life of Self-Censorship," *San Francisco Chronicle of Higher Education,* September 21, 1983.

25. Rubén Zamora, interview with author, San Salvador, June 26, 1990.

26. Desruisseaux, "Salvador's Jesuit University."

27. Ellacuría, "Los retos del país a la UCA," p. 158.

28. Ibid., p. 165.

29. The phenomenon is discussed in Chapter 10. A comprehensive analysis of the emergence of the popular movement of the 1980s is given by Mario Lungo Uclés in "La constitución de un movimiento de base amplio y su papel en la construcción del proyecto popular," a paper written for publication in English by EPICA, Washington, D.C., 1991. See also Lungo's *El Salvador en los años 80: Contrainsurgencia y revolución,* (San José, Costa Rica: EDUCA-FLACSO, 1990), pp. 158–68.

30. Introduction to Joaquín Villalobos, "El estado actual de la guerra y sus perspectivas," *ECA,* no. 449, March 1986, p. 169. The disclaimer did nothing to dissuade the *Diario de Hoy* from running an article on May 29,

1986 attacking the Jesuits for being, as the headline proclaimed, "Completely in agreement with Joaquín Villalobos."

31. Mayorga, "Recuerdo de diez Quijotes," p. 11.

32. UCA board member, interview with author, Guatemala City, September 5, 1991.

33. Rodolfo Cardenal, interview, April 10, 1991.

34. "La cuestión de las masas," Editorial, *ECA* no. 465 (July 1987), pp. 415–34. Interview, Jerez, February 18, 1991.

35. Ungo, interview, December 15, 1990.

36. "Consideraciones justificativas y aclaraciones del Manual de Organización de la Universidad Centroamericana 'José Simeón Cañas,' " *ECA* nos. 324–25 (October–November 1975), p. 691.

37. Ellacuría, "Los retos del país a la UCA," p. 165.

38. UCA staff member, interview with author, San Salvador, September 22, 1991.

39. Sobrino, "Inspiración cristiana de la universidad," p. 701.

40. Jon Sobrino, *The True Church and the Poor* (Maryknoll, N.Y.: Orbis Books, 1984), p. 19.

41. Mayorga, "Recuerdo de diez Quijotes," p. 17.

42. For a full bibliography, see Hasset and Lacey, *Towards a Society that Serves Its People,* pp. 383–89.

43. Rodolfo Cardenal, "Ser jesuita hoy en El Salvador," pp. 1021–26. Among the contemporaries of Martín-Baró in Chicago were two Jesuits, Dean Brackley and Michael Czerny, who would in 1990 lend their services to the UCA after the assassination of their brothers in November 1989.

44. Adrianne Aron, "Martín-Baró on Psychology and Politics," presentation at conference on "The Thought of El Salvador's Murdered Jesuits," Swarthmore College, November 17, 1990, manuscript, p. 1.

45. Former student of Martín-Baró, interview with author, San Salvador, September 29, 1991.

46. Former student of Martín-Baró, interview with author, San Salvador, September 12, 1991.

47. Martín-Baró, *Acción y ideología,* p. viii.

48. Ignacio Martín-Baró, ed., *Psicología social de la guerra* (San Salvador: UCA Editores, 1990), p. 13.

49. Martín-Baró, "Hacía una psicología de la liberación," *Boletín de Psicología* no. 22 (San Salvador, 1986), pp. 219–31.

50. Ibid., pp. 226–27.

51. Martín-Baró, "El papel del psicólogo social en el contexto centroamericano," conference given in October 1985. Reprinted in *Revista de Psicología de El Salvador (RPES),* no. 35 (January–March 1990), p. 58.

52. Martín-Baró, *Psicología social de la guerra,* p. 14.

53. Martín-Baró, "El papel del psicólogo social," p. 59.

54. Ibid., p. 61.

55. Martín-Baró, "Guerra y salud mental," conference given in June 1984. Reprinted in *RPES,* no. 35, January–March 1990, p. 78.

56. Arely Hernández, interview with author, San Salvador, October 9, 1991.

57. Martín-Baró, "De la guerra sucia a la guerra psicológica: El caso de El Salvador," first published as "From Dirty War to Psychological War: The Case of El Salvador," in A. Aron, ed., *Flight, Exile and Return: Mental Health and the Refugees* (San Francisco: CHRICA, 1988). Reprinted in *RPES,* no. 35 (January–March 1990), pp. 109–22.

58. Martín-Baró, "La violencia política y la guerra como causas del trauma psicosocial en El Salvador," conference given in October 1987. Reprinted in *RPES,* no. 35, p. 90.

59. Ibid., p. 90.

60. Ellacuría, "Los retos del país a la UCA," p. 162.

61. Martín-Baró, *La opinión pública salvadoreña (1987–1988)* (San Salvador: UCA Editores, 1989), p. 7.

62. For its documentation of popular support both for the Church-backed National Debate and the ARENA party in the 1988 legislative elections, respectively, ibid., p. 2.

63. Martín-Baró, "La encuesta de opinión pública como instrumento desideologizador," *RPES* no. 35 (January–March 1990), p. 11.

64. Martín-Baró, *La opinión pública salvadoreña,* p. 79.

65. Martín-Baró, "La encuesta de opinión pública," p. 21.

66. Martín-Baró, "Guerra y salud mental," p. 82.

67. Segundo Montes, "La situación de los salvadoreños, desplazados y refugiados," *ECA* no. 434 (December 1984), pp. 904–20.

68. Segundo Montes Mozo and Juan José García Vásquez, *Salvadoran Migration to the United States: An Exploratory Study,* Center for Immigration Policy and Refugee Assistance (Washington, D.C.: Georgetown University, 1988).

69. Juan José García, interview with author, San Salvador, September 29, 1991.

70. For a full bibliography see Hasset and Lacey, *Towards a Society that Serves Its People,* pp. 390–94.

71. J.J., "Los dólares 'perdido' en el correo," *ECA* no. 411 (January 1983), pp. 58–59; Juan José García, "Segundo Montes, *El Salvador 1989,*" *ECA* nos. 505–6 (November–December 1990), pp. 1065–67

72. Full results were published in two volumes by Montes, *El Salvador*

1986: Desplazados y refugiados and *El Salvador 1986: En busca de soluciones para los desplazados* (San Salvador: IDHUCA, 1986).

73. Montes and García, *Salvadoran Migration to the United States,* p. 36. One consequence of the presence of these monies within the Salvadoran economy—even when largely restricted to the informal sector—has been the lack of a need for the devaluation of the Salvadoran *colón.*

74. Segundo Montes, "El problema de los desplazados y refugiados salvadoreños," *ECA* nos. 447–448 (January–February 1986), p. 53.

75. "La Esperanza: Brilla el sol en Colomoncagua y San Antonio," *Carta a las Iglesias* (February 15–28, 1989), p. 11.

76. "Reclutamiento forzoso y sangriento en Jayaque," *Carta a las Iglesias,* January 16–31, 1989, p. 6.

77. Ellacuría, "The Task of a Christian University," p. 150.

CHAPTER 9

1. Remarks by David Robinson, El Salvador Desk Officer, U.S. Department of State, Congressional Research Service seminar, "El Salvador in 1991," Washington, D.C., April 1991.

2. Col. Mauricio Vargas, interview with author, San Salvador, January 16, 1991.

3. Chidester, interview, February 8, 1991.

4. Lawyers Committee for Human Rights, "The Jesuit Case: The Jury Trial (*La Vista Pública*)" (New York, September 1991), p. 33.

5. Cited in "El terrorismo del estado," *Proceso* no. 454 (November 28, 1990), p. 2.

6. Ellacuría, "Trabajo no violento y violencia liberadora," p. 87.

7. Jesuit communiqué, *ECA* nos. 505–506 (November–December 1990), p. 1079

8. Documento de trabajo, "Acuerdo sobre fuerza armada," (manuscript, November 1990).

9. Mena Sandoval, interview, January 5, 1991.

10. Secretary of State Baker, ABC Television's "This Week," January 6, 1991.

11. "Justification for Presidential Determination on Release of Aid to El Salvador," U.S. Department of State (Washington, D.C., January 1991), p. 1.

12. Thomas Long, "Salvador Aid Harms Peace Bid, Critics Say," *Miami Herald,* January 19, 1991.

13. Alvaro de Soto, "U.N. Negotiations Not among Casualties of War in El Salvador," *Wall Street Journal,* January 11, 1991.

14. U.S. Government, 1991 Foreign Operations Act, Section 531(c)(1)D.

15. "Some military officers have provided sketchy or contradictory testimony," the report said, "and the absence of full cooperation by all military officers has raised questions about possible involvement beyond those currently indicted." U.S. Department of State, Report on El Salvador Required under the Foreign Assistance Appropriations Act of 1991 (Washington, D.C., January 15, 1991), p. 9.

16. Walker, interview, February 5, 1991.

17. José María Tojeira, interview with author, San Salvador, June 26, 1990.

18. Waghelstein, "El Salvador: Observations and Experience in Counterinsurgency," p. 27. A CIA document described the Jesuits as "The dominant intellectual force on the left," and recounted how Ellacuría "once boasted that as many as 100 UCA alumni belonged to an FMLN faction." CIA, "Religious Groups and their Tires to the FMLN," 1990, U.S. document declassified November 1993, Washington, D.C.

19. Duryea, U.S. Army Military History Institute Interview, pp. 25–26. Ellacuría was described as representing the "extreme left wing" of "elements of the Church which have openly sided with the insurgents."

20. U.S. official, interview with author, Washington, D.C., May 8, 1991; U.S. official, interview, April 8, 1991.

21. Chidester, interview, February 8, 1991.

22. Six were military advisers, two embassy officials (Chidester and Janice Elmore), and the ninth Maj. Buckland's sister Carol. The nine would eventually be questioned under the Letters Rogatory process, see pp. 284, 358–359.

23. The officers were Major Samuel Ramírez, who had been posted with the Atlacatl in November 1989, and Lt. Col. Fred Berger, to whom he had allegedly confided, in early December 1989, the involvement of the Atlacatl in the Jesuit murders. An edited transcript of the Ramírez interview would eventually be presented to the court in June 1991; the Berger interview was never released. U.S. embassy/State Department cable, November 21, 1990, U.S. documents declassified November 1993, Washington, D.C.

24. In April 1991 a cable from the State Department to the U.S. embassy in Rome contained points to be raised with "appropriate Vatican officials." Criticizing statements made by Tojeira and Estrada as "unfounded and outrageous," the cable claimed they "seem to fit a pattern

of attacks against the USG by the Jesuit communities in El Salvador based on innuendo, supposition, and outright lies." State Department cable, April 17, 1991, U.S. document declassified November 1993, Washington, D.C.

25. Walker, interview, February 5, 1991.

26. Chidester, interview, February 8, 1991. Shaufleburger had been waiting in his car for his girlfriend when killed by the FPL.

27. U.S. official, interview with author, Washington, D.C., April 29, 1991. Both the notes kept by Jesuits present at this meeting (see below) and a telephone interview with Aronson himself on September 14, 1992 in which he described the meeting as "not unpleasant . . . it wasn't overdramatic" suggest this view to be exaggerated by dislike of Tojeira.

28. "Reflections on meeting with Bernard Aronson, Assistant Secretary of State," October 4, 1990, ACAPSJ.

29. Ambassador William Walker, interview with author, San Salvador, March 26, 1991.

30. U.S. military officer, interview with author, San Salvador, March 21, 1991.

31. Lawyers Committee, *Underwriting Injustice*, pp. 126–33.

32. Walker, interview, March 26, 1991; Clifford Krauss, "U.S., Aware of Killings, Kept Ties to Salvadoran Rightists, Papers Suggest," *New York Times*, November 9, 1993. U.S. embassy/State Department cable, August 21, 1990, U.S. document declassified November 1993, Washington, D.C.

33. Jim McGovern and Bill Woodward to Hon. Joe Moakley, "Staff trip to El Salvador," January 7, 1991, p. 1.

34. Ibid., p. 6.

35. Mena Sandoval, *Del ejército nacional al ejército guerrillero*, p. 11. The estimate of the CIA investment was made by Schwarz in "American Counterinsurgency Doctrine and El Salvador," p. 2.

36. Source close to the military, interview with author, San Salvador, April 11, 1991.

37. See p. 392 for a discussion of the CIA's assessment of Ponce in the early 1980s.

38. U.S. colonel, interview with author, February 11, 1992.

39. Arms Control and Foreign Policy Caucus, *Barriers to Reform*, p. 13.

40. Charles Lane, "The Pilot Shark of El Salvador," *New Republic*, September 24, 1990.

41. U.S. military officer, interview, March 21, 1991.

42. U.S. Congress, House Committee on Foreign Affairs, Subcommittees on Human Rights and International Organizations, and on Western

Hemisphere Affairs, Hearings, January 24, 1990, (Washington, D.C.: U.S. Government Printing Office, 1990), p. 47.

43. U.S. embassy/State Department cable, September 4, 1990. U.S. documents declassified November 1993, Washington, D.C.

44. Walker, interview, March 26, 1991.

45. Congressional aide, interview with author, Washington, D.C., May 20, 1991.

46. Salvadoran colonel, interview, March 15, 1991.

47. CIA cable, May 15, 1990, U.S. document declassified November 1993, Washington, D.C.

48. Col. René Emilio Ponce, interview with author, San Salvador, January 18, 1991.

49. U.K. journalist to whom remark was repeated by Salvadoran colonel, interview with author, San Salvador, November 12, 1991.

50. Salvadoran officer, interview with author, April 24, 1991.

51. U.S. official, interview with author, San Salvador, July 9, 1991.

52. Walker, interview, March 26, 1991. U.S. embassy/State Department cables, October 30 & November 13, 1990. U.S. documents declassified November 1993, Washington, D.C.

53. Walker, interview, March 26, 1991, cable of November 13, 1990 as cited above.

54. Lawyers Committee for Human Rights, "Update on Investigation of the Murder of Six Jesuit Priests in El Salvador" (New York, March 25, 1991), p. 13.

55. Transcript of the video declaration of Maj. Eric Warren Buckland, Washington, D.C., January 12, 1990. Unless otherwise stated, citations that follow are also from this transcript.

56. Buckland, transcript of U.S. Department of Justice interview November 19, 1990. Within the Human Rights Instruction in the 0–3 Command and General Staff Course at Fort Benning's School of the Americas, one hour is devoted to the study of Liberation Theology.

57. Buckland, transcript of U.S. Department of Justice interview, November 19, 1990.

58. A State Department memorandum drafted by Peter Romero on December 3, 1990 revealed an assessment of this recantation never hinted at by officials in interviews. The Justice and Defense department officials had believed that Buckland was "trying to be truthful," but it was "also their opinion that Buckland either had prior knowledge or felt that there were 'signs' that he should have recognized that led to the Jesuit murders." "Buckland interview on November 19, 1990," U.S. document declassified November 1993, Washington, D.C.

59. Col. Mark Hamilton, interview with author, San Salvador, October 16, 1991.

60. U.S. military officer, interview, March 21, 1991.

61. U.S. official, interview with author, San Salvador, August 21, 1991.

62. Shirley Christian, "Salvadoran Army Angers U.S. Advisers," *New York Times,* August 5, 1991; U.S. military officer, interview with author, Washington, D.C., February 11, 1992.

63. U.S. official, interview, August 12, 1991.

64. Buckland, transcript of U.S. Department of Justice interview, November 19, 1990.

65. Jim McGovern, interview with author, Washington, D.C., April 29, 1991; Joe Blatchford, telephone conversation with author, Washington, D.C., May 2, 1991.

66. U.S. official, interview, April 29, 1991.

67. Hannan and O'Connor document, untitled and undated but c. February 1991, pp. 2, 4.

68. McGovern, U.S. official, interviews, April 29, 1991.

69. Congressional aide, interview with author, Washington, D.C., April 22, 1991.

70. Walker, interview, March 26, 1991.

71. Generals Ponce, Zepeda, and Rubio; Colonels Montano and Vargas letter to Minister of Justice René Hernández Valiente, February 22, 1991.

72. U.S. embassy/State Department cable, March 13, 1991. U.S. document declassified November 1993, Washington, D.C.; Clifford Krauss, "Salvadoran Army Vows to Press Jesuit Case," *New York Times,* March 14, 1991.

73. Walker, interview, March 26, 1991.

74. With over 12 percent of the popular vote, the Convergence won 8 out of 84 seats in the National Assembly; a ninth was won by the left-wing UDN. See *ECA* no. 509 (March 1991) for an analysis of these elections.

75. Clifford Krauss, "U.N. Aide Assailed in Salvadoran Talks,' *New York Times,* February 1, 1991.

76. Judy Aita, "U.S. Assures U.N. of Support for Salvadoran Mediation," USIA release, February 1, 1991.

77. Alvaro de Soto, interview with author, New York, April 27, 1992.

78. Under Salvadoran law, constitutional amendments must be approved by two consecutive assemblies. Amendments had to be passed before April 30, which was the last day in which the outgoing assembly could be in session.

79. Mexico Agreements, April 27, 1991 (New York: U.N. Department of Public Information).

80. See Chapter 6, note 59.

81. Karl, "El Salvador's Negotiated Revolution," p. 157.

82. Officer cited in El Rescate, *Report from El Salvador,* April 29 to May 6, 1991.

83. Salvadoran military officer, interview with author, San Salvador, November 22, 1991.

84. Ibid. Other sources reported this confrontation to Moakley. See Statement of Rep. Joe Moakley, Washington, D.C., November 18, 1991.

85. Press conference, Sidney Blanco and Henry Campos, San Salvador, January 9, 1991.

86. Presentation of Edward Sidney Blanco Reyes and Alvaro Henry Campos Solorzano to the judge of the Fourth Criminal Court, San Salvador, May 6, 1991, p. 6.

87. Their court appearances were on May 29 and 30, respectively, *Proceso* no. 476 (June 5, 1991), p. 8.

88. Lawyers Committee for Human Rights, "Jesuit Murder Update," (New York, August 1991). One confrontation was allowed, but never took place because one of the officers was in the United States for training.

89. Moakley, et al. to President George Bush, Washington, D.C., June 5, 1991.

90. Jim McGovern, interview with author, San Salvador, June 28, 1991.

91. At a Salvadoran Press Corps Association breakfast, San Salvador, July 2, 1991.

92. Moakley, interview, May 8, 1991.

93. Transcript of the statement by Rep. Joe Moakley to the House Subcommittee on Western Hemisphere Affairs, Washington, D.C., April 11, 1991, p. 2.

94. Jim McGovern, interview with author, Washington, D.C., April 22, 1991.

95. U.S. official, interview, April 29, 1991.

96. William Walker, interview with author, San Salvador, July 11, 1991.

97. Jim McGovern, interview with author, San Salvador, September 27, 1991.

98. See Arnson, *Crossroads,* pp. 260–61 for an account of how this and a subsequent trip to Santa Marta contributed to the FMLN's sense that "very powerful sectors of the Congress were pushing for negotiations and bringing the administration along."

99. Leonel Gómez, interview with author, San Salvador, July 20, 1991.

100. Rep. Joe Moakley, Remarks at the University of Central America, San Salvador, July 1, 1991, p. 6.

101. Moakley, interview, February 6, 1992.

102. Moakley, Remarks at the UCA, p. 7.

103. Response by Rev. Jon Sobrino SJ to the Remarks of Rep. Moakley, UCA, July 1, 1991, p. 1.

104. Moakley, Remarks at the UCA, p. 8.

CHAPTER 10

1. Ellacuría, "Las difíciles negociaciones en El Salvador," *El País* (Madrid), October 7, 1983.

2. Samayoa, interview, April 3, 1992.

3. Ellacuría (titles in translation), "A Process of Mediation for El Salvador" (1981); "Ten Theses on the Process of Negotiation" (1983); "Are There Solutions for the Crisis in El Salvador?" (1984); "A New Framework of Solutions for the Problem of El Salvador" (1986); "Proposals for a Solution Following Esquipulas II" (1987); "Dialogue in the Hundred Days of Cristiani" (1989). See bibliography in Hassett and Lacey, *Towards a Society that Serves Its People,* pp. 373–82.

4. Ellacuría, "Análisis ético-político del proceso de diálogo en El Salvador," *ECA* nos. 454–55 (August–September 1986), pp. 727–54.

5. Ellacuría, "FMLN, El límite insuperable," *ECA* no. 446 (December 1985), pp. 890–97.

6. "Communicado del Ejército Secreto Anticommunista (ESA)," *ECA* n. 418 (September 1983), p. 834. CIA / State Department, "Briefing Pope on Right-Wing Terrorism in El Salvador," October 27, 1993, U.S. document declassified November 1993, Washington, D.C.

7. "Communicado del ESA, atribuyendose las acciones terroristas del 6 de septiembre de 1983," *ECA* no. 419 (October 1983), p. 903.

8. On May 9, 1986, Defense Minister Vides Casanova told Ellacuría that the government had already fended off thirteen coups. *Notebooks,* no. 102.

9. Senior official in Duarte government, interview with author, San Salvador, June 22, 1991; Ellacuría, *Notebooks,* no. 9, October 12, 1984.

10. Ellacuría, *Notebooks,* no. 10, October 19, 1984. "Los militares y la paz social," Editorial, *ECA* nos. 429–30 (July–August 1984), pp. 475–90.

11. Ibid., pp. 480–81.

12. Eugenio C. Anaya, "Crónica del mes: octubre y noviembre," *ECA* no. 434 (December 1984), p. 929.

13. Tomás R. Campos (Ellacuría), "Las primeras vicisitudes del diálogo entre el gobierno y el FMLN-FDR," *ECA* no. 434 (1984), p. 903.

14. Gersón Martínez, interview, March 18, 1991.

15. Former member of FPL Political Commission, interview with author, San Salvador, March 12, 1991.

16. "La responsibilidad de las 'terceras fuerzas,'" Editorial, *ECA* no. 394, August 1981, p. 750.

17. Ellacuría's *Notebooks* include details of twelve meetings (ten of them held in Managua) with relatively large groups of people (generally five to six) between mid-1984 and his death. That the meetings were often called when the FMLN was particularly unhappy with the position assumed by Ellacuría and the UCA obviously contributed to the differences expressed within them.

18. Samayoa, interview, April 3, 1992.

19. See for example Tomás R. Campos (Ellacuría), "El FDR-FMLN ante las elecciones de 1984," *ECA* nos. 426–27 (April–May 1984), p. 287.

20. *ECA* nos. 426–27, April–May 1984, *passim*.

21. Ana Guadalupe Martínez, interview, April 4, 1992.

22. Ibid.

23. Elizabeth J. Wood, "Civil War and Reconstruction: The Repopulation of Tenancingo, El Salvador (1986–1991)," (manuscript, Department of Political Science, Stanford University, May 21, 1991).

24. Conferencia Episcopal de El Salvador, "Reconciliación y paz," and "Respuesta del FMLN-FDR a la carta pastoral de la CEDES," *ECA* nos. 443–44 (September–October 1985), pp. 743–50.

25. *El Mundo,* July 25, 1983.

26. Fidel Chávez Mena, interview with author, San Salvador, December 12, 1990; Abraham Rodríguez, interview with author, San Salvador, January 19, 1991.

27. Ellacuría, *Notebooks,* no. 63, September 19, 1985.

28. In 1983 differences within the FPL came to a violent head with the murder of the second-in-command Ana María, and the suicide soon afterward of "Marcial," Salvador Cayetano Carpio. Leonel González became the leader of the FPL.

29. J.S., "Visita de Mons. Rivera a Chalatenango y Guazapa," *ECA* nos. 443–444 (September–October 1985), p. 703.

30. Ellacuría's own account of the negotiations around the kidnapping of Inés Guadalupe Duarte is given in Tomás R. Campos, (Ellacuría) "Lectura política de los secuestros," ibid., pp. 684ff.; *Notebooks,* nos. 62–77, September 14–October 24, 1985.

31. Ellacuría, *Notebooks,* no. 73, October 24, 1985.

32. Campos (Ellacuría), "Lectura política de los secuestros," p. 691.

33. Ellacuría would note that Noriega offered his cooperation at every level, "without any show of egoism or imposition." *Notebooks,* no. 76, October 22, 1985.

34. Differences between Rodríguez, representing Duarte, and Rey Prendes, representing the PDC (and more inclined to call the guerrillas' bluff), were complicated by consultations with Chávez Mena and Alejandro Duarte and hurried telephone calls to Duarte and Vides Casanova in El Salvador.

35. The number of wounded had increased from 96 to 101. The FMLN dropped its demands for the release of the 29 union leaders and abandoned its attempt to have the government explain the fate of the nine "disappeared"—one of whom was Aguiñada's son.

36. Campos (Ellacuría), "Lectura política de los secuestros," p. 699. Wichsnewski had assured Ellacuría that both Cuba and Nicaragua were in favor of a rapid solution to the kidnapping.

37. Ibid., p. 692.

38. Ellacuría, *Notebooks,* no. 84, December 5, 1985.

39. Ellacuría, *Notebooks,* nos. 39 and 42, May 21 and 27, 1985.

40. The talk was given in a Forum at the UCA on November 14, 1985 and published as "Replanteamiento de soluciones para el problema de El Salvador," in *ECA* nos. 447–48 (January–February 1986), pp. 54–75.

41. Ellacuría, "Replanteamiento de soluciones," p. 68.

42. "It is a political proposal with its political subject hidden," Rubén Zamora told Ellacuría, only half in jest, "because the political subject is you Jesuits." Zamora, interview, April 12, 1991.

43. *Diario de Hoy,* September 6, 1986.

44. Rubén Zamora, "The Popular Movement," in Anjali Sundaram and George Gelber, eds., *A Decade of War: El Salvador Confronts the Future* (London: CIIR and New York: Monthly Review Press, 1991), pp. 182ff.

45. Ana Guadalupe Martínez, interview, April 4, 1992.

46. Samayoa, interview, April 3, 1992.

47. What remained of the UPD had split from the UNTS at the end of 1986 and was itself reformed into a new association of organizations, supported by AIFLD and backing the Duarte government, called UNOC, the National Worker and Peasant Union.

48. "La cuestión de las masas," Editorial, *ECA* no. 465 (July 1987), p. 425.

49. Rubén Zamora, interview, April 12, 1991.

50. FMLN *comandante,* interview with author, San Salvador, April 4, 1991.

51. *Diario de Hoy,* November 19, 1985.

52. *Prensa Gráfica,* May 7, 1985; *Diario de Hoy,* August 18, 1988, January 25, February 16, March 3, 1989.

53. Conferencia de Inteligencia de Ejércitos Americanos, "Estrategia del movimiento comunista internacional en Latinoamérica a través de distintos modos de acción" (manuscript, Buenos Aires, 1987), p. 9.

54. Salvadoran political figure, interview with author, San Salvador, March 25, 1991.

55. Edgar Chacón, interview by Enrique Ortego, "Los Jesuitas estaban en la mira," *Proceso* (Mexico City), November 20, 1989, p. 37.

56. Washington lobbyist, interview with author, Washington, D.C., May 10, 1991. Ellacuría's English was much better than he would let on. He preferred, however, not to give an interlocutor the advantage of confronting anything less than his precise, articulate, and occasionally devastating Spanish.

57. Cited in Arnson, *Crossroads,* p. 120.

58. CIA Directorate of Intelligence, "The Political Role of the Catholic Church in Central America," December 1988, p. 5. U.S. document declassified November 1993, Washington, D.C.

59. *Chicago Catholic,* May 30, 1986.

60. Walker, interview, March 26, 1991; Washington lobbyist and translator at 1986 meeting, interview, May 10, 1991.

61. Ellacuría allowed himself a brief footnote to his record of the opinions expressed by Kirkpatrick in their meeting: "In a later conversation with Chávez Mena, she told him that she had been impressed by our discussion." *Notebooks,* no. 104, May 15, 1986.

62. *Diario de Hoy,* July 8, 1987.

63. *Diario de Hoy,* May 29, 1986.

64. Television interview cited in *Diario Latino,* September 4, 1986.

65. *Diario Latino,* September 6, 1986.

66. Ibid.

67. At about this time, Castillo Claramount was named general secretary of the PDC. "ELLACURÍA WAS NOT TO BLAME," read the caption on a cartoon in *El Mundo,* September 8, 1986.

68. *El Mundo,* September 11, 1986.

69. *Diario de Hoy,* September 19, 1986.

70. Ignacio Martín-Baró, "Los medios de comunicación masiva y la opinión pública en El Salvador de 1979 a 1989," *ECA* nos. 493–494 (November–December 1989), p. 1082.

71. Ellacuría, "El Salvador en estado de diálogo," Editorial, *ECA* no. 453 (July 1986), pp. 525–33.

72. "Dos horas en el juicio," *Carta a las Iglesias,* October 1–15, 1991, p. 14.

73. "Punto de vista," Channel 12 television, September 1987.

74. This and following citations from video transcript of the television broadcast cited above.

75. Ernesto Cruz Alfaro, "Crónica del mes octubre–diciembre," *ECA* nos. 457–58 (November–December 1986), p. 1937.

76. Referred to in "Punto de vista" and interview, (former Spanish) Ambassador Fernando Alvarez de Miranda, San Salvador, September 24, 1991.

77. Ellacuría, "Caminos de solución para la actual crisis del país," *ECA* no. 462 (April 1987), p. 302.

78. "El plan Arias," *ECA* no. 461 (March 1987), pp. 252–54.

79. "FMLN-FDR Propuesta," May 26, 1987, *ECA* no. 463 (May 1987), p. 403.

80. "Punto de vista," transcript.

81. Ambassador Edwin Corr interviewed in Manwaring and Prisk, *El Salvador at War: An Oral History,* p. 449.

82. Martín-Baró, *La opinión pública salvadoreña,* p. 90.

83. The Truth Commission was unable to reach a conclusion as to who was responsible for Anaya's murder. Truth Commission Report, p. 167.

84. Col. Reynaldo López Nuila, interview with author, Miami, May 30, 1991.

85. W.Z., "La ley de amnistía y la reconciliación nacional," *ECA* no. 468 (October 1987), p. 712.

86. U.S. Congress, "Bankrolling Failure: United States Policy in El Salvador and the Urgent Need for Reform," Report to the Arms Control and Foreign Policy Caucus by Sen. Mark O.Hatfield, Rep. Jim Leach, Rep. George Miller (Washington, D.C., November 1987).

87. Ibid., p. 3.

88. Already limited by the military's control of its execution, the final blow to agrarian reform came as the assembly voted to end transfers of land under Phases I and III and refused to approve Phase II.

89. Chris Norton, "The Hard Right: ARENA Comes to Power," in Sundaram and Gelber, *A Decade of War,* pp. 196–215. FUSADES cannot be exclusively identified with ARENA. A major conduit for AID monies, its concern with economic modernization extends beyond the limits of individual parties. For an overview of the structural change within the ruling classes of El Salvador in the 1980s, see Lungo Uclés, *El Salvador en los 80,* pp. 109–43.

90. "1988, un año de transición para El Salvador," Editorial, *ECA* nos. 471–72 (January–February 1988), p. 5.

91. Ellacuría, *Notebooks,* no. 189, November 20, 1987.

92. Msgr. Arturo Rivera Damas, "Esquipulas es una esperanza," *ECA* nos. 469–70 (November–December 1987), p. 863.

93. "Carta de invitación del señor arzobispo de San Salvador," in *Debate Nacional 1988,* San Salvador, 1988.

94. *Diario de Hoy,* July 13 and August 9, 1988.

95. "El significado del debate nacional," Editorial *ECA* nos. 478–79 (August–September 1988), p. 713.

96. *Diario de Hoy,* July 11 and August 9, 1988.

97. "Debate nacional 1988, documento final, no. 58," *ECA* nos. 478–79 (August–September 1988), p. 743.

98. "Los candidatos y la paz," *Carta a las Iglesias,* October 1–15, 1988.

CHAPTER 11

1. Ellacuría, "Una nueva fase en el proceso salvadoreño," *ECA* no. 485 (March 1989), pp. 183–84.

2. *El Mundo,* March 9, 1989.

3. Ellacuría, "Una nueva fase en el proceso salvadoreño," pp. 167–97.

4. Ellacuría, *Notebooks,* nos. 243 and 255, April 10 and May 31, 1989. Three years later, while receiving an honorary doctorate from St. Joseph's University, Philadelphia, de Soto would describe his mediation of the Salvadoran negotiations as being "inspired to a large extent" by this "epiphanic" meeting with Ellacuría.

5. FMLN, "Propuesta para convertir las elecciones en una contribución a la paz," *ECA* nos. 483–84 (January–February 1989), p. 133.

6. Ellacuría, "Una nueva fase en el proceso salvadoreño," p. 175.

7. Ellacuría, *Notebooks,* no. 216, May 17, 1988.

8. Ellacuría, *Notebooks,* no. 219, May 21, 1988.

9. Villalobos had no memory of the meeting described in Chapter 5, p. 141.

10. Ana Guadalupe Martínez, interview, April 4, 1992.

11. Francisco Javier Ibisate, interview with author, San Salvador, November 11, 1991.

12. Ellacuría, *Notebooks,* no. 233, August 30, 1988.

13. Ibisate, interview, November 11, 1991.

14. Joaquín Villalobos, "Perspectivas de victoria y proyecto revolucionario," *ECA* nos. 483–84 (January–February 1989), pp. 11–52.

15. Ellacuría, *Notebooks,* no. 237, March 5, 1989.

16. The consultants were Greer, Margolis, and Mitchell and Associates, Inc.

17. That violence had included the killing of two journalists, the wounding of a third, and the firing on a vehicle carrying a fourth who had been wounded in crossfire and died en route to a hospital.

18. Ellacuría, "Una nueva fase en el proceso salvadoreño," p. 184.

19. Statement by Press Secretary Fitzwalter on President Bush's telephone conversation with President-Elect Alfredo Cristiani, March 22, 1989, *Public Papers of the President* (Washington, D.C.: U.S. Government Printing Office, 1989) p. 299.

20. The slogan *La alegría ya viene* was lifted, together with other elements, from the successful "No Campaign" rejecting the rule of General Pinochet in the 1988 Chilean plebiscite.

21. Ellacuría, *Notebooks,* no. 244, April 12, 1989.

22. Ellacuría, "Una nueva fase en el proceso salvadoreño," p. 188.

23. See the Americas Watch Report, *A Year of Reckoning: El Salvador a Decade After the Assassination of Archbishop Romero* (New York, March 1990), pp. 69–76, for a discussion of the assassinations of Miguel Castellanos, Francisco Peccorini, José Roberto Garcia Alvarado, José Antonio Rodriguéz Porth, Edgar Chacón, and Gabriel Payes.

24. Alvaro Antonio Jerez Magaña, *La infiltración marxista en la Iglesia* (San Salvador: Editorial Dignidad, 1988); Monsignor Freddy Delgado, *La Iglesia Popular nació en El Salvador* (privately produced, San Salvador, 1989).

25. *Diario de Hoy,* January 25, 1989.

26. Aronson remembered that he found both Ellacuría's conviction that this was the time to bring an end to the war and the fact that he was critical of the FMLN's assassination campaign "hopeful." Telephone interview, September 14, 1992 and Ellacuría, *Notebooks,* no. 243, April 10, 1989.

27. Interview, translator, San Salvador, June 10, 1991.

28. "Decisión 88," Channel 6 television, September 28, 1988.

29. ACAN-EFE cable, March 16, 1989.

30. *Diario de Hoy,* April 13 and 16, 1989.

31. Letter of Segundo Montes to ARENA, *El Mundo,* April 14, 1989.

32. *Diario de Hoy,* April 20, 1989.

33. "Vísperas violentas," Editorial, *ECA* nos. 486–87 (April–May 1989), pp. 292–93.

34. *El Mundo,* May 30, 1989.

35. "Crónica del mes—mayo–junio," *ECA* no. 488 (June 1989), p. 503.

36. "Vísperas violentas," pp. 285–86.

37. Communiqué broadcast on Radio Venceremos, cited in Americas Watch, *A Year of Reckoning,* p. 70. Privately it had been established that the FAL was responsible for both.

38. Ellacuría, *Notebooks,* no. 256, June 9, 1989.

39. Salvadoran Press Corps Association Breakfast, April 21 1989, transcript.

40. *Diario de Hoy,* May 7, 1989.

41. CBS television archive in television documentary "A Question of Conscience" (New York, 1990).

42. *Diario de Hoy,* July 3, 1989.

43. Friend of Ellacuría, interview with author, San Salvador, June 22, 1991.

44. *El País,* July 28, 1989.

45. "Ignacio Ellacuría, SJ," *Noticias SJ* (December 1989), p. 12.

46. UCA staff member, interview with author, San Salvador, September 25, 1991.

47. A.C., "Los asesinos de Jürg Weiss," *ECA* nos. 483–84 (January–February 1989), pp. 92–96.

48. UCA staff member, interview, September 25, 1991.

49. S.M., "A propósito del informe de la delegación europea sobre el asesinato de Jürg *ECA* nos. 486–87, April–May 1989, pp. 365–67; High Command statement, Ibid., pp. 405–10.

50. Montes went to ask Ponce's permission for Vargas to take part in an UCA Forum planned for November. He commented afterward on Ponce's mild manner and concluded that, "he was someone with whom one can talk." UCA staff member, interview, September 25, 1991.

51. Interview included as archive material in CBS News's "60 Minutes" on "The Jesuit Murders," April 22, 1990, transcript.

52. Ramos, interview, November 20, 1990; Sobrino, interview, March 7, 1991.

53. *ECA* nos. 490–91 (August–September 1989).

54. Ellacuría, *Notebooks,* no. 265, August 17, 1989.

55. Cristiani invited individuals from the Christian Democrats and the Convergence to participate in this commission, but the invitation was declined as they had been invited *only* as individuals and not in representation of their respective parties.

56. Salvadoran political figure, interview with author, San Salvador, June 22, 1991.

57. Ellacuría, *Notebooks,* no. 265, August 17, 1989.

58. UCA staff member, interview with author, San Salvador, October 2, 1991.

59. Ellacuría, *Notebooks,* no. 256, June 9, 1989.

60. Ellacuría, "El diálogo en los primeros cien días de Cristiani," *ECA* nos. 490–91 (August–September 1989), p. 684.

61. *Prensa Gráfica,* July 22, 1989 and August 15, 1989.

62. Davíd Escobar Galindo, interview with author, San Salvador, March 25, 1991.

63. Rubén Zamora, interview, April 12, 1991.

64. Beneke, interview, March 26, 1993.

65. *El Mundo,* September 16, 1989.

66. Ellacuría, *Notebooks,* no. 268, September 12, 1989.

67. Rolando Alvarado, interview with author, San Salvador, November 15, 1991.

68. UCA staff member, interview, September 25, 1991.

69. Ellacuría, *Notebooks,* no. 260, July 20, 1989.

70. Ellacuría, "El diálogo en los primeros cien días," p. 690.

71. The account of this meeting is based on interviews with Antonio Cardenal and Ana Guadalupe Martínez, March 19, 1991 and April 4, 1992, and with individuals to whom Ellacuría recounted details.

72. Ana Guadalupe Martínez, interview, April 4, 1992.

73. Antonio Cardenal, interview, March 19, 1991.

74. "El diálogo entre el gobierno y el FMLN en Costa Rica," *Proceso* no. 405, October 18, 1989, p. 2.

75. "Viaje del Padre Ellacuría," memorandum dated October 20, 1989, Office of the Rector, UCA.

76. "El diálogo entre el gobierno y el FMLN en Costa Rica," p. 4.

77. "Crónica del mes—octubre," *ECA* no. 492 (October 1989), pp. 865ff.

78. Adviser present at the meeting, interview with author, San Salvador, January 19, 1991.

79. Ellacuría, "El desafío de las mayorías populares," *ECA* nos. 493–94 (November–December 1989), p. 1078.

80. Rolando Alvarado, interview, November 15, 1991.

81. Jerez, interview, February 18, 1991; de Sebastián, interview, January 21, 1992. Ana Guadalupe Martínez explained in her interview (April 4, 1992) that the FMLN had wanted to ask Ellacuría whether he would undertake the mediation of the short period of negotiations they envisaged as the likely outcome of their victorious occupation of San Salvador.

82. Ignacio Ellacuría to Colonel Juan Antonio Martínez Varela, November 9, 1989, photocopy, AIE.

83. Cited by Julio Fermoso, Rector of the University of Salamanca, "Homage of the Universities of Spain to the Martyrs of the UCA," June 18, 1990, AIE.

84. Letters Rogatory interview (U.S. Department of Justice, Washington, D.C., August 1991), p. 14. In Court Record.

85. Society of Jesus, "Cronología del asesinato de los Jesuitas en El Salvador," November 17, 1989, in *Carta a las Iglesias* (November 16–December 31, 1989), p. 7.

86. "El asesinato de los jesuitas (1)," p. 8.

87. Fermín Saínz, interview, November 27, 1991.

88. Carmen Castro, in the UCA auditorium, November 15, 1990.

89. Interview, Juan Antonio Ellacuría, San Salvador, November 18, 1990.

90. *Avuí,* November 15, 1989, cited in the Lawyers Committee, "The Jesuit Case: A Year Later," p. 16.

91. Rolando Alvarado, interview, November 15, 1991.

92. Estrada, interview, February 2, 1991; UCA staff member, interview with author, San Salvador, March 11, 1991.

93. Martín-Baró's account of the search was published in *Noticias SJ* (December 1989), ACAPSJ, p. 53.

94. Rolando Alvarado, interview, November 15, 1991.

95. Saínz, interview, November 27, 1991.

96. Alicia Martín-Baró, interview with author, San Salvador, November 15, 1990.

CHAPTER 12

1. José María Tojeria, "El caso de los jesuitas dos años después," *ECA* nos. 517–18 (November–December 1991), p. 1033.

2. The deserter, Pvt. Sierra Ascensio, would be tried in his absence.

3. None of the reforms would take place before a cease-fire, and the issues still to be resolved before that became possible were among the most intractable: the reform of the armed forces and the division of territory between two sides.

4. Shirley Christian, "As Talks Falter, Salvador's Warring Sides Turn Back to Guns," *New York Times,* August 16, 1991.

5. *Diario de Hoy,* May 13, 1991.

6. U.S. official, interview with author, Washington, D.C., February 11, 1992.

7. The vote went 56 to 43, *Congressional Record,* July 25, 1991, p. S10873.

8. "There is one serious problem in the negotiations," one U.S. embassy official would say in an interview on July 9, 1991, "the mediator. I mean he is a nice guy—we went out for pizza—but he has no clue."

9. Clifford Krauss, "U.S., Soviets Write to U.N. Chief in Joint Effort to

End Salvador War" (New York Times Service), *Miami Herald,* August 17, 1991.

10. Lee Hockstader, "Cristiani as Peace Catalyst," *Washington Post,* January 2, 1992.

11. The FMLN demanded either the dissolution of the Salvadoran army or the fusion of the two armies into one combined force; both were completely unacceptable to the government delegation.

12. "El contexto de la cita de Nueva York," *Proceso* no. 488 (September 18, 1991) p. 15.

13. Lands in excess of the legal limit held by private owners, and surplus land in the hands of the state would be redistributed to landless *campesinos* and small farmers. In the conflictive zones, where land had been worked by members of the FMLN's civilian base, land reform was postponed in deference to the near insoluble issue of "territoriality" that had threatened to derail talks earlier in the year. "Los Acuerdos de Nueva York," *ECA* no. 515 (September 1991), pp. 867–71.

14. Oscar Santamaría and Roberto Cañas, respectively, on Channels 2 and 12 of Salvadoran television, cited in El Rescate, *Report from El Salvador,* September 23–30, 1991.

15. COPAZ would include two representatives of the government (one from the armed forces), two from the FMLN, and one each from each political party or coalition with a seat in the National Assembly (ARENA, PCN, MAC, PDC, Democratic Convergence, and UDN).

16. The author was present among the international observers of the trial. Her observations form the basis for the account that follows.

17. U.S. official, interview, August 21, 1991.

18. McGovern, interview, September 27, 1991.

19. U.S. Jesuit, interview with author, San Salvador, July 3, 1991; Congressional aide, interview with author, Washington, D.C., December 18, 1991.

20. Tojeira in a press conference on July 30, 1991.

21. Letters Rogatory interview (U.S. Department of Justice, Washington, D.C., August 6, 1991), p. 15, *Court Record.*

22. U.S. official, interview, August 12, 1991.

23. *Diario Latino,* September 5, 1991. Moakley also urged Cristiani to speak out against an amnesty in an open letter dated September 3, 1991.

24. See the Lawyers Committee pretrial report, "The Jesuit Case: The Jury Trial" and Americas Watch, "The Jesuit Trial: An Observer's Report" (New York, December 13, 1991) for detailed accounts of the legal background to the trial.

25. Salvadoran businessman, interview with author, San Salvador, February 18, 1992.

26. Salvadoran official, interview with author, San Salvador, November 27, 1991.

27. Benavides and Tomás Zarpate Castillo were also charged with acts of terrorism; Avalos Vargas, Pérez Vásquez, and Amaya Grimaldi with acts of terrorism and acts preparatory to terrorism; and the three lieutenants with acts of terrorism, acts preparatory to terrorism, and planning and conspiracy to commit acts of terrorism. The deserter Sierra Ascencio was charged only with the murders of the two women. Cases against the lieutenants for the planning and conspiracy of terrorist acts and against Lt. Col. Camilo Hernández and Lt. Mendoza for their role in the coverup would be heard by the judge at a later date.

28. Information provided to the Moakley task force by the Pentagon, see "Interim Report," addendum.

29. Channel 12, Salvadoran television, cited in El Rescate, *Report from El Salvador,* September 23–30, 1991.

30. Tojeira, interview, October 15, 1991.

31. The wives of both Gen. Ponce and his deputy minister for public security, Col. Montano, were present. On the day before a peaceful demonstration by staff and students of the UCA had been prevented from entering even the outer gate of the heavily guarded court.

32. Interviews on Channels 6 and 12, Salvadoran television, cited in El Rescate, *Report from El Salvador,* September 23–30, 1991.

33. U.S. official, interview by author, San Salvador, October 16, 1991.

34. Questions from the summary of the *minuta* prepared by San Salvador's Fourth Criminal Court, September 28, 1991.

35. *Prensa Gráfica,* September 30, 1991.

36. Lee Hockstader, "Judge in Jesuits Case to Flee El Salvador," *Washington Post,* September 30, 1991.

37. The Americas Watch observer, for example, described the verdict as "a stunning blow to justice" proving "how little the Salvadoran judicial system actually works," "An Observer's Report," p. 1.

38. *Diario de Hoy,* September 30, 1991.

39. Mauricio Gutiérrez Castro, interview with author, San Salvador, November 13, 1991.

40. *El Mundo,* September 30, 1991.

41. The source was a man of good standing with the U.S. military; he came forward through concern that the contents of the letter could harm the Salvadoran military.

42. Hamilton, interview, October 16, 1991.

43. Salvadoran colonel, interview with author, San Salvador, October 16, 1991. A DIA cable of October 2, 1991 confirms this view in its analysis of the military reaction to the verdict: "For months there has been a growing sentiment that Benavides 'needed' to be found guilty." U.S. document declassified November 1993, Washington, D.C.

44. Joe Moakley, "Justice Disserved in the Jesuit Murders," *Washington Post*, October 14, 1991.

45. Retired from the air force in January 1990, Bustillo had been appointed military attaché to Israel. It was a posting he never assumed, preferring to travel between his residence in Miami and El Salvador.

46. U.S. official, interview, October 16, 1991.

47. Salvadoran political figure, interview with author, San Salvador, October 8, 1991.

48. This description draws on the statement of Rep. Joe Moakley, Chairman of the Speaker's Task Force on El Salvador, November 18, 1991, and on interviews with task force staff in 1991. One Salvadoran officer who served under Benavides told the author that Benavides "only said yes because he is so insecure," interview with author, San Salvador, November 22, 1991.

49. Long since on the public record was Col. Ochoa's suggestion that Benavides had been obeying orders given him by a small group of officers who stayed behind in the *Estado Mayor* after the large meeting on the evening of November 15, 1989. See Chapter 6, p. 176.

50. Moakley Statement, November 18, 1991, p. 3.

51. See Chapter 9, p. 283.

52. Salvadoran officer, interview, November 22, 1991.

53. Moakley Statement, November 18, 1991, p. 3.

54. Captains Alfonso Chávez García and Carlos Herrera Carranza were killed in circumstances that led fellow officers to believe the army responsible. Chávez García was the commander of CEAT, an elite unit dependant on the *Estado Mayor*. Allegedly he was approached before Espinoza and asked to lead the operation against the UCA. He had refused, the story went, but had been left knowing too much—and also being known to know too much. On May 1, 1990, while leading an operation within San Salvador, he was killed by a single shot to the back of his neck. Herrera Carranza was the captain who interrupted the meeting in the DNI on the morning of November 16, 1989, with the news of Ellacuría's death while "resisting arrest." His position as chief of operations of the DNI led to speculation that he had "known everything" about the murder of the Jesuits. He was shot in the back outside Gotera in Morazán in November 1990.

55. Moakley, interview, February 6, 1992.

56. The source had been D'Aubuisson, who requested a private meeting with Arthur Sedillo, the special investigator brought down from Mexico by Walker, to tell him of Bustillo's remarks in the air force on November 15, 1989. CIA cable, December 10, 1989, U.S. document declassified November 1993, Washington, D.C.

57. Rick Chidester would remember "trying everything in the world to get him to talk to us," and also that the agency intermediaries found him "credible." Chidester, telephone interview, February 13, 1992. CIA cable, June 9, 1990, U.S. document declassified November 1993, Washington, D.C.

58. The "non-paper" was presented with Dietrich's démarche of July 19, 1990. U.S. embassy/State Department cable, July 27, 1990. U.S. documents declassified November 1993, Washington, D.C.

59. U.S. embassy/State Department cable, October 30, 1990, U.S. document declassified November 1993, Washington, D.C.. Chidester, telephone interview, February 13, 1992

60. William Walker, interview with author, San Salvador, February 19, 1992.

61. Walker's version of these events was complemented by those of two other sources.

62. Salvadoran officer, interview with author, February 11, 1992.

63. Moakley Statement, November 18, 1991, p. 6.

64. William Walker, interview with author, San Salvador, November 6, 1991.

65. Moakley Statement, November 18, 1991, p. 1. A book-length rebuttal of the task force's work by an entity calling itself the Central American Lawyers Group (*The Rule of Law in Wartime El Salvador: The Jesuit Case in Context,* Miami, September 1991) provided an added incentive for Moakley to go public. Inquiries in San Salvador suggested that one of the lawyers within the group was Dr. (and Colonel) Roberto Escobar García, closely connected to the military High Command.

66. Tojeira, "El caso de los jesuitas dos años después," pp. 1034–36.

67. "La Universidad Centroamericana 'José Simeón Cañas' en el segundo aniversario de nuestros mártires (1989–1991)," *ECA* nos. 517–18 (November–December 1991), p. 978.

68. "Un proceso de mediación para El Salvador," Editorial, ECA nos. 387–88 (January–February 1981), pp. 5, 16.

69. *Prensa Gráfica,* October 19, 1991.

70. Carroll J. Doherty, "Short-Term Funding Deal Avoids Sticky Issues," *Congressional Quarterly,* (Washington, D.C., October 26, 1991), p. 3138.

71. "Fuertes ataques contra ONUSAL," *Proceso* no. 494 (November 13, 1991), p. 13.

72. La Cruzada Pro Paz y Trabajo, paid advertisement in *Diario de Hoy* and other newspapers, November 4, 1991.

73. Channel 12, Salvadoran television, cited in El Rescate, *Report from El Salvador,* November 4–11, 1991.

74. Shirley Christian, "Salvador Rebels to Halt Attacks," *New York Times,* November 15, 1991.

75. IUDOP, "Los salvadoreños ante los procesos de privatización y de paz en el país," Press Release, December 5, 1991, p. 8.

76. Clifford Krauss, "Panel Links Chief of Salvador Army to Jesuit Killings," *New York Times,* November 17, 1991.

77. Moakley Statement, November 18, 1991, p. 6.

78. Col. Mark Hamilton, interview with author, San Salvador, March 6, 1992.

79. Pamela Constable, "Officer Linked to Salvador Killings," *Boston Globe,* November 18, 1991.

80. *Prensa Gráfica,* November 19, 1991.

81. *Diario de Hoy,* November 22, 1991; (Bustillo also criticized the *New York Times* as "an active voice for the left.") Channel 12, Salvadoran television, November 20, 1991.

82. Communicado del Ministerio de Defensa y de Seguriadad Pública, November 19, 1991.

83. Cited in Martha Doggett, "Justice Is Still Undone," *The Nation,* February 10, 1992, p. 156.

84. Richard Boucher, State Department briefing, November 18, 1991.

85. U.S. officials and congressional aides, interviews by author, Washington, D.C., December 1991 and February 1992. A CIA "Memorandum for the Record" of the November 21, 1991 briefing was deceptively non-committal. It cited just two reports indicating "possible involvement by higher authorities" in the Jesuit murders and maintained that it was still "not impossible" that Benavides acted on his own. CIA Memorandum dated November 27, 1991, U.S. document declassified November 1993, Washington, D.C.

86. Walker, interview, November 6, 1991.

87. Walker, interview, February 19, 1992.

88. Hamilton, interview, March 6, 1992.

89. Chidester, telephone interview, February 13, 1992. Chidester had left El Salvador in May 1991.

90. Hamilton interview, March 6, 1992; U.S. official, interview with

author, Washington, D.C., February 2, 1992. Chidester, telephone interview, February 13, 1992.

91. Jim McGovern, interview with author, Washington, D.C., February 6, 1992.

92. Source close to the military, interview with author, San Salvador, February 17, 1992.

93. Tim Golden, "The Salvadorans Make Peace in a 'Negotiated Revolution,'" *New York Times,* January 5, 1992.

94. Description of January 16, 1992 drawn, in part, from Francisco Andrés Escobar, "De la paz en la dicha suprema: Los acontecimientos de enero de 1992," *ECA* nos. 519–20 (January–February 1992), pp. 69–89.

95. "Discursos pronunciados en Chapultepec y declaración de los jefes de Estado y de gobierno," ibid., pp. 53–68.

96. Alvaro de Soto, New York, April 27, 1992.

97. "Mexico Agreements," April 27, 1991 (New York: U.N. Department of Public Information), p. 3.

98. Within twelve hours of the law's approval, Judge Zamora handed down the maximum sentence of thirty years on Benavides and Mendoza. Although it was instantly appealed by the lawyers for the defense, Espinoza, Guevara, and Camilo Hernández received three-year sentences for conspiracy to commit terrorist acts and, in Hernández's case, for his role in the coverup.

99. The planned reduction was from the armed forces' own assessment of their size at 63,175 men to 31,000 over a period of two years.

100. Salvadoran officer, interview with author, February 11, 1992.

AFTERWORD

1. "Esperar contra toda esperanza," *ECA* Editorial, 534–35, April–May 1993, p. 338.

2. For an overview of the peace process at the time of the elections, see Jack Spence and George Vickers, "A Negotiated Revolution? A Two Year Progress Report on the Salvadoran Peace Accords" (Hemisphere Initiatives, Cambridge, Mass., March 1994).

3. The murders of prominent FMLN leaders that began in the autumn of 1993 led to the U.N. secretary-general's announcement, on December 8, 1993, of the formation of the "Joint Group for the Investigation of Politically Motivated Illegal Armed Groups." See ibid., pp. 4–5.

4. ONUSAL, "IX Informe del Director de la División de Derechos Humanos al Secretario General (agosto–octubre, 1993)" (San Salvador, 1993), p. 21.

5. "Discurso de Boutros Boutros-Ghali, pronunciado el 15 de diciembre, 1992," *ECA* nos. 529–530 (November–December 1992), p. 1090.

6. Presentation of Iqbal Riza at the WOLA/Woodrow Wilson Center conference, "El Salvador: Sustaining Peace, Nourishing Democracy," April 2, 1993, Washington, D.C.

7. Reynaldo Galindo Pohl was a senior statesman who had served as U.N. Special Rapporteur on Iran, Edwardo Molina, a longtime member of the PDC, and Abraham Rodríguez one of the PDC's founders and a close adviser to Duarte.

8. Asked by the *New York Times* what he would do if he were on the list, General Zepeda responded, "I am going to defend myself." Tim Golden, "General in El Salvador Hints Fight Over Purge of Officers," *New York Times,* November 5, 1992. A source close to the Ad Hoc Commission reported a direct threat from Zepeda to one of the commissioners. Interview with author, San Salvador, March 24, 1993.

9. Ibid.

10. Source close to the military, interview with author, San Salvador, March 18, 1994.

11. Letter dated January 7, 1993 from the Secretary-General Addressed to the President of the Security Council (New York, United Nations, released January 9, 1993). One of the 103 officers named by the commission was no longer a serving member of the armed forces.

12. "Esperar contra esperanza," pp. 333–34.

13. Efforts to influence the commissioners intensified as the release date of the report approached, with Cristiani appealing to leaders in Colombia, Guatemala, Honduras, Mexico, Spain, and Venezuela to pressure U.N. officials on his behalf. For a full discussion of the Truth Commission, see Americas Watch, "Accountability and Human Rights: The Report of the United Nations Commission on the Truth for El Salvador" (New York: Human Rights Watch, August 10, 1993).

14. Truth Commission Report, p. 42.

15. These cases included fifteen extrajudicial assassinations and disappearances and four massacres attributed to government forces, five cases of murder to death squads, and eight cases of murder and kidnapping to the FMLN. There were also two cases for which the commission was unable to reach a conclusion.

16. Truth Commission Report, pp. 132–38, 55–59, 60–65, 118–25, and 44–50, respectively.

17. State Department cable, March 19, 1993, U.S. document declassified November 1993, Washington, D.C.

18. Source close to the Ad Hoc Commission, interview, March 24, 1993.

19. According to Douglas Farah, Ponce also "warned" Cristiani not to accept his resignation. "Generals Retire in El Salvador," *Washington Post,* July 2, 1993.

20. U.S. official, interview with author, San Salvador, March 22, 1993.

21. A more detailed account of the events surrounding the murder of the Jesuits than that contained in pp. 44–50 of the Truth Commission Report was that prepared for an earlier draft and published as Comisión de la verdad, "El asesinato de los sacerdotes jesuitas: Segundo borrador," *ECA* nos. 541–542, November–December 1993, pp. 1205–40.

22. Salvadoran officer, interview with author, San Salvador, March 22, 1993. What became of the $5,000 the case contained when taken from the Jesuits has never been determined.

23. The Truth Commission added to the list of military officers implicated in the Jesuit case the name of General Gilberto Rubio Rubio, who as chief of staff joined the other colonels and generals in pressuring junior officers not to implicate their seniors.

24. Truth Commission Report, "Recomendaciones," pp. 185–98.

25. Channel 12, Salvadoran television, March 23, 1993.

26. Gutiérrez Castro's remark cited in Tracy Wilkinson, "Salvadoran Leader Blasts U.N. Report," *Los Angeles Times,* March 19, 1993. Press Release, "Declaración del Presidente de la República, Alfredo Cristiani," March 18, 1993.

27. Francisco Lima was the lawyer, cited in Thomas Long, "Salvador Pardons 2 in Killing of 6 Priests," *Miami Herald,* April 3, 1993.

28. Cited in Guy Gugliotta and Douglas Farah, "12 Years of Tortured Truth on El Salvador," *Washington Post,* March 21, 1993.

29. Mark O. Hatfield, "Salvador's Grievous Loss," *Christian Science Monitor,* March 31, 1993.

30. Benjamin Schwarz, "Of Course We Knew," *Washington Post,* April 8, 1993.

31. Transcript of the statement of Secretary of State Warren Christopher before the Senate Committee on Foreign Appropriations, Subcommittee on Foreign Operations, March 30, 1993, Washington, D.C.; Statement by Secretary of State Warren Christopher, U.S. Department of State, March 24, 1993, Washington, D.C.

32. Letter to the Honorable William J. Clinton from congressional committee chairmen, March 26, 1993, Washington, D.C.

33. Richard W. Murphy and George S. Vest (members), I. M. Destler (academic adviser), "Report of the Secretary of State's Panel on El Salvador," U.S. Department of State, July 1993, Washington, D.C., p. 1. For a full discussion of the report see Arnson, *Crossroads,* pp. 290–95.

34. "Report of the Secretary of State's Panel," p. 29.

35. Ibid., pp. 19 and 64.

36. Ibid., p. 11. The declassified documents were drawn from the files of the Central Intelligence Agency, the Department of Defense (including Defense Intelligence Agency), and the State Department.

37. State Department cable, February 19, 1991, U.S. document declassified November 1993, Washington, D.C.

38. See Chapter 9, note 41. The State Department's refusal to deliver to the Truth Commission the briefing document originally prepared for them, was recounted in an interview with a Truth Commission source, Washington, D.C., April 2, 1993.

39. CIA/State Department, "Briefing Paper on Right-Wing Terrorism in El Salvador," October 27, 1983, U.S. document declassified November 1993, Washington, D.C.

40. CIA Directorate of Intelligence, "Memorandum requested by Vice-President Bush," January 20, 1984, U.S. document declassified November 1993, Washington, D.C.

41. Walker, interview, March 23, 1991.

42. Cited in Jefferson Morley, "The Jesuit Murder Mystery," *Washington Post*, July 18, 1993.

43. CIA cable of August 17, 1990. Other cables containing the raw intelligence on which this assessment is based include: a CIA cable of early May 1990; CIA cable of May 22, 1990; CIA cable of June 20, 1990; U.S. embassy/State Department cables of August 13, 14, and 16, 1990; two DIA cables of August 27, 1990; a CIA cable of September 19, 1990; U.S. embassy/State Department cables of October 30 and December 3, 1990 and March 18, 1991; a CIA cable of July 10, 1991; and a State Department cable of December 3, 1990. U.S. documents declassified November 1993, Washington, D.C.

44. The CIA documents refer specifically to a "Memo dissem report" of June 29, 1990.

45. See Chapter 6, p. 184.

46. U.S. Embassy/State department cable, August 14, 1990, U.S. document declassified November 1993.

47. DOD/Southern Command documents, "Note to SouthCom," February 10, 1991, U.S. documents declassified November 1993, Washington, D.C.

48. U.S. Embassy/State Department cable, February 19, 1991, U.S. document declassified November 1993, Washington, D.C.

49. See Chapter 9, pp. 279 and 282.

50. U.S. embassy/State Department cable, February 19, 1991, U.S. document declassified November 1993.

51. "Generals Retire in El Salvador." Generals Zepeda, Rubio Rubio, and Vargas retired with Ponce. Although Vargas had been named by neither commission, his role in the negotiations meant that some in the armed forces held him partially responsible for the commissions' existence in the first place. From the presidential office Vargas continued to work on the peace accords; Ponce was awarded a position in ANTEL, the state telephone agency; Zepeda assumed a shady role as "military liaison" with the ARENA party.

52. For background to the elections, see Jack Spence and George Vickers, "Toward a Level Playing Field? A Report on the Post-War Salvadoran Electoral Process"(Hemisphere Initiatives, Cambridge, Mass., January, 1994).

53. "Second and Third Reports of the Secretary-General on the United Nations' Observer Mission in El Salvador, Electoral Division," February 18, 1994, Section 19, p. 6 and March 18, 1994, Section 7, p. 3 (New York, United Nations, 1994).

54. ONUSAL Press release, "Declaración del jefe de misión sobre el desarrollo y los resultados de les elecciones" (San Salvador, March 21, 1994).

55. The author was present in El Salvador during the elections.

56. Both cited in Douglas Farah, "Salvadorans Await 2nd Voting Round," *Washington Post,* March 22, 1994.

57. Results from letter dated 21 April 1994 from the secretary-general addressed to the president of the Security Council (New York, United Nations, April 1994).

58. An election-day profile in the *Washington Post* cited former U.S. embassy officials and businessmen who said that "there is only anecdotal evidence that Calderón participated in violence. But he maintained close ties to those who did." Douglas Farah, "Likely El Salvador Victor Is Right's Unlikely Successor," *Washington Post,* April 24, 1994.

INDEX